Will,

Happy 12th Birthday

Hope this helps you take your first 5 wicket haul!

Lots of love,
Uncle Matt, Aunty Jacqui & Poppy xxx

BOB WOOLMER'S
Art and Science of
CRICKET

This edition first published in 2008 by New Holland Publishers (UK) Ltd
London • Cape Town • Sydney • Auckland
www.newhollandpublishers.com

Garfield House, 86–88 Edgware Road, London W2 2EA, United Kingdom
Cornelis Struik House, 80 McKenzie Street, Cape Town 8001, South Africa
Unit 1, 66 Gibbes Street, Chatswood, NSW 2067, Australia
218 Lake Road, Northcote, Auckland, New Zealand

New Holland Publishing is a member of Avusa Ltd

Copyright © in published edition: Struik Publishers 2008
Copyright © in text: The Estate of the late Robert Andrew Woolmer, Timothy Noakes, Helen Moffett 2008
Copyright © in photographs: as accredited

Reproduction by Hirt & Carter Cape (Pty) Ltd
Printed and bound by Tien Wah Press (Pte) Limited, Singapore

2 4 6 8 10 9 7 5 3 1

All rights reserved. No part of this publication may be reproduced, stored in a retrieval system
or transmitted in any form or by any means, electronic, mechanical, photocopying, recording or otherwise,
without the prior written permission of the copyright owner/s.

PUBLISHING MANAGER: Linda de Villiers
EDITOR AND CONTENT CONSULTANT: Tom Eaton
DESIGNER: Beverley Dodd
COVER DESIGNER: Russell Woolmer
PRINCIPAL PHOTOGRAPHER: Carl Fourie
BOWLING GRIPS ILLUSTRATOR: James Berrangé
TECHNICAL ILLUSTRATORS: James Berrangé and Martin Jones
PROOFREADERS: Roxanne Reid, Anthony Sharpe and Joy Clack
INDEXER: Clifford Perusset

ISBN: 978 184773 314 6 (Standard Edition); 978 1 84773 328 3 (Slipcase Edition)

Front cover and spine images © Gallo Images/Getty Images

The authors gratefully acknowledge permission to use copyrighted material from the following: Kerith Aginsky, Justin Durandt, Gallo Images/Getty Images, Janine Gray, Paul Hurrion, Brian Kantor, Alan Knott, Peter Philpott, Marc Portus, Quintic Consultancy Ltd, Martin Schwellnus and Richard Stretch. It has not been possible to trace all copyright holders. Please contact the publishers at the above address in case of errors or omissions.

CONTENTS

Foreword by Richie Benaud **4**

Bob Woolmer (1948 – 2007): a memorial **5**

PART I: DISCOVERING CRICKET **10**
CHAPTER 1: The challenge of cricket **12**
CHAPTER 2: The mind game **26**

PART II: CRICKET TECHNIQUES **86**
CHAPTER 3: Batting **90**
CHAPTER 4: Vision and batting **184**
CHAPTER 5: Bowling **204**
CHAPTER 6: Fielding and wicket-keeping **322**

PART III: THINKING CRICKET **368**
CHAPTER 7: Strategy and captaincy **370**
CHAPTER 8: Statistics: a view of the future? **446**
CHAPTER 9: Coaching **464**

PART IV: CRICKET SCIENCE **524**
CHAPTER 10: Physiology and fitness **526**
CHAPTER 11: Whither cricket? The future of the game **632**

Select bibliography **643**

Index **649**

Acknowledgements **656**

FOREWORD

I had my first proper sighting of Bob in the early 1970s, when he was starting to make an impression in the Kent team, and I was working with BBC Television. He was an elegant player, under the influence of Colin Cowdrey, and he impressed me as being a good thinker on the game. There was no better example of this than in 1974, when, in the semi-final of the Gillette Cup, he bowled his 12 overs for 22, and then steered Kent to victory with 18 not out in a pulsating finish. In the final at Lord's three weeks later, it was Bob who bowled magnificently, and then shared the tense winning partnership with Alan Knott.

He confirmed my impression of his ability and his thinking in the years that followed, and when he played for the World XI in World Series Cricket, he was already thinking ahead into the area of coaching. Captains and coaches, good ones that is, are always a couple of overs ahead of the play; otherwise they find themselves trailing the opposition. Bob's habit of 'thinking cricket' is one of the reasons this is a coaching book different from all others.

It is essential to play your cricket in common-sense fashion. It follows that using a common-sense approach to coaching will provide a wonderful combination. On my first tour of England in 1953, I received the best simple advice from Bill O'Reilly as to the manner in which I should completely revise my bowling technique. It successfully changed my bowling career. So I believe that in the teaching of players, the key lies in watching a man play, detecting his mistakes, and having the ability to correct those mistakes, one at a time. Never forget the simple things.

In Bob's book there is much to ponder about mental skills and strengths, and it comes across that a player must use, rather than waste, his talent. To have a talent that is rarely used is a sad legacy in life; fortunately this was not true of Bob Woolmer's life. He was able to use his cricketing talents to the full, and his book is proof of this. I hope it is a great success.

Richie Benaud
Coogee, New South Wales, Australia, January 2008

BOB WOOLMER (1948 – 2007): A MEMORIAL

Bob Woolmer began life with a cricket bat in his crib; and he died in the service of cricket, on 18 March 2007, at the Cricket World Cup in the West Indies. His sudden death, most probably of heart failure, caused a cloud of speculation and confusion that for a few months threatened to veil Bob's gigantic contribution to the game to which he had given his life.

He had just finished this book, a substantial work that contains much of what he had learnt, pondered and learnt afresh about cricket. It now serves as his legacy; and his surviving co-authors, and the many helpers who worked on it, hope that it reflects, in some measure, the depth and breadth of Bob's wisdom, experience and constantly questioning cricketing mind.

Bob's favourite saying to those dealing with a sporting defeat was, 'It's only a game. Nobody has died.' A modest, transparent and humble man, he would have been overwhelmed by the global outpouring of sentiment at his death. Yet his cricketing reach extended around the globe. He had coached cricketers on four continents, and had played against the world's best on the fifth. In North America, he had helped to prepare the Canadian team for the 2003 Cricket World Cup. In Europe, he played for Kent and England, and coached Warwickshire to a success that remains unmatched in the history of English county cricket. Later, in his role as ICC High Performance Manager, he played a significant role in the coaching of the Holland and Ireland teams. In Africa, he coached Namibia, Kenya, and of course, the South African national team – all while continuing to run his coaching clinics for youngsters in Cape Town; and, in Asia, he tackled with relish the formidable task of coaching the Pakistan side. Bob was fascinated by the nation of Pakistan, its people, their religion and culture, and its cricketers, in whose enormous talents he was a firm believer. In return, he was granted the love of yet another adopted nation, with President Pervez Musharraf awarding him the Star of Excellence (one of Pakistan's highest civilian honours) in recognition of his work of 'great distinction and commitment' for Pakistan cricket.

Many believe that Bob redefined the role of the coach in international cricket. The writer Tom Eaton, who edited this book, wrote in a piece for *SA Cricket*:

'There has been much talk in recent weeks about his legacy ... but [this] is not something friends, family and former players need to cobble together; because his legacy has been growing for the last twenty years, and today it is immense.

'It was Bob, after all, who legitimised the reverse-sweep, encouraging Warwickshire's Dermott Reeve to play the stroke in earnest. It was he who mentored Jonty Rhodes, helping the freakishly gifted South African to revolutionise the role of the fielder in the modern game. It was he who kept the thoroughbred fast bowler Allan Donald firing on all cylinders. It was he who made it not only acceptable, but essential for coaches to use digital media as tactical aides.

'To look at this list is to see a startling collection of achievements: add the reverse-sweep to the fielding revolution; high-class fast bowling to laptop diagnostics, and you have a cross-section of modern cricket. It is, in other words, not a wild exaggeration to suggest that Bob, more or less alone, dragged the sport into the 21st century. Australians may claim (rightly) that it was they who pushed Test run-rates over four per over in 2000, but that escalation was based on half a decade, in the 1990s, of playing high-pressure one-day cricket. And that pressure, one could argue successfully, was injected into the international game by Rhodes at backward point, and Woolmer giving him the license to be brilliant.'

Bob was not a 'how to' coach. He always asked 'Why?' He sought to produce thinking cricketers who understood that there were options. But he would explain why he thought that all the options were not necessarily equal – then leave his charges to make their own choices.

Bob was also a cricketing communicator, who insisted that cricketing concepts be taught with crystal clarity, to the extent of testing them on his wife, Gill. He taught at the highest levels of the game, while never neglecting the lowest, to the extent that it sometimes seems that every male under 45 in Cape Town, whatever his creed or colour, was coached by Bob. And all speak of his dedication and his innovation.

Bob began the final chapter of his 1984 autobiography with the words: 'Cricket has always resisted change. If the game is to survive, we must ensure that it moves with the times.' It was through his constant search for change and improvement that he changed lives.

The lives he affected were not just those of the players he coached. For millions, cricket offers a way into a parallel universe of honour and decency, in which the conduct of a team of athletes is almost always admirable, co-operative and collaborative, sometimes even noble. Because cricket is played over days, not hours, no testosterone- or adrenaline-fuelled rush of brute strength can achieve success.

Instead, the game requires constant, considered strategizing over time. It requires repetitive activity for hours and hours without any loss of focus. Above all, it requires extraordinary amounts of patience and fortitude.

This is the immense attraction of cricket for many – that it showcases not only athletic ability, but character. Part of why women spectators are being drawn to the game in numbers that are overtaking those of male fans is because cricket presents such a compelling and appealing view of men working together towards a common goal – if not to win, then to accept defeat philosophically. Cricket offers the pleasure and comfort, in ever more troubled times, of watching men operating in groups that are not drunk and rowdy and rapacious, but patient, persevering, thoughtful, respectful and honourable.

Of course this doesn't describe all or even most cricketers, but it describes a lot of them – including Bob Woolmer. Former English cricket captain David Gower wrote of Bob: 'There is nobody ... who better represented the high principles of sportsmanship and behaviour that have been traditionally associated with cricket.' And so we remember Bob as he was – a modest, down-to-earth man who was unafraid to express his opinion, and who was universally admired for his warmth, his decency, his sincerity and his integrity. Above all, we remember his enthusiasm and love for his twin passions – his family and cricket.

We close with Bob's own words, written six weeks before his death as a preface to the book he had at long last completed:

'In 1996, Professor Tim Noakes said to me, "You should write down all the knowledge you have gleaned over the years so that people might better understand the game and the passion it invokes." My response was, "Well, why don't we put our heads together and write a different type of cricket book? One that not only reinforces the basics of the game, but gives further insight to those who aspire to play, watch and teach the game, and share the passion it invokes." Thus this book was hatched.

'During the journey of the last ten or so years, and with the aid of many people, we have slowly pieced this manual together. As we did so, we realized the enormity of the task, and also that the game has changed little since its inception in many ways, but in others has changed enormously.

'In those years, I have written and rewritten chapters because my own coaching style has had to change with each role that I have undertaken. It has become extremely clear that there is no right or wrong way to play or teach this game. Inevitably, it is the player who will shape his own destiny either as player or coach. There is no cloning in cricket.

'Yes, youngsters will have role models, but they will still have their own style. Players being taught have to listen and take what is best from that advice and apply it to their game. Also and increasingly, coaches will have to adapt their knowledge to suit the player.

'You can be involved with this game for 15 minutes or 35 years and you will still learn. Those of you who are convinced that you are doing it the right way may find suddenly that "your way" is challenged and that you have to change to suit a youngster or a great player (never give up because he/she may not understand).

'I am indebted to so many who have helped contribute to the book: Alan Knott (the greatest keeper I have ever seen), John Snow, who makes the science and art of bowling so complete, to all the great batsmen I have played with and against and coached for ten minutes or three years – you have taught me so much. To those who inspired me to coach – the first probably Trevor Bailey, through his coaching book, followed by Colin Page (my first first-class coach), who said that I should qualify as a coach! How did he know? Above all to my father, who placed a ball and bat in my cot two days after my birth in the hospital in Kanpur, India, and said "Son, I hope this will be your life." He knew more than any other that this great game would engulf me and take over my whole life.

'This book is not finished; it has just started. We hope that other coaches will respond, and ask us to add to it. We welcome constructive criticism. We also hope that it will inspire some to become players, coaches and more.

'To Tim Noakes, Helen Moffett, Tom Eaton, Clive During, and so many others who have helped to assemble this book, many, many thanks.

'It is a passion; it is a labour of love; it is a never-ending journey.

'This book is dedicated to my wife Gill and my boys, Dale and Russell, who have put up with me for so long, who have shared my passion and helped me to pass it on. To them I owe so much – I cannot thank them enough.'

A NOTE ON LANGUAGE AND GENDER

Cricket is certainly not a game reserved for males. Around the world, children of both sexes play the game with evident pleasure, and are often coached by female schoolteachers; women's cricket is a serious sport with numerous participants and its own World Cup (although, like many women's sports, it struggles with the Cinderella syndrome of being overlooked by sponsors and the media); women are making an impression on the previously all-male enclave of commentating, with South Africa's Cass Naidoo and Barbados's Donna Symonds probably the best-known female commentators at international level; and probably most significant of all, women are beginning to overtake men as the primary television audience for cricket.

Cricket is enjoyed by entire families, and that includes mothers, sisters, aunts and grannies. All three authors of this book hail from cricket-playing families – extremely distinguished in the case of the Woolmer and Noakes lineages – but in Helen Moffett's case, while her father, uncles and grandfathers played school and club cricket, her mother and aunt were enthusiastically involved as scorers. And it was her mother's passion for the game that set her own cricketing imagination alight.

Helen can also attest that Bob Woolmer and Tim Noakes, like many geniuses, focused on the talent before them, rather than the package in which it appeared. Tim works with some of the most gifted scientists, physiologists and athletes in the world – some of whom are women. Likewise, Bob picked the best when seeking expert auxiliary support as coach to two national teams; like Tim Noakes, he knew that talent and intelligence are not bound by physical characteristics.

Yet throughout this book, the authors refer to players (and coaches) as 'he', or speak of bats*men*; one could be forgiven for paging through and thinking it was written for boys and men. This is not the case. Anyone who plays cricket, coaches it, or even just watches it can benefit from the information contained here. However, the truth is that much of the research that Tim Noakes has conducted, studied or supervised has been on male cricketers or athletes; likewise, while Bob Woolmer coached cricketers of every age, ability and station in life, from impoverished children in townships to elite adult superstars, he only ever coached boys and men. Therefore it would not have been an honest reflection of the vast experience of the authors to go through the book writing 'he and she' and 'him and her' every time the gender of a player was mentioned; neither can we offer the airy explanation that 'he' can be read as including 'she'!

We hope that readers will excuse what might look like exclusive language, and use common sense in applying what they learn here to those they coach. For instance, many of the pointers in the chapter on vision obviously won't apply to those visually-impaired athletes who play 'Blind Cricket'; but the techniques of batting and playing shots will remain the same. Exactly the same principle applies when coaching girls or women – while it will be obvious (for instance) that they are not going to be able to bowl as fast as male speedsters (and so may be less likely to get the ball to reverse), everything we say about practising line, length and variation in bowling will apply. In the meantime, we look forward to seeing more women involved in cricket, both on and off the field, in decades to come.

PART ONE

DISCOVERING CRICKET

CHAPTER ONE

THE CHALLENGE OF CRICKET

INTRODUCTION

In 1893, a Rev. Holmes wrote, 'We know as much of the history of cricket as we shall ever know now, and we have been told everything relating to the science of the game. There is no fresh ground to be explored.'

No doubt the good parson is turning in his grave at the astonishing changes the last century has wrought on a game in which he saw no new possibilities. In terms of science and sports medicine in particular, the last several decades have heralded a flurry of research into every aspect of the game.

But cricket as a game casts a long shadow. Those who play it, coach it, administer it, watch and love it are aware, to greater and lesser degrees, that the game to which they devote their time, and from which they gain great pleasure, is complex, rich, intriguing, demanding and occasionally infuriating. In 1993, a *Times* leader stated that, 'Cricket presents tactical complexities undreamt of on the football pitch; it is chess compared to tiddly-winks.' This claim, and similar ones, have been made about cricket for well over a hundred years: in 1905, A.C. MacLaren announced, 'Cricket develops the mind; there is more *thinking* to be done over cricket than over any other game.' In addition, many realize that the game of cricket has accumulated layers of meaning beyond those of a sporting contest. The cricket writer and political analyst C.L.R. James, in his 1963 cricketing classic, *Beyond a Boundary*, penned the now famous words: 'What do they know of cricket who only cricket know?'

The nostalgia associated with cricket, which has spurred hundreds of memoirs involving the smack of leather on willow and cucumber sandwiches for tea, derives from a specific period in the long history of cricket – the late Victorian and Edwardian periods. This was the era of the Grace brothers, of umpires with mutton-chop moustaches, of Gentlemen and Players, of John Wisden's *Almanack* and the last blooming of the British Empire. This latter element was the crucial key to cricket's survival: it transported cricket – literally – into the twentieth century and beyond. It was the fervour with which the inhabitants of British colonies in the nineteenth and early twentieth centuries adopted (and then adapted) the English game that made cricket – once the preserve of minor public schoolboys – a truly international sport.

This eccentric game has not only become a multi-million-dollar enterprise played around the world, but it continues to grow in popularity. More and more countries are fielding cricket teams, and only football is more widely watched on television. Another intriguing factor is that women form the most rapidly growing sector of those who watch the game. Cricket continues to fascinate and engage, in spite of the time it absorbs.

But why is cricket unique? Why do so many find the game irresistible? Conversely, why do some find the game so difficult to understand? Cricket has so many facets that it takes a while to grasp them all. There are almost no other sports in which there are so many variables, in which the player has to continually adapt to such a wide spectrum of constantly changing conditions and aspects of the game. It is a particularly complex and compelling combination of a team sport and a gladiatorial one-on-one challenge (batter versus bowler). Unlike most other games, it can and often does end in a draw, regardless of superb, even heroic performances by individuals and teams. And at the highest level, it is played not just over hours, but days, which demands high levels of concentration, focus, commitment, stamina and doggedness.

> 'Football is about the group domination of space; cricket is about an individual's encounter with time. In cricket, exceptionally diverse levels of competition are imposed upon the individual. He plays directly against a single other batsman or bowler, against the pitch and conditions, against himself, against the needs of the game in terms of attack and defence, and against ten other participants in addition to his immediate adversary. He does this both for himself and in relation to the mood and intent of his team' (Cook and Scott, 1991, p. 153).

HISTORY AND LAWS OF CRICKET

The game of cricket has a long history, and while it is not necessary for players to know exactly how it evolved over the centuries, its past does shed light on the plethora of rules (Laws) that accompany the modern game. A few scholars argue that cricket dates from a game known as 'Creag' referred to in early medieval literature, but it is generally accepted that the first reliably dated reference is one that showed up in the Guild Merchant Book of 1598. Here a merchant was recorded as swearing under oath that a parcel of land had been used for cricket for 50 years: 'hee and his fellows did runne and play there at Creckett and other plaies.' Clearly, they had trouble preserving sportsfields even in those days, and equally clearly, cricket was established in southern England by the end of the sixteenth century.

We know that the game has rural roots, a legacy preserved in the length of the wicket – 22 yards (20,2 metres), or one-tenth of a furlong, an agricultural measurement used when ploughing fields. Balls were bowled underarm towards a target, and then fended off by a batter who wielded a club with a curved end (rather like a modern hockey-stick). He was permitted to hit the ball as often as he liked in defence of his 'wicket', and whether delivered by the bowler, or struck with the bat, the ball travelled along the ground. The original wicket was sometimes a tree-stump, but more generally a little portable gate used for sheep-pens. Initially, both single- and double-wicket games were played, with the former finally dying out in the mid-nineteenth century. Once the game caught on, artificial wickets consisting of two stumps, with a stick laid horizontally across them, were used. The third stump and bails came along after complaints by bowlers who managed to bowl through the wicket without disturbing it. The need for some sort of referee is almost as old as the game, and the word 'umpire' first appears in English as 'noumpere', meaning a 'non-peer' – literally, an odd man out or neutral party asked to adjudicate. An early eighteenth-century illustration shows that by then it was already traditional to use two umpires.

The above would have been the form of the game for much of the seventeenth and eighteenth centuries. Cricket gained steadily in popularity throughout the seventeenth century, in spite of gloomy mutterings by the Puritans, and by the eighteenth century, it was a well-established sport played by adults, and as accepted in urban settings as in the country. It was particularly popular with the aristocracy and landed gentry, with both sexes playing it at home. Formal matches became hotbeds of wagering, gambling, match-fixing and other forms of chicanery, which goes to show that there is nothing new under the cricketing sun.

The game had in the meantime become sufficiently complex to warrant the first compilation and publication of the Laws of the Game in 1744. These form the basis of today's Laws, and continue to be updated, altered and added to when circumstances in the modern game dictate that changes be made. For instance, after the 'bouncer wars' spearheaded by the great West Indian fast bowlers during the 1970s (and picked up by Pakistani fast bowlers towards the end of the 1980s), the Laws were changed to allow for only two bouncers per over in the multi-day form of the game (to howls of outrage from some sides, and sighs of relief by others).

Detailed as the Laws are, so many of the rules of cricket take the form of unwritten tradition that innovations in the game invariably ruffle feathers. Sometimes these innovations become part of the game; for example, there is no rule yet that says batters have to wear helmets when facing fast bowling, yet this has become normative, with only the truly stupid or suicidal going out bare-headed. And sometimes, they lead to frantic additions to the Laws on the basis that certain traditions are intrinsic to the game – as when Dennis Lillee wielded an aluminium bat during the 1979–80 Ashes series, causing consternation among the cricketing establishment. It was discovered that there was no Law saying that bats had to be made of wood, an omission that was hastily amended.

As explained in Chapter 5, changes in bowling, not batting gave cricket the shape and form with which we are familiar today. Towards the end of the eighteenth century, players began perfecting what we would recognize as a 'length' ball, a delivery that bounced once before reaching the batsman. This meant that batsmen had to start playing forward, developing defensive techniques for the first time. Meanwhile, at the start of the nineteenth century, round-arm bowling was pioneered, apparently by a Miss Christina Willes from a prominent cricketing family. The story goes that she was hampered by her voluminous skirts when bowling (the corsetry hoops that were then fashionable would have been the real problem, forcing her bowling arm above hip-height).

In his 1897 *Jubilee Book of Cricket*, the great batsman Ranjitsinhji pinpointed the introduction of round-arm bowling as the moment of transition between old and modern cricket, and certainly the nineteenth century saw the steady rise of the bowler's arm towards its current position. This, together with the new defensive shots the batsmen needed to master in response, led to the development of the straight bat, as shots were now played through the air, not along the ground. By 1864 (when overarm bowling was legalized in the Laws), the game had become one today's players and viewers would recognize as modern cricket.

SOCIO-POLITICAL CONTEXT

On the international stage, cricket is a truly post-colonial phenomenon, with former colonizers and colonized regularly playing against one another, as well as sworn political enemies. India and Pakistan play each other regularly, although at particularly troublesome times, they have had to do so in neutral countries. But in spite of explosive (sometimes literally) political divides, the two countries have toured each other on a regular basis in recent decades. South African sportswriter Michael Owen-Smith described hardened journalists being moved to tears at a one-day game at Eden Gardens in Kolkata, when the Pakistan team snatched victory from the jaws of certain defeat in the last over of the game. After a long and terrifying silence, the 80 000-strong crowd erupted not into boos and cries of outrage, but into a standing ovation for the winning team, which responded by running a victory lap before the applauding masses.

Sport has always had the potential to be a great leveller, and cricket is no exception: it is quite possible for poorer countries to beat richer ones, and at times this has happened with monotonous regularity. Think of the dominance of the West Indian fast-bowling pack attack from the 1960s to the 1980s, in which the descendants of slaves spent nearly three decades harrowing the rest of the Test-playing nations. The history that spread cricket around the world is never quite forgotten – when the England cricket team, fresh from winning the Ashes in 2005, proceeded to a Test series in Pakistan, one wit announced that 'the Sahibs were soundly walloped'.

Sadly, the last two decades seem to show that in cricket, teams from developed countries seem to be outstripping those of developing countries. This is not purely a matter of hard cash: the cricketing industry in Asia rakes in billions of dollars. Rather, it seems to be a question of infrastructure, research and government support. A country with a large middle-class population, and government-subsidized schools with good sports facilities and reliable infrastructure is more likely to produce star athletes consistently. Talent knows no nationality, class or race, but other factors constantly intrude; for instance, South Africa has identified a host of young black fast bowlers with real talent in the last ten or so years. Yet once they begin playing at first-class level, many break down repeatedly with stress fractures. One theory (as yet unproven) is that poor nutrition in childhood means that their frames simply cannot absorb the extra pounding as they play more and more cricket. Young speed-merchant Mfuneko Ngam burst onto the international stage against New Zealand in 2000 – a blistering edge was grassed in the slips in his first over of Test cricket – and with 11 wickets in his first three Tests, the 21-year-old looked set to fill the massive boots of Allan Donald. But heartbreak followed as his classic action, extreme flexibility and genuine tearaway pace were undermined by chronic stress fractures.

Like all sports, cricket is a glittering dream to some, and a source of bitter disappointment to a much greater majority. Those to whom it remains a gentle and gentlemanly game played in whites on the village green might be shocked to know of the dizzying hope and heartbreak the game can engender.

A lack of solid nutrition during his township childhood had cost him dearly, and Ngam's international career was over less than 12 months after it had begun.

Yet the game continues to grow and even thrive in contexts that may seem all but impossible. In dusty and forgotten corners of the globe, in rural villages in India and Pakistan, shanty-towns in the Caribbean, townships in South Africa, and council estates in northern England, there is an army of unsung heroes: the dedicated cricket coaches and teachers who work with bright and talented youngsters even when there is little chance of ever seeing their charges fulfilling their potential.

In countries with a history of 'baksheesh' and kickbacks, families and coaches without influence despair of ever seeing their children given the opportunity they deserve. In South Africa, the country's citizens are still counting the cost of 40 years of systematic deprivation of the great majority under apartheid, and wrestling with the thorny problems of how to establish equity both on and off the playing fields. Sport has been as impoverished as any other arena, and far too many potential D'Oliveiras have been lost to the game forever. Meanwhile, on the Asian subcontinent, being chosen to play cricket at the elite level is the equivalent of winning the lottery – except that the odds are even smaller, and the ticket is a costly one. Promising young players are taken out of school early (and never finish their education), families beggar

MONEY MATTERS: SOCIO-ECONOMICS AND SPORT

It may seem like common sense to note that the cost of playing a particular sport may limit participation by young children in sport in general and in the more expensive sports in particular – and yet this is not always fully recognized.

Australian researchers (Kirk et al., 1997) decided to take a closer look at this issue, and found that families make a much larger contribution to supporting their children's involvement in junior sport than is generally appreciated. Direct costs include buying uniforms and equipment, coaching and membership fees, and the costs of transporting children to venues. Indirect costs include the time adults spend travelling and watching their children play the sport, as well as the time they give to volunteer activities – administration, fund-raising and coaching. The result is that in Australia, those children whose parents are reasonably well off make up the majority of players in most club and representative sports.

The authors concluded that the traditional assumption that (Australian) sport is open to children from all sectors of society is simply not true. There is no doubt that similar (if not far greater) barriers exist in other sports-playing societies. This issue must be addressed if we are to promote equitable sports participation across all social classes.

themselves paying for the best coaching and equipment, and the entire enterprise seldom ends in anything but heartbreak. In the Caribbean, where cricketing morale has been sagging for some time, coaches all too often lose their best athletes to the lure of the American dream.

Like all sports, cricket is a glittering dream to some, and a source of bitter disappointment to a much greater majority. Those to whom it remains a gentle and gentlemanly game played in whites on the village green might be shocked to know of the dizzying hope and heartbreak the game can engender.

However, world events largely beyond our control influence all sports, not only cricket. South Africans are lucky enough to be able to make positive and constructive contributions to the future of the game, and many of those involved with cricket at all levels are doing heroic and largely unheralded work in cricket development. While much still needs doing, it is heartening to see members of the national team and many others conducting coaching clinics in impoverished areas, fund-raising, and helping to develop facilities – certainly one of Bob Woolmer's dreams.

Cricket is thus a game with a rich, complex and at times burdensome history, one that determines its unique political and social context. But there are everyday variables that affect each game of cricket beyond this somewhat sweeping backdrop; variables as peculiar and yet familiar to players and fans as any of cricket's most famous eccentricities.

WEATHER

Cricket is played in summer (although the playing season gets longer every year, spilling well into spring and autumn) and is an outdoor sport. This means that it is at the mercy of the vagaries of the weather. While this is true of every outdoor sport, in which players may have to contend with rain and wind, cricket is unusual in that it cannot be played if rain is falling (in comparison with rugby, for instance). This is for a number of reasons: the bowler cannot control a wet, slippery ball, players may struggle to see the ball, and the playing surface, the pitch itself, must be kept dry to prevent it from becoming dangerously slippery, and sustaining damage that is difficult to repair.

Given the amount of rain that falls in the average English summer, plus the fact that cricket is often played in subtropical countries that have summer rainfall or, in the case of South Africa and Zimbabwe, summer thunderstorms, rain thus becomes a wild card in many games. Because rain holds up play, confining players to the dressing room until the clouds roll away and the outfield has been dried out, it can force dramatic changes in strategy in multi-day games, given that it steals time from the game. A captain robbed of an afternoon's play may well have to declare in order to force a result. Rain can also dictate that a team romping towards victory may have to settle for a draw.

But it is not just the course of the game that is affected: inevitably, and no matter how swiftly the covers are drawn over the pitch, and how effective the rollers (and even huge vacuum-cleaners) are, moisture from rain will have altered the playing conditions. Spin and seam bowlers may find that the ball is 'gripping' the pitch or deviating through the air more dramatically. Batters may find that a pitch on which they were belting out runs has slowed down considerably – and all of a sudden, the game swings in favour of the fielding side.

In the one-day form of the game, rain rules have had to be developed to deal with the situation that arises when rain makes it impossible for the side playing second to bat out their full quota of overs. The calculations that come into play, which involve lowering both the targeted number of runs and the number of overs in which they have to be scored, have been far from perfect. They became notorious at the 1992 World Cup in Australia, when the South African team, newly returned to the international arena after decades of isolation under apartheid, performed with commendable courage and flair, becoming a popular choice for a shot at the final. In the semi-final, they were beaten not so much by their opponents, England, as by Messrs Duckworth & Lewis, the devisers of the programme that calculated the rain rules. With the experienced Dave Richardson and all-rounder Brian McMillan at the crease, with 22 runs to make off 13 balls, victory was possible. But then down came the rain. Only eight minutes of play were lost, but the computer ticked away, first recalculating that 22 runs had to be made off seven balls, then 21 off one delivery! The South Africans were thus denied their shot at their first World Cup final by default. This farcical situation was partly due to strict broadcast schedules. However, there was such an outcry that the 'rain rules' were fine-tuned so not as to set illogical targets in future. This did not prevent the South African side misunderstanding them on home ground at the 2003 World Cup and being bustled humiliatingly out of the competition as a result. They also played a role in the damp squib final of the 2007 Cricket World Cup at the Oval in Barbados, reducing it to a mere exhibition game rather than a real contest between the finalists, Australia and Sri Lanka.

Not only rain, but wind, dew, humidity, cloud cover and even tides can affect the game of cricket, for two main reasons: they affect the pitch itself; and they influence the movement of the ball as it is bowled, either through the air (some bowlers benefit from bowling into the wind, for instance) or off the pitch. This is why experienced cricketers pay close attention to weather reports and conditions, and develop the ability to gauge how these conditions will affect the pitch – a skill that requires considerable canniness, not to say a crystal ball.

THE PITCH AND OUTFIELD

The art and science of preparing a cricket pitch and outfield are extremely complex. A good groundsperson is by definition a botanist, engineer, geologist, agriculturalist, chemist and hydrologist. While the nitty-gritty of pitch preparation and maintenance is an arcane business, involving matters such as drainage, cultivation and cutting techniques, soil analysis, rhizomes, rollers and much else besides, it is an excellent idea to ask local groundstaff to give junior players a talk on the topic, or take them on a guided tour that includes the equipment used.

While not every player needs to understand how a pitch is laid and maintained, all of them will need to learn how to 'read' a pitch. This refers to the rapid (and continuous) assessment of the behaviour of a pitch the minute one begins to play on it. This evolving 'behaviour' of the pitch ('What is it doing now?') is one of the most significant variables in the game. No-one can ever determine exactly what a pitch will 'do' until the first ball is bowled on it, and we have all seen experts do the pitch report and get it completely wrong. What is more, the captain who wins the toss has to decide whether to bat or field depending on the likely performance of the pitch, a decision that can also go horribly wrong if the pitch does not behave as anticipated. This is why it is considered so unsporting to sneak down to the grounds on the eve of a match and bowl a few balls on the competition pitch. In any case, the groundsperson responsible for nursing the pitch to match-readiness, and who will be anxiously running tests preparatory to the last few tweaks (which might include wetting, rolling and brushing before putting it to bed under covers) would almost certainly have stern words with anyone trying this.

Although experience in reading a pitch and the technical ability to adapt as quickly as possible to a specific pitch are paramount, it is worth gathering as much information as possible about the different components of a pitch and its outfield.

The pitch is the 22-yard (20,2-metre) strip with wickets at either end; the outfield refers to the rest of the ground on which the game is played. The latter is roughly oval or lozenge-shaped, and is circled by a boundary rope or marker. The east-west measurement (square of the wicket, in other words) must be a minimum of 140 yards (128 metres), and the north-south measurement needs to be at least 120 yards (109,72 metres) – hence the oval shape. No boundary may be shorter than 60 yards (54,86 metres), but there is no upper limit, although it is obviously not in the interests of the game to have an outfield much bigger than is stipulated in the Laws. But this explains why no two Test venues are exactly alike.

If one could look at a cross-section of a cricket field, it should look somewhat like an upside-down saucer; the pitch itself should be flat, but slightly proud (raised) above the rest of the field, which should slope away evenly. This is essential to allow rain and other moisture to run off the pitch. In other words, all bowlers run in to bowl at a very slight gradient. Of course, each ground varies slightly, with some requiring that the bowler run rather more uphill than others. Others have ends of differing gradients, some are bounded by rivers and estuaries, some are slightly tilted (Lords is famous for its slope – the north-west end of the ground is more than two metres higher than the south-east), and some even have permanent fielders in the shape of mature trees.

An ideal five-day pitch will start off firm, with a little moisture in the soil and even some grass on top, offering consistent and even bounce for the first few days, and pace for both bowler and batter. The outfield should be slightly spongy, to allow for fielders to slide and dive without injury, but should be smooth enough to allow the ball to travel across it at speed. On the second and third days, the pitch becomes quicker as it dries out, becoming ideal for batting. Towards the end of the third day, minute cracks in the pitch should be starting to widen as the pitch dries out, and a fourth- and fifth-day pitch is likely to be dusty and beginning to crumble, slowing the ball down and allowing spinners' deliveries to grip and deviate off the ground. Bounce will become uneven, and there will be scuffmarks made by the bowler's feet as he delivers the ball at either end of the crease. These too can be exploited by spinners, and present a danger to unwary batters.

But there are a thousand subtle variations on this basic theme. It should also be clear that pitches will be prepared differently for the multi-day and one-day forms of the game. (The ideal one-day pitch should resemble a five-day pitch on about the third day of a game – dry, but still lively, and offering even bounce.)

Among the most significant challenges that elite cricketers face is playing on the wide variety of pitches around the world. South African, Zimbabwean and Australian pitches are similarly constructed: they are made of a clay mix known as bulli, which is laid to a depth of anywhere between 300mm and 70mm over drainage layers of gravel and red soil. Test match venues require at least 250mm of bulli, but less is acceptable for club and junior cricket (the deeper the layer, the longer the pitch lasts). This is then usually planted with a hardy subtropical grass, sometimes the same species for both pitch and outfield, but more commonly two different kinds. The type is determined by ability to recover from damage (this is why different grasses are used for golf courses, where grasses sustain very little battering, cricket fields, where there is considerable wear on the grass, and race-courses, where the surfaces are regularly torn up) and the local conditions. For instance, some grasses thrive in coastal, salty or humid zones, but cannot tolerate frost; others are frost-resistant, but develop diseases in wet areas, and so on. In South Africa alone, Newlands in Cape Town experiences rain in winter, dry summers and no frost, while Kingsmead in Durban is hot, steamy

The ideal one-day pitch should resemble a five-day pitch on about the third day of a game – dry, but still lively, and offering even bounce.

and exposed to sea air and heavy summer rains. The Wanderers in Johannesburg meanwhile sees sharp frosts in winter and sudden thunderstorms in summer. Each of these micro-climates demands that different grasses, drainage systems, maintenance routines, cutters, rollers, fertilizers, herbicides and so on, be used. It is also because of all of these elements that a pitch can change from season to season. A cricketer may feel that he has the hang of a particular ground, then discover that the pitch has been relaid, or new turfs have been imported, or even a different watering regime has been used since the last time he played there. Now translate this to the worldwide arena, and one gets an inkling of the tremendous variations found in pitches around the globe – and the exceptional flexibility they demand of those who play on them.

Generally, the more clay in the pitch, and the more compacted the soil, the firmer, faster and bouncier it is, with the bounce tending to be even. This is why Australian and South African pitches tend to be so speedy. There is more sand and organic matter (and less moisture) in subcontinental pitches, which is why they tend to be slower and to crumble more easily, offering opportunities both to wristy batters who like to flick late cuts down to the boundary, and spinners, who want to see as much deviation as possible after pitching, and who like to exploit scuffmarks, dust patches and cracks for this purpose.

English and New Zealand pitches use various forms of winter grass (i.e., grass that remains green throughout winter), usually rye grass, which, together with cooler, wetter conditions, create the green wickets beloved of seam bowlers, and on less well-drained grounds, the 'sticky dog' wickets dreaded by batters.

The impact that pitches have on individual cricket innings is greatly underestimated: a score of 60 not out on a crumbling or sticky wicket is sometimes much harder to achieve than 150 on a fast, flat track. For instance, Rahul Dravid's unbeaten 27 against South Africa at Durban in 1996 was a titanic effort in light of India being dismissed for 66. Batting as he did for 120 minutes, with wickets falling constantly at the other end and the South African seam attack in brutal form on a lively track, was surely as impressive – at least mentally and technically – as a five-hour century ground out on a more placid surface.

Much of the technical advice given to players is actually as much about pitches as shots – as in the old saying 'Thou shalt not cut before July' (see p. 150), or even the adage that the first hour of any game belongs to the bowler. The

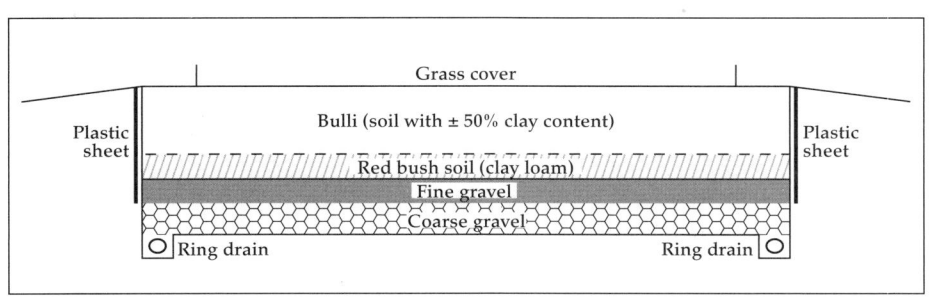

FIGURE 1.1: *Cross-section of a typical southern African/Australian top-level cricket pitch. Note the layering of bulli, red soil and gravel used in construction.*

latter is dominant at this stage of the game because the batter is at this stage trying to establish a strategy not only for playing the bowlers, but also the pitch, and he cannot do so until he has accumulated a certain amount of information about both.

This is why elite cricketers should learn as much as they can about pitches and outfields. For some, this is essential: coaches should definitely bone up on the subject, as should umpires, who are responsible for overseeing the maintenance of the pitch and outfield during the game. They are the ones who call for sawdust (to mop up moisture), chalk for redrawing creases and signal a halt in play and call for covers if it starts to rain. It is also their duty to establish whether a pitch is in sufficiently good condition to allow for safe play. Popular South African umpire Cyril Mitchley, now retired, said that the most difficult moment of his umpiring career was his decision to cancel a one-day international fixture in 1997 at Boland Park on match day, as the pitch did not meet the required standard.

Finally, it is clear that proper preparation of a grass pitch and outfield is labour-intensive, expensive, and requires specialist skills. As a poorly maintained and bumpy grass pitch is useless, if not downright dangerous for practice purposes, artificial pitches are popular, especially at junior and schools level, and in less well-resourced communities. These usually consist of concrete, although tar or compacted sand can also be used. Concrete-based pitches and nets are covered with cricket matting, usually made from polypropylene or polyethylene. Currently, jigsaw-type plastic mats are being

THE PITCH THAT KILLED A TEST MATCH

The opening Test between England and the West Indies at Sabina Park in Jamaica in 1998 became the first Test to be called off in 121 years because of the state of the pitch. After less than an hour's play, with England on 17 for 3, and the batters ducking and diving to avoid the balls deviating off the wide cracks in the pitch, officials decided to abandon the match. In only ten overs, the batters had been hit seven times. Commentators, sponsors and fans were understandably outraged that the pitch was in no condition for an international match. The players kept a diplomatic silence, but Michael Holding and Ian Botham (both of whom created a fair amount of mayhem themselves with bat and ball during the 1980s) used words like 'disgrace' and 'death-trap' to describe the pitch.

What was particularly distressing about this incident was that Sabina Park had an august history as a particularly fast track. It has been the scene for some of the world's most notable batting triumphs – the world's first Test triple century in 1930, Sir Garfield Sobers's record-breaking 365 not out against Pakistan (for 36 years the highest score by a batsman), and Lawrence Rowe's Test debut of 214 and 100 not out against New Zealand in 1972.

promoted, as these have the advantage that they can be removed, leaving the area free for other sports to be played. The problem here is that young players who grow accustomed to playing on these surfaces may struggle to adapt to grass pitches. Junior players who show promise should be enabled to play on grass from time to time.

UMPIRES

Umpires hold a strange place in the cricket pantheon. They have their quirks, they are sometimes suspected of bias (to the extent that neutral-country umpires are now required to stand in all international matches), they can be utterly, disastrously wrong – and yet their decision is law on whether a player is out or not. Their role underlines the fact that in almost no other sport can a player be ejected when he has committed no error – or spared when he is legitimately out. The spectacle of the umpire raising a finger is intrinsic to cricket: it means that there can be no argument, no appealing, not even a hint of dissent (cricketers can be fined if the match referee considers their disappointment to be so visible as to constitute a show of dissent).

One of the great pressures on the twenty-first century game is to replace or at least support umpires with increasingly sophisticated technological aids. We discuss these important developments, and their implications for umpiring and the future of the game in Chapter 11. There have been a few spectacularly bad umpiring decisions in recent years: during the 2006 England-Pakistan Test series, umpire Darrell Hair first docked runs from the Pakistani total for allegedly tampering with the ball, then announced that they had forfeited a game they were otherwise certain to win.

And at the 2007 Cricket World Cup final, with the result a foregone conclusion, the match officials and umpires forced players to return to a darkened, damp field they had abandoned because the ball was no longer visible. Here they were made to play out the final few overs of the game – a performance made meaningless by the fact that the dominant Australians agreed to use only slow bowlers, and the Sri Lankan batters promised not to try and chase the total. These and other debacles are likely to lead to stricter regulation of umpiring at first-class level.

AND THAT'S ASIDE FROM THE GAME ITSELF...

Aside from all these external factors, within the game itself, the multiplicity of variables continues:

- There is a wide variety of bowling forms, discussed in Chapter 5.
- The different types of bowling and different deliveries make up an even wider variety of bowling strategies, discussed in Chapter 7.
- The bounce of the ball off the pitch differs almost every time, even if only by a tiny fraction (see Chapters 4 and 5).
- The ball itself changes slowly but continually, as it becomes steadily more worn and misshapen as a result of repeated contact with the pitch, outfield and bat. Once the new ball is taken after 90 overs, the nature of the game will change once again.
- Adjustments need to be made according to whether batters (in particular) and bowlers are right- or left-handed. In almost no other sport does this have such an impact.
- From the perspective of the batter, there is a wide range of possible strokes to play, discussed in Chapter 3.
- There are also ongoing variables in field placings. It is impossible to protect the entire field against the batter, so these have to change constantly and strategically (see Chapter 7).
- Different forms of the game demand different approaches – strategies for one-day games differ markedly from those for multi-day matches (see Chapter 7).

LADY LUCK

Finally, in no other sport does luck play such a significant role – winning or losing the toss can significantly tilt the game towards one side, depending on the conditions. Rain interrupting play at a crucial stage of play, wind springing up to assist the drift of a spin bowler, dew slowing down the outfield, a strike bowler pulling up at the end of his follow-through with an injury, a batter assailed by cramp, a poor umpiring decision (or two or three), a delivery hitting a crack opening up on the pitch and deviating in a direction that the bowler didn't intend (or that ambushes the batter), the ball hitting the wicket-keeper's helmet and going for five byes, the rare occasions on which a ball grazes the stumps but the bails remain intact (a ball bowled at Pat Symcox when South Africa were touring Pakistan in 1998 went directly through his wicket, passing between two stumps – but neither bail was dislodged, so he remained not out) – the list of bad breaks and strokes of good fortune is endless. This is partly why cricket is a game that tests not only technical and athletic ability, but also character.

And perhaps this explains why old-school cricketers are so fond of quoting Rudyard Kipling's poem 'If', especially the lines 'If you can meet with Triumph and Disaster / And treat those two imposters just the same'!

CHAPTER TWO

THE MIND GAME

INTRODUCTION

Cricket is a game of pressure. The higher the level it is played at, the greater that pressure becomes. However, even an eight-year-old batter or bowler soon discovers the stresses and strains inherent in the game's one-on-one nature. A batter has a partner out in the middle, but when it matters he is entirely alone, facing eleven players all focused on his downfall. Knowing that he cannot afford to make a single mistake, the batter fights a battle that requires skill, concentration, insight and stamina.

Like most sports, cricket has developed a mythology of toughness, full of anecdotes about individuals pushed to the limits of their endurance. Think of tail-ender Brian Close putting his battered body on the line against a murderous Michael Holding in the gloom in 1976 at Old Trafford, where fading light and a pitch with a crumbling top made batting appallingly dangerous; Michael Gatting coming round after having his nose comprehensively broken by Malcolm Marshall and wanting to go back out to bat, too dazed to register that he had collapsed onto his stumps and was out; Dean Jones, vomiting and dehydrated under a punishing sun, being told by a spartan Allan Border that he'd drop him from the team if he didn't push on to a double century; Malcolm Marshall bowling out England with a broken left thumb. The showmen and cavaliers of cricket, men like David Gower and Shane Warne, are admired and adored; but it is the hard men, with their broken noses and wired jaws, who earn the instant respect of their public.

But celebrating the toughness of cricketers, and mythologizing the undeniable pressures of the game at international level, can result in a loss of perspective. This chapter provides an examination of the huge stresses to which players are exposed, but it is important to preface this with a qualification: cricket is a game; and if a game is not enjoyable, or produces more stress than enjoyment, then it is not worth playing.

Perhaps the best way to put cricket's mental pressures in perspective is to quote Keith Miller, the great Australian all-rounder. During the Second World War, Miller flew fighter-bombers for the Royal Air Force, daily risking his life in skies swarming with German Messerschmitt fighter aircraft. Upon his return to civilian life, his cricket career ignited the world's imagination, and his combat record was somewhat overshadowed by his dashing exploits on the field; but he never lost touch with the reality he had known during the war. Late in his life, he was asked in an interview how he had coped with the pressures of cricket. His famous reply serves as a salutary reality-check for those who believe that the cauldron of Test cricket is as difficult as life gets: 'Pressure is a Messerschmitt up your arse. Playing cricket is not pressure.'

This is not to deny that cricket can be extremely draining on the psyche, and the strain on Indian and Pakistani stars like Sachin Tendulkar and Mohammad Yousuf (who carry the hopes of millions of often volatile fans on their shoulders) is immense. But cricketers who talk about the professional game being hard work – implying that they deserve more credit for their labour than most – need to remember that cricket is not hard work. Drilling for eight hours a day two kilometres underground in a South African gold mine is hard work. Cricket is stressful, nerve-wracking, and mentally and physically exhausting; but it is always a pleasure.

CRICKET PSYCH 101

For years many cricketers were uneasy with the idea of the 'psychology' of the game, if not downright terrified by it. For them, it conjured up images of lying on a couch discussing loss of form with someone knowing nothing about the intricacies and subtleties of cricket. The myth in many cricket-playing countries is that 'real' men are always in control of their emotions, and have no need for any of that 'touchy-feely' stuff, let alone any kind of psychological analysis that might imply the opposite.

The sporting extension of this myth is that all sports are physical contests in which mental attributes are secondary. Therefore all the athlete and his or her coach need to do is to train the body, and the mind will somehow magically train itself. This is quite wrong. Although things are slowly beginning to change, until very recently little or no attention has been paid to this vital component of sporting success.

This is especially true of cricket, even though in this game psychological factors are extremely important, even crucial determinants of success. How else does one explain the inconsistent performances of some of the most uniquely gifted players in the history of the game, batsmen such as Daryll Cullinan, Michael Slater and Saeed Anwar? Conversely, how does one explain the consistency of players like Steve Waugh or Gary Kirsten, whom many would agree were not as technically gifted as some whose records are less impressive?

Clearly there is more to cricket than physical strength and technical ability. Once one lifts the lid on a cricketer's psychological state, one has the opportunity to learn about the game and those who play it best in an entirely new way.

Although the one-on-one element is present in many sports, and the combination of individual and team pressure can also be found in baseball, cricket is often played over several days, demanding special levels of concentration, determination and flexibility. A quick flip through a pile of cricketing biographies or autobiographies clearly shows that the nature of the game is such that players cycle from agony to ecstasy and back again on a regular basis. The greatest exponents of the game are anything but exempt from the dramatic swings of fortune that cricket exacts: if anything, it can be much harder to go through a long run drought if you are Brian Lara, or to lose the captaincy if you are Sachin Tendulkar, because everyone knows you have the talent to succeed. But the anguish (and the joy) are intense at even the most junior levels. Cricket is a game in which hope slowly dies, only to flare up again, only to be crushed again, only to bloom again…. And perhaps most baffling of all to non-cricketers, two teams can play their hearts out, with heroic performances by both sides, and the game can still end in a draw. Sometimes this is almost worse than losing, because it can render an extraordinary effort meaningless. It therefore takes

THE MIND/BODY DEBATE

In his book *The Zen of Cricket*, Tony Francis tackled the question that is often asked of top-flight athletes: how much of an athlete's success is based on his or her body, and how much relates to his or her mind?

'I became three times the player by getting my thinking right,' writes Francis. 'In my opinion, cricket at the professional level is played 90 per cent in the brain and 10 per cent with raw ability. Yet 100 per cent of players spend 100 per cent of their time practising the 10 per cent. Why?' (p. 93).

While no-one is advocating that you cut back drastically on your physical preparation, this is a salutary reminder that it is all too easy to overlook mental exercises – to neglect your brain.

a balanced disposition to be able to cope with the highs and lows, to enjoy the good times and to take the inevitable defeats with a philosophic attitude.

One concept the layperson – and the player suspicious of 'shrinks' – should understand is that good cricket psychology need not be mysterious. It falls into two categories: mental skills and psychosocial skills. Mental skills come into play during the game itself (and to a lesser degree, during practices), and can be incorporated as part of a player's game plan. These skills can be taught, practised and mastered just like any other skill: although some players are more naturally gifted in this department, everyone can develop mental skills if they are committed enough to put in the time and effort. Psychosocial skills come into play when the wider world impinges on the player. These will determine how he or she handles personal stress (such as family problems, for example) and unusual circumstances (such as touring).

The need for strong psychosocial skills is especially pertinent to elite players, who face unique and complex stresses: the pressures of touring, long spells away from home (often in foreign countries), being in the company of the same fifteen or so players continuously for months on end, continually disrupted routines and unfamiliar faces, the deteriorating relationship between players and the press (especially the tabloid elements), and the relentless glare of media publicity that blows small or even non-existent incidents out of all proportion.

Perhaps most dangerous of all is the 'rock star' syndrome, in which a player rockets to fame in a very short space of time. There is instant recognition by the public and media, at the same time that the player suddenly possesses more money than ever before, along with unprecedented numbers of 'groupies' throwing themselves at him. A young player, still trying to identify his role in the team and in society, can suddenly find himself facing a host of temptations, all in the glare of the spotlight, and with a voracious media waiting to tear him off the pedestal it has helped to build.

Of course, it is not just elite players who have to deal with pressures that are both everyday and unusual. Every cricketer is human, and faces day-to-day stresses that will shape his or her performance in the field. Whether it's a schoolboy worried about his parents' divorce or a club cricketer facing retrenchment at work, stress outside the game will always influence the way the player performs, not least because of the high level of concentration cricket demands.

This can be a blessing in disguise: those who are anxious or even miserable can sometimes lose themselves in a game, especially one in which they have the power or skills to make an impact. Unhappy people, who feel they have lost control of their lives, may find that cricket is the one aspect of their existence where they are still masters of their own destiny. Schoolteachers who coach junior teams will all be familiar with the boy who is shy, introverted, insecure, hesitant and not very good at his academic work, who suddenly turns into a calm, focused leader or dashing, skilful player on the cricket pitch. This aspect of escapism – the ability to leave behind the 'real' world with all its threatening and complicated problems – is one reason why players from disadvantaged backgrounds, whether inner cities, council estates or townships, can and do overcome the odds to perform at higher levels of the game.

Indeed, research by American sociologists has shown that inner-city teenagers in that country dream of escaping to a better life via two avenues: music and sport. Very similar patterns can be seen in most cricket-playing countries. The current decline of cricket in the West Indies has prompted some to suggest that more young players are leaving the Caribbean in search of non-sporting work in the United States, or else are turning to basketball as a potentially more lucrative option; but certainly in Asia and South Africa, the lure of professional cricket is a major motivating factor for millions of boys and young men (and increasingly, young women).

In short, it must be remembered that cricketers have always come from a vast medley of cultures, backgrounds and political mindsets. Considerable psychosocial skills, and no small amounts of common sense and sensitivity, are required by both players and coaches to overcome everyday hurdles. Just one or two questions, a telephone call and a friendly agreement could have averted one of the game's more telling incidents, in which the Sri Lankan team had to play a one-day international in South Africa on empty stomachs. Despite being told that the team comprised Buddhists (who were vegetarian), Hindus (to whom the cow is sacred) and Muslims (who could not touch pork), the national airline taking them to a day-night game served meat lunches on the flight, with no vegetarian substitutes on offer. The Sri Lankans endured this slight without complaint, but a less composed team – perhaps tired and hungry and at the end of a long tour – could easily have levelled ugly accusations at the host nation.

The brouhaha over the 2000 Carlton and United one-day triangular between Pakistan, India and Australia provides a good example of just how fast and furiously the mud can fly. The series came on the heels of two Test series in which hosts Australia had comprehensively beaten first Pakistan and then India. Both series were marred by some controversial (in a couple of cases, shockingly bad) decisions by Australian umpires against the visitors. Even the Australian public, usually quick to label grumbling tourists as excuse-makers, admitted that at times it seemed as if the home team had twelve members on the field: eleven players plus one umpire.

Matters were not helped by a sustained and poisonous sledging campaign by the Australians, which was seen as entirely unnecessary given that the home team was playing so well. But acrimony turned to rage when complaints about bias became accusations of racism. Suddenly the one-day series degenerated into a circus, with umpires defending themselves against charges of racism (they took the unprecedented step of releasing a statement denying racial or home-team bias). Much to their credit, no players from any team took their words off the field. However, the media, commentators, team managements and cricketing bodies of the three countries showed no such restraint, and the yelling took quite a while to die down.

This kind of situation can blow up as easily in one's own backyard as on international cricket tours, as seen by the furore caused in 1999 when, during a first-class game in South Africa, a white player thoughtlessly recommended bowling a 'coolie creeper' to a batsman of Indian descent. More recently, former Australian batsman Dean Jones was instantly fired from his commentating job for announcing, 'The terrorist's taken another wicket,' as South Africa's bearded Muslim batsman, Hashim Amla, held onto a sharp chance. Jones apologized profusely, and Amla was relaxed and gracious about the incident, but it provided a glimpse into the assumptions swirling around beneath the friendly camaraderie of cricketers. Ingrained prejudice will out, whether deliberate or not, and it can emerge anywhere, whether in a friendly or inter-schools game or a Test match.

Today's players and coaches therefore need special reserves of tact, sensitivity and diplomacy – psychosocial skills usually associated with considerable maturity. Players face more complex racial, cultural and religious situations than ever before. This can be bewildering, but unfortunately the old innocent attitude – 'We're just here to play cricket' – no longer cuts much ice, as Mike Gatting learnt the hard way during the last 'rebel' tour to apartheid South Africa by English players. Whether they like it or not, elite athletes are the ambassadors of the twenty-first century, and cricketers are not exempt. If anything, their burdens are heavier because their visits to foreign countries last much longer than those of most other sportsmen and women.

Sir Donald Bradman said that cricket was a metaphor for life, and he spoke the truth. Cricket is more than a straight bat or bowling a good line or length. It is played by people: complex individuals with unique psychological profiles and personal traits. Bradman and his contemporaries might have shown you the door if you had tried to talk to them about psychology, but they were no strangers to it. What we call psychological strengths and mental skills, they would have called common sense, tact, diplomacy, courage, cunning, and street smarts: all qualities our grandparents believed to be innate.

Changing times and new sensibilities have shown that in this regard, Bradman's generation might have been wrong: the apparently God-given qualities listed above can be learned and developed. Of course, some cricketers will never learn to be tactful, just as others will never learn to be sensible, but training goes a long way: South African international players tend to field more awkward questions than most,

What we call psychological strengths and mental skills, our grandparents would have called common sense, tact, diplomacy, courage, cunning, and street smarts.

THE MIND GAME   31

given that country's highly racialized past, and they usually do a creditable (if not always very articulate) job of answering difficult questions on sensitive topics.

There are also particular situations that coaches and players are likely to be confronted with that might not be unique to the game of cricket, but are particularly associated with sports and other performance-related activities. One is the problem of the gifted player who suffers from nerves to a crippling degree; another is the problem of 'pushy parents', who live vicariously through their children's sporting successes and subject them to unrealistic expectations and pressures. Young players who are gifted enough to play at elite level can also present special problems, as they are faced with the need for extreme discipline and an austere lifestyle at just the age where it is natural to start kicking over the traces. There is also a growing problem of burnout, whether it is the elite cricketer who is worn out with the county or international treadmill, or the star of the school team who is called upon over and over until he loses enthusiasm for the game.

If you as a player or coach take anything from this chapter, we hope it will be a heightened awareness of the value of psychology in cricket (and indeed in all sports), and a sense that understanding the inner workings of the mind of an athlete is not only a valuable process (rather than one to be treated with suspicion and derision): it is essential for those cricketers who want to reach the very highest level of the sport.

MENTAL TOUGHNESS

Successful cricketers are more psychologically complex than they might like to admit. Some elite cricketers minimize their performances throughout their career, insisting that their only role in the team is to do their job. A few gifted individuals flaunt their self-confidence, even coming across as arrogant, but most are modest, quick to give credit to their fellow players. Nevertheless, one psychological trait shared by all the great players is a palpable toughness.

Whether it is the refusal to be cowed by pain and intimidation, or the ability to remain focused and skilful under pressure, or simply being able to stay cheerful and optimistic throughout a long losing tour, mental toughness elevates those who have it above the rest. A hardened, highly trained mind does make the difference between the good and the great, especially in the furnace of international cricket. Australian fast bowler and quintessential 'hard man' Dennis Lillee, whose career spanned the years 1969 to 1984 (an exceptionally long time to keep bowling at top speed), was under no illusions as a young player about the nature of the conflict in which he found himself:

WHAT IS THE IDEAL MENTAL MAKEUP FOR PLAYING CRICKET?

Batters and bowlers are fundamentally different psychologically. The ideal batsman is patient, a stickler for detail in terms of his skills, and is only truly happy when batting: it's all he wants to do, all day, every day. The ideal bowler, on the other hand, is aggressive and stubborn. All the great bowlers have been supremely aggressive: whether fast like Dennis Lillee and Curtly Ambrose or slow like Shane Warne and Derek Underwood, they all wanted to get batsmen out, seeing bowling as a gladiatorial challenge. Batsmen can be just as aggressive – Ian Chappell was as confrontational as any paceman, sledging the bowlers regularly – but you have to have the skill and courage to back up your words: don't let your mouth write cheques your bat can't cash!

To succeed at the top level of any sport, you also need to be somewhat of a Jekyll and Hyde character, with two apparently opposite personalities. This is something encountered over and over again in international cricket: the affable, easy-going, soft-spoken bloke off the field who turns into an aggressive brute once he takes up bat or ball, almost maniacally intent on winning. The great player will never do anything devious to win, but within the laws of the game, he comes at the opposition extremely hard.

What you learn is that there are weak people and there are tough, strong people… [T]here are two games going on out there, a mind game as well as a physical game of cricket, and you must never let anyone dominate you. The tough survive and the weak do not. It was an interesting lesson to learn, especially at my young age' (Lillee and Harris, 2003, p. 30).

If mental toughness gives the individual the edge, then it gives the team as a whole an overwhelming advantage. Over decades, it has become abundantly clear that if two teams of equal physical and technical skill meet each other in ideal conditions, with a pitch that does not favour either side, it is the side that is mentally stronger that will prevail. This was never more evident than in the final of the 1999 Cricket World Cup: Pakistan, having swept through the tournament with a flurry of superb performances, collapsed in disarray against the Australians, who had scrambled doggedly to the final after some very ordinary performances in the preliminary rounds of the competition.

Lack of mental toughness can also be the underlying cause when a team lets victory slip from their grasp – for example, when they have the other side in disarray, but allow the tail to wag. In 1995 at Newlands in Cape Town, England found themselves being held up by a tenth-wicket pair of Dave Richardson and Paul Adams, a delay that was threatening to swing the match – and the still drawn series – back in South

HOW SANDY GORDON DEFINES MENTAL TOUGHNESS

Dr Sandy Gordon is probably the most respected cricket psychologist in the world today. Certainly he is the most prominent, having worked with and conducted research on the Australian, Sri Lankan and Indian teams, among others. His official title is a mouthful: Senior Lecturer in Sport and Exercise Psychology and Sport Sociology, at the School of Human Movement and Exercise Science at the University of Western Australia, Perth. This innovative department was one of the pioneer sports science faculties in Australia, and it is not entirely coincidental that Sandy Gordon's career here has overlapped with the Australian team's steady rise to world dominance in the last two decades or so. He cites his international colleagues Jones, Hanton and Connaughton in defining mental toughness as follows:

Having the *natural* or *developed* psychological edge that enables you to:
- *Generally*, cope better than your opponents with the many demands (competition, training, lifestyle) that sport places on a performer;
- *Specifically*, be more consistent and better than your opponents in remaining determined, focused, confident and in control under pressure.

Africa's favour. The teenaged Adams, a number 11 batsman through and through, should have been snuffed out in minutes. Instead, the capacity crowd were on their feet, relishing the sight of a pugnacious teenager with more courage than technique driving and deflecting paceman Devon Malcolm to distraction. The faster Malcolm bowled, the faster the ball went down the leg side or over the slips, and by the end of the afternoon, the pair had added 73 runs in 65 minutes, and England were a day away from losing the match and the series. A steelier bowler and captain might have slowed everything down, taken the pace off the ball, bowled straight, and stopped feeding the batsmen their favourite shots (the cut for Richardson, the leg-glance for Adams).

Some players have a natural affinity for mental toughness, but just like technique, it is something than can be learned and developed. Gary Kirsten, for example, insisted that he was not a natural cricketer, but through self-belief and determination (developed over years) he made himself invaluable to South Africa as an opening batsman – an extremely difficult role, and not one he had been groomed for in his early career.

One of cricket's recent myths, fuelled largely by Australian national pride, is that Australians are tougher – mentally and physically – than anyone else in the world. This is harmless wishful thinking (unless it begins to be clouded with pseudo-scientific theories on genetic superiority). The reality is that Australians are identical biologically and neurologically to their English counterparts, a group they traditionally consider to be weedy and complaining specimens; and yet twenty years of domination of England by Australia (interrupted briefly but spectacularly in 2005) provides overwhelming evidence of a different psychology, of dramatically heightened mental toughness. More specifically, it is evidence of a culture of toughness, passed down through generations of cricketers; in other words, of *learned* toughness. In the words of Sandy Gordon, 'While an inestimable amount of mental toughness is undoubtedly *caught* (socialized), some of it can also be *taught* (coached)' (2005, p. 5). In Australian cricket, it is clear that this toughness is both 'taught and caught'.

By the end of his career, Steve Waugh was the poster-boy for mental toughness in cricket. Regardless of their nationalities and allegiances, his contemporaries would always name him as the man they'd pick to bat for their lives. And when Waugh walked out to bat at number five or six for Australia, the apprehension of the opposition was often clearly visible, either as a tensing of the shoulders, or as a sudden flurry of field-setting and hand-clapping, as if it were the first morning of a Test, and Waugh an opening batsman. And in all the ways that mattered, he was: an immovable wall for the first hour of his innings, and then a rockfall once he had his eye in.

Waugh was a nervous starter: he wouldn't hook or pull, as a result often looking uncomfortable against the fastest bowlers. His strokeplay was businesslike. None of his shots looked pretty. And yet for long periods he was rated – officially and unofficially – above contemporaries Sachin Tendulkar and Brian Lara, two of the most elegant and naturally gifted batsmen the game has ever known.

Yet this was the batsman selected in mid-1980s as an all-rounder, a dashing and attacking player considered less technically sound – and much less gifted – than his twin brother Mark. The transformation from showman to bedrock of the team was extreme, and entirely self-wrought. Waugh was a self-made champion, who recognized that mental toughness could be learned. More than that, he learned to see discipline and toughness as not only a means to an end, but an end in itself. In the words of sportswriter Greg Baum, Waugh saw 'a well-executed defensive shot against a craftily delivered ball as a victory in itself, and something that could be even more demoralizing to a bowler than a boundary'.

TURNING CRITICISM INTO SUCCESS

Some players crumble in the face of criticism. Feeling that they are being unfairly persecuted, they become paranoid, aggressive and reckless, daring their coach or teammates to confront them so that they can fly off the handle all over again.

However, most international players have the strength of character, determination and ambition to turn criticism into success, no matter how hurt or angered they may

If two teams of equal physical and technical skill meet each other in ideal conditions, with a pitch that does not favour either side, it is the side that is mentally stronger that will prevail.

Adversity will bring out a player's true character. The weak will fold, and the strong will deliver.

feel. This is a special quality, a component of mental toughness that is not always recognized. If you can master it, whether through hard work or more easily by virtue of your personality, you are indeed fortunate.

Bob Woolmer recounted an incident during his tenure as coach of the South African side, when a gifted player turned failure, criticism and anger into spectacular success. On a 1999 tour of New Zealand shortly before the World Cup, there was political concern back in South Africa about the racial composition of the team, leading to instructions from cricket administrators that white players be dropped to make way for emerging black talent. This brought to a head a long-standing grievance on the part of gifted batsman Daryll Cullinan. Bob recalled: 'My relationship with Daryll was good at the time, despite the underlying tension dating back to the tour of Australia in 1997, when he had thought I had spoken inappropriately to the media about his difficulties with Shane Warne. Getting on in years, and with a history of being dropped whenever the team hit a rough patch, Daryll was understandably jumpy about the orders coming through the telephone from back home. He'd stroked a century in an early tour match, but his second dig – a scratchy 20-odd, devoid of his usual timing – happened to coincide exactly with the telephone debate. No doubt assuming he was going to be the sacrificial lamb, he sent a younger player to let me know he wanted to see me. What followed was a huge row, two hours of recrimination focusing mostly on those headlines back in Australia, and how I had no confidence in his batting. Of course nothing was further from the truth, but Daryll was incensed. We worked hard to thrash the matter out, but with the first Test looming, I was worried that his mental and emotional state might undermine his game. Five days later, Daryll broke Graeme Pollock's record for the highest Test score by a South African batsman, making 275. I couldn't help feeling that he had taken all the criticism he had soaked up over all the years, and focused it into one huge and resounding rebuttal.'

Cullinan's new record didn't stand for long: Gary Kirsten equalled it ten months later, in a marathon innings against England, and in 2003, Graeme Smith surpassed both men. But once again these extraordinary efforts weren't simply cavalier innings by men without a care in the world. Kirsten's place in the team was in serious jeopardy in 1999, with just 158 runs coming from his previous seven innings, and his painstaking, match-saving innings was the consummate reply to those calling for his head. Likewise Smith, barely in his twenties, had had to endure months of sniping in the media both by journalists and former players, who heaped scorn on his appointment as captain and called into question his batting technique. Big double-centuries at Edgbaston and Lords put an end to that. Smith had transformed negative energy into good, using the goading of his critics to fire him to great heights.

Media criticism and public disapproval are not the only factors a tough player can turn into sources of motivation. Sometimes there is nothing like a huge hostile crowd to challenge a cricketer. South African spinner Pat Symcox and Australia's Steve Waugh (who, after he had taken a controversial catch to dismiss Brian Lara during Australia's 1994 tour of the West Indies, walked out to howls of disapproval every time he played) were invariably pumped up in these circumstances, and relished confronting – and silencing – the crowd. Allan Donald's entire body language changed when he went onto the field; opening the bowling in front of 40 000 partisan spectators in Pakistan, for instance, the pace bowler became visibly more aggressive and charged-up. Later he revealed that he 'lived for moments like these'. Shane Warne, ever the psychological warrior, told his teammates that he considered the intense booing he received in South Africa in 1997 as a sign that the crowd loved him! While apparently contrary at first glance, this statement reveals Warne's insight: apart from pulling the rug out from under the South Africa fans (who were now, thanks to Warne's statement, unwillingly praising him every time they booed him), he had recognized that they loved to hate him, a token of real respect for his talent and the danger he posed to the home team's batsmen.

It would seem, therefore, that there is nothing like adversity to bring out a player's true character. The weak will fold, and the strong will deliver. However you respond to criticism, always remember: criticism is crucial for progress. But not everyone has the iron will to turn destructive criticism into success: if you criticize others, make sure it is constructive criticism: that it doesn't simply pose questions but also suggests answers.

BASIC MENTAL TECHNIQUES

There is more to cricket psychology than simply racking up life experience. The elements that make so many Westerners uncomfortable with psychology relate to the specific techniques often taught to athletes and other achievers to control nerves and heighten achievement. This collection of techniques is known by psychologists as Neuro-Linguistic Programming, and they can be used by anyone who has to perform in public on a regular basis, whether they are singers, athletes, lecturers or politicians. The techniques are not as esoteric and mysterious as the name may suggest, and while superstars may be able to afford to consult the kind of specialists who give training in this field, they are based on simple relaxation, breathing and visualization techniques. These are techniques any coach can teach and any player can master, and they are described in the pages that follow.

The resistance to these practices comes from cultural stereotyping, as well as the macho cult that often surrounds athletes. Many are suspicious of relaxation exercises because they associate them with hypnotism (itself a much misunderstood tool – see p. 45 for an account of how Wasim Akram's wife, a psychologist, would hypnotize him before key matches). Breathing techniques are mistrusted because the ill-informed associate them with yoga, meditation and Eastern or New Age religious practices. And visualization involves getting in touch with inner emotions – a notion that make some athletes feel uncomfortable. However, these fears and doubts simply reflect complete ignorance of what is involved, as well as unwarranted prejudices concerning unfamiliar cultural practices. Indeed, yoga is extremely useful to many cricketers, fast bowlers in particular, as it helps them maintain suppleness during the off season. Similarly, meditation does not mean that saffron robes and incense are obligatory; in fact, a growing body of medical research shows that meditation may have the capacity to lower both blood pressure and pulse rate, and to reduce stress significantly. In other words, anyone can benefit from the techniques involved and their physiological effects.

These three simple techniques – breathing, deep relaxation and visualization – are highly effective secret weapons for any athlete. They have been used by millions in Asia and elsewhere for thousands of years to heighten focus, concentration and clarity. Today's practitioners find that they relieve stress, control anxiety and nervousness, and can lift depression as well. Research shows that these techniques can cause changes in blood pressure, muscle temperature, heart and respiratory rates and in the electrical wave patterns of the brain. Moreover, it seems that they increase the time spent in delta-wave or deep sleep, thus guaranteeing more refreshing sleep. The following are basic introductions to these tools.

BREATHING CORRECTLY

This may seem ridiculous: surely we all know how to breathe? We do, but the reality is that most of us breathe less efficiently under stress or during exertion, heightening the effect of the stress. Breathing is one of the human physiological activities that while automatic, is also within our ability to control. Many automatic physiological responses, such as the speed at which our heart beats or our intestines digest food, are beyond our control. But the rate and depth of our breathing, even though it is involuntary, can be altered through conscious effort.

The ideal way to breathe involves belly-breathing or yoga breathing. When we are tense or short of breath, we tend to suck air into the upper part of the trunk, causing visible movement of the upper chest. However, this only partially fills the lungs, and we have to keep snatching quick, short breaths to get the required oxygen. Belly-

In many parts of the world, breathing techniques are a means of managing pain.

breathing, however, involves the diaphragm rather than the chest muscles. Try it by sitting or standing comfortably with one hand placed loosely on your stomach, over the navel. Now breathe in slowly through the nose, concentrating on sucking the air down into the lower part of the trunk. Your chest should remain almost motionless, but you should feel your belly push or balloon outwards as you inhale, and sink back as you exhale. Repeat it until you are certain you can differentiate between this and chest-breathing. If you are not sure, any singer or actor, or anyone who does yoga, will be able to show you the difference. Spend five or so minutes breathing like this several times a day. Breathe in and out slowly through the nose (as a variation, you might like to try breathing in through the nose and exhaling through the mouth). There is no need to take very deep breaths (this could make you dizzy); breathe normally, without forcing the pace.

Used before or during a match, this form of breathing is an effective way of containing and controlling anxiety or agitation: while it obviously won't alter the circumstances causing the stress, it will counter-balance the tendency to become anxious, which will affect your skills. It is also a good way to calm yourself and so prevent your heart and pulse rate from racing uncomfortably. Almost all performers will carry out some form of breathing exercise just before going out to face the crowds (in the case of singers, actors and professional public speakers, it's essential). For athletes, it is a valuable tool for managing the pre-performance jitters. It is also an extremely handy technique to use at the crease as a means of calming yourself and refocusing between balls.

If you're still sceptical, consider that in many parts of the world breathing techniques are a means of managing pain, and are taught as a major tool for coping with labour pains during natural childbirth. Still not convinced? Try this simple experiment. Lean over to touch your toes, taking the stretch to the maximum. Stop when the tension in your muscles borders on discomfort. After a few seconds, breathe in deeply through the nose right to the diaphragm. Now exhale slowly. As you do so, the tension will leave your muscles, enabling you to stretch a few centimetres further. If you repeat the exercise, your muscles will stretch even further. This lets you feel how correct breathing releases muscle tension. It should always be part of your stretching routine.

DEEP RELAXATION

Respected batsman and servant of cricket Colin Cowdrey, who captained England and Kent during the 1960s, once said that a batsman should be like a wrestler: quick on his feet, but with an upper body that is entirely relaxed until the moment of impact, allowing him to move quickly and decisively when he needs to. The more tense a wrestler is when he's attacked, the more slowly and clumsily he'll move; and the same applies to batsmen.

Of course, this is much more easily said than done: it's not easy to face a bowler like Dennis Lillee or Shoaib Ahktar without tensing up! However, staying loose against fast bowling is one of the best skills you can develop. Correct breathing techniques, described above, will help, and so will the ability to relax deeply off the field and control relaxation at will on the field.

One of the most basic methods of attaining deep and beneficial relaxation is to use what is called the progressive relaxation technique. There are several variations, but they follow the same general pattern. Progressive relaxation is particularly effective for those who struggle to sleep, especially before or during a match. Once you have mastered the skill, you might well be able to dispense with other aids to sleeping while on tour.

The method works as follows: first contract, then relax muscle groups throughout your body, working systematically through the entire body. The aim is to make you consciously aware of what the disparate sensations of tension and relaxation feel like, so that you can identify tension in any part of your body and deliberately relax it before it 'sets in' and gets a grip. All too often, we become aware of physical tension in our bodies only after discomfort sets in, and by then, our muscles are in knots, and it is much more difficult to relax them.

If you have mastered belly-breathing, then you are already halfway to mastering this technique. To practise it, find somewhere quiet and warm, ideally a carpeted bedroom with the curtains drawn. Switch off your phone and make sure you won't be interrupted. At first, try it out on the floor, not a bed. Lie down full-length, slipping a pillow under your knees to provide support for the lower back. You might also want to place a folded towel or flat pillow under your head.

Once you are lying comfortably and breathing correctly, begin by pointing the toes of your right foot and clenching that foot as hard as possible. Isolate and work only these parts of the body – no other part of your body should tense up. Concentrate especially on keeping the jaw and shoulders loose. After a few seconds, relax your toes and foot, and consciously feel the tension ebb away. Repeat the sequence. Now do exactly the same with the other foot. Now use this technique to work your way up the body, alternately tensing and then relaxing each major muscle group in turn, ending with the head and jaw. You should work the feet, calves, thighs, buttocks, stomach, lower back, chest, upper back, hands and arms, shoulders, neck and jaw. Keep checking that you are isolating the muscles, and focus on the sensations of tension and release. You can also reverse the sequence, moving from head to toe. Some find it easier to begin with the hands and arms: as long as you move sequentially through the entire body, and don't skip any sections, the order does not really matter. The whole process should not take more than 10 to 15 minutes. Next, allow yourself to relax completely for five minutes before getting up. Don't be surprised if you doze off.

Practise this at least twice a day. After an exercise session, you will find it a valuable adjunct to your stretching routine. The ideal time is just before you go to sleep. You will feel the results in a few weeks, but make sure you have mastered the technique before a match – it is unlikely to be much help if you try it for the first time at two in the morning before an important innings.

But apart from the physical benefits, do not underestimate the mental boost that physiological relaxation can bring. Mental fatigue and burnout are growing problems not just for cricketers, but for all athletes (not to mention many other professionals). Refreshing and resting the body can also help pre-empt mental staleness and tiredness.

When should cricketers use these strategies? If they seem strange at first, practise them in private at home, rather than testing them for the first time in a crowded dressing room just before going in to play. Visualization (see below) and relaxation strategies can be used the night before a game as part of the preparation process. Shortly before bedtime is a good time, but make sure you are not too exhausted. Once you feel comfortable with the deep breathing exercises, you might like to incorporate them into your warm-up and dressing-room routines.

As these tactics become second nature, you will be able to use them increasingly on the field – for example, as part of your set-up routine when you arrive at the crease. Visualization exercises that involve clearing the mind are particularly useful between deliveries, especially if there is quite a bit of action (catches being dropped, near run-outs, sledging). Peter Philpott refers to this process as 'thinking inside the circle' (banishing all distractions outside the circle); Bob Woolmer called it 'clearing the table': all the detritus of a dinner party is cleared away, leaving a white tablecloth; or else a clean white sheet blots out all distraction, the ball coming out of it clearly visible and ready to be hit (see p. 60 for more on Bob's visualization techniques).

VISUALIZATION

This builds on the breathing and relaxation skills already mastered, and is a key ingredient in Neuro-Linguistic Programming. Once you are breathing correctly and completely relaxed, you need to learn how to empty your mind. (You will immediately remember that you have urgent chores to do or phone calls to make, but persevere – distracting thoughts are normal when you first begin these exercises. If you really struggle to focus, you might want to ask an experienced person, such as a therapist or meditation coach to 'guide' you the first few times. However, the joy of this technique is that you can perform it alone, anywhere and anytime.) Some practitioners suggest you focus on the breath flowing in and out of your body, perhaps even visualizing it as a favourite colour.

Your next task is to recall a specific moment in your playing career when everything was going well: the first time you made a century or significant milestone, a day when your batting was smooth and fluent, a match in which the ball was leaving your hand perfectly, and swinging or spinning so viciously that you felt you could bowl all day; the afternoon you thumped the opposition's strike bowler back over his head for the winning runs; the hot morning you spun around to take an almost impossible catch at full lunge. Now try to recapture that moment in precise detail: what you were wearing, what ground you were at, what the weather was like, the smell of the grass, the expressions on the faces of your teammates, the sweet smack of the bat on ball, the elation of watching your leg-break drift, the sting of the catch on your palm, and the exact emotions you felt. Relive those feelings as intensely and accurately as possible, until the sensation of delight, success and skill is firmly imprinted in the forefront of your mind. Don't let modesty intrude: feel and believe in your brilliance at that moment. Relish the joy that the game can bring. Believe that you can do it all again, knowing how it feels. Try to pull this past moment into the present, so that the confidence it engenders spills over into your next performance. Once you feel confident and positive, slowly bring yourself back to the present moment, continuing to breathe slowly and deeply. The idea is to bring those positive feelings into the present moment, so that the memory of your past performance has an impact on your current performance.

This is obviously just one example of how using this kind of imagery works: players should be encouraged to develop their own mental pictures. This helps them mentally to rehearse their game in an optimistic and reinforcing way.

While acquiring this skill (and wearing down any instinctive resistance you might have to the process), you'll need to practise it at least twice a week. You could conjure up different memories each time: the more positive reinforcement, the better. Because the technique is fairly intense, once you have mastered it, it is best to save it for moments when it's really needed. It's a useful exercise for the night before an important innings or game, particularly for players struggling with fear of failure or loss of form. It puts them in touch with their talent and positive feelings about the game, and helps break the spiral of anxiety and gloom that invariably accompany a slump in performance.

It can also be extremely handy after a poor performance or disastrous mistake. We discuss some guidelines to preparing mentally for a game in the following sections, but there is almost nothing to offer the cricketer who has failed humiliatingly and publicly, or lost a match for his team through a crucial error. Truisms like 'it's only a game' (no matter how sensible) are unlikely to be of much comfort in circumstances like the time the Australian side had to prevent Pakistan from making one run off one remaining delivery to avoid losing a Test match, and wicket-keeper Ian Healy not only missed stumping Inzamam ul-Haq, but let the ball go through for four byes – a rare moment when the tough-as-nails Australian was seen in tears. And then there was the heartbreak for the South African team and their nation in the last over of *that* semi-final in the 1999 World Cup.[1]

We are hardly suggesting that imagining past glories is going to be a universal panacea in moments of such intense anguish; but as a technique to help recoup and get back out there to play the next game, it is certainly better than brooding over what might have been, or shuffling around apologizing to your teammates, haunted by guilt.

We fully understand that this technique will initially go against the grain of most cricketers, who often have it drummed into them from an early age that arrogance and big-headedness are cardinal sins. Unlike some athletes, cricketers are acutely aware that their successes are seldom entirely their own doing: bowlers in particular know that they rely on fielders for many of their wickets, and gifted batsmen know that a wily old hand playing the anchor role at the other end, or a brave tail-ender stubbornly sticking with them, is what makes so many of their centuries or match-winning performances possible. Nevertheless, the purpose of this exercise is not to brag to yourself, but to feel vividly the full extent of your talent and the possibilities it holds.

Visualization can include a secondary skill – that of autogenic phrase training. This is simpler than it sounds, although it takes practice. The athlete first has to master the technique of deep relaxation. Then, at a moment of intense visualization, he or she will repeat a certain affirming phrase (such as 'I'm going to take five wickets next time I bowl' or, less specifically, 'I feel confident and strong' or 'I'm going to help my team win'). Sports psychologists might also encourage their clients to repeat their chosen phrase last thing at night before a big game. The idea is to associate the phrase with your optimum state of deep concentration and readiness to play the game. Eventually, this can become a mantra you can recite (quietly!) in the dressing room or even on the field. Doubters should note that this technique has been shown

---

[1] Allan Donald says he got over the distress and embarrassment of his role in the final run-out that cost South Africa a place in the final by watching a replay over and over again on television until it no longer devastated him. Psychologists call this technique 'flooding'. It worked: he says that within a few months, he was able to 'laugh at the memory'.

to induce beneficial changes in muscle temperature, in heart and breathing rates, and in the brain's electrical activity (Noakes and Granger, 1995).

These techniques are excellent tools for anyone who needs to perform at consistently high levels. It is now time to turn our attention to the specific skills needed for cricket, and to focus on the mental components of the game itself, as well as those mental skills and stratagems that can be learnt and practised.

THE PSYCHOLOGY OF BATTING

Who'd be a batsman? Nine possible ways of being dismissed, no second chance, the stress of knowing that each ball could be your last and walking off on your tod stared at by everyone. Being out is so immediate, so final, like nothing else in sport, and yet batsmen have to suppress their exasperation for at least two minutes before letting it all hang out in the dressing room.

Simon Hughes, *A Lot of Hard Yakka*

As so neatly expressed by Hughes, the batsman's lot is such a tough one because there are no second chances: cricket is one of the few sports in the world today where just one mistake can mean that your effort is over. In other games, you can miss the goal, fail to convert a try, serve a double fault – and carry on playing. Cricket has the rare distinction of being a game where an umpire can send a player back to the dressing room, not for cheating or beating up another player, but for making a simple error. No quarter is given: you cannot ask for clemency while you are still getting your eye in and settling at the crease, you cannot plead poor light or the distraction of a plane flying overhead, and if you are a specialist tail-ender, you cannot ask the opposition's demon paceman (who is practically snorting and pawing at the crease in anticipation of your wicket) to give you a gentle ride. Even worse, you can – and, at least once a season, will – be dismissed through no fault of your own, but simply because the umpire makes an error.

Finally, to add insult to injury, at the elite level you cannot vent your frustration – whether caused by your failure, your over-zealous batting partner, or a trigger-happy umpire – without risking serious financial penalties. Any show of disappointment within range of the dozens of zoom-lenses around a Test venue will be beamed straight into the match referee's hutch, and from there straight into your bank balance. This is perhaps the one aspect of cricket that heavily discriminates against batsmen rather than bowlers: a bowler whose appeal is turned down can scowl, clutch his hair, rub his chin ruefully, perhaps collapse in a despairing heap on the pitch, and

PARTNERSHIPS WIN MATCHES: THE BOWLER AND THE PSYCHOLOGIST

Wasim Akram is one of only fourteen players in the world who has achieved the double of 2000 Test runs and 200 Test wickets; he is Pakistan's highest ever wicket-taker, and for six years he held the record for taking the most one-day international wickets. Of course, sheer talent and excellent mentoring accounted for much of his success – Imran Khan and Javad Miandad both groomed him for great things in his youth. However, for the latter half of his career, he had a secret weapon: his wife, Huma. A respected and sought-after psychologist and practitioner of Neuro-Linguistic Programming, she coached her husband in deep relaxation and visualization skills, even hypnotizing him before matches. In interviews with Helen Moffett, both described how this worked. Wasim explained, 'This is not like Paul McKenna does it! What she does is to put me to sleep for twenty minutes while she describes the sea. Even though I'm asleep, I can still hear her, and when I wake up, I am completely fresh again.' Huma described it more scientifically: 'The techniques I use – and anyone can benefit from them – enable him to experience deep relaxation and positive reinforcement at the same time.' In Wasim's autobiography, Huma goes into more detail:

> *Image-building and positive affirmations are the main part of my technique. They would be helpful to any sportsman and are quite simple to do. I reaffirm positives and eliminate all negative aspects. I'll ask Wasim to imagine a previous situation in a game where he's been successful, and suggest he incorporates that into the following day's play. Never talk about the opposition or your teammates…. Indirect hypnosis is all about encouragement; there's no compulsion – that's why it's best to use conciliatory terms like 'if you would like to'…. The best work I do with clients is when they're awake, relaxed and susceptible. The voice tone must be soft and even. It's good to insert pieces of factual information at times. So when Wasim has started to visualize a day when he has performed well, I can say, 'That was the day you took eight wickets.' Then I'll try to get him to explain his emotions that day, while underlining his success. The idea is to tap into that feeling of achievement and well-being so that he'll be able to channel those positive thoughts into the next day's play. A lot of golfers approach an important round in the same way (Akram and Murphy, 1998, pp. 175–76).*

To these techniques, Huma added autogenic phrase training, so that last thing at night, her husband would repeat 'I am the best bowler in the world' five times before dropping off to sleep. Many might find embracing this kind of self-belief difficult, especially in cultures that discourage arrogance or self-aggrandizement. Yet it gives extraordinarily talented players an extra edge – think of the apparently undentable self-confidence of players like Viv Richards and Shane Warne. Of course, this kind of mantra is no good if you're middling at best as a performer: Huma noted that she had the luxury of taking talent for granted in her most important client! Lesser players might prefer repeating a phrase like 'I am confident and relaxed' or 'I am well-prepared and strong'.

Failure in the game, especially for batsmen, is the norm and success the exception.

even gently challenge the umpire's decision. (He might just ask, 'Where was that one going, Ump?' but everyone on the field knows he's actually saying, 'You might have thought it was missing leg, you blind geriatric incompetent, but anyone with half a brain and a passing knowledge of the Laws of cricket could see it was hitting middle halfway up!') But a batsman need only loiter in his pitch a second too long after being dismissed, or raise his eyebrows in genuine surprise, or swish his bat at the ground in disgust, and he is pilloried. It is not surprising that bats and dressing-room furniture sometimes have to bear the brunt of all this pent-up rage….

FEAR: KNOW THE ENEMY

Being dismissed, in other words, is not pleasant. And as something that can happen at any time (either for a good reason or a vastly unfair one), ending both his participation in a match or perhaps even his career, it is feared by any sensible batsman. But failure is a complex concept, and can differ hugely from person to person: a score of 25 would have been a wretched failure for Sir Donald Bradman, but Australian strike bowler and rank tail-ender Glenn McGrath would be rather pleased with it. Indeed, even this example can be misleading, since a hard-fought and unbeaten 25 by a batsman in an innings of 80 all out can be seen as a (somewhat grim) success.

As failure is a personal idea, so too is fear, an emotion largely dependent on the batsman's own personal psychology and background: it is unwise to assume that all batsmen fear failure, as will be discussed shortly. Instead, it is important to understand the fears that crop up most commonly among batsmen, and to analyse those most appropriate either to yourself (as a batsman) or your players (as a coach).

1. Fear of failure

This is perhaps the most common way in which batters get themselves out: the fear that dogs every batsman on his journey out to the crease, whether niggling apprehension, or full-blown terror. It's a fear drummed into the players from early on, even by those who have overcome their fears and succeeded at the top level: Colin Cowdrey, former England captain, used to tell young players, 'The most important ball you'll face is the first ball. Why? Because it could be your last!' But that's bogeyman talk.

It is important to identify the specific bugbears that haunt individual players as they walk out. Each player's fear of failure can be exacerbated by different things. For some, a huge hostile crowd booing and throwing firecrackers can be completely demoralizing. For others, a certain kind of field-placing can get the butterflies fluttering. It is therefore important for every batsman to identify his own fears, so that he and his coach can work on them. For instance, is he unsettled by certain grounds or types of pitch? Are there any bowlers (either individuals or types, such as left-arm bowlers, or leg-spinners) he hates facing? Is he afraid of letting the side down? Has there been insufficient time to prepare for the innings? Has he left a favourite piece of equipment or a talisman behind? Is he distracted by family troubles back home?

Having identified these fears, coach and captain can address them accordingly and in a targeted way. Mike Brearley, arguably one of England's finest Test captains, noted that different folks need different strokes: all-rounder Ian Botham performed best when 'riled', so Brearley would try a bit of dressing-room teasing to get him going (even yelling insults when Botham was bowling innocuously). The immovable opening batsman Geoff Boycott, on the other hand, needed reassuring no matter how well he was playing. Graeme Pollock was another superb batsman who nevertheless appreciated being reminded that he was a fine player.

The way that the coach and captain (and other team members) handle failure by a batsman is also crucial, especially in the case of younger players. If a player has been dismissed for a low score or a duck and has trailed miserably back to the dressing room, the worst mistake the coach can make is to come down hard on him. There are some players who will immediately approach the coach and ask him to tell them where they went wrong, but many will need reassurance at this moment. If they've been dismissed by an unplayable ball, say so. If they lost their wicket making a mess of their shot, or falling into a bowler's trap, ask them where they think they went wrong, but not necessarily right away. It may be wise to save this kind of analysis for the next practice session. Bear in mind that cricket is such a high-skill activity, with such a small margin for error, that failure in the game, especially for batsmen, is the norm and success the exception.

Tactical responses to failure will also differ depending on the level of cricket being played. A schoolboy whose heart is really set on rugby, for example, might play deliberately casually or badly, and require some straight talk in response; and most youngsters or inexperienced players will need a diagnostic explanation of the reasons for their dismissal. At the first-class level, however, players do not actively try to fail, nor are they generally unaware of the mistakes that have led to their dismissal. Unless a player has been truly irresponsible, there is no point in criticizing a poor performance.

This does not mean that failures and shortcomings, even those that are apparently trivial, should be ignored. They should be carefully noted and the reasons why they happened discussed with the players, so that the necessary steps can be taken to reduce the likelihood that they will recur. In other words, the coach's response to poor performance should always be diagnostic. It is senseless to apportion blame to individuals in the heat of the moment, and coaches should make sure that other team members do not do this either.

In fact, negative criticism (especially if it does not offer any solutions) can cause fear of failure in an otherwise confident player. One of the reasons put forward for the consistently disappointing performance of the England team between 1995 and 2000 – a team which included lavishly talented players like Michael Atherton, Graham Thorpe, Graeme Hick and Devon Malcolm – was that they were regularly exposed to negative criticism, both by the English press and team management. Devon Malcolm is perhaps one of the saddest examples of a great talent wasted for lack of encouragement (the very opposite of encouragement, in fact) at critical times. Simon Hughes, former Middlesex bowler and cricket analyst, is in complete agreement: praising Mike Brearley's superb man-management, and his ability to make his teammates feel '10ft tall', he writes, 'Compare that with the treatment Devon Malcolm received from the England management in South Africa at the end of 1995. They shamelessly sniped at his technique, almost as if they suspected all the township adulation was going to his head and he needed taking down a peg.... No wonder he had a lousy tour' (*A Lot of Hard Yakka*, pp. 46–47).

Remember that the long-term strategy is to prevent one failure from becoming a string of failures (fear of failure becoming a self-fulfilling prophecy) and ultimately a loss of form. So if necessary, dole out a bit of comfort and chalk the whole thing up to experience. Even the world's most brilliant batsman has days when he will fail. The important thing is to learn from the experience, and not to be haunted by it in the next innings or match.

2. Fear of success

At first glance, this may seem a contradiction in terms. Like most athletes, cricketers are generally extremely competitive, and you would assume that winning is always their primary goal. However, this is not always the case: strangely enough, fear of success is sometimes closely related to fear of failure.

If you plot the career of most elite athletes on a graph, you will find that the initial curve towards success is a steep one. It is once they experience the rarefied air at the top that the curve reaches a plateau (if the player is lucky); but often it starts spiralling downwards. This is because success carries burdens: the burden of being the first, the best, and above all, the burden of the expectations of others, once a standard of consistent excellence has been set. The higher the expectations, the greater the pressure, and the greater the fear of failure. Sometimes failure, no matter how agonizing, is the devil you know.

Another psychological aspect to consider is that players may be reluctant to overtake or beat a favourite hero or sporting idol. Those who hold records are often revered national heroes: think of players like Graeme Pollock (the highest-

STEVE WAUGH AND THE FIVE LESSONS OF FAILURE

In December 1996, Steve Waugh revealed to cricket writer Greg Bauer the psychological strategies he had used to turn personal failure into triumph. The result of this conversation was a searching article, and one worth summarizing here for its insights into how the contributing factors of failure can be transformed into the stepping stones of success.

Bauer describes how after Waugh made a duck in the first innings of a Test against India in Delhi in October 1996, he went on to use all the errors he had made as the platform for his subsequent 67 not out (ground out over two days), no mean score on a traditionally tricky subcontinental wicket in the second innings.

After failing in the first innings, Waugh listed all his mistakes that went into his duck. The list was a catalogue of avoidable blunders: he had been watching the match on the television monitor, and had thus exaggerated to himself the dangers of the pitch (which was admittedly in a dreadful condition – umpire Peter Willey described it as the worst first-day pitch he'd encountered); he had been caught up in the noise and bustle of a dressing room full of visitors, instead of preparing mentally for what was to come; he had left behind the lucky red rag that he always liked to have in his pocket when batting; he had not formulated a strategy against India's spinners, who were making the most of a pitch that heavily favoured spin; and finally, he went out agitated, intimidated, and expecting to fail.

As a veteran campaigner, Waugh knew what steps to take after his first-innings failure. Rather than dreading his next innings, he put together a strategy for coping based on the advice of people he trusted and respected.

- That night, he phoned two people: first, his former captain and teammate, Allan Border, to ask for technical advice; and second, his wife, knowing she would give him the personal support and affirmation he needed.
- Waugh paid very careful attention to all the aspects of the Indian innings, carefully observing how the more successful of their batsmen managed to deal with the frightful pitch without losing their wickets.
- He gave himself a pep talk about over-reliance on his lucky red rag, telling himself, 'If I've got it, it's nice to have it here. But it's not going to play my shots for me.'
- On the day of his second innings, Waugh withdrew into a corner of the dressing room, and studied the field while perfecting the details of his plans for the bowlers, giving himself plenty of time and space to prepare for his turn at the crease.
- A vital part of Waugh's approach was not to allow the prospect of facing any bowler

to intimidate him. According to Bauer, Waugh said of Kumble, 'He's probably the best spinner in the world on that type of wicket [and yet] it was almost as if I wanted to get down [to] his end and face him.' He had a strategy for playing him all figured out, and was prepared to play a waiting game until he saw an opportunity to score. Waugh has described this as the most satisfying aspect of Test cricket: facing a really good bowler and taking the game to him. (He made headlines in South Africa during the Australians' 1997 tour when, after receiving a peppering from Allan Donald that left him black and blue, commentator Trevor Quirk made the mistake of offering him sympathy on national television. The answer was uncompromising: 'Don't feel sorry for me, mate. That's what I do and that's what I enjoy. That's Test cricket at its best.')

A logical and not particularly ground-breaking series of realizations and events, you might say. But in each of these lay the kernel of larger lessons, which Waugh was experienced enough to recognize, and adapt to his current situation. The lessons are worth learning:

LESSON NO. 1: NEVER BE TOO PROUD TO ASK FOR HELP.

We could add Lesson No. 1a to this: don't be afraid to look outside your own camp for help. Waugh found some useful ideas for playing leg-spinner Anil Kumble from an article in which South African captain Hansie Cronje described his team's strategy for playing Kumble's unique brand of fast, bouncy and barely deviating spin. It is also worth noting that a quiet chat with a supportive non-cricketing friend or relative – someone who believes in you, knows your strengths and can affirm them – can be a great psychological boost, even if they don't understand much about the cricket skills involved.

LESSON NO. 2: DON'T UNDERESTIMATE THE BENEFITS OF LEARNING FROM THE OTHER SIDE DURING THEIR INNINGS.

Waugh's careful observation of how the Indians were coping with the conditions paid dividends. All too often, when the opposing batsmen are getting on top of the situation, we see the fielding side's heads going down. They might be better occupied observing what it is that the successful batsmen are doing right, and planning their next innings accordingly.

LESSON NO. 3: USE GOOD-LUCK CHARMS AND PERSONAL RITUALS TO BRING YOURSELF UP, NOT DOWN.

An astonishing number of top cricketers are superstitious and cling to certain rituals before or during a match. During India's 1996/97 tour of South Africa, Sachin Tendulkar insisted on wearing a special set of pads, once owned by Sunil Gavaskar, regardless of their increasingly battered appearance. Viv Richards always insisted on leaving the dressing room and taking the field last when his side was fielding. Shane Warne believed that his lucky number was 23, and was greatly heartened at the least sign of it (such as on his hotel room door). The psychological benefit of lucky charms and special rituals can be great if they boost the confidence and comfort the player (or, as an added bonus, rattle the opposition); but their absence should not be allowed to make any difference.

LESSON NO. 4: FIND OUT WHAT WORKS FOR YOU IN THE DRESSING ROOM (OR ON THE BUS TO THE GROUNDS, IF YOU'RE AN OPENER) WHILE WAITING TO PLAY. THEN STICK TO IT.

Waugh had played enough cricket to know what worked for him, and by withdrawing into a corner to plan his strategies, he was retreating into a familiar and effective working space. Don't allow distractions if you know you need quiet. Don't brood if it makes you tense. If you know that you have done everything possible to prepare and you find that studying the game is making you more, not less nervous, then find something absorbing to do. (Other preparation methods are discussed in the rest of this chapter and in Chapter 7 on Strategy.)

LESSON NO. 5: RELISH THE CHALLENGE OF FACING A CLASS BOWLER.

Of course, this is easier said than done! Yet if the player, coach and captain have all done their job, no player should walk out to face a bowler without a strategy for playing him. And this means that the bowler is not testing you; you are testing yourself against that bowler. The distinction is a fine, but vital one. It means that in the final analysis, it is not the individual bowler that is causing the problem, but your approach to him.

This is closely related to perhaps the greatest hurdle of all: batsmen who put themselves under pressure. If they walk out to the crease intimidated by the way the game is going, the pitch, the bowler, and above all, believing that they will fail, they don't stand a chance. Waugh freely admits that he got himself out in the first innings against India because he put pressure on himself and went out expecting to fail. When preparing his gear for the second innings, however, he packed enough changes of clothing to last right through a day of batting – a symbolic way of indicating to himself that he believed that he would not go out, and would bat right through the innings.

scoring South African batsman until Daryll Cullinan overtook his record in 1999) or Sir Garfield Sobers, whose record for the highest ever score by a Test batsman stood for 36 years. When Brian Lara finally broke this record in 1984 at the Antigua Recreation Ground, his emotions were intensely mixed – he had dethroned a man he idolized.

Watching Gary Kirsten go out the very next ball after equalling Cullinan's record with the bat, one couldn't help wondering if fear of that lonely spot at the pinnacle, or reluctance to dislodge his friend and teammate from his position of glory, perhaps played a subconscious role in his 'soft' dismissal. By that stage of the innings, with the exhausted Kirsten having played through two days to reach his 275, English captain Nasser Hussain was lining up practically every member of his team to have a go at Kirsten, and the bowler who finally strangled him down the leg side was the part-time swing bowler Mark Butcher, certainly no demon with the ball. Both the bowler and Cullinan, who was watching from the balcony, looked considerably more distressed at the dismissal than the batsman!

And sometimes the price of success is too high. The only place to go after reaching the top is downwards. After coming from behind to win the 1992 World Cup, members of the Pakistan team at that time admit that after the initial joy and glory, they went through their worst patch of low morale and team in-fighting ever. Many players felt that they had now 'done their duty'; others felt that there was nowhere to go from that point. All struggled with feelings of flatness and staleness, in spite of the almost hysterical adulation that greeted them everywhere they went. They also responded badly to the expectations that they would now play like the world champions they were. Worst of all was the expectation that they would never lose another match. Logic flew out of the window, and their inevitable losses were seen as betrayal, lack of patriotism and worse: there was no longer any excuse for losing – they were the best in the world, weren't they? The penalties for losing matches thus increased massively: players had their relatives attacked, their houses stoned, and saw their effigies burnt. (This kind of response is by no means restricted to the Asian subcontinent: think of the hysteria and hanging of effigies after English player David Beckham was blamed for his country's exit from the 1998 football World Cup.)

The fact that the Pakistan team simply rolled over and played dead in the World Cup final against Australia in 1999 undoubtedly had its roots in the repercussions of their previous win. The Pakistan team is notoriously mercurial, and Australia were the better team on the day – they peaked at exactly the right time, whereas the Pakistan team had probably peaked a week too early. Nevertheless, with the exception of a few players, they did not even put up a fight. So-called 'choking' could perhaps be nothing more than fear of success. Although the prolonged doldrums in which the West Indian team has languished for the last decade stems from a variety of different causes, one could perhaps argue that one of these is the backlash of all those years in which they dominated, even terrorized, the rest of the cricketing world. Their problem is certainly not lack of talent, but lack of morale and application. Similarly, the Sri Lankan team also went through a spell of indifferent form after their 1996 World Cup win, and folded completely in 1999 under the pressure of being the ex-champions. It took them a decade to bounce back (after working with mental toughness expert Dr Sandy Gordon), and at the 2007 World Cup, theirs was the only team that presented any real challenge to the rampant Australians.

Therefore, coaches should not discount the possible negative repercussions of a win. The more exalted the win, the more likely it is that players will need to be carefully talked down from the heights. There is no doubt that the Pakistan team would have benefited from debriefing after their 1992 win, strange as it may seem.

3. Fear of physical injury

This is a very real fear, and a sensible one, too. Every year, serious injuries (and every few years, death) result from contact with a hard red leather ball travelling at speeds in excess of 140km per hour. Although the menace of the West Indies fast bowling 'pack' has diminished over the years, no-one will forget the 1970s and 80s, when going out to face Australians Jeff Thomson and Dennis Lillee or the West Indian quartet of Michael Holding, Malcolm Marshall, Andy Roberts and Joel Garner was like 'standing on the M1 at rush hour and trying to dodge the traffic' (Geoffrey Boycott's rendition of the ordeal). The feisty Allan Lamb spoke for many batsmen when, describing playing against the West Indies at the peak of their fast-bowling dominance, he said it was the only time in his cricketing life that he felt relieved to get out – alive. He claimed that many players believed that it was only a matter of time before the bullet that had your name on it found you.

Here modern players have an advantage over their predecessors in that protective equipment is being constantly updated and new devices developed. Better still, it is now regarded as sensible, rather than 'sissy' to take full advantage of whatever protective gear is available.

Watching footage of past matches, the modern viewer is appalled (but not unimpressed!) by the risks some players took. As recently as 1993, West Indian captain Richie Richardson took top marks for foolhardiness – and bravado – when he faced the pace attack of Wasim Akram and Waqar Younis on a badly prepared and extremely dangerous pitch in a game at Newlands, wearing nothing more in the way of armour than pads, a box, and a floppy hat. (This was the notorious one-day game in which almost more wickets fell than runs were made, and the groundsman responsible was ultimately sacked.) Allan Donald was another potentially lethal paceman Richardson went out to face sans helmet, much to the bowler's annoyance – he had to fight scruples about sending down bouncers. Donald describes how, when bowling to Sultan Zarawani of the United Arab Emirates in the 1996 World Cup, the latter flatly refused to wear a helmet, even though the opposing team begged him to do so. The result was inevitable: 'I bounced him, and he took it straight on the head. His hat fell off, his hair stood on end – I truly thought I'd killed him.'

Viv Richards was another player who refused to don a helmet, not even when notorious scalp-hunters were bowling, speed merchants like Dennis Lillee, Jeff Thomson, John Snow and Safraz Nawaz.

Today, such valour would be regarded as foolhardy. However, it seems that one of the ingredients that makes a good batsman is no small dose of courage, and fear of injury is perhaps more of a problem for the tail than for established batsmen. This makes perfect sense: if a bowler of the calibre of Makhaya Ntini or Matthew Hoggard gets hurt at the crease, the implications, both for them and their sides, are grave. On South Africa's 1998 tour of England, the host team's worst nightmare came true when a ball bowled by Allan Donald broke Darren Gough's finger at the crease, thus removing England's strike bowler from the attack for six weeks.

This is one of the reasons it remains important not to neglect batting skills (especially defensive skills) when coaching bowlers. Even if they will never be masters with the bat, feeling confident of a few good strokes can be an important part of their armoury as they go out to face an opposing bowler on the rampage. Indeed, an uncharacteristically good innings by a tail-ender can have a far-reaching psychological effect on the opposition: we have already mentioned Paul Adams' resistance against England in 1995, and perhaps no single stroke by a tail-ender resonated further than Matthew Hoggard's glorious cover drive for four off Brett Lee in the fourth Test at Trent Bridge in the 2005 Ashes series: the sight of a rank rabbit stroking probably the fastest bowler in the world to the fence provided an enormous boost to the already buoyant spirits of England.

An increasingly common variation on fear of injury seen today is not so much the fear that the bowler will detach one's head from the rest of one's body, but the fear of playing with a slight or suspected injury. The days when players like Kepler Wessels (South Africa's first post-apartheid captain) limped out to the crease, gritting their teeth against the pain of a chronic injury, are all but over. While some may mourn the demise of the heroism involved, from a medical point of view, it makes far more sense for an injured player to rest.

But what of those little niggles and aches? In today's world of professionalism and packages, with so much emphasis placed on the limited 'shelf-life' of cricketers, every professional athlete fears accidentally exacerbating a minor injury and ending up on the examining table, hearing the dreaded words, 'surgery or at least six months rest'. However, the lines between mind and body become very blurred at this stage. How can the coach, captain, team physiotherapist or even the player tell whether the alarm induced by that little twinge in the shoulder or hamstring is related to the fear of failure and a subsequent and submerged reluctance to play?

One strategy that might help to clear things up is to find out whether the player feels relief or disappointment at the thought of missing a few games while his injury is investigated. If he expresses frustration and disappointment, rest him. If he admits to a sense of relief, however, it might be worth digging a little deeper to find out what else is going on. Is he feeling mentally burnt out? Is he just not enjoying the game right now? Is the anxiety caused by his real or suspected injury casting a shadow over other aspects of his game? Is he worried about his place in the side? Troubles at home? And so on. Obviously, this should be done in a way that is non-threatening and doesn't put further pressure on the player.

4. Fear of loss of form

In many ways, this could be described as a more serious and complex version of fear of failure. It occurs after a batsman has already experienced one or more failures, and is gazing into the black pit of potential loss of form. If he has a vivid imagination, he already sees himself dropped from the side, perhaps losing sponsorship or earnings, disappointing his family and loved ones, and so on. If he is an international player, he will not be helped by the media, which will instantly label two consecutive low scores as 'a loss of form' and then trumpet this from the sports pages. (The relationship between elite players and the media is growing increasingly complex. As elements within the media grow rapacious for 'dirt', the once-friendly feelings that prevailed between the Press box and the dressing room are being replaced by increasing distrust and even hostility. We provide further discussion of how to handle media pressure later in this chapter.)

The tactics for combating fear of loss of form are similar to those for fighting fear of failure, but need to be applied persistently and over a period of time, if necessary. Sometimes, however, it might be best to take the pressure off a player by resting him for a game or two, or by letting him feel his way back in less high-profile or 'visible' matches. It's important to keep stressing the big picture: loss of form happens to every batsman at some stage of his career. It might be helpful to talk to, or study the tactics of batsmen who have bounced back after experiencing loss of form. For example, Gary Kirsten regularly cycled through nasty patches of single-digit scores followed by sublime spells of 50-plus scores during a distinguished career. He went through a spectacular slump in the first half of 1997, but came back to show excellent

Loss of form happens to every batsman: this too shall pass!

form in the second half of the same year, playing flawlessly in difficult conditions in Pakistan, where he joined the elite group of openers who have carried their bat through a completed innings. Early in 1998, he became the first South African batsman to achieve an average of over 50 for one-day-international games, no mean feat for someone the South African sports media had all but written off several months earlier. During England's Millennium tour of South Africa, the papers were at it again, speculating that he would be dropped after a lean spell, not yet having learnt that if Kirsten produced half a dozen low scores on the trot, the next century was on the horizon. He answered his critics in the most satisfactory way, grinding out the above-mentioned record-equalling 275.

What is important is to help a batsman understand that loss of form is not necessarily the end of the world. If this bogey is put into perspective before the player succumbs to his worst nightmare, it might even be possible to go back to normal before being sucked into a downward spiral of low scores and increasing despair. Remember the old saying: form is temporary, but class is permanent. Even if you are not a class act as a batsman, at least the first part still holds true: this too shall pass! Similarly, coaches should always encourage players who are experiencing a bad patch to see the bigger picture, reminding them of the talents that won them a berth in the side in the first place. Sometimes the right word of encouragement and a bit of perspective can help more than all the technical fine-tuning and fiddling that many desperate players (and their coaches) resort to.

Bad form comes to every batsman. Even the best and most consistent in the world have gone through long trots of standing rooted in the crease and hanging their bat out at everything outside the off-stump, or leaving a gap between bat and pad, or dragging cut-shots back onto their stumps. For gifted and experienced players, good technique comes automatically, so although a technical problem may prompt or exacerbate loss of form, the root cause is almost invariably mental. Many coaches can confirm that after a shocking performance in the middle, a struggling batsman's glaring technical faults evaporate the minute he enters the nets. Because batting especially is a reflex that occurs at a subconscious level, the more the mind tries to override those reflexes, the more likely it is that errors will develop. It is thus vital to help the failing batsman to correct the erroneous thinking patterns that have developed as the result of repeated failure. This is not to deny the need for constant vigilance and innovation on the technical side; rather to stress that a more holistic approach almost always pays off when addressing loss of form.

MENTAL STRATEGIES FOR BATTING

We have discussed the importance of players' psychology in understanding success and failure; we have introduced you to useful mental techniques for relaxing and focusing (which batsmen, bowlers and fielders can all use to great effect); and we have examined the chief fears inherent in batting, and how to come to terms with those fears.

But batting is not simply about coping, or trying to make the best of a difficult situation. Like everyday life, it is about much more than survival: it is about attacking, adapting, controlling and compromising. As a batsman you want to be able to cope with whatever is thrown at you, and to be mentally and emotionally prepared for all possible scenarios; but you also want to be in a position to start dictating terms, or imposing your own personality and psyche onto your innings and indeed the match.

The following strategies are therefore both mental tools and physical techniques that have a direct impact on your psychology, to allow you to transplant your mental preparation into the physical art of batting.

PREPARING FOR AN INNINGS

Mental preparation for batting is all about routine. Rituals, physical sensations (like hitting up in the nets) and emotional responses (nerves, excitement) should all be familiar, and as such, welcome and calming, a well-known sequence of events that give you the feeling of being guided towards your innings in a predictable way. Imagine an airliner on its final approach: the landmarks near the airport are its early familiar signs, a reassuring sight for the pilot. Then the lights on the runway straighten out into a strip, allowing him to go through the well-practised routine of straightening up the aircraft. Finally, once the wheels touch down, the familiar bumps and thumps, the routine of reversing thrust and applying the brakes, all come as second nature. The plane is safely down.

In many ways, your preparation routine represents the landmarks and runway lights: familiar moments and feelings that do as much subconsciously to get you 'down on the runway' – or well on the way to a big score – as you do consciously. So whatever your routine is, respect it. If it works for you, don't change it or try to adopt the routines of famous players just because they're successful.

Also don't underestimate the value of familiar physical sensations. Psyching yourself up is all very well, but nothing is quite as reassuring as the feeling of leather on willow, which is why virtually every Australian venue now has nets down outside the dressing room. Most elite players who are waiting to bat in a game will go down during lunch or a break in play and hit balls, just to get into the routine.

In fact, any activity that takes hand-eye co-ordination is a good idea before going out to bat: table-tennis, informal games of indoor tennis (make sure you can pay for any broken windows!), and bouncing a ball off a wall can all get your body and mind working in a way that will facilitate better batting. Stretching is also helpful, and a little jog around the dressing room won't hurt either. Even though you're not likely to be throwing yourself around at the crease in a way that makes a first-ball hamstring strain likely, rather be safe than sorry. Besides, in one-day cricket you'll be expected to sprint twos and threes from the outset.

Whatever you do, don't read before batting. Reading accustoms your eyes to moving left and right while focusing on a very short fixed distance, rather than focusing on random lengths between one and about 20 metres directly in front of you. To this end, a useful exercise is to glance up at a point 20 metres away, to condition your eyes to focusing quickly. Also try to watch an invisible ball as it comes towards you from that distance. If you do look at a book or magazine while waiting to bat, continually glance up from it to an object further away.

Many players develop routines over years, unconscious patterns that they follow year in and year out. But if you haven't – or you aren't aware that you have, and need further reassurance – consider turning your normal match preparation into a routine that can steady and focus you as you work through it. Check this ritual carefully for gaps; hone it and polish it. It can range from details as small as drinking no coffee the night before a game to a session of sophisticated analysis of video footage of the bowlers you will be facing the next day. Draw up a checklist, preferably with your coach, of the various aspects of preparation that you can pay attention to. These could include:

- **The likely state of the pitch,** what it might do over the next few days (if you are playing over several days), and what batting strategies are best for it.
- **The weather reports** (not just whether the match might get rained off, but wind speeds and directions, humidity levels, etc.).
- **The opposing side:** an analysis of their bowlers' strengths and weaknesses, and a game plan for playing each one (do not neglect the change bowlers by focusing only on the strike bowlers); and an analysis of their fielding side (how good are they? How fit? Who are the danger men, who is carrying an injury, who is left-handed? etc.).
- **The grounds:** are there practice facilities, and what standard are these? Is there anywhere to warm up? What are the dressing rooms like?
- **Refreshments:** check out the supply of foods and beverages that you consider essential. If you know that lunch is likely to be a lottery, make sure to pack

something nutritious that you enjoy. Take your own fruit, beverages, and favourite snacks if necessary.
- **Your gear: is it in perfect order?** Check your boots, bat and helmet especially carefully ahead of time. Make sure that everything you need is in your coffin, clean and tidy, so that there are no energy-sapping last-minute panics, and you don't have to borrow from your teammates or go out to bat looking a mess.
- **Team talks: are you alert, open and receptive to the guidance of your captain and coach?** Do you have sensible questions and suggestions? Or are you overawed or bored, having heard it all before? Try to cultivate a fresh, positive attitude, regardless of whether you are a newcomer or an old hand, and keep an open mind. Younger players will especially appreciate the input of more experienced players, who might have played these particular bowlers or on this pitch before.
- **Have you asked your family for support,** and are your personal affairs in order? Be sensible: the night before a big match is not the time to try and thrash out important family decisions, or to go out on an important or first-time date.
- **Have you packed something light and undemanding to keep you occupied** in case you spend all day in the dressing room waiting to play (or, alas, after you have played)? Remember that rain might hold up play, too. Books, magazines and cards are a good idea, or take a laptop and catch up on e-mails. An interesting point here: Bobby Simpson banned the use of personal stereos (Walkmans, in the pre-iPod era) by the Australian team in the pavilion during matches, as he felt it cut players off from each other, and alienated them from what was going on. This is a valuable hint: don't take anything into the dressing room that is more absorbing than the game.

The most important aspect of all this preparation is not to create extra stress or fuss, but to be pro-active in avoiding anxiety. If you are about to play an innings, you don't need surprises, especially not unpleasant ones, to disrupt your focus. Arriving at the grounds to discover that there is one cold shower for 22 players, for example, can be unnerving as well as irritating. You do not need the extra stress of discovering that you've brought the wrong pair of boots, or that you've forgotten to pack the snack bars you usually eat during breaks.

Once again, this all looks like common sense. Yet an amazing number of players, even at the elite level, skip practical elements of preparation, and go out to play feeling harassed, rushed and flustered. Poor preparation is not only likely to cause practical problems; it is an unnecessary drain on your mental resources.

Whatever you do, don't read just before going out to bat.

THE WOOLMER WAY: VISUALIZATION FOR BATTERS

As discussed earlier in this chapter, visualization can be a highly effective tool in centering yourself before an innings or match, or in putting you in a positive and confident frame of mind. But as part of your pre-innings routine, it can also serve another much more practical purpose: it can tighten up your technique, help you see the ball earlier and better, and get your shots working before you even set foot on the field.

It is a skill that you should practise in the nets first: it starts with 'clearing the table', wiping everything out of your mind and being left with only a large white tablecloth, hanging as if on a washing line. All your problems, worries, niggles and distractions are gone. All you see is a clean white expanse, a huge mental sightscreen. Now imagine the ball coming at you out of that sheet. Enlarge the ball with your mind; perhaps take it up to beach-ball size. Slow it down. The ball is the only thing in your mind. Watch and study its trajectory as it comes slowly towards you. Is it a leg-break, drifting into your pads and dropping at the last minute? Is it a fast outswinger, coming through flat and fast and ducking away late?

Now picture your shot. See how your body reacts to the delivery, the feet moving the hips and the hips moving the torso, the arms getting into position, the hands guiding the bat. Play the perfect shot to that delivery: remember, you have all the time in the world, and the ball is big enough to hit it wherever you want.

Once you've developed this technique for going into net sessions, take it into matches. The night before is often the best time for a good visualization exercise. If you're going to be facing a leg-spinner, see Shane Warne bowling at you, the ball drifting in, and react by watching with your mind's eye as you step inside it and hit it through the off side. If you're opening the batting, visualize how you leave the ball, sharply and smartly, and how you play straight, chasing nothing wide and cutting out all cross-bat shots. Now sleep on it.

The next day, while waiting to go out to bat, run through those images again. Now that you've seen what the ball is doing, adapt your mental pictures accordingly. If it's a low and slow wicket, close your eyes and see yourself stepping out to a flighted ball, timing your shot to perfection all the way back past the bowler. If it's fast and bouncy, imagine what it looks and feels like to step nimbly back and into line, feeling the ball thud sweetly into the meat of your bat at chest height.

Waiting to bat: dealing with nerves

Routine will put you in the right frame of mind, but it can also calm you when the butterflies are lifting off en masse. For instance, knowing that your kit is laid out exactly as you want it can go a surprisingly long way in making you feel potent and centred. This is especially important if the ball is moving around or batsmen are ducking and diving: normal big-match jitters can suddenly escalate as fear makes itself felt. Bob Woolmer remembered waiting to go in next against the West Indies in 1976: 'Holding and Roberts had just bounced Brian Close and John Edrich, and although it was a balmy 78 degrees outside, I remember that my hands were ice cold from fear – fear of failure and injury. I had to dispel that fear by knowing that I was prepared, that everything was in its place, and also by visualizing knocking the ball away off my chest and becoming angry with the bowler. The intensity of fear in the modern game is greatly reduced by padding and restrictions on bouncers, but in those days it was a matter of confrontation, and you had to bully yourself into winning.'

There's a dream that every batsman has had at some stage: a wicket falls, and you're stuck in the toilet, without your pads on, or else you're all kitted up but you can't find your gloves anywhere. This perennial nightmare serves one important function: it reminds the batter to be organized. And organized is something that describes almost all international players. Test teams never panic when a wicket falls. Indeed, unless the ball that claimed the wicket was phenomenal, or the pitch played some spiteful trick on the departing batsman, the rest of the players in the pavilion hardly react at all. Pakistan's Inzamam-ul-Haq was a fine example of this: he was entirely serene while waiting to bat, and when a wicket fell, he would assume a faintly resigned expression, get up, and walk out to do the business for his team. His serenity came from experience. International players have done this many hundreds of times before. They know what they need to do; and they know that although the first 20 minutes are likely to be rough, what follows will make it all worthwhile.

Which is not to deny that international batsmen get nervous: on the contrary, the stakes cannot be higher than they are in a Test or one-day final. It's knowing what to do with those nerves that sets elite players apart, and the familiar routines described above will feature prominently. In the South African dressing room in the 1990s, Daryll Cullinan ritually cleaned his bat; Allan Donald whitened his boots, regardless of whether they needed it. Other players prefer to follow the game as it unfolds. Jonty Rhodes found that following the game on the television monitor helped him to prepare both psychologically (getting his own mental state in order) and tactically (orienting his upcoming effort in relation to what his team needed him to do). Steve Waugh, as we have seen, shunned the TV monitor, instead preferring to watch the game 'live', carefully noting field positions and pitch conditions.

FORTY WINKS

There's being relaxed before an innings, and then there's Viv Richards. While most of his fellow batsmen tried to breathe deeply or jogged around the dressing room to shake off nerves, the West Indian great was more likely to be found catching some shut-eye: 'One of the great things about going to sleep before I batted was that I had a picture in my mind of what the opposition could do, and only the outgoing batsman could further influence me. What could be very unnerving would be watching a turning ball or a fast bowler going past the bat; from the pavilion it could look ten times as quick or be turning far too much. That's when it starts playing tricks with your mind. That was another reason why I preferred to sleep. It was never as hard out in the middle as it looked from the pavilion' (Richards and Harris, 2000, p. 116).

It is interesting that Richards mentions having a picture in his mind of what the opposition could do: he was, without engaging with any of the terminology, visualizing. Which brings us back to the usefulness of the mental strategies discussed earlier in this chapter. Indeed, sitting padded up in your chair is the time when relaxation and visualization techniques can really come into their own. Hopefully you will have done deep relaxation exercises the previous evening, and some visualization before falling asleep; but sitting on the players' balcony is the ideal time to shut your eyes, and once again go through the motions in your mind, or, like Richards, enter into a mental and visual simulation of what the opposition are likely to throw at you.

BUILDING AN INNINGS

You have now arrived at the crease, jogging and swinging your bat to warm up as much as you can before you face your first ball. Your mouth is dry and your pulse is racing, so make sure you follow a set pattern to steady your nerves: exchange a few words with your batting partner, take a long hard look at where the fielders are, give the wicket an exploratory prod (if for no other reason than just to slow things down and to work the tension out of your wrists and arms), take guard, and let the umpire know you're ready.

Having just taken a wicket, the bowler is pumped up, the slips are applauding and perhaps sledging you – the odds are entirely stacked against you. But this is normal, and should be of no concern: from a technical point of view you know exactly what to do next. It is the mental aspect of batting that now takes precedence, dragging you and your technique through those first torrid overs.

At this moment, your primary task is not to give your wicket away. Once you've seen off the first ball, you'll have a new job: not scoring runs. Indeed, your job description now demands that you not look for runs for the next ten or fifteen minutes, longer if you're playing a Test match. Be under no illusions about the fact that the bowler has the upper hand right now. Whether you respect his skill or not, at least respect his advantage for now: you can start your reply later.

In fact, if there is a good principle of batting, it is to respect the bowler at all times. Remember that no matter how many mistakes he makes, he will be allowed to continue playing (until his captain takes him off, anyway); whereas one mistake on your part, and you could be heading back to the pavilion. This goes for all the bowlers you will face; so often one sees a well-set batsman – who has resisted and survived a barrage from the strike bowlers – tamely surrender to a more innocuous change or part-time bowler. This is partly because the batsman's concentration is broken by the change, but also in part because he has made the mistake of relaxing his guard, and taking runs for granted.

Once again, in terms of mental strategy while batting, it is important to set up mini-rituals between deliveries, especially those that have turned you inside out, or struck you on the body. The minute the ball is no longer in play, some players like to walk down the wicket to chat briefly with their batting partner. This is both courteous and an important element of communicating ongoing strategy. It can also be helpful if you struggle with a sense of isolation, as it is a reminder that you are part of a team. It can also be a way of shrugging off the glare of the bowler or the catcalls of the close fielders.

Alternately, you can try the technique perfected by South Africans Gary Kirsten and Jacques Kallis, especially when they are playing themselves in: between deliveries, they walk away from the wicket for a few steps in the direction of square leg, isolating themselves from the ruckus all around, deliberately withholding eye-contact from members of the fielding side, gazing into space instead. Kallis in particular gives a convincing impression of total deafness – a tactic that invariably curbs the enthusiasm of zealous sledgers.

If you are struck by a ball and are shaken, avoid the bowler's eye – he does not need to see your consternation. Step away from the wicket, and try belly-breathing (see pp. 38–39 above) for a few seconds. Make a conscious effort to relax and congratulate yourself on still being at the wicket. If you have received a really nasty blow and are seeing stars, the bowler will probably dash down to check that he hasn't killed you, or the close fielders will help you to your feet. If it is simply a matter of excruciating pain, the unwritten rule is that you will be given a sip of water and a few minutes in which to recover. (If there is any chance that you have incurred an injury beyond bruising, the responsible medical official must come onto the field to check that you are fit to go on playing.) With all this going on, it is essential that you learn how to switch back into the zone of concentration before facing the next ball – it might be a good idea to revert to the rituals you use at the start of an innings. Bob Woolmer found that being struck by a

If there is a good principle of batting, it is to respect the bowler at all times.

delivery always made him intensely angry, an emotion he would control and channel into a brilliant answering shot as soon as the opportunity presented itself.

If you have just narrowly escaped trouble after playing a loose or risky shot, do not berate yourself; simply eliminate that shot from your repertoire for the time being (you can bet that the bowler will do his best to get you to repeat it, so don't give him the satisfaction). Whatever you choose to do, develop some small ritual that helps you regain composure and re-establish concentration whenever something happens to fluster you and break your focus – whether it is a near run-out, an unnerving bouncer, or the gut-wrenching wait while the third umpire considers whether to give you out or not. Remember that if you lose your concentration, your wicket won't be far behind. Take deep breaths, re-adjust your gloves, mutter a mantra to yourself, whatever it takes until you have cleared your mind and reminded yourself of your goal and strategies.

DANGER POINTS

At certain times batsmen are more vulnerable psychologically, and therefore more likely to lower their mental defences and make an innings-ending mistake. These moments – known as danger points – are usually caused by lowered intensity and a dip in concentration, usually when the game pauses, or distractions like time constraints and weather conditions start to intrude.

Drinks breaks and impending breaks in play are two of the most consistently detrimental danger points for batsmen. The former breaks the batsman's rhythm, forces him out of his 'bubble' or zone, while it gives bowlers a chance to recharge and rest tired legs. The latter is particularly hazardous: with just 15 minutes to bat or a few more overs to see off, batsmen stop playing each ball on merit, instead looking ahead to the break. Not only does this mindset undermine concentration and focus, but it can also change the way a batsman plays. With safety in sight, one of two things can happen to the batsman: either a nervous tightening up ('I can't lose my wicket now!') or an unravelling of technique coupled with uncharacteristically loose shots ('I've got this far without too many problems, and I could do with a couple more fours before I head in').

Over-confidence is always a threat, but it can be particularly damaging once you have reached your half-century. Indeed, a score of 60 or 70 is one of the most dangerous: you've found your rhythm, you're fully warmed up, your eye is in, you're not even hearing the sledging any more, so naturally you start thinking that you're in control. Two minutes later, when a wide half-volley comes your way, you feel confident enough to chase it, forgetting that it was precisely by leaving those types of deliveries that you reached 70. You nick off, and it's all over. Remember, just because you feel good, it doesn't mean that you'll magically be balanced or in

Bob Woolmer pulls one away to the boundary en route to a match-saving 120 against Australia in 1977's Jubilee Test at Lord's. Wicket-keeper Rod Marsh and slip Rick McCosker watch it fly.

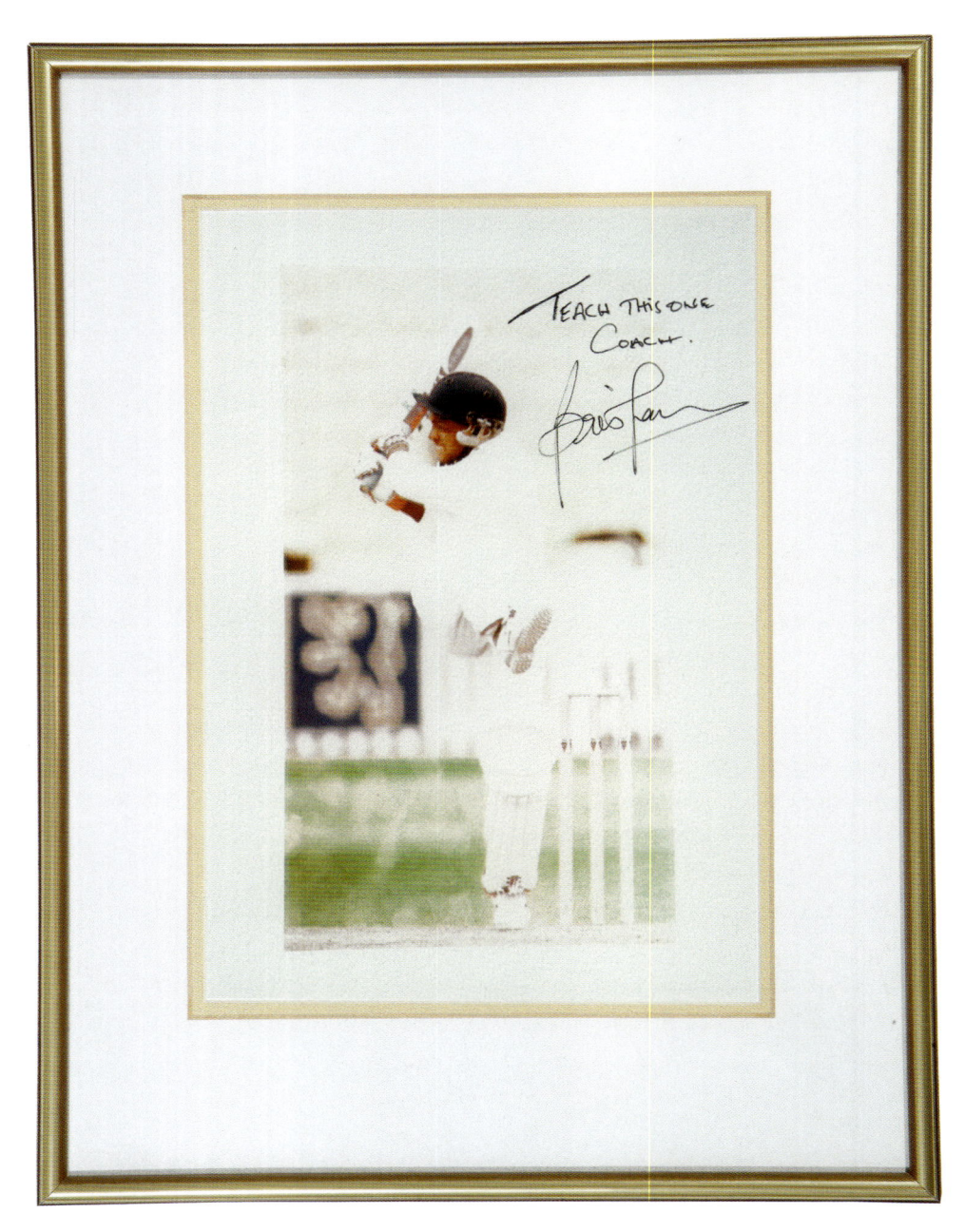

Teach this one, coach… Brian Lara in full flow for Warwickshire, where he was coached by Bob. This photograph, with cheeky autograph, hangs on the wall in the Woolmer's home in Cape Town.

position for a risky shot. A wide half-volley is just as dangerous when you're on 80 as when you're on 8.

In order to reach 70 (before nicking off!), you will have overcome another danger point, but many batsmen are not so lucky. The batting milestones – multiples of 50 – have tripped up almost every batsman in the history of the game, and these milestones are something you will need to learn how to manage. A disproportionate number of batsmen get out in the high 40s and 90s, or between 100 and 105; indeed, Australia's Michael Slater made something of a trademark out of being dismissed in a variety of heartbreaking ways in the mid- and high 90s.

Failing to pass a milestone – falling short – is the result of increased pressure, while getting out shortly after passing it is the result of suddenly released pressure. Both an increase in and release of pressure destroy concentration, as a barrage of non-cricketing thoughts suddenly intrude: what does this score mean for my career and my earnings, I hope my family is proud of me, and so on. If, like Slater, you specialize in getting out in the 90s or at other milestones, all the baggage of that record of failure begins pressing upon you. Scoring those three or four runs suddenly becomes the most difficult task in the world: the ball starts moving around like a boomerang, the opposition seems to have sixteen fielders, and you seem unable to move quickly enough, as if you're chest-deep in water. These feelings have nothing whatsoever to do with your fitness or technique: it is your mind – and only your mind – holding you back.

Different players have differing strategies for dealing with the pressure of milestones. Some, who have the talent and confidence, throw caution to the wind and attack – Sri Lanka's Sanath Jayasuriya has a penchant for reaching Test centuries with boundaries. (It should be said that Slater rarely went into his shell in the 90s, and had some of Jayasuriya's luck come his way, his career might have followed a different path.) However, walloping your way through the nervous 90s, or going from 88 to 100 Viv Richards-style with two powerful blows, is not necessarily a good tactic. Not only can this bring about your dismissal, but it may be difficult to regain your focus and start building from scratch once you have attained your century. Remember there is no shame in getting those last ten runs in singles.

The best approach is to wipe the slate clean after every delivery. If you're on 47 or 93, play exactly the way you did when you were on 12: play each ball on its merits, and forget it as soon as it's past. Precisely the same applies when you're on 104 or 210: the way you played on 12 must have had some merit (after all, it's got you this far), so why not stick to a winning formula? There is only one ball you need to worry about – the next one – and your score is completely irrelevant to how you deal with that delivery.

A wide half-volley is just as dangerous when you're on 80 as when you're on 8.

Nobel Peace Prize winner and great cricket fan, Archbishop Desmond Tutu once said, 'How do you eat an elephant? Mouthful by mouthful.' The same applies to batting. How do you safely navigate the approach to a milestone, and move serenely to the next one? Run by run.

SLEDGING

Some of the more practical psychological techniques for facing a good bowler are outlined in Chapter 7 in the discussion on batting strategy; but surely the most mentally taxing – or at least emotionally unsettling – thing you are likely to encounter at the crease is the practice of sledging. The term's origins are already being blurred by myth, but according to Ian Chappell, the word first cropped up as jargon in the mid-1960s in Adelaide, where players' efforts to chat up women were derided by their teammates as having all the subtlety of a sledge-hammer – the offending bloke was subsequently dubbed a 'Percy' or a 'Sledge', thanks to the soul singer's domination of the charts at that time with the song *When A Man Loves A Woman*.

Banter, good-natured ribbing and even fairly stringent verbal assaults have always been part of the game: players of past generations often relished dishing out some 'how's-your-father', and some of cricket's greatest witticisms have been born in the heat of verbal jousting. One of the most famous – and probably apocryphal – describes Viv Richards, then playing for Somerset, getting worked over by Glamorgan paceman Greg Thomas. Richards is supposed to have played and missed, upon which Thomas jeered, 'It's round and it's red, in case you were wondering.' A few balls later, Richards dispatched the bowler's delivery over the ropes and away into the stands. Chewing his gum nonchalantly, Richards strolled past the discomforted bowler, remarking, 'You know what it looks like. Now go and fetch it.'

But it was the Australians, first under Mark Taylor and then Steve Waugh, who developed sledging in its modern form. Termed 'mental disintegration' by Waugh, it was a deliberate and planned tactic of abusing an opposing batsman in whatever way was most likely to unsettle him. Often this was done in a fairly good-natured way. Kosie Venter, a particularly chubby Free State cricketer, was resolutely refusing to leave his crease when batting against Shane Warne in a tour match. 'Throw him a Mars Bar, Warnie!' suggested a helpful Australian fielder. 'Maybe he'll come down the pitch for that!' Likewise, Gary Kirsten was spotted chatting flirtatiously to a few of the Australian players' girlfriends on tour. The next time he walked out to bat, he was greeted as 'Tom Cruise'. And perhaps the most famous 'chirp' of all came from gritty Australian wicket-keeper Rod Marsh, who welcomed Ian Botham to the crease by asking, 'How's your wife and my kids?'

But sledging can be extremely hostile and psychologically disturbing: one devout

Christian had his religion attacked, while rumours abound that a batsman whose wife had recently died in an accident had comments flung at him about her. Australian captains and coaches have defended the tactic, claiming that it is a legitimate weapon as long as it's not taken too far, but the debate on sledging remains lively.

Which is not to say that Australians haven't been trumped at their own game from time to time. When Daryll Cullinan made his comeback against Australia after a long lay-off, he was met by an almost salivating Shane Warne – his nemesis in previous encounters. 'I've been waiting almost two years for this!' said Warne. Cullinan's reply: 'Looks like you spent them eating.' And perhaps one of the finest responses ever on a cricket field came from England batsman James Ormond. Walking out to the crease, he was greeted by Mark Waugh, who expressed the opinion that there was no way Ormond was good enough to play for England. 'Maybe not,' said Ormond, 'but at least I'm the best player in my family.' Ouch.

Whatever your personal opinion of the use of aggressive – and often foul – language, the fact is that sledging is here to stay, and players need to know how to deal with it.

As a rule, it's the batsmen who are on the receiving end: it's a very brave (or very foolhardy) batsman who dishes it out to the fielders or bowler. Some batsmen have done this – Ian Chappell being perhaps the most ferocious exponent of sledging from the crease – but invariably these have been players with the talent and mental toughness to get away with it. Sledging has one tactical purpose: to disrupt the concentration of the batsman, and to rile him into making a mistake.

Your response to sledging should depend on how easily it does or does not affect your focus. Temporary and selective deafness is an extremely useful tool. However, how you respond will depend largely on your personality: more pugnacious players relish a bit of banter between balls, and feel that the strutting involved keeps them on their toes. For example, it was a grave tactical error to sledge Steve Waugh: it just made him play better.

Generally, there are two golden rules that need to be observed regarding sledging:

- **Never – ever – dish it out if you can't take it.** Also remember that cricketers have long memories: a youthful outburst can come back to bite you a decade later.
- **Never get personal or ugly.** You can rattle a batsman's cage as effectively with good humour or sarcasm as you can by casting aspersions on his parentage.

Indeed, possibly the most effective type of sledging is never directed at the batsman, instead taking the form of banter between fielders (the case of Kosie Venter and his

A SIGN OF RESPECT?

Jonty Rhodes pointed out that the Australians he played against only sledged those batsmen they considered good players: in his mind, therefore, being sledged was a sign of respect. There is some logic to this: when bowlers and fielders have failed to conquer a batsman's technique, the last resort is to conquer his mind. In other words, the batsman who is being sledged may well have proved to be technically superior to the bowling on offer.

hard-spun Mars Bar is a good example). Talking about, rather than talking to, the batsman not only oozes contempt for his presence at the crease, but also constantly reminds him of his isolation. Some batsmen even start trying to engage fielders in conversation to alleviate this sense of being cut off, to which the most devastating response is either mild surprise – as if the fielders have just noticed the batsman's existence for the first time – or complete silence, in which he is entirely ignored.

As this shows, sledging can overstep the bounds very quickly and easily, and it is important for batters to understand that they don't have to endure verbal abuse that is particularly vicious or inappropriate. There are also certain tactics that are completely unacceptable. For example, no fielder should approach you in the middle between balls, or while you are changing sides, in order to hurl abuse at you. Similarly, no bowler should ever yell directly at you immediately after dismissing you, or make as if to chase you off the field, giving you a 'send-off'. Indeed, Shane Warne was heavily fined for his notorious outburst after dismissing one of cricket's great gentlemen, the South African opener Andrew Hudson.

If you feel that sledging is going too far, the best way to handle it without appearing a snitch or a whinger, is to approach the opposing team's captain and suggest that things are getting out of hand. If that doesn't work (or if he is the chief culprit – rare, but not unheard of), you will have no choice but to speak to the umpire. Vicious or intense sledging of very young or inexperienced players is not acceptable either: if the umpire doesn't look like intervening, the onus is on the more senior batsman at the crease to protest at the treatment being doled out to his partner. The corollary to this is that youngsters who are new to the team and still earning the respect of their peers should not try to impress with their wit and skill at sledging. Keep your mouth shut until you know your way round and have proved your worth with the bat or ball. Always bear in mind popular all-rounder Ravi Shastri's response to Australian twelfth man Mike Whitney, who was brutally sledging the Indian: 'If only you could bowl as well as you talk, you wouldn't be twelfth man!'

RACIST SLEDGING

We might all assume that racist sledging is utterly unacceptable – it has no place in the great game of cricket. It therefore came as a shock when a young Irish researcher discovered that 51% of cricketers in a survey that included 115 players claimed that they had noted a racist element in sledging, either occasionally or frequently (Johnston, 2003). When these findings were presented at the 2003 Congress of Science and Medicine in Cricket, they made headlines in the South African press. Of course, Dennis Lillee's penchant for referring to Bob Woolmer as 'yer Pommie bastard' might well be considered racist, but even so, these findings are sobering. All cricketers have a responsibility to make it crystal clear that racist sledging is intolerable, and should voice this opinion firmly and loudly should they encounter it.

Finally, remember that by far the best way to calm things down on the field is to apologize. It costs nothing, and earns the respect of your opponents.

THE PSYCHOLOGY OF BOWLING AND FIELDING

Most of what we have said about mental preparation for an innings applies to all cricketers. However, once they walk out onto the field, the emphasis shifts according to the differing roles of the players. The bowler's job is to take wickets, while the wicket-keeper and fielders must stop runs and catch anything that comes their way. Once again, assuming that technical, physical and strategic preparations are all in order, and every member of the fielding side has a plan in mind for each batsman, the question is: what mental strategies do the bowlers and fielders adopt?

Although their technical task is to take wickets and stop runs, their mental goal must be the domination of every batsman who steps onto 'their' field. Batsmen have to accept that there will be times when they must concede an advantage or give ground in order to survive. However, the bowlers and fielders can – and should – try to overpower the batsman at all times, whether by all-out attack, or frustrating defence.

BOWLING: THE MIND GAME

Bowlers' emotions are more clearly evident than any other player's, and most use this to their advantage by building up a ritual designed to 'psyche out' the batsman. We have all seen how bowlers who have nearly taken a wicket or tied a batsman up in knots let their opponent know how narrowly he has escaped, either verbally or through a most expressive gamut of facial expressions and body language. Some bowlers put a lot of effort into their post-delivery performance, whether it's shouting instructions to the fielders, appealing noisily, or cursing when a loose delivery is punished. All this sound and fury is likely to intimidate the batsman, especially if he is newly arrived at the crease. As we've said, it seems as if the bowler is in the driving seat – but is he?

Consider this: a batsman who is out of touch will usually be dispatched back to the pavilion in double quick time; but a struggling bowler has to finish his over, no matter what sort of punishment he is receiving or how many no-balls or wides he is spraying around. An out-of-form batsman's misery can be ended in a single delivery, but there is nowhere for a bowler to hide. Almost all bowlers' biographies and autobiographies describe the unique agonies of this kind of humiliation.

Simon Hughes describes the longest ever over as follows: 'An extraordinary disease suddenly afflicted Gladstone Small. In his third over he sent down eleven no-balls in addition to five legal ones and was in such a state by the end of it he opted to deliver the last off a three-pace run-up. It was a wide…. "Well, captain, you asked for three good overs to start with," the bowler said wryly afterwards, "so I gave you them all at once"' (*A Lot of Hard Yakka*, pp. 89–90).

Even if the suddenly incapable bowler's captain hastily takes him off, he has to hang about in the field knowing that he will be needed again, and wondering if he will once again perform poorly.

How then to respond if you have bowled a poor ball? For one, try not to stand around tearing your hair, or gazing sadly after the ball that the delighted batsman has drilled to the boundary. Instead, as soon as the ball is no longer in play, turn around and head back to your marker. A tiny but crucial psychological edge is gained when the batsman cannot see your face after he has played a good shot. Batsmen also point out that bowlers who get back to the job as briskly as possible do not allow the player at the crease as much time to recover and collect themselves before the next delivery. Of course, this is tricky if you are a speedster with a long run-up who also needs every second of recovery time between deliveries. But perhaps one useful mental trick here is that if you have bowled a bad ball, turn your back on the batsman as soon as possible. If you hang around grimacing and cursing, the batsman will have won that round in the ongoing psychological battle between the two of you.

Top bowlers have said that one mental strategy they find useful is a variation of the old trick of wiping the slate clean. Wasim Akram, known for being halfway back to his run-up mark by the time his previous ball had been collected by fielders, says, 'Once a ball has been played, that delivery is over. Banish it from your mind – there is nothing you can do about it. Focus purely on the next ball. Always think one ball ahead, never one ball behind.' So remind yourself of your strategy and stick to it – get right back to the game plan. Visualization can be as effective for bowlers as for batsmen.

Getting psyched

The psychological preparation for batting is, as we've described, a fairly complex ritual of relaxation, conditioning and focusing. Batting is a deft art, and concentration is paramount. Bowling on the other hand, is deft only up to a point. We don't want to libel any of the great fast bowlers, but bowling fast is to batting what sneezing is to singing: an explosive force of nature channelled along hopefully useful lines, rather than a neatly planned and executed series of movements.

Bowling is, in other words, violent, which batting is not. And as in most sports where players must perform acts of controlled violence (such as boxing, rugby and gridiron football), bowlers can benefit greatly from 'psyching themselves up' before they take the field.

One of the more extraordinary sights Helen Moffett witnessed (while in the players' pavilion during a one-day international between Sri Lanka and Pakistan) was Wasim Akram and Waqar Younis psyching themselves up in the break between innings: 'The Pakistani champions sat down for a cup of tea together in the pavilion, and proceeded to enter into a long but relaxed discussion on the pitch and various strategies for the batsmen. Over a period of about fifteen minutes, their conversation (now switched from English to Urdu) became increasingly animated and steadily louder. Their body language progressed from relaxed poses to increasing readiness for action, with much waving of arms. After a while, they leapt to their feet and began pacing the very limited floor space with increasing speed. They continued to gesture at the television monitor (which was playing highlights from the unimpressive Pakistan innings) and to raise their voices until they were shouting. It was clear that they were not arguing with each other, but hyping one another up to perform, and the effect was undeniably menacing – they seemed like two caged tigers, to the extent that those sitting nearby began shrinking down in their chairs.'

Shortly afterwards the Pakistan team went out to defend a mediocre total, and Wasim and Waqar duly ripped through the Sri Lankan top order with utmost venom and almost indecent speed. They took the first six wickets between them, leaving the spinners to mop up the rest. Sri Lanka were bowled out in the 36th over, a hundred runs short of their total, and Wasim was judged Man of the Match.

Of course, psyching oneself up to this pitch of intensity is not infallible, and it can never be a substitute for correct technique or talent. But it does point to an extremely important mental difference between batsmen and bowlers that both

'Once a ball has been played, that delivery is over. Banish it from your mind. Focus purely on the next ball. Always think one ball ahead, never one ball behind.' – Wasim Akram

IN THE GRIP OF THE YIPS

Scientists at the University of Sheffield undertook a detailed study of what is often called the 'yips' in bowlers. This is a term borrowed from golf, which they defined as involuntary movements that take place in the performance of fine motor skills – which promptly become not so fine. The 'yips' don't refer to indifferent or poor bowling, but rather to the apparently total and sudden loss of technical skill – as clearly happened to the unfortunate Gladstone Small in the 18-ball over described on p. 70. They concluded, to no-one's surprise, that this disruption of a learned skill has little to do with technique, and everything to do with the mind, and is a self-perpetuating problem – bowlers who experience it find their self-confidence severely undermined as a result. Rather than the frustration experienced by a bowler who has sent down a loose delivery, bowlers with the 'yips' describe feelings of intense embarrassment, shame and powerlessness. The authors of the study speculated that bowlers with the 'yips' were experiencing a severe form of 'choking', but acknowledged that they couldn't establish why the problem initially occurred (Bawden and Maynard, 2001). It would seem that this problem should be approached as a mental one. Further investigation into mental toughness training increasingly holds out hope to bowlers afflicted in this way.

should be aware of. At the beginning of a batsman's innings, adrenaline is his enemy – it can tempt him into rash and loose shots (it is later that it benefits the batsman, once his shots are flowing). However, at the beginning of the bowler's innings, adrenaline is his friend: it can give him that critical extra edge or 'killer instinct'.

As a bowler, learn how to make excitement work for you. The moment you are most likely to take a wicket is immediately after getting one: not only will you have a new batsman in your sights, you will still be experiencing the 'rush' and heightened physical sensations triggered by the previous wicket.

In fact, it is surprising that hat-tricks (taking three wickets with three successive balls) are not more common: no doubt this is because of the perception that they are extremely rare and difficult to achieve. However, in terms of the bowler's heightened psychological and physiological condition, and the advantage this gives him, they should happen more often than they do. Think of the bubbly Sri Lankan bowler Lasith Malinga, who burst into prominence when he took four wickets – three of them belonging to senior and established South African all-rounders – in four balls at the 2007 World Cup. At the time, the young fast bowler wasn't even aware that he was the first person in international cricketing history to achieve this feat. It is possible that his very freshness contributed to his extraordinary achievement, with no weight of expectation to trouble his mind.

Focus

As we have already explained, batters and bowlers need to concentrate in different patterns – the batsman switches on and off during his entire innings, to preserve his most intense focus for when he faces a delivery. A bowler focuses throughout his entire over; even as he marches back to his mark, he is continually assessing the conditions, the plans he has for the batters in the middle, the kind of field he wants, and more. However, even here there are subtle gradations in his concentration.

One of the best coaching manuals ever written, Peter Philpott's *The Art of Wrist-Spin Bowling*, represents one of the first efforts by a bowler to explain the 'mind game' of bowling, and his chapter 'Mind and Body' remains required reading for all interested in this aspect of the game. Philpott advises bowlers, once they have chosen their delivery, to clear their minds of everything except 'what you want to bowl and where you want to bowl it' (p. 88). It sounds so simple, but it takes what he calls 'close focus', as well as the ability to ratchet levels of concentration up and down the scale: 'As we steady ourselves before delivery, we begin to concentrate fully, doing so through approach, delivery, follow-through and the play that follows. Then when the ball is dead, we relax partially, and walk back whilst reviewing the last ball, the overall plan and the next ball. Back to the mark, steady yourself, make your decision on your next ball, then concentrate totally. At the end of the over, we relax [and] turn our concentration powers totally onto our fielding duties. But, between each ball, we switch to a brief semi-relaxation.'

Philpott goes on to note not only that sustained concentration is demanded by cricket like no other game; he points out the corollary – that to sustain such concentration requires 'the ability to relax and switch rapidly from concentration to relaxation and back. You will need to develop both skills as a [bowler]. Practise them like any other skills' (p. 89).

Philpott, himself drawing on the wisdom of the Australian swing bowler Bob Massie, suggested a useful technique for working on the 'close focus' needed for bowling, which he called 'the Circle of Concentration' (see Figure 2.1). It's very simple: 'Draw a circle and inside it write down all the things over which you have control when you are bowling. These are the only things you should think about. Now write down all the other things a bowler often thinks about as he is bowling. Put them inside the circle if he has control over them, outside if he has no control. [This circle] emphasizes once again that the core of successful concentration is to home in on those things over which you have control, and to eliminate from your thinking anything over which you do not have control' (pp. 92–93).

You will of course recognize the similarity of this mental technique to the white sheet or tablecloth visualized by batters – all of which point to the importance of ruthlessly eliminating every kind of distraction in order to maintain optimum focus and concentration.

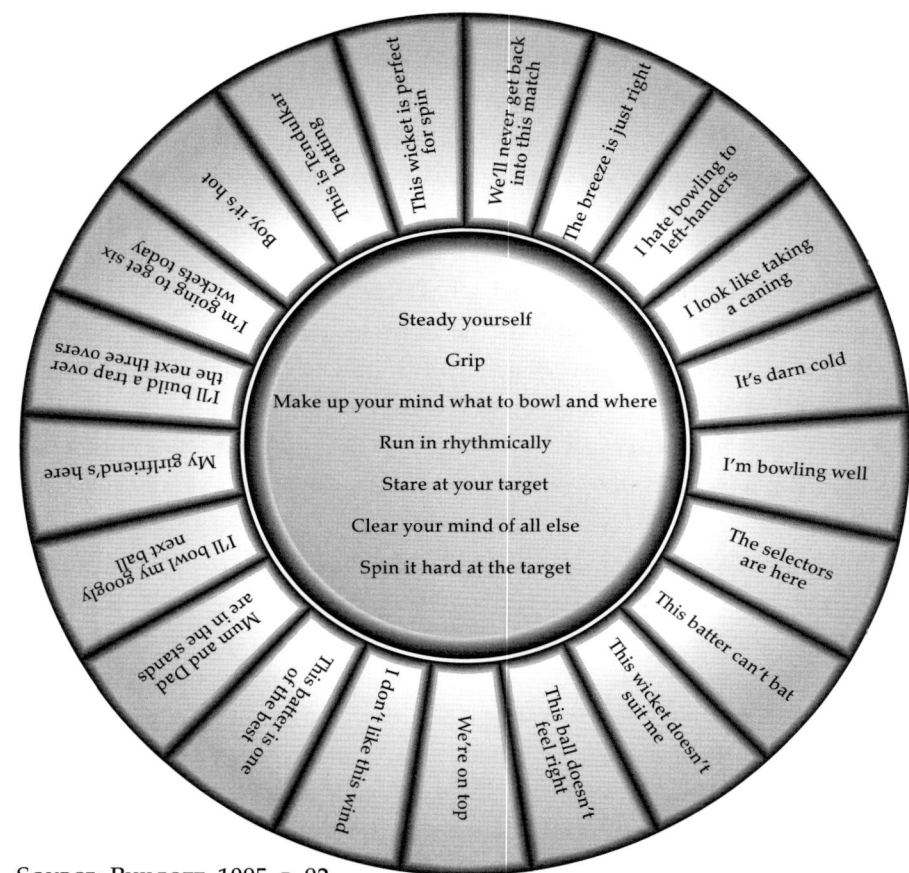

Inside the circle:
Steady yourself
Grip
Make up your mind what to bowl and where
Run in rhythmically
Stare at your target
Clear your mind of all else
Spin it hard at the target

Outside the circle (distractions): This wicket is perfect for spin; We'll never get back into this match; The breeze is just right; I hate bowling to left-handers; I look like taking a caning; It's darn cold; I'm bowling well; The selectors are here; This batter can't bat; This wicket doesn't suit me; This ball doesn't feel right; We're on top; I don't like this wind; This batter is one of the best; Mum and Dad are in the stands; I'll bowl my googly next ball; My girlfriend's here; I'll build a trap over the next three overs; I'm going to get six wickets today; Boy, it's hot; This is Tendulkar batting.

SOURCE: PHILPOTT, 1995, P. 92
FIGURE 2.1: *Peter Philpott's Circle of Concentration – think inside it, not outside!*

Staying in the game

Every bowler, even Gladstone Small on the grim day described above, finishes his spell at some stage. If he's lucky, or a confidant of the captain, he might get moved to cover or mid-on; but if he's like the vast majority of bowlers, he'll be exiled to the outfield, either somewhere on the square boundaries or at fine leg. Thus banished, it is very easy for a bowler to start drifting mentally: he's tired, the day is hot, and he's miles from action, with his next spell an hour away. So how does the bowler stay focused?

The answer lies in the ability to switch on and off (or to scale focus up and down, as described by Peter Philpott above). Batsmen need to switch off after each delivery, to walk away and rest, before switching on again. For them this happens with every ball they face; but bowlers need to be in the zone, switched on, throughout their spell. However, when you're done and you're loitering at fine leg, you need to switch off. This doesn't mean a blank or zombie-like state: too many bowlers switch off completely, gazing off into the distance as catches plop down a few yards from where they've been daydreaming. Strive for a passive alertness: don't live the game through the bowler who's currently bowling, but don't drift away either. Instead, think about your tactics, or how to work out a particular batsman, while you get your breath back and rebuild your energy for your next spell.

FIELDING: COPING WITH FAILURE

It happens to every cricketer at some stage: the critical catch dropped, the ball sneaking through the fingers or bobbling over the leg to cross the boundary rope. Everyone knows that 'catches win matches', and if the game is subsequently lost – or it is your error that loses the match – it can be very difficult not to blame yourself. All too often, the fielder goes out to his next game or session of play feeling guilty and demoralized.

A little perspective may help here. As any doctor will tell you, when a patient dies as the result of medical errors, there is almost never one single error that determines the result. Rather, it is the progressive accumulation of many small errors that ultimately tips the balance in the favour of death. When a match is lost, the same principle applies. Even if you let the winning runs or byes slip through your desperately grabbing hands, the truth is that if the batters on your team had posted a higher total in their innings, these would not be the winning runs. Chris Scott, the Durham wicket-keeper who dropped Brian Lara on 18 at Edgbaston in 1994, no doubt felt increasingly wretched as the West Indian maestro marched on to 501 not out, but the massive score was not his fault: the bowlers had something to do with it too!

So instead of retreating into your shell when you make a serious error in the field, remind yourself that a single exceptional performance by any member of the team can still win the game for your side. Try to be that player, rather than sinking into gloom and self-doubt.

Once again, the response of the captain, coach or senior players is vital. The captain in particular should take immediate action if the offending player is visibly distressed or withdrawing into himself, particularly if the bowler has been unable to contain his anguish or wrath: a comforting pat usually speaks volumes, or a few brisk and positive words: 'You'll catch the next one.' If the bowler has vented his spleen, he should offer a few words of apology once he has calmed down – although not all are this generous-minded. If the culprit is inexperienced or a newcomer, a senior player might offer something like 'It happens to all of us' or 'Welcome to the club.' Other players will usually take their lead from the coach and captain: if the coach is dancing a jig of fury on the balcony, and the captain is looking daggers, the rest of the team will follow suit. So try to cultivate a look of sunny unconcern, or an expressive shrug. Sometimes the best medicine can be gallows humour: a captain who manages to turn disaster into a joke ('I see you're lulling them into a false sense of security!') is more likely to keep the mood of the team upbeat.

As with any failure, diagnosis is valuable; blame is not. Criticizing individual players is valid only if their error was the result of lack of commitment or gross carelessness. If either the coach or the player feel that extra catching or fielding practice is necessary, especially if players are unused to fielding on the current surface, then by all means tackle the problem. The key is to be constructive, never destructive.

PSYCHOSOCIAL SKILLS

The nature of cricket is such that it tears at the nerves of all participants.

David Frith, By His Own Hand

As explained at the beginning of this chapter, the elite or professional cricketer needs more than mental skills to handle the peculiar stresses of the modern game. Of course, as we have also discussed, what we might call psychosocial skills, an earlier generation of players would call common sense – or at most, 'life skills'. Certainly tact, flexibility, honour, a sense of humour, patience, an ability to see the big picture – all these components of what might also be called 'emotional intelligence' – will be of immense help to the cricketer, especially one playing at higher levels of the game. Many great cricketers and cricket lovers have commented on how cricket prepares one for life; and as the British humorist Jilly Cooper pointed out (perhaps rather idealistically), 'Cricketers are often patient, kind, loyal and long-suffering – great husband material.'

Many cricketing wives might disagree strenuously with her, but there is no doubt that cricket offers more than the usual challenges of sport, as well as several that are unique to the game. If these challenges are successfully overcome, such experiences can stand players in excellent stead in all aspects of their lives, including their families and their non-cricketing careers.

Here we focus on specific problems that, while not unique to cricket, present perplexing problems to elite cricketers in particular.

EMOTIONAL FATIGUE

We have already mentioned burnout, or emotional fatigue, a problem that has at times stumped even players of the calibre of Sir Donald Bradman, who once felt so worn down by the demands and dreams of a nation that he seriously considered chucking in his cricketing career. But it's not only the great and the good that suffer: the star junior bowler or batsman who is trundled out at every turn, and repeatedly expected to win the match, will eventually feel jaded and resentful. During some of Brian Lara's slumps in form, it was clear from his body language as he trudged out to the wicket that he resented feeling pressure to win matches all on his own.

However, even if each player takes responsibility for the success of the team, everything possible has been done to prepare for a season, and the team functions well together, the pressures of international cricket at higher levels of the game are such that situations of emotional fatigue are unavoidable – especially now that cricket seems to be played all year round. We believe strongly that players should rest completely for at least two months of the year; likewise, the playing season itself should last no more than seven months. There are compelling physiological reasons for this (see Chapter 10), but the psychological reasons are equally important.

THE PSYCHOLOGICAL CHALLENGES OF TOURING

Touring is exhausting. The body is subjected to more than its fair share of aeroplane cabins, dreary hours on plastic chairs in airport lounges, dragging luggage around (or filling in forms because it has gone missing), still more hours in buses stuck in traffic, strange beds, the shock of sharing a room with someone other than one's spouse (especially if they snore or talk in their sleep), jetlag, endlessly disrupted routines, unfamiliar food and the little bumps and snags of being in strange surroundings (not knowing the name of the local brand of aspirin, for example, or where to buy it). And that's before you've tried playing cricket.

Not only is touring a recipe for emotional fatigue; cricket tours by definition last much longer than the average sporting tour, usually months as opposed to weeks. Obviously, being away from home and all its familiar routines, friends and loved ones, constantly moving from hotel to hotel, wasting hours in transit (South African bowler Shaun Pollock calls it the 'hurry up and wait' phenomenon), constantly adjusting to foreign climes and conditions – all these factors and more will take their toll on the sunniest of characters.

HOW TO BE A HAPPY TOURIST

As has been pointed out, even the most positive attitude and an infectious sense of humour can't offset the effects of jetlag, being woken by a stranger stumbling into your hotel room at 3am before a Test match (international cricketers seem to attract more than their fair share of would-be burglars), an upset stomach caused by unfamiliar food, or the news that the flight to your next destination has been indefinitely delayed.

However, you can opt to be sensible. International cricket tours are marked by tales of Test cricketers who decided to pig out at the seafood buffet or eat in a dodgy restaurant, with disastrous digestive consequences. Follow the same rules as tourists: in developing countries, drink only bottled water and (if you want to play it really safe) stick to vegetarian food. Many international cricketers claim that hotel food is fine, and shudder at the thought of consuming food from a kiosk or café, but be aware that exposed buffets stewing away all day on hot plates in the hotel can be a recipe for food-poisoning. Fresh-made food prepared in front of you is generally a good bet.

Some players love the opportunity to travel and relish trying out new and exotic cuisines. At the international level, cricketers who rush out into the streets as tourists rather than hiding out in their hotels can do wonders for inter-country relations. Shortly after South Africa's re-admission to international cricket, fast bowler Fanie de Villiers endeared himself to hundreds of thousands around the world through his enthusiasm for exploring and seeing the sights when touring other countries. Steve Waugh is another who took on the role of 'ambassador' for the Australian team, visiting not only tourist sights, but historic and humanitarian venues as well. His trips behind the scenes of the countries he toured led to lasting bonds and even charitable projects, making him a figure of international respect above and beyond his skill with a bat.

Even if you aren't particularly interested in museums and scenic vistas, it is not a bad idea to learn a little about the countries marked for touring; learning basic greetings and courtesies in local languages is always appreciated. Moreover, ignorance is not bliss in foreign countries: it is illegal to consume alcohol in Pakistan and some states of India, and what you might consider light-hearted and harmless flirting may well be construed as intention to seduce or the beginnings of marriage negotiations in some countries. By all means, interact with locals, especially if that's what you enjoy, but never assume that your status as a visiting athlete gives you the right to flout local laws or religious or cultural norms.

HOME ADVANTAGE

For those who doubt whether the phenomenon of home advantage exists or not, the statistics are incontrovertible: home teams win more than 50% of their matches, regardless of the sport.

Why this is so is open to interpretation. Self-belief may be a key element: a 1998 study (Terry et al.) found that male rugby players report higher levels of self-confidence, and lower pre-match anxiety, when competing at home than when away.

Another factor could be the influence that a large and wildly partisan crowd can exert on an umpire or referee. At lower levels of the game, umpires have been threatened, burnt in effigy, and even shot at by outraged local fans convinced that their home-team stars have had a rough decision against them. Even in international cricket – which has tried to sidestep the issue with neutral umpires – it takes a very brave umpire to give Sachin Tendulkar out LBW in front of 100 000 Indian fans at Eden Gardens. Bob Woolmer remembered playing in the Currie Cup in South Africa, and hearing bowlers complain that Graeme Pollock was never given out LBW; likewise, there were stories that Hanif Mohammed was never given out in Pakistan.

Leg-before decisions are often the most contentious and give rise to the most bitter recriminations, largely because of all umpiring decisions, they are the most subjective. Not surprisingly, many pundits have assumed a clear link between LBW decisions and home advantage; however, an early study by Samper and Mobeley in 1981 produced some intriguing results. The researchers analysed every umpiring decision given in every Test match since the inception of Test cricket in 1877 until 1980. They drew five final conclusions:

- Visiting batsmen have been out LBW more frequently than have home batsmen, though the only countries where the home/away difference is statistically significant are India, Pakistan and South Africa.
- Australian umpires are more reluctant to raise the finger in support of LBW appeals than are umpires in other countries, a fact which applies both to home and to visiting batsmen.
- In the West Indies, home batsmen have been more prone to LBW dismissals than home batsmen in other countries.
- In New Zealand, visiting batsmen have been less likely to be given out LBW than batsmen visiting other countries.
- In India, visiting batsmen beware: you are more likely to be dismissed LBW than in any other country.

In other words, only two traditional stereotypes – that Indian umpires are trigger-happy with LBW decisions, and that Indian, Pakistani and South African umpires

Cricketers on tour who rush out into the streets as enthusiastic tourists can do wonders for inter-country relations.

are biased in favour of their own teams – were born out with statistical evidence. The other findings seemed to fly in the face of conventional wisdom, particularly the conclusion that in the West Indies it was in fact the *home* batsmen who were in danger of being rather too hastily shot out.

While these findings have little bearing on modern Test cricket, where neutral umpires stand, they nonetheless serve to challenge public perception about this or that nation's propensity for producing crowd-pleasing umpires. However, this is not to say that umpires and referees are not pressured into overlooking home-team mistakes, or being overly harsh on visitors.

More recently, Jones et al. (2001) evaluated 6 361 umpiring decisions in 2 992 games in English Club cricket, defining an umpiring decision as one in which the umpire was required to give a subjective decision. Their hypothesis was simple: since these games are played in front of relatively few spectators, there should be no crowd influence on umpiring decisions.

And so it proved to be. Home teams did win 57% of their decided matches, but there was no difference in the proportion of total umpiring decisions, or in each of four categories (leg before wicket, catches by the wicket-keeper, stumpings and run-outs) for either home or away teams. Home advantage, this study seems to suggest, is less a result of biased umpiring than the product of increased confidence (a knowledge of local conditions, familiarity with the ground and its surrounds, a sense of well-being gained from being close to home with all its positive connotations) and reduced stress (no enervating international flights or bus journeys, no unsettling worries over getting kit and supplies to the venue).

SEX: THE UNMENTIONABLE SUBJECT

A delicate issue that is never discussed, but often in the minds of administrators and coaches, is that married players (whose spouses do not or cannot accompany them on tour) are expected to be celibate, sometimes for months on end. If they are not (and every international cricketer knows that opportunities for straying present themselves), they run the risk of media exposure, embarrassment, pain and, at worst, marital strife and disruption, all conducted long distance and often in a cruel glare of publicity, with no chance of popping home to patch things up.

If anyone has any illusions about the potential for psychological stress and misery (for all involved) held by the unmentionable topic of sex on tour, they need look no further than the frank chapter that Allan Lamb's wife Lindsey contributes to his 1996 autobiography. She described her misery as she was doorstopped by the press in the wake of England's 'sex and drugs and rock 'n roll' tour to New Zealand in 1984, in which her husband's off-field exploits featured prominently: 'When you go shopping

TOP: *For many fans in Asia, cricket is more than a game. In war-torn and economically depressed Sri Lanka, it offers an escape into a world of hope, glamour and heroism – here embodied by national treasure Muttiah Muralitharan on a billboard as he prepared to break Courtney Walsh's record for the most Test wickets in 2004.* **BOTTOM:** *But with huge expectations placed on Asian teams, failures are keenly felt. Here Pakistani fans burn posters of senior players after their team's dramatic early exit from the 2007 World Cup in the West Indies.*

The gentleman's game. **LEFT:** *India's first superstar played for England, and was literally royalty. Prince Kumar Shri Ranjitsinhji, known as Ranji, seen here circa 1910, scored 24 692 first-class runs in a career spanning almost 30 years. His impact on the game was lasting, and he is widely credited with establishing the late cut, leg glance and backward defensive as legitimate shots.* **RIGHT:** *In a slower era, a telegram is delivered mid-innings to the man who would come to define cricketing greatness – Sir Donald Bradman.*

you think everyone is pointing at you and whispering about you…. Nobody, not even Allan, could know how deep the scars are.' She concluded sadly but bluntly, 'I knew I loved Lamby, and still do, but I don't trust him.' But to this, she added a feisty postscript: 'I would take Lamby to the cleaners if it happened again, he wouldn't know what hit him. I'm older and stronger now, and he'd end up believing that a corrugated cardboard shelter under Waterloo Bridge would be Buckingham Palace by the time I'd finished with him' (*Allan Lamb: My Autobiography*, pp. 146–47).

And the subtitle of the autobiography of Lamb's 'partner in crime', Ian Botham, says it all – *Don't Tell Kath* (his wife). And it is not only the family men who suffer: single players can also get themselves into some serious tangles while far away from home, and missing their partners.

Even an apparently innocent action might have hurtful repercussions: some years ago, a nubile young lady approached Shane Warne as he fielded on the boundary at the Wanderers Stadium in South Africa, and begged him to autograph the 'upper part of her upper back leg', as he put it. The damsel flashed her knickers, Warne obligingly signed – and earned an angry long-distance rebuke from his heavily pregnant and understandably upset wife, who was watching the incident on TV back home thousands of miles away. In the years that followed, Warne did much worse than pat a few bottoms on tour, and his marriage is now over as a result.

A growing problem is that international players have in the past few decades begun to attract 'groupies' in the same way that rock stars and movie actors do. While some might wonder what is so bad about crowds of adoring fans, there are darker sides, especially with the less salubrious elements of the press hanging about to pounce on any 'kiss-and-tell' story that presents itself.

Players may find that rare evenings off and outings that are much needed as a break from the rigours of the game are marred by interruptions and demands from impetuous fans. While elite players are by definition public figures, who should always try to maintain a courteous and obliging attitude to fans, especially young children, they may not appreciate the attentions of effusive young women while trying to enjoy a restaurant meal with their spouse. A childhood friend of a former South African bowler often admired for his good looks recounts that when she was in London at the same time as the touring South African team, she accompanied her friend on various social outings. Even though their relationship was not romantic, she found to her amazement that she was sometimes approached and verbally attacked by jealous fans. She admitted that the experience would make her think twice about marrying a star athlete.

The fitness coach for an international team bewailed the impact that 'groupies' were having on the younger and more impressionable team members: 'They

Young cricketing stars are getting the dangerous message that any woman is theirs for the asking.

THE MIND GAME **81**

are learning to have no respect for women, especially Western women. They are also getting the dangerous message that any woman is theirs for the asking,' he complained. It does not have to be spelled out that glamour and status can go to the head of an international athlete, with sometimes disastrous, even tragic consequences. Mike Tyson was not the first and is unlikely to be the last sports star to find himself in prison for rape, and Makhaya Ntini had what some considered a narrow escape when his rape conviction in 1999 was overturned on appeal.

Heavy-handed attempts to play chaperone or schoolmarm by coach and management can make things even more strained and awkward: none of this adds up to a happy atmosphere while touring. The best solution by far is to allow spouses and partners to visit players during prolonged tours, or to allow touring players brief spells of 'home leave', if practical. Costs will naturally be a factor here. Of course, every individual is different: some players will cope with long periods of celibacy without difficulty; others might consider this an undue hardship, and some may have no intention of practising fidelity, whether at home or abroad. The most sensible approach is to address the matter frankly with players and consult them on how long they think it is reasonable to be deprived of the company of their spouses while on tour. Administrators should be frank and even-handed about the budgetary constraints; they should also be open to compromise.

If it is agreed that spouses and other family members can accompany players for part of their tour, the timing of their arrival should be carefully planned, however; they should not arrive the day before an important match, when their presence is likely to distract players. They should rather arrive immediately after a match.

POINTING PLAYERS TOWARD PSYCHOTHERAPY

As a coach, the fastest and easiest way to alienate a player is to suggest, out of the blue, that he needs to get professional psychological help. You might as well just label him a loony, and ride him out of town on a rail. As noted in the introduction to this chapter, most players still regard seeking psychotherapy, or any kind of emotional counselling for that matter, as an admission of weakness, something that reveals them as less virile than their teammates. This is why you need to be very careful about when and how you suggest these avenues to players struggling with various psychological problems.

The following are some common scenarios when it is appropriate to guide a player towards professional help. However, be sensitive to his personality and situation:

WHEN IT ALL GETS TOO MUCH: SUICIDE AND CRICKET

In his fascinating if sobering book, *By His Own Hand*, David Frith looks at the high rates (compared to other athletes) of suicide by former cricketers. Most of those who chose this route were faced with financial ruin, family problems, poor health and romantic disappointment. A frighteningly high proportion were alcoholics, many of whom had begun drinking during their years of cricketing success. Nevertheless, he suggests that another factor might be 'the inability to cope when the athletic peak is passed and the adulation vanishes'. As Peter Roebuck writes, 'For how does a man manage who, from 20 to 35, enjoys the applause, the spotlight and the rapture, and for whom, midway through his life, all is suddenly silent?'

South African off-spinner Pat Symcox, now a commentator, articulated this particularly poignantly some years after his retirement: 'When you're a member of the team, you can walk in and out of the dressing room without knocking. Once you've left, no matter how well you know the guys, you have to knock – you can't just walk in. I'll never forget what it felt like to have to knock for the first time.'

There is no doubt that first-class cricket can absorb the best years of a player's life, then leave him middle-aged and unqualified for much else. There is a need to ensure that elite cricketers are encouraged to get skills and qualifications that can enable them to make the transition to post-cricket careers. Not every top-level cricketer will be able to become a coach, commentator or sports writer.

But Frith is not convinced that something about cricket itself (or giving it up) predisposes certain vulnerable individuals to suicide, pointing out that almost all of the 80 subjects in his book (all of whom played cricket, many for a living, and all of whom killed themselves) were prey to significant stressors, and very likely disturbances of the chemistry of the brain. Nevertheless, he adds: 'Cricket's virtues are renowned. Played well, it gives thrilling satisfaction to the performer; it also gives vast spectator pleasure; and – to those who need it – it offers broad scope for warm companionship and comfort. Withdraw the first and last of these, and the void created presents itself as a potential hardship at best and fatally damaging at worst.'

He goes on to observe: 'Half-hearted cricketers are extremely rare. This game gets a grip on people such as only religious fanatics might comprehend.... So many retiring cricketers talk about "putting something back into the game", when what they need most is a continuing connection with the familiar pastime or profession which has given them so much pleasure, pride or even pain for 20 or 30 years' (pp. 254–55).

if he's in no state even to admit he has a problem, suggesting he seek help may make matters worse.

- **When a player has experienced any major life trauma** (such as bereavement), the coach might suggest counselling in a mild and non-threatening way. Of course, this should not be the coach's responsibility: such a suggestion should come from family members, the player's doctor or religious advisor, or close friends. But it can be very hard for men in most patriarchal cultures to acknowledge that they need emotional help, and it might sometimes be easier for them to see a professional if they can insist that 'Coach thinks my game is being affected'. In cases like these, the coach should proceed carefully and tactfully, keeping a watchful eye out for signs of disintegration.

- **If there is persistent inappropriate abuse of alcohol or some other substance,** to the detriment of the player's game, decisive action must be taken. Here the coach, preferably together with the team's medical advisor, needs to be firm in pointing out that the player's place in the side is at risk, as addicts are generally in profound denial, at least initially.

- **Being dropped is usually a player's worst nightmare.** Players who are facing the disappointment of not being selected for a national or other team, or who have been dropped, should be given space to vent their true feelings. A neutral figure such as a sports psychologist can often facilitate such expression. This will also help players maintain a semblance of calm and dignity when explaining the situation to sponsors, the media and the public.

- **If a player seems to have developed a profound and serious psychological block about some aspect of the game,** and is experiencing persistent loss of form as a result, and all other methods of dealing with the situation have failed, offer the option of consulting a sports psychologist. For example, the player may fall apart when faced with a particular bowler, or he may be in the excruciating position of captaining the team while suffering from miserable form (a nightmare that puts him in good company, this scenario having been endured by, among others, Mark Taylor, Michael Atherton, Alec Stewart, Brian Lara and the late Hansie Cronje).

- **If a player performs well at practices and in 'low-profile' games, but consistently fails in front of a crowd,** or if a player suffers from nerves to a distressing and debilitating extent, professional training in relaxation techniques (as discussed earlier) may be indicated.

CONCLUSION

The last words should go to two cricketers who played cricket as hard as the best, but who exuded joy and enjoyment on the field. Even with their teams on the rack, they seemed to radiate a confidence that came from understanding the bigger picture, a sense that there was a world beyond the stadium in which they now found themselves.

The first is South Africa's poster boy for fielding, Jonty Rhodes. In a widely circulated interview, he was asked what lessons had most influenced his career. His sporting mindset had been fashioned, he replied, by a coach whose inevitable response to those moments when his team's fate appeared to be beyond salvation was: 'Ah, but it's good to be alive!'

The second is a player who has already been quoted – but Keith Miller's famous observation really says it all: 'Playing cricket is not pressure. A Messerschmitt up your arse is pressure!'

PART TWO

CRICKET TECHNIQUES

What does it take to become a great cricketer? Simply stated, it involves a high level of skill, as well as all of the attributes that go into the making of any great athlete, such as a natural flair for the game, a good eye and quick reflexes, as well as the willingness and patience to persevere.

A great deal of athletic ability is now also an essential component for success, as is the ability to maintain fierce, unbroken concentration for hours at a stretch. Finally, enjoyment and love of the game, the ability to perform both as an individual and in a team context, and a hunger for success are all essential parts of the mental make-up of a potentially great cricketer.

If all these qualities are present in the young cricketer, what he (and, increasingly, she) will need to learn are the technical rudiments and necessary skills of the game, how and when to use those skills, and – obviously – the rules of the game.

All aspiring cricketers need to learn how to field, but in modern cricket it is essential that players also master the basics of bowling, whether pace or spin, and perhaps even learn rudimentary wicket-keeping skills. Due to the increasing demands of the one-day game, the modern cricketer needs to be adept in at least two of three disciplines. We see time and again how players with two strings to their bows are invaluable to their teams. Whether they are bowlers who are able to perform heroics with the bat, such as Wasim Akram, Andy Flintoff or Shaun Pollock, or wicket-keepers who average over 40, such as Adam Gilchrist, they are crucial if a team is to be successful. One need only point to South Africa's Pollock, Lance

Klusener and Jacques Kallis, a line-up of all-rounders who dominated in the late 1990s, to underscore this point. South Africa also fielded Mark Boucher (equally tenacious as a wicket-keeper and batter), and Jonty Rhodes, a hard-working batsman who raised standards of fielding to a new high in the last decade of the twentieth century. Australia's Michael Bevan was rated the world's top one-day batsman in the mid-1990s, but he was probably also the most useful. He was not only a sparkling, fast-scoring finisher and comfortably the best fielder in the Australian side, but he was adept at getting breakthroughs as a change bowler.

In the four chapters that follow, we intend to deal with those elements of cricket that can be learnt, practised, and hopefully mastered – the techniques of the game. However, we want to stress that there are many interpretations of correct technique and how it should be taught: different coaches may demonstrate or describe a certain skill differently.

The techniques described here are tried and tested, based on many years of experience. They worked for Bob Woolmer, first as an all-rounder who played for Kent and England (and the Wisden Player of the Year for 1976); and then as a coach for Warwickshire, South Africa and Pakistan. His exceptional coaching abilities were recognized by the International Cricket Council, which appointed him their High Performance Manager, responsible for bringing affiliate members up to international standards. In terms of the successes that first Warwickshire and then South Africa and Pakistan achieved under Woolmer's tutelage, his methods have proved their value. We hope you will benefit from them as well.

CHAPTER THREE

BATTING

Of all cricket's skills, batting is the most glamorous. At the highest level of the game, scoring runs and not being dismissed will bring fame and glory of a kind that is possibly unique in the world of sport. In the 1930s, the cricketing world regarded Sir Donald Bradman with the kind of awe reserved for monarchs and film stars; and Brian Lara's 375 against England in 1994 earned him similar status. At the summit of batting achievement lies immense prestige.

But batting is the skill that will also take the most time to learn and perfect. This process begins with understanding the *how* and *why* of the art. Unfortunately, too many coaching manuals still focus on the how without explaining the why.

Batting is difficult, and anyone who walks out to the crease to bat will discover three immediate problems: judging length, judging line, and being able to move properly; or, more specifically, getting balanced to deal with that line and length. Batting in cricket is not a natural movement like slugging a baseball: even a child with good ball skills will struggle to bring bat into contact with the ball, especially if the ball bounces high.

Many young batters aren't exposed to the deviating ball, because young bowlers aren't able to move it off a straight line. When you first set out to bowl, the ball goes straight to the batter. If it does deviate, it's probably doing so into the side of the net! Young bowlers only start being able to spin the ball when they are nine or ten – and if they are able to bowl true leg-spin at that age, it confuses the batsmen completely because they've had little or no experience of such dramatic changes in line.

However, when you move to a higher level of the game, the skills of batting – picking line and length, balance, shot selection, shot execution – have all been mastered and become second nature. At this level, the only thing that keeps batsmen from scoring freely is deviation.

But what of the highest level? Why don't all Test batsmen score triple-hundreds regularly, especially on pitches that don't help the ball to deviate? Here the enemy is almost always mental pressure. It takes more than talent to excel: when Brian Lara took the world record for the highest Test score for the second time (400 not out in April 2004), his effort required immense concentration, application, desire and skill.

Test batsmen are good enough to look for swing, to see the shine on the ball, to look at the finger position at the point of delivery, and to check the angle of the seam. But movement off the seam will always remain a problem, because it happens so fast and so late. If you're facing a Glenn McGrath and you've committed to a particular line, and the ball jags back or away, there just isn't time to adjust. If you're lucky, you'll miss. If not, the scorecard will show J. Bloggs, caught Gilchrist bowled McGrath.

On English wickets of the past decades, a lot of batsmen were able to play a line, see the ball deviate, and adjust in time, because the wicket was slow. But in Australia or South Africa, where pitches tend to be quicker, a batsman may see the ball move, start to adjust, but only have time to get an edge on it and nick off a catch. Sides who tour these countries have to learn to play inside the line of the ball – in other words, not to follow the ball, as they would in countries like India and Pakistan, which generally have slower pitches.

It *is* possible to play the seaming ball. As with all sports, the messages sent to the brain by the eyes dictate how the body will respond, and the response from the body is conditioned by how you've practised or trained yourself. There are days when you find you can play the swinging or seaming ball with ease, when you're so still and balanced that if the ball seams away, you can adjust and hit it through the covers. But there are also days when batting just seems impossible.

When everything does go right, when you're able to play every ball on its merit, and place it just where you want it to go, it is usually the result of being in what sports psychologists call your *ideal performance state*. (Laypeople talk about being in a bubble or 'in the zone'.) And once you are in that state, you become oblivious to everything around you except the ball you are facing. Everything seems to slow down, giving you plenty of time to react.

This is often evident in Tests. Dashing strokemakers such as Chris Gayle or David Gower will keep the bowlers in the game all the time, offering chances. But when batsmen like Ricky Ponting or Sunil Gavaskar enter the zone, bowlers just don't know what to do to get them out. In the end, their only option is to break down that bubble, through verbal intimidation or by distracting them by mixing up the attack.

But these tactics are dealt with in Chapter 2. For now, it is important to learn enough about the art of batting, especially the how and why of batting, to be able to reach that zone.

THE PRINCIPLES OF BATTING

In 1851 the Reverend James Pycroft set out six golden rules of batting in *The Cricket Field*. In 1980, England match-winner Ian Botham did the same, proving that 130 years had done nothing to alter the principles of good batsmanship.

	PYCROFT	BOTHAM
1	Sight of a ball depends on a habit of individual attention both before and after delivery.	Concentrate.
2	How characteristic in the ease and repose of their figures – no hurry or trepidation. How little do their heads or bodies move!	Keep your head still and get it over the ball.
3	By standing close up, and playing well over your wicket with straight bat, and throwing, by means of the left leg, the body forwards, over a ball rising to off stump, you can make an effective hit from an off-bailer without lessening your defence.	Get behind the line.
4	One of the best leg hitters is Dakin, and his rule is: keep your right foot firm on the ground: advance the left straight at the pitch, and as far as you can reach, and hit as straight at the pitch as you can.	Get your foot to the ball when you play forward.
5	The bat, though properly 4½ inches wide, is considerably reduced when used across the wicket: *so never hit across the wicket.*	Bring the bat through straight.
6	Let your arms do the hitting.	Extend the arms when you play shots.

Source: Synge and Anns, 1987, p. 115

THE SCIENCE OF BATTING

Batting is a science, one that uses a number of skills:

- *Visual and neurological skills* – watching the ball, judging where it goes, processing this information (a lightning-swift unconscious process), decision-making and shot-selection.
- *Physical and biomechanical skills* – creating the correct body movements so that shot-making corresponds with the length and line of the ball, timing the hitting of the ball.
- *Psychological skills* – dealing with the elation and depression associated with scoring a hundred or a duck.

On a more practical and step-by-step level, the skill of batting requires the batsman to watch the ball from the bowler's hand, judge where it is likely to pitch, move the feet and body into position to hit it, and then choose the correct shot to either score or survive. All this while the ball travels in excess of 140km per hour, leaving the batter 0.4 of a second to respond to a hard leather ball weighing 156 grams, a missile that can break bones – and even kill.

This is why a batsman's courage (and his luck) can determine success or failure. However, no top batsman relies on courage and luck: he relies on his technique, and his understanding of what he does, and when and why he does it.

THE BASICS OF BATTING

Coaches and commentators talk about sticking to the basics, but what does this actually mean? As illustrated, both Botham and Pycroft, 130-odd years apart in time, identified six basic aspects of batting that they believed to be vital. It is perhaps simpler to cut this list down to five basic principles. If these are adhered to, they will give all batsmen the best possible chance of succeeding at the highest level.

These five basic principles of batting are:
1. Watch the ball.
2. Keep your head still on release of the ball.
3. Judge length accurately: line will change with swing and spin.
4. Allow your hands to lead your body and feet into the correct position.
5. Select the correct shot.

1. WATCH THE BALL

The eyes will give the brain the first clues as to where the delivery is going to land and therefore start your decision-making process. So when should you start watching the ball? This differs from batsman to batsman; however, the pre-delivery clues are often there if you know where to look for them.

How early a batsman starts watching the ball (during the bowler's run-up, during his gather) is a matter of personal preference, but it is vital that you are watching the ball as it leaves the bowler's hand: look for the shine, the position of the seam, what the fingers do and where it is released. The release position determines the length of the delivery, and being able to use visual clues will help you to decide (correctly!) whether to go forward or back. For example, some bowlers hold the ball deep in their fingers – almost against their palm – when bowling a slower ball, while Shane Warne's flipper was held in the end of his fingers.

2. KEEP YOUR HEAD STILL – BE BALANCED

Stand up as straight as possible, too. If you crouch… and then have to straighten up as you play the ball, your eyes will be on a different plane, and you will look at the ball from a changing angle, just when you need concentration most. Imagine a rifleman moving his head up as he fires, and you will see what I mean. You should keep your eyes at the same height from the ground right through the shot, whether with bat or gun, if it is accuracy you want.

Learie Constantine, *The Changing Face of Cricket*

Despite being over half a century old, this advice from one of the masters of early West Indian cricket is still absolutely correct: all coaches will implore a batsman to stand still when the ball is released, and indeed to remain still for up to 2/100ths of a millisecond afterwards. A motionless head means your eyes can focus on the ball, and this will enable you to see where it is going and where it will land. The reflex action that follows – reflex because it has been drummed into you through practice and repetition – will be more precise as a result.

Against great fast bowlers, a batsman often doesn't have time to get properly balanced or become entirely still as the ball is delivered. He needs a quick reflex movement to get him ready, both physically and mentally, to play the correct shot. This movement creates a batting rhythm, which helps him get into an advanced position to deal with the ball landing in a particular area (an area which is often only guessed at – or hoped for!). If the ball is not in that area, he can easily transfer his body into a second position. For example, his first movement could prepare him

> ## NOW YOU SEE IT, NOW YOU DON'T
> The question of vision and the role it plays in batting is the new frontier in sports medicine and cricket science. New research is fuelling and stimulating debate over whether batters are actually watching the ball (in a strictly physiological sense) all the way out of the bowler's hand down to the pitch. There are indications that in fact the eye/brain connection makes a lightning-swift and involuntary jump from the bowler's hand to where the batter's brain estimates the ball is most likely to pitch. This information is particularly important for coaches, as well as batters who like to understand every aspect of their game. As this fascinating new material falls somewhere between physiology and the technique of 'watching the ball', we have included it in a separate chapter immediately following this one. For now, however, concentrate on watching the ball with unwavering focus.

for short deliveries, but still enable the fallback option of transferring his weight forwards, allowing him to deal more quickly with fuller deliveries.

This pre-delivery movement is known as a rhythm or trigger movement. When playing in the Asian subcontinent, where pitches are slower and batsmen have more time to react, trigger movements can become more of a shuffle. Pre-delivery movements are discussed in more detail on pp. 118–122.

3. JUDGE LENGTH

It's an all-too-common exchange:
   Coach: 'What happened there?'
   Player: 'It kept low, coach.'
   Coach: 'Don't you think you might have gone forward?'

The player walks off in a huff, but fortunately, with more video analysis available, coaches are able to win these kinds of arguments by proving to their players that they were going through their trigger movements as the ball was on the way down to them. In other words, the batsman hadn't decided yet whether to go forward or back.

It may seem obvious, but for a batsman to be successful, he has to be able to make the correct decision: going forward to a bouncer or back to a half-volley leads inevitably to dismissal, not to mention embarrassment or even injury. The short ball aimed at the chest and above will bounce too high for a comfortable and controlled forward shot, and the ball will either hit the glove or the body, leading either to a catch in the gully region or injury. Going back to a ball of good length or a half-volley will cause the ball to rush onto the batsman, beating his hurried defensive adjustments, and he will be bowled or out LBW. This is what made Warne's flipper so lethal: its flight and top-spin persuaded batsmen to play back, expecting a long-hop, only to have the ball skid onto them and trap them LBW.

In short, being able to move forward and back correctly greatly increases the chances of success; therefore early and accurate judging of length becomes vital.

4. MOVE INTO THE CORRECT POSITION

Coaches always talk about getting the feet into the correct position, but they should really include the hands and the body in that statement: the feet may move, but other parts of the body don't always go where they should! For example, when playing forward, the head, front shoulder and foot should move together, either in line with the ball when defending, or next to the ball when attacking.

Of course, a batsman can still score runs if his feet are in the wrong position, and many players have swung wildly and been effective: we've all seen tail-enders get away with murder. However, as in any racket or ball sport, it is better to get the feet moving correctly, as balance and a good base will make sure that the shot is correctly executed.

Good footwork simply aids good balance. To illustrate how body mechanics work, and how big a stride you really need when playing forward, try the following exercise: stand with your feet together, arms folded across your chest. Now lean sideways towards the point on the pitch (or the carpet) where the bowler would be aiming, until you are about to topple over. Notice just how far your front leg has to move to prevent you from falling and restore your balance.

Batting is essentially a sideways game, played along parallel lines. The ball travels on one line and the bat should meet the ball on that line. This means that the body should therefore travel along a parallel line next to the ball. Whether or not this happens depends almost entirely on getting the feet into the correct position.

To make sure that this particular point is clear, think carefully about what terminology you use. Bob Woolmer said he always cringed when hearing coaches yell, 'Get your foot to the pitch of the ball!', as this would imply that the batsman should get his foot to exactly where the ball pitches. This of course is a total misnomer, as following this instruction would mean the ball bouncing on the batsman's instep!

There are two basic points to remember when playing forward:
- when attacking, get beside the ball and give yourself room to hit it;
- when defending, get your head, front shoulder and foot into line with the ball.

PITCH-PERFECT SHOT SELECTION

The condition of the pitch often dictates shot selection, but what are these conditions? Slow pitches, pitches with uneven bounce, fast pitches – what distinguishes each one, and how do they affect batting?

Pitches are discussed in more detail in Chapter 1, but when discussing shot selection, it is important to cover the basic differences in pitch conditions. A slow pitch is one on which the ball grips as it pitches, either because the pitch is wet and soft, or dry and dusty (sometimes even crumbling, as is often the case in Asia). On such pitches, a 120km/h delivery can slow down to around 105km/h on contact, while on a fast pitch (whether hard-rolled clay, as at Sabina Park in the 1980s, or a slippery green-top like the Wanderers in the same decade), the ball arrives at the batsman's end apparently as quickly as it left the bowler's hand. While there is minuscule deceleration due to friction, to the batsman, the difference is negligible.

This apparent speed off the pitch is described as the ball 'coming onto the bat' or 'sliding on', and is largely a product of the batsman's reflexes: by the time the ball pitches, the batsman has already made a prediction as to how fast the ball is 'coming on' to him, and has already started to swing the bat in anticipation of the ball's arrival. If his prediction is wrong, and he swings too early, the chances are that he will claim that the pitch is slow and is 'holding' the ball back. However, if the deceleration of the ball is minimal, or he's reading the pitch well and his prediction is good, he'll find he has time to select the correct shot, and time it well.

But international batsmen can't allow themselves to be restricted by pitches that don't seem to 'come on', and so they learn to play differently on different surfaces. No two countries share identical soil conditions, or indeed conditions such as humidity, cloud cover and dampness, all of which affect swing and seam. (These factors will be discussed more fully in Chapter 5, which covers bowling.)

It is therefore important to have practised a wide range of shots for all conditions, and then to choose the appropriate shots for each ball and each surface.

5. SELECT THE CORRECT SHOT

Peter May, the brilliant batsman who dominated English cricket during the 1950s, said that for every question the bowler asks the batsman, there is an answer. In other words, for every type of delivery, there is a correct shot. Whether or not you get the answer right depends on how well you have trained yourself to respond automatically.

Of course, some players are so good that they no longer need to provide orthodox answers to the bowlers' questions. The two Richards, Viv and Barry, were among the exceptionally gifted batsmen who could hit the ball wherever they wanted: a half-volley a foot outside off stump would normally go through the covers, but Sir Viv was just as likely to plant it between mid-wicket and square leg, such was his ability.

But for those not blessed with such superhuman gifts, scoring runs is much easier if you have the necessary options to deal with the variety of positions in which the ball lands. The more shots you have – and the more you are 'grooved' to pull out the right shot for the right ball in the right conditions – the better off you will be.

Field settings also control shot selection. If a batsman is limited in his array of shots, it allows the opposition to bowl to a set field. This often causes frustration that ultimately leads to a rash shot and dismissal. Good captains and bowlers will quickly notice any weakness in a batsman's array of shots or defensive technique and exploit it in this way.

WRAPPING UP THE BIG FIVE

The five principles of batting outlined above are the cornerstone of a successful career as a batsman. These techniques must be learnt and practised until they enter the subconscious and become reflex actions. This kind of conditioning takes time – between seven and ten years, depending on how hard and often the individual practises. But by the end of that time, reactions will be instant – known as 'grooved'.

TIMING THE BALL: CRICKET IS A TWO-HANDED GAME

'Woolmer! You're using too much bottom hand!'

Many batsmen will have heard a similar cry from their coach. Unfortunately, this debate doesn't usually go much further: as a young player, Bob Woolmer was often tempted to reply, 'All right then, tell me how you want me to use my bottom hand!'

The problem is not so much 'too much' bottom hand as incorrect use of the bottom hand. Over the years, coaches have neglected the importance of the use of the bottom hand. Bob Woolmer recounted: 'I asked a group of 50 coaches to raise their hands if they thought batting was controlled by the top hand: almost all raised a hand. I then asked them to think about the drill of hitting high catches for fielding practice: which hand did they use? Top or bottom? All answered that they used the bottom hand. And so I asked them again: which hand controls the shot? The debate started afresh!'

Batting is two-handed, like golf and hockey. However, everyone has a dominant hand (90% of people are right-hand dominant), which is most clearly evident when they throw or write or play one-handed games like tennis. It is this dominant hand that provides the power and timing while batting.

In baseball, or when playing a two-handed tennis shot, hand dominance is not a problem: both a home-run to left field and a cross-court backhand winner use simple biomechanics, with the waist and shoulders turning as the arms swing across the body. It doesn't matter if either hand comes off the bat or racquet after impact: indeed, in both sports the shot will remain effective if played one-handed, with either hand – only the power of the shot will be affected.

But the shape of the cricket bat forces the batsman to swing his arms in a pendulum movement, thereby forcing the hands and arms to work together. Both hands have separate axes (our shoulders), and so they have different swing planes, separated by a distance of anything up to 80cm, depending on how broad the shoulders are. For example, your left arm can swing out in line with your left shoulder at 90 degrees, but try to swing your right arm out in line with your left shoulder at 90 degrees, and suddenly your chest gets in the way.

A bat held with two hands together will hang immediately under your eyes, and in a direct line down the centre of the body. But this vertical position is the only time on the bat's pendulum swing path that the two hands will be in equilibrium: before impact it is natural for the top hand to lead the bat, while the untrained batsman will want to use his bottom hand on impact.

This would not be a problem if our arms swung on the same axes, but because the bottom hand is swinging on a different axis to the top hand – and is usually stronger and more co-ordinated – it can destroy the top hand's direction at the crucial moment of impact.

This is what coaches have warned against for generations. But by turning the bottom hand into a bogeyman, they have also overlooked a simple biomechanical principle: the top hand starts the shot on the backswing, and the bottom hand finishes the shot (first with impact, then with follow-through).

In other words, it is the bottom hand that completes the shot and creates both timing and power.

It might be useful to visualize the path of the swing as resembling the hull of a 19th-century man-of-war boat. The backswing towards the stumps is the high bridge and captain's cabin; the hitting area is the flat bottom; and the follow-through is the prow of the boat. It follows

FIGURE 3.1 *The path followed by the swinging bat*

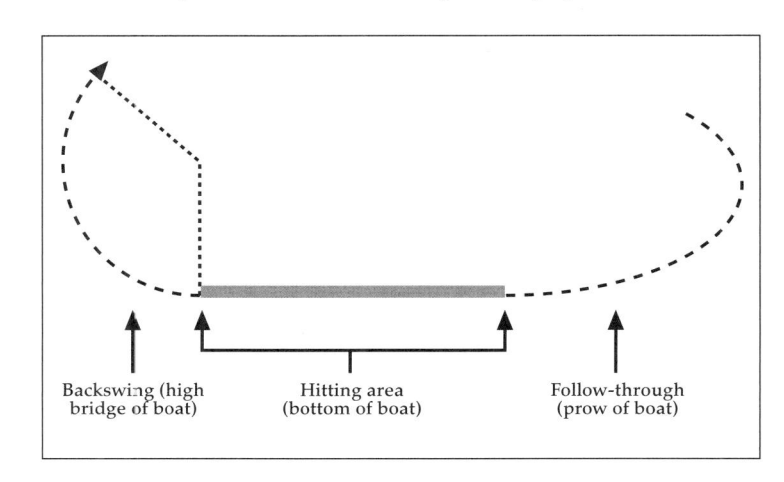

Backswing (high bridge of boat) | Hitting area (bottom of boat) | Follow-through (prow of boat)

BATTING   99

logically that the longer the 'bottom of the boat', the greater the contact point and hitting area will be. The follow-through begins once both hands have travelled along the 'bottom of the boat' for as long as it is physically possible to do so, and then begin lifting because the bottom hand (attached to the back arm) can no longer match the top hand's swing path.

Another way of imagining a successful stroke through the hitting area is to visualize attaching a paintbrush to the end of your bat, and then trying to paint a straight white line while leaning forward into the front-foot drive position. The longer and straighter the line, the better the hitting area.

There is of course no denying that in many players – in some cases, even at international level – the bottom hand influences the top in a negative way, either taking the bat across the line of the delivery, or overtaking the top hand when driving (which will usually induce errors such as missing the ball or scooping it into the air for an easy catch). The bottom hand will also rotate according to its natural biomechanics: if it cannot reach the ball on the bounce, the hand tries to compensate in order to keep the ball down and starts to turn over (the palm rolls down towards the ground). This movement will of course prevent the full face of the bat making contact, and sometimes guarantees a fresh-air shot, much to the batsman's chagrin and the fielders' amusement.

But instead of issuing vague warnings about the dangers of the bottom hand, coaches must recognize that the dominant hand is not going to go away, and that more attention therefore needs to be given to teaching the bottom or dominant hand to work correctly along straight lines.

In summary, always remember that both hands must trace the same path. Wherever the ball goes, both hands must follow it.

LEFT OR RIGHT, TOP OR BOTTOM?

Some batsmen who are generally right-handed, but who have been taught to bat left-handed, find themselves struggling to pull and cut.

Diagnosing this problem once again concerns the bottom hand: the right-handed 'left-hander' sometimes struggles to pull or cut because his bottom hand – in this case his left hand – is not his dominant hand, and is weaker than his right hand. For batsmen with this problem, the pull shot will have to be timed rather than powered. The same applies to right-handed batsmen whose left arm and hand are stronger. Weight training and specific training drills can also improve the strength and co-ordination of the weaker hand.

Former England opener Nick Knight is a good example of a right-handed left-hander: left-handed at the crease, but right-handed at everything else. He hated sweeping, which was natural, as his bottom hand was not the dominant hand; but as soon as he tried reverse sweeping, he found it easier and became extremely successful at this shot. This was not surprising, given that he was now using his dominant hand to hit the ball.

TIMING IS EVERYTHING – CHOOSING A BAT FOR YOUR CHILD

If your child announces that he (or she) hates batting and wants to give up cricket, don't automatically assume it's because of bad coaching or unpleasant teammates. The chances are he's miserable because he's too weak to lift the bat you've given him!

Alarming statistics have shown that the upper body strength of South African children has decreased by over 50% in the last ten years. To investigate this claim, a Western Cape high school known for its cricket conducted a long-term series of tests, and found even more startling results. In 1990, 80% of their under-14 boys tested could do ten or more pull-ups. In 2004, only 10% of them could do one or more pull-up!

As physical education becomes less and less of a priority in South Africa and a growing number of countries around the globe, and as sedentary childhoods revolving around PlayStations and junk food become more prevalent, these statistics are going to get worse.

Of course, children aren't helped by the cost-cutting tactics of their parents. It's an almost universal excuse: the boy's only nine, he's growing like a weed, there's no way I'm spending hundreds of pounds or dollars (or thousands of rands) on something he'll outgrow in a year! The result? Small boys are given bats half as tall as they are, that they have no chance of swinging, let alone learning to play controlled shots with.

The ideal length for a bat is the inside measurement of the batsman's trousers, regardless of whether he is 3 feet or 6 foot 5 inches tall. Bats that come up to a boy's hip or waist will do irreparable damage to his technique – not to mention his pleasure and interest in the game.

The weight of the bat must also be carefully considered. Naturally, some children are stronger than others, but as a general rule of thumb, children over the age of seven fare best with bats that weigh no more than a kilogram. A good yardstick is to ask the child to lift the bat in his non-dominant hand (i.e., his left hand if he is right-handed), and to hold it out horizontally with his shoulder for one minute. If he can do this without strain or difficulty, the weight is correct. Exactly the same precautions apply when choosing bats for girls.

Finally, look for the grain size. These are the individual slats of willow running down the length of the blade. Anything above eight grains or strips visible on the face of the bat means it's a good bat. Don't worry about knots.

And remember, no matter how well made and how expensive they are, bats break.

However, physical strength seems to be a major factor in the success of players with non-dominant bottom hands. Both Matthew Hayden and Lance Klusener are right-handers who bat left, and as many contemporary bowlers have learnt, both can hit the ball a long way. In fact, both players seem to have unusually strong bottom hands, despite these being their 'weak' hands in theory.

Hand-dominance is an essential developmental stage in children – babies who fail to pick one hand to favour over the other can develop emotional problems as they grow older. But it is possible that parents and coaches will in future begin to train both hands for co-ordination and strength, with potentially revolutionary results: a generation of ambidextrous cricketers.

BATTING TECHNIQUES

No-one will ever persuade me that there is one method of batting which can be imposed on young cricketers by the book. Let the mind of the youngster fly… show him a big field with no fielders, no barriers, no batting rules, and let him whack the ball in all directions.

Sir Vivian Richards

Many experienced coaches agree with the great West Indian's philosophy, but it is worth remembering that Sir Viv himself followed all of the basic principles of batting, even if these came to him naturally. If he had not had an instinctive grasp of the foundations of batting, he would not have been successful. For example, Richards' head was always still as the ball was delivered, which greatly aided his uncanny ability to pick the line and length early; and he also played with a very straight bat.

No matter how gifted a batsman, and how easily improvisation comes to him, the fact remains: the higher the level of cricket played, the more a batsman has to strive to be technically perfect in judging length, shot selection and shot execution.

However, before you face your first ball, there are three essential preparatory techniques that you need to create your 'ready position' or 'set up'. They are:

- **Guard** – where you stand;
- **Stance** – how you stand;
- **Grip** – how you hold your bat.

TAKING GUARD

Your guard shows you exactly where to stand as you take up your position at the wicket. More specifically, it gives you your bearings: you can't keep looking behind you to orient yourself with your off stump, and marking your guard gives you the confidence of knowing where your off stump is. This sense of where you are in the crease, and where you are in relationship to the stumps, is vital for judging line, and for deciding which balls to play and which to leave alone.

Most batsmen have been guilty of playing at too many deliveries: how often have we heard a commentator or coach saying, 'He needn't have played at that,' as a batsman trudges back to the pavilion, having been dismissed off a careless and over-expansive shot? Sir Garry Sobers simplified this idea by pointing out that if at the start of your innings, you align yourself to play only at balls that are on line with the stumps, leaving any deliveries that go wider, you are less likely to edge the ball. It seems obvious, but this ability to judge – visualizing your stumps, and knowing when they are in danger and when not – is essential in building an innings. The batsman who fails to work on developing this judgement is far more likely to play at balls he should be leaving alone, or to end up leaving balls that go on to hit the stumps.

In terms of defence therefore, it is important to understand that you only need to defend your stumps, and, when the ball bounces, your body and face. Playing away from the body – fending out or driving with the bat at arm's length – can and will lead to catches in the slip cordon. Likewise, defending square of the wicket to cover and extra cover is inadvisable: if the ball is rolling to cover, the chances are you met it outside off stump; and if it's outside off stump, and not an appropriate ball for trying to score off, what are you doing playing at it?

Which guard you choose is up to you: you know your strengths and weaknesses, and how accurately you are able to visualize where your stumps are behind you. However, whichever one you settle on, remember that your guard must allow for any pre-delivery rhythm or trigger movements, whether they be a back-and-across movement, a two-footed hop across the stumps like Brian Lara, or a quick front-on walk into line like Shivnarine Chanderpaul.

1. Leg stump

This guard is often preferred by better players, especially if they know they are strong on the off side, because it frees up the arms and allows the batsman to hit the ball from the stumps to the off side. The batsman also knows that any ball directed at his pads is now a free hit, as he is standing outside the line of leg stump and can't be out LBW.

When taking leg-stump guard, hold the bat up straight so the umpire can align its edge with leg stump, and then use the bat or your spikes to mark a line on the crease. (On scuffed and battered older pitches, it might be useful to use Chanderpaul's method of hammering a bail into the pitch, so that the position of your stump is visible as a small hole rather than a scuffmark among many other marks.) Now when

The leg-stump guard

you stand with your toes on this line or mark in a relaxed and fairly upright stance, your head will be over your leg stump.

Remember, though, that your head's position is likely to change during pre-delivery movements: even if you don't move around at the crease very much, you are likely to crouch, which will push your head and eyes further towards middle or off stump. Therefore, it is important to be aware of how and where your head and eyes move, so that you can stay confident about the whereabouts of your off stump. This advice holds true for all the stances.

Outswing bowlers can find it extremely difficult or frustrating bowling at batsmen who show them their stumps, which is exactly what the leg-stump guard does. If he aims at the stumps and the ball does not swing, the delivery ends up drifting into the pads, which any batsman worth his salt easily tucks away for runs. If he starts the ball on off stump, and it does swing, it allows the batsman to free his arms and hit through the off side. Also in your favour, if you choose this guard, is that if the ball swings in or moves off the seam to hit your pads, the umpire can normally see middle stump, which suggests to him that the ball was probably going on to miss leg stump. Even some doubt must go in your favour, and your innings continues.

Bob Woolmer recommended that all players learn to bat using this guard, although the final choice is a matter of personal preference. However, there are risks involved. Freeing the arms to hit a ball off middle or off stump is fine, but if that ball seams or swings late, you're going to be bowled. You also need to be a very fine judge of line and length if you're going to leave deliveries while your stumps are exposed.

The leg-stump guard is most useful when facing inswing bowlers and off-spinners on turning wickets. It can sometimes also be useful for facing reverse swing in the later overs of a match.

| LEG-STUMP GUARD ||
BENEFITS	RISKS
• Bowlers have to aim at the stumps: straight deliveries open up the leg side, and outswingers enable the batsman to free his arms with no risk of being bowled. • Umpires can be swayed by seeing your middle stump and are unlikely to give you out LBW.	• Exposed stumps can make you vulnerable to being bowled – you will need to watch line and movement carefully.

2. Middle-and-leg or 'two legs'

Taking middle-and-leg – or 'two legs' as it is also known – means that you are two inches nearer off stump. This might not seem like much, but many players feel more comfortable with the stumps behind them and their legs and body providing a kind of security blanket. Once again, the feet line up on this guard. Assuming that you have a conventional stance, the off stump should now be under your eyes.

Traditionally, there are two different ways of asking for the middle-and-leg guard – you can present either the face of the bat or its edge to the umpire.

This guard is particularly suited to players who are comfortable playing on both sides of the wicket. There are not many risks involved, although depending on how one plays, there is a possibility of being out LBW, as the body and legs are more in line with the stumps. However, this is a good guard with which to start your cricket career.

| MIDDLE-AND-LEG GUARD ||
BENEFITS	RISKS
• Off stump is in line with the batsman's eye, giving him a better sense of where off stump is. • Opens up leg-side scoring opportunities.	• Increases risk of being out LBW.

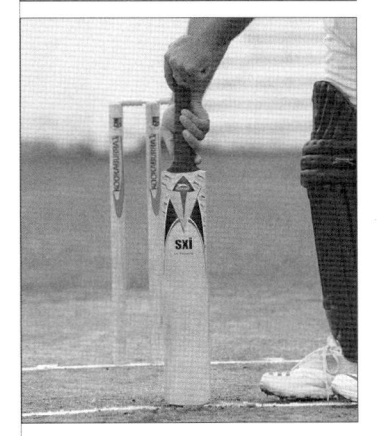

'Two legs', using the edge or face of the bat

3. Middle or centre

This guard favours batsmen who are strong off their pads, and who expect to make most of their runs on the leg side.

In this stance, your eyes will be on a line just outside off stump, making it easier to leave deliveries that start on that line. Many batsmen who take a middle-stump guard feel that they know exactly where their stumps are, while the opposite is true of bowlers: the sight of the batsman's legs and body standing squarely in front of the stumps – often hiding them entirely – tends to bother bowlers, who like to feel that they have a chance of knocking back the odd stump.

However, the risks inherent in this guard outweigh its benefits. The most obvious is the increased danger of playing around deliveries and being trapped LBW. In fact, this stance – in front of the stumps – might even provide bowlers with a target. Secondly, the batsman's eyes might be on a 'safe' line outside off stump, but that

'That's middle!'

BATTING 105

doesn't mean he won't be tempted into playing at balls he should be leaving alone: deliveries that are well wide of off stump suddenly seem to be on a good driving line, and he can end up nicking innocuously wide balls. Finally, there is the danger of moving too far across in the crease and exposing your leg stump. We've all seen batsmen move their weight towards off stump, looking to glance or pick up the ball over mid-wicket, only to be bowled round their legs.

MIDDLE OR CENTRE GUARD	
BENEFITS	RISKS
• Opens up leg-side scoring opportunities. • Batsman's body and legs block the bowler's view of the stumps, which can frustrate him or upset his line.	• Increased risk of being out LBW. • Invites shots outside off stump. • Can expose leg stump.

ADVICE FOR LEFT-HANDED BATSMEN

It is always vital to know where your off stump is, but in modern cricket this is especially true for left-handed batsmen. Until recently, left-handers have enjoyed something of an advantage in cricket. This is because in order for a right-arm bowler to hit the stumps, he needs to swing the ball in (an ability in short supply in the present-day game), and most straight deliveries from a right-arm bowler aimed at the stumps must pitch outside leg-stump, leaving the batsman immune to LBW appeals. Finally, if the bowler strays onto off stump, the eventual line of the delivery gives the left-hander room to free his arms and hit the ball through the off side.

However, in the last decade or so, more bowlers have been coming around the wicket to left-handers, a method most famously and successfully used by Glenn McGrath against Brian Lara and Gary Kirsten in the late 1990s. The change in angle changes the line of off stump for the left-hander, and many southpaws find it difficult to adjust. The result is that left-handers are now as vulnerable as right-handers to being bowled, and also cannot leave the ball quite as easily as before.

Left-handed batsmen need to be even more aware of their off stump than right-handers. They also need to learn to adapt their guard and stance to cope with the challenges posed by right-arm bowlers going around the wicket. For example, it is now common for left-handers to open their stance, in other words, to stand more chest-on to the bowler. These counter-tactics used by batsmen are examined more carefully in the discussion of stances available to batters on pp. 111–18.

THE GRIP

The importance of the grip cannot be overstated: this will regulate how you swing the bat back and forwards (the biomechanics of shot-making); affect how and where you make contact with the ball; and dictate how you deal with the many variations in the bowling coming at you.

The prevalence of extremely fast short-pitched bowling in the 1970s and 80s, often aimed at the head and body, saw widespread experimentation with grips as batsmen tried to find controlled ways of keeping the ball away from their throats and faces. The advent of bouncer restrictions and the near-mandatory use of helmets at first-class levels of the game have changed this trend again, with batsmen no longer having to play high as often, and therefore not having to alter their grips too much.

But the arrival of one-day cricket presented its own challenges to traditional grips, with batsmen required to adapt and improvise their repertoire of strokes almost as a matter of course, whether working ones and twos to keep the run rate ticking over, or slogging quick boundaries.

Of course, improvisation with grips is nothing new to cricket, as evidenced by this description of the Edwardian maestro and maharajah, Ranjitsinjhi:

> *When he is making a stroke his hands play up and down the handle like a violin player's on the strings of his instrument… his grip is almost entirely with finger and thumb* (C.B. Fry, quoted in Synge and Anns, 1987, p. 84).

The great Ranji (as he was generally known) seems to have been as adept at improvising as any Jonty Rhodes or Michael Bevan of the twentieth century.

Being able to adapt has its place, but remember that the most important function of any grip is that it must enable the batsman to swing the bat in a straight line to hit the ball, and allow both hands to swing the bat parallel to the shoulder line. One way of checking this is to try swinging the bat like a pendulum along a straight line (preferably marked along the ground), first with the top hand, then the bottom hand, and then both together. Ensure that your feet are parallel to a line going directly down the pitch from stump to stump. If your grip is correct, the bat will follow a straight line, and both the top and bottom hand will work together. If you find that your hands force your shoulders to dip or sway, then the grip is incorrect, and an adjustment will have to be made.

It is vital that your grip feels comfortable and natural: it should enable you to hit freely all round the wicket. Once you have mastered the orthodox or basic grip, described over the page, you can make minor adjustments until you feel satisfied with the way you are hitting the ball. It is important to find out what works for you.

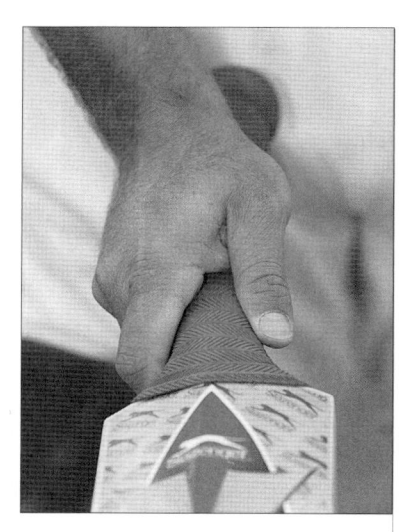

1. Orthodox grip

The natural inclination when picking up a bat is to grip it with an 'O' grip: that is, with each hand gripping the handle as one would grip the rungs of a ladder. This is often necessary when children are bought a new bat that is too heavy for them.

However, children should be taught a basic position that enables them to deal with all circumstances, and in this case the ideal grip – one that is widely taught by coaches – is the orthodox or 'V' grip.

Hold the handle with your hands not too far apart (two fingers' width is a good guideline), with the inside of the bottom arm forming a natural extension of the handle. The natural 'V' formed by the thumb and first finger of both hands should be aligned just off centre towards the outside edge of the bat. The knuckle of the forefinger of the bottom hand must point down the middle of the bat, with the knuckle above the thumb of the top hand pointing down the same line. The top hand should hold the handle firmly, while the bottom hand should be relaxed: imagine a young bird, and hold it tightly enough not to drop it, but loosely enough not to crush it.

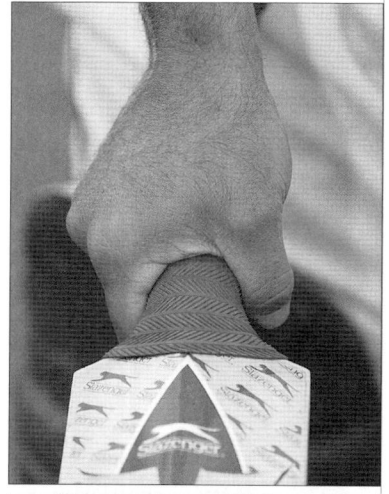

The orthodox grip – note that the handle is not being 'strangled'

2. The 'O' grip

The 'O' grip is very popular, perhaps because it feels more natural and more potent than the 'V' grip (this is how cavemen must have held their clubs!); but unless it is understood, it can and will cause problems, specifically when the bat is lifted or swung back.

Because of the firmness of the all-finger grip, when the bat is lifted, the elbow of the back arm slides past the bottom of the ribcage. This causes an inverted 'T' angle comprising the bottom arm and handle.

The bottom hand then slips underneath the handle, which chokes the movement of the bat and cuts down the size of the hitting area. On the downward arc, the bat starts to swing across the body, dragging the head and right shoulder down: without perfect timing, this will lead to the batsman being bowled or edging the ball into his stumps. The 'O' grip can also stifle driving opportunities on the off side through extra cover, as well as making it very difficult to play off the back foot square of the wicket.

However, it can be used with great success: some extremely prolific run-scorers (Donald Bradman, Graeme Smith and Mohammed Azharuddin, among others) have shown that if you work out where the ball can be hit safely, you can excel with an 'O' grip.

LEFT AND MIDDLE: *The choked 'O' grip forces the right elbow to move along the underside of the ribcage, with the right forearm forming an inverted 'T' with the bat handle.*

3. The Knott Grip

A further variation is the adjusted grip first used by John Edrich, and then adopted by Alan Knott in an effort to cope with the hostile fast and short bowling of Dennis Lillee and Jeff Thomson during England's 1974/75 tour of Australia. This grip helped Knott to play 'high'; in other words, to get the bat up to defend against the excessive pace and bounce that the fearsome Australian duo were generating on green and generally uneven pitches. As the grip suggests, ducking was not an option, given that the ball was rising off a length not short enough to get underneath!

This grip first evolved in front of a long mirror – the old-fashioned version of video playback. Visualizing the bounce of the ball, Knott studied the response of his hands as he adjusted the height of the bat. The first problem he encountered with the orthodox grip was that he could only reach a certain height. Therefore, he was inhibited in dealing with the ball that 'gets big' – the delivery that rises disconcertingly off the pitch, usually off an area just short of a good length on a fairly bouncy pitch, that is too full to duck beneath, but comes on too quickly to hook.

By adjusting his grip so that the top hand slipped around the back of the handle until the back of the hand was facing backwards, he found he could 'periscope' up another foot, which made the rising delivery playable. The one drawback was that the method restricted his ability to drive the ball straight: because the grip choked the free-flowing movement of the arms in the straight drive, Knott found himself push-driving for a single or two runs at best, instead of drilling the ball to the boundary rope.

However, this carefully thought-out method helped the England wicket-keeper-batsman play some fine innings during his career. Bob Woolmer counted himself among those many players who were better able to cope with ultra-quick bowling with the help of this grip.

The limiting effect the grip has on certain strokes isn't necessarily a bad thing: it certainly restricts impetuous batsmen, who might otherwise play too many adventurous shots too early on. In fact, this grip might be considered a handy means of starting to build an innings, especially against pace; once settled at the crease, you could revert to a more orthodox grip.

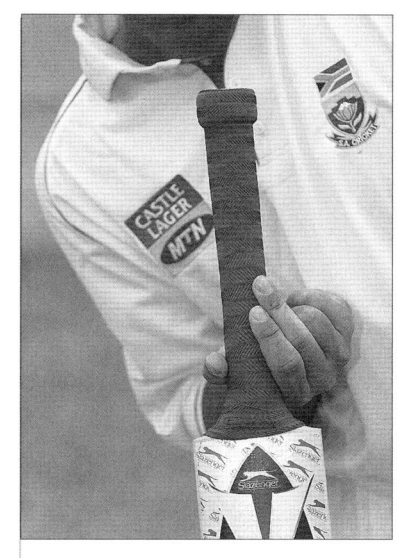

The bottom hand loosens and allows the full face of the bat to be offered in defence, while…

…the top hand offers a light but firm support, and is ready to lift the splice well above the batter's face.

BATTING 109

Hingeing

A final crucial aspect of any grip is your ability to hinge, without which the backswing is impeded (try holding the bat as in the first picture – 1 – and swinging it back). This should be an automatic movement when lifting the bat behind you in your backswing. As shown in 2, the top hand should control the backward path of the bat while the bottom hand acts as a support. Children who have bats that are too heavy for them will grip the bat harder with the bottom hand, and will immediately find themselves unable to swing the bat in a straight line towards the ball.

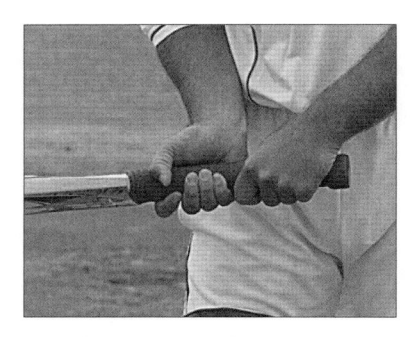

1: *Choked grip (all the fingers are around the bat handle)*

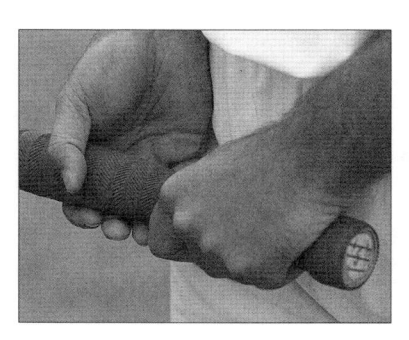

2: *Hinged grip, close-up view*

3: *Hinged grip, releasing three bottom-hand fingers to a resting position*

Summing up grips

- Players should make sure they master the orthodox grip before they begin experimenting. Hands should be in the correct position – if in doubt, check them against the illustrations above.
- The top hand should hold the handle of the bat firmly.
- The bottom hand should support the handle of the bat, rather than squeeze it: the hands and arms must be flexible and not rigid.
- Your grip must enable you to swing the bat like a pendulum along a straight line.

SOFT HANDS

No doubt you will have heard the expression 'soft hands' used to describe certain delicate shots or deft defensive strokes. In essence, this term refers to the opposite of what we have warned against in this section: 'choking' the bat, or squeezing it too hard, with disastrous effects on both your backswing and forward swing into the shot.

Hingeing is the first step in playing with soft hands: as shown in 2 and 3 opposite, rather than gripping the bat handle like a club, the bottom hand simply acts as a guide. The bottom hand quite literally holds the bat 'softly' (remember that baby bird!).

Soft hands are a defensive aid only: when hitting the ball, you will need all the force and timing that the bottom hand can provide. But when it is necessary to take the pace off the ball, soft hands are vital. By releasing the bottom hand, the impact of ball on bat is greatly diminished, which translates into the ball dropping quickly to the ground, rather than popping up to a close fielder in the case of spin bowling, or carrying to the slips off a fast bowler.

The results of not playing with soft hands are most clearly seen in beginners, who often loft easy catches to silly mid-on and mid-off because the bottom hand has forced itself past the top hand, scooping the ball into the air.

Using soft hands also means playing the ball with relaxed arms, allowing it to come on to the defensive shot, and giving with the arms as the ball arrives. Ride with the ball, don't force or punch at it. Try to relax and 'give' as the ball arrives: instead of trying to hit the ball, visualize trying to hold it on the bat for a moment before guiding it down or away.

An excellent way to develop the ability to play with soft hands is to try catching a tennis ball, thrown from three or four feet away, on a racquet without letting it bounce off. This teaches you to receive the ball with flexibility, rather than being braced or rigid.

THE STANCE

The most important consideration in choosing a stance or 'ready position' is that you must be comfortable. You must be able to move backwards or forwards quickly, easily and smoothly and you must be relaxed. Whatever stance you choose, keep your eyes level and ensure that your body weight is slightly forward of centre. (Imagine a line through your body from the head through the groin, and move your head slightly forward of that line.) This slight forward weighting will gain you vital milliseconds when the ball arrives: it is easier and therefore quicker to move back by rocking off the front foot; and the weight has already shifted to assist in the movement.

Try to 'soften' your heels – take the weight off them, but don't lift them. This should move your weight onto the balls of your feet, which in turn allows you to move forward and back when you need to. Experiment until you find out what works for you, and then practise it until you are satisfied.

1. Orthodox or sideways stance

The orthodox stance shown here is probably the best option when you first begin playing cricket. The feet should be shoulder-width apart and parallel to the batting crease. Now make sure that not only the feet, but also the knees, hips and shoulders are all parallel to the crease. Once the body is correctly lined up, roll the upper body forward, and 'sit down' slightly, so that the hands come to rest on the top of the front pad, with the bat resting on the ground.

Head, shoulder and front hip should be over the front foot, keeping the eyes level. The front elbow should point down the wicket, and the knees should be bent to allow movement forwards or backwards. It is important to keep the upper body relaxed, especially when facing quick bowlers. The position of the feet must allow the body to be in a balanced position; this enables you to move backwards and forwards with equal ease. Remember: you must feel comfortable.

It is also worth experimenting with the front foot. Sometimes by opening it up to the bowler, you will be able to move beside the ball instead of in front of it. Being beside the ball allows room for the bat to swing down the line of the ball, while if the foot goes across the line, the bat will have to swing around the front foot.

The orthodox stance: the upper body is balanced and relaxed, and the head, front shoulder, hip and knee are comfortably aligned over the front foot.

2. Wide stance

The first noticeable aspect of this stance is that the head is now slightly in front of the centre line, and in a position that is recommended by most students of the game for the reasons of weighting already discussed.

This is a stance favoured by many successful and hard-hitting batsmen. Graeme Pollock, Lance Klusener and Graeme Smith of South Africa, as well as Adam Gilchrist of Australia, have all adopted a wide stance. Not coincidentally, both Pollock and Smith are tall men, and it is a stance that seems to be particularly effective for taller batsmen, as it is less taxing on the back.

The theory behind a wide stance is that the batsman will have to move less to get to the ball, thereby eliminating movement-related errors. To play forward, you make only a sideways adjustment, and to play back, you simply rock the weight off the front foot. In effect, you've gone both forward and back before the ball is bowled, which can create enormous frustration for bowlers, and free you to score off a wider range of deliveries. If its mechanics are thoroughly understood, and it is practised diligently, this can be a very effective stance.

The wide stance: weight is pushed forward, player is ready to drive with minimal foot movement, or to rock back to play aggressive cross-batted shots.

BATTING 113

3. Open stance

The open or front-facing stance is still sometimes censured by coaches and commentators as technically unorthodox, and yet over the years it has been successfully adopted by a host of great cricketers, including Ken Barrington, Jim Parks, Peter Willey, Shivnarine Chanderpaul, Lance Klusener and Mohammed Azharuddin.

Instead of standing with his shoulders at a right angle to the wicket, the batsman opens up his front shoulder so that the line from front to back shoulder points roughly towards second or third slip.

This stance is based on the principle that standing slightly more front-on to the bowler gives the batsman a better view of the ball. The explanation for this is that just as you have a dominant hand, you also have a dominant eye, one that transmits visual signals to the brain more quickly and effectively than the other. This means that if you bat right-handed, and your right-eye is dominant, a side-on stance means that your dominant eye is having to squint away to the left over the bridge of your nose, or at least look down a line that is slightly outside that of the ball. Opening up the stance, so that there is a more direct line of sight from your right eye to the bowler's hand, can give you a better picture of the delivery. The same applies to left-eye-dominant left-handers.

A further argument for this stance is that it makes the batsman stronger on the leg side. However, in order to gain these advantages, he has to make a large movement across the stumps if he wants to drive an off-side half-volley. This extra distance he has to cover will take precious time away from his balance and shot-making processes, and may lead to a false shot outside off stump. Off-drives might not be the only shots to suffer: standing too square on can severely limit a wide variety of strokes on the off side.

There are thus advantages and disadvantages to an open stance, and you need to weigh these carefully.

Whether you stand tall with your bat off the ground (top), or take a more traditional crouch with the bat on the pitch (bottom), the open stance gives you a clearer and longer sight of the ball.

4. Feet close together

If you've ever watched early film footage of cricket from the 1920s, or paged through a book of photographs of the likes of Bradman and Hobbs, you'll have seen that this used to be a very popular stance. Very few batsmen adopt this stance today, because it reduces balance; however, 70 or 80 years ago, before the advent of dangerously fast bowling and bouncy wickets, batsmen didn't need to develop as wide a range of defensive movements and shots as they do today.

It is interesting to note that those who adopted this position opened the front foot slightly and kept 60% of their weight on the back foot, ready to get forward. This was a hangover from the days of underarm bowling, when batsmen could just stay on the back foot and hammer the ball to all parts, as there was very little pace involved.

Still, before being too critical of this stance one should remember that it worked for Bradman, who faced his fair share of quick men on uneven, uncovered wickets…

Bradman's trademark stance, with the bat face pointing at square leg and his feet almost together.

5. Closed stance

In a closed stance, the batsman's front shoulder turns towards mid-off. The line of his toes likewise points in this direction.

This stance is included here more as a warning than a recommendation: it is fraught with potential problems.

Firstly, the closed position of the body may well encourage the player to move forward and across the line of the ball, which will lead to an early foot movement known as 'planting'. This sees the batsman move outside (to the off side) of the ball, and then try to play around his 'planted' foot, usually with disastrous results if the bowler is accurate and intelligent.

Secondly – and this is more rare than players fumbling around their front foot – is the problem of batsmen allowing their back foot to slide towards the leg side. Visualize yourself stepping straight back while standing in a closed stance: you're going to head towards fine leg. In other words, you're going to expose your stumps and put yourself out of reach of off stump.

A closed stance can often be the result of poor weighting: too much weight on the front foot can turn the shoulder towards the head. This is also caused by tension and nerves, which cause the batsman to crouch too much onto the front foot. Coaches need to be on the lookout for this, and should always stress comfort and relaxation in the set-up position.

Lines gone wrong: here the player's eyes are no longer level, and to play straight, he will be forced to come around his front foot.

BATTING **115**

6. Standing tall with high backlift

This is a modern stance, pioneered by Tony Greig and then adopted with success by, among others, Mike Brearley, Graham Gooch and Clive Rice.

The stance differs from all the others discussed so far in that the batsman does not 'sit down' or crouch at the wicket, but instead stands in an upright position. Rather than resting on the ground, his bat is lifted high behind him as the ball is delivered, ready to follow through.

Those who swear by this stance say it is more restful on the back than the crouching position. In theory, the stance helps the batsman to be properly balanced, enables him to play the rising ball more easily, and stops him from toppling towards the off side, thereby preventing LBW decisions. However, this theory is flawed, as is discussed in the section on pre-delivery movements. Another potential danger is the increased vulnerability to the fast yorker: standing tall can mean that the batsman has less time to get down quickly and dig out the ball.

Summing up stances

- The orthodox stance is generally a wise place to start.
- Don't be afraid to experiment until you find the stance in which you are (a) most comfortable and (b) best able to play all your shots.
- Taller batsmen may find a wider or more open stance helpful.
- Whichever stance you choose, make sure it allows you to get into position quickly and easily.

Even though the player is no longer resting on his bat, he is still balanced, centred and in a good position to move forward or back.

ADAPTING YOUR STANCE TO COMBAT BOWLING TACTICS

Your guard and stance offer you security: together, they form your blueprint for successful and safe batting. However, it is the job of the bowler to erode your comfort zone and break through your defences. Intelligent or highly skilled bowlers can turn your tried and tested set-up position into a liability with just a few deliveries. When this happens, it is essential that you have the confidence and foresight to adapt in order to stay in the game. The following are some scenarios in which you might consider temporarily altering where and how you stand.

1. Leg-spin – Shane Warne ripping it out of the rough

Leg-spinners bowling over the wicket into rough is a far more common sight in cricket today than twenty years ago. To combat this tactic, stand outside leg stump – in other words, offer your exposed stumps to the bowler. Make sure to stand inside your crease, as this will cut off the angle that might allow him to bowl you around your legs. Standing outside the leg stump means you won't be tempted to play around your front pad. This also applies to a left-arm spinner.

Showing your stumps to the turning ball might seem risky, but the slightest error in line or length by the bowler means that you can free your arms and hit through the off side. In other words, the bowler is under pressure because he's turning the ball into your hitting arc. If you were standing in front of your stumps, the same delivery would force you to push out around your front leg, opening you up to all kinds of dangers, such as an LBW shout, catches to silly mid-on, or a nick to the keeper.

When you play straight to the leg-spinner turning it out of the rough, play with the spin towards the off side. But when you play across the line with a horizontal bat, always hit against the spin: if you try to pull or sweep a ball spinning in the same direction that the bat is travelling, there is a tendency to rush the wrists past the ball, whether over or under, which can result in the top-edge popping up, or the bottom edge dragging back onto the stumps, or even the back of the bat making contact with the stumps.

Most importantly, when you hit the spinning ball, hit it hard. Be committed. Don't flick after it – it's all too easy to nick off this way. In this respect, Pakistan's Mohammad Yousuf is superbly gifted: use him as a good example of how to drive with the spin. Otherwise you can't go wrong emulating V.V.S. Laxman in his stellar 2001 series against Australia in India, in which he obliterated the bowling of Shane Warne in spite of some frightening rough outside his leg stump.

2. Fast and tall – Big Bird building up a head of steam

Joel Garner, the West Indian known as Big Bird, stood at around 6 foot 8 inches tall, and it was this height that made him so difficult to play. If you tried to get into line with his bowling, you were always fending the ball from chest height; but he also bowled a brutal yorker, and if he slipped that in, you ended up playing around your legs.

The easiest way to combat this kind of attack is to stand outside leg stump, and to stand deep in the crease so that the yorker becomes a playable delivery. Anything on off stump or outside becomes a free hit or is easily left, and therefore all the pressure is switched back to the bowler.

3. Southpaw danger – Wasim Akram swinging it in from over the wicket

Bob Woolmer was being severely troubled by the left-arm inswing of Garry Sobers, until he was introduced to a useful technique by Colin Cowdrey. Cowdrey advised him to open up his stance by putting the toe of his back foot on off stump, and the toes of his front foot on leg stump. He then told him to align every shot back towards the stumps at the bowler's end – and to leave everything else. This included cutting out all shots square of the wicket. According to Cowdrey's method, the angle of delivery from Sobers would slide the ball past the face of Woolmer's bat onto the off side: playing with an open face (as Woolmer had been doing) could only lead to a snick to the slips.

In short, instead of playing the inswinger to extra cover, focus on playing it back down the wicket. All you've got to worry about then is the one that goes straight on, but because your stance is open, you'll probably miss it.

4. Keeping the slips interested – Makhaya Ntini sliding it across left-handers

This operates on exactly the same principle as above. The problem arises when left-handers see right-handed batsmen going back and across, and copy them. But going back and across only opens them out and makes them prone to nicks; or else the front foot goes across too far, and closes them off, which also leads to nicks. It is essential that left-handers keep the normal comfortable angle of their body intact, and stand still. If they move, it must be a rhythm movement that helps them to keep the angle, such as two steps forward, or to the side.

PRE-DELIVERY (TRIGGER) MOVEMENTS AND BAT-LIFT

Taking guard, finding a suitable grip, and establishing a comfortable stance are all part of your technical preparations for batting, but now that the bowler is actually on his way towards you, you need to get ready for the next step: that is, actually receiving and hitting the ball. This is where you begin to generate rhythm movements, or 'trigger' movements, as they are sometimes called – those instinctive actions you take to ready yourself and to squeeze out an extra fraction of a second before playing a shot or defending.

Many coaches will tell you that you must stand still at the crease in order to judge line and length correctly, and they are absolutely correct in principle: this is one of the keys to successful batting. But how are you supposed to stay still when the thunderbolts start crashing down at you, courtesy of Michael Holding, Waqar Younis, and others of the speedy fraternity?

The simple and frank answer is that you can't. We simply are not able to think or move quickly enough to be able to react with strength and precision once the ball has pitched. In other words, you need to develop a series of movements that take place *before* you hit the ball. Used correctly, these give you more time, and when playing fast bowlers, even a millisecond can spell the difference between an outside edge and a sweetly timed drive through the covers. Furthermore, these movements will also help you to develop that vital but often elusive asset for successful batting – rhythm.

1. Bat-lift and backswing

It seems self-explanatory that in order to hit the ball, you need to swing the bat backwards before swinging it forward; but the lifting and backward swinging of the bat are more important to your pre-delivery movements than simply as agents of leverage.

As their respective names imply, there are two movements involved in preparing to play a stroke: the reflex action of lifting the toe of the bat off the ground (bat-lift), and then the decision as to how much power you need for your shot (whether attacking or defending), which you then translate into a decision as to how far back to swing the bat (backswing).

Watch any great player and you will see this two-part action clearly, especially when they face quicker bowlers: first there is a bat-lift and then a backswing.

The bat-lift – whether a quick tap of the toe of the bat into the pitch or the feet, or a small ripple of movement through the wrist that gets the bat moving off the ground – happens simultaneously with the pre-delivery movement of the feet and body. The timing of these movements is of course entirely individual, but most batsmen share similar movements: a bend in the elbows as the bat lifts, a crouching movement and a setting of the neck, a bending and tensing of the knees. Bob Woolmer referred to this as the 'ready' position.

Ian Chappell, one of the stellar batsmen of the latter half of the twentieth century and a knowledgeable coach, describes these movements as 'unweighting'; that is, getting your weight and momentum moving in such a way as to be ready to go forward or back, depending on the delivery. Most of the great batsmen, from Donald Bradman to Jacques Kallis, developed their own methods of unweighting, according to individual preference. Interestingly, unweighting is usually only seen at the start of an innings, or against the new ball; times when the batsman needs his technique to be working at top efficiency, and when he needs to be more alert than ever. It's no

THE GREAT BACKLIFT DEBATE

Most coaches believe that if the bat does not come forward in a straight line, then the backswing must be altered until it does: countless young batsmen have been told at some stage or another that their bat is coming down from somewhere near second slip, and that they'll never be successful unless they straighten up and fly right.

It is indeed vital to bring the hands down in line with the ball, and young players should certainly be encouraged to get the fundamentals right.

But Tony Shillinglaw's challenging study of Donald Bradman's backlift has opened up a fascinating debate on the matter. This is discussed in more detail at the end of this chapter, but Shillinglaw simply pointed out that Bradman – the most consistent run-scorer in the history of the game – brought his bat down at an angle: down from the much-maligned second slip position. Bradman was in fact far from unique in this respect: further investigation has revealed that strong batsmen such as Shahid Afridi, Adam Gilchrist and Ricky Ponting all share this trait.

The key movement, however, comes during the forward swing of the bat: a subtle but definite turn of the shoulder that straightens the path of the bat towards the line of the ball.

Straight back, or towards the slips and gully? Why not look at what today's best batters are doing? What everyone agrees on, however, is where the bat needs to end up!

coincidence that many batsmen also open their eyes very wide when unweighting, an indication of their extra alertness.

During the correct bat-lift, the front shoulder should be pointing at the ball, while the head must be absolutely still, the arms and shoulders totally relaxed, and the hands under the eyes.

The 'ready' position is crucial, as this will determine your ability to judge line and length, and it is from this position that you will decide whether or not to play at a delivery. But the backswing is as important. This is created by the shoulder turning, moving the hands into a high position, ready to hit the ball hard.

Against real pace it is vital to pick the bat up early and not too high (especially at the beginning of your innings), as this will allow you time to play the ball, as there will be less distance for the bat to travel to reach the ball.

2. Rhythm and pre-delivery movements

Batting rhythm comes from balanced, easy and minimal foot movements. Against genuine pace, these need to be made a fraction of a second before the bowler releases the ball. Against slower or medium pace bowlers there is more time, but the earlier the movement, the more time you will have to play the shot. In other words, the key to any foot movements is when (and not how) they are made.

There is a variety of movements you might like to try:
- Moving your back foot back and across towards the off stump; then transferring your weight back to the front foot as the bowler releases the ball; then making the final movement, having judged length, and playing the appropriate shot.
- Moving the front foot forwards (but not to the off side) a fraction before the bowler bowls, initiating your movements and response to the delivery as above.
- Picking up the back foot and front foot in turn and spreading them a little wider, without sideways movement, again just before the ball is released.

These are just three common ways in which rhythm is generated. Once rhythm has been achieved, these movements tend to fall away: by the time you are settled and well on your way to a century, you'll find that you are standing perfectly still, and the ball will look like a balloon.

Some players prefer to mix and combine these movements, depending on the speed of the bowling or the pace of the pitch, but as a rule of thumb, most players tend to use the back-and-across method on fast, bouncy pitches; and usually push forward on slower pitches (perhaps taking a couple of steps down the track as their unweighting movement). Once again, the longer they bat, the less they move.

Remember, it's not wise to go back and across to a spinner, since this leads to two changes of line (first your eyes, then the ball as it spins). Rather go forward or back on a straight line, especially when the ball is turning.

Chappell's definition of unweighting holds that there has to be a transference of weight from one foot to another if movement is going to be possible, in other words, you need to create momentum. Try experimenting with your own weight transference: put all your weight onto the back foot and try to move back. Not so easy! This clearly demonstrates that if you are going to move backwards, then your weight has to transfer onto the front foot and vice versa.

Every batsman will eventually develop his own unweighting movements. It is important that a player experiments until he finds a method that suits him. Coaches should also refrain from coaching only one movement or set of movements, especially their personal favourites!

The illustrations on the next page provide some practical examples of the principles and techniques described in the previous sections.

BATTING 121

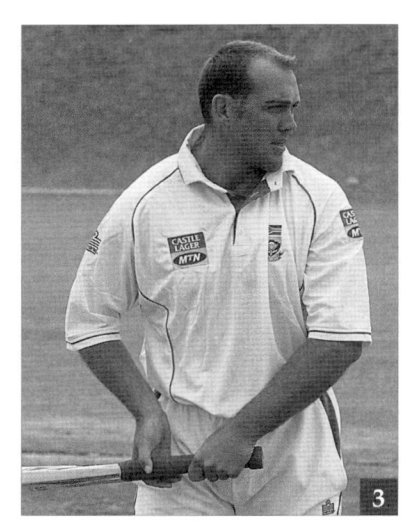

1. *Lifting the bat into a 'ready' position as the bowler approaches. This movement is used by many of today's top batsmen. From this position it is easy to defend and attack. It is important to be relaxed in this position, and to time the bat-lift together with any pre-delivery foot movements.* **2.** *Note how in this front view the bat is going towards the slips. At this juncture, it is not important to lift the bat straight over the stumps; rather, aim for a relaxed lift off the ground. The arms must not tense up.* **3.** *Arms relaxed, hands under the eyes, head still, watching the ball, knees bent ready to make the reflex decision.*

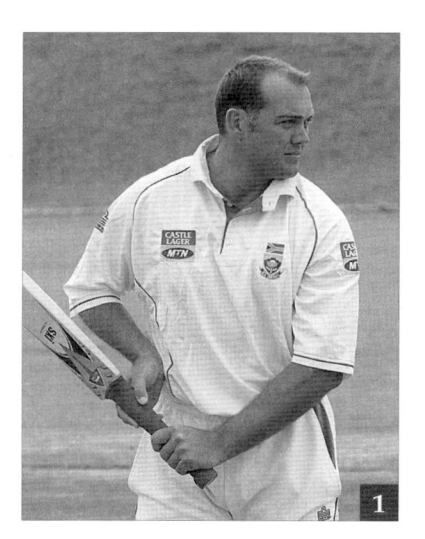

1. *The swing before the batsman is about to hit the ball. The shoulder turn will push the arms back and into the correct position so that the bat comes down straight. To get more power as you swing the bat back, the front wrist should 'cock' – the face of the bat will turn out towards point. Some batsmen turn the bat inwards at this moment. This is not recommended!* **2.** *Going back and across just before the bowler bowls is known as a rhythm or trigger movement. This movement is used by many players to give them more time against pace, and to allow them to get in line with the stumps earlier.* **3.** *The front foot press: the front foot is pressed forward and towards the off-stump. The danger here is that one can be 'trapped' and have to play around the pad.*

122   CRICKET TECHNIQUES

THE SHOTS

If you want to write a novel, you need a good vocabulary and a firm grasp of grammar. A Test match innings is a cricketer's novel, created slowly and carefully for his own pleasure and that of his teammates and supporters; and in this instance, shots are his grammar and vocabulary. Without a cricketing vocabulary, you simply can't craft an innings: like many people who are not good writers, you might have a splendid idea (a match-saving defensive innings, a match-winning century), but without the nuts-and-bolts grammar, you won't know where to start.

What follows is an explanation of every possible batting shot – the full repertoire. Whether you should play them all is another matter entirely. Too many batsmen fail because they play all the shots all the time. Just as a novelist adapts and restricts his or her language according to the subject matter and reader, so the batsman must discipline himself and learn which shots are appropriate to which conditions and circumstances.

How many shots should you have? The simple answer is: all of them. Some Test batsmen have managed at international level with an apparently limited range of strokes – South Africa's Kepler Wessels (who played for Australia as well) is a case in point, as is Steve Waugh, who slowly but surely *eliminated* shots from his repertoire during his long and distinguished career – but even such players have enough shots to get by. Younger batsmen can sometimes feel pressured into learning and playing strokes that don't suit their game or temperament, just as others can become lazy or inhibited, afraid of extending their options and relying instead on the small range of strokes they know and trust. If you are uncertain of where you stand, memorize this basic yardstick: if you can score on both sides of the wicket, stop getting yourself out, and manage not to get bogged down against spin – then you have enough shots.

Of course, there are some shots that you must have, especially at higher levels. During England's tour of South Africa in 2005, Kevin Pietersen dealt destruction and mayhem to the home-team's bowlers in the one-day series; yet at no stage was his inability to cut tested. This weakness was successfully exploited by Warwickshire earlier in his first-class career: they simply put on a left-arm seamer who bowled short and wide outside Pietersen's off stump, and he holed out to gully every time, rarely reaching double figures. He has since worked on that aspect of his game and gone on to be a phenomenal shot-maker at international level, but for a time, it was a huge gap in his armoury, and effectively made him irrelevant as a front-line batsman.

Training and practice are everything in shot selection. By learning the shots, learning (as Peter May put it) the correct answer to every question asked of you, and practising them over and over again, you will be able to react effectively and powerfully when the time comes.

STRAIGHT BAT SHOTS

Many traditional coaching methods have been overtaken and outdated by the rapid development of the game in recent decades, but it's unlikely that coaches will stop telling batsmen to play straight anytime soon. Playing straight, with a vertical bat, both defensively and when attacking, is the essence of batting. All the masters of the game have played straight, which is all the evidence you should need to encourage you to learn and master the straight bat shots.

Playing straight also makes mathematical sense: on the face of an upright bat there is six times the area in which the ball can make contact than there is on the bat that is held horizontally. In other words, it is considerably easier to hit the ball with a straight bat.

One of the most commonly seen dismissals is caused by playing across the line of the ball with the bat at an angle, usually resulting in a catch in the slips or the ball being dragged onto the stumps. Right-handed left-handers – batsmen who bat left-handed but who are right-handed – are more susceptible to playing with an angled bat, because their bottom hand does not have the strength or co-ordination necessary to swing the bat straighter. As discussed in the section on grips (pp. 107–110), it is up to the bottom hand to adapt its grip if the bat is going to be allowed to straighten.

Experiment with your own bat by wrapping more and more fingers around the handle: you will notice how the bat's angle changes as you add more fingers to the grip. Players with weaker bottom hands will inevitably want to have more fingers on the handle for comfort, which tends to cost them in the long run.

It's been stated here before, but it's worth repeating: training the bottom hand is a vital part of coaching the art of batting. It's been dormant for 90 years, and that's 90 years too long!

1. THE FORWARD DEFENSIVE

One often hears that teaching the forward defensive shot to young cricketers can dampen their enthusiasm for the game. We disagree. In fact, teaching young players cricket shots without first ensuring that they master this one is tantamount to teaching them to ski or roller-blade without first showing them how to stop.

We would be the last to discourage a young player from hitting the ball – after all, the nature of the game demands that runs be scored. However, if bowlers consistently bowl a good length, then batsmen will have no choice but to meet their deliveries with appropriate shots. This being the case, the argument for learning the forward defensive is very strong. Without this skill very few innings would last very long, a sure-fire way of killing a young player's interest in and enjoyment of the game.

Statistics show that during an average innings of 100 (if such an innings can ever be called average), the forward defensive shot comprises nearly 70% of all shots offered during that innings. This was well illustrated by Jacques Kallis's anchor innings of 95 against India in Bangalore in February 2000, which enabled South Africa to win by an innings and 71 runs. Kallis faced a gruelling 359 balls, almost twice as many as faced by the next-highest scoring batsman. He later remarked that halfway through the innings, he thought he was too tired to play one more forward defensive stroke, underlining that this stroke is the foundation on which most innings are built.

The forward defensive is just that: the first line of defence for your stumps. And just because it is a basic and unglamorous stroke, don't assume it is easy. In essence, you are defending a target that is 9 inches (22,86cm) by 28 inches (71,1cm), from a missile the size of a jaffa orange (hence the exclamation, 'That ball was an absolute Jaffa!'), with a bat that is 36 inches long, 4 inches wide and weighs at least two and a half pounds. In theory, it's easy, but in real life, it is much harder than one expects.

When to play the shot

The forward defensive is played to a ball that cannot be driven, and that is too full to go back to. It is played when the bowler is attacking the stumps, as opposed to bowling in the 'corridor of uncertainty' (see p. 244). In other words, it is played to a threatening delivery on a good line and length. Remember that a good length ball will differ according to the height – and therefore the reach – of the batsman, the pace and bounce of the pitch, and often the position of the game (for instance, two identical deliveries can look dramatically different if the first arrives with your team on 450 for 3, and the second arrives in the final session as you try to hang on for a draw). A rough guide for what constitutes a good length ball is usually something around three metres from the batting crease.

There is an old saying: 'If in doubt, push out.' This is based on the assumption that the umpire will not give you out on the front foot, so the further forward you go, the more likely you are to be given the benefit of the doubt in case of LBW appeals. With the advent of technology, which has made umpires less inclined to give batsmen the benefit of the doubt, this adage has become a little ragged, and there have been some shocked batsmen walking back to the pavilion, who felt certain they were practically doing the splits when the ball hit their front pad!

However, if the ball is moving around a lot off the seam or keeping low, it is better to try and meet it early to prevent movement, just as a goal-keeper in football might narrow the angle to make the shot harder. Hence the advice to 'get to the pitch of the ball to smother the spin.' If you're at the pitch of the ball and it deviates, it can only deviate into the middle of your bat, or at most an inch either side of the middle.

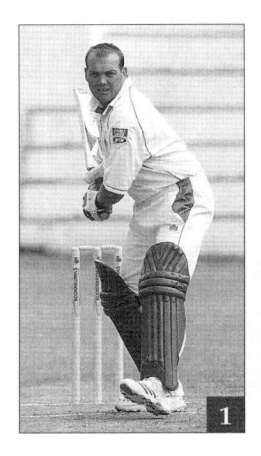

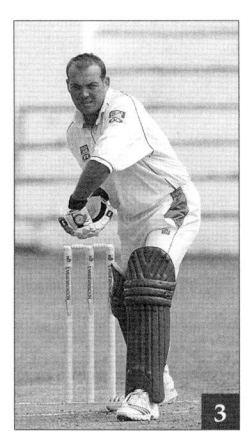

Playing the shot

Watch the ball out of the bowler's hand, and pick line and length as soon as possible, with the head kept absolutely still (1). Take a comfortable stride towards, and just inside, the line of the ball; keep the eyes level, swing the bat back and over the stumps by making a small front shoulder rotation. Cock the wrist of the top hand and release the fingers of the bottom hand, holding only with thumb and first finger (2). At this moment, the face of the bat should be slightly open and the backswing should take the top hand back past the knee. The front hip should be balanced over the front foot, and head and shoulder should be together (3).

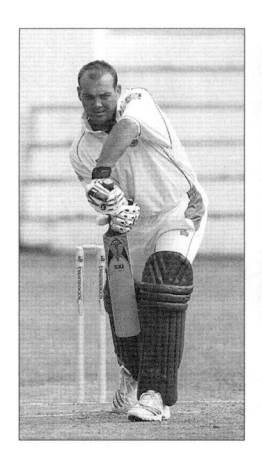

At the moment of impact, the heel of the back foot is raised to allow the batsman's weight to get forward: don't leave the heel on the ground, as this causes poor balance. Rotate the front shoulder towards the ball, and allow enough room with your front foot to enable the path of the bat to meet the path of the ball. It is important to remain sideways on, and to bring the bat down straight and square to the line of the ball, travelling parallel to the initial position of the shoulders, past the back pad (so that the ball cannot nip through) to join the front pad. The bottom of the bat and pad must be kept together, with the hands high over the ball. The body should be balanced, with the hip over the front foot and only the toe of the back foot resting on the ground for stability (4 and 5).

As you play the stroke, the top hand should be dominant, remaining in front of the bottom hand (this will angle the bat and keep the ball down), while the bottom hand releases the full grip so that only the thumb and forefinger remain to guide the bat into position.

Meanwhile, keep the top elbow high, the head and eyes over the ball, and the eyes on the ball (for as long as is possible), which at this point should be bouncing onto the bat and then rolling harmlessly away.

Remember, don't make any effort to force the ball away: you should feel that your bat is an impenetrable, immobile wall rather than a blade.

Practising the shot

A mirror is an excellent tool for practising the various phases of the forward defensive: watch every part of yourself as you make the shot – feet, shoulders, elbows and hands. Then practise in degrees of progression, first with a partner throwing underarm with a tennis ball; then throwing a cricket ball underarm; then overarm bowling with a cricket ball; and then finally a bowling machine. If you don't have access to a bowling machine, get your partner to throw (or bowl, if he is consistent enough) at the correct length. If you make a mistake judging length, try to stay in position and survive.

Whether you use a mirror or video footage to examine your technique, it is important to try to 'feel' the correct positions, to train your body to assume the correct positions until they become second nature. Make sure that you start at a slow, manageable pace so that the accent is on the correct body shape. As you become better at the shot, gradually increase the pace of the ball until finally reaching competitive levels. Also remember to practise the shot against spin and seam wherever possible.

Common problems

- **The extra-cover defensive:** a common error, in which the batsman pushes out towards extra cover with an angled bat. This technique presents only half a bat to the line of the ball, and any movement off the pitch or through the air will either find an edge, nip between bat and pad and bowl you 'through the gate', or miss the bat altogether, which can be psychologically disconcerting, and will certainly unleash a torrent of commentary from the opposition!
- **Hard hands:** pushing hard at the ball while defending. This can create a variety of problems, the most dangerous of which is that if the ball hits the edge, it will carry comfortably to the slips. Likewise against spin, the hard push will give the ball the impetus to fly neatly into the hands of the fielders around the bat. Even

if you evade these dangers, the ball will still travel too quickly to the infield to enable a single to be stolen. Finally, if you push out past the front pad, a gap (the infamous 'gate') will appear, and any inward movement by the ball will take it through and into your stumps. This is especially true on slow pitches where the ball 'holds up' on the surface. In other words, don't confuse the forward defensive with the defensive push, which is a legitimate shot used when the batsman is trying to push the ball into a gap for a single or to steer the ball off the back foot down to third man. However, even this shot, a product of one-day cricket, is fraught with danger and it is often punished by dismissal. In fact if you're going through a lean trot or a run of bad form, don't even think about playing it.

- **Defending across the line:** bringing the bat down across the line is a common fault and needs to be eradicated early on. What looks like a good forward defensive ends up with the bat carrying on across the pad, with the result that the batter is either bowled (off the outside edge or simply past the outside edge), or caught behind off the outside edge.
- **Bent back knee:** to get forward and over the ball properly, your back knee needs to be fairly rigid, with your back leg stretched out behind you, toes on the ground and heel in the air. When the back knee is bent, the entire shot becomes more upright, leading to serious trouble.

The cause of this error is an incorrect body position: the body is out of control, largely because there is no balance being provided by the back knee, which means there is no guarantee that if the ball moves, the body will be able to respond. Most obviously, the bat is stuck behind the front knee and can't go any further if the ball turns or seams in towards the pad, which will almost certainly end in an LBW dismissal.

Geoffrey Boycott, one of the most dogged defenders of a cricket ball in history, was very clear on how to play the forward defensive: 'Do not push out in hope. Do not be in doubt. Make up your mind. Be positive.' As Boycott knew, being positive doesn't necessarily mean going hard at the ball with bat, body and hands. It means that the decision to defend can be a positive one.

TO PAD OR NOT TO PAD?

Pad play – the tactic of pushing the ball away with the pads, pretending to play, but keeping the bat well clear of actual contact with the ball – is often used in conjunction with the forward defensive. It can be an important defensive strategy on turning pitches in the subcontinent, and was also a major factor in English cricket for years, on the uncovered pitches once called 'sticky dogs'.

Pad play is still very much in vogue against spinners, as it is very difficult for an umpire to give the batsman out LBW if the ball is turning prodigiously: on a turning pitch, with the ball pitching outside off and spinning in, it can be a life-saver. To pull it off correctly, you need to make sure that the ball is covered by your pad, with your bat tucked in behind it, so that to the umpire it looks as if you're about to play it. When it does turn, you subtly shove the ball with the front pad and then finish by playing a forward defensive shot well after the ball has gone, hopefully with enough panache and determination to deceive the umpire into thinking you've played a bona fide shot! Be warned, however, that pad play is not readily tolerated by modern umpires, and often makes them more inclined to favour bowlers' LBW appeals.

On pitches where the ball is moving around a great deal, whether through seam or spin, it is more advisable to look to play the ball, only taking the bat out of the way at the last minute if the delivery does too much. This way, if the ball goes straight on, you can play it comfortably.

Colin Cowdrey's advice to a young Bob Woolmer was clear: always make an effort to hit the ball, and leave it at the last minute if necessary. He called this method 'playing to leave', and found it preferable to leaving the ball and then trying to adjust to hit it at the last moment.

2. BACKWARD DEFENSIVE AND BACK GLANCE

When a boy at Rugby, 'Plum' [Warner] first heard the down-to-earth maxims... most apposite for the leg glance: 'Lean on her, Sir' and 'Smell her, Sir, smell her'. Together, these phrases might better advise the budding batsman how to play the stroke than the many words, diagrams and photographs that have been published in the coaching books over the last fifty years (Synge and Anns, 1987, p. 85).

Aggressive fast bowling reached a peak in the late 1970s as the pace attacks mounted by the West Indian and Australian bowlers put batsmen through the mill, the likes of Michael Holding, Joel Garner, Dennis Lillee and Jeff Thomson taking the game by the scruff of the neck and shaking it. Severe injuries were common, and tensions often flared, with accusations of bullying bandied around. The introduction of batsman-friendly laws and rapid improvements in the quality of helmets and other protective gear has meant that the fast bowling threat has been reduced in the modern game. Nevertheless, the short, rising delivery is still very much in vogue today.

This is why it is essential for every batter to master the backward defensive, to cope with deliveries that bounce steeply off a good length. Indeed, many aspiring young cricketers have been found wanting at the higher levels of the game because of their inability to cope with the rising ball. Schoolboys must learn to play off the back foot, as during their formative years they will have mostly played forward, due to the innocuous pace of the bowlers they will have faced, and the low, slow pitches they will have played on. Schoolboy bowlers lack the strength and height to generate pace and bounce, and as a result young batters never have to face balls bouncing dangerously at their chests and throats, and can play forward most of the time.

These factors conspire to leave batsmen one-dimensional, lacking the variety of shots necessary to become exceptional players. At the highest levels of the game, any inability to play a particular shot will be ruthlessly exploited by bowlers able to land the ball precisely where they wish. This is why it is essential to learn and become proficient in all the possible cricketing strokes from a young age.

When to play the shot

Backward defensive: while the forward defensive shot protects the stumps, the backward defensive is mainly used to defend the body against balls pitching short of a good length and bouncing to waist height and above.

Back glance: this is played to a shorter ball that rises or cuts back towards the front hip, stomach or groin. Younger and more inexperienced players often jump away to the leg side instinctively when the ball cuts back into their mid-section, instead of playing it off their hip. This evasive action often results from having been hit a painful blow in the past, which is why it is so important that youngsters wear thigh-pads, a box, and ideally a chest pad as well.

Short-pitched bowling tests the courage of all players. Backing away is the first sign of fear, unless it is done for a specific reason (making room to play an attacking shot, usually in one-day cricket). As soon as the batsman displays fear, the bowler will smell a wicket, knowing that he has unnerved the batsman. Apart from renewing the energy and focus of the bowling, the batsman who backs away exposes his stumps and opens himself up to a wide variety of dismissals: being bowled, edging the ball into the stumps, being caught in the slips or gully, and so on.

Being able to get into line is an important skill to have in the multi-day game. It takes courage, but it also sends a strong message both to your teammates and to the opposition: Ian Redpath and Brian Close were two international players who were particularly admired for being willing to take the ball on the body without flinching.

Playing the shot: backward defensive

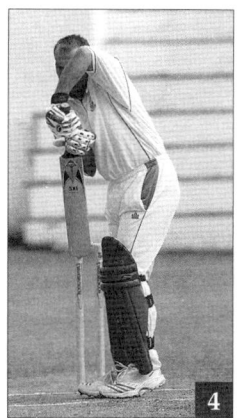

The initial movement of the backward defensive, as shown in the second frame, is for the back foot to go back and across towards the off stump, with the head behind the line of the ball and the shoulder pointing at the trajectory of the delivery. Be careful not to get your head outside the line of off stump: there's no point risking an edge defending an area that isn't threatening either your stumps or your body.

The third frame shows how the front foot then slides back and rests on its toe next to and just behind the heel of the back foot. This will help you balance, since all the weight will now be on the back foot. Initially, the front shoulder should be pointing at the line of the ball. The bat should swing through in a straight line towards the ball's trajectory. (The path of the bat comes from just inside the line of the right shoulder.)

Coaches teaching the backward defensive must make it clear that the ball will be bouncing above waist height, and that defending the body will be more important than defending the stumps. Therefore it is crucial that young batsmen are also taught how to leave the ball off the back foot as part the learning progression of this shot.

Alan Knott's 'periscope' grip (right) is described in the section on grips (see p. 109), and his method might be worth practising along with the conventional backward defence. Release three fingers of the top hand, holding the bat with thumb and first finger. This allows the bat to be raised higher to cope with the excessive bounce.

Few school players will be facing balls that get that high, but in more competitive cricket, some of the quick men can get the ball up frighteningly high and fast. Facing bowlers like Michael Holding, Bob Woolmer found he had almost no time to deal with the ball: playing a normal defensive shot could mean the ball hitting and breaking his forearm. The grip shown here helped him lift the bat above shoulder level so that the handle was above his eye line, enabling him to keep the ball down. A rather grim advantage is that this exposes the fleshy part of the arm, which is less susceptible to a fracture.

BATTING

YOU'RE SO SQUARE!

No coach or commentator can mention the backward defensive without immediately drawing fire in a debate that has raged for decades: whether or not the shot should be played sideways or square on.

The reality is that both methods can be successful, and both methods can be disastrous. In the end, perhaps it's wisest not to be dogmatic about which is better; instead, allow the height of the bouncing ball to dictate the best way to play the shot.

For example, if the ball is bouncing controllably and you're looking to attack, then sideways is the better option, as this allows the bat to swing through the correct path. If the body is in the way (square on), then the bat will come down from the direction of gully and swing out in a 'U' shape towards the ball. Thus contact will be limited, and you're more likely to get an edge than to score. But if the ball nips back, it becomes tricky to play sideways on, as the body is in the way of the bat.

There is no final answer: Ken Barrington, the famous defensive England batsman, preferred the square-on method, as did Sir Donald Bradman; Ted Dexter preferred the sideways method. Let's agree to disagree!

Playing the shot: back glance

The first movements of the back glance are essentially those of the backward defensive: a step back and across to get into line with the off stump (1 and 2). However, if the ball nips back towards your body, it is time to turn the defensive shot into a run-scoring one.

Turn the body square on, and move the bat across your body into the line of the ball. Stop when that line has been reached – in other words, have the bat waiting for the ball to arrive, rather than pushing out at the ball (3).

If possible, don't go further outside your body than your front pad: it is just as dangerous to play outside your body on the leg side as it is on the off, and few dismissals are as frustrating as being strangled down the leg side.

132 CRICKET TECHNIQUES

The hands then rotate down with a firm twist of the wrists, deflecting the ball down to fine leg (4 and 5): at this point the bottom hand should be holding the bat only with thumb and forefinger. As the ball makes contact, the bat is slightly angled, and as the shot is completed, the left foot goes backwards, allowing you to turn completely. The hands remain over the ball with the top hand in front of the bottom one. The bat has now turned, and the ball has run away to fine leg, allowing you to trot through for a single, or, if the contact was finer and the ball speedy, adding another four runs to your total.

If you are going to play the back glance safely and effectively, there are two golden rules to remember:

- **Keep your eyes glued to the ball throughout** (don't flinch or blink as the ball rises up towards your face).
- **Never play across the line.**

Like all the shots, the backward glance can become a reflex if practised enough.

Practising the shots

Start by practising the movements in front of a mirror to ensure that everything is correct and moving as it should be. Next, ask a partner to throw a tennis ball from a distance similar to where the ball might pitch; that is, up at your body from a point low to the ground short of a good length (1). Focus particularly on stopping the ball and allowing it to land at your feet. When you are confident that the shot is working, move on to using a cricket ball, first thrown up at you, and then bounced at you at pace (2).

Once the backward defensive is well on the way to becoming grooved, start combining it with the back glance. Be warned: this will not be easy, and the movement of the leg glance will take some co-ordinating, but practice and patience will help to eliminate the fear factor. Remember to use a thigh pad and good pair of gloves: coaches don't always have the most accurate throwing arms!

Mastering the backward defensive and the back glance will remove the temptation to back away to leg. In addition, like the glance off the front foot (to be discussed shortly), the back glance is extremely useful for picking up steady singles.

An interesting development of the back glance is found on the Asian subcontinent. Players from India and Pakistan are traditionally extremely wristy (meaning that their wrists are very strong and yet highly flexible, allowing them to work the ball into angles more forceful players struggle to pick out). Since the back glance employs the wrists, and Asian pitches tend to be less bouncy, players in this region find it far easier to connect well with back glances. In India and Pakistan, the shot has transformed into something of a leg clip that goes behind square leg, providing rich pickings in terms of boundaries.

1. *Flicking the ball up off the pitch at the body to simulate a rising delivery.*
2. *Bouncing the cricket ball at the body, a more typical 'throw-down'. (Note that Kallis is lifting his bat in the direction of the slips, not directly backwards.)*

However, if mistimed, it can easily bring about a dismissal, since the ball remains in the air for much longer than it does after a conventional glance. This Asian variation has in fact given rise to a new fielding position, a slightly deeper forward short-leg specifically designed to catch that clip shot.

Common problems with the backward defensive

- **Defending towards cover:** we have already highlighted the dangers of playing a forward defensive towards extra-cover, and a similar flaw often creeps into the execution of the backward defensive: a tendency to play back defensively to balls rising well outside the off stump, and to push out towards the off side. The danger here is similar to that of the extra-cover forward defensive, as any away movement will mean an edge to the slips.

  This is a common fault, and one caused mostly by coaches remaining adamant that the batsman should be sideways-on when defending. They are right in insisting that the first movements should ensure that the body is in a side-on position, but they should accept that the final defensive shot is played front-on; in other words, in a square position.

- **Grip too tight:** holding the bat too tightly with the bottom hand will almost always lead to an awkward body movement – the head will bend to the right, forcing the eyes outside the line of the ball. Furthermore, if the ball hits the hands at any pace, and the fingers are clenched and unable to move quickly, broken bones can result, with the dreaded result of a six-week absence from the game.

FRONT-FOOT DRIVES

Of all the pleasures cricket provides, and in all the satisfaction gained from playing shots correctly, few things match the thrill of drilling a straight cover or on drive through the field to the boundary. For batsmen, driving is as good as it gets.

When to play these shots

All the shots listed here are played to a half-volley or a low full toss. They can also be played on the up, which means hitting the ball as it rises off a good length. However, hitting on the up should be informed by the state of the pitch: you need to be confident of the ball's bounce and carry before you start playing cavalier shots on the up.

1. OFF DRIVE, STRAIGHT DRIVE

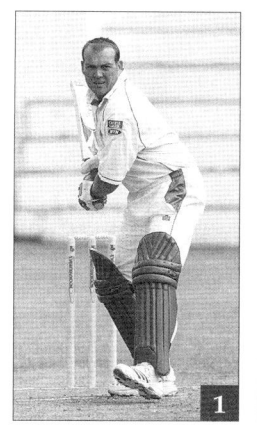

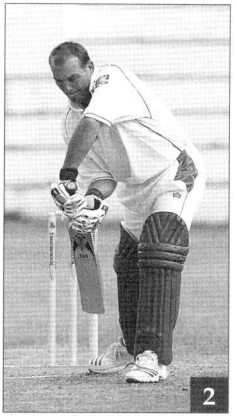

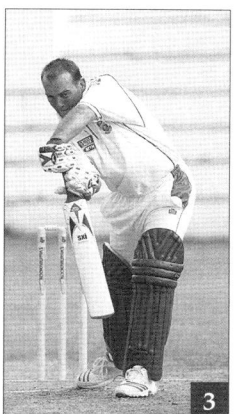

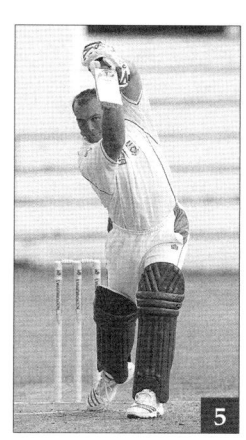

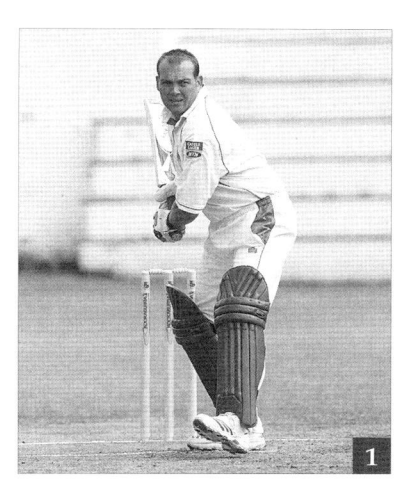

Take a balanced step forward towards the bowler (1), with the weight on the front leg and the heel of the back foot raised, so that you can place your front foot beside the pitch of the ball. The back foot should roll onto the toe, and not swivel; if the back toe swivels, it causes the body to square up, which will hinder the execution of the shot and make the hands work across the body, leading to a nick to the slips.

Swing the bat down in an imaginary line from the toe of your back foot to the pitch of the ball. Make contact under your eyes (as in 2), making sure the wrist of the top hand is in front of the bottom hand (2 on the right) if you want the ball to go along the ground.

BATTING 135

Depending on your swing and the momentum of the shot, you can use the check-drive follow-through, favoured by batsmen such as Colin Cowdrey, Jacques Kallis and Sachin Tendulkar.

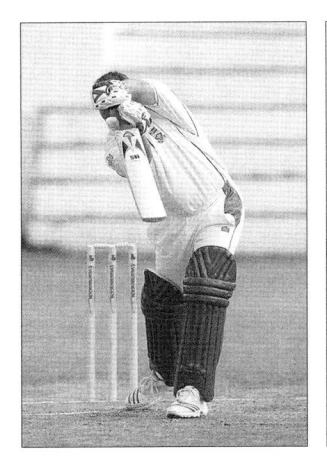

The front elbow pivots up high, and the bat is stopped in its swing before rotating up past the horizontal and over the shoulder (as shown above). As we will learn later, the value of the follow-through is largely diagnostic; it indicates that the batsman has played the shot fluently and correctly, maintaining good balance throughout. It reminds the batsman (and the bowler!) that the batsman is in control of his shots.

An alternative to this approach is the follow-through drive, named thus as the drive is allowed to 'flow' naturally through its entire motion without being checked. At the top of the drive the wrists 'break' (5 below), causing the hands to turn inwards towards the leg side.

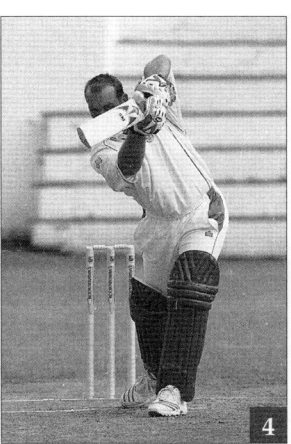

Frames 3 and 4 show the final position of the follow-through drive: the wrists have rolled over and through, and the bat handle is now facing where the ball has gone. This is a very complex wrist movement, sometimes referred to as 'wringing the dishcloth' because of the twist of the wrists required. Unless this is practised regularly and perfected, it can lead to problems: a common fault is to turn the wrists too early in the shot and therefore end up mistiming the ball, getting an inside edge as the bat face starts to come across the line of the delivery.

This method was favoured by greats such as Bradman and Hutton, and in the modern era, Rahul Dravid (among others) demonstrates this follow-through with great panache.

2. COVER DRIVE

All drives come from the same base: they differ only in where you want the ball to go. The cover drive is played later than the straight drive and the on drive. Allow the ball to come past the front foot, turn the front shoulder to the area you wish to place the ball, and then ensure that the hands work on the same line, hitting and guiding the ball through the cover region.

Be wary of driving square of the pitch too early in your innings: misjudging the length of a delivery can bring the slips and gully into the game, and send you out of it. Remember that when using an angled bat, you are using only half a bat – sometimes even less – when playing through the covers. Timing and balance have to be perfect if this shot is to be successful: inefficient balance and technique – or undisciplined hands – can all too often lead to a slip catch.

Poorly co-ordinated hands will also cost you dearly on slow pitches: the hands rushing past the ball will often bring an inside edge down onto the delivery, and in turn onto your stumps.

The full flow of the cover drive. The angle here is deceptive: the batter has played the ball almost under his eyes.

BATTING **137**

3. ON DRIVE

The on drive is one of the more difficult front-foot strokes, played to a delivery pitched up on middle- or leg stump: many batsmen prefer not to commit to an attacking stroke with their wickets under threat, and opt for a defensive push instead. Indeed, very few international batsmen have made this their trademark shot, although Sachin Tendulkar is particularly strong straight down the ground between the bowler and mid-on, an indication of his superb ability to judge length, and his perfect balance at the crease.

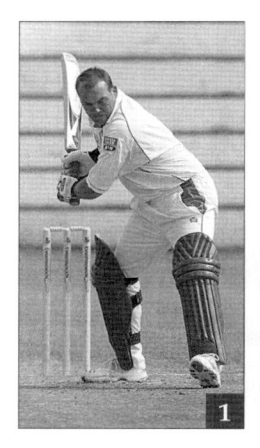

Make sure that your shoulder points towards the ball, then move your front foot just outside the line of the ball, i.e., towards the on side (1 and 2). Make contact under or just in front of your eyes: the on drive is played fractionally earlier than the cover drive, and you need to time it perfectly so that you are not reaching for the ball, but also not too late on it, killing it into the pitch at your feet (3). Don't play across the line of the ball: try to hit it back past the bowler on the on side, rather than working it square through mid-wicket (4 and 5).

DRIVING ON THE UP

Hitting the ball a few milliseconds after it has pitched and bounced is risky, but to the well-set batsman on a good pitch it can pay excellent dividends, as well as having a dramatically demoralizing effect on the bowler and his captain. Most drives can be played on the up, but for the purposes of this discussion, we will examine two: the on drive and the check drive.

The on drive played on the up requires extreme skill, an even-paced surface and excellent timing. Make sure that you play the shot towards mid-on: the ball may well squirt off the bat and go square of the wicket, but the bat path must remain in the well-documented 'V' between mid-on and mid-off.

The shot begins with both feet brought together on or about leg stump: this will allow the ball slightly more room to come at you. The bat is swung normally, but instead of timing the stroke to meet the ball under the eyes, the shot is 'early', so early in fact that the ball is struck about two feet in front of the eyes. This requires fantastic hand-eye co-ordination, and if properly executed, oozes class. However, beware if the ball swings late: movement after the shot has begun can easily result in edges, or missing the ball completely, and the resulting ignominy of being clean bowled.

If you're trying to perform this stroke and failing, don't despair: it requires immense skill and timing, and conditions also have to be perfect if you're to play it with absolute confidence.

The second drive that is hit 'on the up' is the push or check drive. This is normally played to a good length ball (as opposed to a half-volley) where more control is needed; in other words where the ball isn't squatting down on a full length and begging to be hit. It is a shot best restricted to a good surface with true bounce.

Basically it is a stiff-armed push, which comes with its own dangers: if the ball 'stops' on the surface (slows dramatically), it is almost impossible to stop your swing, with the result that the ball is played far too early, and usually loops up to a grateful cover or mid-off fielder.

So why play the check drive at all? The answer lies in its history. Because pre-Second World War batsmen had a tendency to roll the wrists early in the follow-through drives, coaches – and many players – set about developing a drive that would keep the face of the bat on line with the ball for longer. This, together with the advent of heavier bats, which gave more value for less impact, resulted in the modern check drive.

In other words, it is a modern version of the traditional drive, which was developed in the 1950s to overcome the problems sometimes experienced in executing the more flamboyant and complicated drives preferred by the likes of Don Bradman, Jack Hobbs, Len Hutton and Wally Hammond. Nonetheless, the classic wristy drive played properly has a larger impact area, cutting down the risk of late movement. The push drive is extremely vulnerable to late movement of the ball.

Therefore, like any shot, it has to be practised a great deal. The push drive is more often used in one-day cricket to nudge the ball into gaps, and it is worth remembering that looking to score, especially by playing on the up, will always be more dangerous than putting away a true half-volley.

Having said that, it is worrying to note that the check drive has increasingly crept into the four-day game, where it often leads to soft dismissals: we see players caught in the covers and at gully, as batsmen become vulnerable to a well-bowled slower ball. Instead of trying out this shot on a tricky track during a cat-and-mouse four-day game, rather wait until conditions are perfect – a good pitch with no seam movement, a soft ball, and spread field – before trying it out.

Practising the shots

The most effective way to practise all the variations of the front-foot drive is to use progressive training. This is a system that gradually builds skills upon skills in a manner that makes sense both in terms of the batsman's thought processes and his biomechanics, until finally the complete shot has become a reflex action. When the batsman recognizes a specific delivery, his progressive training will mean he is fully equipped to know how, when and why to play the shot he has selected.

The following general routine can be applied to almost all the drives described above.

- **Start with a stationary ball placed on an upside-down paper cup** (there should be a small rim on the base of the cup to prevent the ball from rolling off).
- **Practise the mechanics of the shot by placing your feet in the correct position,** and then hit the ball, allowing the arms to work.
- **Move back into your stance position.** Now move your feet into the correct position and hit the ball. (Coaches can also set up targets for batsmen to hit, such as gaps between cones, if these are required.)
- **Get your coach or partner to roll a ball towards you,** and put your foot alongside the ball and hit it through the target area or back to the roller.
- **Introduce timing:** get your partner to stand next to you on the off side (leg side if you're practising the on drive), and have him drop a tennis ball on a driving length. Move your foot alongside the pitch, but hit it only on the second bounce, as illustrated in this sequence.

- **Now progress to underarm throws:** get your partner to throw from about three metres in front of you, and hit to both the off side and the on side (so as not to kill the thrower!).

140   CRICKET TECHNIQUES

- **Send him back to throw from about 15 metres away, overarm.** It's very important that he throws accurately; if necessary, threaten him with a few straight drives to get him focused!

- **Progress to a bowling machine, working on each length for a period of time** – bowling machines groove shots, and shouldn't be used to simulate random deliveries on random lengths.
- **Finally move into a conventional net with standard net bowlers.**

One of the most fundamental processes you can discover in progressive training is how transferring your weight increases power in the shot, and how best to execute this transfer. The easiest and best way to experiment with this is to practice what Bob Woolmer called one-foot driving. The idea is not to stand on one foot and try driving, but rather to hit the ball and then lift up the back foot a split second later. This will allow you to feel the effect of the weight transference.

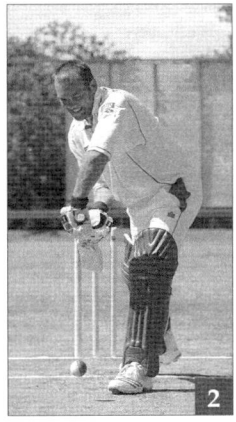

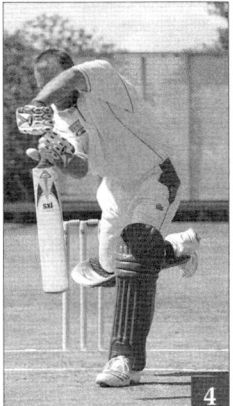

Move into position as you normally would, and play the drive (1 and 2). As you make contact, lift your back foot off the ground: as illustrated, you should be able to balance on your front foot (3, 4 and 5). If you fall forward from this position, you will know that your weight is not properly transferred – your shots will be suffering as a result.

A common problem: turning inside-out

This can happen when you try driving at a ball in front of you. Reaching for the ball has the effect of turning the body to a more square-on position in the crease, with the front shoulder facing square leg and the back shoulder aiming at cover point. Once the shoulders move, the hips follow. Suddenly your bat is forced to come down from gully along the line of your body, and then somehow move out again towards the off side.

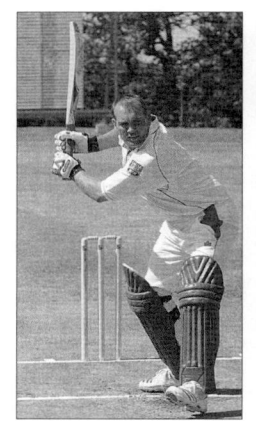

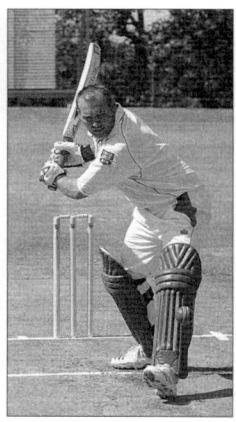

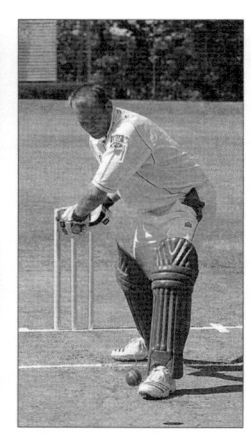

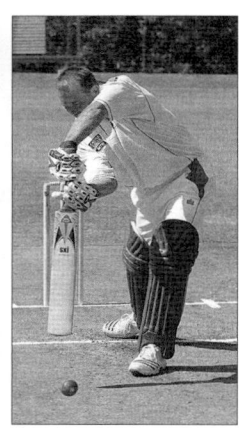

This is known as batting 'in to out' or 'inside out', and instead of swinging through the line, you will find yourself slicing the ball. Obviously, this position can be useful when playing the ball square on the leg side, but if you are driving the ball on or just outside your off stump, the poor swing of your bat will cause severe problems. The solution is simple, however: play alongside the ball, and play along parallel lines as explained before.

CROSSED LINES: HITTING STRAIGHT AND ACROSS THE LINE

Coaches spend a great deal of time telling batsmen to 'hit straight' and to 'play through the line', but Bob Woolmer (who owned up to being one of these coaches) knew that an eleven-year-old, a fifteen-year-old and a Test player will all present different interpretations of what those instructions mean. So what exactly are we talking about when we encourage batters to play through the line of the ball?

When the ball leaves the bowler's hand, its trajectory creates a line in your mind's eye that points to where it will pitch. Any movement will change the line slightly, but in general it continues through to the wicket-keeper, unless there is some intervention by the batsman, who will intercept that invisible line with the invisible line of his own swing.

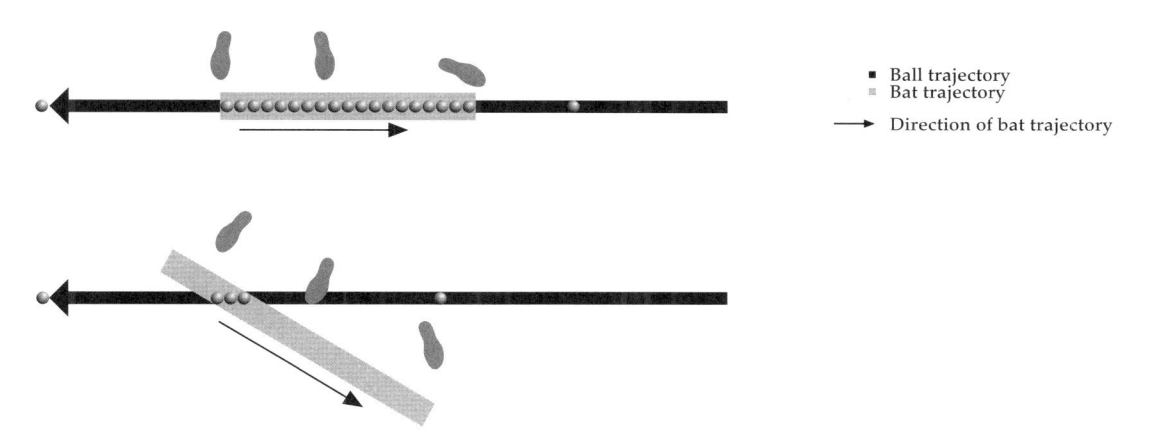

FIGURE 3.2: *The lines followed by bat and ball*

In order to play a shot correctly, the bat line must meet the ball at the contact or crossing point (see the top line in Figure 3.2) but must remain on that line to execute the shot. The challenge that arises when playing across the line is that the hitting area becomes much smaller (the bottom line in Figure 3.2). More skill and timing is required to play sideways, which is why bowlers strive for lateral movement. This also explains why the measure of a skilled and world-class batsman can be judged by whether he has mastered the ability to play across the line.

Hitting a cover drive means that the hands and bat must follow through on the shoulder and feet line; this is vital if they are to make contact. Any change to the swing will almost certainly result in failure to make contact – or an edge.

Summing up the drives

- When driving on the front foot, make sure that the weight is transferred forward, through the hip and knees into the foot.
- As a general rule when driving, keep the back foot still with the heel lifted. Use it as the fixed point in the shot, while moving the front foot around in a half-circle. This will enable you to drive in an arc from point to mid-wicket.
- Get your foot down the wicket towards and beside the pitch of the ball, with your toes pointing at the ball.
- Leave yourself enough room to swing the bat.
- When you pick up your hands and move them back into the backswing, your shoulder will turn a little: do not panic! This turn is vital, since it is your shoulders that will determine the direction and timing – and therefore the power – of the shot.
- Remember that the essence of the drive is a swing, not a punch.
- On impact, your hands must be over the ball, arms straight and wrists slightly cocked to keep the bat straight.
- Hit through the line of the ball. Now relive the sweet sound of willow cracking into leather, and enjoy the applause.

COMING DOWN THE WICKET

Changing the bowler's length is one of your most valuable weapons, in all forms of the game; and coming down the pitch is one of the best ways of doing this. The chassis, the shimmy, the glide, the two-step, going on the charge, hopping out, running down the wicket: call it what you will, but coming down the wicket has proved its worth over and over again, whether against Test match spinners or medium-pacers in a one-day match.

They say you might as well be stumped by 5 yards as by 5 inches, and there is some wisdom in this: if you are going to come down the pitch, do so boldly, and remember that you are doing it not to escape from a bowler, but to intimidate him. You are the hunter, not the prey. Five yards down the track, you are sending out a very aggressive signal, and you will definitely force the bowler to change his length and rethink his approach.

Playing the shot

When you come down the wicket, do so at the ball: begin your movement the instant the ball leaves the bowler's hand. Come down slowly to begin with and be prepared to defend if you have to, without forgetting that your intent is aggressive. If (and only if!) the ball is in the correct place, can you then hit it safely over the top or along the ground. Above all, keep your head still and watch the ball throughout: it's easy for beginners to let their heads roll back as they 'tee off', usually resulting in a mis-hit or a complete miss.

There are a number of methods of coming down the wicket, ranging from the chassis and the glide to a slow walk down the pitch with the bat in the ready position. Some players simply run down. However, the sequence illustrated here represents a more conventional approach.

Your first movement is important: the first stride with your front foot will determine how far you go. Don't be timid in this respect: make sure you come a long way down the wicket, pointing your shoulder towards where you expect the ball to pitch (1). Obviously your height will determine how far your front foot can move: tall batsmen will need to measure or restrict their stride, while shorter players can stretch out. Experiment and find the best method for you.

Frame 2 shows the 'slide', the feet coming close together. This is easier than picking up the feet, but it has two major drawbacks: firstly, your head will come over its original height, which will distort your view of the ball and interfere with your judgement of its flight; and secondly, the shuffle limits the distance you can advance down the pitch.

Here the batsman has crossed his back foot behind his front foot, a movement called the 'chassis' (3). This means that when he reaches out with his front foot to the pitch of the ball, he'll have an extra six inches at his disposal. This method also helps to keep the eyes and head level, which preserves the batsman's set-up and helps him play correctly, both then attacking and defending.

One of the disadvantages of using this 'cross-over' method is that it can take you to the leg side of the ball and away from the line; and if the bowler sees you coming, he might be able to adjust and bowl the ball just wide of your reach, exposing you to a stumping.

Frames 4 and 5 show the completion of the shot, as the weight is once again transferred forward, in this case into an attacking stroke. Notice how far the front foot has come from its starting point in the first frame: by staying nimble, the batter has advanced a good three feet up the track, radically disrupting the bowler's length.

Common problems with coming down the wicket

- **It's going straight up in the air:** players who have had success in the past with coming down the wicket suddenly find that when they go for the big shot they end up skying the ball and being caught. This is purely a problem of timing and co-ordination: the batsman is getting under the ball rather than hitting it. Remember, as you get into the shot, you must rotate the front shoulder so that your hands can swing through the ball. If you don't rotate your shoulder, you will find that the bottom hand will come through the shot far too quickly, and the ball will go straight up in the air. As mentioned many times already, the bottom hand is key to hitting the ball a long way: anyone who's hit high catches at fielding practices will know this. So whether you are hitting over the top or trying to clear the field, it is important that the bottom hand is working properly to provide power and timing in the shot.

- **I'm not getting to the ball:** footwork is the most important aspect of coming down the pitch – more specifically, the distance between your front foot and your back foot. If you make small, hesitant movements, you aren't going to get to the correct hitting area. If the ball is turning, swinging or seaming, and you're stranded short of where you need to be, you're going to be in trouble. If this happens, quickly try to find a way to bale out of the situation: sometimes the only solution is to try to stop the ball, and hasten back to your crease.

THROWING THE KITCHEN SINK AT IT

It's worth remembering that just because you are coming down the pitch, it doesn't mean you have to hit the ball out of the ground. If the bowler sees you advancing and changes his length, you are perfectly entitled – and in fact required – to play defensively if the ball is not there to hit. This is why it is important that you do not give any visual clues as to when you might be leaving the crease, but rather advance after the ball has been released.

Indeed, dummying and coming down the pitch are all part of the game when trying to upset a spinner's length; but many batsmen don't practise this skill, and are therefore uncomfortable doing it in match conditions. Just like any skill, it is vital that you practise and gain confidence.

If the ball is a half-volley, then go ahead and hit it: your momentum will carry it a long way. If you want to hit it for six, lean back slightly, get the hands underneath the ball, and carry them right the way through. Here it's forgivable if the bottom hand overtakes the top hand, since you're trying to gain upward momentum. In fact, when you decide to unleash the bottom hand, give it the 'kitchen sink' treatment – don't choke or give up on the shot before it's gone all the way through.

Be careful, though, of trying to hit it too hard: you can get too far underneath the ball.

4. FRONT-FOOT GLANCE

The leg glance off the front foot, while not glamorous, is a useful one to have in your repertoire of strokes. The Nawab of Pataudi and the great Ranjitsinjhi were famous for using variations of this shot, and it stood them in good stead: the wristy glance is an effective way of harvesting steady runs by working the ball around, and more specifically, working it backward of square on the leg side.

When to play the shot

The front-foot glance is best employed when you are receiving deliveries of a fairly full length on your pads, or fractionally outside of them on the leg side. Anything along this line is essentially a risk-free single begging to be taken. Alternatively, it can be a manufactured stroke in the context of a one-day game, working a straighter delivery fine on the leg side to take advantage of fine leg being up in the circle. In general, it is a safe stroke to any delivery that comes in to you, whether an inswinger or an off-spinner bowling to a right-handed batsman.

Playing the shot

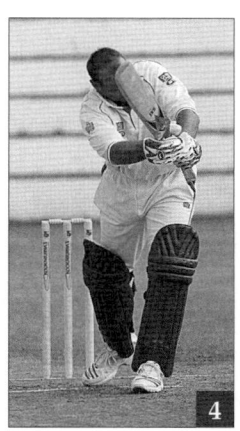

Go forward as you would for a forward defensive stroke: your head should be right over your front foot, with your weight going forward (1). As the ball swings in, bring the bat down in front of the pad, and rotate the wrists towards the leg side and slightly downwards (in order to angle the ball onto the ground) (2). Control the bat with your top hand, and allow your bottom hand to take the soft route, with only two fingers on the handle so that the bat can be turned without obstruction, glancing the ball off the face and away for a handy single (3, 4 and 5).

Be aware of your balance when playing this stroke: less experienced batsmen often topple forward if they miss the ball, which can be a gift to the alert wicket-

BATTING 147

keeper, lurking in the hope of a stumping down the leg side. Remember to keep the bat upright and in line: if you play across the ball, you risk getting a leading edge (which will carry to the bowler, especially if you've twisted the bat hard in your hands) or being given out LBW.

5. THE PICK-UP

The pick-up is the glamorous cousin of the leg glance. If the traditional front-foot glance is all about wrists, timing and balance, then the pick-up is all about brute strength and an overpowering bottom hand.

Playing the shot

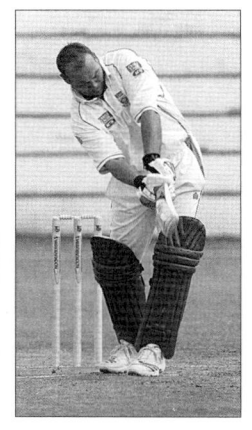

The easiest way to explain the wrist action of this shot is to point to a tennis forehand loaded with top-spin. Bring your feet together, wait for the ball to arrive under your eyes on or outside leg stump, and then launch it behind square with a strong flick of your wrists, almost as if you were trying to impart top-spin on the ball. Gary Kirsten used the shot to great effect in the 1996 World Cup in Asia: on slow pitches, against spinners and medium-pacers (most memorably the part-timers of the United Arab Emirates), Kirsten peppered the mid-wicket and deep-backward-square boundaries by picking up anything bowled at a suitable length, including balls on or outside his off stump.

6. THE BACK-FOOT DRIVE

It may seem incongruous to group this stroke here, along with front-foot drives and pick-ups, but the back-foot drive is something of an anomaly among cricketing shots. It is the only attacking stroke played off the back foot with a straight bat, and it therefore bridges the divide between the attacking front-foot shots played with straight bats, and the attacking back-foot shots played with horizontal bats.

The back-foot drive played well is almost always a sign of a very good (or even great) batsman. Bowlers in the top echelons of the game are getting stronger, fitter and faster all the time, and to score off them, given the miserly lengths they bowl, takes some doing. The back-foot drive, or 'back drive' as it is also known, allows those few batsmen who have mastered it to help themselves to more runs than the fast bowlers of the world would like. But it takes superb judgement of length and excellent control of both hands to pilfer short and nasty stuff for runs while forcing off the back foot.

When to play the shot

The back drive is played to a ball that pitches short of a good length, but relatively close to the body, giving no room to cut. Be certain that you are mentally and physically prepared before you start trying to play it: first get your eye in and get accustomed to the pace and bounce of the pitch – otherwise any extra bounce could take the outside edge.

Playing the shot

1. Start to turn your front shoulder towards the ball as it comes at you. 2. Turn your shoulders fully round with your backswing, and be ready to hit the ball hard once you've identified whether or not the back drive is a viable shot for the delivery. Move your back foot back and across in line with middle- and off stump, with the toes pointing to backward point. 3. Bring your bat down to intersect with the line of the delivery. Keep your front elbow high, the bat remaining close to your body, and let your front arm lead the shot. Stay balanced, with a still head and eyes fixed firmly on the ball. 4. Hit the ball under your eyes. The elbows of both arms should make a cradling movement, as if you are rocking a baby vertically. 5. Follow through with a controlled punch, like the check drive on the front foot. Keep the bat on the line of the ball, and go up on the toes of the back foot to give more emphasis to the shot.

BATTING 149

Practising the shot

As with the front-foot drives, progressive training can build the shot into your armoury until it becomes second nature. Use a stationary ball at stump height, first to learn the basic principles of the shoulder, arm and hand movements. Then add in foot movements, and then enlist a partner to throw a ball underarm from the usual length – which in the case of the back drive is about six to eight metres from the bat. This is the ideal way to practise, as most pitches (apart from concrete) have varying bounce, and without consistent bounce while practising this shot, you can become extremely frustrated.

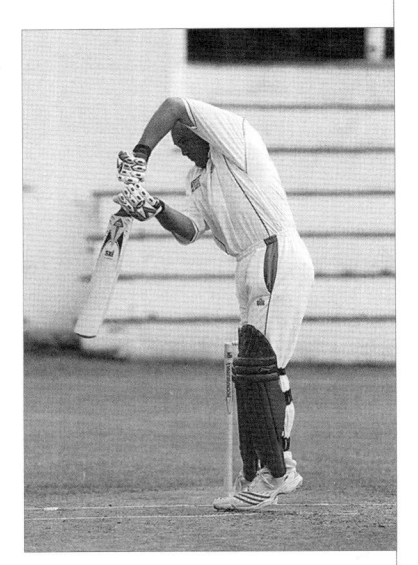

Common problems with the back drive

- The most common fault associated with the back drive is the inability of some batsmen to play the stroke with bent arms in the 'cradle' formation (left) because of the height of the ball. In these cases the body opens up and becomes too square on, which in turn prevents the bat from following the correct line.
- Secondly, some batsmen assume that because the ball generally goes quite square off a back drive, they need to play it square. This is not the case: the natural angle of the stroke – even one aimed at mid-off – will take the ball square; and trying to help it can only make you vulnerable to getting an edge and being caught behind.
- Most successful back-foot drivers have powerful arms and upper bodies: judicious weight training can help to make you a better driver off the back foot.

The 'cradle' formation: imagine rocking a baby in your arms, but now turn the baby so that it stands upright.

CROSS-BAT SHOTS

THE CUTS

'Sunshine, thou should not cut until July!'

So said the legendary Yorkshireman Wilfred Rhodes, giving (presumably unsolicited) advice to a young player who played a cut too early in the season. What Rhodes meant was that playing cut shots was a dangerous business until pitches dried out and became firm in the summer sun, and the ball started coming onto the bat. Today it remains a dangerous shot if not played correctly, but one that is highly productive if practised.

It is a shot that has spawned numerous variations: cuts off the back and front foot, the late cut (favoured by so many in the early 1900s), and more recently the upper cut, slicing fast bowling over the slips and away towards third man. This shot in particular was born of desperate times, as Tony Greig and Alan Knott tried to find ways of scoring off Lillee and Thomson on the ferocious pitches of Australia that didn't involve hooking, pulling, or getting in line more than was absolutely necessary!

Even the apparently formal, traditional variations of the shot have been adapted and experimented with over the years: the late great Denis Compton used to give himself room by moving his back foot outside leg stump to a straightish delivery, and cutting on length rather than line.

But if there is one general piece of advice that holds true for most types of cut, it is that offered by the stalwart South African batsman, Peter Kirsten, when Bob Woolmer asked him what made him such a good cutter. 'If you're going to cut, cut hard,' was his reply.

This advice is worth following: if the ball is rising, follow the rise and cut up. If the ball is levelling off or dropping, cut accordingly.

1. SQUARE CUT OFF THE BACK FOOT

This is a great run-scoring shot, both fun and tricky to play, but it is also a dangerous stroke that induces a large number of dismissals, with the batsman often out caught in the gully or the slips. So play it sparingly, and only to deliveries that are conducive to the cut shot. As with all cross-batted shots, be wary of attempting it on pitches of uneven bounce. Remember to keep the bat parallel to the ground: if you don't, the shot becomes even more risky than it is already.

When to play the shot

The cut is played to a short ball that is at least an arm's length outside off stump when it reaches the crease. If it's a delivery from a pace bowler, you need to craft the shot entirely from gentle timing. If you're facing a slow bowler, hit it as hard as you can. But in both cases, make sure that you've chosen a short ball that gives you enough time to get into the correct position: arms fully extended, a yard away from you.

Playing the square cut off the back foot

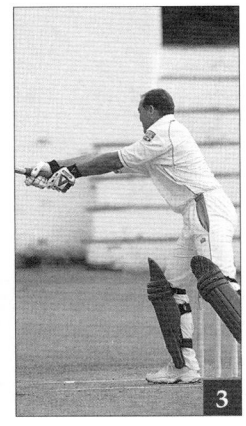

1. As you recognize the ball to cut, you should start turning your front shoulder towards it, which initiates the back foot's movement. 2. Your back foot should move across the pitch and ideally your toes should point down towards third man. This allows you to hold the correct shape, and to get the right hip out of the way. At the same time, your hands should be in position above shoulder-height, which will allow the correct bat path during the shot. 3. Make contact with the ball at arm's length for maximum effect and power. Your weight must transfer from the front foot onto the back foot, and the back knee needs to bend slightly for control. This is the toughest part of the shot to master (and to coach), as the final part of the shot relies on a quick wristy rotation of the hands commonly referred to as 'rolling the wrists'. 4 and 5. The start and end of the shot are similar in that the arms are bent on impact, straightened to guide the ball, and then bent again. As the shot finishes, focus on keeping your shoulders square to the ball as your hands and arms do the work.

2. SQUARE CUT OFF THE FRONT FOOT

As with the square cut off the back foot, this shot is played to a wide, short ball outside the off stump, normally on good wickets when the batsman is set and ready.

Playing the square cut off the front foot

This variation of the cut uses very similar arm and wrist movements to the cut off the back foot. Move your front foot across the stumps so that it points to cover: this will ensure that the front shoulder has turned in order to allow your arms to swing.

Keep the bottom hand above the top hand as the bat moves into position to strike the ball: this will keep the bat parallel to the ground. At the point of contact, keep your arms straight and your weight over your front leg. Immediately after contact, roll your wrists.

The full follow-through ensures that there is no body turn. If you have completed the shot correctly, the bat handle will be pointing in the direction of the ball.

3. THE LATE CUT

The late cut is one of the more delicate shots, and although it is no longer as popular as it once was, it remains a thing of beauty whenever it is played. In tactical terms, the late cut is almost identical to the reverse dab (a delicate reverse sweep).

When to play the shot

The late cut is played to deliveries just wide of off stump that are too full to play at with any of the more conventional cut shots. The batsman also needs some pace on the ball: the spinners' arm-ball is often the ideal delivery at which to play the late cut. It is often the safest and most rewarding shot to play to a spinner or medium-pacer when there are no slips in place and the keeper is standing up: guiding the ball almost out of his gloves past off stump and down to third man for a single is delightfully cheeky, as demonstrated often by Pakistan's Javed Miandad.

Some coaches warn against late-cutting off-spinners, instead recommending that the shot be reserved for balls that are short of a length and headed towards third man. On tracks that offer the off-spinner plenty of turn they might have a point, but on a flat track with little turn, it can be extremely lucrative to late-cut the off-spinner.

Playing the late cut

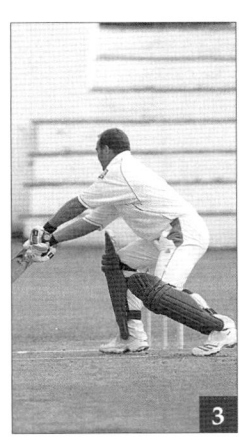

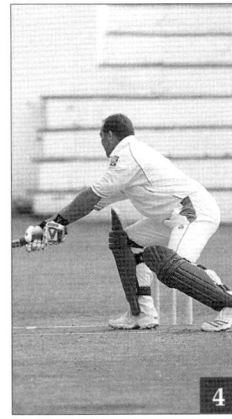

1 and 2. The back foot goes back and inside the line of the ball. 3–5. Lower your body by bending your knees, as the further the ball is pitched up, the lower it will stay. Keep your eyes locked on the ball, as this is a shot based entirely on timing – try to play the ball as late as possible, so you're almost dabbing it out of the wicket-keeper's hands. The actual strike should resemble a tapping motion, as though knocking a stump into the ground with the face of the bat. Wait and let the ball go past your body: you'll be amazed at how much time you have. Once you've spotted the gap between backward point and the keeper, use the pace of the ball to run it down to third man with soft hands. When the ball bounces lower (or higher) than the knees, bend to adjust to that height. The secret is to keep your hands above the ball.

PRACTISING THE SHOT

The late cut is not easy to practise unless you have a true surface like concrete or carpet. However, with the help of two friends, you can get the feel of the shot well enough: ask one to throw to you on a good length a foot outside your off stump, and get the other to play wicket-keeper. Without alarming the volunteer behind the stumps too much, work on trying to tap the ball down gently just before it reaches his hands, with your back foot pointing at him.

Common problems with cutting

- **Uneven bounce:** poor or uneven pitches make cutting dangerous, as the slightest variation in bounce can cause you to top-edge a cut behind the wicket, or bottom-edge the ball into your stumps.
- **Poor body position and poor use of the arms:** the mechanics of the cut shot are very specific, and many players see the stroke merely as an opportunity to lash out square on the off side, without paying due care to the role of their bottom hand, the rotation of their shoulders, and the position of their feet. Study the two sequences below.

154 CRICKET TECHNIQUES

Notice how in the first, poor foot and shoulder positions cause the batter to hit over the ball by many inches. In the second, the back foot goes further to the off side, while the toes point at gully, rather than backward point. This helps the hips rotate further, which in turn helps the shoulders to rotate better. The result: a crisp, cracking cut.

- **Wrists don't rotate:** the power, timing and placement of the cut shot comes from the rapid rotation of the wrists at the point of impact, not from the swing of the arms. In fact, there should be negligible arm movement in the stroke, and the wrists should be allowed to whip through, rather like cracking a whip.

If the second and third problems continue to dog you, and you continue to be dismissed when you play cuts, perhaps eliminate the shot from your repertoire until you have spent more time practising it.

THE HOOK AND THE PULL

There still seems to be some confusion in the minds of many players and junior coaches as to the difference between the hook and the pull, and a brief distinction should be drawn here.

The hook is played to a bouncer or a ball aimed above chest height. Hooking usually sends the ball behind square, but this will also depend on the line of the ball as it is delivered: the straighter and faster the delivery, the finer you will have to hook it. Likewise, if is outside off stump, it is possible to hook it in front of square.

The pull, on the other hand, is played to a ball that is shorter and usually slower, and as such, the foot movements required of the pull are easier to manage. For example, the pull is often used against spinners or medium-pacers who have dropped one short.

Both shots, however, are played with straight, fairly rigid arms, which provide the power and the control.

1. THE HOOK

The hook shot can be played to a bouncer or short-pitched delivery aimed at your head. It is an extremely risky shot, and you must be confident that you can cope before you attempt it; once you play this shot to a fast bowler, you have thrown down the gauntlet and you can expect him to bowl you a few more bouncers – or alternatively, change his length and pitch the ball up more.

The success of the hook shot is often dictated by the height of the ball. The higher the ball when it reaches you, the more likely it is to rocket up off the face or back of the bat, providing a catch for the wicket-keeper, or – as bats gets heavier and meatier – a high catch for fine leg or third man.

Playing the shot

Hooking requires perfect concentration. Watch the ball as it comes to you. Keep your head and eyes very still. Do not blink, flinch or look away! The moment you take your eyes off the ball, you are effectively blind and a sitting duck, liable to be hit on the helmet or the back of the neck.

1–3. The first movement for the hook shot sees the back foot going back and just outside the line of the ball. The front foot then joins the back foot, but has no weight on it and can lift off the ground easily and move in conjunction with the swing of the bat. Keep your balance slightly forwards of the centre of your body, and try to position the shoulder inside the line of delivery, with your hands as high as possible in the backswing. As you move backwards, extend your lower arm as far in front of you as possible, and retract the top hand by flexing the elbow of the upper arm. 4. Make contact in front of your eyes with arms held out straight, while your whole chest pivots around, followed by your legs and feet. If possible, try to hit the ball just inside the line of your head, to avoid injury should you miss or deflect the delivery back towards you. 5. Follow through by spinning like a ballerina in Swan Lake! And to make sure you don't end up a dead duck, try to hit down on the ball as you swivel. Sometimes if the ball grows too 'big' on you, this will be impossible, but most balls of chest-height can be controlled in this way.

Practising the shot

Start with tennis balls, and have your coach or a friend throw them accurately at your head from about 10 metres away. Gradually increase the pace and then move on to the hard ball. Add a helmet for protection when doing this, and be prepared for the odd knock. Move onto overarm throwing, and then finally to a bowling machine. Increase the pace and make sure that you watch the ball all the way.

Common problems with hooking

- **Hitting the ball too hard:** if the hands move too quickly through the line of the ball (which can happen when you're pumped up and playing for your life against a pumped-up paceman), you can end up mistiming or splicing the ball to a nearby fielder. Or, in the worst-case scenario, you can be through the shot too soon, and take a painful blow to the body.

    You can combat this by being in control of the shot from start to finish. Rather than hitting the ball, concentrate on helping it round, using the pace of the ball rather than your own speed and strength. This is another distinction between hooking and pulling: when you pull, you hit the ball; but when you hook, you simply help it on its way.

- **Playing at balls bouncing too high:** some batsmen have a reputation for being 'happy hookers', players who compulsively chase short balls around their shoulders and faces. Bowlers mark them down for special treatment, and, if the umpire isn't being particularly strict, the bouncers start flying.

    If you find yourself halfway into a hook shot to a ball that has suddenly got too big on you, the most important thing to do is to get the bat out of the path of the ball: either raise or lower your arms, just as long as your bat isn't near the ball. Alternatively, bale out of the shot by bowing your head and simultaneously swinging your hands down very quickly as you turn, allowing the ball to go over your head. If neither of these options is available, get your bat out of the way, close your eyes and think of Brian Close, and take it on the body for the good of your team!

- **Old-fashioned stomach-churning fear:** nobody wants to get hit, especially not in the face or on the head, and sometimes batsmen flinch or look down as they play this stroke, usually with exactly the results they feared! Remember, if you are wearing a helmet, playing a hook shot is not likely to be lethal. Always wear your helmet when practising this shot as well as playing.

    If you intend continuing to play the hook shot, try to learn the signs that bowlers give off when they are about to bowl a bouncer: some have a faster run-up, others call codes to their captain, others just look very keyed-up and seem to be exuding fire and brimstone! And there's always the telltale sign of two fielders posted out for the hook behind the wicket.

TO HOOK OR NOT TO HOOK?

Steve Waugh decided to stop hooking altogether, as did his brother Mark. Bob Simpson, one of Australia's best batsmen, once gave Steve Waugh some interesting advice: 'You do not necessarily have to look good against fast bowling – the secret is to survive it!'

Viv Richards used to go for the hook straight away to unsettle the bowler and show his mental strength. During World Series cricket in 1978, Australian speedster Len Pascoe bounced Richards at the beginning of the innings – in his own words, 'to attempt to unsettle him'. Viv took him on and smacked ball after ball to the leg boundary. Ian Chappell pointed out to the bowler that Viv was enjoying this passage of play and suggested that Pascoe pitch it up to him instead. The bowler did so, and Viv calmly smacked him back over his head for four more – a classic duel of tactics and dominance.

The real trick is to pick the right kind of surfaces (even and true bounce) and the right pace of those bowlers who are 'hookable'. Avoid hooking really fast bowlers – but if you decide you want to take them on with this shot, wait until they are tired.

2. THE PULL

Playing the pull shot well from an early age will give the young batter a big advantage. Most young bowlers tend to drift down the leg side and bowl short, inviting the pull shot. At higher levels of the game, playing the pull shot is more often than not dictated by a field setting that favours the off side. The batsman then looks at ways of manipulating the ball into areas where runs are more freely available.

Playing the pull is probably the most natural shot in the game. You swing as though chopping down a tree, smacking a blanket or a rug hanging on a washing line. In fact many coaches, when teaching a youngster to play for the first time, start by teaching the pull, which always stimulates young batsmen. It's fun to hit the ball hard!

When to play the shot

This shot is played to a short ball (commonly called a 'long-hop') delivered by a medium-pace or slow bowler, going down the leg side at waist height.

The shot may also be played to a slow short ball pitching outside the off stump. This is a bad delivery and the batsman should take full advantage by putting it away to the boundary.

Playing the shot

Remember the fourth principle of batting: 'Move your feet into the correct position.' In order to play the pull shot both well and successfully, the feet need to move into position quickly, establishing a firm base.

1. The first movement takes the back foot back and towards the middle or leg stump, making sure that you go back onto the toe of that foot (which should be pointing up the pitch or towards mid-off). This enables you to pivot, allowing the front foot to move out towards the square leg umpire. **2.** To make sure the ball is hit hard, the backswing has to be high and full. Contact has to be made in front of the eyes, so the head must move into line. Foot movements enable this; the wider the ball, the wider the front foot movement. The toes of the front and back feet should end up parallel to the return crease. This will ensure that the ball can be hit in front of the wicket (square leg). **3 and 4.** The bat should make contact with the ball in front of the eyes: on contact, the arms should be straight for maximum power. Immediately after contact, roll the wrists to keep the ball on the ground. **5.** The final part of the shot is the follow-through. Weight should transfer from the back to the front foot to keep the ball down and to ensure maximum power.

Practising the shot

Once again, progression training is key. In this case, try using a ball on a stump, as illustrated below: get the position right, then the feet, then the whole movement, and then graduate to tennis- and cricket balls.

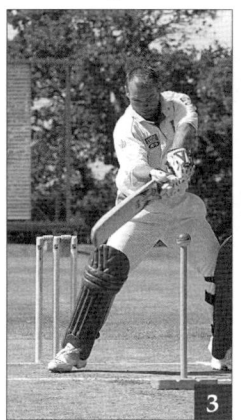

Common problems with pulling

The most common error that creeps into the pull shot is that foot movements are too slow, and therefore do not get the head in line with the ball. Making contact with bent arms and the weight remaining on the back foot also reduces power, with the ball being mis-hit up in the air.

An important element of the pull shot is to make sure that the bat is parallel to the ground, not at an angle. It's a common mistake to have the bat at a 45° angle, which increases the risk of top-edging the ball into your face. As in any run-scoring shot, if you do not feel right at the last moment, bail out of the shot and aim to survive.

Generally, however, the pull is one of the easier cricket shots to play. For this reason, it is a handy basic shot to teach at junior level, as it will enable younger players to score runs.

THE SWEEP SHOTS

If you want to force the spinner to change his length, but you don't want to advance down the wicket and risk a stumping, sweeping can be the way to go.

Jonty Rhodes

Rhodes's point here is something all batters must bear in mind, rather than taking unnecessary risks: the sweep's primary objective is to change the bowler's length.

Despite what a dwindling pool of die-hard sceptics might say, the sweep is a genuine cricket shot. It has a proud and growing pedigree, as more and more batsmen both great and ordinary hone and practise it. By now, it has been used on dozens of occasions to destroy bowling attacks, specifically those based on spin.

Mike Gatting's ill-fated reverse sweep in the 1987 World Cup final against Australia is still held up by critics of both the reverse sweep and its slightly more respectable sibling, the standard sweep, as an example of why it is dangerous. What is seldom mentioned, however, is that Gatting tried the shot on the very first ball he faced from new bowler Allan Border. Was the demise of Gatting – and eventually England – the result of the sweep, or of a batsman not taking time to get used to a new bowler? Likewise, nobody mentions Graham Gooch sweeping his way to 80 in a World Cup semi-final against Pakistan, or Gordon Greenidge using the shot to win a Test against England with an over to spare, after David Gower had been criticized for declaring too late.

However, despite these successes, it is hard to deny that the sweep is a higher-risk shot than most: first, because you're always taking a chance playing across the line;

and second, because certain umpires have decided that it's an inherently risky and unwise stroke, and are more inclined to listen to the appeals of bowlers when you're sweeping than to judge their appeals on merit.

But ask any spin bowler what he thinks of the sweep, and he will tell you that it does have the effect of messing up his length, and if played well, it can make it very difficult for him to contain the batsman. Because the sweep is played to a good length ball, it reduces the bowler's options, forcing him to bowl more quickly or slowly, which in turn forces him to change his length. Remember, you're sweeping to force him to change his length: it's no use sweeping once an over and leaving him settled for five balls out of six.

Heave-ho!

Any cross-batted shot into the leg side has the potential to reach or clear the ropes for a four or six, and to many young batsmen, the sweep seems an invitation to try for a boundary. Bob Woolmer encouraged batsmen who played sweep shots to hit down: the object is to change the bowler's length, and scoring a boundary keeps you on a strike and gives the bowler a chance to settle.

However, you can sweep the ball to the boundary, whether with a violently hit conventional sweep or the more glamorous slog sweep. Australia's Matthew Hayden is a prime example of someone who has perfected what can be called the 'bludgeon

WITH OR AGAINST SPIN?

The principle behind lifting the ball into the stands is the subject of ongoing debate: namely, do you hit with the spin, or against it?

All the good sweepers will tell you that it's safer to hit against the spin. Their reasoning? You are hitting into the 'final' line of the ball, in other words, the line the ball is going to take until it hits your bat, as opposed to a line going (infinitely far) away from your bat as the ball spins away.

The mechanics of this were touched on earlier, when discussing how best to alter your stance when facing a leg-spinner pitching it out of the rough, but it bears repeating. When you sweep, there is a natural tendency to rush your wrists through the shot as you see the ball turning. The result is that the bat overtakes the ball, and you can end up top-edging as you rush under the delivery, bottom-edging as you skim the top of it, or even lobbing the most embarrassing of catches up off the back of the bat.

In short, if you sweep with the spin, make sure that you smother the spin by hitting down on top of it.

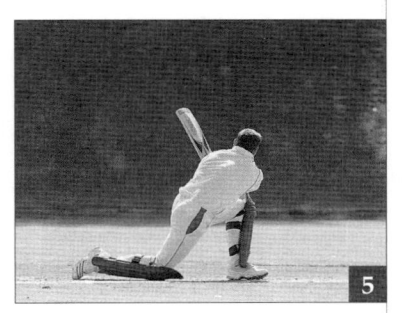

sweep': a conventional, technically correct sweep, hit extremely hard. Throwing the kitchen sink into the shot has two advantages: firstly, and obviously, it has the power behind it to take it to the boundary and beat any outfielders who might run down a ball rolling more slowly; and secondly, it almost automatically removes short leg from the equation. Most short legs are simply not fast (or brave!) enough to get down to a ball hit that hard, which usually leads to the man being removed, and the pressure on the batsman being lifted.

In order to sweep the ball for six, you need to get into a position that allows you to hit the ball into the air. This technique – the above-mentioned slog sweep – is discussed on pp. 165–66.

Malice aforethought

Many coaches and critics criticize the sweep for being a premeditated shot. But it has to be: it is an attack on the bowler, rather than a response to a specific delivery.

Of course, it is dangerous to play it too early, since the bowler will be able to adjust, whether by bowling more quickly (the arm ball) or more slowly (to create more bounce), both of which will make the sweep shot much more difficult. In these cases it's important that you have a form of counter-attack, such as the defensive sweep, described on p. 164.

However, an early movement into the shot, with the back knee already on the ground as the ball leaves the bowler's hand, will allow you to move the front foot around according to whichever sweep you need to play. For example, if you place the front foot inside the line (i.e., the off side) of the line of the ball, you will be able to guide the ball fine. If you stay on the leg side of the ball, you will be able to hit the ball squarer, and so on.

1. ORTHODOX SWEEP

When to play the orthodox sweep

Former England captain Mike Brearley summed it up nicely: 'On an excellent pitch, it's folly to play the sweep when runs can freely be had by driving; but on a "turner" or a pitch where the ball does not come on for the drive, the sweep may be the most effective, even the safest shot.'

It is important when learning to play the sweep that you identify the length you should play the full sweep to. If you reach out in front of you with both hands on the bat and touch the ground, you will see the best position for the ball to pitch. Play to the length of the ball – in other words, the length you'd also normally consider a forward defence.

Playing the orthodox sweep

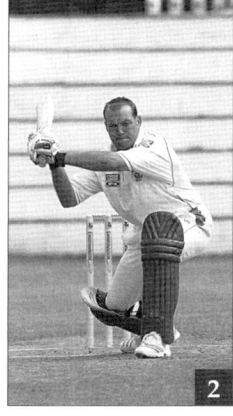

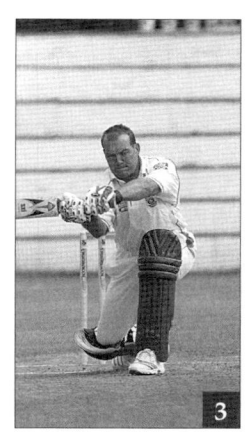

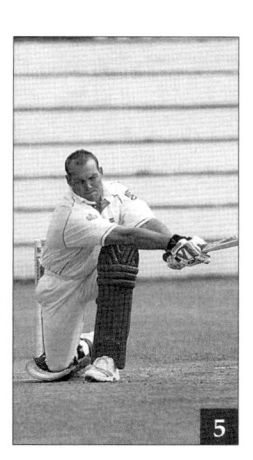

Study the sequence on the opposite page together with this front-on sequence for a clearer picture of the correct technique for the sweep shot. 1. Make sure that the position you get into is comfortable and has a solid base, so that when you swing the bat, the shot will be balanced and controlled. The height of the bat swing depends on how hard you want to hit the ball. Here the batsman is looking for the full sweep. 2. Note the position of the back knee and the front foot: the knee is just inside the line of the front foot to create balance. The front leg is almost vertical, and the head is over the top of the front knee. 3. Swing the bat parallel to the ground, keeping the head forward. 4. Make contact with the ball with your bat parallel to the ground, and your arms as near to parallel as you can manage without losing control or power. Your arms should also be at full strength now for maximum power in the shot. Also notice that the head has now moved slightly forward over the knee. At the point of impact, the bottom hand's wrist rolls over the top hand, and the arms will begin to bend and swing over the front shoulder. If you have swung the bat correctly from the very first position of the swing (1), your follow-through should look like that in 5 in the side-on sequence.

Common problems with sweeping

When troubleshooting the sweep shot, two problems keep cropping up.

- **The head stays behind the knee.** Instead of pushing their weight forward and reaching a balanced position on their back knee, batters tend to hang back, going down onto their pad with the head still in the position shown in 1.
- **The bat is held at too great an angle to the ground.** The ideal sweep shot has the bat sweeping past across the line of the delivery almost exactly parallel to the ground. However, many batters bring the bat through at 30 or 45 degrees to the ground, which means they have no control over the shot, and greatly increase the risk of a top edge popping up, either to the wicket-keeper or close fielder, or into their own faces.

2. DEFENSIVE SWEEP

There are many varieties of sweep, and a particularly useful variation of the orthodox sweep is the defensive sweep, sometimes referred to as a paddle. The shot was christened the 'defensive sweep' by Alan Knott, who became a fine exponent of it. He used it simply as an option for picking up singles very fine down the leg side, but it can be used to good effect in the one-day game: with fine leg up, it can run away for four.

When to play the defensive sweep

Good spin bowlers will work as hard at undoing you as you are working at undoing them. Sometimes – especially if you've premeditated the sweep and have made a miscalculation – you can find yourself beaten by flight or spin, thoroughly committed to the orthodox sweep, and more or less stranded unless you take sudden action. That action is the defensive sweep.

A good example of this is when you've gone down to sweep, and the bowler has slipped in a fuller, quicker arm-ball, and you're staring down the barrel of a potential LBW appeal.

Playing the defensive sweep

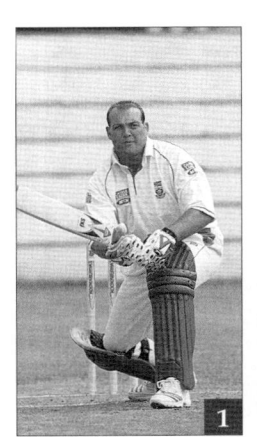

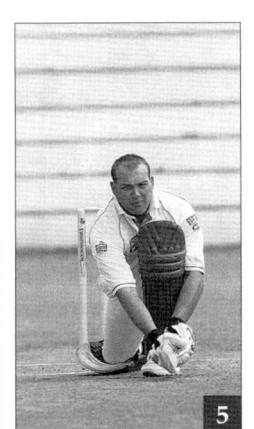

The set-up position and early execution are identical to those of the orthodox sweep as outlined above (1 and 2); but instead of hitting out at the ball, pull your hands back, as close to your front foot as possible. Lay the back of the bat on the ground, and angle the face to where you want the ball to go (3, 4 and 5).

The ball will then slide off the face down to short leg, the pace of delivery – rather than your arms – providing the momentum.

The defensive sweep is very much a get-out-of-jail shot, but it can be used intelligently – and cheekily – to score runs where there are not usually any fielders.

The reverse defensive sweep (see sequence below) gives you the option to score on the off side in similar situations: simply change the angle of the bat.

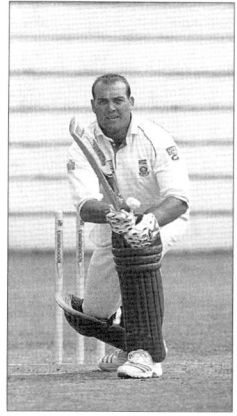

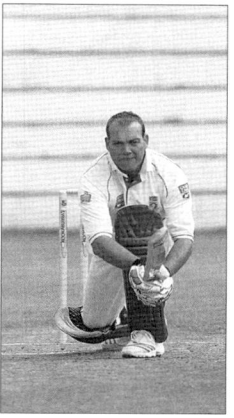

3. SLOG SWEEP

Hitting a sweep shot for six requires a different body position, since you need to create more room for your hands and arms. Don't forget that every time you lift the ball into the air, you're at risk.

When to play the slog sweep

This shot is played when you want to hit the ball over the infield with the intention of sending it for six. Sometimes, it is played to score much-needed runs as fast as possible during a hectic run chase; at other times, it is used to gain a psychological edge over a bowler, or to remove him from the attack entirely. Hansie Cronje was one of the first international batsmen to perfect the shot, and when he used it against the much feared Shane Warne in 1993, the runs he scored were far outweighed by the sense that South Africa wasn't entirely in awe of the Australian.

Likewise, in 1998, Cronje went after Muttiah Muralitharan, probably the best off-spinner the world has ever seen, slog-sweeping him to all corners of Centurion Park. Muralitharan was taken to the cleaners, and Cronje went to what was the fastest 50 in Test history at that time. His runs greatly helped South Africa's cause, but the dominance he asserted over the Sri Lankan strike bowler was much more important.

Playing the slog sweep

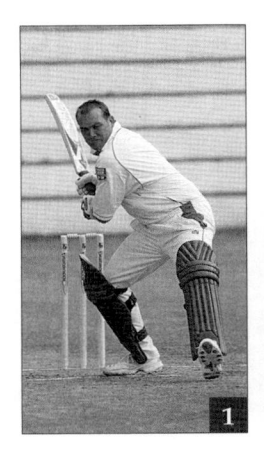

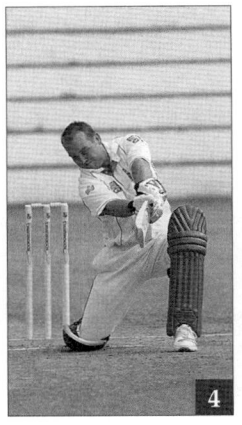

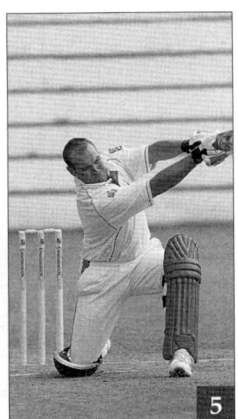

The slog sweep is an extension of the sweep played to a ball wider of the leg stump. In other words, you're always hitting against the spin, either to a leg-spinner or an orthodox left-arm spinner. Left-handers slog-sweep off-spinners.

Splay your front leg out towards the leg side (1). This allows room for the arms and hands to get under the ball. Keep your arms straight, in order to maximize power in the shot (2 and 3). Then follow through expansively: don't check the shot or stop the bat in line with your front knee (4 and 5). If struck correctly, they'll be looking for the ball twelve rows back.

4. REVERSE SWEEP

It's worth pausing for a moment to discuss why this shot crawled out of the woodwork, why it causes so much consternation, and how it came to be accepted (more or less) as part of the game.

The first myth that needs debunking is that the reverse sweep is a very recent innovation. This is simply not true: it has been used since the early 1970s, and perhaps even earlier. Mushtaq Mohammed played it against Bob Woolmer's swing bowling, and Gordon Greenidge used it to great effect in the 1976 Jubilee Test, playing for the Rest of the World.

It was Dermott Reeve, however, who made it famous (or infamous), when he used it as a tactical weapon to break the fielding regulations that were stifling English one-day cricket in the early 1990s.

At that time, one-day international cricket regulations had recognized the need for a free flow of runs, and had restricted the number of men permitted on the leg side to just five. However, English one-day cricket had not yet adopted this rule, and an off-spinner could bowl at leg stump with as many as seven men on the leg side.

Not surprisingly, it was extremely difficult to score against this kind of tactic. Reeve simply exploited this convention by playing the reverse sweep, forcing the field to change accordingly. Little did he know how well his unorthodox shot would work, or what the ramifications would be.

Bob Woolmer (then the Warwickshire coach) and Reeve decided to let the entire team practise the shot, and Reeve endorsed the tactic in a team meeting. Woolmer was in complete agreement, and set about working out how best to teach the shot.

Unfortunately this decision didn't reach Warwickshire's second eleven coach Neal Abberley: Bob Woolmer remembered wandering over to the nets one day to see a tearful Roger Twose stomping away across the tarmac. Woolmer asked what the problem was, and was told that Abberley had expelled him from the net for practising the reverse sweep!

Woolmer apologized to Abberley for the breakdown in communication, but he recalled that although his colleague accepted his apology, he couldn't help feeling that Abberley was initially dead set against the shot.

Woolmer himself had doubts, but Reeve was a good salesman. When the time came to put the plan into action, it had an immediate impact: the opposition's disdain for the shot saw Warwickshire exploit it to the maximum for two years. During this time visiting sides came and went with the attitude that Reeve's team were lucky, insane, stupid, crazy – Woolmer heard it all.

The result for Warwickshire was a Nat-West trophy at Lords in 1993, two out of three one-day trophies in 1993, and the championship and two more trophies in 1995, the year after Woolmer left the county to coach South Africa.

The statistics speak for themselves. During those years, Warwickshire managed on many occasions to score at over six runs an over against spin – three runs an over more than their opposition. If ten overs were bowled by spinners, that translated into a 30-run advantage.

Woolmer's departure, and Reeve's retirement, saw Warwickshire gradually stop using the sweep, and the lessons learnt were either forgotten or abandoned. When Woolmer returned in 2000, he found reverse-sweeping dead and buried as a tactic, and sweeping in general so discouraged that the level of one-day cricket played had regressed.

However, when English teams did finally accept one-day international rules, the shot – and the sweep in general – did become less effective, partly because it was now an option open to all. It remains a very useful means of disrupting bowlers and upsetting teams.

When to play the reverse sweep

The shot is best employed against a good-length ball, usually (but not necessarily) outside the off stump, against a bowler defending the leg side.

Ideally, there should be a gap behind square on the off side, around backward point. With the reverse sweep, you're looking to sweep the ball through that gap.

Playing the reverse sweep

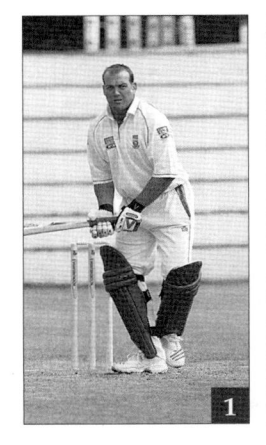

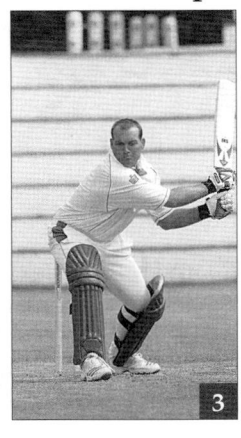

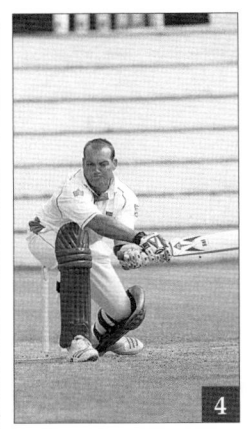

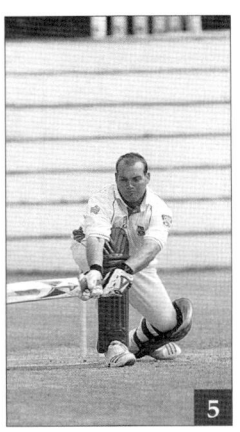

The early movements in the shot are basically those of the orthodox sweep (1). However, these are followed by a turnover: the bottom hand comes directly over the top hand (2), and the face of the bat turns towards the off side.

The grip dictates that the shot starts from the leg side, with the bat following through to the off side (3, 4 and 5). This sequence ends before the follow-through, but the reverse-sweep follow-through can be just as expansive as that of the conventional sweep.

Variations

The front leg can get in the way of the hands, as can be seen above, so you might want to experiment with some other variations.

1. **Start with both feet in the crease and open up the stance.** Place the back foot down the pitch, as if you're about to hit a two-handed backhand in tennis or squash (make sure that the front foot stays behind the batting crease to prevent the stumping). Now hit across the line, bat parallel to the ground. This is the method originally used by Dermott Reeve and Jonty Rhodes.

2. **Rhodes gradually altered how he played the shot, and ended up reverse-sweeping as follows.** He jumped into the backhand squash position – effectively taking up

the stance of a left-hander – making sure both feet were inside the crease. Now he could either play the reverse sweep, or the shot discussed next – the reverse hit or reverse pull.

These variations illustrate how the reverse sweep has changed over the last half-decade, as more and more players use it and adapt it to their own requirements. And Dermott Reeve should take the credit for all of it. Apparently he is looking forward to the day a cricket book is published with a reverse sweep shown on the cover!

5. REVERSE HIT

As one of the quickest and most nimble international batsmen of his generation, Jonty Rhodes had the time to adjust his shots at the last minute. As a result, fans would often see him go down to reverse-sweep, only to jump into a more upright position as the ball bounced higher, and pull the ball away 'left-handed'. Such was his timing and strength that many of these 'reverse pulls' carried for six over gully – or 'short fine leg' as it became.

When to play the reverse hit

This depends largely on the field placing, and the lengths and lines the spinners are trying to bowl; but essentially you're playing the shot to break the shackles after a few maiden overs or dot balls; and above all, you're trying to upset the bowler's rhythm.

As a disruptive weapon, it is almost unparalleled. When Dermott Reeve first used the shot against Ravi Shastri in a match between Warwickshire and Glamorgan, fetching a ball from the rough outside his leg stump and smashing it out of Edgbaston, the Indian all-rounder was so shocked, he complained to the umpire that Reeve was batting left-handed. Shastri's composure in tatters, he soon became expensive and was taken off. Warwickshire won the match. Similarly, Brian McMillan used the shot to lift Muttiah Muralitharan out of Nairobi's cricket ground, a move that upset the Sri Lankan spinner's rhythm considerably.

Playing the reverse hit

As the ball is released, the back foot moves forward and just inside the line of the ball. The hands are reversed (as in hitting a reverse stick cross in hockey). Then bend your knees, and emulate the position of a backhand shot in squash. Swing through the ball with a hard follow-through: the power in the shot can be awesome.

The Rhodes version

Jonty Rhodes' version of Reeve's reverse hit resulted in some serious damage to bowling figures. His variation was similar in all respects to Reeve's, but instead of changing feet and turning hand over hand, he simply jumped into a square-on position, and played a 'squash backhand'. If you would like to learn to play this stroke, remember to keep your knees flexed to adjust to the height of the ball after it has bounced.

Practising the shot

The first thing to stress is this: if you've decided to learn to play the reverse hit, then you can't practise it enough.

The best ways of grooving this shot in your repertoire are progressive training and repetition. Remember, it is a shot that takes flair and confidence, and if you get it wrong, don't expect many sympathetic voices in the dressing room.

WRAPPING IT UP

This chapter covers all the cricket shots you are ever likely to play. Of course, as the following chapters will show, there is much more to playing the game (and playing it well) than simply learning this 'vocabulary' of shots.

But now you have the basics – defensive and attacking shots, straight- and cross-batted shots, as well as the stances, guards and grips from which to launch your own match-winning performances – or simply survive.

As we have repeatedly emphasized, it is no use poring over the instructions given here and studying the photographs unless you go out with bat and ball and practise each part of each shot over and over and over again. Each movement must be correctly practised, with careful attention paid to each part of the body. Slowly, the pieces will start to come together into the makings of a confident and correctly played shot. Focus on grooving just a few shots at first, and making these the cornerstone of your batting before going on to master, say, the hook shot or the reverse sweep.

The role you play in your team will also determine your focus. If you are the team's strike bowler, unless you are a genuine all-rounder, your focus should be on defensive shots and tactics, and on honing one or two run-making shots that will enable you to scramble a single and give the strike to the (hopefully) more recognized batsman at the other end. Likewise, if you open the batting for your team, you will have to have excellent defensive skills, but also the ability to cope with short-pitched and vicious bowling. Middle-order batters should have a range of shots for playing spinners.

But even once you have a rich repertoire of shots at your disposal, your cricket apprenticeship is just beginning. In the next several technical chapters, we will look at the game all over again, from the perspective of the bowler, wicket-keeper and fielders. And before we move on to this, we will make a scientific examination of the role played by vision in batting, a new realm of insight into the game we are only just beginning to explore.

If you are primarily a batter, it is essential that you understand the technical craft of all these aspects of the game, and choose to excel in at least one other (if not two) arenas of the game. As noted elsewhere, a batsman becomes invaluable to his team if he is also a dynamic fielder, and a handy change bowler as well.

And technique is only half the battle; as you begin to string your shots together into a carefully judged and useful innings, other qualities will come into play: mental strength, focus, physical fitness, experience, strategy (i.e., the ability to assess each stage of the game and respond appropriately in tactical terms), knowledge of the pitch and conditions, team skills, and so on. Even something as apparently minor as what you drink in the breaks in the game can have an impact on your batting. This is the allure, the special magic of cricket – no matter how gifted an athlete or technically brilliant a batter you are, there are always a dozen variables to contend with – or to use to your advantage.

BRADMAN'S UNRECOGNIZED LEGACY: HIS 'ROTARY' BATTING METHOD

Is it possible for one man to be correct but to have been ignored? This is the question that Lancashire county cricketer Tony Shillinglaw poses in his 2003 book *Bradman Revisited: The Legacy of Sir Donald Bradman*. (Shillinglaw played cricket at the Birkenhead Park Cricket Club, the same club for which Tim Noakes's father played in the 1930s, one of those remarkable coincidences that keep cropping up in cricket lore.)

Shillinglaw's hypothesis is that Sir Donald Bradman was the greatest cricketer of all time not because of some biological advantage that was never identified in his lifetime, but because the solo cricket games he invented and practised in his backyard during his boyhood in the small South Australian village of Bowral produced an almost unique batting method. Yet because this method of Bradman's conflicted with the batting orthodoxy that began to be taught after the Second World War – especially through the influence of the MCC coaching manual within the Commonwealth nations – it became convenient to label Bradman as a 'one-off genius' whose unorthodox method could and should not be adopted by those who lacked Bradman's allegedly uniquely superior biological attributes. What worked for Bradman, so the story goes, cannot possibly work for any other player, now or in the future.

And there the debate might have rested, if not for Shillinglaw's persistent worry that perhaps the legacy of the Don's genius was going to waste. This despite the fact that Bradman's book on cricket, *The Art of Cricket*, is considered to be the 'bible' of cricket coaching – in the words of another legendary Australian player, Richie Benaud, it is the 'most brilliant coaching book ever written and illustrated'. Yet nowhere in his book does Bradman suggest that his batting method was unique, much less a superior solution to the challenges faced by batsmen; nor does he clearly identify what differentiated his method from that taught in the MCC coaching manual.

Indeed, only the most eagle-eyed reader would detect that Bradman's batting style was fundamentally different from the traditional one. It is a measure of the man's humility that when Bradman's 'secret' was presented to him by Shillinglaw shortly before his death, his only comment was: 'I have read Tony's [Shillinglaw's] words with interest and some embarrassment because I lay no claim to the expertise with which he credits me.'

In his book, Shillinglaw builds his case that this 'secret' of Bradman's was the development of what indeed might be the ideal batting method. He assembles his arguments according to the following facts.

Donald Bradman was never coached. Even more interesting, he had never even witnessed a first-class cricket match until he found himself playing first-class cricket for New South Wales. And he did not read books on cricket by other well-known players. Up till the age of seventeen, he played almost no formal cricket. By then, the method he had devised was uniquely his own. And unlike many young players who found that unorthodox techniques worked for them at the beginning of their playing careers, Bradman never found it necessary to change his method as he rose up through the ranks of the game.

Despite never having been coached, Bradman's rise in cricket was meteoric. He played his first cricket match when he was eleven years old on a dirt pitch at his junior school in Bowral, South Australia. He scored 55 not out. During the remainder of his school years, he played two more matches on a concrete pitch covered with coir matting. He scored 115 and 72 in those matches, both times not out. So in the only three competitive matches he played during his entire school career, Bradman scored 242 runs without losing his wicket.

At thirteen, Bradman played two matches for the Bowral senior team, scoring 37 and 29 – once again without losing his wicket. By the time he left school at age fourteen, he had played in all of five matches and had never even practised on a grass pitch. Yet he had scored 308 runs without once being dismissed.

Bradman's serious cricket career began three years later when he became a regular member of the Bowral first team at the start of the 1925/26 cricket season. In the interim, he had played three more matches, bringing his grand total of completed innings to eight. Yet he completed the season by scoring 1 318 runs at an average of 101,3 – including a District record score of 300, and another of 234 not out against a team that included the gifted leg-spinner Bill O'Reilly, whom Bradman would later name as the greatest bowler of all time. Of that innings, O'Reilly would later write: 'I could not assimilate the knowledge that a pocket-sized schoolboy could give me such a complete lacing.'

This astonishing sequence led Shillinglaw to ask the question: 'What led a seventeen-year-old, who up until then, was the scorer of only 375 runs in his life, into having the capacity to immediately reach such a peak and go on to produce the phenomenal batting record the cricketing world is now familiar with, without ever having a significant lapse in form at any level he played?' Given that Bradman never adapted his technique, a style that was set before he ever played a first-class match, his unique batting methods warranted closer scrutiny.

Bradman taught himself not how to play cricket, but how to control a fast-moving ball, a crucial distinction. This principle informed his own coaching approach: 'Coaching should deal with what to do with the ball, not so much as how to do it. The coach must have sufficient intelligence not to be dogmatic but to discern what method is best for the pupil.' Hitting rather than thinking about how to hit is perhaps best understood in terms of the evolution of the human brain. We evolved the archaic brain pathways necessary to control complex movements – the 'what to do with the ball' components – long before we developed the pathways to analyse *how* we do it. Evolution has thus provided us with all the brain pathways necessary to bowl, catch and hit the cricket ball without engaging the higher brain centres that control thinking – and which evolved only much later. Moreover, these archaic brain pathways are best developed by incessant practice.

The training method that Bradman evolved arose as a game to keep him occupied after school. This game, which determined the batting method he developed, was dependent on the exact dimensions of the backyard of his parent's home in Bowral. Bradman himself described it thus: 'At the back of our home was an 800-gallon water tank set on a round brick stand. From the tank to the laundry door was a distance of about eight feet [close to three metres]. The area underfoot was cemented and, with all doors shut, this portion was enclosed on three sides and roofed over so that I could play there on wet days. Armed with a small cricket stump (which I used as a bat) I would throw a golf ball at this brick stand and try to hit the ball on the rebound. The golf ball came back at great speed and to hit it at all with the round stump was no easy task.'

This became an intricate game, in which the young boy worked out how wickets would be lost and boundaries scored. Using this system, he played 'Test matches' in which he batted for all the players on both sides.

With hindsight, Bradman conceded, 'This rather extraordinary and primitive idea was purely a matter of amusement, but looking back over the years I can understand how it must have developed the co-ordination of brain, eye and muscle which was to serve me so well in important matches later on.'

Bradman also taught himself to field almost by accident, developing 'another form of amusement' in which he threw a cricket or golf ball at a low pole fence, with rounded poles lying horizontally. Only if the ball struck the poles at a certain angle would it return to him at a catchable height: 'Obviously this also developed the ability to throw accurately, because if I missed the selected spot, it would mean a walk to retrieve the ball.' Perhaps as a result of the skills that he developed in this fielding game, Bradman became one of the best fielders of his day and one of the most accurate throwers from close distance.

Bradman developed an unorthodox method of batting as a result of this self-training. In particular, his grip was unusual. The face of his bat was closed and the tip of the bat rested between his feet, touching his left toe (see p. 115). This contrasts with the more usual method in which the bat face is more open, parallel to the crease, facing the bowler (see p. 114). Since Bradman's bat faced towards mid-wicket rather than directly up the pitch, so his grip rotated further round (clockwise) towards the back of the bat when viewed from above. As he described: 'Notice that the inverted V formed by the thumb and first finger of the right hand is straight in line with the insertion of the handle down the back of the blade.' In this position, his grip is rotated about 90° clockwise (backwards, when looking from above) and sometimes even further from the more traditional grip.

Nevertheless, in his cricketing 'bible', Bradman fails to emphasize how radically his grip differs from that which is conventionally taught. He evades the debate by stating: 'I refuse to be dogmatic about one's grip, because I believe various holds can be satisfactory. So much depends on the batsman's methods…. I refuse to condemn an unorthodox grip just because it is different. The use of wrist and arms and the method of stroke production cannot be stereotyped.'

Elsewhere, he wrote, 'I am more inclined to teach boys what to do than how to do it – so long as there is no fundamental or glaring error. Better to hit the ball with an apparently unorthodox style than to miss it with a correct one.'

Of course, here he could be describing himself – he was the most successful striker of the ball in the history of cricket. Yet before he established himself internationally, he was considered not only unorthodox, but an 'ugly, half-cock player', in the words of one commentator. Another wrote of the young Bradman, '[He] was one of the most curious mixtures of good and bad batting that I have ever seen… He will always be in the category of the brilliant but unsound ones…. He does not correct mistakes or look as if he were trying to do so.'

An uncritical reader of Bradman's *The Art of Cricket*, who had never seen Bradman bat, could be forgiven if he or she failed to appreciate just how different

Bradman's stance and grip and his initial movements were compared to what has been taught for the last 50 years. Of course, it was because Bradman's batting technique was so unorthodox that he had to grip the bat differently.

Bradman argued only that the position of his left hand produced what in golfing terms is known as a 'slightly shut' face, the benefit of which is that it keeps the ball on the ground, especially when playing on-side strokes. In other words, the further forward (nearer to the plane of the bat face) the left (top) hand holds the bat, the more likely it is that the ball will be struck in the air when playing shots on the on side. Indeed, Bradman was meticulous in keeping the ball down when playing cross-batted shots on the on side, aiming to hit the ball almost directly to the ground when he played the hook and pull shots.

Bradman was not blind to criticism or closed to experimentation, writing: 'I experimented, worked out the pros and cons and eventually decided not to change my natural grip.'

But the more radical component of Bradman's method was that **the initial movement of his bat during the backlift was towards second slip and not directly backwards towards the wicket** – as prescribed by the original MCC coaching manual. Greg Chappell, considered by many to be the second greatest Australian batsman after Bradman, observed that Bradman achieved this initial movement merely by cocking his wrists with his forearm muscles, without any movement of his shoulders and upper arms. The value of this is that it minimizes weight redistribution resulting from this initial movement.

Bradman was clearly conscious of the unorthodoxy of this method, and defended it as follows:

Reams of matter have been written about the necessity of taking one's bat back perfectly straight. Some coaching books even advocate taking the bat back towards the stumps. Well now, this is the sort of illustration which proves the need for intelligent coaching as distinct from strict rule of thumb.

Don't let me be misunderstood. I am all in favour of a straight bat at the right time and place, but technique must be the servant, not the master.

Too many players fail because their thoughts are concentrated on where their left elbow is or where something else is, instead of on hitting the ball.

I was never conscious of my backlift and I did not take any particular notice where the bat went until I saw movie shots of me in action. Then it was clear my initial bat movement almost invariably was towards the slips.

> *This was accentuated by my grip and stance and perhaps it should have been straighter, but to me, anyway, the important thing was where the bat went on the downswing.*
>
> *For defensive shots the bat should naturally be as straight as possible, but for a pull shot, for instance, a perfectly straight backlift would make it far harder to execute the stroke.*
>
> *The basic technique of a straight bat is sound for defence but there should be all possible emphasis on attack, on the aggressive outlook. Think of some of the great batsmen and you will find very few who did not depart in some degree from orthodoxy.*

Bradman considered that the key to correct batting was to be in the correct position at the top of the backlift, a position he reached shortly after ball release and at the exact time when he would be tracking the ball during the first 120 milliseconds of its flight, calculating, in his subconscious mind, not just where the ball would pitch but more probably exactly where in its flight he would strike it. But in *The Art of Cricket*, Bradman does not explain exactly what that position is. Instead, he offered the opinion: 'If we could take moving pictures of all leading batsmen in action, particularly when they were not conscious that a camera was focused on them, I think we would find the majority of them take the blade rather more towards first or second slip. That initial movement probably allows a flexibility which the strictly orthodox does not.'

Here the term 'probably' is a measure of Bradman's reluctance to force his ideas on others. There is no doubt, however, that he was convinced that the conventional method made it much more difficult to play cross-batted shots towards leg. So perhaps his modesty has not served the game well. However, in a letter to Shillinglaw written near the end of his life, Bradman wrote more forcefully: 'The perpendicular bat theory virtually eliminates pull shots (which can only be played with a cross bat) and square cuts (except by angling the blade) which, in turn, is a recipe for giving catches in the slips.'

Also revealing is Bradman's suggestion that the batsman whose backlift might point towards the slips would have to be filmed unawares. The inference is that if he knew he was being observed or recorded, he would revert to what he had been taught and hence considered to be correct. This suggests the damning power of the accusation of 'unorthodoxy', an accusation that has exercised a peculiar hold over the game for decades.

Shillinglaw draws a parallel to the career of Wally Hammond, a contemporary of Bradman's, who was at times considered his batting equal. Responding to the statement that he would never play for England because he was too 'unorthodox', in particular because he played with a bat that was not vertical, Hammond modified his game to restrict his leg-side cross-batted shots. This might explain why his Test match batting average, acquired in a career that overlapped with Bradman's (1928–1948) was 58,45 – compared to Bradman's 99,94.

In an introduction to the re-release of his 1934 coaching film, Bradman stated that the standards of fielding had increased substantially since his era, but he was silent, perhaps intentionally, on the current state of batting and bowling compared to his day. However, he did note that 'In batting, there are very many competent players but for some reason, maybe coaching, the emphasis seems now to be more on forward play. There are fewer batsmen who are predominantly back foot players. Hence we don't see as many cut shots and pull shots. One cause seems to be the tendency to use heavier bats. These are fine for the pendulum-type shots but militate against strokes across the line of flight.'

Bradman's initial motion was to move the bat and hence the centre of mass of the batter plus his cricket bat, away from the body towards point. Thus his weight was also transferred in the same direction, that is, onto the balls of his feet. In contrast, the 'orthodox' technique, in which the bat moves backward, initially transfers the weight onto the back foot from which it is extremely difficult to perform any shot other than one off the front foot. So to play backward requires a secondary movement that returns the weight to the balls of the feet. Perhaps one factor contributing to the dominance of front-foot play in world cricket is because of the weight transfer to the back foot resulting from a backlift that goes towards the stumps. Alec Bedser, the great English batsman, came close to the nub of the matter when he noted that Bradman's backlift and downswing created a 'flow' towards the ball – what today we might more scientifically describe as a rotary movement of the bat as it travelled along the continuum from backlift to downswing.

As a result of his unusual technique, Bradman was considered 'unorthodox'. In the words of Shillinglaw: 'His "genius" could be understood as a concept but it defied rational explanation. The accepted concept of orthodoxy could not be challenged by one man, no matter how outstanding.' Furthermore, since Bradman was unorthodox, it was considered inappropriate even to consider studying his 'ugly' method. Shillinglaw includes a 1933 correspondence that offers this gem: 'At the other end was Bradman. And if his partner shone in orthodoxy then the little champion positively sparkled in unorthodoxy. Balls that according to all the tenets of cricket should have been handled with a meticulously straight bat, were rudely dispatched boundary-wards with a blade that artistically flashed across the line of flight without recording the suggestion that the user thereof was indulging in the "cross-bat" so despised by the orthodox confreres of the willow... Never was the mastery of Bradman more exemplified than in that single off-theory over of Thompson's [sic] when every ball was cracked to the unprotected leg, while the covers presented the appearance of an over starched paddock of flannel-clad fieldsmen.'

One advantage of Bradman's technique was that it allowed balls pitched even far outside the off stumps to be pulled to leg. This presented those who bowled to Bradman with significant problems. South African bowlers in particular suffered from Bradman's batting onslaught. In five innings against the South Africans, Bradman scored 806 runs, once not out, for an average of 201,50 with four hundreds. It is perhaps not surprising, then, that the most detailed description of what it was like bowling to Bradman has been provided by the South African bowler A. J. Bell. The hapless Bell bowled to Bradman in seven matches, often for an entire day, without once claiming his wicket. Shillinglaw quotes from Bell's autobiography to highlight the difficulties bowlers faced in choosing the best line and length when bowling to Bradman:

One pitches a good length on his leg stump and the ball gathers another coat of paint off the pickets of the fine leg boundary.... If you bowl just short of a length on the off pin he takes great pains over his shot and is content to push it down the gully for a single, or just out of reach of the unfortunate fielder.... We tried for four and a half months to get him caught in the slips by bowling short just outside off stump. His wonderful placing and command over the ball made life absolutely untenable.... He seems to know what kind of ball you are going to bowl and where you are going to bowl it. He makes up his mind in a flash and does not hit the ball to the fielder as a great many do, but places it just out of reach and grins cheerfully.... His hook shot is incredible. He steps right back onto his wicket (one does not see much wicket when he is batting) and cracks the ball plumb in the middle of the bat.... When he does mistime the ball [rather, when his prediction of the exact trajectory and position of the ball was incorrect, as this is the more probable error – authors' insertion]*, and this is very infrequently, the ball does not shoot up in the air... but drops harmlessly on the ground. This is due to the fact that every shot he plays, he intends the ball to hit the ground just a couple of yards from his feet. In all his shots he seems to turn the wrist over so that on the completion of the stroke the face of the bat is towards the ground.*

Bell also noticed that Bradman never attempted to score in front of the wicket when facing fast or medium bowlers who were fresh. Rather he 'glides the ball down the leg side or hits it like a bullet between point and third man'.

Bradman considered adopting other techniques but found these limited his run-scoring ability: 'I allowed my bat to rest on the ground between my feet simply because it was a comfortable and natural position. It is regarded as more orthodox to teach a pupil to rest his bat behind his right toe. This position encourages a straighter backlift, is perhaps sounder for defensive play, but I feel it has greater limitations in versatile stroke making.'

Shillinglaw concludes that the recognized 'orthodoxy' is based on a pendulum motion of the bat in which the batter's first priority is defence of the wicket, whereas Bradman's focus was on attacking the bowler and dictating terms to him. It is the latter approach that seems to have been adopted by the current generation of exceptional Australian batsmen.

Why has orthodoxy survived in the modern coaching manuals whereas no mention is made of Bradman's technique and how it fails to conform to this orthodoxy? Shillinglaw notes that it has been much easier to dismiss Bradman as a 'one-off' than to challenge the orthodoxy. Nevertheless, he feels it is imperative that we investigate why one individual was able to have a test average 30% better than the next best average in the history of the game. Biological factors alone cannot explain this significant a difference – they do not differ by 30% between the very best and the next best human in any particular activity.

In fact, a fundamental teaching in science is that it is dangerous to presume a cause unless it has been proven. Since we have no evidence that Bradman was biologically superior, we must entertain the possibility that Bradman's brilliance might have been the result of his superior and unorthodox batting technique.

Shillinglaw concludes: 'Bradman appeared to select every stroke and continue its motion from the same advanced position of perfect balance.' The advantage of this has to be obvious. Once his subconscious had selected the type of shot to be played, the forward swing of his bat could be adjusted to accommodate either a defensive shot with a straight bat or an attacking shot with a cross-bat. There was no need to produce a different sequence, depending on the nature of the delivery. For example, to hit a pull shot from a straight backlift requires the bat to move laterally away from the ball before it can begin to move towards the ball. No such limitation exists in the Bradman method, where the swing of the bat can rotate according to the dictates of the ball.

WHAT THE CAMERA REVEALS

Further evidence of this is provided by extensive analysis of film footage of Bradman, including his coaching video. What is of significant interest is that he played shots in Test matches that were not repeated in his coaching video. Typically, these were cross-bat shots off the back foot to all parts of the field. These are not listed among the 'orthodox' batting shots included either in his video or in his book on coaching.

His stance and grip, as discussed above, were unorthodox. Nevertheless, his head and body were absolutely still at the time of ball release. The only observable movement immediately before ball release was the beginning of his backlift. At the moment of ball release, the tip of his bat had reached the level of the top of the stumps.

His backlift was achieved by cocking his wrists without moving his upper arms or shoulders and was directed towards second slip/point. This enabled the transfer of weight to the balls of his feet, not onto his back foot. As a result, he was able to move onto either the back or front foot to play his strokes. However, he preferred to play back, except when the ball was extremely full, or he was stepping out of his crease to attack a spin bowler.

The direction of his backlift allowed Bradman to achieve a constant, repeatable 'set' position from which he could execute all his straight- and cross-batted shots. In the case of a straight-batted shot (a drive to the off side, for example), his bat would return to the line of the stumps as it came forward. As a result, by the time it struck the ball, the blade of the bat was straight and headed in the direction in which the ball was to be driven. This technique, in which the bat rotated through a circle in the course of the backlift and forward stroke, has been termed Bradman's 'rotary' method by Shillinglaw. Our most recent analysis shows that, without exception, all the great batsmen of the past – including W.G. Grace, Graeme Pollock, Garfield Sobers, Viv Richards and Brian Lara – all followed this technique, as do all the current batsmen in the all-conquering Australian team of 2007.

In contrast, if the ball was short enough to pull or hook, Bradman's backlift would continue until it was above the level of his shoulder. From there the bat would travel directly to the point where it would strike the ball. As the bat was travelling on a downward path, the ball would be struck towards the ground. By rolling his wrists, Bradman made doubly certain that he did not hit the ball into the air.

Finally, when driving on the front foot, Bradman rotated his upper body and struck the ball as if he was playing a golf shot, a phenomenon seen in many modern players who are powerful strikers of the cricket ball – most notably the Australians Matthew Hayden and Adam Gilchrist.

Indeed, our unpublished study of eight of the current top batsmen in world cricket in 2006 (including Ricky Ponting, Jacques Kallis, Mohammad Yousuf, Inzamam-ul-Haq, Kevin Pietersen, Damien Martin, Herschelle Gibbs and Andrew Symonds) reveals that none lifts his bat directly backwards at the start of his backswing. Indeed it is difficult now to find a leading Australian batsman who does not lift his bat towards the slips, suggesting that finally in his own country, the legacy of Bradman is being honoured not just in memory, but in the practice of the sport he dominated.

Shillinglaw proposes that formally recognizing, accepting and adopting the 'rotary' batting style would provide the true and lasting legacy of Sir Donald Bradman as his gift to the game of cricket.

IF BRADMAN IS CORRECT, WHAT DOES THIS MEAN FOR THE COACHING OF YOUNG CRICKETERS?

1. **Learning to control a fast-moving ball must be the first requirement.**
   If Bradman's brilliance resulted from the hundreds of hours that he spent playing his boyhood cricket matches, then perhaps young children should be encouraged to learn cricket first by hitting a tennis ball against a wall with a cricket bat. Then they should graduate to using a golf ball and a cricket stump. Once they have mastered that technique (as Bradman did), they can begin to learn the nuances of cricket. Interestingly, Bjorn Börg, five times Wimbledon champion by the age of 24, has said that he learned to play tennis by hitting the ball against the wall for hours each day. To win a 'point', he had to return the ball ten times.

2. **One reason why orthodoxy and over-coaching fail might be because they do not develop the art of controlling the fast-moving cricket ball at the right age as effectively as a simple game (like those Bradman invented) does.**
   There is now considerable evidence that there are key periods when the brain 'learns' certain skills. If there is no exposure to that skill during

that key period of brain development, then that skill will never be properly mastered. For example, the ability to play a specific musical instrument probably requires that the child be exposed to these activities from a very young age. Similarly, the fact that Bradman spent most of his childhood playing his imaginary cricket matches suggests that the optimum period to develop these skills is probably from the age of seven onwards – perhaps even younger.

3. Shillinglaw strongly believes that 'the very minute a young player is told to stand with his bat open-faced behind his rear foot, the battle is lost. From this position the only natural movement is straight back. Bradman's style of batting cannot be adopted from this stance.'
This opinion needs to be seriously considered by future generations of cricket coaches.

4. Bradman's ultimate secret was that his technique allowed him to play a wider range of strokes than are usually described in classic cricket texts.
His less conventional strokes (which looked more like golf or tennis shots) are becoming increasingly common in the repertoires of twenty-twenty and one-day batting maestros such as Matthew Hayden, Andrew Symonds, Yousuf Khan, V.V.S. Laxman and others.

POSTSCRIPT: BOWLING TO THE DON

Perhaps the final word belongs to the man reputed to be the fastest bowler in history, Australian Jeff Thomson, in an interview with television personality and cricket lover, Michael Parkinson. Thomson remembered Bradman, then in his late sixties, attending the opening of a new cricket field. Two aspiring cricketers, on the verge of selection to the state team, had asked if they could bowl to him, and the old warrior agreed.

At first 'the young men bowled respectfully at him, aware both of his age and the fact that he had neither pads nor gloves. But when Bradman started playing shots, they quickened up and eventually were bowling flat out… the quicker they bowled, the harder Bradman smote them to the boundary. It was bloody magnificent. All my life I had looked at his record and thought – how can anyone be twice as good as Greg Chappell? That day I found out.'

CHAPTER FOUR

VISION AND BATTING

'The brain is a better cricketer than you'll ever be.'
Greg Chappell, *Cricket: The Making of Champions*

While technique and tactics have been central to cricket manuals for over a century, the physiology of the game is relatively new in the popular consciousness of the game. Even today's increasingly sophisticated players and audiences, who have a layperson's knowledge of stress fractures and rotator cuffs and bone spurs (all Greek to players and fans of a generation ago), nevertheless still refer to the 'Magic Spray' that comes out when a player gets a nasty knock, a name that only half hides in humour the rather superstitious relationship the public has with sports medicine.

Still, physiology has entered the public debate, and will stay there: from the media to the stands, discussions abound over players being over-bowled, backs that won't stand the strain of particular actions, shoulder and wrist movements that will help or hinder the run-scoring ability of the latest up-and-coming international star, and so on.

It would seem, then, that cricket manuals and popular discourse have finally caught up with the game's development: that we are now discussing everything that needs to be discussed. But this is not so.

One crucial – perhaps even fundamental – physiological aspect still needs to be understood and incorporated into the teaching and playing of the game: vision. In fact, so important is vision in cricket, and so great its potential contribution to the game, that we believe it merits a chapter entirely to itself, independent of the general discussion of physiology in Chapter 10.

INTRODUCTION

Bowlers should be taught how to disguise critical cues, present false clues, increase the number of possible relevant clues, vary all the dimensions of speed, swing, flight and direction, and finally provide the critical clues as late as possible (Stretch and Bartlett, 2000).

More than almost any other human activity, sport illustrates the ruthless Darwinian process of selection. Those without the necessary skills fail to advance to the next level of competition, and remain at the level at which they are competent. Those who have the necessary aptitudes, whether physiological or psychological, advance.

There are many selective factors that will determine the level to which a cricketer can advance: concentration, desire, courage, application, fitness and so on. But the most obvious, at least for batters, are the dual but different abilities of their subconscious brains to process information quickly enough to deal with incoming fast deliveries, and precisely enough to play the deceptive flights and spins produced by slow bowlers.

Without these capabilities, often simplistically labelled 'hand-eye co-ordination', a batter will never reach the highest levels of sport. This is the law of the sporting jungle, and it applies across the board. The reason that some international batsmen have a batting average in the 30s while others average in the 60s may well hinge on these subconscious mental abilities – the ability of expert batters to see clues in the bowler's run-up and delivery action, and to predict the future path of the ball with an accuracy that defies understanding, simply by tracking the first few metres of each delivery's flight. Batting will always be easier for those who can subconsciously select the relevant visual information and process it more quickly, thereby having more time to choose the most appropriate shot and execute it with exquisite precision.

But the great irony that this chapter will explore is that ultimately, the batter must hit the ball *without knowing exactly where it is*, nor indeed precisely when it will be there. Similarly the close-in fielder must catch the ball without knowing exactly where it is, nor the exact moment that it will arrive in his grasp.

In other words, successful batting and consistent catching are, at the moment of impact, based almost entirely on blind assumption; yet most top players make this predictive leap with an accuracy of timing and position that cannot be equalled by any human-made system.

To review the raw split-second data of what actually happens (in terms of vision and decision-making) when batters execute a shot is to wonder how any batsman survives more than one delivery. Using information gleaned in the first third of each delivery's flight, he must predict the moment at which the ball will reach him

The great irony is that ultimately, the batter must hit the ball without knowing exactly where it is, nor precisely when it will be there.

Batting is timing; bowling is upsetting timing.

with an accuracy of 2–4 milliseconds, and with a future positional accuracy in three-dimensional space of 1–2 centimetres in any direction. In other words, he needs to know *exactly* when and where the ball will arrive to be played. As predictions of the future go, these are extraordinarily specific: the tiniest error in predicting either the future arrival time of the delivery, or its exact position at that instant, or indeed the correct movement of the bat, will usually result in dismissal.

And yet at the highest levels of the game, batsmen make correct decisions, and almost perfect predictions, for dozens, if not hundreds of consecutive deliveries. This is largely because they have removed one of the unknown factors from their unconscious calculation processes: their own movements. As seasoned international players, their technique and the biomechanics of their batting are grooved and practised to such a degree that they know exactly how they will respond to certain deliveries. But the need to predict, to launch a stroke at a point in space without being certain that the ball will ever arrive in that point at the right time, cannot be removed by practice, and it remains the greatest threat to top players. It is the errors in their predictions, often caused by misreading and misunderstanding their visual senses, which lead to their dismissals.

However, this is not simply a struggle between a batsman and a point in space in which the ball may or may not show up: there is an agent provocateur at work here! If batters are trying to gain the clearest and most accurate visual sense of the future position of the ball, then bowlers are equally determined to obscure that sense. In fact, a good bowler is one who is able to produce deceptive visual information during his approach and delivery, misleading signals that will persuade the batter to play a stroke where the ball mysteriously is not. As an American baseball pitcher said: 'Hitting is timing; pitching is upsetting timing.' Exactly the same principles apply to batting and bowling. Batting is timing; bowling is upsetting timing.

In this way, cricket has evolved 'to produce a balanced contest between the visual-motor skills of the batsman and the strength and skills of the bowler. Batting is possible (or batsmen would refuse to play), but not all the time (or bowlers would refuse to play). The abilities of the best batsman against the fastest bowlers reveal the limits of the (human) visual-motor system' (Land and McLeod, 2000).

Those limits, and their breaking-points, have become cricketing lore – think of Harold Larwood shocking Australian cricket into the twentieth century in the 1932/33 Bodyline series, Jeff Thomson eliciting a boycott by the Indian team in 1977/78, and Curtly Ambrose annihilating England with figures of 8 for 40, with the rest of the team retired hurt, at Port of Spain in 1994.

But how do great batters continue to achieve with some consistency what might appear to be impossible? And how do the most skilled bowlers exploit the natural limits of the human visual-motor system to their best advantage?

THE VISUAL CHALLENGE POSED BY FAST BOWLING

In the early 1980s, Tim Noakes and his colleagues at the University of Cape Town wanted to establish whether batters differed in their ability to process early information about the delivery in order to make accurate choices about which stroke to play.

They enlisted the help of former South African Test player Peter Kirsten, a batsman widely recognized as one of the best players of pace bowling in his generation. However, they soon discovered that even Kirsten was unable to hit the ball when it was delivered by a bowling machine at speeds in excess of 130km per hour. Yet out in the middle, Kirsten had comfortably dealt with deliveries travelling in excess of 150km per hour. This simple experiment proved that an expert batsman needs to observe the bowler's run-up and delivery if his brain is to compute the delivery's future trajectory when travelling at speeds of more than 130km per hour. In other words, the batter relies heavily on a kind of visual early warning system, here referred to as advance cues, during the bowler's approach and delivery. Without these cues, he becomes increasingly less able to face genuine pace with any degree of confidence.

The switch of the indoor lighting was then linked to the bowling machine Kirsten was facing, so that the lights were turned off at the moment the ball left the bowling machine. The results were telling: even if he had sight of the ball for as little as the first 100–200 milliseconds before the light faded (of the approximately 550 milliseconds of the ball's flight), Kirsten – and presumably a player of his class – could predict the trajectory and exactly where it would pitch with 70% accuracy.

Lesser batsmen, however, were less successful, and less inclined to wait around to see if their predictions had been correct: some provincial bowlers asked to bat in these testing conditions simply ran from the wicket as soon as the lights died down.

On the basis of these results, the researchers drew the simple conclusion: a superior ability to predict the ball's trajectory early in its flight is probably a genetic gift innate in all 'natural' batsmen, and is simply developed to an exceptional degree in cricketing geniuses such as Sir Donald Bradman, Sir Garfield Sobers, Graeme Pollock, Barry Richards, Brian Lara and Sachin Tendulkar. This was not a novel suggestion. Bill Ponsford, who batted with Bradman in the 1930s, said, 'Don sees the ball two yards earlier than the rest of us' (Fingleton, 1946). Similarly, Garry Sobers described early detection as central to his success: 'I was never coached. I had a simple approach, based on the theory that if a batsman picked up the ball early enough, he could position himself to play whatever shot he thought the ball deserved' (1996, p. 78).

'Don sees the ball two yards earlier than the rest of us.'
– Bill Ponsford on Donald Bradman

However, the Kirsten experiment revealed that even a world-class batsman needed substantial visual information for shot selection: even though he could predict the trajectory of the delivery with just 100–200 milliseconds worth of information (before the lights went out), and even though his predictions of line and length were remarkably accurate, the best he could manage in response to the delivery was a defensive parry. He had simply not received enough information to be able to make a confident enough prediction about the ball's position relative to him to commit to an attacking stroke.

The conclusion drawn from this experiment is that Kirsten needed to see more than just the first quarter of the delivery's flight if he was to judge its final position and time of arrival with sufficient precision to play an attacking shot.

DEFENDING IN THE DARK

Why could Kirsten play a defensive stroke but not an attacking one? The answer lies in his straight bat. When you are defending with a vertical blade, you don't need to predict the final position of the ball on the vertical plane with any accuracy: whether it hits your bat 1cm or 40cm off the pitch, it is still a safe shot. Nor is timing important, since the ball is meeting you, rather than you meeting it.

ADVANCE CLUES: THE BATTER'S EARLY WARNING SYSTEM

The explanation for Kirsten's dilemma – his inability to play an attacking shot to deliveries travelling at more than 130km per hour – was the absence of advance cues in the experiment. An impassive, immobile bowling machine reveals little about the nature of the delivery it is going to produce: an increase in the pitch of its motor might suggest a quicker ball, and the point on the pitch at which it seems to be aimed should give some clues about the length of the delivery; but even these were removed from the scenario in the author's experiment, as batsmen were given earplugs and the machine was hidden behind a sheet, the ball appearing through a specially cut hole.

In other words, batsmen who participated in the experiment found themselves starved of the advance cues they were used to in match conditions. As already stated, the bowler is trying to deceive the batsman into a false shot. Like a poker player, he is trying to make the batter read his intentions incorrectly. But like so many poker players, he is simultaneously betraying a wealth of information through tiny subconscious signals, most of which he doesn't know he is broadcasting.

The following are just some of the ways in which he is telegraphing his intentions as he kicks off from his mark:

- **The speed of his run-up** – the faster the approach, the faster, or shorter, the delivery might be.
- **The point of delivery with regard to the popping crease** – tight against the stumps, and it might be a slower ball fishing for an LBW appeal, or an outswinger. Wider of the stumps, perhaps a fast yorker speared in at middle stump.
- **His grip** – the ball deeper in his fingers suggests a slower delivery.
- **The angle of the seam and shiny side of the ball** – most international bowlers try to hide this information from the batsmen, sometimes by cocking their wrist down over the ball until the point of release, or by holding their other hand over it, as mastered by India's Javagal Srinath and Pakistan's Wasim Akram.
- **The speed of the arm movement prior to and at the moment of releasing the ball.**
- **The exact position in space and the precise moment at which the ball is released** – in quick bowlers, a fractionally later release signals a short ball. Spinners who are looking to give the ball plenty of air to generate more drift and bounce might release it fractionally early.
- **The action of the wrist at the moment of release** – a wrist snapped straight down can signal a bouncer, while a quick snap down to the left or right, or a pushing action, can indicate an outswinger or inswinger, or a cutter. The position of the wrist is also critical to reading leg-spinners.
- **The position of the front shoulder at the moment of delivery** – a dropped front shoulder almost always signals a short ball.

It seems that batters use advance cues predominantly to predict length. Thus, having bet his wicket and his innings on a particular length, he then makes his initial movement either back or forwards.

BREAKDOWN OF THE BATTER'S RESPONSE TO A DELIVERY

As the bowler runs in, the batsman begins his search for anticipatory cues that will allow the earliest possible detection of the future flight pattern and velocity of the delivery. As stated above, the clues he is most urgently seeking are those that will hint at a possible length, to reveal whether his initial movement must be forward or back. It is probably that the very best batsmen in the world have already predicted the length of the delivery (with considerable accuracy) by the time the ball is released.

A striking example is that of Brian Lara, who was asked whether he had been nervous at the point in his innings when he had equalled – but not yet beaten – Sir Garfield Sobers' world record score of 365, when batting against England in Antigua in 1994. He conceded that he had been anxious for the first two deliveries (dot balls). But, he said, as bowler Chris Lewis ran in for the third delivery, he lost his anxiety:

he knew during Lewis's approach to the wicket that the delivery would be short. In fact, Lara was in position so early for the hook shot that took him to the new world record, he almost stood on his stumps.

Once the ball has been released, the batter views it for as long as he needs to make a decision on the exact stroke he will play. This is known as the viewing time (VT).

Having decided which stroke to play, the batsman then experiences a latency time (LT) during which his motor response to the delivery is organized and the necessary information travels via the various nervous pathways from his brain to his muscles. This latency time approximates what is known as the 'reaction time' and lasts about 180 milliseconds. Finally, the LT phase ends when the brain's commands finally reach the muscles, and initiate a response from those muscles that produce the batter's specific stroke. This is known as the movement time (MT).

THE DIFFERENCE BETWEEN GREAT AND GOOD

To the dependable amateur opening batsman, who faces the new ball every week for his club, this might all seem very removed from his experience of batting in the real world. After all, if one is talking about analysing batsmen's reactions to deliveries, then one is suggesting that all batsmen react in more or less the same way. And having faced the odd first-class or even retired Test bowler, our batsman is under no illusions about his own abilities: viewing times, latency times and such things are fine in theory, but he knows that there is simply no way that his reactions can be compared to anything even vaguely approaching those of a Bradman or a Sobers. Of course, he's quite wrong. The fact is that there is no evidence that superior batsmen have quicker reaction times or even superior visual skills. Rather, it is the way in which elite batters use the same information available to all batsmen that sets them apart.

Using a temporal occlusion study (one in which they allowed batters to see only part of the flight of the ball), Abernethy (1982) and Abernethy and Russell (1984) found that top batsmen can make accurate shot selections from shorter viewing times than less good batsmen. Furthermore, they suggested that more skilled batters are better at generating useful information from advance cues than less good batters.

The implications of the study were clear: the fundamental difference between elite batters and those with average skill is the ability of the elite to know where the ball is going even before it is delivered. England off-spinner Jim Laker confirmed this hypothesis when he said that 'Bradman seemed to know where the ball was going to pitch, what stroke he was going to play and how many runs he was going to score' (Williams, 1996). Greg Chappell, one of the great Australian batsmen to follow Bradman, has written: 'As the ball left the bowler's hand, all I saw was the ball and the bowler's hand. This gave me all the clues I needed to gauge the line, length and type of delivery' (2004, p. 146).

These authors also found that superior batsmen extracted more information from any equivalent viewing time and were therefore better able to cope with a reduced viewing time when facing a fast bowler. In contrast, when viewing times were reduced, less skilled batsmen were unable to respond appropriately – much as the weak batters ran away when the lights went out during the study in Cape Town.

In other words, batsmen succeed or fall by the wayside not because of their ocular and mental equipment, but because of how successfully or not they use that equipment. It is their brain 'software' that makes the difference, not their 'hardware'. Since these pioneering studies, a number of others have evaluated the use of visual information by batters. Penrose and Roach (1995) showed that skilled batsmen were significantly better than the less skilled at using advance cues to predict the subsequent line (radial variability) of bowling deliveries. They evaluated this by showing batsmen videos of different deliveries that ended 80 milliseconds before the bowler released the ball. This is known as the video-occlusion technique.

As more information was provided, less skilled batters increased their predictive ability, so that if more than the first 80 milliseconds of the delivery was shown, the predictive ability of the less-skilled batters was the same as that of the skilled batsmen. However, the longer decision time of the less-skilled batsmen left them with less time to take up a balanced position and to execute the appropriate cricket shot with the necessary control. The authors concluded that one of the keys to batting is the art of selective attention – the capacity to attend only to those crucial cues which predict the future line and length of the delivery, while ignoring the other cues that provide irrelevant information. They propose that batters learn to identify the most relevant advance and ball cues and concentrate exclusively on those clues, to the exclusion of all 'irrelevant' information.

More recently, in 2005 at the University of Cape Town, Sharhidd Taliep, Lester John and Tim Noakes, together with other researchers, measured the electrical activity of the brain in expert and novice batters while they watched video footage of inswing, outswing and slower deliveries. They found that the brains of expert batters needed about 10% less time (405 versus 445 milliseconds) to detect the outswing deliveries and about 12% less time (438 versus 495 milliseconds) to detect the inswing deliveries. In addition, expert batters had much greater alpha wave activity in the brain at the instant of ball release, indicating that they were more focused ('in the zone') at the moment the ball left the bowler's hand. This instant is what Greg Chappell calls the moment of 'fierce focus'. He notes that as a player, 'I used fierce focus for the shortest possible time because it required a lot of mental energy' (2004, p. 146).

The fundamental difference between elite batters and those with average skill is the ability of the elite to know where the ball is going even before it is delivered.

THE SACCADE HERESY

'Watch the ball!' It is a command as old as cricket, repeated mantra-like by coaches on five continents, and drummed into every child who has picked up a cricket bat. It has stood batters in good stead for almost 200 years, proving its worth on countless ovals, whether rustic cow pastures or Test venues packed to capacity. And it seems to have almost no foundation in reality.

The heretics were Land and McLeod in 2000. What they suggested went entirely contrary to traditional wisdom on vision: batsmen, they said, do *not* in fact watch the ball onto the bat. Using sophisticated video technology that recorded the direction of the batsman's gaze as well as his head movements, they observed batters facing a bowling machine. The results were revealing.

Batters kept their heads and eyes still for the first 140 milliseconds after the ball was released. Then they suddenly shifted their gaze downward by 7,5° in a rapid non-tracking movement known as a saccade, so that their eyes were looking at the spot on the pitch *where they expected the ball to pitch*.

The eyes then rotated upwards (relative to the head) for 300 milliseconds while the head moved downwards through the same angle, the eyes remaining fixed on the pitch where the ball was expected to bounce. Once the ball had bounced, the head and eyes quickly moved down in order to track the latter part of its flight. This occurred from about 350 to 550 milliseconds after the ball's release, after which the ball was no longer accurately tracked as the ball travelled progressively further 'ahead' of the batter's gaze. As a result, the eyes did not follow the ball for the last 100 milliseconds of the delivery.

How long had the batter watched the ball? 140 milliseconds after release; another 200 milliseconds after the ball had bounced: a total tracking time of around 340 milliseconds. And yet the delivery took 650 milliseconds to reach him. The numbers defied the coaches' mantra. The batter had had his eye on the ball for just 52% of its flight.

Did any batsmen watch the ball onto the bat? Certainly, the fuller the ball, the longer batsmen observed it before the first saccade. But a full, uninterrupted sight of the ball, with no saccade, happened only when the best batsman in the test group received a full toss. However, this did not imply that better batsmen did not need to make saccades. On the contrary, the study showed that when playing normal, bouncing deliveries, this batsman made his initial saccade earlier than the less gifted players.

Naturally, laboratory conditions can create artificial circumstances: the visual performance of these batters was studied for a relatively short time, and it is possible that the tracking patterns might have changed as they played themselves in. Perhaps, after an hour or two of batting, the batters might have been seeing the ball 'as big a football', and tracking deliveries for a greater proportion of their flight.

Nevertheless, the evidence suggests that batsmen do not watch the ball all the way onto the bat, no matter what seasoned veterans might claim. But is this a reason to scrap 150 years of coaching dogma? Should coaches start urging their young players to 'saccade after 140 milliseconds'? Of course not. Even if batters are not literally watching the ball all the way onto the bat, they should still be trained to try.

FIGURE 4.1: *Tracking the cricket ball*

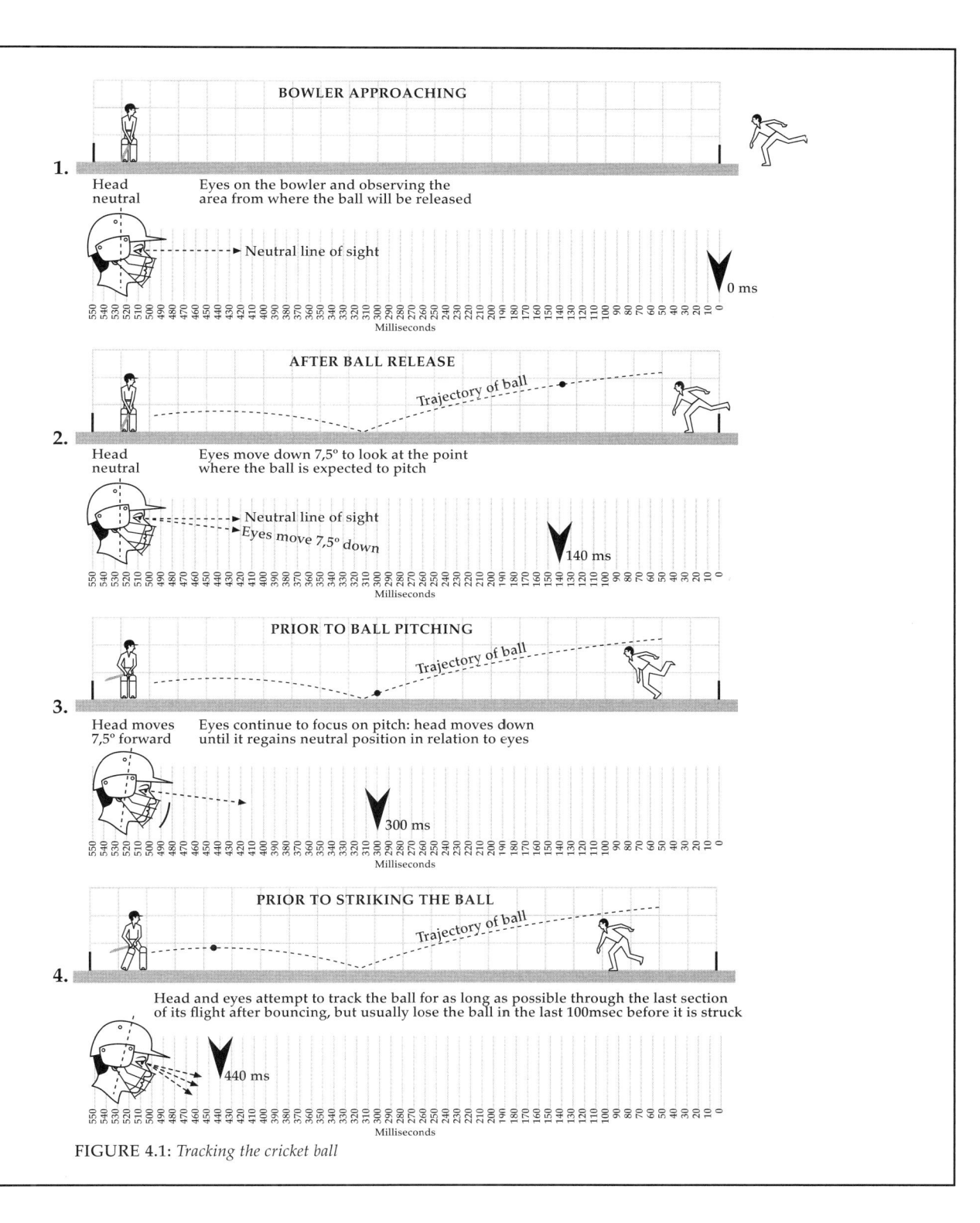

THE LIMITS OF REACTION TIME

Experiments like those reviewed on the previous pages have shown that batsmen tend to watch the bowler's arm and hand as he runs in, no doubt searching for some of the advance cues already mentioned. As the bowler braces into his delivery stride, the batsman performs a saccade from the bowler's hand to the area above and to the right (for a right-hand bowler) of the bowler's hand – in other words, the area from where he expects the ball to be released. Almost like a 'cut' in a film, the change of view is apparently instantaneous. As already outlined, the batsman then watches the delivery for a short time, but long enough to predict where the ball will pitch. Once he has made his decision, he performs another visual saccade, this time focusing on the place on the pitch where he has predicted the ball will land.

Figure 4.2 shows one of the crucial differences between good and great batters: because a batsman is unable to react to any deviation in the final 200 milliseconds of a delivery's flight, the earlier he can perform the saccade, the more swiftly and accurately he can respond to the delivery.

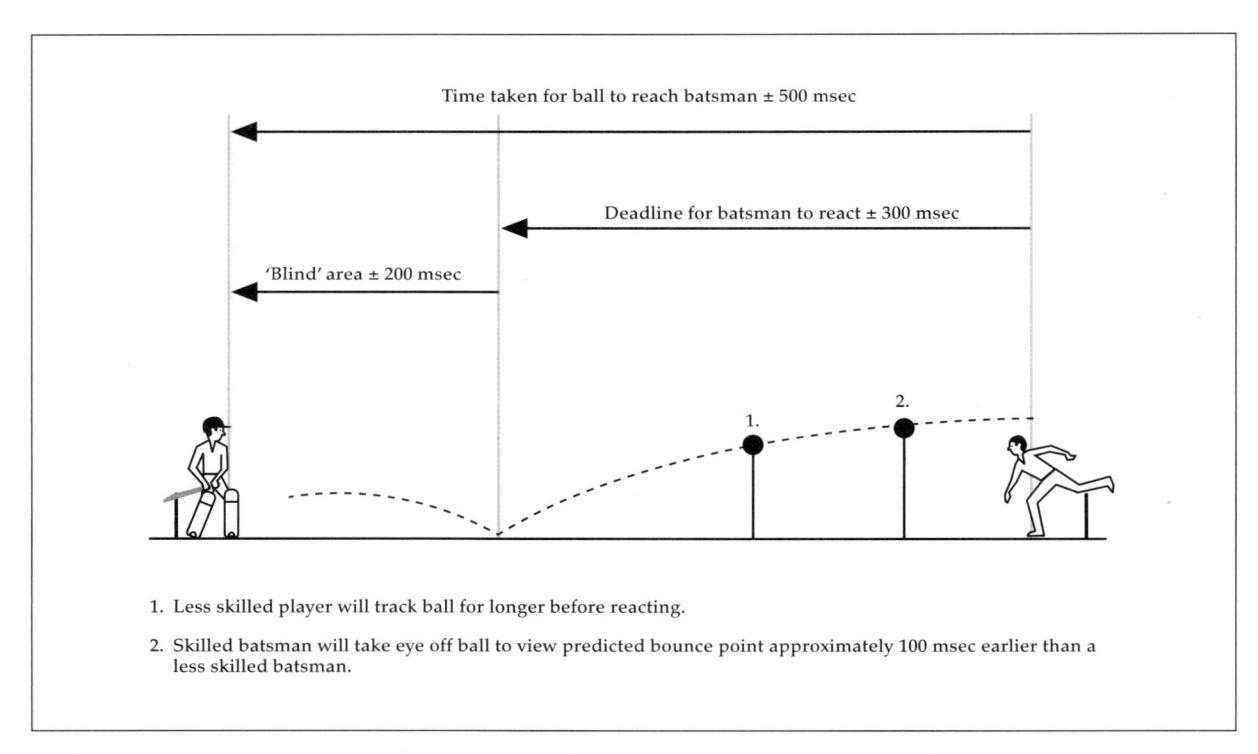

1. Less skilled player will track ball for longer before reacting.
2. Skilled batsman will take eye off ball to view predicted bounce point approximately 100 msec earlier than a less skilled batsman.

FIGURE 4.2: *The visual responses (in milliseconds) of skilled and less skilled batters to the delivery of a good length ball. The more skilled batter will perform the saccade from the ball to the anticipated area it will pitch fractionally earlier.*

So why is the saccade an automatic reflex? Why do we make no conscious attempt to track the moving ball? The answer lies in the physiological limits of the human eye: we are physically unable to follow an object that requires our eyes to alter their angle of observation at more than 70° per second (Ripoll and Fleurance, 1988; Bahill and LaRitz, 1984). If anything moves across our field of vision at a greater speed, our brain takes control, predicting a point at which the object will appear in the immediate future, and performing a saccade to take the eyes to that point.

The ball has now landed, and the batsman watches it off the pitch, able to respond to any new visual information he might receive about deviation or bounce. But only up to a point: all batsmen have a point of no return, a point beyond which they are simply unable to respond to any late deviations (see Figure 4.3). The human nervous and muscular systems just don't move quickly enough. This also explains why fast bowlers are so feared, and why a delivery that pitches about 200 milliseconds before it reaches the batter is considered such a valuable one.

This frontier of reaction time, beyond which the batsman is more or less paralysed by our species' relatively lumbering reflexes, is found around 170 milliseconds before

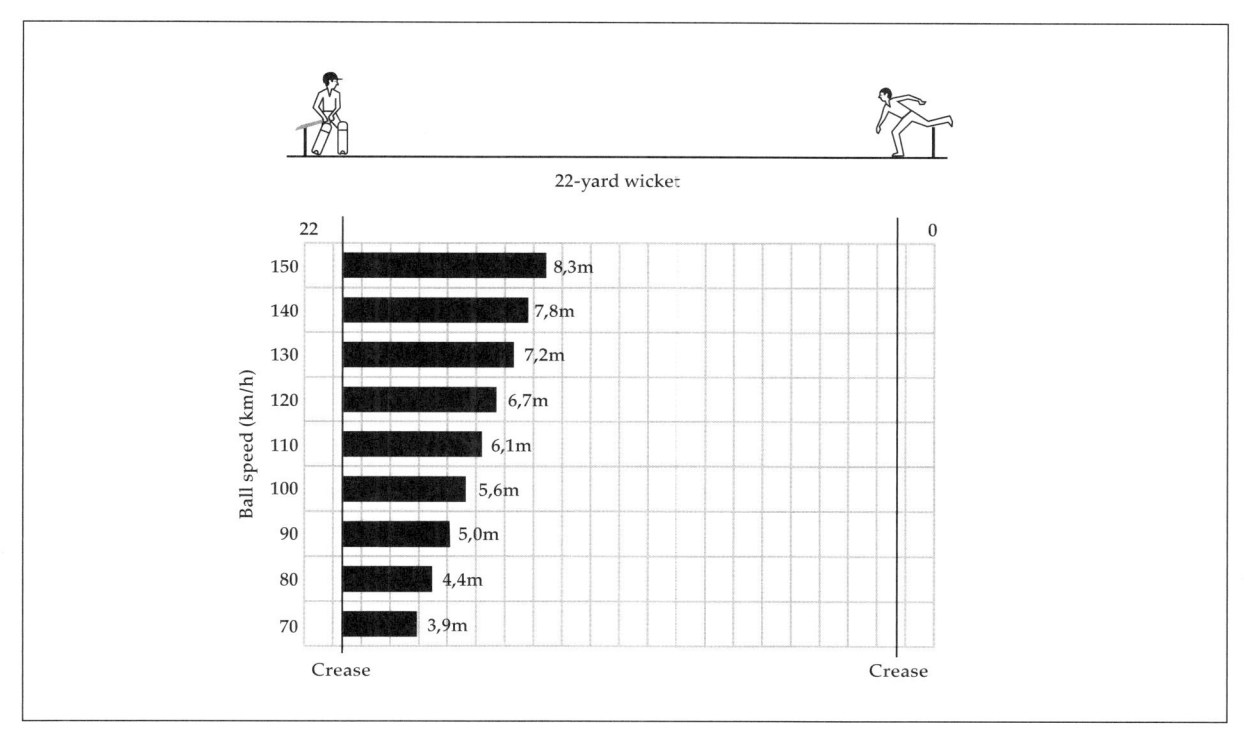

FIGURE 4.3: *This shows the distance the ball travels in 200 milliseconds when bowled at different speeds. The 'blind' or black area shows the distance the ball travels while the batter is still unable to 'compute' information and translate it into a new action.*

VISION AND BATTING 195

> *Any delivery that makes an unpredictable movement less than 200 milliseconds from the batter is physically unplayable.*

the ball reaches his hitting zone. Clearly, this refers to time rather than distance: 170 milliseconds against a pace bowler would leave the ball many metres further away from the bat than it would against a spin bowler. This figure – 170 milliseconds – has been termed 'one visual reaction time' (in other words, the smallest unit of reaction time) and was determined in a novel study conducted by Peter McLeod in Oxford in 1987.

He asked three English international batsmen, Wayne Larkins, Peter Willey and Allan Lamb, to bat on a matting wicket under which a series of wooden dowels, invisible to the batsmen, had been placed. Deliveries that pitched on flat matting naturally behaved predictably, coming through to the batsmen with only the conventional and expected deviations (bounce and negligible lateral movement). But balls that landed on one of the dowels deviated dramatically to either side. McLeod then filmed the batsmen, paying special attention to their reaction to these unexpected deviations – a hasty sideways movement of the bat in an effort to play the new line of the ball.

The conclusions were absolutely clear: under no circumstances was any batter able to adjust his stroke in less than about 170 milliseconds after the bounce of the ball. Thus McLeod (1987) concluded that 'one visual reaction time' is about 170 milliseconds. He further concluded, in line with legendary Australian spinner Clarrie Grimmett's suggestion, that a good length delivery should be defined as one which pitches too close to the batter for him to be able to respond to anything the delivery does off the pitch. Interestingly, in the late 1920s this was called a 'blind length' delivery.

Further study has slightly adjusted the above number: we now know that 200 milliseconds is the absolute cut-off period after which the batsman is hamstrung by his reactions. In other words: any delivery that makes an unpredictable movement less than 200 milliseconds from the batter is physically unplayable.

However, McLeod's findings raised an interesting question: how, he wondered, is it possible for a batsman to occupy the crease for hours on end without losing his wicket, when during that time he will receive perhaps a hundred or more 'unplayable' deliveries – in other words, balls that have pitched within 200 milliseconds of him?

He concluded that good batsmen, especially those facing quality bowlers able to make the ball deviate late, adopt two general strategies:

- They get as close to the pitch of the ball as possible, so that even if it deviates after pitching, it will not have moved far enough to beat the edge of the bat.
- They play defensive strokes with 'soft hands' (discussed in more detail in Chapter 3), so that if the ball deviates and takes the edge, it will not have the momentum to reach fielders.

RAGE AGAINST THE DYING OF THE LIGHT

It has saved batsmen and Tests and enraged and enthralled spectators for generations. Despite rigorously policed schedules and over-rates, and multi-million dollar broadcasting deals, the modern game can still be brought to an abrupt halt by a batsman's inability (real or pretended!) to see through the gloom of an approaching evening. But why are batsmen 'offered the light'?

Fergus Campbell and colleagues (1987) from the University of Cambridge showed that reaction time becomes increasingly prolonged as the light fades beyond what is termed bright, and even before the light is perceived as 'dim'. They describe the conditions in the transition between bright and dim, as 'gloom'. The effect of gathering gloom on reaction time is dramatic. Luminance is measured on a log scale of 100 000 to 0cd/m^2 (cd = candela, a unit of light), with 100 000cd/m^2 being full light and 0cd/m^2 complete darkness. Values of between 1 000 and 100cd/m^2 represent light conditions described as 'gloom' – the point at which we begin to turn on car or house lights. It is within this range that human reaction time begins to slow. Campbell's study found that with each unit reduction in luminescence below bright light, human reaction time was reduced by 33 milliseconds. From a delivery from a fast bowler, this would translate into a travel distance of about 1 metre (another look at Figure 4.3 will remind us why 'gloom' is so potentially dangerous to batsmen).

This means that a batter would be less able to respond to a deviation in the ball's trajectory late in flight or after it pitched. The normal reaction time is about 170–200 milliseconds in good light, so that the batter is unable to respond to any deviation by the ball during the final 170–200 milliseconds of its flight. In bad light, the further slowing of reaction time means that the initial flight will take longer to detect, so that the batter will take longer to calculate the ball's trajectory. As a result, like Peter Kirsten batting in the dark, he will be less and less able to play attacking strokes, and will be forced to play defensively to those deliveries he did not 'see'. On top of this, he will be unable to respond to deviations in the ball's trajectory during the final 210 milliseconds of its flight, compared to 170–200 milliseconds in good light. So the bowler will be able to bowl shorter (by about a metre) and still have the ball treated as if it is of a 'good length'. Thus the bowler is able to be less accurate in his length while still curtailing scoring.

The biological explanation is that in bright light, the rod photoreceptors in the retina do not relay useful information to the brain. Cone receptors discriminate between colours in bright light, while rod cells are designed for black-and-white vision in poor light. The rods lack the discriminatory capacity of the cone cells, but as the light fades, they become increasingly active. It is assumed that the increasing activity of the rods cause this progressive delay in reaction time – they do not function as fast as do the cones.

THE VISUAL PITFALLS OF FLIGHT

The detection of the nature of a slow delivery requires visual and brain skills that are quite different to those required for predicting the future length and direction of a fast delivery. For example, a slow delivery may take about 900 milliseconds to reach the batsman. If the visual reaction time is 170 milliseconds and the movement time is 200 milliseconds, the batter still has nearly 600 milliseconds to observe the delivery before deciding how to play it.

But while he now has the luxury of being able to watch the ball for up to 600 milliseconds, he faces a new obstacle: flight.

For generations, spin bowlers have known that batsmen struggle against deliveries given plenty of 'air'. Common cricketing dogma has provided plenty of explanations for this phenomenon: the high trajectory forces the batsman to lift his head; the longer flight time allows the ball to spin and drift; the steep angle of descent will generate tricky bounce; and so on.

Certainly these factors might contribute to their fair share of dismissals, but the threat posed to batsmen by a looping delivery starts long before the ball drops onto the pitch and starts deviating away from the bat. It starts in his eyes; in an inherent weakness in his visual system. For the human brain is unable to predict the exact landing position of a delivery that, for a significant portion of its flight, moves above the horizontal direction of the gaze. (This suggests that instead of telling spinners to get the ball above the batsman's eyes, coaches should be telling them to get it above his eyes *for as long as possible*.)

In the case of a 'flighted' delivery, this is because during the early part of the ball's flight, its image on the retina provides only poor cues to the batsman as to exactly where the ball is in space, and therefore how far away from him it is, and how fast it is approaching (Regan, 1992; Regan, 1997). As a result, the batsman, while still able to predict accurately the exact arrival time of the ball, won't be certain of exactly where it will be in terms of its length at that moment (Regan, 1997).

While every ball delivered starts above the batter's horizontal eyeline, this weakness is not exploitable by fast bowlers, since the trajectory of a fast delivery will always be downwards from its point of release. This means that the batsman generally knows exactly from where in space a fast delivery will begin its descent.

Regan (1997) suggests that the slow bowler exploits this visual weakness in three ways: 'First, he delivers the ball in such a way as to prevent the batsman from predicting where the ball will hit the ground until it is too late to react correctly. Secondly, he forces the batsman to rely on the inadequate retinal image information obtained early in the ball's flight by delivering, with no discernible change in body posture or action, balls that dip or alternatively change direction after bouncing. Thirdly, over the course of several deliveries, he allows the batsman to learn a particular relationship between the early part of the ball's trajectory and the point where the ball hits the ground, and then changes the relationship with such art that the batsman does not detect the change' (pp. 550–51).

To study how and why good batsmen overcome these limitations, Renshaw and Fairweather (2000) tested their ability to detect the five different deliveries typically bowled by wrist spinners: off-breaks, leg-breaks, flippers, top-spin and back-spin.

They reasoned that a slow delivery bowled at 18m/s (65km/h) will take 200 milliseconds to travel 3,6 metres. Since, as has been explained, batsmen are likely to be unable to respond to any new information in the last 170–200 milliseconds of the delivery's trajectory, they will be unable to respond to the direction that the ball turns after pitching if the ball pitches 3,6 metres from the batsman – the definition of a good length delivery.

Since so many good deliveries from a bowler like Shane Warne pitch in this area, Renshaw and Fairweather concluded that skilled players of spin bowling must be able to predict the future direction of the spinning delivery on the basis of information detected from the bowler's action and updated during ball flight.

To evaluate this possibility, they used a temporal occlusion technique to evaluate the ability of different levels of batsmen to detect five different spinning deliveries under two conditions: (1) when they watched on videotape either the bowler's run-up and ball delivery throughout its flight up to the moment of ball contact; and (2) when only the bowler's run-up and the first 80 milliseconds of flight were shown, during which the ball would have travelled about 1,6 metres.

They showed that expert batters were better able to distinguish the different types of deliveries than less good players. They also found that for all groups, detection rates (percentage of deliveries correctly identified) were best for the leg-spin (90%) and googly (52%) deliveries, but were considerably less good for the flipper (32%), back-spin (23%) and top-spin (12%) deliveries. Surprisingly, viewing the full flight of the delivery did not add any further predictive value in the case of these deliveries. Hence predictions were equally good or poor (in the case of the flipper, back-spinner and top-spinner) regardless of whether only the delivery action and the first 1,6 metres of the flight were observed, or if the entire flight (approximately 15 metres) was viewed.

This study shows that essentially all the relevant information that the batter requires is provided in the spin bowler's action. Thus the batter makes his prediction of what the ball will do on the basis of advance cues in the delivery action. In addition, it seems that if the ball lands 3,8 metres or closer to the batsman, he is unable to play it 'off the pitch'. Rather he is playing it on the basis of his prediction made at the time of

The brain is unable to predict the exact landing position of a delivery that, for a significant portion of its flight, moves above the horizontal direction of the gaze. So instead of telling spinners to get the ball above the batsman's eyes, coaches should be telling them to get it above his eyes for as long as possible.

All the relevant information that the batter requires is provided in the spin bowler's action.

ball release. Of course, if the delivery is just short enough so that the batter can detect even a fraction of its trajectory after pitching, he will easily be able to play it 'off the pitch', placing it wherever his skill level will allow.

These authors also conclude that the more similar the bowler's action is when he delivers different deliveries, the greater the difficulty the batter will experience in detecting the nature of the delivery. This is why the leg-break and googly are more easily detected – they have the most distinctive delivery patterns and are also the most frequently bowled deliveries, so that batsmen are more used to playing and hence detecting them. In contrast, the delivery action for the flipper, back- and top-spinner deliveries are more similar, increasing the difficulty the batter will have in differentiating them. This has previously been shown in the detection rates for different tennis serves; it is more difficult to distinguish between those serves that are the most similar, for example, flat and slice serves (Goulet et al., 1989).

The authors make the compelling argument that all the information necessary to play each delivery is available to all batters and there is no time constraint when playing spin bowling. Thus those who are skilled at playing spin bowling are better able to extract that information. This comes through experience, but could clearly be enhanced by the use of video occlusion techniques. However, the focus should be on the bowler's action rather than on the delivery's subsequent trajectory. Meanwhile, the advice to bowlers is that they need to be taught to bowl many different deliveries from nearly identical actions.

In a follow-up study, Renshaw et al. studied the accuracy of prediction of batters facing the same five deliveries, but under visual occlusion conditions in which parts of the bowler's upper body anatomy were progressively removed from the video display. In the first condition, all the bowler's body parts were visible throughout the delivery stride; in the second condition, the bowler's arm and wrist were removed from the last delivery stride onwards; and in the third condition, the bowler's whole body was removed from the delivery stride, leaving only the ball visible during the delivery and flight phase. The authors found that for the leg-spin and the top-spin deliveries, there was no added advantage of seeing the bowling action – the flight alone allowed the batters to make similarly successful predictions. This is surprising, as it suggests that the leg-break delivery can be predicted with equal probability by detecting either advance cues, as discussed earlier, or by seeing only the flight of the delivery. This unexpected finding probably reflects the general familiarity that the batters have with facing leg-break bowlers.

In contrast, seeing only the flight reduced the accuracy of detecting the googly by about 50% to just over 20%; the flipper by about 30% from 35% to 25%; and the back-spin delivery also by more than 50%.

So the more complex slow deliveries that are bowled less frequently are detected with much greater difficulty. When facing those deliveries, the batter requires all the information available – both the bowler's action and the flight – to increase the probability of a successful prediction. But the probability of a successful detection remains rather low for the less-frequently bowled deliveries, and is almost no better than guess work.

One suggestion might be that bowlers should bowl these more complex deliveries more frequently, at least until the batters become as equally good at predicting those deliveries as they are at detecting leg-spin and googly deliveries. (Bowlers might disagree with this course of action!) Of course, it is not only the direction of turn that the bowler uses to deceive the batter. He must also be able, subtly, to alter the 'flight' of these different deliveries in order to extract the most from his art.

Another component of the superior performance of the elite becomes apparent when they process sports-specific visual information. In a classic study, Chase and Simon (1973) showed that experienced chess players were able to recall the positions of the chess pieces on the board with high levels of precision if the pieces had been left in place during the intermission of a real chess game. In contrast, if the pieces were randomly placed on the chessboard, experts were no better than novices in recalling the positions of the pieces. The explanation is that the experts recognized the pattern of play in the real game and thus could recall the position of the chess pieces on the basis of their historical knowledge of how that particular game was progressing at the time it was interrupted. By replaying the game in their brains, they were able more accurately to replace the pieces that had been removed from the real game (Allard et al., 1980).

Similarly, expert baseball and field hockey-players are better able to recall the positions of players when shown slides showing the development of a particular game situation. But without evidence that they could interpret as a developing play, they were no better than novices in recalling the exact positions of different players (Starkes, 1987). This is because expert players have a store of knowledge collected over the years they have played the game. They then compare any new information about a developing play with that old information in order to predict what is about to happen. In addition, they scan the playing field for the most relevant information, and use that information to make better predictions of what is about to happen than do novices.

In summary, these studies provide scientific proof for the contention made by Whiting in 1969 that: 'The expert will not only need to watch the ball for less of its flight, but he will also require less time to discriminate, programme and make decisions on the information that he receives' (p. 35).

SEEING RED: COLOUR-BLINDNESS AND CRICKETING ABILITY

As its name suggests, red-green colour-blindness affects the ability to see the colours red and green. Given that cricket involves a red ball leaping up off a green background, you would be forgiven for assuming that batsmen suffering from red-green colour-blindness are in for a rocky – and painful – ride.

To test this assumption, orthopaedic surgeon Nicholas Goddard (who himself suffers from red-green colour-blindness and a self-declared inability to strike the bowled cricket ball), and his colleague Dominic Coull, then at the Royal Free Hospital, London, tested 280 of the 306 professional cricketers who were playing county cricket in England in 1992.

They found that whereas 8% of the general population are colour-blind, only 4% of English professional cricketers are similarly affected. Was this the result of natural selection, with red-green colour-blind cricketers finding themselves disadvantaged and therefore less likely to turn professional? Perhaps. But the fact that there was still an appreciable number of red-green colour-blind first-class players suggests that this is a disability that can be overcome by cricketers.

In fact, the study found that the batting averages of those cricketers with red-green colour-blindness were no different from those with normal colour vision. Nor did the batting averages of colour-blind batters in one-day cricket improve after the white ball had been introduced into English Sunday League cricket, which might have been expected, given that the white ball is easier to pick up.

So it would seem that colour-blindness probably selects against a career in professional cricket; but those with red-green colour-blindness who do make it into professional cricket do not appear to be significantly disadvantaged, suggesting that they are able to compensate for what, superficially, would appear to be a significant disadvantage.

SUMMING UP

All cricketers need to understand that whatever mental activities of importance take place after a bowler begins his run-up occur in the primitive parts of the brain collectively known as the subconscious. The bowler cannot pitch the ball in a particular area through his conscious actions, just as the batter cannot execute a shot by thinking about it as he plays the shot. Nor can the fielder consciously decide how to catch a ball, whether it be a sharp chance in the slips or a high catch in the outfield that seems to hang in the heavens forever.

The best bowlers, batters and fielders in the world do everything better than their peers. But at the core of their success is the ability of their subconscious brains to process visual information, available to all, more accurately and more rapidly than others. They then use their superior motor skills to bat, bowl or field better than all others. But to allow their subconscious brains to do the job most effectively, all cricketers must resist the natural human response to believe that the conscious brain should be involved in the process. The brain hardware (or 'wetware') that evolved in our mammalian ancestors to control these responses developed long before the relatively new parts of our brains that control our thoughts and our ability to analyse events and draw conclusions. A monkey swinging gracefully at speed from the branches of one tree to the next does not stop to calculate the muscular forces needed to ensure that she reaches the branches of the next tree. She just lets it happen. If she had the higher brain functions found in modern human beings, she would realize that evolution had ensured that the basic motor functions necessary for her continued survival had been hardwired into the archaic parts of her brain millions of years earlier.

It is the descendants of these 'primitive' motor responses that allow cricketers to complete the extraordinary actions that they each do reflexively on the cricket field, *without* conscious thought.

It is important to grasp that cricketers perform best when they allow their subconscious brains to do those functions for which nature designed them, rather than crowding out reflexes – a result of the natural tendency of the conscious brain to take control.

So it is no wonder that cricketers, batters especially, perform best when they enter 'the zone' (described in Chapter 2). In this state, their subconscious brains can best attend to the great visual and motor challenges posed by this unique game. Indeed, one of the fascinations of cricket is that it seems almost to have been designed to test the limits to which humans can develop these archaic brain systems.

CHAPTER FIVE

BOWLING

INTRODUCTION

Opening batsmen who faced the pace attacks of the West Indies or Australia in the 1970s will look grim as they recall harrowing half-hours, or show off scars and crooked fingers, insisting that nobody ever worked so hard or experienced such suffering in the history of the game. Cavalier middle-order batsmen might make snide remarks about bowlers being hired thugs who do nothing but stand at fine leg all day looking tired. But the reality is that bowling is, and always has been, the toughest part of cricket.

Pointing out that it takes twenty wickets to win a multi-day cricket match has become a favourite cliché in recent years, but what this means for the bowler is hours – and sometimes days – of toil, under the hot sun, or fighting a slippery ball and a headwind, knowing that his entire side (and sometimes his entire country) is waiting, with varying degrees of impatience or even desperation, for him to take a wicket.

And even if he changes the course of a game with a well-timed breakthrough, his lung-bursting efforts will almost certainly be overshadowed by a batsman. Brilliance by a batsman almost always represents a headline-grabbing century. Brilliance by a bowler might be two hours of miserly line and length for a return of 1 for 40 off 25 overs on a flat wicket against a pair of settled batsmen. Hardly the stuff of television highlights packages.

Bowling is a sporting vocation that takes great fitness, stamina and skill, but also great strength of character. It will never be as obviously glamorous or rewarding as batting. And yet nothing is more rewarding for the fast bowler than seeing the stumps fly or the batsman flinch, or, in the case of the spinner, seeing a batsman beaten in the flight and stumped yards out of his ground. Even the workhorse medium-pacer takes no less delight in seeing the ball nip or swing away, finding the edge, and carrying safely to the wicket-keeper, or jagging back to thump into the front pad plumb in front.

For millions, the quintessential cricket experience would be to watch Sachin Tendulkar or Brian Lara (or, in days gone by, Viv Richards or Sunil Gavaskar) stroke their way to a century with their characteristic blends of power and grace. But it is no less extraordinary or moving a sight to see a class bowler on song – an Allan Donald or Wasim Akram steaming in on those days when they are all but unplayable, when even the batsmen cannot help admiring their perfect combination of power, pace, accuracy and planning, as well as that extra touch of throttle that elite fast bowlers seem able to conjure up when the going gets tough. Similarly, being present to watch Abdul Qadir or Shane Warne or Muttiah Muralitharan dismantle a batting line-up, imploding the opposition's plans and dreams with pressure and guile, is an experience to relish.

No coach or teacher should ever make the mistake of nurturing batters at the expense of the bowlers. Encourage children to bat and bowl, and keep a sharp eye out for those who seem to especially enjoy bowling. Remember: batters are the 24-carat gold in your team, but a truly gifted bowler will be the jewel in the crown.

A BRIEF HISTORY OF BOWLING

The action of bowling is an unnatural and apparently illogical one. Why, an American observer might ask, doesn't the bowler simply throw the ball pitcher-style at the wicket in front of the batsman? Why deny himself the benefit of the huge leverage of a bent-arm throw, and deliver the ball at high pace without all that running in, over after over?

The answer to those questions lies in the history of the game, a history in which batsmen have, for various socio-economic reasons, always had the upper hand. Thus to understand the modern bowling action, it is important to investigate its history and evolution.

The *Oxford Dictionary of Cricket* suggests: 'It is arguable that the evolution of cricket has to a very large extent been determined by developments in bowling, rather than by developments in batting.' As explained in Chapter 1, for several generations after the dawn of the game, the bowler simply rolled or tossed the ball along the ground, using an underarm delivery. The next change was the invention of the ball that bounced only once on its way to the batsman (what might be called a 'length' ball), and this dominated games of the mid-eighteenth century. It forced batsmen to fundamentally change their technique, and cricket became a game in which batsmen played forward and began defending, rather than standing back and swiping at the ball, much as hockey players do today.

But things really began to shift at the beginning of the nineteenth century, with the development of the round-arm delivery technique, in which the arm is held straight and more or less horizontal to the ground. Some enterprising historians have suggested that this change came about partly because women (who played the game recreationally) couldn't throw underarm while wearing wide skirts, hoops and crinolines. However, it is also likely that the effectiveness of the new style impressed bowlers. From about 1807 onwards, this kind of bowling was increasingly seen in official matches. Legislation lagged behind, but the round-arm delivery was finally given the imprimatur in 1835, with the stipulation that the bowler's hand could not rise higher than his or her shoulder. Of course by then, many bowlers had discovered that raising the arm above the level of the shoulder (with the wheeling effect that would look familiar to us today) made this form of delivery still more effective. In essence, round-arm bowling was a step en route to overarm bowling.

The crunch came in a notorious match in 1862, when Ned Willsher of Kent was repeatedly no-balled for bowling overarm by umpire James Lillywhite (ironically, the same Lillywhite who had previously been no-balled for bowling round-arm during his career as a bowler). It was a drastic action, but one calculated to force an institutional change. It took two years and much bureaucratic peevishness (a familiar situation for any follower of the modern game's politics) before the MCC finally voted to change the Law. The vote eventually went 27–20 in favour of the new technique, and the Law was changed in June 1864. The principal reason for the change, it was argued, was that bowlers were having problems taking wickets with the 'older' styles of delivery.

There have been other changes in the Laws of the game in the last 50 years that have had an impact (sometimes literally) on the bowler: for example, the reduction of deliveries per over from eight to six, no doubt a welcome relief to fast bowlers. But the most controversial change for bowlers in this time has been the no-ball Law, introduced in 1968, which is largely responsible for so many of the foot- and back injuries currently ravaging the game at the highest levels. The reason is simple: since all bowlers have to cut the batting crease with their delivery stride, it means that they all land in and around the same place on the wicket as they get into their action. With three, four, or even five right-arm bowlers landing on the same square foot on the umpire's left, the landing area quickly becomes dented, then rutted, and finally concave. Bowlers must then either avoid this hole in the wicket, or must bite the bullet and land in it. Either way, they are forced to change the angle at which their foot is landing, thereby creating different forces in the body.

Prior to the introduction of this Law, bowlers could drag their back foot across the back crease, taking pressure off the front foot, as well as opening up a far greater landing area for their front foot.

This chapter discusses the standard of 'classic' bowling action, but if history has taught us anything, it is that what is standard today will be quaint and anachronistic in a hundred years time – if not much sooner. We might be presenting a current standard, but we are well aware that bowling actions are still evolving. Socio-economic circumstances are constantly changing, fewer and fewer children are getting access to physical education at school, and the lifestyles of most middle-class youngsters have never been more sedentary. The implications of these changes for bowling action are profound: as bodies become weaker and more prone to injury, actions will adapt and change accordingly.

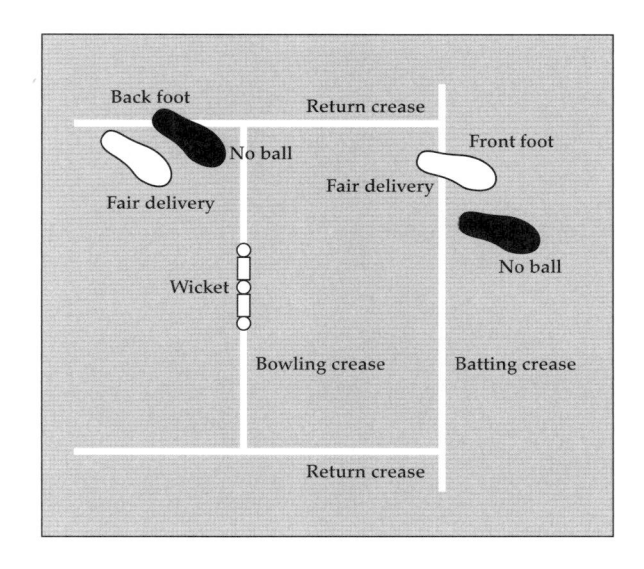

FIGURE 5.1: *The 'legal' position of the feet when bowling according to current Laws*

New forms of the game are also influencing the old art of bowling. Limited-overs cricket has made accuracy – and the ability to bowl yorkers – essential, while even shorter versions, such as 20-over cricket, is bringing the medium-pacer to the fore, bowling on a length that is difficult to get under, and offering no pace for the batsman to use. But shorter, more frequent games and bigger winners' cheques also mean that bowlers are more tense, less likely to be bowling without having found a rhythm, and therefore putting substantially more stress on their bodies.

This is why this chapter begins with a discussion of the bowler's action, since this is the foundation upon which a bowler's skills are built. Too many coaches are lax in their approach to coaching bowling, perhaps a result of there being so many different methods in circulation. But most of these are based purely on trial and error, or personal experience, rather than on hard facts or research. There is a real need to establish baseline principles for teaching the basic bowling action.

So how does the basic action of bowling work? What is a sideways-on action? What is a mixed action? The answers to these questions are the first steps in fulfilling your bowling potential.

THE BASIC ACTION

Whether you bowl quick outswingers or looping off-spinners, the basic aspects of the bowling action are the same. As the great English fast bowler John Snow (whom Bob Woolmer considered the best bowling coach in the world) points out, it is only the amount of effort put into the action, and the variation in wrist and finger movements, that define which type of bowler you are.

To describe this basic bowling action in words is rarely helpful, since it ends up sounding like a highly complicated manoeuvre and can discourage young players from ever trying it. To be fair, the five distinct movements that make up the bowling action are fairly complex, but when seen as parts of a smoothly executed whole, they all make sense.

The bowling action is built on three foundations: momentum, balance and timing. Momentum carries you to the point of delivery; balance allows you to be in control of your movements as you bowl the ball; and timing controls the finer nuances of the delivery, such as line, length and flight. To understand how important momentum and balance are in the bowling action, roll a coin along a table-top, and imagine that it represents a bowler, his arms and legs spread out to touch the edge of the coin. Any jerky or unco-ordinated movements, and the coin will begin to wobble, eventually losing momentum and teetering over onto its flat side. Bowling is no different: any interruption to the smooth cartwheeling action of the delivery, and the ball will go nowhere.

The bowling action, from the moment the bowler leaves his mark at the start of his run-up, until he jogs to a stop at the end of his follow-through, is a smooth and continuous effort; but for the sake of teaching, practice and analysis, we have broken it down into five distinct phases. These are:

1. The run-up and jump into the beginning of the gather

The front arm extends high (to the edge of the imaginary coin or cartwheel); the body turns sideways; the back foot is parallel to the crease; the head looks over the front shoulder; and the ball tucks in near the chin and points towards the target. John Snow says that at this point you are 'bringing your limbs, body and wits together like a boxer smoothly readying himself to throw a punch'. (Allan Donald had a famously 'low' gather, so in this picture the front arm is relatively low.)

2. The set-up

The gather is completed. This is the start of the uncoiling spring effect: the front knee is brought upwards, so that the body rocks back; the bowling arm now begins to extend towards the bottom of the coin or wheel (see also side-on panel 3 on the opposite page – again, no two actions are identical).

3. The unfold

The bowler 'unwinds' towards the target; the front foot comes down and forward with the front arm (both arms are now virtually parallel to the ground); the head begins to follow the front arm down over the top of a braced and straightened front leg. Some 'give' in the front leg is acceptable to prevent injuries, as long as the front leg straightens out again at the moment of delivery. The bowler's eyes are fixed on his target.

BOWLING 209

4. The delivery

The head is level and the eyes in line with the chosen target; the bowling arm swings up and through the full extent of the coin, with the ball being released at the top of the arc, as the arm is about to swing down again. The bowling arm follows through fully towards the batsman, which is vital when getting the ball to swing, seam or spin: don't catapult the ball out of the fingers.

5. The follow-through

The body completes its 'circle' (with a turn of the hips) and the bowling arm follows the same path as the front arm. Allow momentum to drain away by running some way down the pitch if necessary: fast bowlers can actually injure themselves by stopping only three or four paces after their delivery. Snow explains that this stage is 'merely a relaxation and expending the energy of the delivery', which carries you off the wicket.

Many bowlers trying to bowl faster believe that they need to leap higher into their delivery stride, and push off to extraordinary heights. However, both bowlers and coaches should take note: it is height of the delivery that is important, not the leap. Keep your shoulder and arm as high, and your body as vertical, as possible throughout the delivery.

Another useful guideline – and a helpful coaching tool – is that of 'bowling downhill'. To get the effect of bowling with your weight going towards the target, and what it feels like to bowl over your braced front knee, imagine bowling down a slope or even a flight of steps. Perhaps even try this on nearby steps, going through your action as you rock from a higher step to a lower, and then onto the third step down with your follow-through. You should never feel as if you're running and bowling uphill.

SIDE-ON VERSUS FRONT-ON ACTION

The sequence discussed and illustrated above describes the classic 'side-on' bowling action, which is considered by many to be the ideal way to bowl: the body remains sideways-on to the target from the moment the back foot lands until the front foot hits the bowling crease; the bowler sizes up his target by looking over his front shoulder; and during the actual delivery there is a strong and sudden rotation of the hips, which generates power.

However, some bowlers prefer to have their chests facing the batsman during their jump and gather, and this is called a front-on action. Technically speaking a 'front-on delivery' is a misnomer, since all bowlers face the batsman chest-on at the moment they release the ball, but in the quick, smooth delivery action, the chest-on gather and jump look dramatically different to the side-on action.

Front-on actions are often regarded with considerable suspicion by coaches. Common criticisms are that this action restricts the bowler's ability to swing the ball away from the right-hander, and that the lesser degree of rotation in the hips means that there is less power behind the ball. Of course those who employ this second argument usually fail to recognize that the greater the turn of the hip, the more things can go wrong with the action, especially if there is not enough momentum in the bowler's run-up.

Certainly many of the most famous chest-on bowlers haven't been famous for their outswingers, and have tended to spear the ball into the pads. But when this group is headed by bowling legends like Malcolm Marshall and Wasim Akram, one should be very careful about dismissing it as an 'incorrect' action.

In fact, there is absolutely no reason why a coach should ever try to change a chest-on action to a side-on action if the chest-on action is working for the bowler and producing wicket-taking deliveries. Besides, research suggests that fundamentally changing an action that is already ingrained is almost impossible. The authors estimate that the most a coach can implement is a change of around 5% or less to a bowler's action – which is not so much a change as a tweak here and a fine-tune there. However, it will simplify matters when teaching bowling from scratch to ingrain a side-on action.

For a perfect illustration of the difference between a front-on and a side-on action, see the colour plates of Malcolm Marshall and Waqar Younis – two stellar bowlers who epitomized their respective actions.

THE DANGERS OF A MIXED ACTION

While a front-on action may be considered unorthodox, there is nothing 'wrong' with it. A mixed action, however, can be downright dangerous, and all coaches should be on the lookout for it. A mixed action is one in which a bowler combines front-on and side-on postures in the same action, and this coaches *must* correct – ruthlessly if necessary – as soon as they see any hint of it.

When delivering the ball with a mixed action, the bowler lands his back foot (and therefore aligns his lower body) as if for a front-on delivery, the back foot pointing generally in the direction of the batsman. But he then twists his shoulders and upper body into a side-on position during the delivery stride. (The reverse can also happen.)

This high-speed contortion puts enormous strain on the lower back, which is being forced to rotate excessively, as the hips and shoulders are travelling in opposite directions; worse still, this strain is being exerted at the most vulnerable moment of extension – i.e., the point at which there is most strain on the spine. This leads almost invariably to injuries of the lower spine, including disc degeneration, bone bruises or even fractures. These can cut a promising bowler's career short, but yet more serious, can have crippling effects in the player's later life, years after he has ceased to play cricket. Many bowlers persevere with mixed action because it can be a very good way of generating pace and swing, but they do so at a cost: chronic injury almost always results from this action. We explain the exact injury consequences, prevention and rehabilitation techniques in the section in Chapter 10 on intrinsic injuries commonly found in fast bowlers.

Coaches must know what a mixed action is, and then be able to spot and diagnose it. In this regard, video footage is helpful, but if you lack sophisticated equipment, the simplest way to check for mixed action is to ask the bowler to perform three normal deliveries in succession.

1. **During the first delivery, check the position of the feet and hips.**
2. **During the next, observe the position of the hips and shoulders.** (This should be enough to establish whether the two are in tandem or rotating in opposite directions.)
3. **The purpose of the third delivery is to ensure that you haven't missed anything, and confirm your diagnosis.** If you are in any doubt, consult an expert – preferably before the bowler has to pay a visit to an orthopaedic surgeon.

We discuss the biomechanics of bowling below and in Chapter 10. For a more detailed discussion on laying a healthy and sustainable foundation for young bowlers, see Chapter 10.

BOWLING OFF THE WRONG FOOT

Coaches may recommend this or that action, but a bowler adopts a particular action primarily because he finds that it suits him, is effective, and is comfortable enough to repeat for 30 overs a day. The result is not always a textbook side-on gather, delivery and follow-through, and one distinctive anomaly is the bowler who 'bowls off the wrong foot'.

The action is unmistakable: it looks awkward, based heavily on a strong, extremely fast rotation of the bowling arm, and a sort of flurrying hop rather than one powerful delivery stride and pivot. Mike Proctor was one of the most famous bowlers of this type. Batsmen found him more than a handful, as they had to deal not only with his express pace, but also his highly disconcerting action – the ball being released somehow later than they were expecting. This fact, that the ball was delivered fractionally after the front foot had touched down (so that the next stride was already beginning), gave the impression that the bowler was bowling off the wrong foot.

But as the sequence of Australian Max Walker below shows, this is an optical illusion. Walker lands on his back foot and transfers his weight onto his front foot as he bowls, just like most bowlers. There is a lovely high action, and a full follow-through. But where most bowlers plant their front foot and pivot over it, Walker – and most of the other 'wrong-footed' bowlers – transfer much less weight onto the foot, instead touching down more on their toes than their flat foot.

© QUINTIC

If the action is settled and grooved, and is producing good results for a young bowler, it should not be tampered with. In fact, the 'wrong-footed' bowler may even be sparing himself future injuries, since he spends much less time on his front foot, and is therefore not exposing his front knee and hip to repeated strain when he lands.

Sohail Tanvir, the young Pakistani medium-fast bowler, is the latest exponent of the 'wrong-footed' action. In his case, he combines his unorthodox delivery stride with the left-arm front-on action of probably the best left-arm fast bowler of all time, his countryman Wasim Akram. Hardly surprisingly, Tanvir is collecting a number of scalps at present. It remains to be seen whether opposing batsmen will learn to read him and respond appropriately.

THE RUN-UP

The nuances of the art of bowling have long been celebrated and coached, with pundits and commentators waxing lyrical about braced front knees, high actions, strong spinning fingers, beefy delivery strides, and so on. Yet in all of this close examination and discussion, strangely, the run-up has often been overlooked. Perhaps this has been because to those not versed in bowling, it seems a fairly simple and unglamorous activity: after all, why should bowlers be praised for running along in a straight line?

And yet every so often bowlers have come along whose talent and presence has forced even the most determined thrill-seeker to acknowledge that the run-up can be as dramatic as any fizzing leg-break or steepling short ball. Michael Holding, a medium-distance runner in his youth, became known as 'Whispering Death' as he cruised in smoothly and silently (umpires said they often couldn't hear him arriving at the crease), swaying as he ran, a sight many batsmen recalled as mesmerizing. Equally electrifying was Wes Hall, with a long-curving run-up, looking like a steam-train about to run over the batsman; and those who faced the uncomfortably fast Mike Proctor reported being thoroughly intimidated by his enormously long approach.

Not all bowlers indulge in distance and pace. John Price of Middlesex 'turned the corner', apparently running from mid-off towards the umpire, and then suddenly straightening. Derek Underwood would deliberately disappear behind the umpire before jumping out, almost ambushing the batsman. Bob Woolmer remembered facing Garry Sobers, 'so languid and easy in his run-up that it seemed impossible he would bowl at anything other than gentle medium pace, only to have the ball whistle past the bat.'

Were these great bowlers who happened to have great run-ups? Or were they great bowlers because they had great run-ups? The second question seems the more pertinent. In fact, it is not an exaggeration to say that the entire bowling action – and therefore the success of the bowler – is dependent on the run-up.

Yet many younger or inexperienced bowlers arrive at their run-ups through an almost arbitrary process, often marking out 'about fifteen longish strides' from a point more or less in the neighbourhood of where they're likely to be landing. At net practices, this haphazard approach becomes even more pronounced, with bowlers jogging in off wildly erratic approaches, alternating between energetic sprints of 20 metres and bored, lazy strolls of a few paces.

Still others are badly influenced by superstar role models. Having watched Shoaib Akhtar run in from 30 metres, young players can be lured into steaming in from a point well beyond their physical capabilities, arriving at the crease out of breath and in no condition to unwind into a good bowling action. Similarly, many aspiring spin bowlers have mistaken Shane Warne's apparently leisurely walk to the wicket for lethargy, not realizing that the Australian derived his power from his action and exceptionally strong forearms and fingers. So his fans mistakenly choose to take only two or three steps, instead of six or ten, or however many their particular action requires.

Perhaps they are simply being confused by the apparent contradiction of the run-up: it is vital to get it exactly right, to groove it perfectly until it becomes endlessly repeatable; and yet it is an entirely individual process. Inside about 20 metres, there is no 'ideal' run-up that a coach can enforce or train, and yet a great number of things can go wrong during this crucial phase of the bowler's task.

In other words, the run-up will always vary from bowler to bowler. Try to work out what feels right and comfortable for you. However, there are certain general guidelines that apply to all bowlers.

- Try to hit your mark at the beginning of your run-up accurately.
- Build your pace while running (or, if you are emulating Warne, walking) in – there is no need to sprint flat-out from the very first stride.
- You should hit your ideal running speed about three or four strides before the point of delivery.
- Your run-up must allow you to release the ball at maximum momentum, yet while you are still able to control the delivery.

The last point is crucial: bowling is largely about momentum, and this momentum comes entirely from your approach. Roll a coin along a flat surface, and watch how it begins to wobble once it loses its momentum: having travelled in a straight line (like a bowler delivering a ball with a grooved, balanced, side-on action) it now veers off either to the left or right – the equivalent of a bowler 'stalling' at the end of his run-up, and spraying the ball down either side of the wicket as he tries to force it through.

The sequences on the next page show a run-up that is more or less perfect: smooth, balanced on approach, gaining momentum from a strong, high leap and gather, which then allows the bowler to power through the crease beautifully.

WORKING OUT YOUR IDEAL RUN-UP

So what is the 'ideal' run-up? In a nutshell, it is whichever distance allows you to reach maximum momentum while still being in control of your movements.

Remember, just because your run-up is based on when you feel ready to bowl, don't assume that this feeling is a vague, variable undefined whim. Just as a long-jumper's approach needs to be measured out exactly, so too does a bowler's, both for purposes of momentum, and for the obvious reason that your front foot needs to cut the popping crease.

A note to coaches, however: if a young bowler is genuinely quick, don't be too hard on him if he bowls no-balls. Being overly strict about where his foot lands can often inhibit a young tearaway, and early in his career it is far more important that he learns to bowl quickly and accurately than to be concerned about whether he gives away a few extra runs in the form of no-balls. Later, of course, once he has learned the necessary control, he will need to be more disciplined!

216 CRICKET TECHNIQUES

> ### WHEN, NOT WHERE
> Bob Woolmer recalled: 'I was once observing West Indies seamer Vasbert Drakes, then just nearing the end of a superb career for Border in South Africa. Drakes seemed to be bowling too many no-balls for my liking, and I felt certain the veteran could bowl even better. I asked Drakes to demonstrate his run-up on a field, without stumps or any target at which to bowl, and told him to bowl as he would ideally like to – in other words, to deliver the ball at the precise moment he felt his momentum and control peak. I then watched to see if Drakes landed on the same place each time he delivered. In 90 minutes, the West Indian barely landed on the same spot twice. He had simply never worked his optimum running speed out in his own mind. Drakes was running in, seeing the white line of the crease approaching, and then putting in an extra stride before trying to get power behind the ball with his body rather than his momentum.'

The best way to calculate your optimum run-up is as follows:
- **Stand on the batting crease at the non-striker's end,** with your back to the wicket (i.e., facing in the direction of your run-up).
- **Push off and start running towards the outfield.** Start just behind the crease so that the same foot hits the crease every time you cross it. It doesn't matter which foot crosses the line, as long as you remember which one it is.
- **Run into the outfield, and bowl whenever your feel ready and comfortable** – you will feel when that is, almost as if a cork is working itself loose in you and getting ready to pop.
- **Ask a friend or teammate to mark the spot where your front foot lands when you bowl.** Repeat this process a few times to ensure that your rhythm is correct. This point now becomes your imaginary bowling crease at the end of your ideal run-up.
- **Walk back from that point to the popping crease, counting the number of ordinary steps it takes you to get there.** This is your optimum run-up.

RUN-UPS FOR FAST BOWLERS

Although there is no ideal length for a fast bowler, it seems that most fast bowlers run in from anywhere between 15 and 30 metres. Perhaps because the elite club of men who can bowl dangerously quickly is particularly macho, shorter run-ups have sometimes been frowned upon and derided as somehow inferior, but many bowlers have been deadly off 15 metres. Wasim Akram's approach was famously short, yet in his heyday he was one of the quickest bowlers in the world, and late in his career he

> ## WOOLMER VS JUMBO JET AKHTAR
> Run-ups hit the headlines in 2004 when Woolmer was quoted as wanting Shoaib Akhtar to shorten his run-up, while the Pakistani paceman in turn insisted he needed his long run-up, just as a jet aircraft needed a long runway to get airborne. The press made a meal of it, seeing a newsworthy conflict, but in reality Woolmer's suggestion had less to do with Akhtar's personality than technique and tactics. Under Woolmer's tutelage, Allan Donald had shortened his run-up because he felt he could bowl at the same pace off a shorter run for longer, which translated into longer spells. But Shoaib was taking around four and a half minutes to bowl an over, and Pakistan was getting fined for slow over-rates. Besides, anyone who runs in off 30 metres needs to be as fit as a triathlete to sustain it for 30 overs a day, and Akhtar's body was not always up to the demands he placed on it.

could still swing the ball both ways with superb rhythm. Richard Hadlee was another example of a fast bowler who continued to be as effective as ever off a shortened run, even if a journalist did complain that 'New Zealand's heaviest artillery was operating off a pop-gun run-up'. If a pop-gun run-up results in over 400 Test wickets, it can't be all bad.

Run-ups are measured in yards or metres, but it is as useful to think of them in terms of time: you might be releasing the ball at the spot you feel most comfortable, but you're also letting go at the *moment* you feel most comfortable. How bowlers push off into their run varies dramatically – some take lots of small steps very closely spaced, other begin by walking, others are sprinting by their third stride – and so it is difficult to find any kind of average duration. However, if we measure them from the point that the bowler hits his stride and settles into his rhythm, we find that the average length of a seamer's run-up is between 3,5 and 4 seconds. In other words, from the point he hits his stride and feels as if he's 'cruising in', to the moment of delivery, is 4 seconds or less.

When working with Allan Donald, Bob Woolmer found that the South African's ideal 'cruising time' was 2,74 seconds, after which he was at optimum pace to hit the crease: at 2,8 seconds, everything was ready to let go of the ball. Obviously players aren't able to count 2,8 seconds exactly while running in at full tilt, but Woolmer and Donald found that counting strides (with Donald's eyes shut so as to feel the optimum moment better without being distracted by the crease or other visual snags) got him as close to his ideal time as possible. In Donald's case, it was nine strides, and so he grooved his run-up and delivery accordingly: his delivery could be counted out as 9-jump-10-11.

Remember that just because you've found a length that suits you, don't be afraid to experiment with adaptations now and then during your career. Donald and Hadlee are examples of great fast bowlers who cut back their run-ups, often for less significant matches such as one-day games, purely to save wear and tear on their legs and backs, and then found that they were taking as many wickets – if not more – as before. Dennis Lillee even practised two run-ups: his standard long approach for full-tilt hostile pace, and another shorter one for those days when he knew his captain would need him for longer spells than usual.

RUN-UPS FOR SPINNERS

When Shane Warne dominated England in his first Ashes series in 1993, and then exposed catastrophic weaknesses in the techniques of South Africa's batsmen in 1994, he transfixed the sporting media. Much of the publicity he received focused on the extraordinary amount he turned the ball, the drift he got, his ear-studs and bleached hair, his sledging, and of course The Ball he bowled to Mike Gatting – a delivery that would set the tone for the next decade (we analyse it in depth on pp. 305–7).

In fact, in all the media attention and myth-making that always surrounded Warne, it is easy to forget that one of the aspects of his game that most startled and surprised pundits was his run-up. Batsmen and spectators alike were used to seeing spin bowlers jog in, or at least walk in quickly before breaking into a short jog just before they delivered. But Warne's slow walk, as menacing as any 30-metre run-up by a fast bowler, seemed quite new. This, allied to his phenomenal control and wicket-taking ability, completely revitalized the approach to a spinner's run-up.

Of course what Warne's run-up illustrates best is that, as with fast bowling, there is no ideal approach for the spinner. In fact, it could be argued that spinners present an even greater variety of run-ups that their quicker colleagues do. Warne's walk stands in sharp contrast to the run-ups of bowlers like Doug Wright, a superb wrist-spinner for England and Kent, who came in with a fast, bounding run off 14 metres, or Indian impresario Anil Kumble, who bobs and bounces his way to the crease. South Africa's Paul Adams had almost no run-up at all, getting into his action off no more than three or four steps.

In general, the spinner's run-up is worked out according to the same principles as those of the seamer: while momentum is naturally no longer an issue, the point of delivery must still come when the bowler feels most ready – balanced and rhythmical – to release; and the spinner's foot must likewise cut the crease. However, it differs in one major respect from that of a fast bowler: purchase.

The fast bowler's foot is the hinge of a lever or the anchor of a catapult. Some fast bowlers who seem to 'bowl off the wrong foot' (discussed on pp. 212–13) hardly even

When trying to diagnose problems with any bowling action, observe the bowler in action from the feet up.

seem to need to plant their front foot. But most of a slow bowler's turn – the amount he spins the ball – comes from the purchase he gets with his front foot, as he turns on the ball of that foot during his delivery.

Slow down the big turner's delivery action, and you will see that his foot lands and then grips the pitch, only after which the twisting momentum of the body's action begins to drag it round. Some spinners try to bowl the ball as they land – often standing on the tip of their front foot – which results in very little spin, or none at all. This is a very common problem among young bowlers, and coaches needs to notice when the hand is coming over in relation to when the foot is landing. If the front foot is down, planted, and ready to rasp round with the body's motion, he'll spin the ball. If he's landing as he bowls, he won't. South Africa's Claude Henderson was a prime example of this. Bob Woolmer noted, 'I first saw him as a promising 18-year-old who wasn't spinning the ball, and it was only after watching Henderson's feet rather than his arms and hand that I realized this was a general problem with spinners. I got him to bowl against his foot, rather than over it, and the result was impressive turn.'

Conventional manuals would no doubt cover this and related problems in a discussion on the bowling action, but many technical faults in spinners are directly linked to the run-up. For instance, left-arm spin bowlers have a destructive tendency to put their front foot over towards backward point or gully, which results in them trying to bowl around it. Suddenly, because of their unnecessarily angled arrival at the crease, it looks as if they're not spinning the ball at all. This is because they're spinning it onto a straight line, and the batsmen are hammering them to all parts of the ground.

In other words, it is the run-up that determines your position at the point of delivery, and the angles you are going to bowl. A good run-up and a good delivery position will mean getting more spin without changing your action.

RHYTHM AND SPEED

John Snow holds that the run-up has two phases. The first starts with an initial push or effort, translating into the first paces of your run, which gets you into a rhythmical running stride. The second phase sees you settle into your rhythm and gather the momentum that will drive you through your action. More importantly, the second phase of the run-up provides you with balance, which allows you to control and sustain all your movements throughout the gather and delivery.

This is a good analysis of the average run-up, but the issue of speed also needs to be addressed. Just as no two bowlers have identical run-ups, so no two people run at the same speed. How you approach the wicket and prepare for the gather is affected by many external factors: whether you're bowling uphill or downhill, how strong the wind is and what direction it's blowing, the length of the grass, the hardness (or bogginess!) of the ground, and so on. This is why you should always practise your run-up in the outfield before you bowl, to get your rhythm and to get a feel for the conditions.

The speed and rhythm of your run-up is also affected by your mental and emotional state. Perhaps it's your debut or a final, and you're excited with adrenaline flowing; or it might be your hundredth game and you're suffering from the 'Oh God, do I have to do this all again' syndrome. Maybe you bowled 30 overs yesterday, and your body is screaming for mercy.

In short, speed and your rhythm are not only hugely variable from one bowler to the next, but can even change from day to day with the same bowler. However, in over 120 years of Test cricket, only the genuinely quick bowlers have run in very hard – men like Dennis Lillee, Allan Donald, Waqar Younis, Brett Lee and Malcolm Marshall. The rest have tended to cruise in off rhythmical smooth approaches.

A rhythmical run-up is one in which both feet start from the same places, and then repeatedly hit the same areas when running in. You'll have seen this in some Test matches, where a particularly long or angled approach begins to stand out from the others on the outfield by the fourth or fifth day, each footmark scuffed or worn, a sign that the bowler has been hitting the same marks over after over.

ADAPTING TO CONDITIONS

An optimum run-up is just that: it assumes that you're playing in ideal conditions, running in on a firm, level field on a fine day; but of course this isn't always the case. Conditions vary, and sometimes – particularly early and late in the season – they can be anything but perfect.

Being able to judge your run-up while taking conditions into account is therefore an important skill. Remember, your run-up itself shouldn't change: only change how you run. For example, if you're bowling into the wind, you're going to have to run harder, but not faster. If you're bowling with the wind, ease off a fraction.

You should also consider shortening the length of your run-up depending on the length of the grass and the hardness of the outfield. Grounds in Australia tend to be very soft, due to the sand-based soils used there for speedy drainage, so while your knees and ankles will be saved a pounding, your thighs will tire much more quickly than on a harder surface. Likewise, the grounds in Asia are rock-hard, providing plenty of spring in your step as you run in, but exerting much more strain on your joints.

Finally, bear in mind cricket's idiosyncratic conditions. Most southern hemisphere grounds are concrete bowls, engineered, built and planted from scratch, but in

England one can still find venues – even Test venues – that are simply expanses of village green that have been developed, complete with inclines in line with or across the pitch. In cases like these, take special care to practise your run-up thoroughly on the outfield to get a feel for its quirks.

THROWING

Any child old enough to throw a ball will have learned that the fastest, most accurate, and most economical way to propel the ball from here to there is to bend the arm back to the ear and then to straighten the elbow with some force, while transferring his or her weight forward with the throw. Baseball pitchers and fielders, who have pushed the art of throwing to its furthest extreme, get enormous speed and distance on their throws without taking more than a few steps, if that many. Indeed, every year dozens of pitchers in the professional leagues of the United States and Cuba send down fast balls as quick as anything bowled by just a handful of elite Test fast bowlers, without taking more than a single exaggerated step towards their target.

In light of this, and given the hundreds of kilometres that bowlers cover in a career of long run-ups, it would seem that bowling is both an unnatural and uneconomical action. But bowling is no more about speed and economy than batting is about hitting a ball a long way: baseball bats can propel a ball more than 100 metres into the bleachers, but if baseball's laws allowed for scoring behind the catcher, batters would find it almost impossible (or at least very dangerous) to try late-cutting or sweeping deliveries.

And it is here that the crucial difference between cricket and baseball arises. Baseball batters have two tasks: firstly they must prevent the ball from travelling through an invisible two-dimensional strike zone hovering a foot or two over home plate; and secondly, they must put bat to ball with only a very limited number of opportunities to do so, to get off base and get the scoreboard moving. These two tasks are inextricably linked: defence of the strike zone requires a stroke at the ball. They cannot opt to defend for three pitches and then attack.

Clearly theirs is not an easy task. But defending an imaginary target, even when having to play injudicious strokes in order to do so, is still considerably safer than having to defend a real one. A small strike zone means predictable lengths (all full tosses!), and generally predictable lines: in fact, the skill of batting in baseball lies largely in predicting or reacting to subtle, extremely rapid changes in line. A batter defending three stumps against a baseball pitcher would be in grave physical danger: no longer having to guide the ball through the strike zone, the pitcher could set about removing the batter in whichever (violent) way he saw fit, whether by breaking his toes with a yorker or by hurling a beamer directly at the body in the hope of sending him reeling back onto his stumps. Naturally even the threat of these injuries would be enough to get a batsman backing away and exposing his stumps, an easy target.

So thanks to the strike zone, baseball is an even contest between batter and pitcher. It is interesting to cricketers to see the outrage that often greets a pitcher hitting a batter on the body, either deliberately or by accident: entire teams pour out of the dugout and brawls are not uncommon. In cases of injury, lawsuits have even resulted. This would be unthinkable in cricket where blows to the body are not only common, but actively encouraged by aggressive captains and teammates. But the fury of baseballers in such cases stems from the equilibrium being broken, as an unfair advantage is claimed.

Cricket's batsmen are much more heavily padded than baseball's batters; and bowlers have long since worked out that the best way to hit the stumps or force an error is to bounce the ball rather than to bowl it on the full. Nonetheless, the dangers outlined above would still make bowlers the overwhelming favourites in cricket if throwing were the norm. A handicap is therefore necessary for bowlers. Instead of reducing the size of their target (and introducing penalties for missing the target as in baseball), cricket has adapted by reducing the bowler's speed. The result: a century-old ban on throwing, and the birth and flourishing of the peculiar straight-armed pitch we know as bowling.

Of course very few bowlers 'throw' deliberately: the universal condemnation of 'chucking', ingrained in every bowler since his or her first backyard game, makes it anathema. Besides which, unless throwing is regularly practised, it is extremely difficult to get right in the heat of battle without being noticed by the opposition and the umpire. Those who do throw the ball (perhaps trying to bowl an express bouncer) can expect to be no-balled. In this regard, club cricketers perhaps have an easier time of it than Test bowlers, as they don't face Code of Conduct violations, and feel free to launch lunchtime diatribes at offending bowlers, or to stop play to complain to the umpire.

However, no-balling Test bowlers has become increasingly fraught. The furore surrounding the controversial action of Muttiah Muralitharan has been protracted and heated (with the Sri Lankan even boycotting a tour of Australia for fear of being no-balled out of matches), while Pakistan's Shoaib Akhtar and Australia's Brett Lee have both been accused of throwing their faster bouncer. (We discuss Muralitharan's case and others like it in much more detail on pp. 234–37.) But these three cases pale in comparison with the treatment meted out to South African fast bowler Geoff Griffin, whose distinctly crooked elbow saw him no-balled out of Test cricket for good during a 1960 tour of England (see the photograph included in the colour plates).

In cricket, a handicap is necessary to even out the contest between bowlers and batters – otherwise the former would have the advantage. Instead of reducing the size of their target (and introducing penalties for missing the target as in baseball), cricket has adapted by reducing the bowler's speed.

However proscribed and demonized, throwing persists in the modern game. It is becoming less common in first-class cricket, thanks to good coaching and rigorous policing, but nonetheless some bowlers continue to deliver the ball with a curious 'kink' in their arms, often appearing as nothing more than an especially flexible action or a subtle wobble in their forearm.

Here it is important to understand that throwing is not the result of a wicked bowler wishing to gain an unfair advantage. Instead, it is almost invariably the result of incorrect technique, and poor coaching. Coaches must be on the lookout for this wobble in young players so that it can be corrected before it becomes a problem: an adult action that includes a throw or 'chuck' will be almost impossible to correct.

Most at risk are young bowlers eager to bowl fast, but who don't yet have the strength, flexibility and co-ordination to do so. As they make the final effort, starting to 'heave' the ball down the wicket, the exertion will cause their trunk, shoulders and chest to turn and swivel both excessively and momentarily too soon, forcing the arm to bend and then release with a catapult effect. This is not only illegal, but also poses great risk to the bowler: the exaggerated arch of the back that results is likely to cause injury. If a young player persistently throws the ball, the coach should persuade him to try his hand at medium-pace or spin bowling instead.

THE GREAT CHUCKING DEBATE

Since the legalizing of round-arm bowling in 1830, cricket has struggled to define what constitutes a throw, or as it was originally termed, a 'jerk'; but the simmering debate came to a head in 1960, when the MCC ruled as follows:

> *A ball shall be deemed to have been thrown if, in the opinion of either umpire, there has been a sudden straightening of the bowling arm, whether partial or complete, immediately prior to the delivery of the ball. Immediately prior to the delivery of the ball will be taken to mean at any time the arm has arisen above the level of the shoulder in the delivery swing. The bowler will not be debarred from the use of the wrist in delivering the ball.*

The definition is clear and seemingly watertight: bowlers whose elbows are locked in full extension before 'the arm has arisen above the level of the shoulder in the delivery swing' are bowling legal deliveries. But things are not that straightforward. The Law on throwing, both in its original and amended forms (see opposite page), has a major flaw: it depends on what the umpire is able to see ('in the opinion of

All bowlers are now permitted to straighten their bowling arm up to 15°, which has been established as the furthest extension possible before becoming visible to the naked eye.

224 CRICKET TECHNIQUES

The faces say it all as slow bowling is reincarnated in 1993 at Old Trafford. Shane Warne's first ball in Ashes cricket is widely regarded as the single greatest delivery in the game's history.

Bodies in motion. **TOP:** *Sir Donald Bradman, perhaps the finest cutter the game has ever known, was still a force to be reckoned with in 1948, his final year of Test cricket. Here wicket-keeper Godfrey Evans and slip Bill Edrich watch and learn at Trent Bridge.* **BOTTOM:** *New Zealand fast bowler Shane Bond shows extreme commitment and athleticism to hold onto a magnificent caught-and-bowled chance off Australia's Cameron White in Wellington in 2007.*

> ### BUT DOES BOWLING WITH A BENT ELBOW REALLY HELP THE BOWLER?
> Robert Marshall and Rene Ferdinands performed calculations at Waikato University, New Zealand, in an effort to address this question, providing and publishing scientific proof (in 2003) that bending and extending the arm during delivery does indeed increase the velocity of the delivery, largely through the increased internal rotation of the joints. Their calculations showed that the benefits of bowling with a bent arm are substantial: bowling with an arm flexed at 20° would increase the speed of the delivery by about 10km/h for slow bowlers, and by about 30km/h for fast bowlers.

either umpire'). Furthermore, the human eye is unable to spot a straightening of the elbow of less than about 10–15° during this phase of the delivery. In fact, it has now been shown that only extremely specialized scientific analysis can accurately identify a true 'chuck' – see the spread on pp. 228–33 for more details.

However, during the 1990s, increasingly sophisticated biomechanical analysis indicated that it was physiologically impossible to bowl with an entirely straight arm – a very small degree of flexion of the elbow was inevitable. The Laws were amended to allow the following: a bend of not more than 10° for fast bowlers, 7,5° for medium-pacers and 5° for spinners. But this too had to be abandoned after the Muralitharan controversy boiled over.

On 1 March 2005, the International Cricket Council (ICC) published its new guidelines on bowling actions, after a panel had analysed video footage of all the bowlers who had participated in the 2004 Champions Trophy. The panel steering the new guidelines featured former international cricketers, several of them bowlers such as Michael Holding, Angus Fraser and Tim May. It was widely assumed in the media that this pedigree would encourage acceptance of the new rules in the cricketing world. In the words of Sunil Gavaskar, the change to the Laws was 'a cricketing decision, proposed by cricketers for cricketers'. Cynics and critics took a different view, suggesting that it was a cricketing decision proposed by businessmen for the benefit of just one cricketer, Muttiah Muralitharan (a claim we examine more closely later).

The new regulations included an overhaul of the processes that had been used to identify and deal with suspect actions, and also focused for the first time on throwing at junior levels. However, at its heart was a dramatic new change in the Law: all bowlers would now be permitted to straighten their bowling arm up to 15°, which had been established as the furthest extension possible before becoming visible to the naked eye.

This was a remarkable departure from past recommendations, which had suggested that fast bowlers be allowed to straighten their elbows up to 10°, fast-medium bowlers up to 7,5°, and spinners up to 5°. The sudden 10-degree bonus for spinners further raised the suspicion of those who believed the entire development had been for the benefit of the Sri Lankan off-spinner – and, to a lesser extent, Indian off-spinner Harbhajan Singh.

The politics can be disputed, but what is beyond doubt is that any degree of extension of the arm will provide an advantage to the bowler. The changes to the Law, publicized as a firm measure to solidify and control the issue of throwing (a kind of legal firebreak, giving ground in order to stop further advances), may well have the effect of promoting throwing. Allow a bowler to flex up to 15°, and he will try his utmost to flex at 15° in order to gain the advantages that extra flexion provides. The changes to the Law may also lead to dramatic changes in the bowling action of spinners – from side-on to front on.

Marc Portus, a senior research scientist employed by the Australian Cricket Board and a specialist in fast bowling, has developed a system by filming bowlers in actual cricket matches, from which he is able to produce an image of the bowlers' skeletons (see panel below). By filming ten international fast bowlers and two first-class players from five different nations, he was able to calculate the extent to which their elbows extended (straightened or 'jerked') as their arms progressed from the horizontal (frame 1) to the vertical (frame 4) immediately after ball release. Bear in mind that the Laws (which initially stated that the elbow should not extend during this period of the

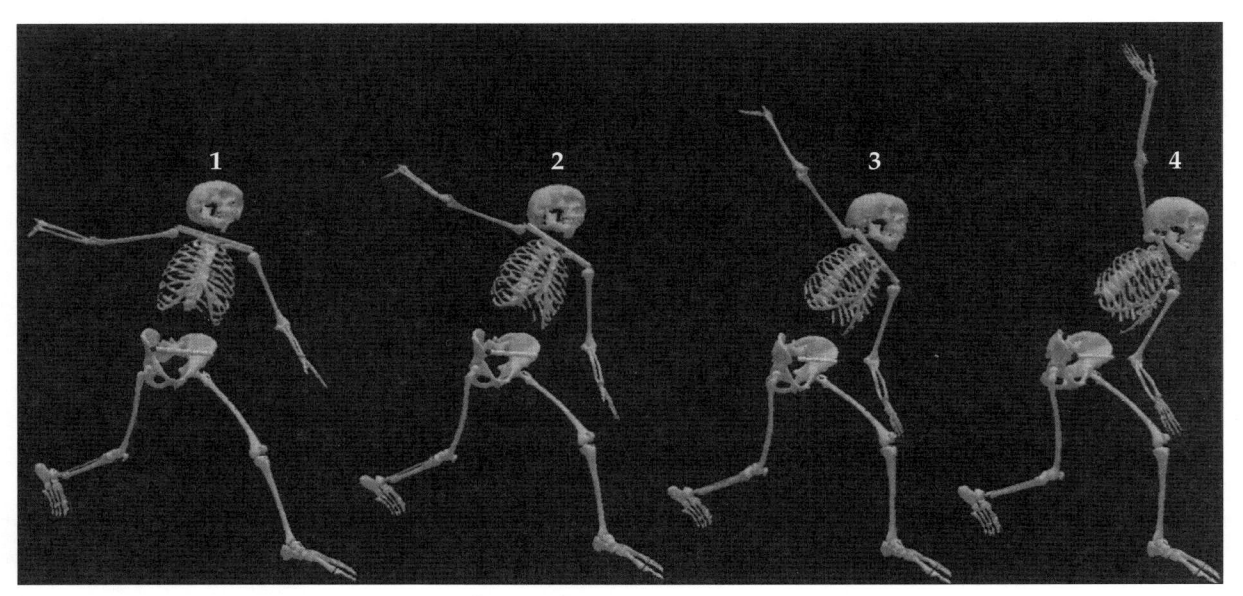

SOURCE: MARC PORTUS, 2003, AUSTRALIAN CRICKET BOARD

delivery) were amended to allow an elbow extension of 10°. But Portus found that of the 34 deliveries from the 21 bowlers he analyzed, 13 (38%) exceeded the 10° limit set by the ICC (see Figure 5.2 below). Interestingly, the majority of these bowlers were considered to have impeccable bowling actions when judged by the naked eye. Clearly, the naked eye is unable to see a great deal of 'jerking' in some of the world's best bowlers.

On the basis of his findings, which he presented at the Second World Congress of Science and Medicine in Cricket, Portus proposed that the ICC should consider extending their tolerance threshold to 16° (as shown in Figure 5.2). With this tolerance level, only 6 of the 36 deliveries (14%) would have been classified as illegal. The ICC subsequently increased the tolerance level to 15° (Portus et al., 2003).

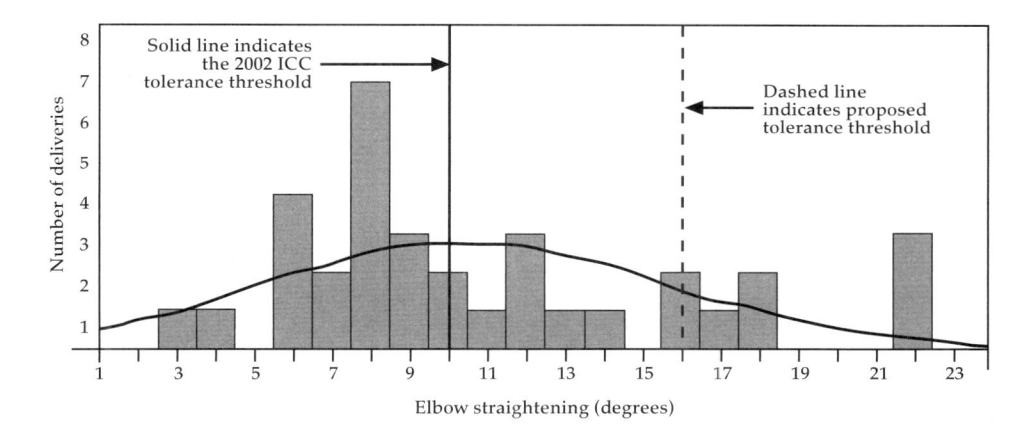

FIGURE 5.2: *Differing tolerance thresholds for elbow extension by fast bowlers, showing the proportion of deliveries considered illegal according to different tolerance thresholds*

Another problem with the MCC's original 1960 definition – indeed, with the entire debate currently agitating the sport – is that it focuses only on the result, and not the cause, of the throwing action. Throwing begins in the lower body and the trunk, with the upper arm only responsible for completing the action. Thus a true definition of throwing must include analysis of the action of the lower body and trunk. This assertion has revolutionary implications for the game, in particular coaches and administrators. However, as often happens when the game of cricket faces change, there is a tendency to cling to tradition, and many have yet to get to grips with the implications of Portus's findings.

SEEING THINGS: THE 'CARRYING ANGLE' – OR WHY THROWING CAN'T BE DETECTED BY ON-FIELD UMPIRES OR CAMERAS

The calling of Muttiah Muralitharan and certain other bowlers for 'throwing' in recent years presented the ICC with a challenge: it was now necessary to *prove* that these bowlers did actually 'throw' according to the current regulations. The ICC thus commissioned a series of biomechanics laboratories around the world to undertake such testing.

Among this group was a testing centre at the University of Cape Town/ Medical Research Council Research Unit for Exercise Science and Sports Medicine at the Sports Science Institute of South Africa in Cape Town, South Africa.

In the process of testing a number of bowlers with suspect actions, Kerith Aginsky, a PhD student in cricket biomechanics, noted that all had a similar fixed anatomical abnormality, known medically as a large 'carrying angle'. This is commonly found in women, but is less common in men. This abnormality causes the lower arm (below the elbow) to deviate from a line drawn down the centre of the upper arm. This can clearly be seen in the photo below of a bowler standing with his arms fully extended to his sides. In his case, the deviation is 17° from the vertical, so his 'carrying angle' would thus be 17°.

Aginsky wondered whether this carrying angle might contribute to the illusion of a thrown delivery in a bowler who was in fact bowling legally – in that he was not extending his elbow by more than 15° during the bowling action. She noted that Muralitharan also has a large carrying angle, and that he had reportedly been able to bowl effectively even with a brace on his elbow which prevented excessive elbow extension. This further suggested that Muralitharan's action, proven scientifically to be legal, might appear to be illegal because of an optical illusion, and that the latter might be influenced by the presence of his large carrying angle.

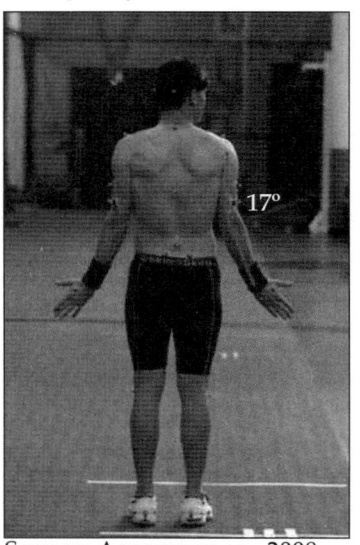

SOURCE: AGINSKY ET AL., 2008

To test this hypothesis, Aginsky and Tim Noakes used the opportunity provided by working with South African spinner, Johan Botha, who was being investigated for a suspect bowling action (Aginsky et al., 2008). Botha, like Muralitharan, has a large carrying angle. By using high-speed cameras and sophisticated biomechanical analyses, it was possible to establish that Botha's action (which, after much remedial work is now legal, as he extends his elbow by less than the cut-off value of 15° for both his off-spin and doosra deliveries) nevertheless gives the illusion of a throw, especially when viewed either on the field by an umpire standing at one spot for the entire delivery action, or when viewed in two dimensions from a single camera position. It was also established that the essential problem is that the bowling action occurs in three planes, whereas video footage in particular represents movement as if it occurs only in two planes. This explains why the illusion of a throw can occur in the action of bowlers like Muralitharan or Botha, both of whom have large carrying angles.

Scientifically, the 'throwing' movement of interest to the ICC is the extension of the elbow by more than 15° during the bowling action. The movement of flexion/extension occurs in the plane best seen when the elbow is viewed directly from the side, so that bony protrusions (epicondyles) at either side of the elbow joint point directly at the viewer or the camera (see below).

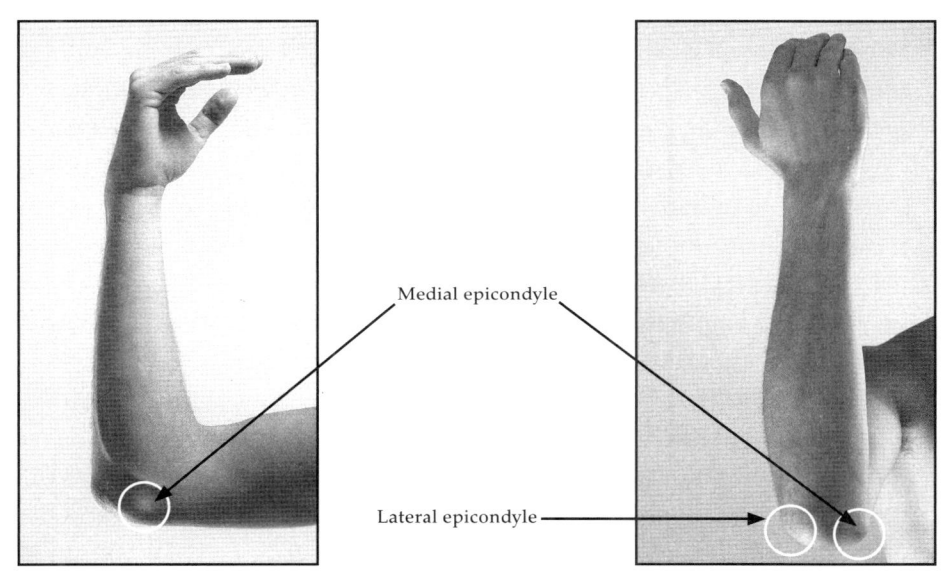

View of the elbow showing the medial and lateral epicondyles, either of which must be at 90° to the viewer if throwing is to be detected with the eye or camera.

In contrast, when the elbow joint is viewed directly either from the front or from behind, the exact degree of elbow/flexion cannot be determined (because this movement is occurring in the plane at 90° to the viewing plane). However, any abnormal angle that is seen will relate to the carrying angle, since this angle can only be properly viewed from directly in front of or behind the elbow (at 90° to the epicondyles).

The important lesson from this explanation is that whenever one views the elbow in order to detect 'throwing', one must first check which view of the elbow one is seeing. If one is viewing the elbow from either directly in front or behind, the angle that is seen is the carrying angle. Only if the elbow is viewed directly from the side, can one be absolutely certain that one is viewing the movement of elbow flexion/extension.

What this means is that for an umpire to be able to identify a 'thrown' (illegal) delivery, he must be able to observe the elbow in such a way that he views only the movement of flexion/extension throughout the bowler's delivery action. This means that throughout the bowling action, he must be positioned at exactly 90° to the side of the elbow so that either of the elbow epicondyles points directly at him. This in turn means that if he (or a camera recording the bowling action) stays in the same place, then the elbow must remain in the same plane (at 90° to the viewing position) for the entire duration of the bowling action. If the elbow rotates out of that plane during the bowler's delivery action, then what the umpire sees (or the camera records) will no longer be solely the result of elbow flexion/extension. It is exactly these circumstances that favour the illusion of a throw, even when the elbow has not extended during the bowling action. This is because when the bowler's arm is at the horizontal position in the delivery stride, the elbow joint is pointing directly upwards, so that a viewer positioned exactly at right angles to the batting crease will see only the flexion/extension angle of the elbow (see Figure 5.3 opposite).

However, when the bowler's elbow goes beyond the vertical at the moment of ball release, the elbow has rotated by about 90°. As a result, at the moment of delivery, the epicondyles of the elbow no longer point across the pitch in a line parallel to the batting crease. Instead, they now point down the length of the pitch. As a result, the only position from which the flexion/extension angle of the elbow can be observed at the point of delivery is either directly behind or in front of the bowler.

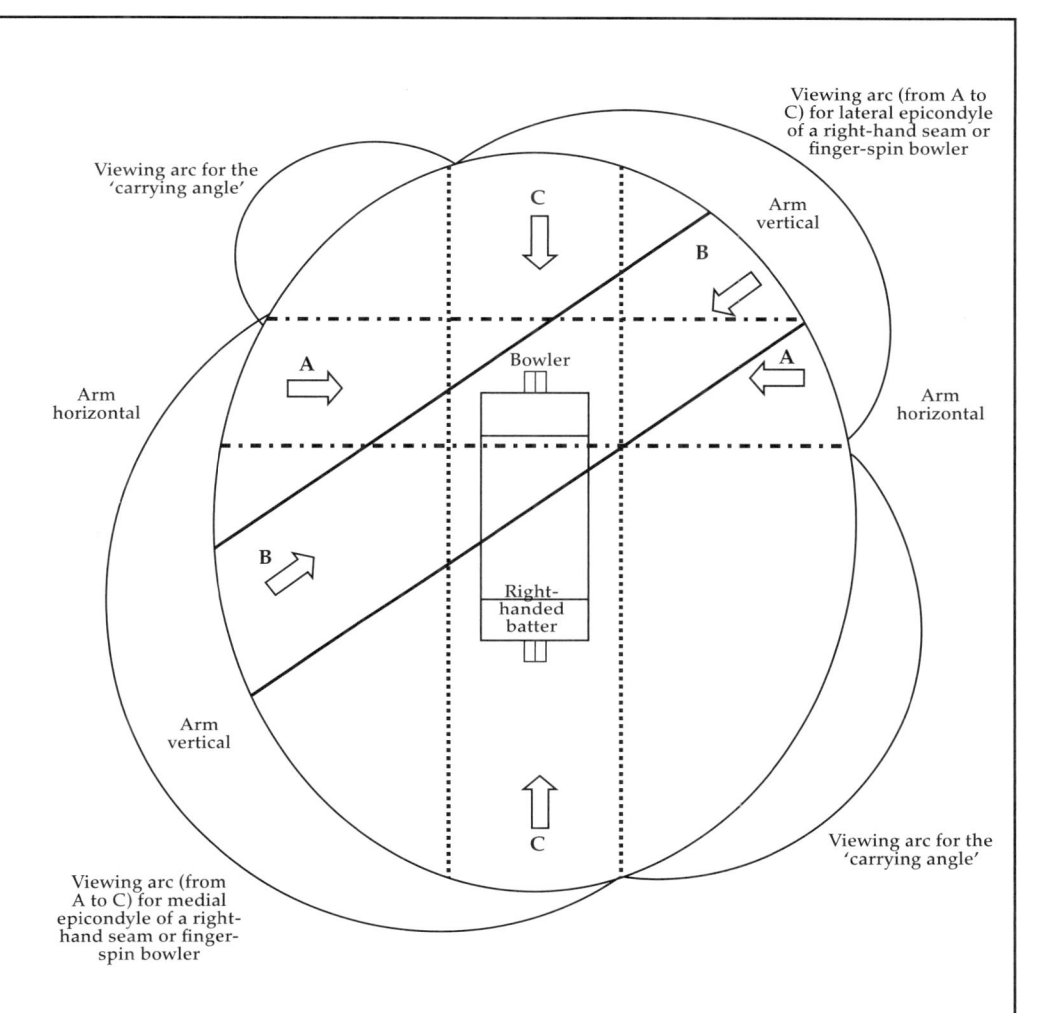

A: Directions from which elbow flexion/extension can be detected when arm is horizontal during the delivery action (position 1 in panel on page 226).

B: Directions from which elbow flexion/extension can be detected when the arm is vertical before releasing the ball (position 4 in panel on page 226).

C: Directions from which elbow flexion/extension can be detected at the moment of ball release.

FIGURE 5.3: *Viewing arcs for detecting throwing at different moments in the bowler's delivery action*
SOURCE: AGINSKY ET AL., 2008

It follows that the extent to which the elbow extends during a bowling delivery can be determined only by comparing the angle of flexion/extension when the arm is horizontal (by viewing the elbow from the mid-off or mid-on positions – A in Figure 5.3) and at the moment of ball release (by viewing the elbow from a position directly in front of or behind the bowler – C in Figure 5.3). Since no human umpire can be in both positions within the approximately 100 milliseconds that it takes for the arm to move that distance, no human umpire is ever in a position to call a bowler for throwing during the actual course of play. The only way for a human umpire (or a camera) to stay at exactly 90° to the elbow joint (so that any elbow extension during the bowling action can be detected), would be for him to be transported in an arc from mid-off to behind the wicket-keeper as the bowler's arm comes forward in the delivery stride. Similarly, a camera (or set of cameras) used to detect 'throwing' would also have to travel through that arc in about 100 milliseconds.

Given that neither of these techniques is available during matches at present, our proposal (Aginsky et al., 2008) is that bowlers with apparently questionable actions should no longer be 'called' during the course of play, given that it is not possible to detect a thrown delivery simply by observing with the naked eye. Instead, the bowler should be referred for expert biomechanical analysis at an ICC-accredited laboratory. If such testing shows that the extent of elbow extension does indeed exceed the ICC criteria, only then should the bowler's status as a 'chucker' be made public and remedial action begun. There is no doubt that real damage has been done (sometimes unjustly) to bowlers' careers in the past by umpires and referees insistent that their action fell beyond the bounds of legality.

What is it about the actions of Muralitharan and Botha that makes it seem 'obvious' that they are 'throwing' to those who view video clips of their bowling actions? The answer is that it is an illusion caused by their large carrying angles when viewed in two dimensions from a single vantage point, typically from a camera positioned either directly in front of or behind the bowler's arm.

If we consider the view from directly in front of either of these bowlers, we would first see the right hand appear above the horizontal, followed by the elbow. But at this stage, the front of the elbow is pointing directly towards the viewer. Thus any angulation that is apparent to the viewer cannot be due to elbow flexion/extension, since this cannot be seen from the front of the elbow (as already explained). Thus any angulation that is seen can only be the result of the carrying angle. However, if the bowler has a large carrying angle (as do Muralitharan and Botha), the viewer will have the impression that the elbow is bent as it comes forward.

However, as the elbow approaches the vertical, the upper arm begins to rotate through 90° so that at the point of release, the elbow is seen from its side, that is, with one of the epicondyles pointing directly towards the viewer. In this position, the angle that is observed is the flexion/extension angle; the carrying angle is not seen in this view and has consequently 'disappeared'.

So, because the upper arm rotates as it moves forward during the bowling action, a viewer from either in front or behind the bowler will first see the carrying angle appear and then suddenly disappear as the arm reaches the horizontal. This will give the unwary viewer the impression that the elbow has straightened, causing a 'throw' or 'chuck'. In this way, the illusion of a throw is created in those bowlers with large carrying angles like Muralitharan and Botha, even when they do not extend their elbow more than the legal amount permitted by ICC rules.

Finally, there is one additional factor complicating the detection of the 'thrown' delivery, especially by the modern generation of spin bowlers. Data shows that spin bowlers like Muralitharan and Botha not only extend their arms during their bowling actions; as their arm moves forward from the horizontal towards the vertical, the elbow initially flexes (bends backwards) before beginning to extend (bend forward) rapidly, as each bowler 'flicks' the elbow to impart maximum spin to the delivery.

This means that an umpire wishing to detect a throw by a modern spin bowler would have to detect when the elbow reaches its maximum degree of flexion (sometimes before the arm reaches the vertical position), compute that angle, and then subtract that angle from the elbow angle at ball release. If the final number exceeds 15°, then the ball has been 'thrown'.

Obviously, no human would be able to detect with certainty this range of movement, happening as it does in such a short time, even if they were somehow able to be in exactly the right positions at both moments (maximum degree of elbow flexion and ball release). Only sophisticated biomechanical analysis is able to perform the necessary calculations.

THE SPECIAL CASE OF MUTTIAH MURALITHARAN

When the Sri Lankan match-winner was first no-balled for throwing, during the Boxing Day Test in Melbourne in 1995, his supporters were quick to allege home-team bias on the part of umpire Darrell Hair – no stranger to controversial decisions. The Australians were threatened by the emergence of a world-class spinner to rival Shane Warne, they insisted, and had reacted accordingly. But when Hair called Muralitharan again in one-day games in Brisbane and Adelaide in 1999, calling his action 'diabolical', the accusations became even more charged, with racial bias being alleged.

For a decade, Sri Lanka's cricketing pride has been largely built around Muralitharan. Chaminda Vaas was a tireless presence with the new ball in Test and one-day matches, and Sanath Jayasuriya had electrified the game in the 1996 World Cup, but it was Test victories that mattered, and the spinner stood alone as their match-winner, often single-handedly bowling his team to victory with endless spells as his colleagues rotated at the other end. An accusation of what boiled down to cheating against their champion bowler was an attack on the national pride of an entire country. Sri Lankans were livid.

However, more objective commentators were not convinced that Hair had acted in error. Bishen Bedi, the great Indian spinner of the 1970s, who had one of the cleanest, most classic actions in the game's history, didn't pull any punches when he wrote, 'If Muralitharan doesn't chuck, then show me how to bowl. He looks like a good javelin thrower.' In August 2007, Bedi confirmed that he was gunning for Muralitharan's reputation when he declared that the Sri Lankan would probably reach 1 000 wickets in Tests, but that those wickets 'would count as mere run-outs' in his eyes.

But the accusations of racist bias looked increasingly troubling as first Pakistan's Shahid Afridi was accused of throwing his fast leg-break, and then Indian Harbhajan Singh's doosra raised eyebrows. Australian umpires and purists remained as rigid as ever, refusing to countenance a slackening of the Laws regarding the straightening of the arm (despite coming under pressure from critics to investigate the action of their own Brett Lee – like Shoaib Ahktar, accused of throwing his fast effort ball). By 2003, their dogmatism was widely regarded in the Asian cricket world as stemming from a mixture of insecurity and racism, the former apparently fuelled by an historic series win for India against Australia the same year, the scintillating final Test as loaded with nationalist pride as it was with sparkling cricket.

By 2004, the atmosphere of suspicion between white and Asian cricketing administrations had intensified. It did not help that of the sixteen bowlers reported by umpires standing in international matches for a suspect (throwing) action in the preceding decade, the vast majority were from Asian Test-playing countries. Only one player each was referred from Australia, England and South Africa. Meanwhile, the ICC's move to Dubai, a strategic shift away from London and Sydney, and the

> 'If Muralitharan doesn't chuck, then show me how to bowl. He looks like a good javelin thrower.'
>
> – Bishen Bedi

apparently insatiable appetite for one-day cricket in Asia, were all fertile soil for conspiracy theorists who believed that Asian cricket's financial clout, nationalism and an ever-hungry Asian television audience would see the Laws on chucking bulldozed to suit the politics of the day. The March 2005 change – which essentially legalized Muralitharan's action – came as no surprise to them.

However, those more deeply involved with the Sri Lankan's case found answers less easy to come by. The first complicating piece of the puzzle appeared when Muralitharan's action was investigated at the University of Western Australia and the Hong Kong University of Science and Technology, and the results were published in the scientific literature in 2000. The findings (Lloyd et al., 2000) revealed that Muralitharan has a congenital abnormality of his elbow, making him unable to extend his elbow fully. In medical terms, he has a fixed flexion deformity of his elbow of 37°, which means that he is unable to bend his elbow through the final 37° to the fully straightened position. The implications of this were intriguing: the spinner was, it seemed, literally unable to straighten his arm, and was therefore physically incapable of chucking. In addition, Muralitharan has a large 'carrying angle' (see photograph on p. 228), which makes it look as if he throws regardless of whether of not he actually extends his elbow during his bowling action, described in detail below.

Which is not to say that he doesn't flex his elbow at all during his delivery. Sophisticated biomechanical observation and analysis show that the spinner's elbow angles 180 milliseconds before ball release (arm aligned vertically downwards); 107 milliseconds before ball release (arm horizontal); and at ball release for each of his three deliveries: off-spin (Figure 5.4a), top-spin (Figure 5.4b) and leg-spin (Figure 5.4c).

Muralitharan is literally unable to straighten his arm, and is therefore physically incapable of chucking.

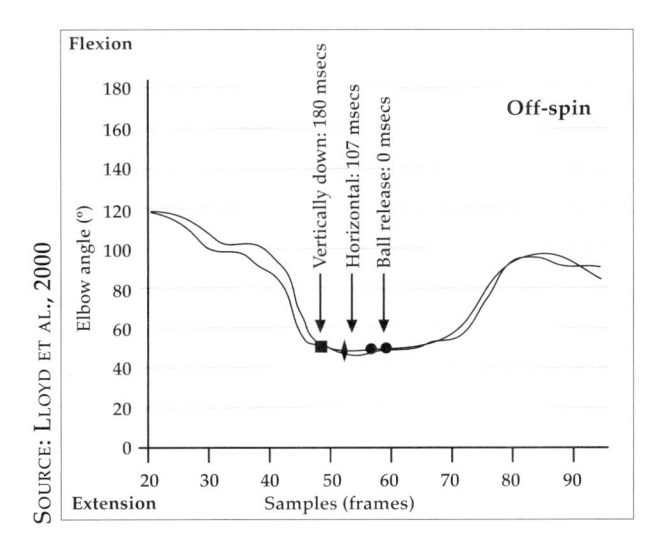

FIGURE 5.4A: *Degree of flexion when Muralitharan bowls off-spin*

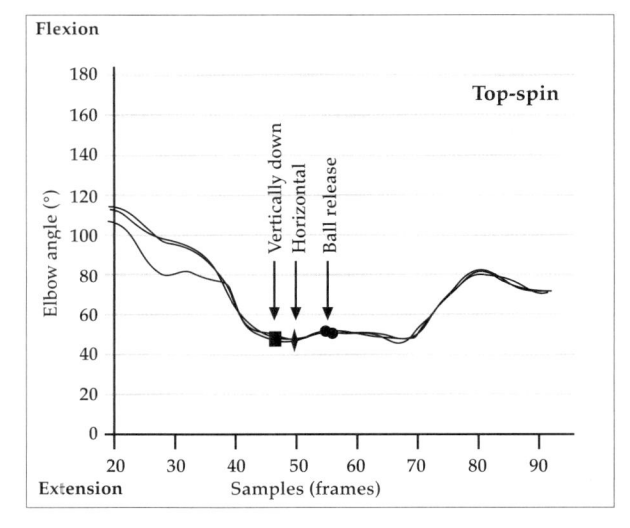

FIGURE 5.4B: *Degree of flexion when Muralitharan bowls top-spin*

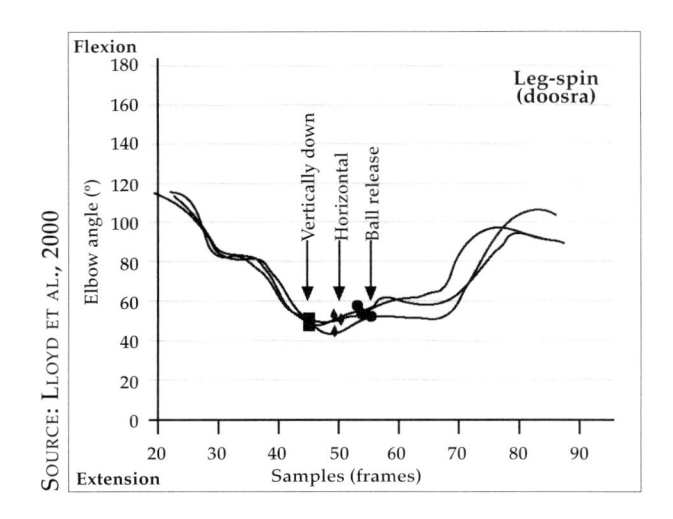

FIGURE 5.4C: *Degree of flexion when Muralitharan bowls leg-spin*

These results show that virtually all the extension in Muralitharan's elbow occurs before his arm enters the final 180 milliseconds of his delivery action, as his arm passes from pointing vertically downwards, through the horizontal and vertically upwards to the point of ball release; that he bowls with his elbow bent at about 45–50° of flexion; and that his elbow hardly extends at all during the final 180 milliseconds of his delivery action. Furthermore, in that arc of the delivery movement, his elbow actually flexes 3,5° when bowling the off-spin and top-spin deliveries, and 7,9° when bowling the leg-spin delivery. Note, however, that this action is opposite to the one used in defining a throw. Thus, since a throw is conventionally defined as an *extension* (straightening) of the elbow during this phase of the delivery, Muralitharan clearly does not throw if this definition is followed. According to the authors of the study, 'the elbow is essentially at full extension from when the upper arm is aligned horizontally until ball release, and no extension of the elbow occurs during this epoch; therefore, he does not throw' (Lloyd et al., 2000, p. 980).

However, in purely scientific terms, this conclusion is not entirely correct since Muralitharan does not bowl with his elbow 'essentially in full extension'. Rather, he keeps his elbow flexed by about 13° from its 'essentially fully flexed position' and then he bends (flexes) it a further 3–8° as he bowls.

Whether you consider Muralitharan's action an illegal aberration or a legitimate technique that will give slow bowlers a fighting chance in a game increasingly stacked against them, the fact remains clear that modern spinners have redefined the way the ball is released and spun. Also beyond dispute is that these spinners are seen as role models and icons by a generation of young cricketers. There are literally thousands of young Muralitharans and Harbhajans bending their elbows and bowling leg-breaks with an off-spin action throughout the Asian subcontinent and elsewhere. Indeed, during the Under-19 World Cup in 2004, no fewer than six spinners were sent home for remedial work on their actions.

Purists and the anti-Muralitharan lobby might insist that this was an admirable piece of police work – that these players and their coaches needed to have certain rudimentary facts of cricketing life explained to them. But in the opinion of Bob Woolmer and his co-authors, the action taken against them was a last act of desperation by the old cricketing order, trying to turn back the rising tide. What we are seeing is not a degeneration of coaching, but rather an evolution in bowling, similar to that of the mid-1880s, when underarm bowling gave way to round-arm bowling.

If you don't like it, don't blame coaches or Asian cricket, and certainly don't blame Muralitharan. If you want to blame something, look no further than covered pitches, helmets, heavy bats, shortened boundary ropes and smaller grounds. Cricket is simply shaking itself back into some sort of equilibrium, and for the first time in almost 30 years, finger-spinners are back in the game.

RHYTHM AND ACCURACY

As mentioned earlier, John Snow believes that rhythm is the bedrock on which all bowling is built: rhythm gives you balance, which gives you control, which allows you to get yourself into the right position to bowl.

It is not surprising, then, that when a bowler finds himself struggling on one of those days when nothing seems to be coming together, he is likely to tell his captain that he 'can't find his rhythm'. Whether slow or quick, bowlers need a rhythm as much as batsmen do, perhaps even more so, since a batsman can get through a lean patch by scratching odd singles or leaving the ball. A hopelessly 'out of synch' bowler, however, is likely to be hit out of the park and then dropped from the attack.

Bowling rhythm is an overwhelming sense of everything working as it should, a feeling that the body, ball and bowling crease together make up a well-oiled machine that simply needs to be turned on and let loose. It could even be argued that a superb rhythm is the bowler's equivalent of the Ideal Performance State (as discussed in Chapter 2).

GETTING YOUR GROOVE BACK

But all good things must come to an end, and all bowlers lose their rhythms at one time or another. This can happen for a variety of reasons. The bowler might be stiff or unfit, or bothered about some aspect of his action, or worried about a niggle that might presage a full-blown injury. Perhaps some family matter is weighing on his mind, or he thinks he is being over-bowled and feels resentful, or he is simply jaded after playing too much cricket for too long.

Some bowlers spend longer in the nets, breaking down their actions with their coach, or watching video footage of themselves; those who aren't professionals can afford to leave the game for a week or two to try and 'detox'. (We discuss the problem of bowlers 'getting the yips' more fully in Chapter 2.)

But some of the great bowlers developed their own unique methods for recovering or maintaining their rhythm. Richard Hadlee would ask a fielder he trusted (or the wicket-keeper) to watch him for any obvious causes. In the meantime, he'd ask his

Rhythm is what gives you balance, which gives you control, which allows you to get yourself into the right position to bowl.

> 'Forget what your arms, legs, shoulders and body should be doing. If your rhythm is right, they will look after themselves.'
>
> – Peter Philpott

captain to take him off briefly and then bring him back on (the equivalent of getting back into bed so that one can get out again on the right foot). Dennis Lillee would jog up and down the field, visualizing himself as a steam engine building up power; and Australian wrist-spinner Peter Philpott would envisage his rhythm, trying to hear it and feel it, and then 'count' himself back into it.

The important point is not to go on trying to force your rhythm to return: Lillee and Philpott's colourful methods also point to the importance of visualizing the ideal performance state (discussed in more detail in Chapter 2). The irresistible mental picture of hard man Lillee trotting up and down the outfield, possibly muttering 'I think I can, I think I can', is testimony that even the most macho player can benefit from visualization.

Indeed, Philpott's thoughts on rhythm are vital, and bear repeating:

> *Forget what your arms, legs, shoulders and body should be doing. If your rhythm is right, they will look after themselves. For this reason, it is a worthwhile exercise at practice – but only when you are bowling well – to 'listen' to your approach, visualize your run-up, and 'hear', 'feel' and 'see' the rhythm of your bowling. Awareness of your own personal rhythm when you are bowling well becomes valuable when you are not. Rather than worrying about where your arms and feet are… concentrate only on your rhythm. Get it back to what it should be… and it all comes back together.*

Captains should recognize that they can play a vital part in getting their bowlers into a good rhythm: if your strike bowler is struggling, the answer may be as simple as taking him off and bringing him on again later, as Hadlee sometimes requested. Consult with him, and call on him once the pitch, overhead conditions, wind direction and end are more to his liking. We've all seen bowlers who were taken to the cleaners during their first spell come back and almost immediately take a breakthrough wicket. Often, this is simply a matter of finding their rhythm. If the captain stays supportive and relaxed, this should not become an entrenched problem.

RHYTHM AND ACCURACY: WHICH COMES FIRST?

Accuracy is conditioned by the position of the bowler's head. If his rhythm is right and his head is in the right position, the ball will go where he wants it to: the head needs to travel horizontally along a plane as he bowls, and when the player's rhythm isn't working, the head can fall away or remain too upright.

Some coaches encounter young spin bowlers who can turn the ball a long way, but who aren't accurate. They assume the child has to make a choice between spin and accuracy until he works out his action and develops his own rhythm. But once again, this is a failure to understand that accuracy comes from the head: whether you bowl looping leg-breaks or fast outswingers, if your head travels smoothly along the horizontal, you'll land the ball where you want it to go.

Bob Woolmer had a simple way of demonstrating this: 'When I want to make bowlers (especially young leg-spinners) aware of what their heads are doing – and therefore what is happening to their accuracy – I ask them to head-butt my hand. I put my hand out, fingers up and palm towards him (rather like a policeman telling the traffic to stop) and ask the player to bowl at me without the ball. However, I insist that he hits my hand with his forehead. The results are usually remarkable: bowlers can aim with their arms and shoulders and hands, but get them to hit a target with their heads, and they go to pieces! Most fall away to the off side, or they're too high and go down the leg side.'

Remember, the stillness and the position of the head is crucial to becoming a successful bowler.

PRACTISING FOR ACCURACY

A theory gathering momentum is that modern bowlers do not practise enough, a notion perhaps given weight by the lack of accuracy of many bowlers currently playing at all levels of the game.

This waywardness has many causes, such as poor actions made worse by too much one-day cricket – adventurous and aggressive batsmen force modern bowlers to be reactive rather than pro-active – but bowlers must also accept some of the blame. Incorrect head-positions and defective run-ups are all very well, but if you are not practising accuracy, you have no chance of becoming accurate.

To this end, we recommend target bowling, one of the most old-fashioned practice methods in the game, but one that is still highly effective. Start with a rectangular mat (car foot mats are ideal) placed 6 to 8 feet from the batting crease, and one stump to aim at. Gradually reduce the size of the mat, and begin to move it around once your aim starts improving. This way you can practise good length balls, deliveries that are short of a length, bouncers, yorkers, and so on. Repeat this drill for an hour a day (punctuated by two breaks for stretching and replacing fluids) and you should be on your way to being able to land the ball exactly where you want to – or in cricketing parlance, 'having it on a string' in the way a fly-fisherman has his fly on a string and can drop it on any spot he wishes.

Whether you bowl looping leg-breaks or fast outswingers, if your head travels smoothly along the horizontal, you'll land the ball where you want it to go.

LINE AND LENGTH

The bowling action is the sequence of movements that allows the bowler to get the ball up the pitch towards the batsman; but simply bowling the ball in the batsman's general direction is not good enough. In fact of all the major ball sports, perhaps only baseball and basketball require a thrower to hit a smaller target; but in neither of these sports is the thrower who misses his target as severely punished as cricket punishes the wayward bowler. The pitcher who sends a curve-ball into the batter's shins is not likely to be picked up and slammed for a home run into deep left field; and the basketballer who misses a free throw can be fairly certain that the defence under the basket is not going to catch the missed shot and sling it a full court-length for a three-point basket.

In other words, as soon as the action is mastered, it is time for the bowler to shift his sights up the pitch towards the batsman. A good action will make this range-finding adjustment far more easy and natural, but all bowlers must nonetheless understand line and length and practise them until they are second nature if they are to succeed.

But why talk about line and length at all? Surely, if the bowler's task is to send the stumps flying, he should simply focus on landing the ball on the correct length in line with the stumps? Well, yes – if there weren't a batsman between him and stumps, a player trained since he could hold a bat to defend and deflect and clobber! Knocking over the stumps is the glorious ideal of all bowlers, especially the quick men, but they need to remember that there is more than one way to dislodge a batter. Castling a batsman is a rush, but it is just as rewarding to see him tripping over his front foot, plumb LBW, or fishing outside off-stump to nick an outswinger or a leg-break to the keeper or slips, or hopelessly stumped. Each of these dismissals needs to be conceived, plotted and executed. And the key element in their execution is aim – or line and length.

Lines and lengths for bowlers vary according to a number of factors. For instance, a good length on a hard, fast wicket might be considerably shorter than a good length on a soft, damp one. Similarly, a tight line for a leg-spinner bowling to a right-hander is completely different to a tight line for a right-arm fast bowler prying at a left-hander's weakness outside off-stump.

Figure 5.5 shows a very impressive grouping of deliveries to a left-handed batsman, all pitching on a good length, and all in the discomfort zone outside off-stump. But clearly this pattern would be catastrophic for a leg-spinner, to either a left-hander or a right-hander: a good length for a fast bowler, with the ball coming through quickly and confusing the batsman as to whether to play forward or back, suddenly becomes a juicy long hop from the spinner, giving the batsman all the time in the world to cart him through mid-wicket or square leg.

TOP: *The power and the glory of Viv Richards, on his way to 189 not out at Old Trafford. Richards' utter contempt for bowlers, and a fearless on-field persona, set the tone for a decade of dominance by the West Indies.*

BOTTOM: *The usual suspects: perhaps the greatest pace attack of all time, Andy Roberts, Michael Holding, Colin Croft and Joel Garner pose for the camera before putting England through the mangle at Port-of-Spain in 1981.*

© GALLO IMAGES/GETTY IMAGES

© GALLO IMAGES/GETTY IMAGES

Southpaw menace: Left-handers have enjoyed disproportionate dominance in cricket, with left-handed strokemakers over-represented in cricketing lore, and left-arm seamers regarded as nothing short of priceless. South Africa's Graeme Pollock, here tormenting England in 1965 **(LEFT)**, *had a Test average second only to Bradman, while Wasim Akram* **(RIGHT)** *established himself as the greatest left-arm bowler in the history of the game, taking 916 international wickets with the ability to move the ball either way, often at blistering pace.*

Similarly, one shouldn't assume that this is a graphic revealing an experienced bowler like Glenn McGrath working over a left-hander: it could as easily reflect the unhappy results of a frustrated fast bowler trying to blast out a right-hander by bowling around the wicket into his body, but not dropping it short enough, and being picked off pads and thigh-pad for easy singles.

In other words, line and length depend on the pace of the bowler, the pitch, the strengths or weaknesses of the various batters, the type of bowler, and even the weather. Finding the attacking line and length that perfectly suits the circumstances is the real skill of a bowler, and one of cricket's more engrossing challenges.

LENGTH

So all coaches, whether they know what they mean or not, will urge their bowlers to settle on a 'good line and length'. But what do these two terms actually mean?

The length of a delivery is determined by how far up the wicket the ball lands. Since a wicket is 22 yards long, it would seem that there are literally hundreds of possible lengths to bowl, from a yorker landing on the base of middle stump, to the embarrassment of dragging the ball down with the arm and releasing it straight at the bowler's own foot. In reality, only the batsman's half of the pitch contains the range of lengths bowlers should use, since anything shorter can only result in a long hop, or a perhaps a bouncer that balloons safely over the batsman's head. Which of these lengths you use as a bowler depends on your own personal preference and conditioning, and the specific tactics you are employing at the time.

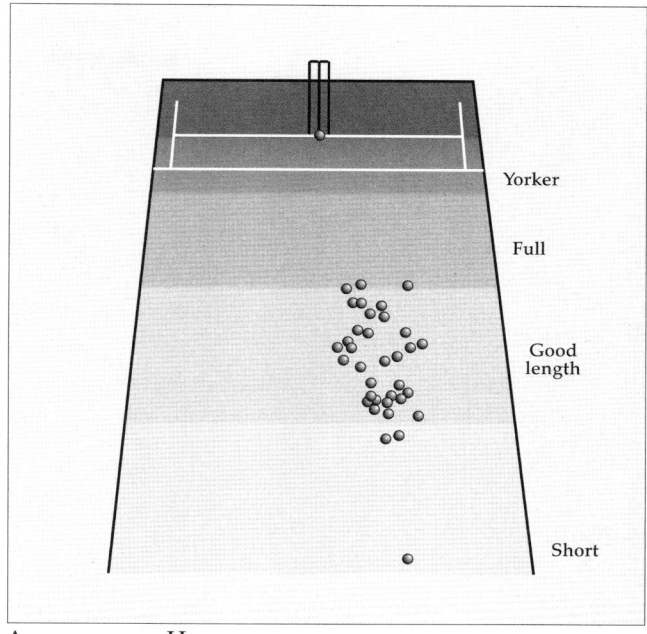

ADAPTED FROM HAWKEYE DATA

FIGURE 5.5: *Good-length deliveries from Glenn McGrath to a left-handed batsman. Note the exceptional control of line as well as length – nothing to drive, cut or pull.*

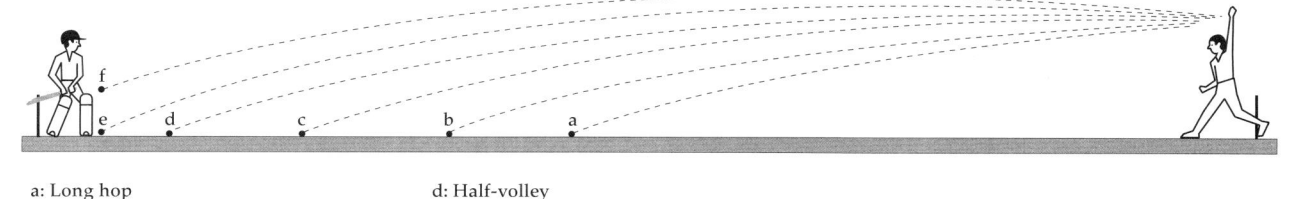

a: Long hop
b: Bouncer (short ball)
c: Good length
d: Half-volley
e: Yorker
f: Full toss

FIGURE 5.6: *Different length deliveries as bowled by a medium-fast bowler.*

Long hop: Sometimes called a half-tracker, this pitches very short, only about halfway down the pitch or perhaps even closer to the bowler's end. It is a delivery that will have your coach and captain tearing their hair out, since it gives the batter plenty of time to pick his shot and smash the ball to the boundary. Cut this ball out of your game completely, unless you are a genuinely quick bowler, in which case (on a good wicket) your long hop is likely to be a bouncer. Even so, fast men like Brett Lee and Allan Donald have found themselves bowling long hops on particularly slow wickets – and paying the price.

Bouncer: Although this delivery pitches on more or less the same length as a long hop, it differs in pace and bounce. Whereas the long hop dawdles invitingly through to the batter at hip-height, the bouncer shoots up off the pitch towards the batsman's upper body or head at tremendous speed, forcing him to evade the ball or fend it off. It is the least subtle and most brutal of the fast bowler's weapons, and is generally used to intimidate. The rules of cricket were changed in 1991 to limit the number of bouncers that could be bowled per over (a move fiercely contested by the West Indies and Pakistan, respectively the undisputed winners and runners-up in the Great Bouncer Wars of the 70s and 80s – a period in cricket history when short-pitched pace bowling, as opposed to spin, swing and seam, became the tactic of choice against batsmen). Today the bouncer tends to be used sparingly to surprise or unsettle the batsman, often before the bowler follows up with a fuller-length delivery.

The West Indian bowlers of the Bouncer Wars era, known as 'ear, nose and throat specialists' by their hapless opponents, not only perfected intimidation, but also concocted a vocabulary that illustrated the pleasure they took in their frightening work. For example, a particularly lethal bouncer was a 'perfume ball', so-called because it gave the batsman a sniff of leather as it hurtled up past his nose. A ball that reared and spat at speed off the wicket was said to have 'done a cobra' on the batsman. And for batsmen desperately looking to get forward and score a few runs? 'If you want to drive, go rent a car.'

Short of a length: This is a ball that pitches closer to the batsman than a bouncer or long-hop, but not close enough to be ideal. Nevertheless, although this can also give the batsman the opportunity to score, it does not give him as much time for shot selection. This means that it can sometimes be effective in preventing the batter from scoring. On an uneven or very bouncy pitch, it can even result in a wicket, as it can rush the batsman into a hasty shot, which gets caught.

Good length: For seamers or faster bowlers, this is a ball that pitches about four metres from the batsman's crease (although of course the exact spot will depend on the condition of the pitch: the slower the pitch, the further up towards the batsman that spot will be). A ball on a good length presents two problems for the batsman:

- he now has less time to decide which shot to play (as there is less time to watch the ball after it pitches);
- he is uncertain about whether to play off the front or back foot. The object of a good-length delivery is thus to create doubt in the batsman's mind.

Half-volley: Usually the half-volley is nothing more than four runs, neatly gift-wrapped and presented to the batsman. On a good wicket, it allows him to drive as the ball pitches, removing the threat of lateral movement, as well as presenting him with a ball bouncing almost exactly into the middle of his bat's sweet spot. However, because batsmen's eyes light up when they see a half-volley, it can make them overconfident, so that they rashly chase wide or swinging half-volleys, resulting in an edge to the keeper or slips. Pitching up the odd half-volley is therefore not a bad tactic. However, you don't want to be bowling them over after over and hoping for edges: that way lies ruined bowling figures and lost matches.

Yorker: A deadly length, especially when bowled at speed. Also called the 'toe-crusher', it usually takes the batsman by surprise, which makes it very difficult to 'dig out'. Because of this element of surprise, and the fact that it reaches the batsman barely a centimetre off the ground, taller batsmen (such as tail-enders) can be particularly vulnerable to it, since it takes them fractionally longer to get down to deal with it. The only reason we don't see more of this great wicket-taking delivery is because it is difficult to get its length exactly right; bowlers striving for yorker-length deliveries often bowl a full toss instead.

Full toss: Another gift-wrapped boundary for the batsman, but this time without any of the risks that accompany reaching for a wide half-volley. The ball does not pitch on the wicket at all, and is effectively a free hit. A full toss from a spinner should – and often does – go for six. However, not all full tosses are necessarily train-wrecks: a low full toss (one that arrives around ankle-height) can be a difficult delivery to get underneath in the final overs of a one-day game. Still, this is a delivery to be avoided.

Beamer: One of the few acts on a cricket field that can get players genuinely angry in an instant. The beamer is a full toss bowled between hip and head height, usually at pace. It is extremely dangerous, since batsmen rarely pick it up (having expected a ball to travel down towards the pitch), and it can cause fatal cardiac arrest if it hits the chest, or equally fatal injuries to an unprotected head. The beamer is unsporting and has no place in the game of cricket.

LINE

Line deals with the direction in which the bowler delivers the ball, and is determined by the target he is aiming for. As with length, this target might vary according to the circumstances and rules of the game, but it will never stray too far from the bowler's primary prey: the batsman and his wickets.

The see-saw battle between bat and ball has never been more clearly illustrated than in Figure 5.5 on p. 241; showing Glenn McGrath bowling on a good line and length to a left-hander, it demonstrates that in cricket, the difference between success and failure is measured in centimetres. Get a ball over the top edge of a flashing cut shot wide of the off-stump, and you've won a moral victory. Get it past the toe of a bat playing the identical shot, and the umpire is likely to call your delivery a wide. You'll be frustrated and the batter will be understandably smug.

As mentioned, you are free to bowl whichever line you feel will produce the best results, but whatever you choose, remember this: it is a cardinal sin for a bowler to bowl a line that benefits the batsman in any way.

Whether this means bowling down the leg side to a player who is strong off his pads, or bowling leg side when your captain has given you an off-side field, you cannot afford to give the batsman an inch. After all, he's not pulling any punches when he hits you to the fence. Also remember that an overly defensive line (which you might believe is frustrating the batsman into playing a rash shot) could be doing nothing more than allowing him to get settled, get his eye in, and costing you a wide or two per over.

This last aspect of your line – accuracy – is a crucial one, especially in the modern limited-overs game. Umpires have become extremely unforgiving, especially concerning deliveries going down the leg side – most international bowlers will know the frustration of being called wide for sending a ball over the top of leg stump. Master your line, and you master your own bowling destiny.

The nuances of line are discussed in more detail in the discussion of bowling tactics in Chapter 7, but it is worth remembering that changing your line is as effective a weapon as any in your arsenal. For some reason younger and less experienced bowlers find it far easier to vary their length than their line, but the two are equally effective, and combined, these variations can be a real handful for batsmen.

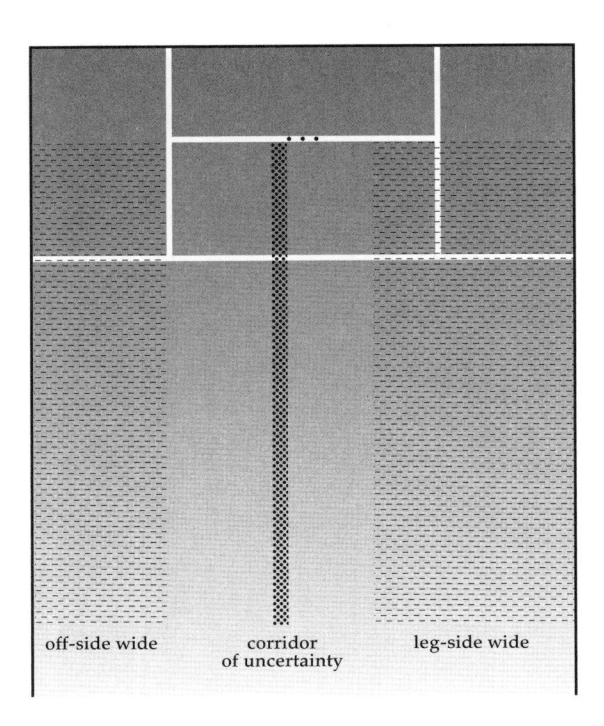

FIGURE 5.7: *Conventional lines for bowling to a right-handed batter (reverse for a left-hander)*

It is a cardinal sin for a bowler to bowl a line that benefits the batter in any way.

244 CRICKET TECHNIQUES

Figures 5.8a and b illustrate how line and length are often used as individual weapons by a pair of bowlers working in tandem. England's Marcus Trescothick was on the receiving end in this case. Peppered by Brett Lee, whose explosive lengths and express pace would have posed problems but at least opened up scoring opportunities, he was also confronted by Glenn McGrath's almost robotic control of line, every ball but the two on the extreme left and right pitching in the danger zone just outside off-stump and on a good, nagging length. In this case, both bowlers exerted pressure in different ways, providing a perfect foil for one another. This combination of pace and precision is an ideal partnership, one that has been extremely successful for such pairs as Donald and Pollock, Waqar and Wasim, Ambrose and Walsh, and even McGrath and Warne.

TAKING AIM

Knowing where you want to bowl the ball as you run in is one thing, but where do you actually aim as you get into your delivery stride?

Most great bowlers say that they look at a spot on the pitch as they unwind into their delivery, although some report simply having a feel for the line and length they're going to bowl, and end up delivering 'blind'. This is largely a matter of personal taste. Bob Woolmer read that Brian Statham looked at the base of off-stump, and duly copied Statham. When Statham wanted to bowl a yorker, he just raised his sights so that he was looking at the top of off-stump. Other bowlers aim for areas on the pitch. Fred Trueman would choose a spot when he wanted to bowl a bouncer, and then try to hit that spot. He wasn't worried about the end-result: by hitting that spot he knew what line the ball would take. He left the ensuing mayhem for the batsman to deal with! Terry Alderman went through a phase when he was almost unplayable bowling to left-handers. He claimed to be aiming at the wicket-keeper's left hand, which would make it very difficult for the batsman to find his off-stump.

One-day cricket has also introduced new challenges for the bowler, as batsmen move around in the crease as the ball is delivered. However, a good rule is to aim to hit the top of off-stump: if you coach young bowlers, drum this into their heads and good results will follow. Naturally, the length for hitting the top of off-stump will vary according to the pitch, but you can't go too badly wrong using this guideline.

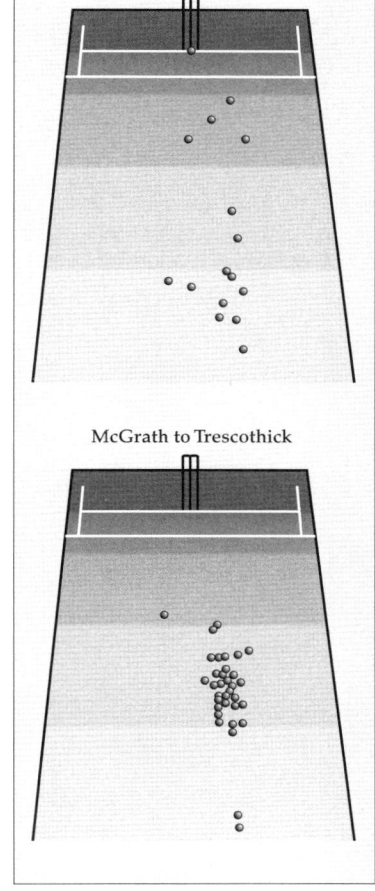

ADAPTED FROM HAWKEYE DATA

FIGURE 5.8A AND B:

Australia works over England's Marcus Trescothick – bombarded by Lee, nagged by McGrath.

MEDIUM-PACE AND FAST BOWLING

Perhaps because they have the same action and bowl the ball seam-up, medium-pace and fast bowlers are invariably lumped together, whether in cricket manuals like this one or by coaches organizing a net session. But the reality is that the two types of bowler are entirely different breeds, each demanding a specific set of physical, emotional and intellectual skills.

Of course, these differences haven't gone unnoticed by opinion-shaping pundits over the decades, with each generation imposing their own cultural norms on each type of bowler. For instance in the late 1890s, anyone bowling genuinely fast would have been seen as something of a ruffian, a working-class brute with more brawn than brain. By the 1950s, fast bowlers were being accorded more respect, but class distinctions were clear: bowling fast was exciting, but not nearly as skilful – or refined – as bowling medium-fast swing and seam. Frank Tyson may have been greased lightning, but it was Alec Bedser who was knighted.

But class distinctions weren't the only factor influencing public debate. Racial stereotypes also came to the fore in the 1960s as the first great West Indian quick bowlers began to appear. Wesley Hall's pace and aggression thrilled English and Australian spectators, but to many – even mainstream media commentators – his ferocity was a reflection of his blackness. The Big Bad Black Bowler had emerged, a stereotypical image that still persists. Even the most painstakingly politically correct commentators imply that there is nothing quite like watching a tall black fast bowler steaming in, whether Michael Holding, Curtly Ambrose, Devon Malcolm or Makhaya Ntini – the implication always being that black fast bowlers are 'in their natural element'.

Of course the famous pace quartets of the West Indies in the 1970s and 1980s did nothing to dispel this impression, even sometimes actively engaging with it as the Caribbean team embraced Black Power and Black Consciousness, giving their cricketing style the faintest of ideological edges. But the stereotypes remained, and many survive intact in the modern game: racialized fantasies that require great spinners to be Indian, histrionic swing bowlers to be Pakistani, dashing batsmen to be Australian, and so on. It is one of cricket's great ironies that modern adults, who would be appalled and embarrassed by assertions that Italians are excitable, Arabs duplicitous and Orientals cruel, suddenly start talking about 'natural rhythm' the moment a West Indian or black South African bowler sets foot on a field!

But the public perceptions of the fast bowler and the seamer have never remained constant for long. By the 1980s – largely thanks to the talented and disciplined heroics of the West Indian pacemen, as well as Dennis Lillee, John Snow, and Imran Khan – the idea of the 'thoroughbred' fast bowler had been established, suddenly imbuing quick bowlers with the class they had always been denied. But at the same time, the elegant and cunning swingers and seamers found themselves demoted in the public eye. In the press and commentary box, they were now referred to as 'trundlers', 'workhorses' or even 'pie-chuckers'. Pace had become king, and swing and seam were admired only when they happened at speed, as performed by Ian Botham or, later, Waqar Younis.

The purpose of this chapter is to give both medium-pace and fast bowlers their due. Current social trends and tastes might make fast bowling more glamorous than the bowling done by less speedy players, but it shouldn't be forgotten that the vast majority of wickets taken every day on thousands of cricket fields around the world are claimed by medium-pacers, just getting the ball to do a little bit. Also remember that a great many world-class quicks mellow in their later careers into medium-pacers of great skill.

So what does it take to bowl the ball seam up, and to bowl it well? The attributes of the genuine fast bowler will be discussed shortly, but they do overlap somewhat with those of the 'workhorse' seamer or swing bowler.

The most essential qualities of the good medium-fast bowler are:
- **Stamina:** Andrew Flintoff (at the faster end of medium-fast) bowled 14 overs on the trot at the Oval in the 2005 Ashes series, a titanic effort for a big man running in hard.
- **Strong stomach, chest and shoulders:** the stronger your stomach muscles, the more resilience your back will have to cope with the huge stresses that bowling seam-up puts on it.
- **Aggression:** this doesn't necessarily have to take the form of physical threat. A medium-pacer pitching up five consecutive swinging half-volleys is showing as much aggressive intent as the fieriest fast bowler trying to knock off a batsman's head. You must want to take wickets.
- **Height:** interestingly, this is more true of seam bowlers than genuine quicks, since those who rely on hitting the seam need to be tall and strong in order to bang the ball into the pitch and get purchase.
- **Patience:** perhaps the greatest attribute of any bowler, slow or quick.

Combine these qualities in a fit, focused and skilled young bowler, and you will produce a more than handy medium or fast-medium bowler. But making a fast bowler is a different matter altogether…

By the 1980s, pace had become king, and swing and seam were admired only when they happened at speed, as performed by Ian Botham or, later, Waqar Younis.

CREATING A MONSTER: THE FAST BOWLER

While there is no denying that bowling fast is one of cricket's most physically demanding tasks, the champion fast bowler is more than the sum of his parts. The great English bowler Fred Trueman summed this up when he said, 'There has never been a successful fast bowler who didn't have fire in his belly… you must be a fast bowler in heart, mind and body.'

But to be a fast bowler in heart and mind, you first need the body. Bob Willis said in order to be genuinely quick, the bowler must have 'the ability to whip his arm over quickly at the time he delivers the ball… unless that ball leaves your hand quickly, you'll never make a fast bowler.' All are agreed that real speed is one of the fundamental assets all quickies need. So how fast is fast?

While a 'fast' delivery is usually clocked at around 140km/h or above, most fast bowlers operate in the speed zone between 130 and 155km/h. Most of the top fast bowlers of the last few decades have all clocked up about the same pace, with one or two able to bowl an exceptionally quick delivery; but to the batsman facing the barrage, the difference between 145km/h and 155km/h is more or less irrelevant, especially if the bowler has got the line and length right.

Arm speed is vital, but the one common trait of all great fast bowlers over the decades is best expressed by the great Wes Hall: 'Man, if you want to be fast, you gotta be loose.'

Suppleness is key to speed, and certainly all the great fast bowlers we've studied, from Trueman to Allan Donald, have been extremely 'loose': in his prime, Donald could sit with his legs straight in front of him and knees locked, and reach 23 centimetres beyond his toes. Michael Holding was all but fluid, and even a muscular 'effort' bowler like Jeff Thomson was extraordinarily lithe. Recalling Thomson's elasticity, Alan Knott said that 'for a big man, he was like a piece of rubber'.

The second asset of the dangerous fast bowler is height. Of course, cricket has a long and splendid history of quick men who were below average height (Malcolm Marshall leads a field that includes Harold Larwood, Ray Lindwall, and Darren Gough), but standing at 6 foot or more will always give the fast bowler an advantage. The shorter men can get the ball to lift dangerously off a length with the best of them, but the tall bowler will always worry the batsman because of the trajectory of his delivery and the steepling bounce. On more rustic or dilapidated grounds, where the presence of sightscreens has become haphazard, facing a tall fast bowler can be a nightmare, especially if the ball is coming down out of dark trees or an overcast sky.

Height not only presents a physical threat, but the steeply bouncing ball can also be extremely difficult to score off. Some of the greatest bowlers in the game's

> *'Man, if you want to be fast, you gotta be loose.'*
>
> – Wes Hall

history have stood well over 6ft 4, men such as Curtly Ambrose, Courtney Walsh, Joel Garner and Glenn McGrath, and it is no coincidence that this elite group also boasts exceptional economy rates, proving almost impossible to score off when they were on song.

The third trait fast bowlers share is athleticism. It may seem an obvious asset, but at lower levels of the game, speed of bowling and athleticism can be confused, as young undeveloped bowlers wreck themselves bowling as fast as they can, while genuinely gifted athletes go unnoticed, bowling spin or medium-pace, or sometimes not bowling at all. A good basic guide for coaches of very young players is a simple foot race: whoever crosses the finishing line first has the potential to be a fast bowler. A rough calculation by a journalist some years ago suggested that during the 1997/98 season, South Africa's opening pair of Allan Donald and Shaun Pollock covered a distance equivalent to three marathons, just in their run-ups!

Strength goes hand in hand with athleticism, and, like the fast-medium bowler, the quick man needs excellent upper body strength and a strong trunk (stomach, hips, hamstring and buttocks), not only to bang the ball down into the pitch 90 times a day, but also to protect him against injuries. Batsmen risk injury from the balls they face, but the fast bowler's injuries arise purely from what he does. No other player is as vulnerable to injury, or as negatively affected by it. A batsman can keep going with the odd niggle or two, but even a minor strain can render a fast bowler ineffective, or remove him from the game altogether.

Fourth in the fast bowler's armoury is his weight: he can't afford to carry any excess fat. This doesn't mean that overweight (or even fat) bowlers can't send the ball whistling around the batsman's ears (almost all batsmen have been worked over at some stage by a chubby steam-engine of a bowler, sweating and blowing as he gets the ball to hum through to the wicket-keeper); but if a fast bowler is to be successful at the top level of the game for any period of time, he needs to shed as much fat (but not muscle) as he can. While not all bowlers should starve themselves in the hopes of looking like Glenn McGrath (dubbed 'the one-iron with ears' by his teammates), it is a fact that any excess weight puts further stress on the body and front leg during the delivery stride.

The fifth attribute of the fast bowler is youth. While spinners tend to improve as they mature, fast bowlers have a limited shelf life. Richard Hadlee, Imran Khan and Courtney Walsh extended their careers well into their late 30s; McGrath's age-defying performances continued until his retirement from Test cricket at 36; and Wasim Akram maintained a lively pace well into his 'autumn years', taking his 500th ODI wicket at the age of 37. But just a handful of men out of hundreds suggests that early mid-life is not a place that takes kindly to fast bowlers.

A rough calculation some years ago suggested that during the 1997/98 season, South Africa's opening pair of Allan Donald and Shaun Pollock covered a distance equivalent to three marathons, just in their run-ups!

Indeed, most of these bowlers don't qualify as genuinely fast: Hadlee and Khan geared down their pace as they grew older, relying increasingly on guile and swing, Wasim's run-up shortened with each passing year, and McGrath was never express to start with. Exceptional fitness, rigorous stretching and a sensible run-up will prolong the fast bowler's career, but he must accept that the clock is ticking once he turns 30, and if he's still letting the ball fly with venom and fire at 33, he's doing very well indeed.

The final trait of the thoroughbred fast bowler – the willingness to work – is perhaps the most important of all, and is best left to one of the greatest of that elite breed to explain:

Nothing in life comes easy, and fast bowling is no exception. To reach the top and remain there you must be prepared for blood, sweat and tears. Blood in your boots after bowling your heart out on rock-hard wickets, sweat in bucketsful left on the training track, and tears of frustration when things aren't going right for you.

To be a good fast bowler you must be prepared for the sacrifices, to make the extra effort in everything you do, to listen and learn at all times, to take the good with the bad, and above all other things to believe in yourself and your ability to bowl out the best batsmen.

There is no easy way to the top, believe me, and that's the way it should be. Those who reach the top and think that the hard work is all over soon find how wrong they are. It's simply a case of work, work, work, and then more work.

(Dennis Lillee, 1982, p. 17)

To sum up, the six vital attributes of the fast bowler are:

- **suppleness**
- **height**
- **athleticism/fitness**
- **low body fat**
- **youth**
- **above all, a fantastic work ethic and huge determination.**

THE DELIVERIES

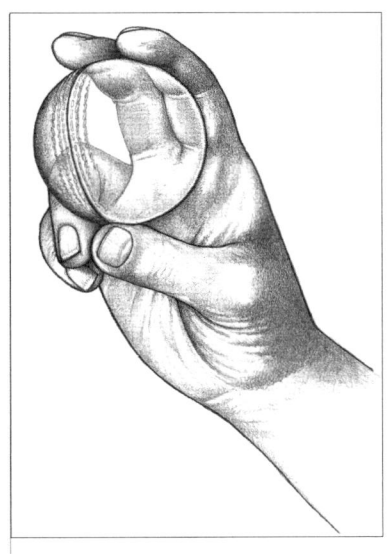

The action provides momentum. It powers the ball down to the other end, and sends it along the line and (to a lesser extent) the length the bowler wants it to go. But it is the wrist and hand that dictate the subtler, more dangerous, variations of the delivery. With a rhythmical run-up and a clean action, you've installed the rocket-propulsion system in the missile; now it's time to attach the warhead.

Variation is nothing without control, and before you begin experimenting with various weapons in the medium- and fast-bowler's arsenal, you must be comfortable with the standard grip employed by all seam-up bowlers.

The first two fingers rest on either side of the seam (or on the seam, if you prefer), with the side of the thumb on the middle of the seam beneath the ball, and the fourth and fifth fingers providing balance. The ball should rest on the last joint of the fingers, with a small gap in between it and the cupped palm of the hand. This space is very important – if you grip the ball too tightly, or wedge it too deep in your fingers, it will leave your hand too slowly, and you are also likely to lose a great deal of control over it.

Standard grip for fast and medium-pace bowling

Gripping the ball too tightly also has negative physiological consequences: it locks your wrist and elbow, and generally tenses the body. This saps speed, flexibility and co-ordination at the moment you need them most – when delivering the ball. A locked wrist also means you'll struggle to seam or cut the ball (discussed further in the pages that follow).

So how does the seam-up bowler take wickets? How does he go from being cannon-fodder, putting the ball on the pitch for the batsman to do as he pleases with it, to being a dangerous, probing, intelligent bowler?

BABY BOWLERS

Those coaching beginners might like to investigate the special cricket balls that have finger-markings that show youngsters the correct places to grip the ball. These are useful aids to those learning both pace and spin bowling.

Do not, under any circumstances, try to teach young boys or girls how to bowl using full-size 156 gram cricket balls in the hope that they will get a 'head start' or 'grow into them': their hands are too small, their fingers too weak, and it will not only wreck their technique, but cause frustration that could turn them against the game for good.

A fast or medium-pace bowler takes wickets in four ways:
- **with seam**
- **with swing**
- **with pace**
- **with his brain.**

The last weapon will be discussed in the section on tactical bowling in Chapter 7; but it depends on a good grasp of the first three. Even out-and-out pace can have its limits of usefulness. Besides, only a tiny proportion of seam-up bowlers playing at any time have the rare combination of physical and technical talents that enable them to be genuinely quick.

The vast majority are medium or medium-fast bowlers, plying their grand old trade with the tried and trusted weapons passed down through generations by the dynasty of seam and swing. From Alec Bedser and Keith Miller to Terry Alderman, from Imran Khan to Shaun Pollock and Glenn McGrath, the more subtle – and intelligent – art of moving the ball off the pitch or through the air is a vital one to master. And like so much else in cricket, it takes hours of painstaking work to add this to your armoury.

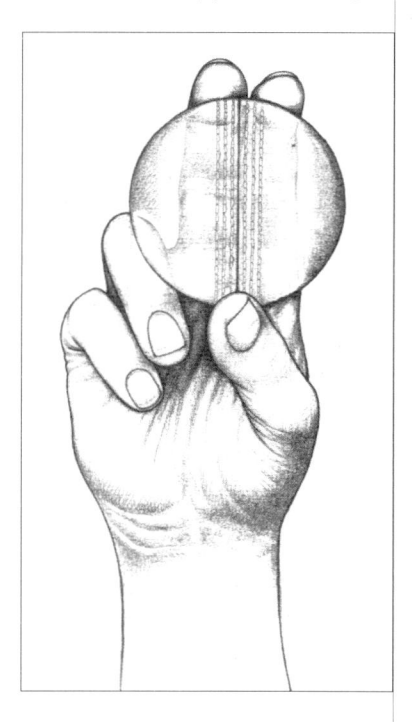

1. SEAM

The seam bowler relies on one of cricket's more ironic quirks: predictable randomness. While the swing bowler or the spinner knows where he wants the ball to end up, the seamer doesn't. In fact he doesn't have the slightest idea where the ball will go after pitching. But neither does the batsman; and when a good seamer is hitting his straps on a helpful pitch, he can be as much as a handful (if not more so) than a tearaway paceman bowling fast away-swingers.

The principle of seam is simple: land a round ball on a proud, angled seam, and it's as good as landing it on an unevenly shaped stone in the pitch. On the right line and length – where the batsman is drawn forward and has little time in which to adjust – the slightest deviation can take the edge or nip back through the gap between bat and pad.

The grip

The grip for bowling seam is almost identical to the standard fast/medium-pace grip. However, there is one important distinction. While the standard grip allows for minor variations in the angle of the seam, seam bowlers need to release the ball with a perfectly vertical seam, and with the wrist held straight behind the ball, to give the seam the greatest chance of landing on the pitch.

Grip for seam bowling

The action

The classic seaming ball is delivered with a very high bowling arm, and a loose wrist that flicks down the seam behind the ball. This 'back-spin' creates stability in the ball's flight and prevents it from wobbling off the vertical, and also allows the seam to grip the wicket when it pitches.

Height is crucial to getting the ball to hit the seam and deviate. Shorter bowlers need to focus on getting their arm up as high as possible, but the ideal seamer is a big, strong man. This is because in order to get the seam to bite and bounce, you need to hit the deck hard. Try to make contact with the ground as hard as possible. Skidding the ball through will not work: the seam will skim the pitch, instead of gripping and jagging away at an unpredictable angle.

Glenn McGrath and Courtney Walsh are two good examples of how important height is to the seamer: the ball comes down from seven or even eight feet in the air, and is banged in short of a length. Walsh in particular had an uncanny ability to land the ball on the seam, even though his deliveries often seemed to be wobbling around dramatically during their flight.

Conditions

Seam bowlers relish wickets with a degree of grip or purchase. This usually means a good covering of grass on a hard, fast surface, and ideally some dampness in the wicket. It is the latter that provides the 'juiciness' one sometimes hears bowlers talking about.

Some countries therefore favour seam bowlers, since the 'standard' wickets prepared there tend towards these characteristics, because of weather conditions or the materials used in the preparation of the playing square. English conditions have traditionally helped seam bowling, but perhaps surprisingly (given its reliance on pace in recent years), South Africa is a true seamer's paradise: grassy surfaces cover much harder tracks than those found in the United Kingdom. This is due to the harder undersoil used by South African groundsmen (usually bulli, a black clay) that makes the ball bounce.

Seam is still viable in countries with much rougher, drier pitches, such as Pakistan and the West Indies, but tends to be a factor only very early on in matches, before the moisture in the pitch has dried out and the ball's seam has been flattened through wear and tear.

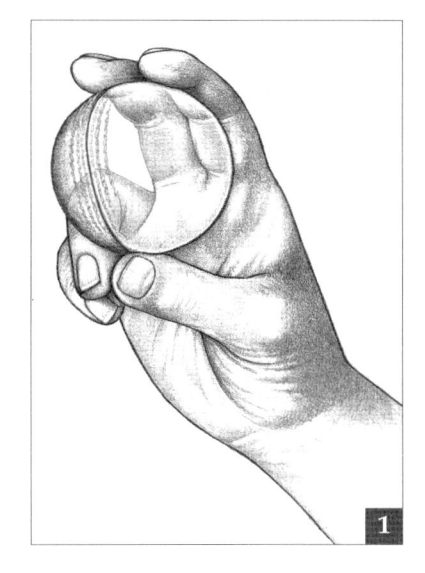

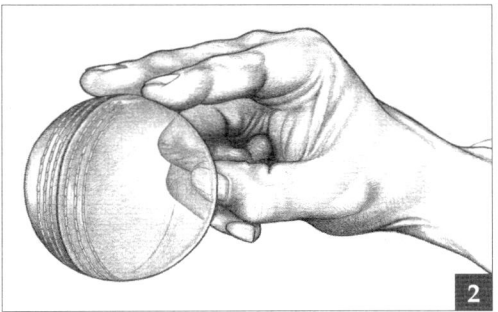

The seaming action, with the first and second fingers imparting equal amounts of back-spin to the ball. Keep the wrist behind the ball to prevent the seam from wobbling in the air.

TROUBLESHOOTING GENERAL SEAM PROBLEMS

- **You're not getting any movement off the seam with the new ball:**
  You're not hitting the seam. Make sure it's leaving your hand with the seam vertical, and that you're flicking your wrist down behind the ball as it leaves.

- **It's seaming too much and the batsman isn't having to play:**
  If the batsman isn't having to play, you're bowling too short. Pitch it up, and the exaggerated movement you're getting will put serious pressure on him.

- **You're not getting any 'zip' and carry off the wicket:**
  Your rhythm is wrong.
  Or your wrist might be too loose. Freddie Brown, who captained England in the 1950s, thought that 'zip' came from action of the wrist, but there is no scientific evidence that backs this up. In fact, a stiffer wrist, flicking through with the arm rather than doing all the work at the point of delivery, seems to help the ball hit the deck harder, and therefore lift off more aggressively. Excessive wrist action or movement can also cause inaccuracy: when Allan Donald put his wrist into a delivery, it could go badly wrong (at pace!) down the leg side. Having said that, they don't get much nippier than South Africa's injury-blighted quick man Mfuneko Ngam, and he can bend his wrist back so that his fingernails almost touch his forearm.
  Another possibility is that you're gripping the ball incorrectly, either too tightly or loosely, or too deep in your fingers.

- **You lack bounce off the wicket:**
  Assuming you're not using a ball in very poor condition on a dusty, slow wicket, it seems most likely that you're simply not hitting the deck hard enough. Hit the deck! Your wrist has to come from behind the ball, and the ball should feel as if it's coming out of the barrel of a gun, rather than sliding out of your fingers.

- **The ball is straying down the leg side:**
  Your head isn't in the right place.

- **You're bowling too full and too short:**
  Your head isn't in the right place.

- **You're suffering from a general lack of accuracy:**
  Your head isn't in the right place.

2. SWING

The perfectly plotted and executed in- or outswinger, curving late in its flight and taking the edge or ducking back into the pads, is one of the most exhilarating experiences a bowler can ever hope for. When bowled well, with good control over line and length, it can be devastating, as the batsman is deceived into playing one line, only to have the ball swing off that line, leaving him groping.

The physics of swing and reverse swing are discussed in detail in the section on the science of swing later in this chapter, but it is important at this stage to have a basic understanding of why a cricket ball veers off its original line under certain conditions.

The ball is made of four quarters, separated into two halves by a proud (protruding) seam. Coaches who explain swing often refer to the seam as a rudder, but it is far more like the prow of boat, 'splitting' the air in front of the ball on its flight; and the two streams of air passing over the two sides of the ball travel at slightly different speeds. The side that is smooth and shiny will present less resistance to the air than the rough side: the resulting low pressure on that side of the ball will pull it in that direction and away from the high pressure. This manifests itself as swing.

This is why bowlers – and fielders – endlessly polish the same side of the ball. Indeed, it is the entire team's responsibility to 'groom' the ball in this way whenever it comes their way, dusting off any bits of grass or mud that might be clinging to

THE PITS

A local rule in South African cricket used to prohibit bowlers from using spit or sweat from their foreheads to shine or dampen the ball, so players resorted to using their armpits.

Naturally this saw an explosion of illicit substances (such as Vaseline and hair gel) being rubbed into armpits and then transferred onto the ball. Even regular underarm deodorants could be fairly sticky.

The end of South Africa's sporting isolation brought it into compliance with the international ruling, which allows for any amount of spit and sweat from the general area of the face to be applied, but bans the use of armpits (a blessing for bowlers and fielders who rub the ball with fingers and then put their fingers into their mouths!).

However, some of the old guard persisted in their devious and pungent ways. Spinner Pat Symcox was chief among the old guard who regularly popped the ball under his arm. These tactics went entirely unnoticed and unpunished on a tour of Pakistan in 1997/98, but a subsequent tour of Australia saw him very promptly pulled up short by the umpires.

the smooth side, and shining it as vigorously as possible. (Before lashing on the spit and sweat, remember that seamers prefer not to let the smooth side get too damp. Swing bowlers, on the other hand, need moisture to clean it and keep it shiny. Check what the bowler and the captain want in terms of 'ball-grooming' before you over-enthusiastically soak the ball!)

A prominent seam and a polished hemisphere only go so far. To swing the ball consistently and well you need:
- **a good basic action,** with the ability to vary it slightly, depending on the delivery you want to bowl
- **a good wrist position**
- **subtle differences in grip**
- **subtle variations on when you release the ball**.

Dennis Lillee, who could swing the ball with the best of them when the situation demanded it, was adamant about what a good swing bowler should do, and his explanation is an excellent starting point:

The most critical part of swing bowling is the way you let the ball go from the hand. If this is not done with a high degree of precision, the ball either will not swing at all or will swing only a little and too early in its flight to be any great danger to the batsman. It starts with the grip of the ball, which should be made by contact of the index and middle fingers on the top of the ball and the thumb at the bottom. This contact should be towards the tips of the fingers and the thumb (what we call 'fingering' the ball), because if the ball is gripped too deeply in the hand, the critical control needed to send the ball away correctly may be lost. The hand should be directed behind the ball at the point of delivery and must not undercut on either side. The ball is sent away with a natural under-spin, and I believe the more under-spin imparted on the ball the later it will swing. The seam should remain vertical throughout the flight down the wicket (1982).

His view that under-spin or back-spin is crucial to swing bowling was illustrated by Australian swing bowler Bob Massie, who took 16 wickets in his first Test at Lord's in 1972. Lillee points out that when bowling, Massie managed to keep the seam absolutely steady for its flight, in no small part due to the large amounts of back-spin he put on the ball with a very whippy wrist action.

THE OUTSWINGER

There is simply no better ball to bowl at a new batsman than a fast outswinging yorker, or perhaps an outswinging half-volley on off-stump. This is a delivery that should be mastered by any bowler who wants to succeed in the game.

Tactically, the outswinger is intended to drag the batsman wide of his comfortable hitting zone, and to have him caught in the slips or at gully. However, many young or inexperienced bowlers make the mistake of getting carried away by the swing, and effectively bowling at the slips! This gives the batsman a pleasant over or two of being able to leave the ball and get settled. The ideal outswinger should be hitting off-stump or just curving away past it. The straighter you start it, the more chance you also have of pinning the batsman in front with an LBW shout, especially if he thinks it's a straight ball and tries to work it off his pads.

The grip

For a right-arm bowler facing a right-arm batsman, the seam is angled towards first slip, while the fingers point down the wicket. Remember that the ball will swing towards its rough half, so in this case, the rough side faces cover. The wrist is angled in towards the body and cocked backwards, while the side of the thumb rests on the seam under the ball.

The action

Outswing starts from 'behind' you. It takes some time to get the feel of when to release the ball for maximum effect, but basically the ball needs to be released from fractionally behind the ear. The hand and body must stay on line – driving through towards the target – and the follow-through must be full and complete.

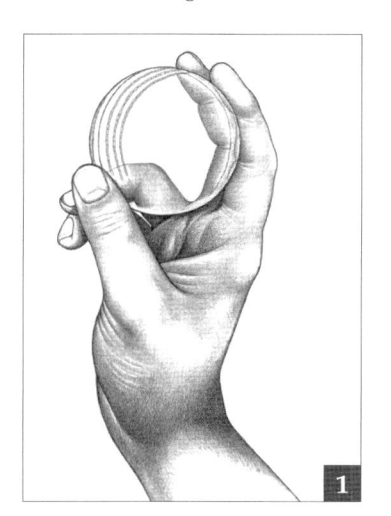

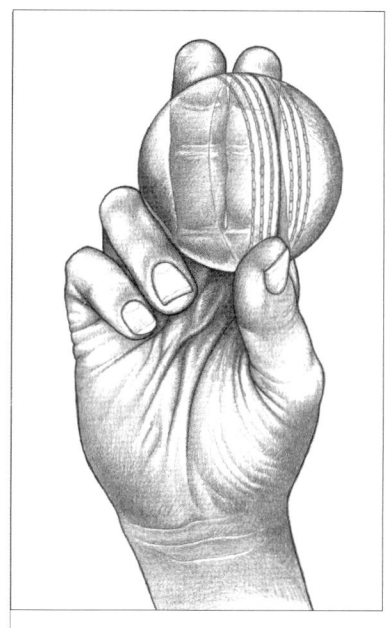

Grip for outswinger

1. *The wrist is cocked for the outswinger – the idea is to snap the ball down from behind your head.*
2. *Here we exaggerate the 'round the pole' movement of the wrist and fingers.*
3. *The wrist snaps down as your fingers and wrist send the ball smoothly down the line of your arm and action.*

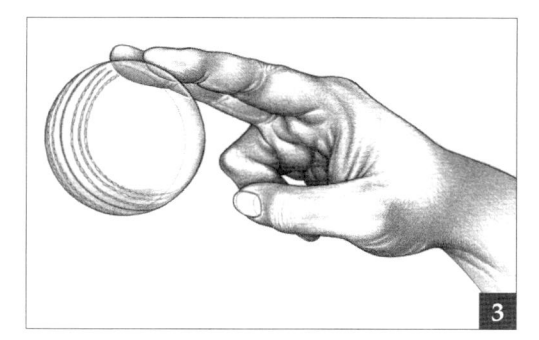

The best way of visualizing the correct arm and wrist action for the outswinger is to imagine putting a pole into the pitch on the bowling crease. Now try bowling around that pole, your arm coming round it on its right-hand side (left if you are a left-arm bowler). Turning your arm in this way will generate swing, but it is also easily spotted by the batsman, who will pick the delivery very early and score at will. So instead of doing it with the arm, go 'round the pole' with your wrist only.

THE INSWINGER

A good inswinger can be the most dangerous of all deliveries, if it is properly planned. For instance, it can be devastating if you've dragged the batsman outside his off-stump with a series of outswingers, and then shoot one back into his stumps or into his pads. As with an outswinger, you should generally be looking to hit off-stump, so start it outside off and let it swing in to hit the top of the stump.

Many bowlers find it easier to bowl inswing because the action does not have to be 'classical', but can be more open. Many young bowlers also take to it early on, thanks to a technical flaw: when they reach the stage in their development when they want to start bowling faster, they can develop an action that falls away early in the delivery stride. This is a natural (if unhelpful) inswing action, and one result is remarkably high numbers of inswing bowlers at lower levels of the game.

Having thus arrived at their action and ability to swing the ball almost by accident, these youngsters often see no reason to change: below a certain age, batsmen simply don't have the technique to cope with the ball coming in to them, and tend to leave the 'gate' open between bat and pad. This means there are wickets galore for the young inswing bowler, but as the batsmen who face him become more skilled, he becomes less and less effective. Eventually he has to learn to bowl the outswinger and correct his action. (At this point alarm bells should ring for the coaches of such bowlers, for it is here that the possibility of a mixed action creeping in is greatest, with all the attendant dangers – see above and Chapter 10 for detailed discussion of how to prevent this.)

Grip for inswinger

The grip

The seam is now angled towards leg-slip for the right-hander, and the flat pad of the thumb (rather than the side of the thumb) now rests on the base of the seam. This has the effect of cocking the wrist forwards.

The action

The inswinger is released 'in front' of the head, with the hand pushed over the ball, almost as a cobra's hood covers its head.

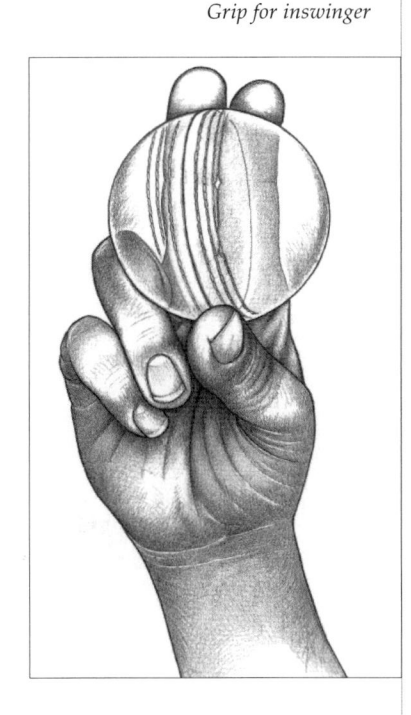

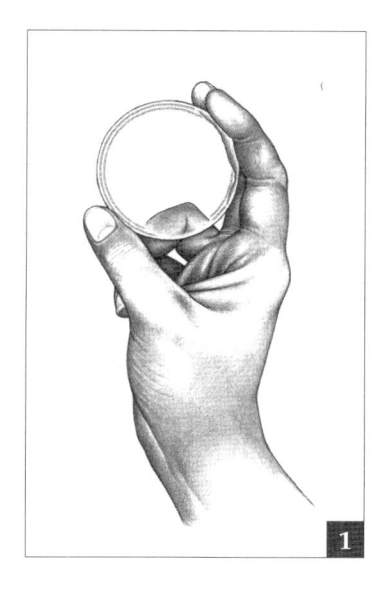

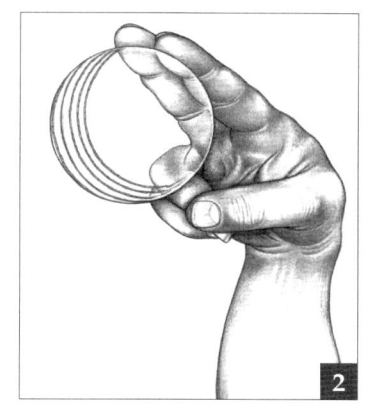

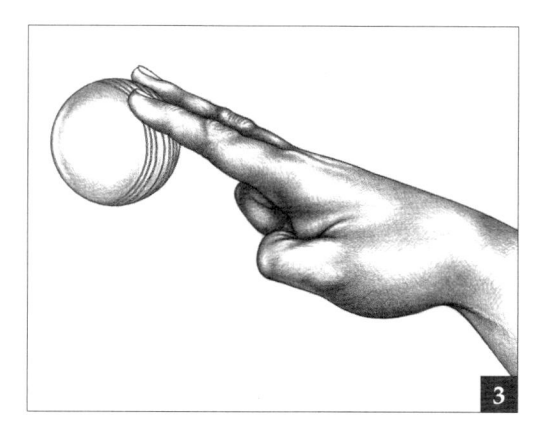

Visualize bowling 'round the pole' as you did for an outswinger, but this time move your arm around it clockwise (around it from the left, if you are a right-hander). Again, let the wrist do as much of the curving as possible, since your arm motion can be easily spotted; and since this is a more awkward and unnatural movement of your bowling arm, it takes less effort to simply move the wrist.

REVERSE SWING

When Pakistan's fast bowlers started getting the ball to swing in viciously and very late during the late 1980s and early 1990s, some of their victims cried foul. Not only were the likes of Imran Khan and Wasim Akram getting prodigious swing with the old ball, but they seemed to be swinging the ball in the opposite direction to where the seam was pointing. To the outraged – but ignorant – batsmen whose stumps and toes had been shattered, it all pointed to one thing: ball-tampering.

There was general uproar (as well as mystification and admiration) in cricketing circles. The fallout included the bitter and much-publicized libel case between Allan Lamb and Ian Botham on one side and Imran Khan on the other, as well as a legal run-in between Lamb and his former Northamptonshire teammate, Sarfraz Nawaz. The Englishmen lost their cases, and slowly the game's conservatives had to concede that the Pakistani bowlers had taken swing bowling to an entirely new level – and they didn't need leather-scuffing bottle-tops to do it either. Some rather more cynical commentators pointed out that it was those countries whose bowlers were the least able to extract reverse swing from their deliveries that had made the most noisy protests during the controversy.

1. *The 'cobra head' is cocked, with the fingers forming the 'hood'.*
2. *The wrist does the work of pushing the ball 'round the pole' (here we have exaggerated the angle of the wrist for demonstration purposes).*
3. *The cobra strikes – this is not so much a snap of the wrist but a strong push, the wrist forming an extension of the arm.*

BOWLING 259

The general explanation of reverse swing is fairly straightforward: a ball that has become extremely scuffed (from travelling around on a rough, grassless outfield) and has been continually polished with sweat on one side, will gradually become heavier on the side being polished. The delivery will then swing towards – rather than away from – that smoother side. The general principle may seem simple, but the practicalities of bowling reverse swing are anything but. It is not enough to pick up a battered ball and assume it will veer in late. The scratches and scuffs on the dry side of the ball increase the drag and allow it to duck in sharp and late when bowled at high speed, but exactly why this is so needs more careful explanation (see pp. 283–84). Moreover, the speeds necessary to get the ball to reverse are usually well beyond the ability of most bowlers. In addition, because the ball swings less dramatically than it does when swung conventionally, it needs to be bowled at a much fuller length; yet the yorker-length delivery is probably the most difficult one to bowl accurately: Waqar Younis was probably the best exponent of reverse swing the world has seen, and he was a master of the blisteringly quick inswinging yorker.

The advantages of being able to 'reverse' the ball into the right-handed batsman are obvious. Not only does it make the old ball a valuable tactical weapon, but it also enables the bowler to thoroughly bamboozle the batter, as he can now bowl what is essentially an inswinger with very little visible change of action.

The grip

The grip for bowling reverse swing is similar to that of an outswinger (see p. 257), with the shiny side pointed in the direction you want the ball to swing, and the seam pointed roughly at first slip. However, instead of having a vertical seam or rudder, the seam 'falls over' slightly. In other words, if you are right-handed, hold the ball as for an outswinger, and point the delivery at yourself. Looking at it as if you are a batter, roll the ball anti-clockwise by a few degrees. The seam should now be lying roughly from just outside your middle finger to roughly outside your thumb.

The action

Almost more than any other fast- or medium-paced delivery, reverse swing invites variation. There is no specific action that can be taught by coaches or learned by young bowlers: if you can make the ball reverse by slightly adapting your own action, don't do anything drastic to your basics. However, it seems that to reverse the ball into the pads, the action needs to be more round-arm (with a lower arm, rather than the vertical seamer's action or the upright slingy action of the in- and outswing specialists). The wrist also falls away slightly to the leg side at the moment of release – the snake-like 'wobble' seen in the wrist of reverse-swing maestros like Waqar and Darren Gough.

BALL-TAMPERING AND REVERSE SWING

Since its arrival on the world stage was inextricably linked with allegations of ball-tampering, reverse swing has always struggled to shake off its reputation as a somehow devious or underhanded tactic. Many of the more conservative pundits continue to dispute its existence, demanding to know how reverse swing into the batsman differs from conventional swing. It is quite possible that some of this surprisingly acrimonious debate is still being fuelled by latent suspicions that reversing the ball is the preserve of cheats.

To make matters worse, these suspicions sometimes appear to have racist overtones. The problem is that the condition of the ball remains integral to reverse swing, and it is no coincidence that the tactic developed in countries with hard, dry outfields almost devoid of grass. As already explained, only a very scuffed ball, and one that has been constantly polished on one side, can reverse: so Pakistan provided ideal conditions for the phenomenon to emerge.

But it didn't help that the only Islamic Test-playing nation at the time was the one that introduced the phenomenon of reverse swing so spectacularly onto the international stage.

This was combined with the apparently 'miraculous' effect of reverse swing. The ball does not gradually begin to reverse – it does so suddenly, and in the hands of exceptionally skilled and speedy bowlers, spectacularly. Batting sides that felt comfortably settled in for a session would find themselves bustled out at humiliating speed once the ball began reversing. Hardliners like Ian Botham still insist that for a side to collapse from 250 for 2 to 280 all out, someone has to be cheating.

The scene was thus set for racial stereotyping that persists to this day, as reflected in the brouhaha over umpire Darrell Hair's declaration that the Pakistan side had tampered with the ball during a Test match with England in August 2006. This set a sequence of events in motion that led to the Pakistan team forfeiting the match (we say more about this debacle in Chapter 11).

However, one can't ignore the fact that many teams do tamper with the ball, speeding up the natural roughening process so that it can start reversing sooner. The prevalence of extremely powerful zoom lenses at international games has largely ended the practice among top teams, but some infamous occasions do stand out, not least for the controversy they caused. Imran Khan announced that early in his career, he'd taken a bottle-top to a ball; England captain Michael Atherton was caught on camera taking what he said was earth from his pocket, and rubbing it into the seam of the ball during a Test against South Africa; and South African captain Hansie Cronje caused indignation when he impaled a ball on the spikes of his boot during a one-day international game in Australia.

Probably the most significant impact the issue has had on the game has been to open up the debate on ball-tampering. In the case of the Darrell Hair incident involving Pakistan, both Angus Fraser and Colin Miller, the UK editor of Cricinfo.com, pointed out that when reverse swing won England the Ashes in 2005, its proponents were hailed as heroes and cricketing geniuses.

In a piece published in Britain's *Independent on Sunday* two days after the forfeited Test, Fraser courageously pointed out that in the course of his career, he had often helped along the scuffing of the ball, or run his fingernails along the seam. He distinguished this kind of 'grooming' from the kind of actions involving resin, bottle-tops, and other more overt interventions. But if the ball was returned to him with a new scuff-mark after hitting the boundary boards, he saw no harm in 'roughing' up the sueded surface created in the process, as opposed to smoothing it down. He also pointed out that such behaviour, whether sanctioned by the Laws of the game or not, was covertly understood to be part of the game, and widely accepted as such. And more pertinently to the case of the forfeited England-Pakistan Test match, he noted that he had never been accused of ball-tampering for his actions.

TROUBLESHOOTING SWING-RELATED PROBLEMS

- **It's swinging without you trying to swing it, and you need to bowl a straighter line:**
  Hold it across the seam. If you're bowling with a two-piece ball and it's swinging uncontrollably, you're out of luck: two-pieces will swing no matter what you try! Four-piece balls can be stopped from swinging by changing your action – straighten up your arm and wrist.
- **It's swinging too much:**
  Change your line and stop making excuses!
- **It's not swinging at all:**
  If the problem is the conditions and not your action, then accept that it's just not going to swing, and start varying your bowling. Change the angle of delivery, and use the crease: bowl from close to the stumps, the middle of the crease and out wide.
- **Your inswingers are drifting down the leg side:**
  You're pushing it, not bowling it. Go back to the basics of your action, and ask your coach to watch you or (ideally) film you.

3. CUT

If there is one constant that runs through these chapters on technique (and indeed the game of cricket itself), it is that even the best-laid plans oft go awry. A track that was hard and bouncy on the first day skids through shin-high on the last day; the uncomfortable humidity that made the ball swing prodigiously in the first session develops into a still, bright, clear afternoon, ideal for batting. Sometimes even your careful homework can let you down: the batsman whom you had been told on good authority was helpless against outswing suddenly reveals a vicious late-cut and supreme judgement of where his stumps are.

As a fast or medium-pace bowler you need to be able to swallow your pride, take a step back, and reassess. Try to impose your will on the conditions, and you'll struggle. Rather ride the game as if you're surfing, keeping alert and mentally fluid.

If the ball has gone to sleep in your hand, or helpful cloud cover has evaporated, taking your ability to swing the ball with it, it's time to alter your approach. In this case, the cutter – whether an off-cutter or a leg-cutter – can be a more than useful substitute for swing.

Be warned: it takes years of practice to 'cut' the ball well at pace, but once mastered, it can be a devastating delivery, as it is effectively the fast bowler's version of a spinning delivery. Batsmen struggle enough with slow leg-breaks and off-breaks: a ball whistling down the pitch and zipping away to leg or off can be too much for many batsmen.

A cutter is also a very effective slower ball, since by running the fingers down the side of the ball (rather than flicking it out of the front of the hand), much of the momentum is bled away, without any change in the speed of the bowling arm.

The grip

Off-cutter: the seam is tilted towards the on side, with the fingers held slightly across the seam. As the ball is delivered, the fingers are brought down the side of the ball by the movement of the wrist. This will turn the ball in towards the right-handed batsman as it pitches.

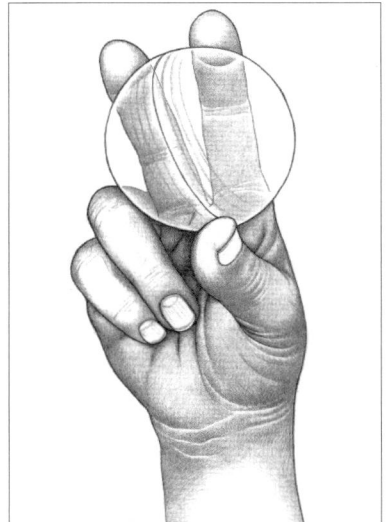

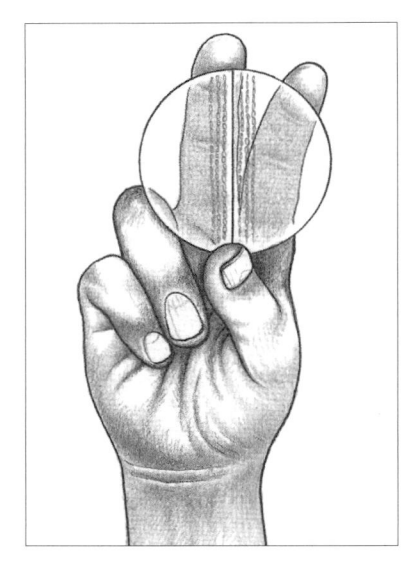

Grip for the off-cutter   *Grip for the leg-cutter*

Leg-cutter: the grip is the same as for the off-cutter, but the seam is now angled in the opposite direction, towards gully. There is less movement in the wrist, and more emphasis on letting the fingers 'fall' over the side of the ball. The faster this movement, the more purchase you're likely to get on the wicket.

The action

The basic action and grips for seam and swing still apply, but the bowler now alters the angle of the seam and pulls his fingers down the side of the ball, making it rotate sufficiently to grip and move after it pitches. (This is also one way of bowling an effective slower ball: the same action is employed, but the hand comes down the side of the ball, automatically slowing it down.) The bowler who intends to cut the ball has both the off-cutter and the leg-cutter at his disposal.

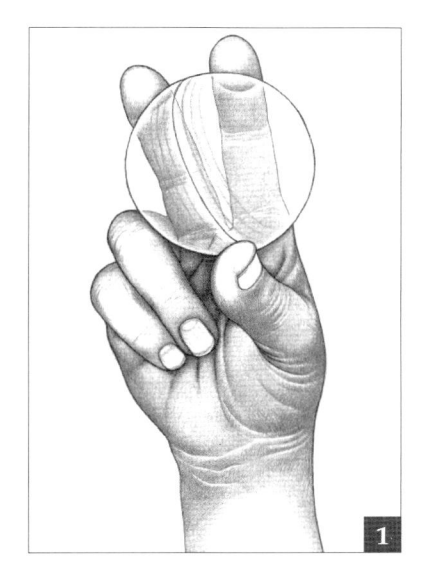

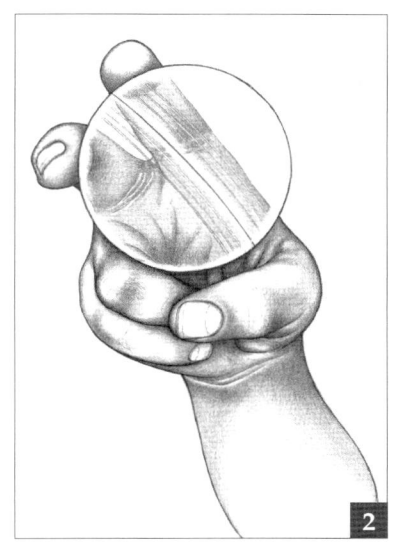

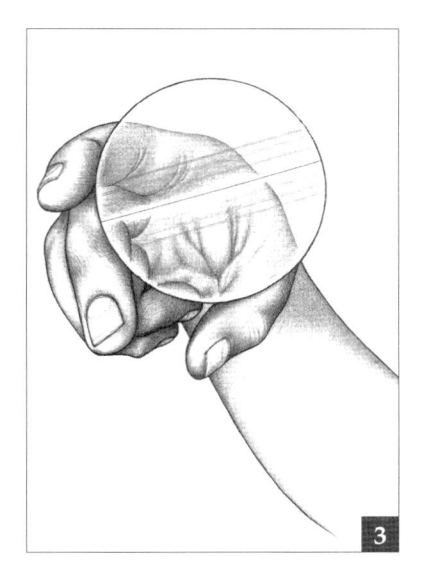

The action for the off-cutter: the fingers 'cut' down the outside of the ball, dragging down the seam to get maximum sideways revolutions (or to take the pace off, if you are attempting a slower ball).

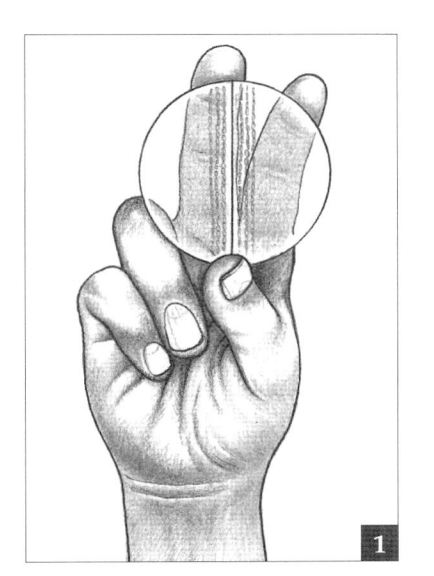

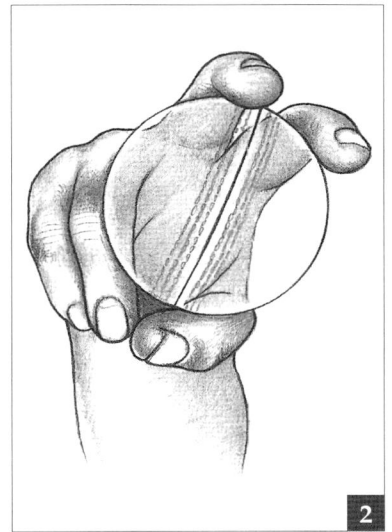

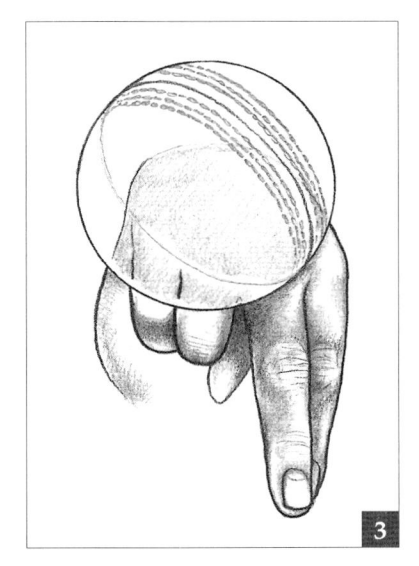

The action for the leg-cutter: the fingers 'cut' down the inside of the ball. Visualize allowing the ball to 'fall' forwards off the side of your fingers, and try not to put too much wrist into the delivery.

BOWLING 265

PRACTISING

No matter how brilliant a fast or medium-fast bowler might be, he cannot hope to get by on his talent alone, as a gifted batsman might be able to do. He must be superbly fit (at the elite level, we believe he needs to be as fit as any tri-athlete) and thus has little choice as to how hard he has to work on his game and fitness.

Indeed, it can sometimes seem as if the pace bowler has got a raw deal. While batting in the nets can be a relaxing or pleasurable exercise for batters, the bowler's standard practice is not much less intense than a match, at least in terms of the exertion he puts himself through in his run-up and action. On top of doing his share in the nets, he needs to practise his own specific skills, attend to his fitness routine, and then somehow find the time and energy for some batting practice as well.

Bowling practice is often repetitive and unstimulating. Trying to hit a single stump as many times as possible is an important drill, but a fairly mind-numbing one too. It is therefore important to find ways of keeping routines fresh and interesting. Coaches should recognize that bowlers are some of the most competitive people in any team, and should devise drills that take advantage of that desire to compete. For instance, the supremely competitive Richard Hadlee would challenge a bowling colleague to see who could hit a single stump the most times with a given number of deliveries.

Making repetition enjoyable is vital, because repetition and hard work are the only ways for the bowler to improve. Practise your repertoire of deliveries thoroughly, and always have an aim, whether to hit the top of off-stump or a particular spot on the wicket. (Off-stump is probably a better option, since different pitches and surfaces require different lengths, and you don't want to get used to one length, only to have it rendered useless by a very different surface in your next game.)

You will need patience and discipline. Practise one delivery at a time, for however long it takes until you are comfortable before moving on, and remember that all the world's greatest bowlers have spent months and years on their own as youngsters, simply bowling. Sometimes it was at batsmen, sometimes simply at a set of stumps. Clarrie Grimmett, the Australian spinner and teammate of Donald Bradman, practised his flipper for fifteen years before he used it in first-class matches!

THE FAST BOWLER'S KIT

There are two basic aspects to any fast or medium-pacer's kit: clothing and boots. While the condition, fit and fabric of his clothing is important for comfort and optimum performance, it is his boots that can make or break him. Each cricketer has one crucial piece of equipment without which he would not only be completely ineffectual, but also in extreme amounts of pain. For the batsman, these are his pads; for the wicket-keeper, gloves. For the quick bowler, these are his boots.

These boots were made for bowling

Unfortunately, cricket boots have been neglected by the scientists who constantly advance and refine running shoes (whether long-distance shoes or sprinting spikes) and football boots. There are some fine manufacturers of cricket boots, but even they have tended to overlook the development of orthotics and shock-absorbing layers in favour of tried and tested techniques passed down more or less intact by nineteenth-century cobblers. And so the injuries continue as the volume of international cricket grows exponentially: ankles, shins, knees and hips damaged because of the economics of cricket, which do not reward investment in the scientific development of equipment.

Boots must be selected according to three important criteria:

1. COMFORT
Your feet will take a beating from bowling 20 overs in a day, and you can't afford blisters and bruised heels when running in.

2. SUPPORT
Ankles, arches and insteps need to be well braced; they should feel almost as if they have been strapped up by a physiotherapist. A low-cut boot may allow your ankle to turn in or out at the point of delivery, a serious injury waiting to happen. Similarly, you need to check whether the boot's manufacturer has developed anti-jarring inserts or supports: nine times your body weight is going through that single piece of equipment every time you land.

3. SPIKES
No fast bowler can risk a half-spike boot with rubber studs in the heel. This is entirely acceptable footwear for spinners, who need to pivot and who are landing with much less force than their fast-bowling colleagues; but the injuries resulting from a slip on landing (a heel stud not replaced, or a rubber cleat not gripping) can be severe. A full set of long spikes is not only a good idea in terms of a bowler's safety and effectiveness, but it is also a good tactical move: metal spikes very quickly destroy the pitch as bowlers follow through, creating rough on a good length outside the left-hander's off-stump. If you have a left-arm fast bowler in your team, even better: the rough is created outside off-stump, giving your spinner a big juicy target. Muttiah Muralitharan, Saqlain Mushtaq and Mushtaq Ahmed were all excellent spinners in their own right, but it didn't hurt their bowling figures to have left-arm pacemen Chaminda Vaas and Wasim Akram roughing up the pitch at the other end.

Modern professional cricketers will have at least three pairs of shoes in their coffin, while professional fast bowlers will probably have more. International quick bowlers often change their boots from session to session, so that they can conserve each pair (keeping the 'spring' in the sole and the ankle-support firm). Bob Woolmer recalled, 'I once had to give Lance Klusener a stern lecture on the importance of a well-stocked shoe cupboard when he tried to borrow another pair of boots just before a match – his own had split and he hadn't brought along a spare pair!'

Nevertheless, financial circumstances often dictate how much kit a player can have, and it is extremely unrealistic to insist that all players have at least two pairs of boots. Bob Woolmer remembered coaching bowlers in South Africa's impoverished townships who were lucky if they had one pair of boots – and these were often held together with duct tape and shoelaces.

However, if you are able to afford it, try to wear your new boots in at the beginning of the season, while keeping at least two other pairs you have already worn in reserve. It is vital for a fast bowler to have confidence in his footwear, to know that he can charge in and slam down his front foot at full throttle.

ROUGHING IT

Don't get carried away! Running on the pitch is forbidden, and if the umpire believes you are doing too much damage to your landing area, he is entitled to order you to change into rubber-soled boots without spikes, or to take you out of the attack entirely. Batsmen aren't exempt either. Those who are deemed to be deliberately running on the 'no-go' area of the pitch (to give their attack some purchase in the next innings) can have their runs cancelled and be similarly ordered to change footwear.

Clothing

The most important consideration here is that you should not stiffen up between overs or spells. If you are doing your job properly, you will be sweating freely, so try to wear cotton or wool, which maintain body heat and are better at preventing chills than synthetic fabrics. Keeping warm and loose is absolutely vital, and even in hot climates fast bowlers should wear a cotton vest or T-shirt under their cricket shirt. Quicks should also put on a jersey or jumper as soon as they finish an over, even if the sun is beating down. If there is even the slightest suggestion of a breeze, it is essential that they do so. Coaches of younger players should keep an eye out for this and nag if necessary.

THE SCIENCE OF SWING

Swing, whether in or out, early or late, has been part of cricket since overarm bowling became the norm over a century ago. Sometimes it is planned, as skilful professional or club cricketers get the ball to leave their hand just right. At other times, it is accidental, with schoolchildren or newcomers to the game experiencing frustration (and mystification) as the ball bends away down the leg side past a very unimpressed wicket-keeper.

And it is not only on the field that swing is an integral, if puzzling, part of the game. Show us a television commentary box or a back page dedicated to cricket or even just a lively debate around a water-cooler, and we'll show you a pundit worrying about the state of swing bowling, or hypothesizing about the core of the ball, or recalling the 'banana-balls' bowled by Ian Botham and Imran Khan in the 1980s.

And yet despite its prevalence in the game and the interest it has always generated among fans, there still seems to be no consensus over *why* the ball swings. In this section, we will explain the scientific facts and principles involved, and in so doing hopefully settle much of the debate.

The most common explanation given for why the cricket ball swings is based on the principle of friction. The theory is that the ball swings towards its rough side because the roughened leather provides more resistance to air flow, which causes friction on that side. The friction causes the rough side to travel more slowly through the air, the smooth side begins to 'overtake' it, and the result is a deviation towards the rough side.

It seems to make immediate sense, but it fails to explain why a new ball (which doesn't have a rough side) swings considerably more than an older ball. More importantly, it fails to take its assumptions to their logical conclusion. For instance, why does the ball, having started to deviate towards the rough side, then magically stop deviating? After all, by the time it reaches the batsman, according to the popular theory, it has deviated only to the extent that the seam is pointing towards the slips, after which it stops deviating.

In reality, if air friction were the sole cause of this deviation, the ball would continue to rotate on its horizontal axis until the smooth side faced forward and the rough side pointed back down the wicket towards the bowler. This would happen over a fairly short distance, and once the smooth side was facing forward, all further rotation or deviation would stop because the air friction on both sides of the ball would now be equal (see Figure 5.9 overleaf for a visual representation of how this would work).

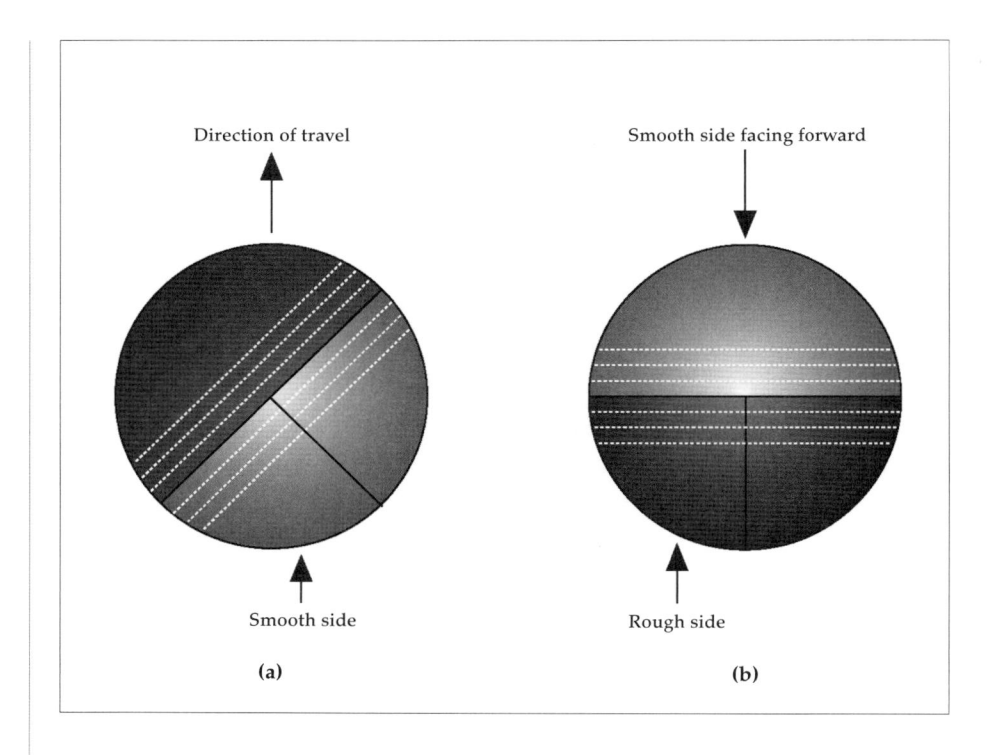

FIGURE 5.9: *If the swing of a cricket ball was caused by increased resistance to air flow over the rough side, the rough side would travel more slowly than the smooth side, causing the ball to rotate (a). This rotation would stop when the smooth side of the ball was facing forward (b). So the ball wouldn't swing, it would simply rotate on its horizontal axis, like the first quarter rotation of a spinning top.*

The traditional explanation, in other words, is flawed. The cricket ball does not simply swing because of friction. Rather, we need to look at the ball's wake, generated in the air around and behind the ball just as a ship creates a wake around and behind itself, and search for the answer in the changes the ball and bowler make to that wake. To do this, we also need to remember that air has mass: if air weighed nothing – for instance, if you were bowling on the moon – the ball would not swing.

THE BASICS OF AIR FLOW AROUND A SPHERE

To understand why a cricket ball swings under certain conditions, it is first important to grasp four fundamental concepts of the physics of ball motion through a medium like air. According to scientists, these are:

1. Patterns of laminar air flow around a sphere (such as a cricket ball) moving at different velocities through the air.

2. The development of turbulent flow in the wake of a sphere moving at increased velocity through air.
3. The boundary layer.
4. The critical Reynolds' number (Mehta et al., 1983).

As a bowler or coach, you will have encountered some and perhaps even many of these aspects already – friction, air flow, and so on – but the following explanations of these four points assume little prior knowledge: this is the physics of the ball's flight starting from scratch!

1. Patterns of air flow around a sphere (such as a cricket ball) moving at different velocities through the air

When any object moves through a medium like air, it experiences a force in the opposite direction to its forward movement. This retarding or drag force is known as wind resistance, and is caused by the energy required by the moving object to force its way between the molecules of air through which it is travelling. Since these molecules of air have mass, and are therefore attractive to other air molecules in their immediate vicinity, they resist any object trying to impose itself on this natural attraction.

Wind resistance increases as the square of the velocity (v^2) at which the object is moving, and is therefore most apparent at higher speeds. A measure of the magnitude of this retarding force can be gauged by comparing how far a sphere would travel in a vacuum in which there is no wind resistance, as occurs in space. Any object launched in space will continue moving at that speed forever or until it hits some obstacle.

Even though a cricket ball is relatively small (compared to a soccer ball, for instance), air resistance has a substantial effect on the speed at which a fast delivery travels over even a distance as short as 18 metres. Thus, a ball leaving the hand of a fast bowler at about 160km/h (44,4m/sec) slows to about 138km/h (38,3m/sec) by the time it reaches the batsman. While some of this loss of speed will be due to the friction off the pitch as the ball bounces, most of it can be accounted for by the effects of wind resistance.

Figure 5.10 shows how air molecules move around a smooth sphere, in this case, a seamless cricket ball, travelling towards the batsman (at the top of the picture). The ball is viewed from above. (The reason why this particular cricket ball does not have a seam will be explained shortly.)

FIGURE 5.10: *The path of air flow around a smooth sphere*

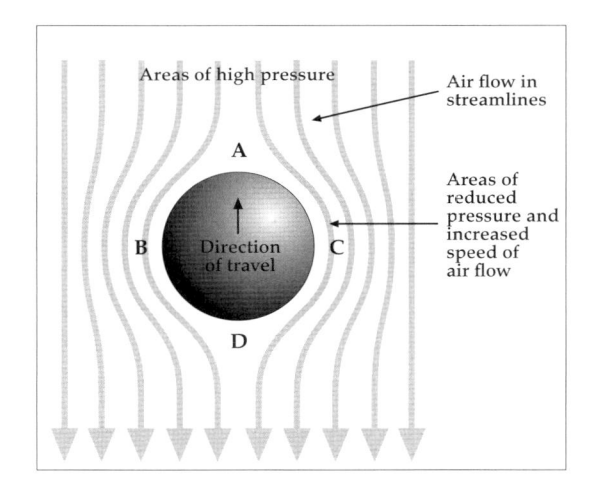

BOWLING 271

As the front of the ball (point A) moves through the air, it forces molecules around the sides of the ball (B – left side of the ball; C – the right side of the ball) until they meet again at point D at the back of the ball. The lines along which the air molecules move are known as streamlines. The flow pattern shown here is described as streamlined or *laminar* flow, since the streamlines remain parallel to each other, even though at the sides of the ball they are compressed closer to one another.

Of special interest to this discussion is the spacing of the streamlines in Figure 5.10 (p. 271): notice how they are wide in front and behind the ball, but increasingly compacted (although still parallel) along the sides of the ball at B and C.

These spaces represent the channels through which the air must flow on either side of the ball. Since the flow pattern in front of and behind the ball is steady (that is, the streamlines are laminar and equally spaced), then the air travelling in the narrowed channels around the sides of the ball must have sped up in order to return to the orderly air flow patterns in the wake of the ball. This means that the air must have travelled faster in order to cover the additional distance around the sides of the ball. Think of what happens when a river flows through a gorge or travels over rapids: the narrowness of the new channel causes the water to flow at a greater velocity compared to the slower pace of the water in the wider part of the river.

The greater velocity of the air travelling around the cricket ball (or the water flowing through the rapids), is caused by a difference in pressure as the air or fluid travels from an area of high pressure (in front of the ball or upstream of the rapids) to an area of low pressure (at the side of the ball or in the narrowest part of the channel), and then to an area of high pressure behind the ball (or in the water below the rapids).

Since the reduction in pressure caused by this increased rate of air flow is similar on both sides of the ball (the streamlines are exactly the same on each side of the ball) there is no side force on the ball. In other words, our seamless cricket ball, with its sides equally smooth, travels in a straight line.

2. The development of turbulent flow in the wake of a sphere moving at increased velocity through air

Figure 5.10 on the previous page shows the idealized (laminar) patterns of air flow around the surface of the cricket ball. But this idealized pattern can only occur if the air travelling closest to the ball surface (and which must therefore travel the greatest distance around the spherical surface of the cricket ball) has enough 'energy' to keep up with the slightly slower-moving air in the immediately adjacent air channel. The air molecules in this channel must not only travel faster, but they must also overcome the forces of friction between themselves and the very thin layer of air molecules which are adhering to the surface of the cricket ball and are therefore enjoying a free ride towards the batter – a privileged position that these adhering molecules are unwilling to relinquish. These frictional forces become increasingly important as the speed at which the sphere is travelling increases.

Thus, as the velocity of the delivery increases, the attraction between these two layers of air molecules increases. This means that more energy is required to ensure that the moving air is able to round the surface of the cricket ball in time to ensure that the flow remains laminar. However, eventually a speed is reached at which the ball is travelling so fast that the air travelling over the surface of the ball is unable to 'keep up' with the faster air flowing in the adjacent streamline next to it. As a result, the air at the ball's surface is no longer able to maintain the pace. Instead, it breaks from the surface, and stops flowing forward. Next, it begins to flow in the reverse direction, that is, towards the ball (Figure 5.11), before beginning to flow in a circular (eddying) pattern in the wake of the ball. Because these eddying currents are moving slowly, they produce an area of greatly increased pressure behind the ball, thereby producing an increased drag that slows down the delivery.

As in the previous diagram, the seamless ball is shown moving towards the top of the page/batter, as viewed from above. Since the air moving over the surface of the ball must travel both the furthest distance around the ball (A to D), and must also overcome the greater frictional forces caused by travelling over the surface of the ball, a speed is reached at which the air molecules in that layer are unable to keep up. Instead, they stop moving forward (D1) and reverse their direction (D2) before beginning the circular movement known as eddying (D3 to D6).

These eddying currents are the bane of all high-velocity sports, as they slow the progress of all fast-moving objects, be they racing-cars, cyclists, downhill skiers and even 100-metre sprinters. The principal focus of the study of aerodynamics is to try to reduce the development of these eddying currents around the surfaces of all fast-moving objects.

FIGURE 5.11: *The development of eddying currents in the layer of air that travels immediately over the air attached to the surface of the cricket ball travelling at high speed*

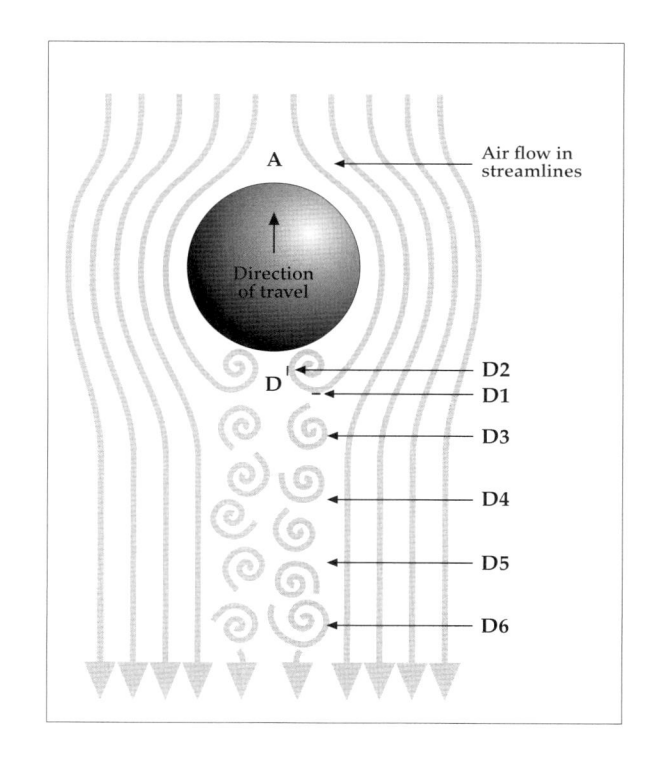

3. The boundary layer

As mentioned above, all objects exposed to air are coated with a thin layer of air that adheres to the surface. Much as a thin layer of water adheres to freshly washed hands and can be removed only by vigorous drying, high-speed air flow wrenches the surface layer of air from the object to which it is clinging. (The air is attracted to the surface of a cricket ball because of the attraction that the molecules of air have for the surface of any object.)

However, once the ball begins to move, the air immediately next to this layer must begin to flow at a higher speed than the air in the adjacent streamline in order to reach the back of the ball while maintaining laminar flow. But the closer the air is to the surface of the ball, the more energy must be expended in order to overcome the attraction for the resting air molecules coating the cricket ball. This layer of air adjacent to the cricket ball, and which is influenced by this effect, is known as the boundary layer. In other words, the boundary layer is that layer of air whose motion is affected by the presence of air molecules on the surface of the cricket ball. The effect of these surface molecules is to increase the amount of energy needed to drive air across them in the boundary layer. At some distance from the ball, this effect is lost and the air travelling around the ball beyond that distance is affected only by the surface geometry of the ball, but no longer by the effects of those surface air molecules (Figure 5.12).

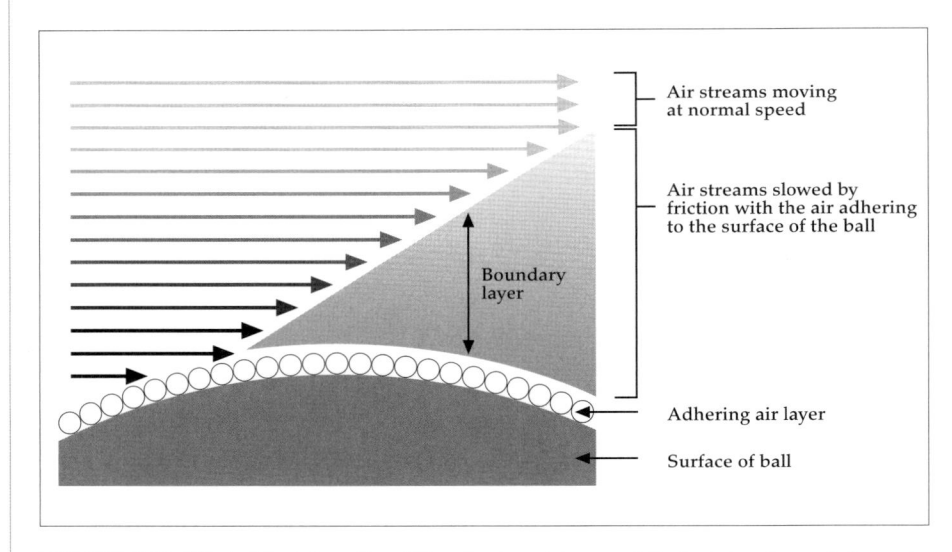

FIGURE 5.12: *Effect of the interaction of the adhering air layer and the boundary layer of air on air flow across a surface*

As described above, as the speed of the ball increases, the air travelling in this boundary layer has increasing difficulty keeping up with the air travelling in those streamlines beyond the boundary layer. Ultimately, a speed is reached at which the air travelling in the boundary layer is no longer able to keep up and, as a result, it separates, causing the eddying currents shown in Figure 5.13 on the opposite page. This is known as the separation of the boundary layer.

At low velocities, this separation occurs near the rear of the ball (Figure 5.13 on the left) but as the velocity of the delivery increases, this separation occurs closer to the front of the ball (Figure 5.13 on the right).

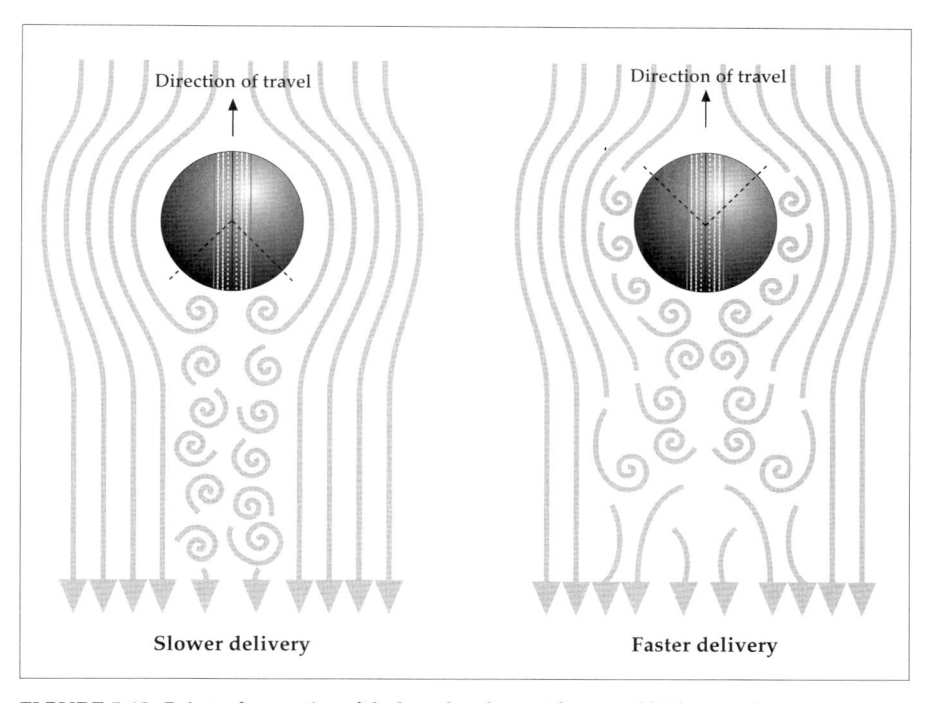

FIGURE 5.13: *Points of separation of the boundary layer at lower and higher speeds*

Note that the points of the separation on the adjacent sides of the ball, both sides of which are equally smooth, occur at adjacent points on the opposite sides of the ball. The point of boundary layer separation is not dependent purely on the velocity of the delivery, but also on the characteristics of the cricket-ball surface, as well as the prominence of the seam and the position of the seam relative to the direction of flight of the delivery.

As we will shortly discuss further, when there is a discrepancy in the point on the surface at which separation occurs, this produces a pressure difference in the streamlines of air travelling on either side of the ball, and the opportunity for swing develops.

4. The critical Reynolds' number

You now know that the drag caused by air resistance on a smooth sphere travelling through the air increases as the square of the velocity (v^2). This means that the drag on a delivery travelling at 40 milliseconds is four times greater than the drag experienced by a delivery travelling at 20 milliseconds.

However, for each sphere there is a specific critical velocity at which the drag due to air resistance is suddenly reduced, so that the sphere can suddenly travel much faster while producing the same drag.

The scientist Osborne Reynolds showed that a specific value, the so-called critical Reynolds' number, must be reached before this phenomenon can occur. Reynolds calculated that at a value over 200 000 (the critical value for the Reynolds' number, calculated from the equation given below), this drag suddenly drops.

The explanation for this phenomenon is that at the critical Reynolds' number, the air in the boundary layer begins to flow turbulently. As a result, air from the boundary layer and from the stream of air travelling immediately adjacent to the boundary layer begin to mix. This means that energy can be transferred from that layer to the boundary layer. The effect is that the air molecules can now travel faster in the boundary layer without losing as much velocity in overcoming their attraction for the surface air molecules. Because of this turbulent flow in the boundary layer, the energized boundary layer clings to the ball's surface for longer, separating only at the back of the ball, reducing the size of the wake of eddying currents trailing the ball. This reduces the pressure in the wake behind the ball, thereby reducing the drag and allowing the ball to travel faster.

The Reynolds' number (R) for any sphere is calculated as:
R = 640vd
in which v is the velocity of movement of the sphere in milliseconds and d is the diameter of the sphere in centimetres.

The diameter of a cricket ball is 7,2 centimetres, which means that the speed at which the critical Reynolds' number is reached is:

$$V = \frac{200\,000}{640 \times 7,2} = 43,4 \text{m/sec} = 156 \text{km/h}$$

However, before bowlers start relishing the prospect of reduced drag should they crank up their pace to 156km/h and above, it should be pointed out that the Reynolds' number is dependent on the smoothness of the surface of this sphere. For this reason, it is difficult to give a precise critical Reynolds' number for a cricket ball (Daish, 1972), because the slightest surface roughness dramatically reduces the Reynolds' number for that sphere. This occurs because the roughness lowers the velocity at which turbulent flow develops in the boundary layer. In bowling terms, a lower Reynolds' number, brought about by surface roughness, means that the ball doesn't have to travel as fast as 156km/h to benefit from reduced turbulence.

Of course, if turbulent flow develops in the boundary layer on only one side of the cricket ball, the point of separation in the boundary layers on both sides of the ball will be different. When this occurs, conditions for swing are developed. The phenomenon of reverse swing especially is dependent on the reduction of the Reynolds' number on the side of an old cricket ball, one side of which is substantially rougher than the other side (this will be explained in more detail below).

The design of the golf ball is the most obvious practical example of the use of this effect to enhance the flight of the ball. The Reynolds' number for a smooth (undimpled) golf ball with a diameter of 4,12cm driven at a velocity of 70m/sec, as achieved by golfers like Tiger Woods, is only 79 000, well below the critical value of 200 000 needed to benefit from turbulent flow in the boundary layer.

But the effect of the dimpling on the surface of a golf ball is to reduce the critical Reynolds' number for the golf ball to velocities that are achievable by human golfers – i.e., velocities of between 50–70m/sec. As a result, the drag is reduced for at least some of the trajectory, allowing the ball to be hit further than would occur without the dimpling. Furthermore, the dimpling also increases the upward lift of the backward spinning golf ball as a result of the Magnus effect (covered in detail in the section on spin bowling on pp. 301–7).

FIGURE 5.14: *Turbulence in the boundary layer around a ball travelling at a speed above the critical Reynolds' number*

WHY THE BALL SWINGS

The phenomena described above may sound fairly complex and somewhat removed from the tussles that go on between batsman and bowler on the cricket field, but they form the foundations of the four vital ingredients necessary for the cricket ball to swing. These are:
- the height of the seam
- the speed of the delivery
- the stillness of the ball's vertical axis
- the angle of seam.

BOWLING 277

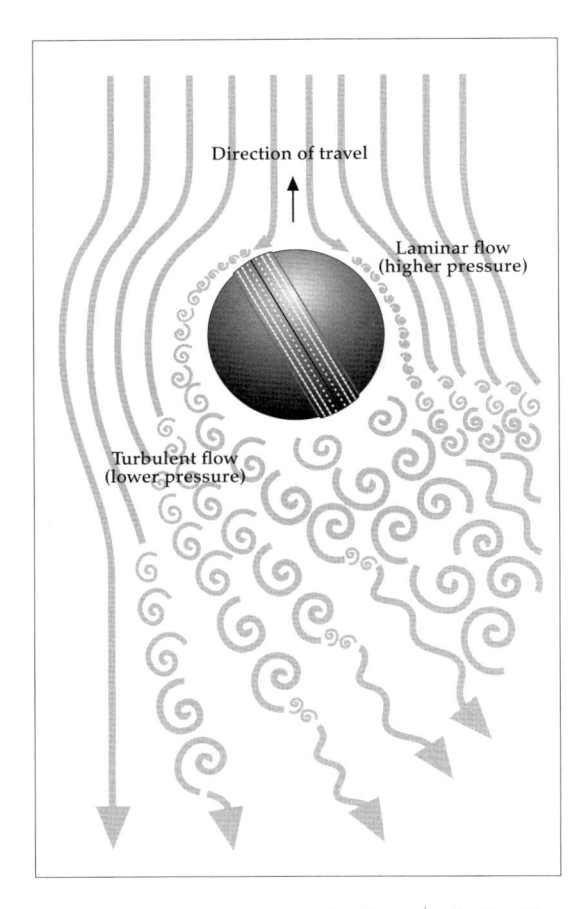

FIGURE 5.15: *The effect of the raised seam on the development of turbulent air flow around a cricket ball*

1. The height of the seam

As any cricketer knows, a new ball swings more than an older one. This is because the seam of a new ball stands proud (raised) above the surface of the ball. In this position, it is able to disturb the smooth flow of air in the boundary layer travelling on the side to which the seam is pointed.

As a result, turbulence is generated in the boundary layer on that side of the ball.

The first theoretical explanation of why the cricket ball swings seems to have been made by a Professor J.C. Cooke of the University of Malaya, who published his findings in the *Mathematical Gazette* in 1955. His explanation was reproduced in 1957 by R.A. Lyttleton, whose explanation was in turn repeated in Sir Donald Bradman's book, *The Art of Cricket*.

Cooke and Lyttleton proposed that swing is caused by the seam producing different flow patterns on either side of a cricket ball that is travelling above a certain critical velocity. Central to their argument is that the boundary layer must separate at different points on adjacent sides of the ball, since this produces the sideways force on the ball that is necessary to produce swing. This differential separation also produces an area of increased pressure in the wake of the ball (greater on one side) that will affect the further trajectory of the ball. In particular, the ball will travel away from the high-pressure area of turbulent flow.

But if the point of separation is the same on both sides of the ball, as shown in Figure 5.13 on p. 275, then the sideways forces on each side of the ball will cancel each other out, and the ball's future trajectory will not be affected other than to be slowed by the drag that develops in the wake of the ball.

However, if the separation point occurs at different points on the adjacent sides of the cricket ball, a pressure differential will be produced in the air surrounding the ball. This will produce a lateral (sideways) force on the ball, and this is what produces swing.

The boundary layer usually separates from the ball somewhere at or beyond the midpoints of each side of the ball, and the actual point of separation is determined by the velocity of the delivery – so that the faster the ball is travelling, the nearer it occurs to the front of the ball (Figure 5.13). Still, remember that if this separation occurs equally on both sides, the flight of the delivery will not be affected.

The key point is that a difference in separation points can be produced by having laminar flow on one side of the ball and non-laminar or turbulent flow on the other side. As illustrated in Figure 5.10 on p. 271, laminar flow is characterized by smooth tiers of air flowing one on top of each other in parallel streamlines. Turbulent flow, by contrast, sees chaotic movement throughout each streamline, as shown in the areas beyond the point at which the boundary layer separates in Figures 5.13 and 5.14.

However, here we encounter a paradox: laminar flow causes the boundary layer to separate from the ball *earlier* than is the case with turbulent flow. This is because during turbulent flow, energy is borrowed from the air in the adjacent streamline, and this extra energy allows the air to travel faster and so stick to the side of the ball for longer.

So one mechanism of producing swing is to produce laminar flow on one side of the ball and turbulent flow on the other. Since the pressure in air moving turbulently is lower than in air moving in laminar flow, a pressure differential is produced which sucks the ball towards the area of lower pressure – the side of the turbulent flow. The effect of a prominent seam, as found in cricket balls, is that it helps produce turbulent flow on the side of the ball to which the seam is pointing (see Figure 5.15).

To illustrate this with a practical cricketing example, consider an outswing delivery to a right-handed batsman, with the seam of the ball aimed towards the slips (Figure 5.16). As the seam strikes the onrushing air on its left side, turbulent flow is produced in the boundary layer so that the point at which the boundary layer separates on the left side of the ball (S_L) moves further to the rear on that side. In contrast, the absence of the seam on the right side of the ball striking the onrushing air allows laminar flow to occur on the right-hand side of the ball. But since laminar flow separates earlier from the ball's surface than turbulent flow does, the boundary layer separates closer to the front of the ball on the right side of the ball (S_R). This is because the turbulent flow 'borrows' energy from the streamline adjacent to the boundary layer, and this allows the boundary layer to 'stick' to the ball surface for longer. The roughness of this surface also reduces the Reynolds' number required to produce turbulent flow, further encouraging the development of turbulent flow. A ball with a rough surface on the left side and a smooth surface on the right will swing more, since the rough left side will allow the development of non-laminar flow at lower bowling speeds than a ball with two shiny sides.

The difference in the separation points on adjacent sides of the cricket ball generates the sideways force that produces the swing. Calculations suggest that the force produced by the difference in separation points caused by a new seam is sufficient to produce sideways movement of up to 50cm during the approximately 16 metres of the cricket ball delivery (Bown and Mehta, 1993; Barton 1982). Add half a

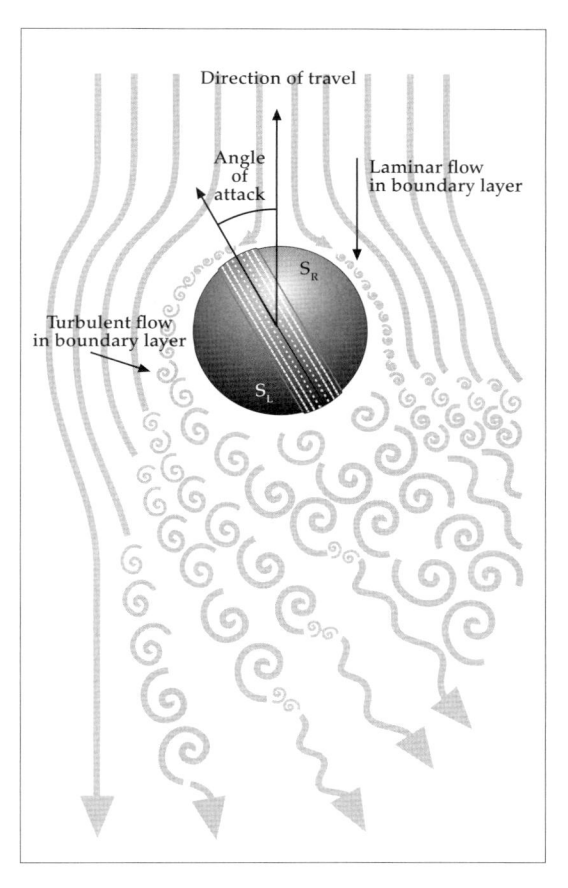

FIGURE 5.16: *The effect of the seam in producing swing away from a right-handed batsman. This occurs at delivery speeds of 80–120 km/h.*

metre of swing caused by the seam alone to another half-metre created by the bowler's action, the overhead conditions, and the pace of the ball, and you have the classic 'banana-ball', speared in at middle-stump and veering away towards the slips. Note that the optimum angle of attack – the angle between the direction of flight and the direction of the seam – needs to be between 20–40° for optimum swing to occur.

2. The speed of the delivery

As already described, in order to swing away from a right-hander, laminar flow must be preserved on the right side of the ball (Figure 5.16). For this to happen, the surface on that side of the ball should be smooth, and it must be travelling at the correct speed. The Reynolds' number will determine at what speed the air flowing around a spherical object will become turbulent: for a cricket ball with a smooth surface, this will be at about 112km/h. At higher speeds, the flow on the smooth right side of the ball in Figure 5.16 will become turbulent, and the boundary layer separation point on the smooth side will move further towards the back of the ball so that the separation points become more similar, reducing swing. This explains why very fast bowlers are unable to swing the ball as much as medium-paced bowlers.

It is also sometimes suggested that the swing that occurs late in the flight occurs because the ball's velocity slips below the critical velocity predicted by the Reynolds' number, so that laminar flow returns on the smooth side of the ball. However, once turbulent flow has developed, it is improbable that it will revert to laminar flow, except at significantly low speeds. Another explanation is that the amount of swing produced by the lateral force is cumulative, producing an exponential parabolic flight path (i.e., a steadily accumulating amount of swing that only becomes visible to the naked eye in its later stages) so that most of the lateral movement will seem to occur just as the delivery approaches nearer to the batsman (Bartlett et al., 1996).

SWING IT INTO THE WIND?

Since most bowlers believe that swing is generated simply by angling the seam and allowing the rough side of the ball to generate friction, they sensibly assume that bowling into a strong headwind will generate more swing. But they're wrong. Remember that swing depends on the ball's speed *relative to the air through which it is passing*. Bowling with the wind reduces the speed of the delivery relative to the air through which it is travelling, which increases a fast bowler's chances of generating swing. Likewise, bowling into the wind increases the relative speed of the ball, meaning that the quick bowler is less likely to get the ball to swing – as explained above.

3. The stillness of the ball's vertical axis

All young bowlers should work hard at getting the ball to leave their hand in exactly the right position, but in the case of seamers, this is not only for reasons of accuracy and pace, but also to enable the ball to swing. The swinging delivery should be bowled with as little 'wobble' around its vertical axis as possible: the less wobble in the seam (in other words, the less the seam veers from third slip to leg gully and back), the more laminar will be the flow on the smooth side of the ball.

While the position of the wrist and the bowler's action are integral to keeping the ball stable on its vertical axis, back-spin is also important: a flick of the fingers down the back of the ball at the point of delivery helps to stabilize the ball. The optimum back-spin speed is usually between 11 and 14 revolutions per second (Mehta et al., 1983).

Dennis Lillee believes that when the seam has been flattened and the ball has lost its smoothness, swing can still be generated as a result of the difference in relative smoothness between the two sides of the cricket ball. However, the seam should now face forward. The Australian paceman also holds that the more back-spin imparted on the ball, the later it will swing. (For more of Lillee's advice on generating swing, see the section on fast and medium-pace bowling.)

4. The angle of seam

The seam must maintain an optimum angle of attack (see Figure 5.16) throughout the delivery. Mehta et al. (1983) showed that maximum swing is produced at a ball velocity of 112km/h when the angle of attack is 20° and the rate of back-spin is between 11 and 14 revolutions per second.

FURTHER MYSTERIES OF SWING

What about the weather?

It is one of cricket lore's oldest and most familiar wisdoms that the ball is more likely to swing in humid or cloudy conditions, but there is still no explanation for why this is the case. Indeed, most puzzling is the fact that a humid atmosphere is less, not more, dense than a dry atmosphere, and should therefore be less, not more, conducive to generating swing. One suggestion is that the humidity either swells the seam, although this is unproven (Mehta et al., 1983), or that it interacts with the varnish of the ball, making it easier for the bowler to grip and thus to impart the ideal amount of back-spin.

Matthew Turner (2002) from Brisbane, Australia, offers a different theory. He suggests that humidity must be separated from the effect of temperature. Even though the humidity can be 100% in Brisbane, the ball hardly ever swings on a hot summer's day. This suggests that heat negates the effects of humidity.

Turner suggests that this may be because heat increases turbulence in the air near the pitch through which the ball is travelling. He suggests that heat produces micro-turbulence in the region of the (hot) pitch surface, which is not recognized as its effects are too slight to be noticed.

His theory is that when the pitch is warm, because the sun is shining without cloud cover, the micro-turbulence that develops in the air immediately above the pitch interferes with the development of turbulence in the boundary layer on the rough side of the cricket ball, and which is so crucial for the development of swing.

His corollary is that when there is overhead cloud, there is less direct sun on the pitch and therefore less heat and less micro-turbulence in the air through which the ball travels. As a result, conditions are more favourable for swing. According to his theory, the ball will swing when the pitch is as cool or colder than the surrounding air.

He also suggests that this might explain why humidity apparently makes the ball swing; this is less likely to be the effect of humidity than the effect of heat on air movement directly above the pitch.

Turner concludes with the advice: 'Look at the weather forecast for the whole game, and look for the best swing conditions if you have swing bowlers, and always bowl if you win the toss after overnight rain' (2002, p. 49).

Or maybe it's the balls

There is another aspect to swing bowling. Since the retirement of Wasim Akram and Waqar Younis, the international arena has seen a remarkable scarcity of swing bowlers, and even those two stellar Pakistanis were almost unique in their day in their ability to make the ball duck in late in its flight. England's Matthew Hoggard had some impressive returns against South Africa and Australia in 2004 and 2005, but many pundits claim that the art of swing bowling is rapidly being lost as real pace and miserly line and length become the norm for the seam bowler.

Even Sir Alec Bedser (regarded by many as the best swing bowler in the history of the game) held a pessimistic outlook about the future of the art: 'We [England] have gradually produced a crop of bowlers who cannot bowl swingers,' he said, an opinion shared by the Test and County Board of England whose assessment in 1993 was that 'the general quality of swing bowling in the [English] domestic game is as low as it has ever been' (Bown and Mehta, 1993).

These criticisms are based on the assumption that a cricket ball will always swing when exposed to the aerodynamic factors already discussed, and that modern bowlers are simply not managing to master the necessary skills to impose those factors on their deliveries. But this ignores the fact that cricket balls themselves have changed considerably in construction from those used even as recently as the 1980s, when Ian

Botham and Imran Khan were swinging the ball to such effect. The Kookaburra balls used today are arguably completely different from those Bedser might have used. It is certainly possible that their design and construction might negatively affect their potential for swing. Having levelled a charge of 'they don't make them like they used to' at modern bowlers, pundits may do well to shift that accusation onto the balls being used. In his 1998 autobiography, Wasim Akram argued that the Reader ball, which he used to such devastating effect during the 1990s, aided reverse swing far more than either the Duke or the Kookaburra ball. He noted that when he captained the Pakistan side, the toss he was most keen to win was for the choice of which make of ball to use during a Test match!

So it seems that further research is needed into the current methods of constructing cricket balls, and how these methods and materials might affect swing.

THE AERODYNAMICS OF REVERSE SWING

The ability to swing the ball in the opposite direction to which it is expected to travel (i.e., in which the seam and roughened side of the ball suggest it should go out) was first perfected by Imran Khan and other Pakistani fast bowlers. Dr Rabi Mehta, who opened the bowling with Imran for the first cricket team of the Royal Grammar School in 1972, has offered the currently accepted explanation of how reverse swing is generated (Bown and Mehta, 1993).

Mehta recalls that sometime after 1980, Khan had informed him that he had noticed that, on occasion, a new ball would swing in the direction opposite to that which was intended. The explanation of Bown and Mehta (1993) is that such 'reverse' swing is possible if the speed at which the new ball is delivered is sufficiently fast.

They suggest that at speeds between about 80 and 120km/h, the seam of the ball is able to produce the turbulent flow on the seam side of the ball as shown in Figure 5.16. However, as the speed rises above 120km/h, the point at which the laminar flow on the smooth side of the ball begins to separate moves towards the front of the ball. Eventually the ball is travelling so fast that the boundary layer strips even before it strikes the seam. What this means is that the seam is now acting as a ramp, directing the air on that side away from the ball, causing the boundary layer to separate earlier on the seam side of the ball – the opposite of what normally occurs in an outswinging delivery (Figure 5.17). This is thought to occur at speeds of 130–145km/h. When this occurs, the sideways force on the ball is reversed so that the delivery bowled as an outswinger, actually swings in (Figure 5.17 on the left).

Bown and Mehta (1993) suggest that the next advance produced by the Pakistani bowlers was the discovery that reverse swing – inswing achieved with a ball bowled with an outswing action and the seam of the ball directed at the slips – could be

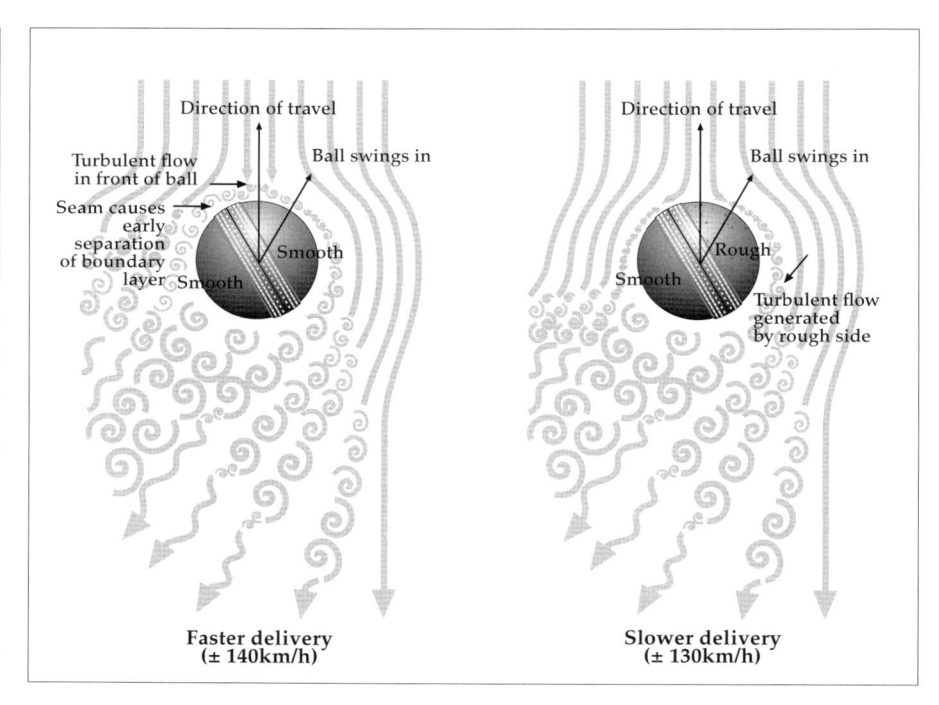

FIGURE 5.17: *The impact of speed and the condition of the ball in bowling reverse swing*

achieved at lower speeds if the rough surface of the ball was bowled facing forward (Figure 5.17 on the right). The effect of the roughened side is to produce turbulent flow more easily at the front of the ball. Furthermore, the rougher the surface, the more marked this effect. As a result, the boundary layer separates further to the back of the ball, thereby causing low pressure on the right side of the ball – conditions that favour inswing, i.e., reverse swing.

Bown and Mehta (1993) conclude that the key to conventional swing is to have one side as smooth as possible, whereas the key to reverse swing is to have one side as rough as possible. A ball with one very smooth and one very rough side provides the bowler with the possibility of producing either out- or inswing with the same action.

IN THE END, THE MYSTERY REMAINS

In the final analysis, all these theories and hypotheses are exactly that: to our knowledge, no-one has yet shown conclusively (using a swinging delivery produced by a swing bowler in a real match) that the factors discussed above provide exclusive explanations for why the ball does or doesn't swing. The explanations given here are based on solid principles of physics, but because it is not yet possible to measure all these variables on a swinging delivery out of doors, the real contribution to the generation of swing of each of the listed theoretical factors remains largely unproven.

SLOW BOWLING

Slow bowling is one of the art forms of cricket. Watching a good spinner, with his leisured and graceful approach and delivery, performing his repertoire of tricks and traps, is to remember that cricket is not just about brute force and pace.

By the 1980s, the art of slow bowling had been all but lost, after two decades of absolute domination by pace attacks. Even those who kept the flame of spin dimly burning – such as India's Bishen Bedi, Pakistan's Abdul Qadir and England's Derek Underwood – were often eclipsed by the murderous quick men; three or four intricately conjured wickets, gained with patience and guile, would be overshadowed instantly by one fiery short ball taking the glove and looping to gully. The consensus seemed to be that spin was in dire straits, perhaps even dying out.

The prospects looked even grimmer with the advent of one-day cricket. Defensive bowling against batsmen who were putting a lower price on their wickets – and therefore far more willing to attack – made all but the best spinners a liability. The final nail in the coffin was hammered in by groundsmen, now equipped with more sophisticated irrigation systems and under pressure to prepare impressively green pitches for television consumption. The damp uneven pitches known to spinning maestros of yesteryear such as Bill 'Tiger' O'Riley, Clarrie Grimmett, Jim Laker, Richie Benaud and Lance Gibbs were a thing of the past.

By 1990, spinners had become luxury selections, a safe option if the four pace men were likely to find the going a little heavy, but certainly not likely to roll a side over with five or more wickets. Some fine finger-spinners did their best to prove the critics wrong, with the likes of Tim May (Australia), Phil Tufnell (England) and Roger Harper (West Indies) regularly chipping in or mopping up tail-enders; but they seldom got the fields they wanted, and if they failed to take wickets, they (or their selection) would come under fire by their media.

In the general climate of gloom and under-achievement in the world of slow bowling, few eyebrows were raised when a young Australian leg-spinner had a nightmare debut at Sydney in 1992 – Ravi Shastri along with the rest of the Indian team left him with the singularly unimpressive figures of 1 for 150. But his captain, Allan Border, along with Australia's selectors, saw something India's batsmen hadn't. One year later Mike Gatting and the cricketing world watched dumbstruck as a viciously spun leg-break drifted outside the Englishman's leg-stump, pitched, and ripped past the outside edge of the bat to hit off-stump. Shane Warne had arrived: brash, iconoclastic, larger and louder than life. Almost overnight, spin (and specifically wrist-spin) became not only fashionable, but glamorous. Young cricketers began dreaming of being the next Shane Warne rather than the next Curtly Ambrose or Allan Donald.

But any renaissance relies on the simultaneous convergence of talents and circumstances, and Warne's emergence coincided with the arrival on the international stage of three exceptional spinners from Asia: India's Anil Kumble, Pakistan's Mushtaq Ahmed, and Sri Lanka's Muttiah Muralitharan (who, although an off-spinner, gets as much turn as a wrist-spinner). By the mid-1990s, the idea of the slow bowler as strike bowler had gained widespread acceptance, and a kind of cricketing arms race had developed around wrist-spin, as each Test-playing country searched desperately for its own match-winning leg-spinner.

Some countries found temporary solutions to the perceived 'leg-spin gap'. South Africa unearthed teenager Paul Adams, while Zimbabwe had some success with Paul Strang, but others were less lucky. England's brief flirtation with Chris Schofield ended in acrimony and failure – not surprisingly, given the lack of development of spinners and the green, lush pitches in that country – while the West Indies' attempts to develop Dinanath Ramnarine and Rawl Lewis sadly came to nothing.

Today spin is surprisingly healthy, given the prevalence of one-day cricket and spin-unfriendly pitches, but its survival should not be taken for granted. Producing match-winning slow bowlers is not a question of money: England and South Africa, two relatively well-resourced cricketing countries, have shown themselves to be incapable of consistently producing even moderately good spinners, let alone strike bowlers; while Sri Lanka, one of the poorest Test-playing countries, has produced not only the phenomenal Muralitharan, but also the extremely capable Upul Chandana. Similarly, Zimbabwe managed to produce Ray Price, a useful finger-spinner, even in the midst of that country's political and economic implosion.

Financial infrastructure, therefore, would seem to have little effect on the emergence of good slow bowlers. Instead, what they need is a supportive school and club system (one in which coaches and captains do not panic when they see their spinners getting hit out of the attack, and in which fielders have the skills to hang onto chances at short leg or in the deep); a fair number of pitches that offer them more than the slick grassy surfaces in vogue throughout the Anglophone cricketing world; and a public appreciation of their craft. Thanks to Warne and Muralitharan, this final requirement is spreading rapidly, but the first two can easily be neglected, fatally undermining one of the game's loveliest arts.

By the mid-1990s, the idea of the slow bowler as strike bowler had gained widespread acceptance, and a kind of cricketing arms race had developed around wrist-spin, as each Test-playing country searched desperately for its own match-winning leg-spinner.

RICHIE BENAUD ON THE ATTRIBUTES OF THE SUCCESSFUL SLOW BOWLER

Not many people can claim to have reached the top of their field in two long careers, but when Richie Benaud retired from broadcasting in 2005, he signed off on a working life in which he rose to eminence as the finest wrist-spinner of his era, became Australia's leading all-rounder of the 1960s (as well a fine and insightful captain), and then went on to entrench himself as the doyen of cricket commentators.

For Benaud, there are five key elements that a bowler must make part of his life and his game if he is to be a successful spinner. These five pointers are taken from the Appendix to Benaud's *Anything but ... An Autobiography*:

1. Patience: Bowling is a tough game and you will need to work on a batsman with your stock ball, sometimes for several overs, before putting a plan into action....

If you take a wicket on average every ten overs in Test cricket, you will have a better strike rate than O'Reilly, Grimmett and Benaud. If you take a wicket on an average every eight overs, you will have the best strike-rate of any modern-day Test bowler, fast or slow.

2. Concentration: Anything less than a hundred per cent concentration running in to bowl is unpardonable. The spot on the pitch where you want the ball to land should be the most important thing in your mind from the moment you turn at your bowling mark.

If someone offered you $20 000 to throw a ball and hit an object nineteen yards away... would you, as you were throwing, look at someone standing close by, or at some other object?

3. Economy: This is a war between you and the batsmen.

Is there some very good reason you want to allow them more than two runs per over?

4. Attitude: Calm, purposeful aggression and a clear mind are needed, plus a steely resolve that no batsman will ever get the better of you over a long period of time....

In other walks of life you want to be mentally strong and on top of the opposition. Is there some particular reason why this should not be the case with your battle with the batsmen?

5. Practice: All practice should be undertaken with a purpose.

You think hard before doing most other things, why should you allow cricket practice to be dull and boring? (1998, p. 284).

THE BASIC PRINCIPLES OF SPIN

The fundamental strategies and techniques of spinning the cricket ball mirror almost exactly those of fast and medium-pace bowling. Everything we have discussed about line, length, bowling with rhythm, picking a target (whether on the pitch or the top of off-stump) and the need for patience, apply as much to spin bowling as they do to seam.

However, there is a profound difference between the two schools of bowling. The fast bowler needs speed through the air, but it is as important – if not more so – that he masters control of lines and lengths, changes of pace, and learns to move the ball off the seam or through the air.

The spinner needs strategic attributes too, but above all else, he must be able to do one thing: spin the ball. Turn – masses of it – must be his aim above all else. He must want to 'turn it square' – make it kick to the leg- or off side at 90° – and he must dream of bowling batsmen around their legs or of getting the ball to skip into middle-stump from two feet outside off-stump, before he even begins to experiment with flight, drift and quicker, flatter deliveries.

So the whole object of the grip and action of the slow bowler is no longer to deliver the ball with the full force of the bowler behind it, but rather to propel it down the wicket in such as way that it rotates rapidly through the air. Whether it rotates clockwise, anti-clockwise, end over end, or around its horizontal axis, and how fast it spins in any of those directions, depends on how it is released and on which kind of bowler has let it go. Sometimes this is done by spinning the ball with fingers, sometimes with a swift rotation of the wrist; the body is always swivelled with the front foot used as a pivot; but whichever method is used, the ultimate goal is 'fizz', that vicious kicking spin that can be heard as the ball hisses through the air just before pitching.

Revolutions are king, but the thoroughbred match-winner needs more, and without a doubt the most crucial among the slow bowler's secondary array of weapons is accuracy. No matter how far he can turn the ball, or how many variations he has, if he is not accurate, he will not be much use. Landing one ripping, fizzing delivery on the perfect spot before sending down five long-hops and full-tosses is a recipe for disaster. Indeed, the career of South Africa's Paul Adams was truncated largely because of his penchant for delivering one 'four-ball' per over, whether an over-pitched googly or a Chinaman dragged down short. Again, Warne and Muralitharan are the ideal models: both have the ability to land a ball on the same spot over after over, or slowly change their line while keeping a single length, working a batsman across his stumps.

The third attribute of world-class slow bowlers is absolute control over the pace of the ball. Batsmen are opportunists, and even those out of their depth against most bowling will quickly recognize that a spinner is bowling at one pace, and will have plenty of time to come down the wicket or play back to predictably looping balls. The slow bowler must be able to alter his pace in tiny, almost unnoticeable increments, either by slowing down and adding more flight, or by speeding up and spearing the ball in flatter.

THE BOTTOM LINE: SPIN OR ACCURACY?

We don't want to give young bowlers an excuse not to work on their control and accuracy, but in the final analysis spin will always be more important than accuracy. The bowler who spins it a long way will always take wickets, because batsmen will still get out to your long hops. But if you bowl inaccurately and don't spin the ball either, you'll get smashed. Master both, and you have the potential to have a profound effect on the game.

Finally, the good slow bowler must recognize that skill and success do not come overnight: while pace bowlers are born, the spinner is a self-made man. He matures later in his career than almost any other cricketer, and that maturity depends largely on how solid his confidence is. An early setback – or, worse, a series of early setbacks – often sees young spinners give up entirely, turning instead to seam bowling or batting. All too often spinners are used as change bowlers, or stuck on for an over before tea. Alternatively, they get a hiding in their first match, and are promptly whipped off by their captain or coach, getting the message loud and clear that they cannot be trusted to explore their new craft. (Imagine if Allan Border had done this to Shane Warne after the latter's fiasco against India in 1992.) If you enjoy spinning, stick to it: with plenty of hard work, and a little luck (a misjudged sweep, a well-held catch in the deep), you will develop the confidence and the skills you need to be successful.

The ideal attributes of a spinner are therefore:
- **prodigious spin**
- **accuracy**
- **the ability to change pace subtly**
- **a willingness to practise and persevere.**

THE ART OF DECEIT

It is not a bad rule, though subject to variations, that you can bowl a batsman out in the first three overs... and after that, you have to trap him.

Learie Constantine, *Cricket and I*, 1933

Fast bowlers force batsmen into errors by beating their reflexes or by unnerving them with the threat of physical injury; seam and swing bowlers beat their man by getting him to commit to a certain line, and then moving the ball off that line too late for the batsman to adjust. But without pace, either of the dangerous or the reflex-beating variety, the bowler is completely vulnerable to the batsman's reactions. Batsmen have to wait for the spinning ball to arrive at the best of times: bowl even slower, giving batsmen even longer to plan their shot, and the result is usually wrecked bowling figures and an early posting to the outfield.

The spinner, therefore, must rely almost entirely on deceit, on persuading the batsman to play the wrong line or length, or to play too early, or not early enough. As a result, spinners have developed their skills and strategies to deceive batsmen about three aspects of the delivery:

- **The exact place on which the ball will land:** Slow bowlers strive to land the ball fractionally further from the batsman playing forward than he expected, or closer to the batsman playing back. Alternatively, they look to deceive the batsman about the line on which the ball will eventually pitch, either by getting the ball to drift (see the discussion of the Magnus effect on pp. 301–7) or by subtly changing their point of delivery on the bowling crease.

- **The exact time at which the ball will arrive:** As we discussed in the chapter on vision, the human brain cannot accurately calculate the exact trajectory of a delivery that spends a part of its flight coming directly towards the eyes, or that travels above the horizontal plane of the eyes. Hence flight and subtle changes of pace go a long way in bamboozling batsmen.

- **What the ball will do after it pitches:** This final point is the Pandora's Box all spinners love opening, and which makes spin such an absorbing spectacle. Whether the ball will bounce viciously at the gloves like a fast Anil Kumble leg-break (or shoot up at the splice like an even faster Shahid Afridi leg-break!), or squat and go straight like Warne's infamous flipper of the early 1990s, depends on the skills the bowler has developed, the strength of his fingers, the integrity of his action, and the keenness of his mind, allowing him to adapt his technique to the pitch conditions.

And it is those skills that we will now explore. Hopefully, they will point you in a direction that will allow you to open your own Pandora's Box, letting the contents loose on a generation of groping, leaden-footed batsmen.

Flight

> *The truth is that no great batsman is likely to be bothered by break, save on unplayable pitches, if he is in no trouble while the ball is coming through the air. [Wilfred] Rhodes gets his men out before the ball pitches; spin with him is an accessory after the act of flight – flight which disguises the ball's length, draws the batsman forward when he ought to play back, sends him playing back when he ought to come forward, and generally keeps him in a state of mind so confused that in time he begins to feel it might be a mercy to get out. Against Rhodes, no long innings has ever been played that did not at the end find the batsman intellectually a little worn and weary.*
>
> Neville Cardus, *A Summer Game*, 1929

The ability to develop and master flight, or 'loop', as it is often called, is an added bonus to any spinner. Anyone who has ever seen a tennis ball dip suddenly towards the ground after a fierce top-spin forehand will understand the phenomenon: loop is created by imparting fierce spin, usually something akin to top-spin (rather than just by rolling the ball out), allied to a quick bowling-arm action and a slow front-arm action.

Of course there are as many varieties of loop as there are gifted slow bowlers. Top-spin will cause a ball to hang in the air before dropping more steeply (and therefore bouncing higher) than the batsman expects; back-spin hurries the ball through lower and fuller, and also keeps low after pitching, thus 'skidding' on to the batsman; while side-spin creates 'drift' in the flight of the ball before it pitches, sending it drifting laterally across the pitch, either into or away from the batsman. This last variation of loop can be particularly devastating if the drift happens in the opposite direction to that in which the ball spins, for instance, the leg-break that drifts off the straight into the pads of the right-hander and then spins across him towards his off-stump.

FLIGHT SCHOOL
Coaches and young bowlers, whether finger-spinners or wrist-spinners, might want to experiment with Ashley Mallet's low-tech method of practising flighted spin: a length of string hung across the net at a particular height, with the bowler then trying to get the ball to 'drop' over the string.

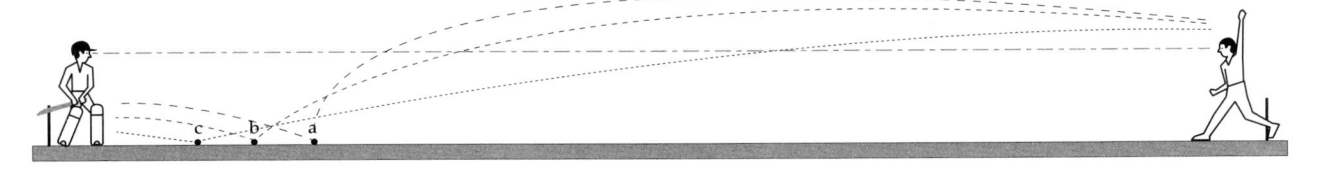

a: Underspin
b: Side-spin
c: Overspin

FIGURE 5.18: *Trajectories and directions that spin bowling can take. Note that all deliveries start above the batter's eyeline. The skill – especially with overspin and side-spin deliveries – is to keep the ball above the eyeline for as long as possible.*

THE DELIVERIES

Spinners are classified according to how the ball leaves the hand, which hand they use, whether they use their wrists or fingers to impart spin on the ball, and in which direction the ball turns. These are discussed in considerably more detail shortly, but a brief 'family tree' may be useful in order to fully understand the different breeds of spinners, and their various skills.

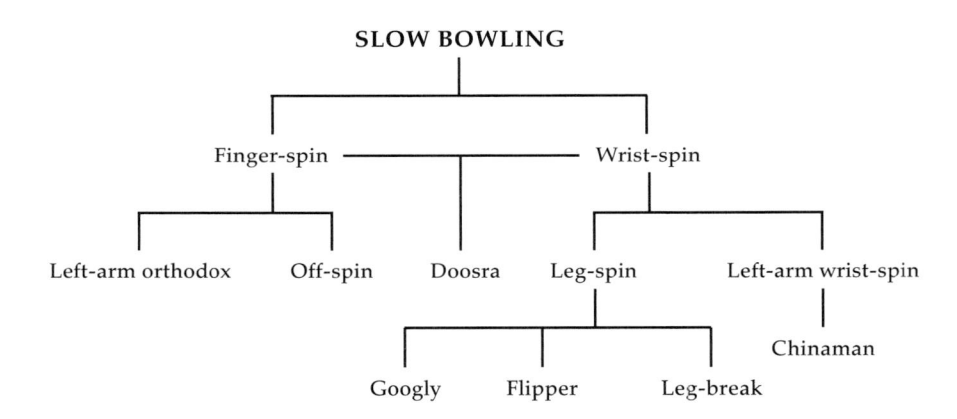

FIGURE 5.19: *The spinner's family tree*

What these various skills entail is dependent on which 'subspecies' the spinner belongs to, or rather on which side of the family tree he find himself (see Figure 5.19 on the facing page).

But most crucial to all spinners are spin and accuracy, and, as explained in the general introduction to this chapter, all control (whether it involves the line and length of seam bowling or the sharp lateral movement of spin) comes from a sound grip, a good release, and above all, a good action.

Thus it is vital to familiarize yourself with the grips and bowling actions of the two main 'subspecies' – wrist-spin and finger-spin – before we progress to a more general discussion of slow bowling.

For the sake of clarity we have separated these two types of bowler, but always remember that the principles of spin – turn, control, patience and cunning – apply to all slow bowlers, regardless of their specialty.

FINGER-SPIN

Somewhat less demanding than wrist-spin, finger-spin represents the natural first step for young bowlers looking to get the ball to deviate. Spin is imparted by a hard flick of the wrist and a quick tweaking of the fingers, as if the bowler were turning a doorknob violently or screwing off the top of a jar; while accuracy comes from a classical side-on action, the arm coming over more or less as it would with a seamer bowling a cutter or slower ball.

> ## WRIST, THEN FINGERS
> Although we carefully distinguish between finger-spin and wrist-spin, it should be noted that these are not strictly accurate descriptions. Both varieties of bowling use both fingers and wrist: the difference lies in which is used first. Finger-spin starts in the wrist and ends in the fingertips, while wrist-spin starts in the fingers and ends in the wrist.

The grip

The best way to illustrate the grip for the orthodox finger-spinner (whether right-arm off-spin or left-arm orthodox) is to demonstrate how to insert the ball into your fingers.

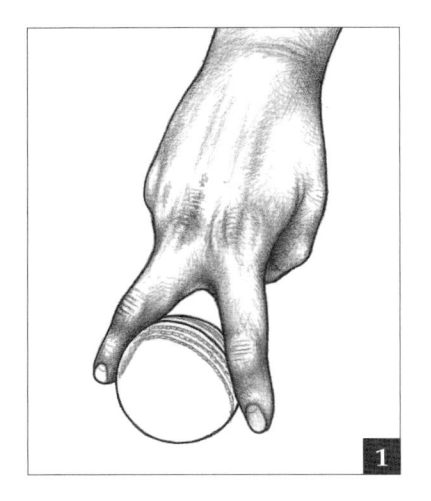

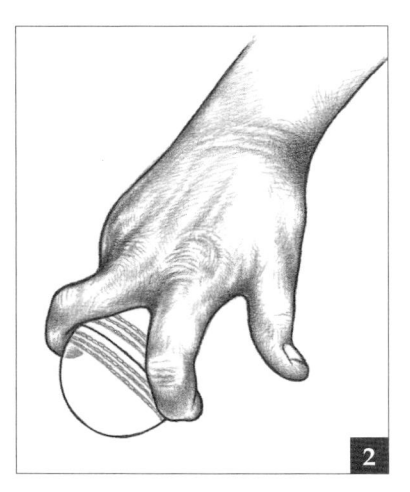

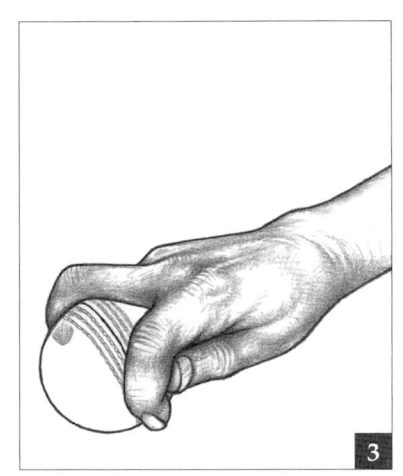

Spread the first and second fingers onto the seam of the ball, ensuring that the main pressure is exerted on the first finger (1). Now fold the hands down behind the ball, bending the fingers (2 and 3).

A useful variation on the orthodox finger-spun delivery is the 'floater', which is intended to beat the other edge of the bat.

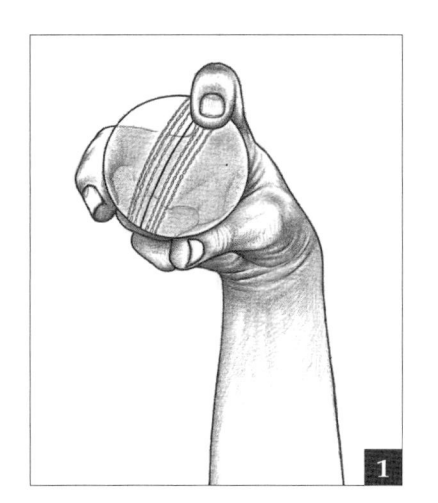

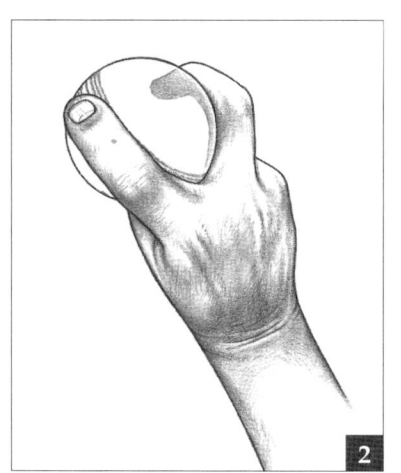

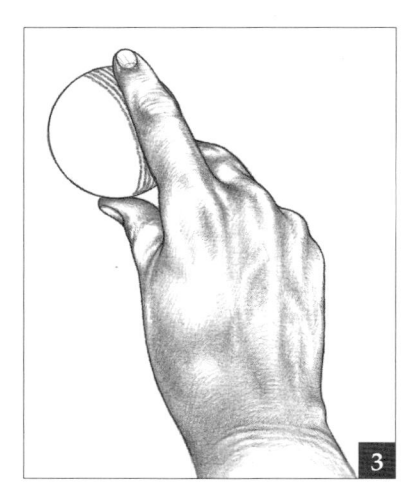

294 CRICKET TECHNIQUES

> If you're playing between showers of rain or on a soggy outfield, and the ball has become wet and slippery, it can be extremely difficult to bowl off-spin as the ball tends to slip out of your fingers like a bar of soap. The solution is to narrow your grip slightly by drawing the fingers a little closer together. Now instead of spinning the ball with your fingers, use only the wrist.

Use the standard spread-fingers grip to deceive the batsman, but instead hold the ball so that the forefinger runs down the seam. The thumb adapts a sidewise position (as for an outswinger – see p. 257). As the ball is delivered, it comes off the ends of the fingers and floats away from the batsman, who may be expecting turn. This opens up the opportunity to get him caught behind or at slip, or even stumped if he walks past the ball. The left-arm orthodox spinner who is turning the ball away from the bat might use the floater to trap the batsman who is playing for turn LBW.

The action

If you were asked to put a marble or ball-bearing on a smooth table and to impart as much spin on it as you could, so that it would whirl around its vertical axis like a top for as long as possible, what would you do? The resulting actions on the little ball would by anything but gentle – no light flicking of the fingers over the edges of the sphere. On the contrary, you would grip it fairly hard, almost pinching it between forefinger and thumb, and then flick it out off the end of your thumb, for an instant pushing down on the sphere and the table as your fingers and hand lifted off and allowed it to spin.

The forces at work in this little exercise are emphatically not gentle. When you grip the sphere prior to spinning it, your fingers are squeezing in from opposite sides, both pushing it down into the table, and at the moment of release, it is pushed either against your thumb or forefinger, depending on how you chose to spin it.

All of which illustrates that spin is about resistance. The cricket ball is not a ball-bearing spinning unhindered in a cushion of oil, or even a wheel spinning on its horizontal axis around an axle. To impart 'rip' on the ball in cricket, you need to grip it, pinch it, squeeze it and tear at it. And that's just your fingers….

During your run-up or early in your action, cock your wrist in towards your body (1). As you release the ball, visualize opening a doorknob in the direction of the spin, and flick out your first finger, imparting downwards 'rip' on the ball (2 and 3).

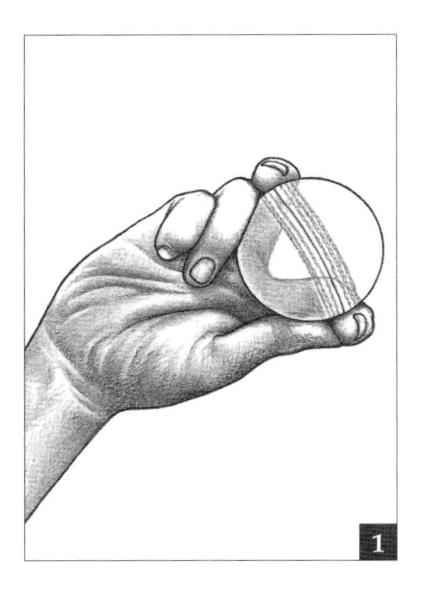

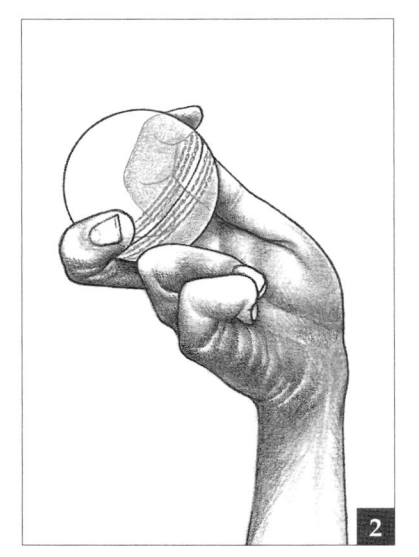

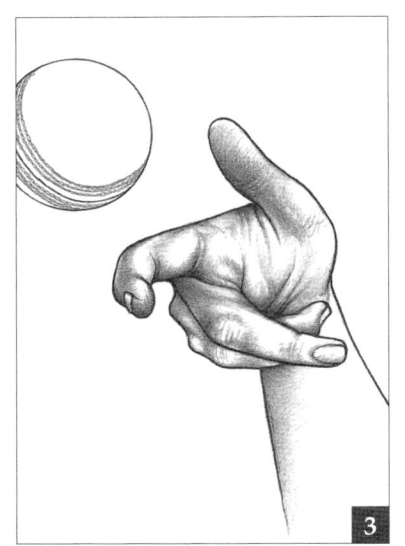

But the spin-generating friction or resistance of your finger dragging down the side of the ball is only half of the picture. When a whip cracks, it is the very tip of the whip that has flicked back on itself to create the sound we hear, but that speed and momentum had to be generated by a flick of the entire whip. In fact, without the fairly slow, leisurely movement in the first few feet of the whip, the 'business end' of the whip would go nowhere at all.

The same applies to finger-spin. If you stood side-on to a batsman with your feet rooted in place and your upper body immobile, and gave the ball the biggest rip you could muster with both fingers and wrist, you would see almost no deviation off the pitch. It might move away off the straight fractionally, but certainly there would be no bounce or 'fizz' off the wicket. Most tellingly, it would bounce slowly and predictably, allowing the batsman to pick his spot.

The reason for this is that spinners, and especially finger-spinners, gain a great deal of momentum and spin from the final pivot of their bodies around their front

All finger-spinners should work as hard as they can at strengthening their fingers, particularly their first and second fingers. This can be done in various ways, but the easiest and often most effective is either to click or snap the fingers very hard, or to screw the ball into the bowling hand with as much resistance as you can muster, as if polishing an apple, spreading the fingers and twisting the wrist around after the fingers.

foot. This has already been discussed in the section on the bowler's run-up, but it is worth repeating: the slow bowler's front foot must land and grip, providing traction around which his body can pivot.

If spinners take one piece of advice from this book, other than that they should aspire to putting revs on the ball, it is this: bowl the ball against your front foot, not around or over it.

Bowling as you land – letting the ball go while still on tiptoe – will produce almost no spin.

Likewise, we have already described the problem seen in many left-arm finger-spinners (left-arm orthodox): positioning their front foot incorrectly and then having to bowl around it, thereby ruining their angle of attack.

The off-break or slow left-arm orthodox action is fluid and rhythmical, but the young bowler should not confuse its fluidity or rhythm with the action of the fast bowler. The fast bowler's run-up and delivery can be broken down into unique actions, but they flow together to form an almost uninterrupted whole. The mistake young spinners can make is to emulate this smooth action, with the result that they bowl as they land.

Instead they need to understand that the pivot – that vital gripping and grinding of the spikes into the bowling crease – is what produces spin, and that it essentially acts as an interruption of the bowling action.

In other words, the finger-spinner's action might be broken down in the following way – identical to the standard seam delivery, except for that one crucial interruption:

Bowl the ball against your front foot, not around or over it.

Run-up; **Gather;** **Set-up;** **Unfold;** **PIVOT;** **Delivery;** **Follow-through.**

© QUINTIC

The panel above illustrates the classic off-spinner's action:
- a pronounced sideways turn in the gather, so that the shoulders and chest are perpendicular to the bowling crease
- superb external rotation of the shoulder
- a high arm, just off '12 o'clock'
- the right knee kicking through with the rotation of the trunk, wrenching the front foot round into its pivot to create spin
- a complete follow-through.

BOWLING   297

VERTICAL DISCUS VERSUS JAVELIN

Just as young fast bowlers are usually urged to learn the 'classic' side-on action, so finger-spinners, whether right- or left-handed, have also traditionally been encouraged to look over their leading shoulder at the target. For over a century, off-spinners have wheeled in, side-on and tall, reaching for the sky with their leading arm before cartwheeling over with high actions and exaggerated pivots on their front foot, as demonstrated in the photographs below.

This shows the orthodox action, with the head dropping away slightly as the shoulder and rigid arm wheel past, a movement reminiscent of a discus thrower, albeit one tilted over towards the vertical.

And then came Muralitharan....

As illustrated above, the Sri Lankan bowls almost entirely chest-on to the batsman, with the result that instead of delivering with the 'vertical discus' action, he almost spears the ball in from above his shoulder, like a javelin thrower. The debate surrounding his highly unorthodox action is discussed in more detail in the section on throwing in this chapter, but we believe that Muralitharan is the first of many bowlers who will use this front-on method of delivery, their ultra-flexible wrists (and elbows) extracting much greater turn and accuracy than the traditional action.

HIGH ARM VERSUS ROUND ARM

We have emphasized that spin is generated by the body swivelling against the front foot (first against the traction provided by the spikes under the ball of the foot, then against the foot as a whole, pressing down heel and toe into the pitch).

But of course it is not your front foot that makes the ball spin, nor even the strong rotation of your shoulders: many fast bowlers have a particularly quick and strong pivot, and they don't spin the ball through the air. Instead it is your arm, combining with the 'whip-crack' of the wrist and hands, which imparts turn.

So why is the body pivot important at all? The answer is a matter of simple biomechanics: the off-spinner flicks his fingers down the side of the ball as he squeezes it out of his hand, but this action would be fairly ineffective without a full downward sweep of the bowling arm, cutting across his body as he follows through.

It makes sense, therefore, that the angle of the arm would have to be that best suited to slicing down the side of the ball and cutting across the body. You don't need to be a spin bowler of any experience to feel that this angle is one just offset from the vertical. Try to slice down next to or under the ball held at '12 o'clock', and you'll drag it straight down, or have to rotate your wrist under it at some point. This is why seamers try to keep their arm vertical, since it is much easier to impart power and pace into a ball by bringing the hand down onto it from directly above.

In other words, the spinner needs to vary the position of his arm from between '10 o'clock' and 'high noon' to change the amount spin he puts on the ball.

Interestingly, almost all the great finger-spinners have had reasonably 'low' arms, coming through at around '11 o'clock'. In addition to an almost round-arm action, these bowlers also kept a slight kink in their elbows: instead of locking the elbow as a fast bowler would, they maintained a slight angle, bowling with a fractionally bent arm that allowed them get beside and under the ball more easily. This also allowed the shoulder muscles to become more involved in imparting spin and force on the ball.

A lower arm action gives you two levers instead of one: first the shoulder, then the wrist.

Remember, there is nothing in the Laws of cricket that says you may not bowl with a bent arm: it is straightening the arm during the delivery that is illegal. Paul Adams (although not a finger-spinner) kept his bowling arm flexed at almost 20° throughout its arc.

The 'classic' action of Saqlain Mushtaq on p. 297 illustrates a standard high action, one that should be encouraged in young bowlers; but even here the arm is coming through at about 'half past eleven'. More experienced bowlers, trying to extract more spin (perhaps bowling in favourable conditions or with a good lead), tend to drop the arm, as illustrated here by the great English finger-spinner Jim Laker.

© QUINTIC

Many modern coaches insist on the more upright 'classic' action, but Laker was able to get prodigious turn, as well as flight and accuracy, from a flatter action. Another considerable benefit of a lower arm position is that it enables you to bowl the under-cutter, a favourite of Laker and Ray Illingworth. It is delivered with an even lower arm than illustrated here, which makes the ball drift away towards the off side.

To sum up, while elements of the finger-spinner's action are sacrosanct, there is room for experimentation with both the position of the body at delivery (side-on or front-on), and the angle of the arm. Try and find what feels most comfortable and is effective for you.

THE AERODYNAMICS OF SPIN AND THE MAGNUS EFFECT

Although warfare in the late-eighteenth and early-nineteenth centuries was bloodier than anything the world had known until then, with massive amounts of firepower discharged over short distances at densely packed armies of men, a remarkably small number of musket-balls and bullets fired actually hit their targets.

Indeed, in his book *Acts of War* (2003), military historian Richard Holmes describes a kind of combat in which kills seemed almost miraculous:

> *The Comte de Guibert, in this respect the most optimistic of the theorists of the horse and musket age, thought that one million rounds of musketry produced 2 000 casualties: one hit, that is, for every 500 rounds... Major-General B.P. Hughes, a modern authority, argues: 'It is impossible to accept that more than about 5% of the bullets that could have been fired were effective, and the rate often seems to have been appreciably lower'* (2003, p. 167).

There were various reasons for this extremely low kill rate: many soldiers threw thrift and discipline to the wind, blindly discharging their muskets in the general direction of the foe, regardless of range. Most were dealing with unpredictable and temperamental weapons. But it was also a simple matter of physics: most shots fired with good aim and within range simply drifted off their intended line, swinging away to the left or right of the target, or swooping up over his head.

It was a phenomenon that troubled generals and their political masters, locked as they were in an expensive arms race in a European continent beset by violent squabbles between nations, each kingdom or empire working frantically to get a technological edge over its enemies.

Not surprisingly, most army leaders had turned not only to engineers, but to scientists and physicists, and a German professor called Heinrich Magnus was duly commissioned by the Prussian Army to study the trajectory of artillery shells. The phenomenon he saw – rotating artillery shells deflecting in the direction opposite to that of their spin – was nothing new to most gunners or marksmen of the eighteenth and early-nineteenth centuries, but it was the German who explained the phenomenon, publishing his findings in 1852, and (unfortunately) accelerating the development of the rifle-barrels of modern firearms.

What frustrated nineteenth-century generals is an entirely familiar sight to modern sports fans. Whether it's Shane Warne's leg-break, a top-spin shot by Roger Federer, a free kick by David Beckham, or Johnny Wilkinson's touch-finder, the Magnus effect features in almost every ball sport, sending balls of all shapes and sizes deflecting in the direction opposite to that of their spin, whether around a vertical, horizontal or diagonal axis. (Of course, amateur golfers might call it something less scientific and more explicit when it sends their sliced drives swinging away into the long grass!)

More than a century after Magnus's first observations, scientist Lyman Briggs (1959) used the Magnus effect to explain why a rapidly spinning (seamed) baseball or a smooth ball without seams both curve in their flight (although the direction of the curve may be different for seamed and seamless balls).

The explanation for the Magnus effect involves the simple principle discussed earlier; air travelling more rapidly over one side of a sphere will produce an area of low pressure on that side. This area of low pressure will then cause the ball to deviate in its direction.

Figure 5.20 shows the air flow patterns around a delivery moving towards the top of the page; the delivery is spinning counter-clockwise in the vertical axis. This delivery is almost impossible to bowl (Clarrie Grimmett may have managed this with his round-arm action, and Warne did so every so often when aiming for a flipper), except for a right-arm wrist-spinner with a very low action, in which he releases the ball from the right side of his hand with his palm horizontal and pointing towards the ground. A left-arm wrist-spinner might also be able to bowl this ball by releasing it slightly later than he would his googly, i.e., with his palm facing up. However, it most clearly illustrates the principles involved here.

FIGURE 5.20: *The aerodynamics of the Magnus effect*

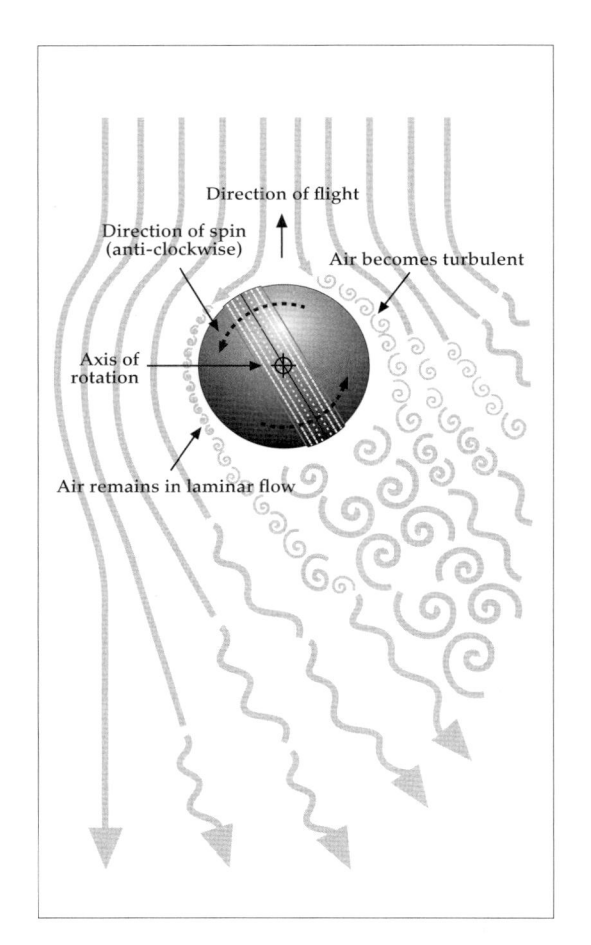

If the contortions and reversed hand positions of leg-spin bowling are confusing, try picturing instead a David Beckham free kick, in which his foot strikes the ball with his right foot on its right side. The spin on the ball is therefore counter-clockwise around its vertical axis, which will cause the ball to swerve to the left late in its flight.

The Magnus effect occurs because the edge of the ball that is turning into the oncoming wind 'trips' the boundary layer, producing turbulent flow in the boundary layer on that side of the ball, the right side in Figure 5.20 (Mehta, 1985). In contrast, laminar flow of high speed occurs on the surface spinning in the same direction as the air travelling over that surface, the left side of Figure 5.20. In contrast to what occurs in the case in the swinging delivery (see Figure 5.16 in the section on the physics of swing), the laminar flow separates from the surface of the ball later than the turbulent flow on the right-hand side of the delivery does. This is because the turbulence is generated by the vigorous spinning of the ball into the face of the on-rushing air (whereas the turbulent flow produced by the seam in the swinging delivery shown in Figure 5.16 occurs across a surface that is spinning backwards, i.e., in the direction of travel – not at 90° to that direction).

As a result, a horizontal force develops towards the left, which pushes the ball laterally through the air in what we would see as 'drift'. Interestingly, the nature of the ball's surface influences the magnitude of the Magnus effect, which is much greater in a fluffy new tennis ball than in a smooth ball – like a cricket ball. This is because the fluffy surface of the tennis ball produces a greater disturbance of flow on the side advancing into the on-rushing air, producing an earlier separation point and hence a greater pressure difference across the ball.

Figure 5.21 shows what is effectively the top-spinner (or a fairly straight doosra) bowled by a leg-spinner or off-spinner: the axis of the spin in Figure 5.20 opposite has been rotated 90° to the left so that the ball is spinning forwards in the horizontal plane directly towards the batsman, who would be on the left side of the page. The delivery is being viewed from the side – i.e., from the off side (mid-off or cover) – of a ball moving towards the left of the page. In this case, the direction of drift is directly downwards, resulting in the delivery 'dipping' or 'dropping' on the batsman, pitching shorter than he would have expected. This delivery will also bounce more steeply.

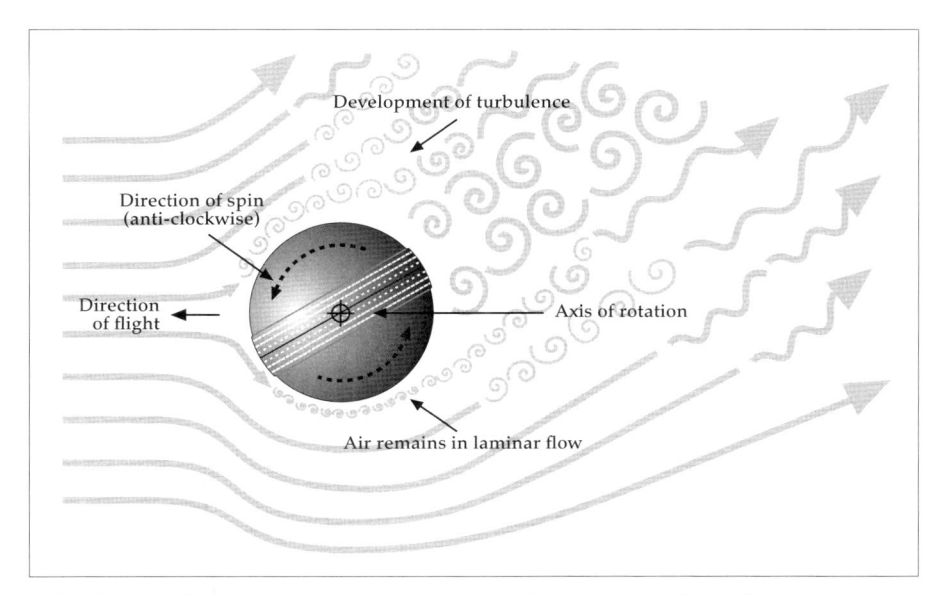

FIGURE 5.21: *The aerodynamics of the top-spinner – which is about to dip steeply*

And if the axis of ball spin is rotated a further 90° to the left, so that the axis of spin runs horizontally through the ball pointing towards the batsman, no drift will occur, as the axis of spin is now in the same plane as the direction of travel – so the effects of the rotation are the same on both sides of the ball (see Figure 5.22). Depending on the direction in which the ball is spinning, the delivery would be either a maximal spinning leg- or off-spin delivery that will turn maximally, but will not drift.

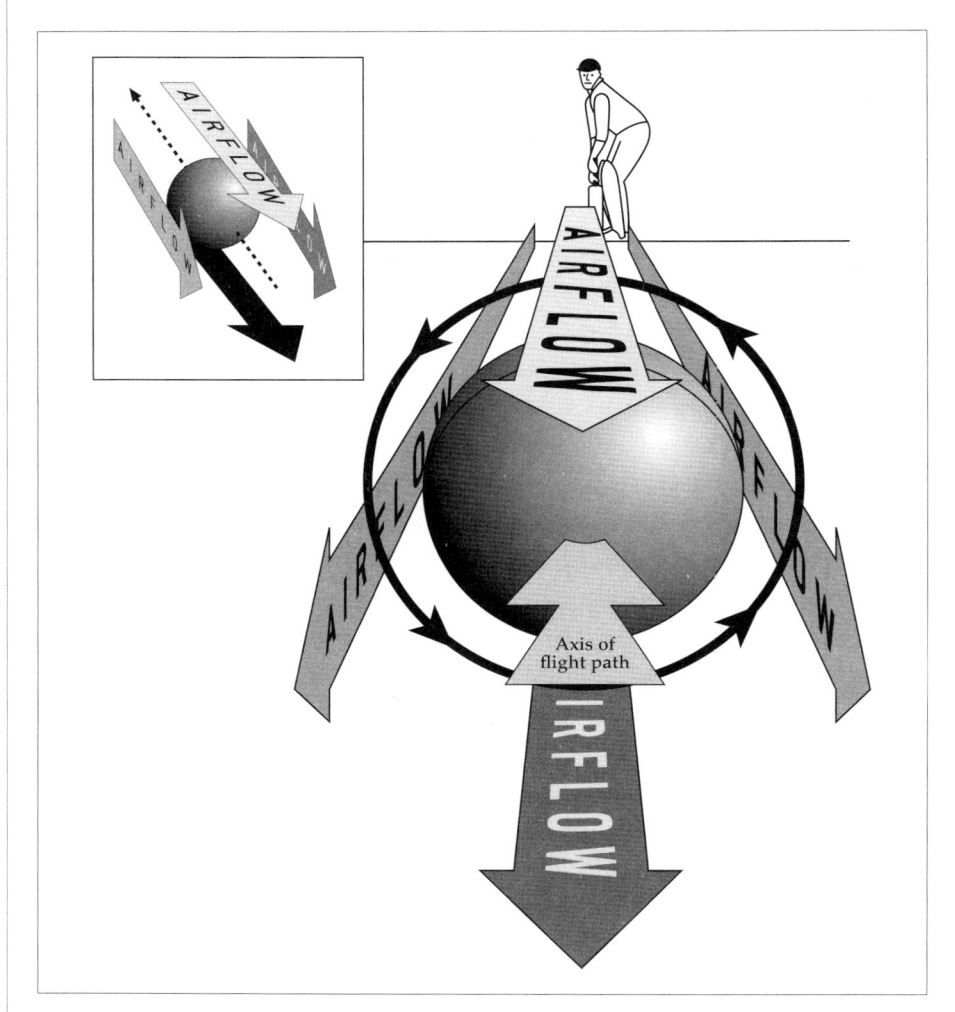

FIGURE 5.22: *Leg- or off-spin delivery in which no drift will occur, as the axis of spin is now in the same plane as the direction of travel*

However, if the axis of spin is angled slightly to the angle of travel, then the Magnus effect occurs and becomes maximal when the angle of spin is at 90° to the direction in which the ball is travelling.

THE MAGNUS EFFECT AND 'THE BALL OF THE CENTURY'

Probably the most famous ball ever sent down in Test cricket was Shane Warne's first delivery in an Ashes Test match. Also referred to as the 'Ball From Hell', the 'Gatting Ball', or simply 'That Ball', it was delivered shortly after 3pm on 4 June 1993 at Old Trafford cricket ground. England looked well set, and the experienced Mike Gatting anticipated no problems facing a green young spinner.

The leg-break Warne bowled to Gatting drifted towards leg, dipping late in its trajectory. The batsman's sensible response was to plant his leg, bat alongside, towards the pitch of the ball – which proved to be the wrong line. The ball pitched outside the leg stump, before spinning back fiercely past the edge of the bat to clip the top of the off-stump. The expression on Gatting's face when he realized his bails had been scattered is one of the classic images of modern cricket. (A similar delivery bowled to South African Herschelle Gibbs in the famous tied 1999 World Cup semi-final was possibly the single most important factor in determining that Australia advanced to the final in that case – last-minute run-outs notwithstanding!)

What happened from an aerodynamic point of view? Generally, a ball moving away from us in the horizontal plane, and spinning from right to left (anti-clockwise) moves to the left (equivalent to the off side in cricket) and not to the right (leg side). This can be seen when a right-sided kicker in football takes a penalty and strikes the ball on its right side (as in Figure 5.20). The ball always curves to the left. But in this case, Shane Warne spun the ball from right to left – yet it deviated to the right (leg side). Had it deviated to the left (as expected), Gatting would have been in line to play an appropriate shot.

In order for the delivery to drift towards leg, the wake of the ball must be disturbed upwards towards the off side. How this happens is not yet well described in the scientific literature. Thus, some speculation is warranted – and illustrated in Figure 5.23 overleaf.

If the axis of rotation of the delivery is in the same direction as the direction of the forward movement of the delivery, then the delivery will not drift (as shown in Figure 5.22). Thus to bowl his 'Ball from Hell', Warne had to have the axis of rotation of the delivery at an angle to its direction

Air flow pattern

Wave deviates upwards and to the left as the ball begins to dip

ROTATION

Ball trajectory curves sideways, down and to the right

Ball turns sharply to left (off)

Ball bounces 2,3m in front of crease

Direction of flight across the pitch

Axis of rotation (less than 90° to direction of flight)

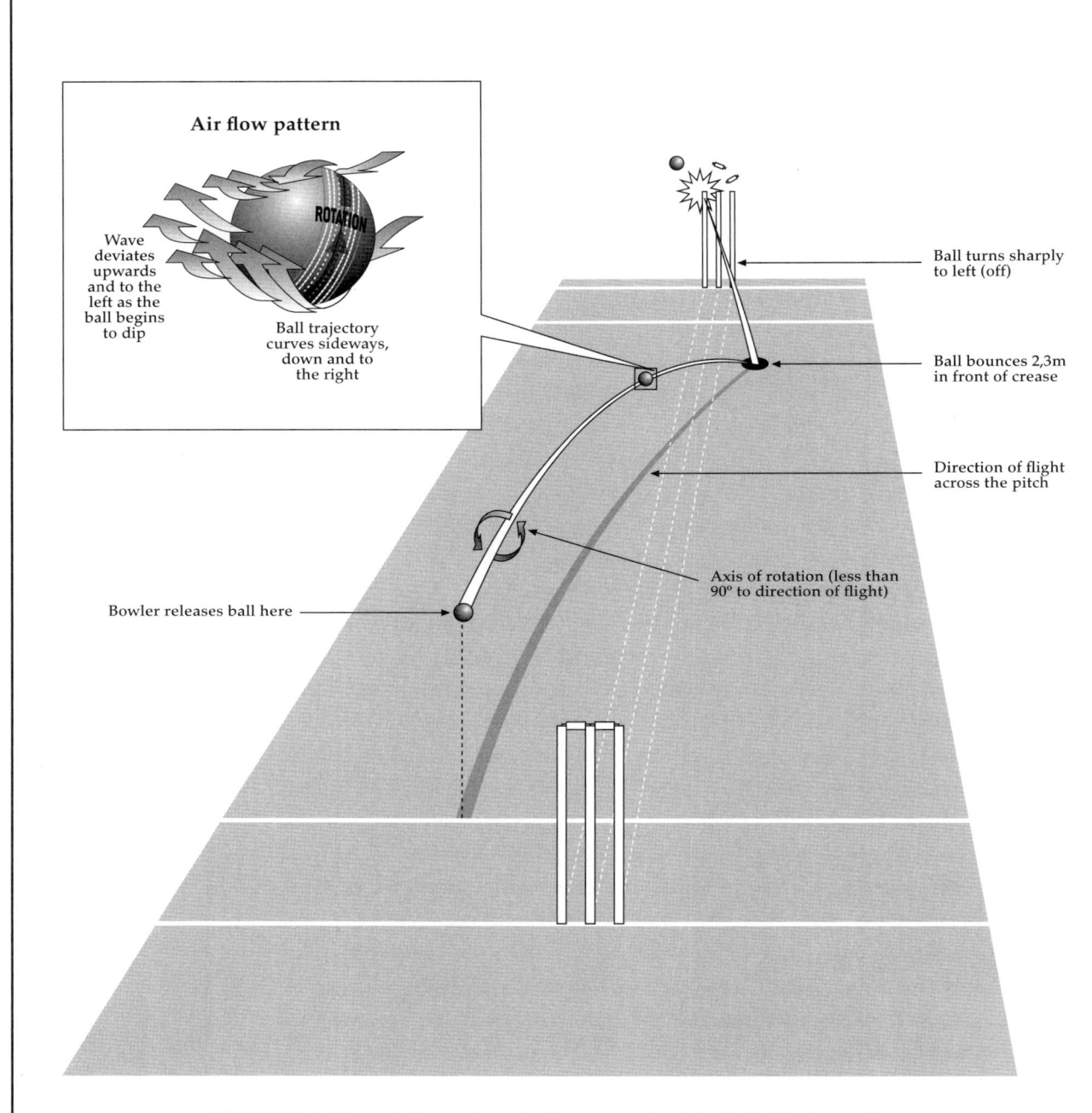

Bowler releases ball here

FIGURE 5.23: *The probable aerodynamic effects that produced the 'Ball of the Century'*

of movement. Most likely, the seam was tilted slightly backwards from the vertical (when seen from above), with the seam on the left side of the ball slightly ahead. In this position, the axis of rotation (seen from behind the ball) is upwards and to the leg side (see Figure 5.23).

For this delivery to drift downwards and to the leg, when viewed from behind, the wake must be disturbed upwards and to the off side. This requires that the air on the leg side and the bottom of the ball must travel faster around the back of the ball than the air travelling on the off side and the top of the ball. This would be explained by the Magnus effect, since the leading edge and top surface of the ball is turning into the onrushing air (towards the off side), whereas the air on the bottom and the leg side of the ball is travelling in the same direction as the spin on the ball. As a result, the air on the leg side and bottom of the ball travels more rapidly, producing the area of low pressure into which the ball drifts and drops.

The challenge for Warne in delivering That Ball was to ensure that the axis of rotation on his delivery was not so far towards the leg side that the Magnus effect would produce purely a downward force (as demonstrated in Figure 5.21 on p. 303); but was also not in the direction of the ball's flight, in which case there would be neither drift nor drop even though the amount of turn would likely be maximal. But this axis of rotation also had to be optimal to produce the degree of turn necessary to beat Gatting's legs, body and bat.

Finally, Warne had to put enough revolutions on the ball to ensure that there was a meaningful difference in the speed of the air moving over the advancing and retreating surfaces of his delivery so that the Magnus effect would indeed be achieved – and so that the ball would turn enough to get past Gatting's defences.

If we are correct in our speculations, and Figure 5.23 correctly illustrates the physics of what occurred that afternoon, then this ball is no longer one of 'mystery'. However, what is in absolutely no doubt is the exceptional degree of technical mastery required to bowl it – as a delivery it truly deserves its monikers 'Ball of the Century' and 'Ball in a Million'. It is little wonder that many consider Warne to be the greatest leg-spin bowler in the history of the game – for more on this, see pp. 317–18.

WRIST-SPIN

A wrist-spinner is a rare breed, possessing a skill that takes years of hard graft and devotion to master. If seam bowling and finger-spin are akin to throwing the ball conventionally (by letting it leave the fingers in the direction desired), then wrist-spin is about trying to land the ball on a small target 18 metres away by effectively losing control of the throw, with the ball slipping out of the side or the back of the hand at the moment of release. Not surprisingly, the thoroughbred leg-spinner is a once-a-generation phenomenon. But even for those wrist-spinners not blessed with the skills (or downright genius) of a Shane Warne or Abdul Qadir, landing a hard-spun 'leggie' on a good length and watching the ball fizz past the bat is surely one of cricket's greatest pleasures.

Accuracy will always be a challenge to young wrist-spinners, but once mastered, the fourfold value of wrist-spin becomes clear:

- **The stock ball of the right-hander turns away from the right-handed batsman.** It is more difficult to make late adjustments to a ball turning away from the body than into it.
- **It allows for the googly and top-spinner,** whereas the conventional finger-spinner can only use the top-spinner or floater as variations.
- **It generates considerably more spin than finger-spin.**
- **It opens up a target area on the pitch that forms the end of the run-up of right-arm fast bowlers bowling over the wicket.** Rough outside the right-hander's leg-stump can be fatal (M. Gatting, b. S. Warne, 1993), while rough outside a left-hander's off-stump can be just as fraught (A. Strauss, b. S. Warne, 2005).

LEG-SPIN

'Leg-spin' or the leg-break delivery has traditionally described the ball that pitches and 'breaks' or spins from the leg side to the off side, just as off-spin or the off-break delivery 'breaks' from the off to the leg. However, left-handed wrist-spinners also qualify as 'leg-spinners' by virtue of having an identical action to right-handers. The left-hander's 'leg-break' is known as the chinaman, and naturally spins into the right-hander. For the sake of clarity and brevity, we will use the term 'leg-spin' and 'leg-spinner' for both right- and left-handed bowlers, to underline the fact that these two 'separate' varieties of bowler are simply mirror images of one another, both letting go of the ball out of the side of the hand with a big rotation of the wrist.

The young leg-spinner is faced with a task considerably more daunting than that of the young off-spinner, who has his thumb and index finger to help him

'Keep it simple: develop a hard-spun leg-break which you can bowl on a perfect length, and make that your stock ball.'

– Richie Benaud

> **LEFT-ARM SPINNERS: A RARE BREED**
> Since left-handers comprise just 10% of the global population, it is not surprising that so few left-arm leg-spinners have risen through the ranks of Test cricket. South Africa's Paul Adams enjoyed a meteoric rise in international cricket, many batsmen finding his contorted action extremely difficult to separate from his more conventional flight and turn; but Adams' star waned as accuracy problems, and an easily identifiable 'wrong'un', made him increasingly vulnerable to attack. Australia's selectors also experimented with Michael Bevan and Brad Hogg: Bevan even enjoyed an extremely brief billing as a Test all-rounder, while Hogg had considerable success in the 2007 World Cup with his conventional chinaman delivery and exceptional accuracy.

guide the ball. This means he needs to keep it simple, and to learn to bowl the basic delivery required by his discipline. For Richie Benaud, the greatest leg-spinner of his generation, this basic delivery was uncomplicated, and he explained it to Shane Warne as follows: 'Keep it simple: develop a hard-spun leg-break which you can bowl on a perfect length, and make that your stock ball.'

It wasn't a revolutionary idea, insisted Benaud, attributing it to Clarrie Grimmett, who preceded him in the Australian halls of leg-spinner fame, and pointing out that it had been his own father's basic philosophy and advice. Being able to bowl the big turning leggie at will and landing it more or less where you intended has two purposes, explains Benaud:

> *First, the bowler is able to take wickets with it and secondly, just as important, if anyone is threatening to hand him a belting, he is able to fall back on it as a defensive measure* (1998, p. 210).

Of course leg-spin bowling wouldn't be half the craft and spectacle it is without all the variations it contains – googlies, flippers, top-spinners and so on – but before we discuss these, it is important to get to grips with the delivery itself and the action it requires.

The grip

The grip for the leg-break, as bowled by a right-arm wrist-spinner. (Left-handed bowlers can simply reverse this.)

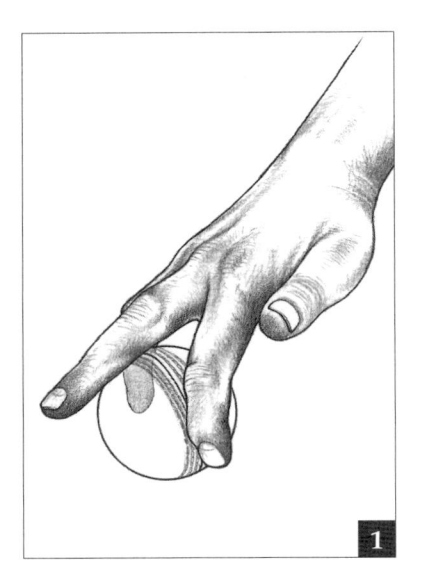

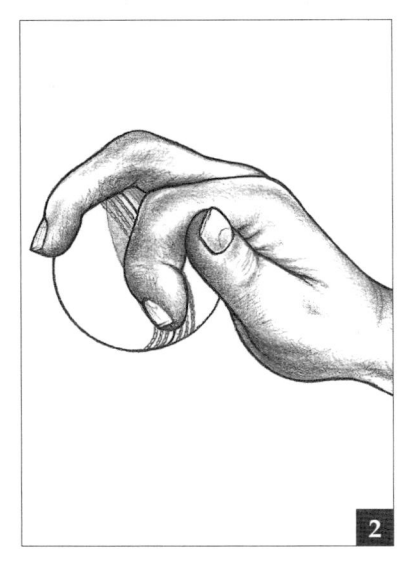

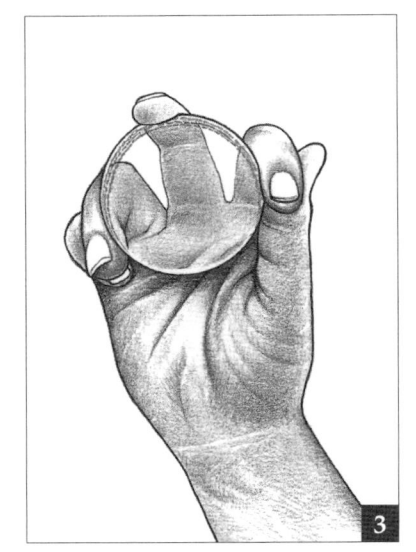

The grip for wrist-spinning does not rely on the pressure points of the fingers as much as orthodox spinning, but relies on a very supple wrist. The grip starts with the first and third fingers running down the seam of the ball, with the second finger resting on top (1). Fold the hand down behind the ball until the thumb is running parallel to the seam (2 and 3).

The action

Cock the wrist down and away from the body (1). As the arm swings over in the bowling action, the wrist flicks open as if you are opening a door anti-clockwise (2 and 3). It is important to keep the bowling arm very high when delivering the ball: this will create the natural in-drift and dip that can be enhanced even more if bowling into the wind. As the bowling arm comes over, the front leg should be braced. The back leg will pivot around it, turning the shoulder towards the batsman.

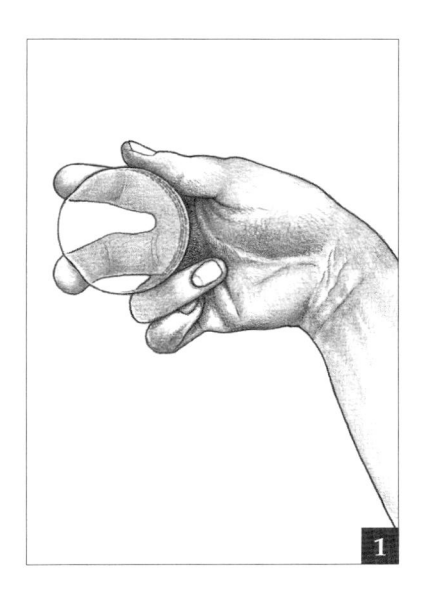

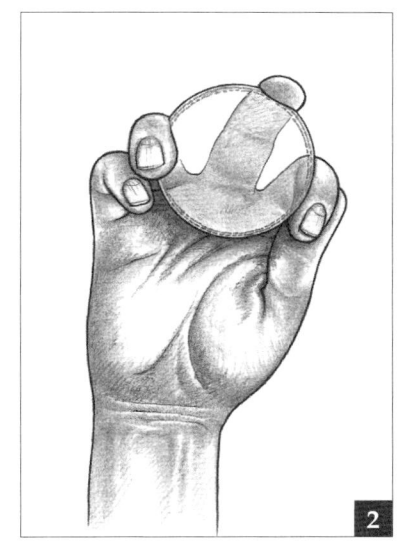

The googly

As stated earlier, the spinner deceives his prey by confusing him about one or more of the following aspects of the delivery:

- **where it will pitch**
- **when it will pitch**
- **where it will go after pitching.**

'Picking' the direction of the spin is something batsmen work very hard at, either by watching the bowler's action and hand, or by watching the ball through the air, so that they don't have to adopt the last-ditch tactic of 'reading the spin off the wicket' – a rather charitable way of describing a desperate attempt to adapt one's shot after seeing which way the ball has spun.

It therefore poses severe problems to the batsman when a particular action (which he has become accustomed to watching, and which always sends the ball in a certain direction) suddenly produces a delivery that goes in the opposite direction. The doubt created in his mind is as valuable as extreme pace or a proud seam: suddenly his early-warning radar – his view of the action and hand – has been 'jammed'.

Which was exactly what B.J.T. Bosanquet realized when, on a tour of Australia in 1903/04 with the MCC, he bowled a ball with a leg-break action that spun like an off-break. The googly had been born. However, it was another seven years before the delivery gained wider recognition. Albert Vogler and Reg Schwarz, the South African slow bowlers who perfected the delivery, have been largely forgotten by popular

BOWLING **311**

cricket lore, but the discomfort to which they subjected the Australians of the 1910/11 tour made it clear that the delivery had arrived to stay (Schwarz, who had studied Bosanquet's methods and who bowled only googlies, took 59 Australian wickets). Today, the variety of names by which it is known is an illustration of how deeply it has entrenched itself into the lore of the game: whether you know it as the 'wrong'un' (because it turns the 'wrong way'), the 'other one', the 'google', or, in Afrikaans, the 'gool-bal', it is a vital and potentially lucrative skill to have as a leg-spinner.

Most great 'leggies' have possessed a decent googly, but some made it their trump card. Abdul Qadir's 'other one' was not only beautifully disguised, but turned an unusually long way. South African Denys Hobson possessed a vicious googly, but his country's politics robbed him of the chance to bamboozle batsmen in the international arena, and he spent his playing days lobbing fizzing leg-breaks and googlies into the howling summer south-easter at Newlands in Cape Town, gaining phenomenal dip and in-drift.

The grip and action

The back of the hand (instead of the ball) faces the batsman at the moment of delivery. Because of the position of the seam as the ball leaves the hand, it turns in towards the batsman with a similar action to the leg-spinner. Since the arm comes over very quickly, even when bowling spin, it can be very difficult for the batsman to pick which way the ball is going to turn. An incorrect observation, a poor choice of shot – and it's all over.

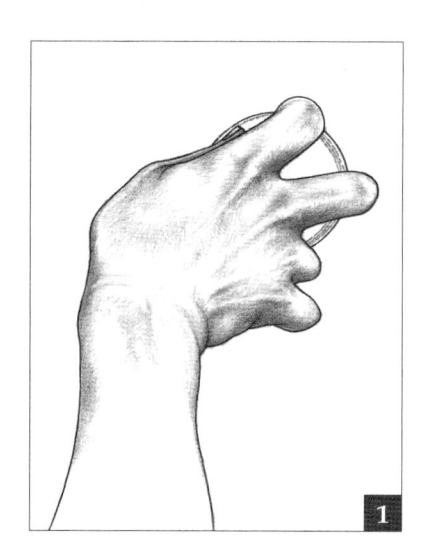

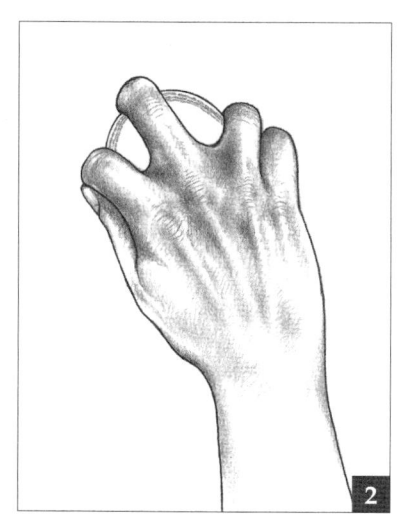

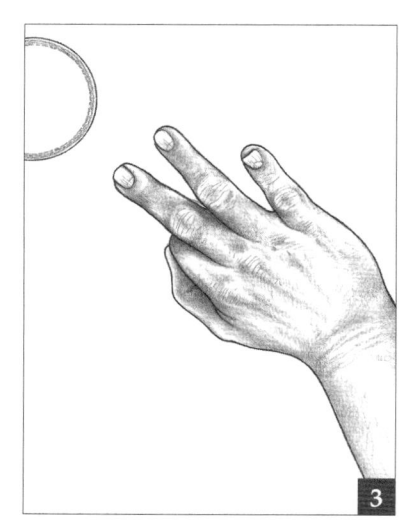

The googly needs a much higher arm than the leg-break, which is best spun with more of a round-arm action. Warne spun his leg-breaks a long way with his arm held lower, but he always struggled to bowl a particularly good googly for the same reason. On the other hand, a bowler like Mushtaq Ahmed, whose googlies could turn as much as his leg-breaks, came over with an almost vertical arm, his head dropping away to allow the arm and shoulder to come over. India's Anil Kumble is another good example of a leg-spinner with a good googly; his high arm reduced the amount of spin he got on the leg-break, but enabled the googly to nip back appreciably.

Peter Philpott, author of the definitive book on wrist-spin bowling, notes that for those starting to practise the googly, it might help to drop the left shoulder (for right-handed bowlers) and open the body. However, he feels that as the bowler gains confidence, and if the wrist, fingers, forearm, elbow and shoulder are doing their job, the action should be no different to that for the leg-break – otherwise the bowler will reveal the delivery to the batsman and lose the element of surprise.

A WARNING TO YOUNG LEG-SPINNERS AND COACHES

A common problem when a youngster starts practising the googly is that his wrist does not return to the basic wrist-spin position, and he loses the ability to bowl the conventional leg-break.

Peter Philpott advises, 'Don't bowl all wrong'uns [googlies] for a week or even a few days.' He prefers his charges to bowl a sequence of different deliveries. He also suggests practising the googly underarm until it has been completely mastered; then moving to roundarm, and then only to overarm. This way the bowler can watch his fingers and wrist in action.

The skill of wrist-spinning is the toughest of all. For any player wishing to master this skill, there has to be a massive commitment to practise.

The flipper

There are two types of flipper: the underhand flipper and side flipper. As demonstrated by Warne in the early stages of his career, the flipper is deadly because it looks as if it's been dropped short, which invites the batsman to rock back to pull it. In fact it is short, but the over-spin on it – or the lack of any spin – means that it doesn't bounce and sit up to be hit, but instead skids onto the batsman, easily trapping him LBW.

The other lethal aspect of the flipper is that it doesn't 'break' to the off side, instead coming on dead straight. This has been the undoing of numerous batsmen who played forward along a leg-break line (allowing for some turn), only to have the ball hold its line and skid past the inside edge of the bat into the pads or stumps. Because it doesn't bounce, if it hits the pads, it is almost invariably inches off the ground, so even if the batsman gets a stride in, he's in serious danger of being given out LBW.

According to Richie Benaud, the flipper is bowled from beneath the wrist. It is squeezed out the fingers so that it spins around its own axis as it travels down the pitch. Benaud warns, 'It should never be used by young bowlers until their ligaments, tendons and muscles are strong enough. It puts far too great a strain on young bodies' (*MCC Masterclass*, 1994, p. 56).

VARIATIONS AND MYSTERY BALLS

Great spinners invent new deliveries every so often – or at least rediscover neglected ones, and rebrand them as something new and terrifying! Shane Warne's 'flipper' was the bane of the cricketing world in the early 1990s, despite it having been invented at least 70 years earlier and used by Clarrie Grimmett. When injury forced him to retire the delivery, he kept working, eventually producing the slider, the 'zooter' and various other unnamed deliveries that may or may not have been 'new' to the game.

Be careful, however, to back up the hype with some sort of potency. South African pundits were all ears when very occasional off-spinner Mark Waugh alluded to his new 'knuckle-ball' on Australia's tour in 1996. The delivery lived up to its name, tossed out of the knuckles of an almost closed fist. Boland batsman Kenny Jackson treated the first one with curious respect, but the rest were given the treatment they deserved, and dispatched to all corners of the Paarl grounds. The knuckle-ball was instantly retired. Having said that, some variations and mystery balls have proved extremely effective.

THE DOOSRA

By 1996, the world's batsmen were quickly shaking themselves out into two categories: those who couldn't play Shane Warne, and those who couldn't play him yet. The Australian had revitalized slow bowling, and with Pakistani leg-spinner Mushtaq Ahmed mopping up everyone Warne hadn't, it seemed that the 'leggie' was the game's new super-predator.

Off-spinners, on the other hand, promised some respite. Difficult to get away, yes, but the traditional finger-spinner suddenly seemed something of a port in a storm of wrist-spin.

But all of that changed when a lanky young Pakistani off-spinner made the ball spin from leg to off. Batsmen could only watch in horror as Saqlain Mushtaq's flighted 'off-breaks' straightened into their pads or jagged away off the outside edge. The doosra had arrived.

The delivery was probably named by Pakistani wicket-keeper Moin Khan, exhorting Saqlain in Urdu to bowl 'the other one' – 'doosra' literally means 'the second one'. There is also some debate around whether or not Saqlain invented the ball, with some claiming the honour for West Indian great Sonny Ramadhin, who also made the ball turn both ways from a conventional off-break grip.

However, there is no disputing that it was Saqlain who first demonstrated the devastating power of the doosra to a global audience, and his dominance in one-day cricket in the 1990s underlines the value of the delivery.

Strictly speaking, the doosra is a weapon of the finger-spinner, but we have decided to include it in this discussion of wrist-spin largely because it behaves like a leg-break, and is delivered with much more wrist and elbow movement than finger action.

When used by masters like Muttiah Muralitharan, it is a complex and difficult delivery, but the simple theory behind the doosra is that it is an off-break with the wrist turned around so that the ball goes the other way, with the seam pointing at first slip instead of leg gully. When you bowl a conventional off-break, your palm and pulse are facing the bowler. When you bowl a doosra, it is your knuckles and the top of your wrist that face down the pitch. Put another way, if you are bowling wearing a watch (which you shouldn't be!), the off-break delivery should show the batsman your watch-strap, while the doosra should show him the time.

However, much of the controversy around the doosra stems from the fact that in order to impart spin, there needs to be some flexing of the elbow, which is why some bowlers have been forced to abandon the doosra altogether – or else water it down so dramatically that it becomes a pointless delivery.

The legalities will no doubt be thrashed out at some stage in the near future, but we feel that it is an exciting development in the game, and in view of the tremendous skill required to learn it – and bowl it on a length – we believe it should be allowed and encouraged.

Richie Benaud's advice to a young Warne was to perfect the hard-spun leg-break as his stock ball: 'I added that it would take him at least four years of extremely hard work to perfect it,' wrote Benaud in 1995. 'He did it in two.'

SHANE WARNE: THE BEST WRIST-SPINNER OF ALL TIME?

In 2000, an elite panel of judges selected five Wisden Cricketers of the Century, players whose spectacular career would represent the epitome of cricketing virtuosity for future generations. The men they chose were Sir Donald Bradman, Sir Jack Hobbs, Sir Garfield Sobers, Sir Vivian Richards, and Shane Warne. The fact that Warne was the only player in the group who has not been knighted for his services to cricket was somehow fitting for a player who, throughout his career, seemed as comfortable with his iconoclastic bad boy image as he was with the mantle of match-winner, mentor and class act.

The bowler responsible for the most famous delivery in Test cricket; the first spinner to reach 500 Test wickets; the first bowler of any kind to reach 600 and then 700; match-winner for four Australian captains; tormentor of England (and the nemesis of South Africa's gifted batsman Daryl Cullinan); Man of the Match in a World Cup final; a self-taught expert in psychological warfare and marketing – Warne riveted and enraged, enthralled and astounded from the first moment he came to the cricketing world's attention.

But the greatest slow bowler of his generation – and perhaps of any generation – had his critics. After all, as well as the illustrious list of accomplishments above, he was sent home from a World Cup series for taking diet pills and thus failing a drug test – and then there was his knack for having his sexual peccadilloes splashed across the tabloids.

Whether it was his love-life, his smoking, his weight, his form, his inability to bowl a good googly, the state of his bowling shoulder, or a one-year ban for taking a banned diuretic, the nay-sayers were never short of a word. If they were to be believed, Warne was past it and a has-been by 1998, then by 1999, then by 2002. By the time the immortal Ashes series of 2005 began, with Warne two months shy of his 36th birthday, there was talk of it being his last series. By the summer's end, he had claimed 40 English wickets, the most in an Ashes Test series since Jim Laker took 46 in 1956, and the fourth most in a five-Test series in the history of cricket.

Halfway through his fifth Test, way back in 1992, things were looking less rosy: a career total of 5 wickets for 451 threatened to end his career before it had begun, and his captain Allan Border's faith must have been wavering. But then came the second innings against the West Indies in that Boxing Day Test, with a haul of 7 for 52, and the rest is a phenomenal history.

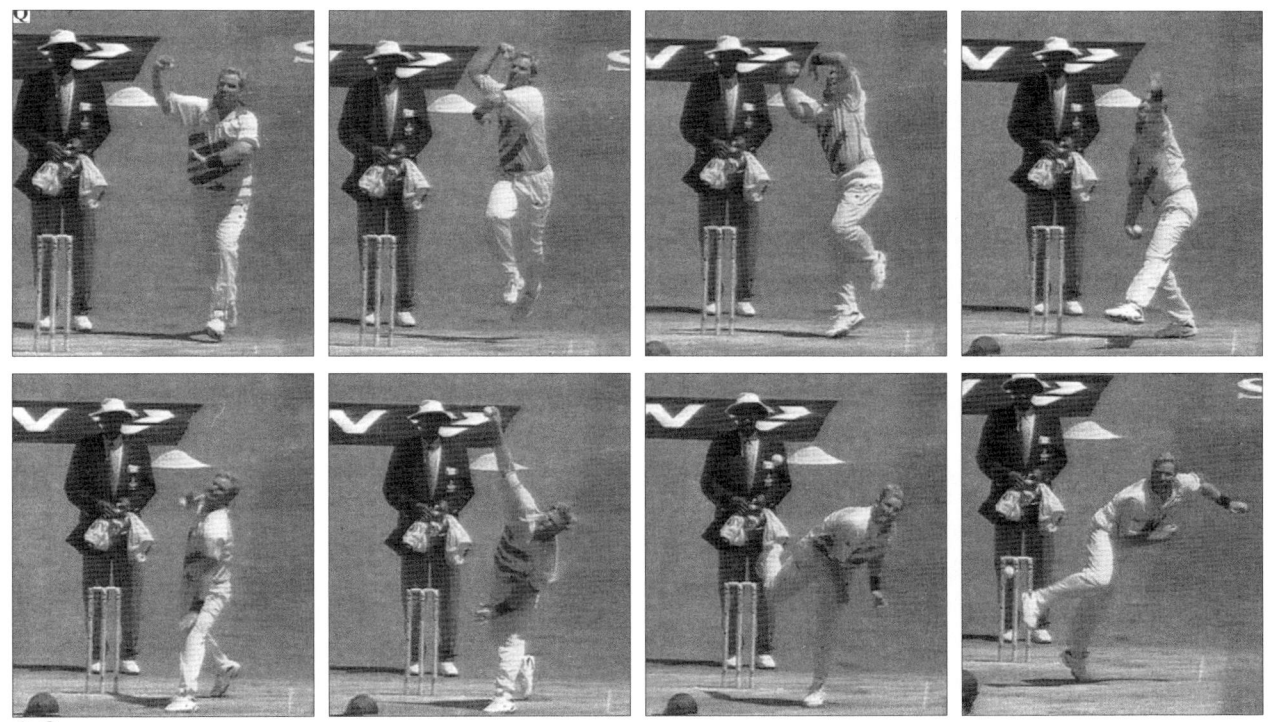

© QUINTIC

WHAT MADE HIM THE GREATEST?

According to Richie Benaud, it was Warne's brain and character as much as his bowling hand that accounted for his success:

> He has the ability, the nerve and the desire. That's close to an ideal combination but not quite all that is needed. You need an enquiring mind, an ability to sift good information from mediocre – and a genuine liking of hard work. The hard work is essential because the first requirement of those odd people who bowl out of the back of the hand is that they must develop that hard-spun stock ball.
>
> Show me someone who just rolls it out of his fingers and bowls accurately, and you can almost guarantee a steady bowler of county or Sheffield Shield standard. But show me someone who spins it hard, with over-spin as well as side-spin, and then develops accuracy through sheer hard work – and you have a young bowler with a real chance.
>
> The other vitally important aspect is that he had the complete confidence of his captain (1998, p. 213).

The brilliance of Warne's action: an extended front arm that doesn't go across his body but instead pulls down in front and to the leg side of his front leg; a superb head position, and a strong, aggressive follow-through.

Or, as was the case, captains: Allan Border had complete faith in his young find, but it was Mark Taylor who gave Warne the licence to attack, inventing the so-called 'Star Wars' field for the spinner, so named because it resembled the claustrophobic channels of the Death Star through which Luke Skywalker has to fly in the climactic sequence of that film, attacked on all sides by fighters and anti-aircraft artillery. In the cricketing version, there are at least two men around the bat in front of the wicket, a slip and gully, and sometimes a leg slip.

Something else worth mentioning is the quality of the relationship Warne had with his keepers, in particular Ian Healy. Healy combined superb keeping skills with a personal style that was immensely supportive of Warne, at the same time as extremely aggressive towards to the unfortunate batsmen – who must often have felt stuck between a rock and a hard place. Healy's most intimidating habit was to swing the ball at the stumps every time he took it, constantly reminding the batsman that if he played forward, he risked a stumping.

To analyze the success of a superstar like the Australian is to perhaps strip away some of the lustre and mystery, but it is nonetheless worth doing. In our view, Warne's greatness could be attributed to the following factors:

- the ability to spin the ball a long way, and to control the degree of turn he got
- supreme accuracy
- variation, guile and drift
- a clean, superb technique
- big bounce due to his wrist action (as much bounce, if not more, than Anil Kumble)
- aggression (as aggressive as any 150km/h strike bowler)
- a very dramatic and plausible style of appealing
- belief in himself
- an easy-going persona off the field (he was popular with most of his teammates)
- excellent publicity ('I've invented a new delivery!')
- a terrific work ethic
- the ability and patience to analyze his opponent technically and mentally.

The antics and negative publicity of Warne's early career (not to mention the sleazier aspects of his private life that emerged later on) have prejudiced many parents against him as a role model for their cricketing children. But as a bowler, he remains the yardstick to which all youngsters eager to bowl spin should aspire.

AND THE LAST WORD GOES TO CLARRIE GRIMMETT

In bringing a chapter on the extraordinary and multi-faceted skill of bowling to an end, we considered the question of legacy – a subject very dear to Bob Woolmer's heart. Bob believed that part of the cricketing coach's duty was to pass on the wisdom learnt from mentors and peers. Australian former Test player, captain and coach Bobby Simpson also stressed the importance of peer influence in cricket, and its relevance to the remarkable success and international dominance of Australian cricket in the current era. Leg-spin bowling, of which Simpson was himself an exponent, is one discipline in which the importance of this peer influence is very clear. Beginning with Bill O'Reilly and Clarrie Grimmett, selected as the two wrist-spin bowlers in Bradman's Best cricket team of all time (Perry, 2001), and extending through Richie Benaud to Shane Warne, Australian leg-spinners have always been among the world's very best.

Benaud has said that he was introduced to the art of leg-spin bowling through the excellent writing of Clarrie Grimmett, the contemporary of Don Bradman; and this legacy of superb manuals on spin bowling has been continued by Peter Philpott, whose *The Art of Wrist-spin Bowling* Bob Woolmer considered one of the best cricket coaching books he had encountered. Fortunately, literature knows no national borders, and young spinners and their coaches don't need to be Australian to benefit from Philpott's book and others like it, enormously valuable compendiums containing a century of hard-earned knowledge and strategy about leg-spin bowling.

But if the writing of Philpott and Benaud have publicized and elaborated on the art of slow bowling, it was Grimmett who literally wrote the book on spin. What follows are selections from his classic texts, *Taking Wickets* and *Tricking the Batsman*, published in 1930 and 1934 respectively. Because these classic works have long been out of print, we believed this is an appropriate place to cite his thoughts on the great skills of bowling as a way to sum up and close this chapter.

GRIMMETT ON FLIGHT:

Grimmett may have been one of the first great bowlers to describe precisely what flight is, why bowlers use changes in flight to deceive the batsman, and why, according to his understanding, such deception is possible.

> *Flighting the ball is one of the bowler's little tricks by which he endeavours to mislead the batsman into thinking that the ball is going to pitch in a different place from that which was suggested by the early stages of its passage from the bowler's hand.*

> *This flighting of the ball is an endeavour to bowl it at different heights in the air, at the same time making it land in the same spot, or drop shorter than it appeared likely to do by its flight.*
>
> *Why should this deceive the batsman, you will ask? If the ball is bowled higher in the air, has not the batsman more time to see the ball? And why is there a possibility that it will deceive him into thinking it will land in a different place?*
>
> *This is easily explained.... Let us take a motor-car coming directly toward us. You will find it is difficult to gauge its speed. Now move to the side of it, so that it crosses at right-angles to you, and you will find it comparatively easy to judge its pace.*
>
> *This is one reason why a ball thrown higher in the air is deceptive. At a certain part of its flight it is coming directly toward the batsman's eyes, and its pace is harder to judge. At the same time, a ball thrown high in the air is also coming at an unusual angle. It is not an ordinary delivery.*
>
> *If, then, the height of the ball's trajectory is varied, it naturally follows that the part of its flight at which the ball is coming directly toward the eyes is different.*
>
> *We, therefore, have a variation which... is valuable to a bowler. It will also be obvious that the longer the ball is in the air the more chance there is of some influence, such as spin or seam swerve, operating.*
>
> *It is also necessary to bowl the ball slower, with increased height of trajectory, to allow for its dropping at a good length.*
>
> *There is something curiously puzzling about a high dropping delivery, particularly a ball that has plenty of spin, and it will often play unexpected tricks.*
>
> *A bowler who uses these devices will find it a great advantage to bowl into any breeze that may be blowing, as this helps to make the flight of the ball more deceptive* (1934, pp. 79–81).

Grimmett did his homework, and saw things from the other side as well: he believed that stereoscopic vision – the use of both eyes at the same time – allowed batsmen to gain a better judgement of the distance, speed and angle of deliveries. In a rare moment of charity for his opponents, he urged batsmen to 'face the ball with both eyes at the same distance from it'. But as a bowler, he saw a chink: 'If a batsman has a one-eyed stance, don't forget to try him well out on the leg side. He is sure to be weak there' (1934, p. 139).

GRIMMETT ON LENGTH:

The leg-spinner was steadfast in his belief that it is the control of length that is the first crucial requirement for the successful bowler – and here his insights apply to all bowlers, not just the slow variety. He believed that young bowlers should be taught to bowl on a shortened pitch until they are strong enough to bowl a delivery of good length on a normal adult-sized pitch. We wholeheartedly endorse this view, which has been widely accepted by English cricket coaches.

Grimmett's advice on practising remains as fresh and useful as it was 70 years ago:

Let me tell you more about length.... Here is a simple method for young bowlers. It will help them to improve. Mark out a cricket pitch the correct length.... Now place a single stump at each end. At varying distance, to suit the particular type of bowler, pin a sheet of cardboard about three feet square on the spot where, as previously described, a good length ball would pitch.

You now have the stage set for an interesting practice or competition, taking in good length and direction.

Try to see how many times with a dozen balls you can hit the cardboard. You'll be surprised to find how really hard it is. There are few bowlers who can hit it consistently three times out of twelve. Yet, with conscientious practice, you will easily improve on this.

This is an interesting method of practice, and one which will appeal to all bowling aspirants, especially the youngsters (1934, pp. 42–43).

Coaches can't go wrong following this handy, low-tech advice. Remember that if cardboard is in short supply, or keeps being blown off the pitch, you can try the Woolmer variation, described earlier, and use a rubber car mat instead.

Grimmett, who continued to play international cricket until he was 44 years old, knew what he was talking about when he said:

Even when a bowler has lost his youth and power to break or swerve a ball, his ability to keep a good length will command respect from the best batsmen. Good length is everything. Without it no bowler will succeed.

A bowler who can retain a good length will reap a harvest of wickets on those days when he gets the assistance of a little rain or when he is on a crumbling wicket, and so will enjoy his cricket better than those who have neglected to lay a solid foundation in this respect (1934, pp. 44–45).

We hope that all bowlers (and their coaches) reading this chapter will find it a foundation from which to explore the many nuances of their crafts, whether it be the ferocity and strength that pace demands, the nagging persistence of the seamer, or the art of deception encompassed by spin. Whichever it is, never forget the mantra of all great bowlers: 'Practise, practise, practise!'

CHAPTER SIX

FIELDING AND WICKET-KEEPING

INTRODUCTION

Traditionalists were appalled by the advent of one-day cricket. It was the end of civilization as they knew it, and they were unanimous in their pessimistic predictions: nothing good could ever come of the new format, and in the end it would kill Test cricket. They were wrong on both counts. It is one-day cricket, not its five-day ancestor, that is having to change and adapt to hold onto its audience (20-20 cricket being the prime example of the shortened game scrambling to keep spectators interested). Meanwhile, more Tests are being played than ever before in cricket's history.

But even the most enthusiastic supporters of one-day cricket could never have foreseen the revolution one-day cricket would trigger: the limited-overs game may have undermined batting techniques and made certain attacking bowling tactics extinct, but it has single-handedly transformed fielding from a sedate accessory to an athletic, exciting and absolutely crucial pillar of the modern game.

This is not to deny a long and grand history of spectacular fielding in cricket. The memory of South African Colin Bland still looms large over the game today, a previous generation still thrilled by recollections of an impossibly fast, supple and, above all, deadly accurate athlete lurking anywhere from cover to deep mid-wicket.

The slip-catching of Bob Simpson may never be surpassed; and the languid, relaxed figure of Clive Lloyd belied an aggressive and lithe genius for fielding.

But it was one-day cricket that ended the fielding comfort-zone. Bland, Simpson and Lloyd in their heyday may have been able to give the modern game's greatest fielders a run for their money, but they played in teams that contained a considerable number of 'passengers', players whose approach to fielding was grounded firmly and comfortably in an earlier era, a time when diving or sliding was seen as somewhat vulgar, and when players could walk off a Test field with their trousers still spotlessly white. Even as late as the 1980s, Test cricketers could get away with a feeble attempt at shoving a boot behind the ball. But one-day cricket – in which every run counted, and in which pressure, more than great bowling, was the key weapon – raised the bar.

Great fielding could not have emerged without the leadership of great fielders, and the popularization of one-day cricket fortunately coincided with the emergence of a new crop of sublimely gifted fielders: had one-day cricket never been invented, the likes of Roger Harper, Mark Waugh, Mark Taylor and Neil Fairbrother would still no doubt have dominated from the outfield and slips. But with a new format that demanded excellence from every player, and with new role models to emulate, even the most ham-fisted fast bowlers began working on their ground fielding and catching.

However, it was the readmission to world cricket of South Africa that proved the final catalyst for the fielding revolution. Not yet blasé about the importance of one-day cricket, and hungry for any victory they could get, the young and athletic South Africans flung themselves at everything, bringing an intensity to their fielding that had not been seen before. Leading the pack was a young batsman by the name of Jonty Rhodes. South Africans knew about his phenomenal skills – the ability to get back on his feet in mid-slide, his staggering anticipation, a knack of catching anything within two metres of him, no matter how fast it was travelling – but it took the 1992 World Cup to make him an international star. His diving run-out of rising Pakistani star Inzamam-ul-Haq propelled him to superstardom, especially in cricket-mad Asia, and a world-record five catches – each more spectacular than the last – against the West Indies in the Hero Cup in Mumbai in 1993 underlined his status as the greatest fielder of his generation, and perhaps the greatest in-fielder in the history of the game.

Today the fielding revolution has transformed Test cricket for the better: there are more consistently excellent fielders playing international cricket now than ever before in the history of the game. And the trickle-down effect of this standard into lower levels of the game has also had a profound impact on how cricket is taught and played. Youngsters still stand in a semi-circle taking catches off the coach's bat, but then it's off for sprint training, and then a spell of diving and sliding. Players can no longer expect to stand in the slips, their arms folded across their paunches!

One-day cricket ended the fielding comfort-zone; it also coincided with the emergence of a new crop of sublimely gifted fielders.

So what makes a great fielder? The best have all shared common traits:
- they keep low
- they're extremely quick across the ground
- they have very powerful throwing arms
- they possess 100% safe hands
- they not only expect the ball to come to them, they hope it does
- they see themselves as an attacking weapon, rather than a defensive tool.

GROUND FIELDING

Catches thrill spectators and feature on television highlights packages, but the lifeblood of fielding is ground fielding, the unglamorous art of rooting around in the dust after rolling cricket balls, or galloping around lonely boundary ropes to save a single. Unglamorous, but priceless: not only does the good ground fielder save runs, but he takes wickets by helping to build pressure on the batters. The ground fielder is the bowler's best friend, and a reliable pair of hands or a swift pair of feet in the deep can lift a side as much as any spectacular spell of bowling or sparkling innings. Ground fielding can be as much an offensive weapon as it is a defensive one. However, before you can attack, you need to learn to defend. This is the default situation not only in many cricket matches (an old ball, a dry pitch and tired bowlers); it must also be your fall-back position as a fielding team if the match is getting away from you.

DEFENSIVE FIELDING

It is often more important to save runs, or make sure the ball does not get past you, than it is to get it in to the keeper quickly. Perhaps the ball has been smashed in your direction, and will certainly go to the boundary if you don't cut it off; or perhaps a bumpy outfield has made ground fielding something of a lottery, with unpredictable bounce making running pick-ups or even sliding too risky. In these instances, you as a fielder are on the defensive, and need defences to match.

Your best defence is the 'long barrier', where the horizontal shin, tucking in tight behind the foot, provides a last line of defence in case your hands fumble the ball. If you are right-handed, your first priority is to get your right foot at a right angle to the path of the ball, as if you are going to stop the ball with the arch of your foot. Then go down on your left knee, tucking it against your right heel, creating a wall across the line of the ball. Use both hands to scoop up the ball, watching it until it is right under your eyes. Jump up by pushing off your right foot, and simultaneously transfer the ball into your right hand. You are now sideways-on, and perfectly positioned to throw the ball in quickly.

Left-handers can mirror these instructions accordingly, as shown below.

The 'long barrier' defence for right-handers   *The 'long barrier' defence for left-handers*

ATTACKING FIELDING

Here the fielder 'pounces' on the ball, rather than using his body as a barrier to halt it. Balance is vital, otherwise you will be collecting grass stains, not the ball.

Attacking the ball in the field

As you approach the ball to cut it off, make sure that you get the right foot (for right-handed players) to the ball (1 and 2). Staying sideways-on, scoop up the ball with both hands (3), using your foot as a second line of defence, 'crow-hop' on one foot into a throwing position (4), and unleash the ball towards the target (5). If speed is at a premium (perhaps there is a potential run-out situation) and the fielder's eye and reflexes are excellent, then the one-handed pick-up 'on the run' is an alternative.

The pitfalls are obvious – if you miss the ball as you grab at it, your foot is not close enough to block the ball. Keeping low and bending the knees are important, and of course, your timing has to be superb. On bumpy outfields, stick to using both hands, with your foot as back-up. In both methods, the value of remaining sideways-on is that you are perfectly positioned to get up, take aim and throw underarm, following through keeping the head moving towards the target (the bowler, wicket-keeper, or stumps).

Using two hands when going hard at the ball should be encouraged at junior level, but if you want to get an edge over the opposition, or you want to run someone out, you also need to practise one-handed pick-ups. Coaches should spend some time rolling balls out to players who then have to pick up either left-handed or right-handed. This also helps fielders learn to transfer the ball into their throwing hands quickly.

In other words, learn the orthodox techniques, but also train for those non-ideal situations that crop up by teaching both hands to work individually. It will give fielders confidence, and a competitive edge. This edge is not always present in school cricket, where players tend to be slower and less skilled, but the earlier you learn, the better.

Trigger movements and stance

Attacking fielders would do well to emulate Jonty Rhodes's trigger movement. Rhodes would walk in conventionally, but as the ball was delivered he would give a single two-footed hop on the spot, almost a bounce. This trigger movement left him balanced, his weight equally spread over both feet, but also primed and energized to move in either direction as required.

Rhodes's trigger movement. Notice that in the second frame both his feet are off the ground as he jumps into a wide stance (third frame), ready to lunge either way.

If you are in the inner ring, you should try to move in a way that Bob Woolmer called 'crabbing', keeping low and moving sideways if necessary. By staying low, you not only cut off the single; you also give yourself a chance of saving the boundary by moving like a goal-keeper. Clearly this doesn't work in the outfield, where out-and-out sprinting is necessary, but in the inner ring you should think of the area around you as a goal-mouth that you're protecting by keeping low and diving left and right.

Chasing the ball and throwing on the turn

When chasing a ball in the outfield, it is vital for your bowler's and team's confidence that you chase hard. Depending on which is your throwing arm (although you should be practising throwing with both!), make sure that you keep the ball on that side of the body if you are going to pick up and throw on the turn. As you reach the ball, pick it up with one hand alongside the right foot (for right-handers). Keeping the body low and still moving away from the wicket, transfer your weight onto your left leg, from which you will pivot and jump. As you leap off this foot, turn your head and take aim with the left arm – this will pivot your body in the direction of the wicket. As you throw with the right arm, both feet leave the ground, so that the turn is completed in the air. Keep your eyes on the target.

FANCY FOOTWORK

Be very careful about fielding with your feet: although it is legal to field a ball or stop it by kicking it or stepping on it, these are not strictly orthodox fielding methods. First of all, cricketers are not necessarily ace soccer players, and will have much less control and accuracy than when using their hands when fielding (although in a one-day game, South African all-rounder Lance Klusener did once effect an exciting run-out off his own bowling by kicking the ball onto the stumps).

Secondly, there is a much higher risk of injury to the player. The West Indian fast bowler Nixon Maclean almost ended his international career in the mid-1990s when he checked a ball that was about to race across the boundary rope by stepping on it. The boundary was saved, but the result was a sprained ankle that kept him out of the game for weeks. During his first match after recovering, he did exactly the same thing – this time without injuring himself, although the team physiotherapist ran onto the field in a state of apoplexy to remonstrate with him!

Finally, umpires are unlikely to smile upon players who regularly stop the ball by stepping on it. Given the storm of controversy that broke when former South African captain Hansie Cronje rested his foot on the ball during a one-day game in Australia, it is advisable that players not consider themselves amateur footballers when on a cricket pitch.

Sliding

The modern art of sliding next to the ball and allowing your momentum to push you to your feet was almost single-handedly invented and perfected by Jonty Rhodes in the mid-1990s: until Rhodes revolutionized fielding in this way, most players would jog along next to the rolling ball and pick it up. While the slide has become ubiquitous, and certainly allows you to get the ball into the air more quickly, be careful of assuming that the old method was automatically inferior. The great South African outfielder Colin Bland has never been equalled in his ability to pick up the ball on the run and get it in flat, hard and accurately. And Clive Lloyd wasn't nicknamed 'The Cat' for nothing, his drooping shoulders and lazy lope disguising a supremely lithe and athletic pick-up and throw. However, the slide is undeniably effective in limiting runs and in setting up run-outs.

Don't slide for the sake of sliding, or just because international players are doing it. Understand how, when and why to slide. Realize that this is a very quick action – down on one knee and up again immediately – rather than a glamorous whoosh across the turf like a football player throwing himself onto the turf in celebration. Remember, you're trying to get the ball back in as quickly as possible.

The most important aspect of sliding properly is to keep your knee out of harm's way. Land on the side of your knee: too close to your kneecap and you risk digging the knee into the turf and injuring it. If the ball you're chasing is on your left side, go down into the slide on your left side and thigh, using your left arm to brace yourself (1 and 2). As you pick up the ball with your right hand, dig your right foot into the ground, using it as a brake, and push yourself up on your left arm at the same time (3). Your momentum will have you up on your feet very quickly, and you'll already be in a position to throw. As you come up, it's important that you take your weight onto the right foot as you stand (4 and 5). Putting weight on the left leg can cause injury, including tearing of the cartilages (Van Hagen et al., 2000).

A variation of this method is now often seen at first-class level (especially in one-day games, where every run counts), and is used when trying to prevent the ball from crossing the boundary rope. This happens when the fielder knows that at the speed both he and the ball are travelling, he will inevitably cross the rope if he slides; yet the ball is travelling too fast to stop by other methods. So he uses the slide-stop method, but instead of picking up the ball and holding on to it for the throw, he flicks or knocks it backwards with a cupped hand, so that its progress to the boundary

The slide. Note the extended right leg visible in the third frame: this is your brake and your traction for getting up as quickly as possible.

is halted, even if he is unlucky enough to slam into the advertising boards. The trick is to get rid of the ball before the body slides over the rope. Ideally, the player performing the heroics should be backed up by a teammate who has followed him closely enough to scoop up the deflected ball, using one of the methods described above, and throw it in as speedily as possible.

Sliding well takes plenty of practice, but you need to be careful about where you decide to practise. Soft, smooth, slippery outfields are ideal: hard, dry surfaces will destroy your trousers (not to mention the skin on your knees and thighs), while sandy outfields greatly increase the danger of your knee digging in. Because of the risk of injury, we recommend that sliding only be practised and used by players who have been correctly coached in this method.

What to watch

Traditional cricketing lore has always insisted that fielders in certain positions should watch specific points. For example, it is accepted doctrine that gully should watch the bat, while first slip should watch the ball. But what is the point of fielding? Are you trying to catch the edge of the bat, or the ball?

A word about fielding close to the bat when a batsman is going hard at a spinner: it's important to remember that the swept ball normally goes up off the bat, not down

WHY WATCH ONLY ONE?

Bob Woolmer recalled Stewart Leary once asking him, 'If you're watching the bat, how do you expect to see the ball?' Once he had begun coaching, Bob worked out a response: 'I think it's limiting to insist that players watch one thing or another: there is room to watch both bat and ball. Whether you watch the bat with your primary vision and the ball with your peripheral vision, or vice versa, you should try to be aware of both simultaneously. I fielded at short leg for nine years, a position in which you're supposed to stay rigidly focused on the batsman. But I found myself watching the bowler (while keeping the batsman in my peripheral vision) for one simple – but very important – reason: I wanted to see the length of the delivery, in order to be able to anticipate the shot the batsman was going to play. If I'd stayed locked onto the bat and pad, and the bowler banged in a short ball and the batsman defended it off his chest or face, I would have been in no position to see what was going on around the gloves. In other words, if I saw it was a bouncer, I was ready to take a catch off the gloves rather than off the boot or pad. Likewise, if I saw it was a length ball and the batsman started shaping to sweep, I could get down and curl into the smallest ball humanly possible!'

into the pitch, so when you need to take evasive action, you shouldn't be jumping up and turning away – that's the easiest way to get a firmly struck cricket ball hammered into your spine or the back of your head! Rather, you should be turning into a very tiny ball and collapsing on the ground. In this position, ignominious as it may seem, the ball is much more likely to pass safely over your head. Conversely, when you're fielding close on the off side, remember that off-side back-foot shots usually go down into the pitch, so be prepared to jump rather than hit the deck.

It's not only close fielders who can benefit from watching the bowler's length. If you're at cover point and you see the bowler drop the ball short, you can be sure the batsman is going to cut. The fuller the length, the finer the cut will be, and the shorter the length, the squarer the ball will go. You can therefore adjust your position and anticipate the ball's probable trajectory before it has even reached the batsman. This was no doubt one of the keys to Jonty Rhodes's astonishing success.

It sometimes happens that you're fielding in the deep, perhaps at deep backward square leg or deep fine leg, and you see the batsman play a big aggressive shot. Suddenly everyone is yelling at you, and a moment later the ball plops down the turf a few yards away. You simply never saw it, but whatever you tell the enraged bowler or frustrated teammates just sounds hollow and lame. However, one way of giving yourself the best opportunity to pick up the flight of the ball from your position in the deep is once again to watch the length: if it's short, you will recognize the hook-shot, perhaps played a little late, and you'll know to expect a high top-edge coming your way – and can start scanning the sky or background. Also learn to trust your ears to tell you how well the batter has made contact: a mis-hit sounds harsh and wooden, and means you should run in, whereas if it's come off the meat of the bat with a sweet crack, you know to hang back.

Anticipation

The greatest fielders in the game, especially those who patrol the covers or other positions close to the bat, often have highly advanced skills of anticipation. Jonty Rhodes, for example, seemed to be able to predict precisely where a ball was going to be struck before it ever reached the batsman. Some of his diving catches seemed to have been anticipated almost supernaturally early, his jump or dive timed to the split second.

Bobby Simpson, himself a superb fielder, recognized this ability but also found it mystifying:

> *The greatest cover and mid-wicket fielders share an uncanny and uncoachable ability to pick the shortest distance to the ball. The mental computer works out speed, angle*

and distance in a flash, the co-ordination between eyes and brain and legs is perfect, the fielder moves intuitively to where the ball is going to be. There must be some sort of radar involved and woe betide the batsman who underestimates it (1996, p. 43).

Similarly, the great Learie Constantine, knighted for his services to cricket, described the pre-emptive magic that great fielders are capable of when recounting a dismissal of Australian Bill Woodfull:

But Chapman's body began to move as Woodfull's feet were placed for the shot; he was half-way there in the split second taken by the flash of the bat on to the ball, which was hit with cracking force and was travelling like lightning; his left hand, shot far out in anticipation, closed round the ball and he had to stagger to save himself from falling headlong in Hendren's lap.... It is said by Australian and English veterans alike that that was the finest catch they ever saw in any land; it is notable mainly because Chapman's hand would have been feet short of the ball if he had not begun to move at the top of his speed and in the abandon of complete confidence before the ball met the bat, but after he had seen Woodfull's body and wrist shaping the stroke to come (Arlott, 1949, p. 200).

Scientists are beginning to explore this mysterious 'radar' in research on the visual challenges of fielding, and it may be that future study will unlock the key to the uncanny anticipatory ability of elite fielders.

THROWING

Getting the ball in from the deep, or attempting a run-out with a direct hit or a low, flat throw into the wicket-keeper's gloves, requires strength and accuracy, but more importantly, a good throwing technique. The throw, like the bowling action, must be smooth, grooved, fluent and repeatable (up to a point: the danger of throwing too hard for too long is discussed in the section on injuries in Chapter 10).

The ideal throw is the one used in baseball, in which the ball is drawn back over the shoulder so that it faces backwards, before the arm unwinds and throws it straight over the shoulder at the target.

But the nature of the game doesn't always allow for ideal technique. Batters steal singles, fielders find themselves on the wrong side of the ball needing to shy at the stumps, or fielders in the deep are wrong-footed by an unpredictable bounce. In these instances, you may need to flick the ball in underarm, or even backhand it at the stumps while you face entirely the wrong direction. These are important skills to cultivate, but if time allows, the classic baseball throw is the ideal.

The most important principles of the baseball throw are worth understanding.
- **The speed and accuracy of the throw will depend on the distance the ball starts from before it is released, and the length of the arm.** This is why an

YOU AND YOUR BOWLER

The relationship between fielder and bowler is one that is often neglected. If this relationship is not actively encouraged or foregrounded by coaches and captains, bowlers can start assuming that fielders are their lackeys, and fielders can start taking the bowler for granted as the bloke who'll do all the work. Or they might resent him when he doesn't bowl to his field.

As a fielder, it is your job to support the bowler. Remember that he's working much harder than you, and on your behalf, so it's your responsibility to make his life as easy as possible. Central to this is watching him at all times: few things are worse than a captain or bowler having to shout in order to get your attention.

Find out how the bowler wants the ball groomed (as explained in the chapter on bowling, a seamer prefers a dryer ball, while swing bowlers generally need one side very smooth or damp). Then give the ball some spit and polish (literally) according to the bowler's wishes every time it comes to you or is thrown to you between deliveries. When you toss it to the bowler at his mark, make sure that you throw cleanly and accurately: fast bowlers in particular will not be charmed at having to jump – or scrabble around their ankles – to take the ball. Ideally, they should just have to put out a hand and have the ball drop into it; but not everyone has the luxury of Jonty Rhodes trotting across, so accurate throws will have to do.

Then there is the matter of etiquette when taking – and dropping – catches. Remember that your performance can lift a bowler, or drive him to despair. England spearhead Bob Willis says he was given an extraordinary boost whenever fielders took sharp catches off his bowling when he was not performing at his best: inspired by his fielders, he would lift his own game. Conversely, when you seem to be dropping everything that comes your way, don't accept personal or hurtful comments by the frustrated bowler. (And the latter should remember the presence of the stump microphone in international matches; everyone remembers Shane Warne's alleged laconic on-field assessment of new teammate Scott Muller – 'Can't bowl, can't throw' – and the ensuing hullabaloo.) A little cursing and a reproachful look might be only human, but the bowler should never attack or blame the fielder, who will be feeling bad enough as it is. Remember that your body language sends an extremely loud and clear message to the bowler about what you think of him as a player: if he gets hit for four, the worst thing you can do is stand shaking your head or showing your frustration. This helps no-one, and can only make matters worse. The bowler will invariably become stressed, tighten up, and lose his control and rhythm.

overarm throw is likely to be speedier than a sidearm throw. However, more force is required for the overarm throw.
- **For maximum speed, the large shoulder muscles must come into action first, followed by the smaller arm and wrist muscles, in a whipping motion.** There are three main levers: the large shoulder muscles, the elbow muscles, and the wrist and forearm muscles. In order for a throw to have maximum force, the body moves in this sequence: hip rotation (pelvis), spinal rotation (back), shoulder motion, elbow extension, wrist flexion and finger extension.
- **In order to achieve optimum results, the force must be applied over a longer time period.** The overarm action allows the application of muscle torques over a longer period.
- **Setting yourself up for the throw:** once again, time may not be on your side, but you should try as far as possible to get into a strong throwing position after picking up the ball. The 'crow-hop' can be useful here – a small hop on one foot to regain balance and to gain control over your body, and also to put power into the throw. This saves the shoulder while providing you with power.

CATCHING

Catches win matches. It's a mantra known to every cricketer in the world, and one repeated so often by coaches and media commentators that it's often overlooked as one of the sport's many clichés. But despite being overused, its truth is as fresh today as it was a century ago. Steve Waugh knew that when he famously told Herschelle Gibbs that he had just dropped the World Cup, after Gibbs took a straightforward catch off the Australian captain during the World Cup semi-final in 1999 – and then dropped the ball as he raised his arm to celebrate. Every Test series has a dropped catch that can spell the difference between victory and defeat, the most dramatic example in recent times being the final day of the 2005 Ashes series: England's Kevin Pietersen survived three dropped catches en route to a match-saving – and series-winning – century at the Oval.

To be a good catcher, you will need:
- excellent reflexes
- a good eye
- good hands
- alertness and anticipation
- a still head.

For those taking running catches or high balls in the deep, speed across the ground will help them get into the right position. Sure-footedness will also help: high catches near the ropes often require the catcher to back-pedal, and those less sure or steady on their feet can trip over themselves or misjudge their distance from the boundary, giving away four runs or spilling a catch.

SOFT HANDS

In Chapter 3 we discussed the technique of playing with 'soft hands', and while catching with soft hands is an entirely different skill, the principle is the same: you are 'giving' with the ball to minimize its impact on your hands so that it does not pop out.

Picture the archetypal bar brawl in a Western movie: the gunslinger who gets punched in the stomach 'gives' with the punch, going back with its force, and in doubling over, 'catches' the fist in his own 'yielding' body. Stuntmen double over for a reason: stand up straight and rigid, and the impact of any blow is increased. More pertinent to cricketers is what happens to the puncher's fist if his victim takes the blow without 'giving' – it bounces off the body, just as the cricket ball bounces out of braced hands.

In other words, learning to give with the ball when taking it is very important. In this regard, repetition is very important, as this is a skill based almost entirely on 'feel' rather than technique. The exercise using a tennis ball described on p. 340 in relation to practising slip catching can also be used for learning to 'give' with soft hands.

HIGH CATCHES

If young players can make deep field catching look easy, then they are on their way to becoming very good cricketers: taking the high ball takes good judgement, concentration and courage. Fielders posted in the deep should focus on the following principles.

- Move swiftly to the area in which you calculate the ball might land.
- As the ball begins its descent, keep your head still and your hands high.
- Once you're in position, keep your knees slightly bent, and your body as relaxed as possible.
- Don't tense up at the last moment: if you take a tumble (especially if you are taking a high catch on the run), a loose body will jar less and enable you to hang on to the ball more easily.
- Don't take your eye off the ball for even a fraction of second – this is one of the major causes of dropped catches.
- As you are about to catch the ball, spread the fingers wide, making as large a surface as possible for the ball to hit. Once the ball makes contact, 'give' with your hands, taking the ball to your chest to absorb the force of the impact.

CUP POSITION: ENGLISH VERSUS AUSTRALIAN

There are two variations on techniques for high catches. In the first, the English method, the fielder holds his hands high and cupped in the direction of the ball, using the fingertips as a guide to the flight of the ball. The backs of the hands should face outwards. This method tends to be used in the United Kingdom, where the majority of catches are made easier by cloud cover.

The English method of taking a high catch

However, in countries where games are more likely to be played with sunshine blazing down on the pitch out of a cloudless blue sky, the Australian method is preferable. Here the fielder once again holds the hands high, but this time with the palms facing outwards towards the ball. The fingers are spread, allowing the fielder a better view of the ball against the light, shading his face while watching it through his fingers. As the ball is caught, the fielder should give at the knees to reduce the impact on his hands.

The Australian method: bend the elbows and take the ball down to the chest

FIELDING AND WICKET-KEEPING 335

Which technique you use doesn't only depend on the weather: many players use both in identical conditions, switching between the two depending on the height of the ball they are catching. You can use the English method up to about rib-height, but lift your cupped hands any higher (to a ball arriving around your collarbone, for example) and it will bounce out into your face. For catches above your head or over your face, the Australian method is an obvious and automatic choice. But for those catches around your collarbone and neck, the choice is less obvious – in catching terms, this is a kind of no-man's-land. The best option for these kinds of catches is a combination of the two techniques, in which you revolve your closing hands around the ball and catch it against your chest – as if you were describing a tubular flower with your hands and then wrapping its 'petals' around each other as it closes.

MINE!

Calling for catches – shouting loudly to your teammates that you are prepared to take a high ball – is very important in certain situations. Indeed, a failure to call can lead to the most horrific injuries, as players (who are staring intently at the ball) can run into each other at full tilt. Just such a collision between Steve Waugh and Jason Gillespie in Sri Lanka left the former with a broken nose, and the latter with a much more serious break to his leg.

Having the confidence to yell 'Mine!' under the swirling high ball is an enormous asset in a fielder. It demonstrates an important mental skill: the desire to catch the ball. Never feel that a catch is someone else's responsibility. Of course, many experience that sinking feeling as the ball is coming down, inwardly regretting that they're in the wrong place at the wrong time, but these are usually the fielders who can be relied on to drop half the catches that come their way.

The rule of thumb when calling is that the fielder running towards the ball is going to catch it far more easily than the player who has to chase out after it from the infield (often looking over his shoulder). However, if it goes straight up in the air, off a top-edge for example, the wicket-keeper should be told to get it, if he isn't already calling for it. He's the one wearing gloves, after all, and if he's looking uncertain, everyone needs to bellow 'Keeper!'.

SLIP CATCHING

The slips are specialist fielding positions, and just as fielders like Jonty Rhodes, Colin Bland and Ricky Ponting made their respective positions in the outfield their own, so other players have stamped their authority on the game through their speed, reach and reliability in the slips.

There have been many fine slip fielders: Brian McMillan and Daryll Cullinan of South Africa, Mark Taylor and Mark Waugh of Australia, Viv Richards and Brian Lara of the West Indies. But perhaps the greatest of them all was Australia's Bobby Simpson. It is not an exaggeration to say that Simpson would sometimes take catches with the ball already past him, and he made no secret of how hard he worked at his fielding, getting people to hit him catches off the face of the bat at extremely short range.

Today the reflexes and range of the slip cordon are constantly worked on by both coaches and players, and apart from the usual dips in the confidence of fielders or teams, slip catching has never been better.

HOW AND WHERE TO STAND

The ideal position for the slip fielder is shown on the right – knees bent, eyes level and hands ready. The knees are bent so that the catch can be taken without having to bend any further, which would cause the head to go down, taking the eyes off the line of the ball.

This position also enables the slip fielder to dive to either side (in the style of a soccer goalie) and also to jump for the high catch. This posture is based on three important facts about slip catching that you should understand and incorporate into your game:

- It is always easier to move upwards for a catch than to go down for it.
- The head must always be kept absolutely still until you have had a chance to judge the catch. Catching opportunities in the slips come very quickly, allowing little time for reaction, so keeping the head still will help.
- You want to keep your hands as low as possible. You want to stay down to come up, not stay up to go down.

Where to position themselves is an almost weekly dilemma for many slip fielders. Almost every one will at some time or another have a grumpy captain flapping a hand at him, telling him to come up or to give himself another yard. Still, an irritated skipper is infinitely preferable to the sight of the ball 'dying' off the edge of the bat and dropping a yard short of your hands, often adding injury to insult by skidding into your kneecap or ankle as you grope forward for it!

The classic slip-fielder's stance

Your distance from the bat should be judged largely according to the pace of the bowler and the wicket: you shouldn't need more than a delivery or two to get a feel for this. However, your spacing in the slip cordon is trickier, and even experienced and international teams regularly get this wrong, with fielders looking accusingly at each other as a nick bisects the gap between them. The best you and your captain can do is judge the spacing according to the strengths and weaknesses of the fielders in the cordon: good divers can stand wider apart, while less confident fielders mean narrower gaps. When in doubt, rather opt for smaller gaps, to guarantee that fine nicks will be caught.

There is only one thing worse for a bowler to see than the edge he has toiled for flying between a desperately diving keeper and first slip, and that is to see the edge flying between keeper and first slip with both fielders standing stock still, looking at the other, each assuming the other would try for it!

To stay friends with your fast bowler, stick to this simple rule of thumb: if it's going between the keeper and first slip, it's the keeper's catch. He's the one wearing the gloves, and he's the one who practised diving and rolling more than any other fielder. Basically, the only thing the keeper shouldn't attempt to grab is a catch headed straight for first slip.

WHERE SLIPS SHOULD STAND TO THE SPINNER

Even though you're standing only a couple of metres from the bat, the danger of the ball dropping short of your hands at slip is just as real as if you were standing 20 metres back to a fast bowler. In fact, all the reasons why a ball from a pace bowler might drop short apply equally to a spinner: a ball played with soft hands; a brush of the gloves; looping 'tennis ball' bounce; a touch of pad as well as bat.

Judge your position at slip according to the speed of the ball and the pitch. Assume the spinner is going to bowl at an average pace, neither flighting it up nor pushing it through flatter, until you get used to the speed at which he's actually bowling. If he has a quicker ball, you'll need to be warned in time so that you can take a step or two backwards (do this subtly: you don't want to telegraph this to the batsman). Perhaps pre-arrange a signal, such as a gesture, or learn to read your spinner's pre-delivery signs, such as a slightly altered run-up or gather. India's Anil Kumble and Pakistan's Shahid Afridi can produce extremely lively pace off their quicker leg-breaks, and the slips need to be alert to the possibility of the ball lifting at their chests or faces.

You'll refine your feel for where to stand as you gain experience, but a basic yardstick is about 2,5 metres from the bat. Any closer than that, and you're going to struggle.

TAKING THE CATCH

The guidelines already discussed in relation to conventional catching obviously also apply to slip catching, although here the ball is likely to be coming horizontally at your body instead of down towards you from an elevated angle. For low catches, dipping or 'dying' off the bat and heading for your shins and ankles, you will clearly need to cup your hands under the ball to scoop it off the grass; for blistering cuts or slogs that have sent the ball screaming for your chest or face, a 'reverse cup' technique is necessary. The iffish ones that come at your bottom rib will probably need the combination capture technique used in the outfield to take balls arriving at neck-height.

A demonstration of the cupping technique used to take a ball coming in at knee-height. Note the bent knees and the head tracking the ball.

However, unlike outfielders, slips also need to take the ball flying past them on their left or right. To guarantee yourself the best chance of hanging on to these chances, pay attention to some simple guidelines.

- Point your fingers away from the body, and create as large an area as possible by spreading the fingers wide.
- As you catch the ball, 'give' back along its path, keeping your hands 'soft' so that the force of the ball closes them.
- Move your head as close to the line of the ball as possible, which will allow you to get your weight behind your movement.
- In the case of wider catches, it might be impossible to get both hands to the ball. In this case, don't slap the ball or clutch at it. Keep it soft!
- If the ball is dropping short, you might have to dive or roll inwards. Similarly,

for the ball that is going quickly, the dive and roll will be backwards. Remember that the purpose of this kind of roll is to cushion the impact of your body on the ground, making it easier to hang on to the ball. All too often slip fielders take staggering catches at full lunge only to have the ball pop out when they hit the ground with their elbows. Even if you're at full stretch, about to do a 'belly flop' on the ground, try to turn your shoulder under you to land on your side or back, as shown in the panel alongside.

PRACTISING SLIP CATCHING

Slip catching is a discipline that needs as much practice as anything else. Fortunately it can be taught and practised in ways that are as enjoyable as they are effective: even the traditional semi-circle of fielders arranged around the coach (who hits catches in random directions off the face of the bat) can be fun.

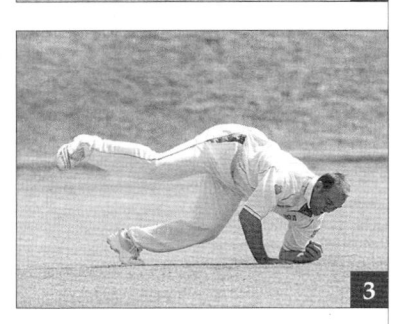

If you have access to any items of the specialized apparatus designed for catching practice, use them as much as you possibly can. The 'cradle' – a boat-shaped frame of wooden slats that sends the ball towards the slip cordon in random directions and at random heights – and the angled net are both very useful, and are in fact better for the fielder than facing catches off the coach's bat, since they include the elements of surprise and pace.

However, perhaps the best method of training catching and reflexes for slip fielders is to replicate a penalty shoot-out. Here the fielder stands in a marked-out 'goal' about 5 metres wide, while the coach hits a soft tennis ball with a tennis racket from a distance of between 10 and 15 metres, trying to score a goal. The use of a tennis ball helps teach the catcher how to 'give' with the ball, as the light weight of tennis balls makes them much more likely to pop out of the hands than heavier balls. After the catcher has taken 50–100 catches with a tennis ball, the coach should revert to a cricket ball – the catcher will be pleasantly surprised to discover how much easier it is to catch a cricket ball.

A perfectly executed dive and roll. The ball has been taken by the second frame; the sequence of movements that follows enables the fielder to maintain possession and control of the ball. Note the inward turn of the shoulder to cushion the impact of the body as it hits the deck.

FIELDING PRACTICE

Fielding is a 'grudge' discipline for many cricketers: unless you're in the slips or in the thick of things at gully or point, it can be dull and tiring. Once the match is over, practising it can seem even less like fun. But fielding needs almost more practice than batting and bowling, because it is the first of your cricketing disciplines that will get rusty in the off season, and the first to disappear entirely if you don't work at it. Bowlers need an over to remember their line and length, a day or two to find their rhythm. Batsmen can get their eye in and get their feet moving within an hour of picking up a bat. But ask either to take a sharp chance in the slips or get down to a rapidly rolling cover drive in the deep after a three-month lay-off, and they'll have problems.

Work hard at your fielding, but also work sensibly. Too many coaches simply hit balls about randomly, or do drills until they or the players get bored. To get the most out of your fielding practice – and to reach levels of excellence you didn't know you were capable of – set yourself goals during the season. Ideally, these should include:

- having confidence in your ability to pick up the ball cleanly
- throwing the ball in accurately from all distances and positions
- catching almost anything that is offered
- never misfielding a ball.

We outline some basic fielding and catching drills later in this chapter, as well as in Chapter 9, but the following is a position-specific routine, to give your practice sessions focus and intensity, as well as developing the specialized skills you will need. You should spend about ten minutes on each of these (less for younger players).

Slip cordon
1. 'Nicks' off the edge of the bat (use three players).
2. Left- and right-hand catching.
3. Diving and rolling technique (use gym mats).
4. High one-handers.
5. Head-high two-handers.
6. Balls coming at awkward heights.

Silly point
1. Correct positioning – use a batsman if necessary.
2. Watching the 'combat zone' – be aware of peripheral vision.
3. Staying down for as long as possible.
4. Avoidance technique, but staying alert for possible rebounds.

5. Positive reactions to calls of 'Catch it!' – don't automatically take cover.
6. Understanding the importance of the position to exert pressure on the batsman.

Short leg (forward and backward)

1. Proper technique – watching the ball or front pad, noting the length of the ball.
2. Catching within reach – reaction work.
3. Simulated catching – three in a group.
4. Diving and rolling – forward and to either side.
5. Avoiding injury – cushioning techniques (such as collapsing into a tight ball with your back to the batsman, or turning and jumping over a hard sweep).
6. Acting as keeper for quick run out to cover.
7. Position of feet.
8. Staying down.
9. Catching the fended-down bouncer.

Gully

1. Practise technique – balls slashed at gully from a thrower.
2. Diving left and right.
3. Rolling and reaction movements.

Inner ring

DEFENCE

1. Dealing with hard hits while walking in from crouched position.
2. Stopping the ball one-handed.
3. Long barrier; body blocking.

ATTACK

1. Pick up and throw on the run in one movement – overarm and underarm.
2. Changing direction of throw on calls of 'Bowler!' or 'Keeper!'
3. Attacking the stumps.
4. Learning to choose the correct option (for example, if a fielder calls from the opposite side because he has the best view of the action).
5. Throwing on the turn (including 'dummying' to discourage the batsman from setting off on a second run).
6. Chasing and sliding to knock the ball back from boundary; knocking ball back so that it is easy to collect.
7. Catching on the run – forwards, backwards, left and right.
8. Catching on the turn – the noise of ball on bat activates movement of fielder.

Outer ring

1. Making ground quickly to the ball, timing foot movements to coincide with the best pick-up and throwing position.
2. Diving or sliding to prevent the ball crossing the boundary.
3. Judgement of high catches using the boundary rope as a guide.
4. Developing the one-bounce throw to gain that extra yard.
5. Practising getting the ball into the air early to prevent the chance of another run.

These are merely guidelines: if you have developed your own effective drills or routines, borrow whatever works for you. But whatever you end up doing, always practise with discipline. As with all elements of cricket practice, half-hearted practising that just goes through the motions is almost worse than not practising at all.

FIELDING – A QUICK REFERENCE

In summary, these are the most important fielding points to remember.

- When in the ring, walk in as if you are a soccer goal-keeper defending a penalty; walk crab-style, and keep low.
- Throwing at the stumps is a vital skill; practise it as much as possible. Use your front arm as a guide, keep your head forward, and look at a point on the base of the stumps that you are aiming for.
- Backing up is crucial: even if you are on the boundary, you should always advance in to help back up at either end. Try and read the situation early.
- Run-outs: stay calm and remember accuracy is essential – always throw the ball firmly and at a catchable height, unless you're aiming for a direct hit on the stumps.
- The slide pick-up and return is the fastest and best method of returning the ball.
- Relay throwing (as in baseball) can be very effective. If the grounds are big, with long distances to the boundary, try and get to an area 30 metres from the stumps, where the deep fielder can throw the ball to you with one bounce.
- Throwing from the deep: in the past, simply getting the ball into the air was a deterrent to the batsmen running. While this is still the case, it has also been proved that it is swifter to pick the ball up on the run, change direction towards the stumps so that your momentum is going towards the area you need to get the ball to, and throw hard either with one bounce or flat to the keeper.
- Throw flat, hard and direct, but be aware that it can sometimes be better to throw with one bounce, especially to the bowler's end.
- Making a real effort to take a catch in a game shows commitment and spirit: don't be shy!

WICKET-KEEPING[1]

INTRODUCTION

The wicket-keeper plays one of the most critical, demanding and thankless roles on the cricket field. Not only must he be supremely fit and focused, he must also be a tactician, a coach and a motivator. He must be prepared to catch or field every single ball bowled in an innings; he must run to the stumps after every delivery; he must dart around the batsman to field defensive prods – all without the chance to catch his breath and rest his legs down at fine leg like the fast bowlers. It is the wicket-keeper who must notice that the batsman is shuffling across his crease or lungeing with a hint of desperation at the spinner; it is he who must encourage and advise his bowlers, reassuring his quick men that they're hitting the gloves nice and hard, or watching their front arm if they've asked him to diagnose a problem in their action. Late on a hot summer's afternoon, with two batsmen well set on big hundreds, with the ball soft and old and the pitch rock-hard, it is he who must persuade his bowlers – and sometimes his captain! – that a breakthrough is just one ball away.

Dave Richardson, South Africa's stalwart wicket-keeper when they re-entered international cricket in the early 1990s, summed it up when he said, 'The wicket-keeper has to keep the spirit of the fielding side up – you can't ever look miserable, not even if you've just let four byes through.'

The demands on the wicket-keeper's concentration, fitness and focus are immense, and it is not surprising that the thoroughbred gloveman is one of the most rare commodities in the game: even the usually impertubable and genial Richardson could look utterly distraught at times, hands on head and heart in boots. The ideal wicket-keeper is agile, focused and skilled enough to catch a ball even when a heavy bat is flashing in front of his face. He possesses a safe and soft pair of hands; he is brave, mentally strong, and has as much stamina as a fast bowler.

Professionalism and a stoic understatement are often the hallmarks of the great keepers – you will very rarely hear the likes of Alan Knott, Ian Healy or Jeff Dujon complain about their lot in life. Which is all the more admirable given that the wicket-keeper is to a certain extent the Cinderella of the side: he works harder than anyone else, maintains extremely high levels of fitness, has to act as cheerleader, nursemaid,

'You can't ever look miserable, not even if you've just let four byes through.'

– Dave Richardson

---

[1] This section relies heavily on the out-of-print 1977 classic *Alan Knott on Wicket-keeping* – still the finest book ever written on the topic. Our thanks to Alan for kindly permitting us to use his material.

and second-in-command; yet his successes are taken for granted, and his mistakes are roundly condemned by all and sundry. A fielder who saves four runs on the boundary is praised for his commitment; the keeper who gets his body behind a badly directed ball down the leg side and saves four byes is almost entirely overlooked. Finally, even if he is a phenomenally successful batsman, he is unlikely ever to be considered the star of the team: even Adam Gilchrist, whose Test batting career often put him on a par with the greatest batsmen in history, was usually overshadowed by his teammates, whether Shane Warne, Matthew Hayden, Ricky Ponting or Glenn McGrath. Similarly, Dave Richardson, who often held South Africa's brittle middle- and lower-order together in the early days after his county's readmission to international cricket, was entirely eclipsed in the public eye by Hansie Cronje, Jonty Rhodes and Brian McMillan.

THE END OF THE SPECIALIST WICKET-KEEPER

Thirty years ago the criteria for the selection of a Test wicket-keeper were straightforward: he needed to be a good team man and a fine tactician, but above all he needed to be an excellent gloveman. Whether standing up to the spinners or standing back to the quicks, he needed the safest and quickest pair of hands in the country, the deftest feet and the strongest back. His batting ability was simply not a concern: if he could score runs in the lower order it was considered a bonus, but otherwise the best one could hope for was a fairly straight bat that could hold up an end for half an hour while the real batsman did the scoring.

No longer. One-day cricket, and the renewed focus on the development of all-rounders, has made it vital for keepers not only to be able to bat, but to lead the batting assault if their team is in trouble. A generation ago, the wicket-keeper-batsman was a rare asset. Today he is a basic requirement. The modern international wicket-keeper must average at least 30 in Tests, and be able to score at six an over in limited-overs cricket, with the strength and ability to hit sixes in the closing overs. The result is a batting line-up that is slowly lengthening: the top six in the batting order is now often a top seven, with the likes of Adam Gilchrist or South Africa's Mark Boucher effectively playing the role of another frontline batsman, with the technique and temperament to see off the second new ball and score big hundreds.

But the foregrounding of batting has been at the expense of glove skills. Adam Gilchrist happens to be a skilled craftsman behind the stumps as well as a phenomenal batting talent, but the reality of the modern game is that teams can no longer afford to

The modern international wicket-keeper must average at least 30 in Tests, and be able to score at six an over in limited-overs cricket, with the strength and ability to hit sixes in the closing overs.

pick the best possible wicket-keeper. These days, most opt for the best wicket-keeper-batsman instead.

Commentator Simon Hughes attributes this change in part to the dependence on fast bowling in international cricket:

This change in emphasis has been hastened by the domination of pace bowling. To pace bowling, keepers spend most of their time standing back – an easier skill than grubbing around to spin standing up to the stumps.

However, a decline in the standard of glovemanship may not be entirely the result of fundamental changes in the game. Wicket-keepers often get the short end of the stick when it comes to coaching, whether at junior or international level, and in a 2002 article in *The Cricketer*, England and Gloucestershire wicket-keeper Jack Russell made no bones about what he saw as deliberate – and potentially costly – neglect:

I simply can't understand why we are neglecting our keepers when millions are being spent on a National Academy and other centres of excellence… if they can afford to employ physiologists and other vital back-up as part of the modern game, surely they can look after the keepers. Or have they become the poor relations of the English game?

A traditionalist view, one might argue, coming from a player whose generation could still afford the luxury of specialist keepers. But the value of good coaching and development for wicket-keepers is constantly being demonstrated, even in one-day cricket.

For instance, in 2001, India decided to accommodate the inclusion of at least one all-rounder down in the order in one-day games. Since that country had (until the arrival of Mahendra Singh Dhoni) a tradition of producing wicket-keepers with profound batting disabilities, they put star batsman Rahul Dravid behind the stumps. The move was an unmitigated disaster. While brilliant in front of the stumps, behind them Dravid turned into a liability, dropping catches, missing stumping chances, and generally helping to create the impression that the team was a B-grade outfit.

The moral of this story is clear: the modern wicket-keeper cannot simply be a glorified long-stop. He needs all the skills of the great specialist glovemen of times past; but he must also bat – and bat well.

WICKET-KEEPING TECHNIQUES

For Alan Knott, the essentials of wicket-keeping could be pared down to just two points: 'the ability to see the ball early, and then to catch it whether it comes in from a delivery, a hit, or a throw-in.'

However, in order to give yourself the best opportunity to implement these two essentials, you need to develop a solid wicket-keeping technique. From your stance and the way you move your feet, to how you catch the ball and anticipate the batsman's movements, your technique will define your success or failure behind the stumps. Wicket-keeping is an art, and like any sporting art, it needs to be learned, absorbed, and then endlessly practised.

STANCE

Where and how you stand as a wicket-keeper is a question of personal taste, but you cannot compromise on comfort: if your stance doesn't allow you to be comfortable, loose and mobile for a full day in the field, you will simply not survive as a keeper.

In the classic stance, your feet are just over shoulder-width apart, with your left foot in line with off-stump (in the case of a right-handed batsman on strike). Your hands hang forwards between your knees, palms upwards and ready, while your arms should be relaxed. Your head and eyes should be level, and as still as possible.

Many wicket-keepers still prefer to stand with their gloves on the outside of either foot. While you must use whichever stance you're most comfortable with – and this one is particularly comfortable – we don't recommend it, since it means you have to move your hands a fairly long way towards the centre to take the ball, which can make you a split-second too late.

However, you should experiment with stances until you find the one that feels best: the game has seen many idiosyncratic stances developed by keepers more concerned with comfort and mobility than textbook illustrations. Some stood with feet together and their knees out to either side; others preferred standing with half-bent knees and their hands outside their pads (giving them a somewhat simian look, it must be confessed!). Wally Grout, Australia's stalwart gloveman of the 1950s and 60s, rested his elbows on his knees, keeping his hands together under his eyes; while the great South African keeper Ray Jennings didn't even squat, instead standing almost upright like a slip fielder.

Whichever stance you end up adopting, remember that it must allow you to move quickly and easily, and mustn't cause stiffness or pain. The mantra of the good keeper should be to keep the mind sharp but the body loose: if any part of you becomes tense or strained, you're more likely to move slowly, spill catches, or injure yourself.

Two of the more commonly seen stances in modern cricket: the classic crouch (top) and the stance with gloves resting on the ground (above).

FIELDING AND WICKET-KEEPING

Most of the leading wicket-keepers in the modern game use the classic squatting position, with their knees fully bent. Many also prefer to have their hands resting gently on the ground. Depending on what feels most comfortable, you can rest your weight either on the balls of your feet, or, for long sessions on hard surfaces, you might like to place the whole of the foot on the ground. Whichever you choose, you should be balanced and stable: no-one should be able to rock you off your feet.

Your stance must also give you the best possible sight of the ball: you need to watch it unblinkingly all the way from the bowler's hand, with as much intensity and focus as if you were batting.

WHY AREN'T GREAT WICKET-KEEPERS ALSO GREAT BATSMEN?

Test cricket has produced many wicket-keepers who were more than useful batsmen. Dave Richardson was invaluable to an inexperienced South African team during the 1990s, while the West Indies' Jeff Dujon and Australia's Ian Healy often hammered the final nails into the coffin after their ferocious top orders had dug the grave. Both men were capable of scoring Test hundreds against the best bowling in the world. Sri Lanka's Romesh Kaluwitharana can even take half the credit for revolutionizing one-day batting, given the ferocity with which he and Sanath Jayasuriya torched the world's bowlers in the 1996 World Cup.

Wicket-keeping and batting success seem to be logically linked. More than any other player, the wicket-keeper gets a feel for the pace, bounce and idiosyncrasies of the pitch. He spends his life watching bowlers, reading spinning balls out of the hand, or analysing the actions of fast bowlers to prepare for quick balls or bouncers. And yet if one thinks of the greatest batsmen of all time, not one is a wicket-keeper. Australia's Adam Gilchrist is the closest thing the game has ever known to a champion batsman who also keeps wicket.

The reason for this dearth of great batsmen in the keeping fraternity has less to do with their ability than it does with their focus. Wicket-keeping demands a major commitment in terms of time, effort, practice and energy – more so than batting. For a player to be great in both departments would take a superhuman effort.

Another factor is a lack of opportunities. Even the best wicket-keeper-batsmen only slot into the order around number 6 or 7, by which time the rhythm of the innings is dramatically different to the way it was for the top order. For the 'real' batsmen, time is not a factor, and all their attention is focused on accumulation and survival. But the wicket-keeper who comes in with just three wickets standing knows he must press on before he runs out of partners, or before his captain declares. Often he needs to sacrifice his wicket in the quest for quick runs. Furthermore, if he comes in with his team well set, there is perhaps less pressure, and more likelihood of a soft dismissal.

STAYING DOWN

Because the basic wicket-keeper stance is a crouch, it is a natural reflex to want to stand up straight when the ball arrives. This is a combination of fear, laziness, and a normal response to any demand for action: fear because of the danger of being hit in the mouth by the ball or the back of the bat; laziness, because standing up is always a relief to tired legs and back; and a normal response because we instinctively want to be upright (albeit a little hunched) when dealing with any sudden and unexpected danger or activity.

However, the key to good wicket-keeping is 'staying down'; that is, remaining in your stance for as long as possible, at very least until the ball pitches. Even when you finally do 'get up' into a more upright stance, your gloves should remain low and grounded. This is why flexibility is so important for keepers: you need to be able to stand bent over with your knees almost straight, but the backs of the hands still on the ground.

If you get up out of your crouch too early, you run the risk of dropping the ball or missing it entirely, especially if it keeps low.

STANDING BACK

It can be a deeply unnerving sight for a batsman to see a wicket-keeper tramp off into the distance and make his mark 20 metres behind the wicket: more than any muscle-bound fast bowler or grassy wicket, it shows him precisely what kind of bowling he's about to face, and that he's about to be put through the mill!

Standing back to the quick bowlers is an obvious decision: you want to give yourself the best chance of seeing the ball and reacting to any deviations in line; you also want to place yourself near the spot where the ball will be dropping to between waist- and knee-height in its trajectory. Exactly how far back you stand will naturally depend on the pace and bounce of the wicket, and will also vary from bowler to bowler.

Knott preferred to give himself a yard or two once his quick bowlers had settled into their rhythm:

> *Most keepers like to catch at about waist-height, when standing back, but I prefer to take the ball at knee-height. This means I can stand an extra yard or so deeper and have that much more time to sight and move after the ball. This can be vital, especially when going for the wide deflections.*

However, early on, before he had gained a sense of the pace of the wicket or worked out exactly what the ball was doing off the seam, he came up to cover all the options:

© QUINTIC

Here Alan Knott is standing back by a good 12 or 15 metres.

> *If an edge comes, it is better to be too near than too far.... The deflection may come to you very quickly and at an awkward height, but at least you have a chance which is denied to you if the ball bounces before reaching your gloves.*

Once you have settled on your position, mark the spot by scratching a small line with your heel or a stud. Give yourself enough room outside the off-stump to allow for any deflections off an outside edge, but also consider the type of bowler you're keeping to: the Shaun Pollocks and Glenn McGraths bowl very close to the stumps and tend to bowl dead straight, leg-stump to off-stump, while bowlers like Malcolm Marshall and Makhaya Ntini deliver from wide of the stumps, their natural angle taking the ball into the batsman's body or even down the leg side. This wider angle will also produce a different variety of outside edge: the edge tends to be thicker, almost a leading edge, with the result that the ball will either fly wider than the conventional nick, or will have less momentum and will start 'dying' in the air sooner. Different bowling angles thus mean different positions for the wicket-keeper.

If you are unsure about how much room to give yourself outside off-stump, or whether to stand straighter in line, go back to basics and position yourself so that you can see the ball pitch on a good length. Knott explains:

> *If you stand directly behind the line of the stumps, you will not see those deliveries pitch because they will be hidden by the batsman's body or bat. To take my position, move across so that when you are squatting, you can see all three stumps at the other end and then go approximately 12 inches wider, so that you can see a gap between the two sets of stumps.... The importance of seeing these good-length deliveries pitching on leg or middle stump is that they might swing late or seam outwards towards the off side.*

Remember, don't let wishful thinking – or nervousness about taking stinging catches – cloud your judgement of the pace of the bowler or wicket: standing too far back won't help anyone, and of all the balls a wicket-keeper must gather, the most difficult and dangerous is the fast ball that bounces a metre or less in front of him.

STANDING UP

Standing up to the stumps (a misnomer, since you should be crouching) is often considered the true test of glovemanship. Whether taking flighted leg-spin pitching on leg-stump and disappearing behind the batsman's body, or having medium-pace swing or cutters thump into your gloves, standing up raises the wicket-keeping stakes dramatically. Reaction times are vastly reduced and deflections are past you in the blink of an eye; the back of the bat is swishing perilously close to your face; dust and grit kicked up by the spinners is spraying into your eyes and mouth; and all this while you keep an eagle eye on the batsman's back foot, hunting for a stumping.

As with standing back, how close you stand to the stumps should be a product of experimentation. However, you want to be close enough to effect a stumping without having to stretch too far or step forward. Knott says:

> I stood as close as was comfortable in that I tried to make sure that my pads were not going to touch the stumps, or the peak of my cap dislodge the bails. By being closer, you can cut down slightly the angle of the edged ball... on the other hand, some feel that if they are a little deeper, it gives them more time to sight the ball.

Whatever you do, though, don't stand wide of the stumps: your head should be as close to the off-stump as possible to give you the best sense of the ball's line. Since you're now close enough to see round the batsman, you should be able to watch even the good-length balls off the pitch. As the ball comes up after pitching, your hands should follow it, with your body coming up out of the squatting position. Although your heels will drop to push you up, keep your weight forward so that you are able to move swiftly without losing your balance.

© QUINTIC

Knott standing up to a slow bowler

STANDING UP TO MEDIUM PACE

A generation ago, many batsmen deliberately stood out of their ground when facing medium-pace bowling, to force the wicket-keeper to come up to the wicket and so reduce his chances of catching any edges. Not many keepers relished this – a misjudged take of a ball travelling at 100km/h could cause serious damage to the face – but the refinement of one-day cricket (in which batsmen are far more eager to come down the pitch) has seen it entrenched as a skill all keepers need to work on.

Bob Woolmer recalled: 'I saw a good example of this while playing for Kent against Leicestershire. Roger Tolchard (Leicestershire and England) was particularly good at mucking bowlers about by coming down the pitch and using innovative foot movements. Alan Knott much preferred to stand back to me as I swung the ball; however, by coming down the pitch Roger was nullifying the swing, so I asked Alan to stand up. The transformation was huge: Roger was no longer confident about coming down the pitch, and I was able to bowl much straighter, which ended with a frustrated Roger holing out at cover or mid-off.'

This tactic has born fruit for many other teams, such as New Zealand (whose slow and medium bowlers, like Chris Harris and Nathan Astle, were then able to bowl dead-straight and get batsmen to lose their cool), and Gloucestershire, which dominated English one-day cricket for five seasons.

TAKING THE BALL

If there is a golden law of wicket-keeping, it is this: expect every delivery to come to you. You therefore need to prepare yourself to take the ball every time the bowler runs in.

Most important in this preparation is the position of your hands. For two-handed catching (which should be your default setting as a keeper), the gloves should form a soft, relaxed cup. The centre of the palms form a natural hollow – your main catching area – while the sides of the hands and fingers form 'walls' that keep the ball in place. This is why you should be careful about over-padding your palms, since it reduces the catching area.

The fingers should be wide enough to ensure a large catching area, but not so widely spread that they become tense. Most good wicket-keepers keep the thumbs clear, and slightly overlap the hands, with the little finger of the dominant hand inside the other hand. However, some simply bring their hands alongside each other, with the little fingers pressed together with no overlap: the great Ian Healy preferred this method, so it does have a considerable pedigree.

With the ball now airborne and hurtling towards your neatly cupped gloves, it is time to start adjusting the direction of your fingers according to the delivery. Never keep them pointing towards the ball as you take it: that way lie serious fractures, split fingertips, and nasty dislocations, as your fingers have nowhere to go but back on themselves or into your knuckle joints. Instead use these basic guidelines:

- For stock deliveries, with the ball coming directly towards you, point your fingers down.

OUT OF LINE

The classic wicket-keeper's take sees him stand directly in line with the ball, his gloves dead centre and low, and then giving down into his stomach or between his legs as he catches the delivery. However, some keepers prefer to get their heads and hands to one side of the line of the ball, which result in them taking the ball with a more sideways-on action, a split second before the ball passes them. As long as your eyes and hands work together, this isn't necessarily a bad technique – South Africa's Mark Boucher has had considerable success with it, and Alan Knott endorsed it as a good way of dealing with deliveries that bounce through at chest-height. However, with the keeper no longer in line with the delivery, any swing after pitching can be very difficult to accommodate, and the keeper can find himself suddenly too close or too far from the ball as it crosses the catching zone in front of his chest. The best way of dealing with this problem is to turn your hip away from the movement of the ball, which gives your hands the room they need to do their job.

- For balls that move laterally to either side, point your fingers to that side.
- For rising balls, point your fingers upwards so that your palms face the bowler – the keeper's version of the 'Australian' method of catching, described on p. 335.

Remember to keep your hands low: stay down while you wait for the ball to bounce, and then raise your hands along the line of the ball – especially if you are standing up to a spinner – with your fingers pointing downwards.

Taking the spinning or medium-pace ball

The fundamental purpose of standing up to the stumps is to be in a position to effect a stumping. You could give yourself a metre – or even two – against the spinners and be in a much better position to take fine edges and deflections; giving yourself five or ten against the medium-pacers would no doubt be a blessed relief; but doing either would immediately neutralize all chances of stumping the batsman.

Thus, throughout the following discussion, remember one simple guiding principle when standing up to the stumps: whichever way you move (off side or leg side), keep one foot within striking distance of the stumps. This will keep your weight more or less where it should be, and you won't be lungeing in vain and missing the bails with outstretched gloves.

When standing up to the spinners or medium-pacers, it is essential that you keep your knees out of the way, so that they do not interfere with your take, or hinder you from 'giving' with the ball. One way is to keep the knees as straight as possible: Alan Knott recommends starting to straighten them (coming out of the squat) as the ball leaves the bowler's hand, while keeping your gloves on the ground until the ball pitches. If you're doing it correctly, you'll look as if you're touching your toes, but with your eyes facing forward to the oncoming delivery.

Some keepers prefer to move one leg backwards a little way. We don't recommend this, however, as it can cost precious microseconds in a stumping situation. Others,

BE READY FOR THE EDGE

'Whether I was keeping to an off-spinner or to a leg-spinner, I would have my hands waiting for the outside edge. This would mean that, for the off-spinner, my hands were on the line of the delivery, but for the leg-spinner, that they were on the *predicted* line: i.e., that the ball would turn and beat the outside edge. Although in both cases the hands are left on the off side, be ready to move them quickly to leg.' – Alan Knott

with particularly loose and flexible hamstrings, spread their knees and keep them bent as they take the ball. If you opt for this position, remember to keep your knees very wide apart, or you'll be in danger of trapping your hands between them.

Tight lines

When preparing to take balls that are coming through just outside off-stump, try to stay behind the line of the delivery. For wider deliveries, Knott recommends a slight alteration:

> *You will have to move your right foot across, trying to make sure you take [the ball] parallel with, or possibly forward but never backwards from, the return crease. This movement brings your head as near to the line of the ball as possible. If the stride feels awkward, you should allow your left foot to follow across naturally, so that you are once again comfortable and balanced. But be careful not to move your left foot so far that you have difficulty in bringing your hands back to the wicket… if the ball is that wide, I keep my head and body slightly inside the line.*

Leg-side deliveries can be tricky, especially if the ball has landed in the rough area created by the bowler's footmarks, or on a crumbling wicket. It is essential that you see the ball pitch before committing yourself to a movement. However, this isn't always possible, and if the ball pitches so close to the batsman that you cannot read it off the pitch, you will at least have judged the flight and moved your gloves into a taking position behind the line of the ball. Knott's technique is worth emulating at times like these:

> *If I see the ball heading for the leg side, I move my left foot slightly towards that side, keeping my head still and peering round the batsman's body to watch the ball pitch. When I have moved my left foot across, my right foot follows, and then I often need to move my left foot again [a sideways chassis], so that I have covered a considerable amount of ground. But my body weight is still slightly towards the stumps… I try never to take my right foot so wide of the leg stump that my hands cannot reach back to the bails.*

Taking the ball down the leg side off a medium-pacer is one of the toughest wicket-keeping skills to master; however, with practice (and courage!), you can make it part of your armoury – you will find it an exceptionally useful weapon.

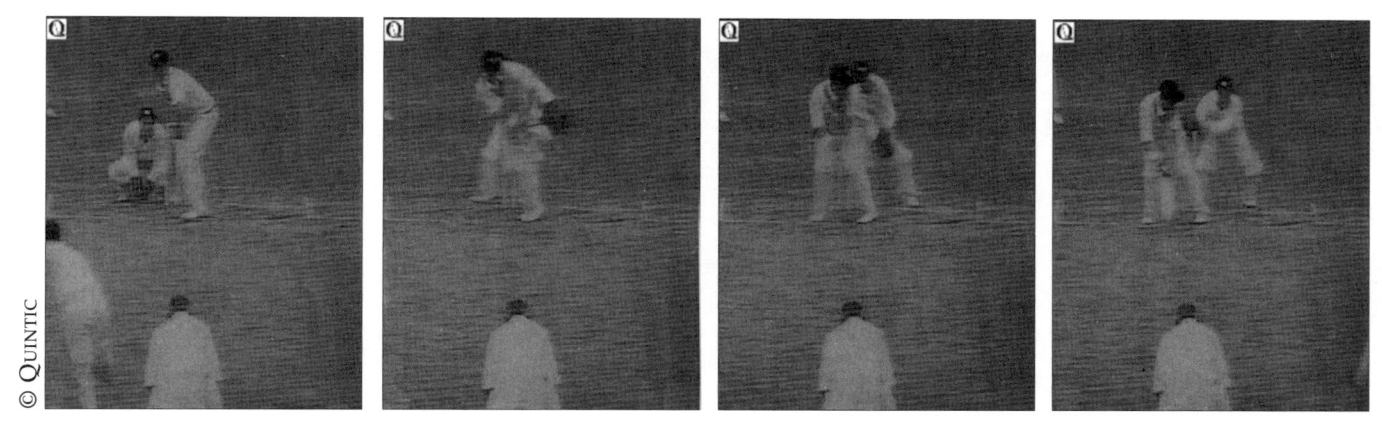

Alan Knott takes a ball from Basil D'Oliviera down the leg side against New Zealand.

Taking it off *that* length

Every wicket-keeper knows that at some stage (perhaps once a match, perhaps once an over!) he'll be called upon to take a ball pitching on that vicious length somewhere between a half-volley and short-of-length delivery. This is the ball that causes even the most seasoned Test keepers to turn their heads at the last minute, eyes clamped shut and face grimacing, as it spits up at the thighs or stomach, kicking up muck into their eyes.

As one of the most experienced keepers in the game, and one who stood up more than most modern keepers (partly because he faced more slow bowlers, but also because he had the skill to stand up to quicker medium-pacers), Alan Knott was no stranger to the dangers of the ball that pitches a metre or two in front of the keeper:

> *The half-volley can be taken just after it has hit the ground, so there is no time for any change of direction, but the ball pitching shorter, especially into the rough, has enough space to become unpredictable. The time left for you to detect any unusual movement is so brief that these deliveries are the hardest to take cleanly.*

There is no more difficult skill in wicket-keeping than taking the ball down the leg side that has pitched on this length, especially on a crumbling pitch: the ball's trajectory after it pitches is variable (it might bounce, skid, or jag unpredictably); you have much less time to react because of its fuller length; and it is obscured by the batsman's body for most of its flight after pitching.

The solution to this daunting challenge is practice, practice and more practice. Put up a set of stumps at the bowler's end of the nets, and ask your coach to throw the ball at the rough the bowlers have created. Of course, some pitches won't allow for this, especially if the bowlers have dug long trenches all over their crease: in these cases, find some rough elsewhere, perhaps on a newer pitch, or simply on an uneven bit of outfield. The uneven bounce, the explosion of fine debris, and the skidding motion of the ball off that difficult length should help you get accustomed to that kind of delivery in a match situation.

STUMPINGS

The golden rule of stumping is simple: take the ball first! Nobody ever made a stumping without the ball in his hands.

Since the idea of the stumping is to knock the bails off the stumps (with ball in hand!) while the batsman is out of his crease, it clearly requires the wicket-keeper to swing his arms and hands back to the stumps from wherever he has taken the ball. Indeed, many keepers prefer to bring the ball back to the bails after every delivery, whether trying for a stumping or not. It can be a useful psychological weapon – Ian Healy used it to great effect – but don't overdo it and accidentally knock off the bails every few deliveries: this won't charm the umpires.

While a swing of the arms is economical, most wicket-keepers prefer to move their entire bodies when going for the stumping. Hands and arms follow knees and legs; never more so than when Jack Russell, taking wide balls, would run at and past the stumps as he swung at them.

Alan Knott points out that bringing the ball back to the stumps with both hands 'means that for all wide deliveries, the body and shoulders must be turned to face the stumps, so that both arms have the same reach towards the wicket.' However, there is obviously more room to play with if you are able to effect a one-handed stumping. While this is a means of carrying out a stumping when you are too far away from the stumps to use both hands, there have been wicket-keepers who have chosen this as a method of stumping.

It is vital that once you have taken the ball with both hands, you are able to transfer it swiftly and easily to the one closer to the stumps, so practise this diligently. While most wicket-keepers prefer to change the ball to their dominant hand (the right-handed Knott found it awkward transferring it to his left hand), it might be useful to practise transferring it to either hand.

CATCHING

Taking the ball obviously implies catching it, but as mentioned in the introduction to this chapter, it is taken for granted that the wicket-keeper will catch those deliveries that are left or missed by the batsman. But the wicket-keeper's catch is something entirely different from his regulation take: his catch always implies that the ball has first made contact with the bat or gloves, leading to a dismissal.

A sharp gather and attempted stumping down the leg side. Notice how the keeper stays within striking distance of the stumps, and quickly transfers the ball to his right hand.

The most important asset good catchers possess are 'soft hands', discussed in more detail in the preceding section on fielding. While the wicket-keeper generally doesn't have the luxury of 'giving' with the ball back into his chest or midriff like the fielder at slip or cover, the principle of catching the ball with soft hands is the same behind the stumps as in front of them: a six-inch recoil with the force of the ball, the momentum of which should close your hands around the ball.

Stiffness or jerkiness is your greatest enemy as a catcher: going at the ball with your hands and wrists (rather than letting it come to you), or remaining braced and rigid as it makes contact with your gloves – all these are one-way tickets to dropped catches. Indeed, early in his career Australian keeper Rodney Marsh was known as 'Old Irongloves' because of an apparent inability to give with the ball. Catches continued to go down until he solved the problem.

One-handed catches

Don't be a hero. One-handed catches are your last resort, to be reserved for nicks that are flying so wide that you need to dive or make rapid ground to either side: trying to be too casual by catching straighter edges one-handed is both ostentatious and risky.

When you go for the ball one-handed, point your fingers outwards and let your head lead your body across to the line of ball. Keep your hands on the line of the ball. For deliveries that need to be taken above or on the same level as your head, use your stronger hand to do the actual catching, supporting it with the other.

Catching two-handed provides a naturally bigger cup, which disappears when only one hand is used. Most keepers, when taking a ball one-handed, will use their finger and thumb, with the ball secured at the base of these fingers. Alan Knott tried to centre the ball under his index finger, making use of the web between the thumb and index finger of his glove:

> *The cup for the one-handed catch has three walls to it. The first wall is formed by the ring and little finger brought upwards facing the thumb, which becomes the second wall. The top of the web [of the glove] then forms the third wall. But the web should not be so taut that you lose the control and movement you need in the thumb, or the ball springs back out; yet if the web is too loose, the ball can easily squeeze out between the forefinger and thumb.*

If you've launched yourself after a ball with one hand, and realize that it is not as far away as you originally judged, as soon as you glove it, bring the other hand down over it as a precaution.

Many keepers like to bring the ball back to the bails after every delivery, whether trying for a stumping or not. It can be a useful psychological weapon, but don't overdo it and accidentally knock off the bails every few deliveries: this won't charm the umpires.

'Alan Knott taught me that the line of the ball should form a T or right-angle to your hand. Imagine a line or laser-beam coming out of the middle of your palm at 90° to your hand. Now take a few one-handed catches and see where that laser is pointing – chances are good it's pointing out away from your body, or else it's hooked back towards your body as your hand closes down on the ball. It should point down the line of the ball.' – Bob Woolmer

Diving and rolling

While most catches that come the way of the wicket-keeper are more or less straight, perhaps deviating a little distance to the right (to the right-handed batsman), there are times when he must fling himself across the pitch or even in front of the slips after sharp deflections and grab the ball inches off the grass. Being able to hang onto edges that keep low is a vital skill of the keeper, but also one of the discipline's most rewarding: few aspects of keeping wicket provide as big a rush as pulling off a diving catch, as illustrated below.

© QUINTIC

Knott dives in front of first slip to pouch a sharp chance.

The ideal position after the roll: glove cupped under and around the ball, arm straight, and free hand cushioning the impact of the dive and roll.

To be a good diver, you will need to develop the strength and suppleness of your legs, particularly your thighs: launching yourself full-length to either side from a squat takes considerable strength.

But what goes up must come down, and you must also learn to roll correctly. The roll is perhaps the most important part of the entire action, since this is what cushions your impact on the ground, thus preventing the ball from popping out of your outstretched glove.

Learn to roll in small stages. Start on your knees, launching yourself to either side from a kneeling position to get a feel for the motions and impacts of diving and rolling. Once you can dive and roll from your knees without spilling the ball, move up onto your haunches. Depending on whether you've caught the ball in front of you (facing the batsman) or behind you (whipping around after it to face the outfield where it was heading), you'll need to turn either your left or right shoulder into the roll in order to land on your side. Whichever way you turn and roll, keep your catching arm (or arms) out as straight as possible so that your elbows don't plough into the turf and jar the ball free.

Overhead catches

The basics of taking the high ball are similar to those outlined in the section on general fielding: the Australian method of catching is still safer and easier than the English version where overhead catches are concerned.

However, the wicket-keeper also has to take his gloves into account. Unless he practises taking overhead catches wearing them, he can easily fall into the trap of replicating what the hands do when not wearing gloves. The result will be clumsiness and a spilled catch.

Alan Knott's personal preference in this case was to place his right index finger and thumb on top of those of the left hand, the centre of the cup now forming where the two index fingers met. He would still usually take the ball with his right hand, with the left hand now forming the side wall, so he would try to ensure that the ball arrived just beneath his right index finger.

The Australian method of taking the ball: in this case Kamran has no choice, as he's either dealing with a beamer, a bouncer off a medium-pacer, or a rotten throw in from the deep!

PRACTISING

Far too many coaches neglect their wicket-keepers shamefully at practice, and some unfortunate glovemen can go through season after season without ever being given the chance to hone their specific skills. Net sessions are rushed, with the focus entirely on batting; space is limited, in which case an entire net dedicated to one wicket-keeper seems like a terrible waste; and the coach might be too busy dealing with problems that seem more pressing – troublesome bowling actions, faulty batting techniques, and so on. If the keeper is fairly reliable, he tends to be ignored as not needing urgent help.

This is a pity, because it is not difficult to combine bowling and wicket-keeping practice, and there are various drills and exercises the wicket-keeper can do to sharpen his skills.

ALAN KNOTT'S DRILLS

IN THE NETS

'I would keep to spinners in a vacant net, asking them to bowl at me individually and exactly as they would in a match…. I would encourage them to pitch quite a lot of balls well up to me, even with the occasional half-volley, so that I got accustomed to taking these rare and difficult deliveries.

'Sometimes I put a stump in the ground to represent the bat. This can give the bowler a better idea of what length to bowl and can also give you deflections off the bat. A colleague batting can be a great help, especially if he plays with a stump or an old cut-down bat.

'I am against going behind the stumps during net practice because a batsman usually has at least three bowlers… bowling at him, giving him a continual run of deliveries, so that the keeper is forever bending up and down. Having to retrieve many of the balls also makes it difficult for him to prepare for the next delivery. Finally, if the keeper wants to stand back, there is rarely enough room for him to do so.'

ALONE OR WITH A FRIEND

'The only ingredients required are a pair of pads, a tennis ball, a wall and a flat surface, such as a yard or garage wall. Stand 10–12 metres away from the wall and throw the ball against it so that on its return it pitches on a length in front of you, and you can take it as it rises from the ground.

'Strap one pad round the other so that they stand up just in front of you and act as a wicket. Pads are preferable to stumps to avoid the risk of injuring the fingers… while practising your stumpings.

'If you have a friend to practise with you, ask him to bat with a stump in front of the pads…. You can even chalk in a crease to add to the realism. The better the player, the more often he will hit the ball, but this is excellent training for the keeper, because when the striker does eventually miss or edge one, you must be ready for it.'

TAKING THE BALL BEHIND A BATSMAN

'You'll need two teammates: a bowler or thrower, throwing the ball to your instructions; and a batsman deliberately missing the ball. Be sure to practise taking balls on various lengths, especially the difficult "intermediate" length discussed earlier, the yorker length, and the full toss. Also get the thrower to mix in a good number of wide balls so that you can practise diving. You must use a gym mat when doing this, especially on hard or indoor surfaces.'

RANDOM DEFLECTIONS

'Put a bat or a stump in the area where the ball is pitching (length-ways works best, rather than across the pitch). Any balls that hit this obstruction are likely to jag to either side unpredictably; and this element of uncertainty makes the practice session considerably more interesting.'

REBOUNDS OFF A WALL

'This is the simplest drill of all. Start with a golf-ball, throwing it against a wall and catching it (without gloves). Then switch to a tennis ball.' As described in the discussion of slip-catching practice, tennis balls have the great advantage of being very light, forcing you to learn a good 'soft hands' technique while not wearing out your palms and fingers. Vary your catching, perhaps alternating between one-handed and two-handed catches.

THE IMPORTANCE OF A VARIED ROUTINE

To this, we would add that during team practices, wicket-keepers should ideally get away from the rest of the squad and work one-on-one with a coach or teammate, going through a lengthy routine that runs them through all the skills they will need in a match. The routine might look something like this:

- **taking the ball from an underarm throw**
- **taking it in the right hand**
- **taking it the left hand**
- **taking it over his head**
- **fielding the rolling ball**
- **fielding the bouncing ball**
- **diving and rolling**
- **standing up out of the roll as efficiently as possible.**

Whatever the routine, the keeper must catch plenty of balls to build his confidence and reinforce his feel for ball on glove.

CAN A WICKET-KEEPER LOSE FORM?

A wicket-keeper's form is his concentration. If he's not concentrating, it means there's something bothering him that needs to be worked out of his system. Unless this is a personal matter (family problems, bad news and so on), this can be done by practice – by taking enough balls. A loss of concentration can also lead to an increase in tension (and vice versa), which causes you to jar and jolt the ball instead of giving with it. Hard work will solve all these problems.

FITNESS

Keepers, like fast bowlers, need to be supremely fit. You will be on the field without respite throughout the entire innings, no matter how many hours (or days) it lasts, and no matter how hot the sun. In the course of an average game, you can expect to do around 600 squats, and, depending on many fast bowlers are in your team, you'll run three or four kilometres as you get up to the stumps after every delivery.

In other words, a rigorous fitness programme, careful and thorough stretching, and a healthy diet are not optional extras but absolute necessities. Everything we discuss about fitness, stretching and nutrition in Chapter 10 goes double for the wicket-keeper. If your back gets particularly tired while you keep wicket, or you are prone to back troubles, you need to focus particularly on core stability exercises, such as those that target the stomach muscles.

When you take the field, you need to be supple and warm, and you also need to have faced an over or two from one of your bowlers to get your eye in: batsmen are at their most vulnerable early on, and you're liable to get a couple of sharp chances in the first few overs. Remember: if 'the first hour belongs to the bowler', as the truism goes, then it belongs as much to the wicket-keeper. Be ready for the chances that will come your way.

THE WICKET-KEEPERS' KIT

Almost more than anyone else on the field, it is vital that the wicket-keeper wears gear that keeps him protected and comfortable. An injury that is serious enough to remove the keeper from the game is an absolute disaster for almost any side: while the unexpected absence of a senior batsman or strike bowler might inspire another player to 'come to the party' by performing exceptionally well, it is not often that a team is able to pull an exceptional back-up wicket-keeper out of the hat. Thus kit that keeps him protected as far as possible from injuries, especially those caused by impact with the ball, is essential. (As with batting, correct wicket-keeping techniques play an important role in avoiding injury, but this is no reason to skimp on protection.) In addition, keeping wicket is a specialist role, and specialized equipment is required.

1. Pads

Modern wicket-keeping pads are small and very light, and are becoming more compact every year. Current designs provide a shortened pad, cut below the knee-roll, and a longer one offering protection above the knee. We recommend the latter (in the interests of having as much protection as possible), but ensure that you tighten the top Velcro strap as much as is comfortable to keep the knee flaps snug against your lower thigh when you stand up straight. Your pads should not feel cumbersome, or knock together as you move (making you waddle). Straps need to be tight, but not so much that they hamper your squatting or interfere with swift movements. Experiment with placement and number of straps until you are both comfortable and able to move speedily and freely, but still have adequate protection.

2. Gloves and inners

These are your most precious pieces of equipment. Look after your gloves and they'll look after you. In fact most good wicket-keepers treat their gloves with a great deal of love and attention: Alan Knott used to take his home with him, and wear them in the evenings (he claimed it kept them supple); and Jack Russell allegedly slept with his under his pillow!

Always use wicket-keeping gloves, padded, with rubber palms and webbing between thumb and index finger: substituting these with batting gloves (or not wearing gloves at all, in a social game, for instance) can result in badly broken fingers, not to mention dropped catches and bowlers tearing their hair.

Comfort is the first priority, and gloves must feel as though they are a part of the hand. Young players should *always* wear them when practising, not only to avoid injury, but in order to get used to handling the ball with them. The thickness of the leather and the amount of padding can vary, so experiment (if you can afford to do so). The thinner the leather and the less padding across the palms and underside of the fingers, the more flexible the gloves will be, allowing the hands more mobility. However, this is obviously at a cost to protection. Alan Knott believes that there should be enough padding to allow the sensation of the ball 'sinking' into the palms, rather than striking them. Too much padding, however, can restrict the cupping motion – you should always be able to feel the ball when catching it.

Kamran adjusts the top Velcro strap to allow him mobility and flexibility, without allowing the pad to flap around or shift on his shin.

PROTECTING YOUR HANDS

Sore hands will make your job a miserable one, so it is worth taking time and trouble to safeguard them. Cricket lore insists that past generations of wicket-keepers slid steaks into their gloves for extra padding (and tells us, with tongue firmly in cheek, that these tenderized and somewhat odorous steaks were then cooked for post-match dinners). No less idiosyncratic, but more animal-friendly, Alan Knott found it useful to insert a strip of plasticine along the base of his fingers: the modern equivalent being especially designed Dermal Pads or 'fat pads', used in exactly the same way. However, children or players who can't afford these extras, or who might not have good quality gloves, can make do with plasticine or plasters without being too greatly disadvantaged.

If you are nursing a bruised or sore finger, you can also try taping it to the adjacent finger – this gives extra support and works especially well in the case of the little and ring fingers. However, when taping two glove fingers together like this, be careful to avoid restricting movement.

As well as adding protection to the gloves, the hands themselves need attention, as it is very easy to dislocate or break a finger if catching the ball awkwardly. The joints of each finger should be taped up (but not too tightly) to offer support. The tape should not be bulky – the taped fingers should fit comfortably inside the gloves. One option is to tape the fingers over the inner glove. Alan Knott also recommends keeping the fingernails fairly long for added protection. Also make sure your gloves completely cover your wrists and the adjacent area: it is extremely painful if this sensitive area is hit with force by a rising ball.

Finally, a word about practices: wicket-keepers should wear full protection and even take extra measures to protect the hands when practising, as this is when they take the ball over and over again in quick succession – which is unlikely to happen in match conditions, except at very junior levels. The same applies when practising stumping: if your hands are going to be colliding with the stumps repeatedly in a short space of time, take precautions to prevent bruising to the hands, or use plastic rather than wooden stumps.

Unfortunately, we cannot tell you that your hands will not be damaged at some point in your playing career. If the average batter leaves three balls an over in the average multi-day match, it means that the average wicket-keeper is going to take over 500 deliveries per match, a few hundred of which will be off quick men. Even the greatest keepers with the smoothest techniques, softest hands, and most cutting-edge equipment, still bruise and break fingers. However, learning correct techniques for taking the ball, and religiously protecting your hands at practices and in matches should go a long way towards minimizing the risks.

Keep a close eye on the rubber facing on the palms: if the dimpling wears smooth or the rubber becomes worn, it becomes harder to hold onto the ball, especially in wet conditions.

Most wicket-keepers also wear thin conventional gloves, known as inners, inside their wicket-keeping gloves. Inners should ideally be made of chamois leather, but if costs are prohibitive or availability is limited, cotton is also acceptable. If you think your hands are starting to bruise, or you're standing back to a genuinely fast bowler, wear two pairs of inners, perhaps cutting off the fingers of the outer pair so that your palms benefit from the added protection but your fingers retain some of their flexibility and sensitivity. This tactic can be especially useful for amateur or school cricketers who don't play every day, and whose hands are therefore not as hardened as those of a professional wicket-keeper.

Whatever inners you use, make sure they have elasticized cotton cuffs, so that they stay snugly on your hand when you whip off your wicket-keeping glove for those attempted run-outs.

New gloves, or gloves that have been sitting in a cold coffin for a week, might be rather stiff and hard, and so it is essential that you get them supple, kneading them to 'warm them up' before a match or practice. Some keepers like to beat their gloves into shape – literally – with the end of a bat or stump to soften the palms. However, never twist gloves, or pull any of the fingers backwards, especially not if they are particularly stiff: sweat and other moisture may have dried and made the leather brittle, and in this state, they can easily tear.

If you wear leather inners, avoid getting them saturated with moisture, since this will make them hard and brittle. However, if they seem stiff when you pull them on, a sprinkling of water may soften them up. Don't overdo it: water on brittle leather can result in a slimy mess that tears extremely easily.

3. Boots

Like every other player on the field, if a wicket-keeper's feet start aching, he will find it increasingly hard to concentrate. Good boots are therefore a necessity, not a luxury; in fact, you should have more than one pair if finances allow. The soles should be well cushioned, so that you feel the pressure of your studs as little as possible.

Depending on your weight and the quality of your footwear, this might never be problem, but it can become a nightmare, as Alan Knott explains: 'When squatting behind the stumps, my weight is very much on the balls of my feet. Four to six hours of this, and I can start to feel every stud position. One remedy is to have two pairs of boots with the studs in slightly different places, which you can change at the end of each session.'

When playing on hard grounds, Knott said he was often tempted to wear rubber-soled boots with no studs and rubber spikes; but this clearly increases the risk of slipping.

4. Helmet and abdominal protector

Modern wicket-keepers have taken to wearing helmets, especially on bouncy or uneven pitches. While some glovemen of yesteryear might frown on this practice, prevention of injury is essential, and it is likely that a specialized, much lighter type of helmet will eventually be designed specifically for use by wicket-keepers.

And of course, don't forget the abdominal protector or box…!

5. Trousers and shirt

The wicket-keeper needs to be supremely comfortable in his clothes. Squatting and standing over 500 times a day will test comfort to its limits, and even the most gentle chafing, or the faintest constriction of material around thighs or back can develop into a nagging – and eventually enraging – distraction, until you are far more focused on your clothing than taking the ball cleanly.

Comfort is obviously entirely subjective: some keepers prefer their trousers to be baggy so as not to restrict their movement; while others find that a tighter fit can offer the thighs and hamstrings a little bit of extra support when squatting. If you prefer the latter option, make sure the seams are strongly stitched, or you are liable to give the slips behind you – not to mention the crowd – an eyeful.

When it comes to shirts, the same guidelines apply as to other fielders. An upturned collar can protect your neck from sunburn or chilly gusts, and long sleeves that cover the elbow are an absolute necessity in allowing you to dive without grazing large areas of skin. Don't be a hero in this department: grazes in the elbow area are likely to be painful, can become septic, and will render you completely ineffective in the field.

Make sure your cuffs don't rub your wrist – again, repetitive irritation can drive you up the wall – or restrict you when you stretch for the ball.

THE KEY INGREDIENTS FOR WICKET-KEEPING: SUMMING UP

In essence then, the successful wicket-keeper:

- has an extraordinary ability to focus
- has endless amounts of patience, and a cheerful disposition
- is formidably fit – as fit as the fastest bowler on the team
- has a stance that is both comfortable and effective
- has a talent for seeing the ball early
- has the ability to take or catch the ball
- is able to work closely with bowlers, standing back or standing up according to their needs
- relishes bats whistling past his face, clouds of dust billowing up his nose, and rolling and diving after deliveries gone sadly astray
- makes sure that he gets to practise his specific skills
- pays close attention to his gear and clothing.

And remember: the wicket-keeper is truly the unsung superhero of cricket.

PART THREE

THINKING CRICKET

CHAPTER SEVEN

STRATEGY AND CAPTAINCY

INTRODUCTION

In this chapter, now that we have some idea of the mental and technical skills involved in the art of cricket, we look more closely at two related crafts. Here we consider what kinds of game strategies would be most helpful to, respectively, those batting, bowling and fielding. We also consider the role of the player called upon to become a master strategist on the cricket field – the captain.

These discussions are combined for a number of reasons. In whatever guise the captain takes the field – he can be an opening batsman, a middle-order batter, a fast or slow bowler, even the wicket-keeper – he, more than anyone else, needs to have a comprehensive grasp of the variety of strategies open to each of his players as individuals, as well as constantly formulating and reformulating his team's strategy. So even though he might open the batting for his side, he needs to understand exactly how his leg-spinner might best take wickets, or slow down the scoring rate.

But this is not a licence for non-captains to skim through this chapter, focusing only on their particular skill. The deeper the understanding of all kinds of strategy by every member of the team, the better this team will function as a unit. Another mistake is to assume you can focus on the stroke-play you enjoy, and leave the 'thinking' up to the captain. You never know when you might be asked to step up and take on the role of captaining your side. Whether it's a small social club, and the usual man has come down with food-poisoning on the eve of a friendly match, or at far more elevated levels, all cricketers should have an understanding of the role and tasks of the captain. Even at international levels, captaincy can be a 'poisoned chalice' (in the 1990s, the sporting media often used this gloomy phrase to describe the job of captaining Pakistan) or a revolving door (look at England's procession of captains during the same period). One day the finger might point your way.

The variety of strategies available to captains, and indeed every cricketer on the field, is part of what makes cricket the magnificent game it is. As we have said before, cricket involves much more than athletic talent and technical proficiency. It's a game in which all the players are constantly thinking, plotting and planning, no one more so than the captain. Mastering the strategies of the game will not only lift your performance; it brings a new level of enjoyment and satisfaction to the game.

THE FUNDAMENTAL CHALLENGE OF CRICKET: THE MATHEMATICS OF TACTICS

What follows is a mathematical outline of some of the challenges that the game of cricket presents. The goal is to dismiss your opponents within the time constraints imposed by the particular form of the game, at a stage when they have accumulated fewer runs than your own team. Only in one-day cricket does there have to be a definite result – multi-day games can end in a draw if one side cannot bowl the other out, regardless of the number of runs made. Thus the classic battle is between run accumulation by the batting side and run restriction/wicket accumulation by the fielding side; and vice versa when the batting and fielding/bowling roles of each team are reversed. The question is, what are some of the (almost infinite) tactics the fielding/bowling team can use to restrict the accumulation of runs while ensuring a progressive capture of wickets? Likewise, how does the batting team accumulate runs without sacrificing their wickets?

Beginning with the bowling/fielding side, their essential problem is that there are simply too few fielders to cover the entire cricket oval and so prevent the batsman from scoring runs. If there were sixteen to twenty fielders, probably the only way the batsman on strike would be able to score runs would be to hit the ball over the boundary, scoring a six – or the equivalent to a home run in baseball. This is because the batsman can theoretically strike the ball in an arc of 360°. (In contrast, the nine players in baseball protect an arc of 90°.) Given an average field size of 30 000m² at famous grounds like Lords in London and Melbourne Cricket Ground (MCG) in Melbourne, Australia, and an average of 18 000m² in the average American baseball field, the comparative 'density' of fielders on a cricket field varies from 0,0003 fielders per m² at Lords and the MCG (eleven fielders minus the bowler and wicket-keeper) to 0,0004 fielders per m² at the Yankee baseball stadium in New York (nine fielders minus the short-stop). This is one of the many reasons why it is rather more difficult to score runs in baseball than in cricket.

Another important difference is that in baseball, the fielder's positions are essentially fixed, whereas in cricket, the nine fielders other than the bowler and wicket-keeper can – at least in theory – field anywhere.

If there was an equal probability that the batter could strike the ball anywhere in the 360° arc, then the fielding positions would be simply located; separated by a constant arc of about 33° (360/11 = 33°). But since the positions of the bowler and the wicket-keeper are fixed at about 0° and 180°, and there is an uneven number (nine) of fielders to cover the remaining angles, the fielding side would have to distribute five fielders to one side of the pitch, each separated by 36° and the four remaining fielders on the opposite side of the pitch, each separated by 45° of arc. (The less mathematically minded would refer to this as a 5/4 field.) In a case like this, the captain of the fielding side would have to devise a strategy to ensure that the batter struck the ball only at multiples of 36° of arc on one side of the wicket, and at multiples of 45° of arc on the opposite side of the wicket. This would ensure that there was always a fielder in place to intercept the ball. That's the theory, at least.

The reality is that it's the bowler's job to send down deliveries that the batsman cannot score off: he must either leave them for the wicket-keeper to collect, or hit them back to the bowler, or to the wicket-keeper, or else directly to one of the other nine carefully positioned fielders. All good and well, but *how* does the bowler ensure that the batsman will either leave or miss the delivery (so that it will be fielded by the wicket-keeper), or strike the ball directly back to the bowler, or to one of the other nine fielders strategically located according to the specific deliveries that the bowler can produce?

At his disposal, the bowler has the following tactics (all of which are discussed in detail later in this chapter, and in Chapter 5): length, line, speed, flight, swing, drift, dip and seam. He can also exploit external factors, or those generated within the game itself – a pitch that is beginning to crumble, a ball that is beginning to deviate through the air because it has become worn during play. He can also take advantage of information he is constantly assessing and revising regarding the batsmen to whom he is bowling, trying to trick, trap, lure or even lull them into making errors.

By correctly combining these factors, he can (a) ensure that the batter has few opportunities to direct the ball away from or past the fielders; and (b) trick the batsman into getting out via any of the ten ways (bowled, caught, stumped, LBW, run out, hit wicket, handled the ball, obstructing the field, timed out, hit the ball twice) in which the batsman can be dismissed.

But this assumes not only an almost inhumanly flawless performance by the bowler; it assumes that he is capable of bowling with absolute accuracy to the field set for him by his captain. The batter will also be constantly searching for opportunities to dominate the bowler and the field – for instance, careful placement of shots 'into the gaps', or coming down the pitch to the bowler in an effort to change his length. Or if he is successful in playing a number of scoring shots, he can force the captain to spread his field, adopt a defensive instead of an attacking field, and so on.

For instance, it will be in the batter's interest to play shots to the side of the field that has only four fielders (roughly placed at 45° of arc). The bowler will meanwhile be sending down deliveries that force the batter to play to the side of the field with five fielders (roughly placed at 36° of arc). Hence the constant battle of wits between batter and bowler, to which the captain is required to respond with appropriate field placings.

THE STRATEGY OF BATTING

The title of this section is hopelessly optimistic. Batting is a scientific art practised in a dizzying variety of forms. Even at the elite level it refuses to be buttonholed – this week privileging technique and patience on a greenish Melbourne pitch, the next encouraging cavalier panache on a flat and dusty strip in Rawalpindi. A batsman can be required to win a match with an innings lasting one delivery, or he might need to bat for ten hours to save a game for his team. The batsman who walks out to open the innings might be playing on the same field against the same opposition as the man who bats at number six, but they can end up playing completely different matches, the opener attacking on a baking pitch under blue skies; while, 24 hours later, the number six batsman has to dig in his heels and play with his back to the wall, desperately trying to stave off a defeat on a suddenly spiteful wicket.

If the relatively well-organized and regulated top echelon of the game is diverse, then its lower levels almost defy categorization. From state cricket in Australia (as close to Test cricket as the first-class game gets) to club and school cricket, to street cricket in South African townships and Indian maidans, to highly competitive beach cricket in the West Indies – batting comes in as many shapes and sizes as batters.

However, just as not all batsmen are created equal, so not all batting techniques and strategies are equally effective. There are no doubt all kinds of nuances to batting in beach cricket – or lounge cricket, for that matter, where hitting the television counts for six runs and nicking the dog means you're out – but being good at these variations of batting is unlikely to count in the true form of the game.

The strategies here are by no means a catalogue of every tactic ever employed by a batsman. Instead, they represent strategies that have worked most effectively for most batsmen most often – although even here generalization is impossible, since cricket has splintered into four-day, three-day, one-day, and now 20-over cricket, and will no doubt evolve again in the next ten years into something entirely unpredictable.

In light of this uncertainty, the best place to start is by returning to the basics of batting expounded in Chapter 3. Here we will explore many different approaches and counter-measures to bowling tactics, but however sophisticated your batting brain becomes, always be prepared to bail out of your tactical battle and return to the technical foundations on which your game should be built:

- watch the ball
- keep your head still on release of that ball (be balanced)
- judge length accurately
- put your feet into the correct position
- select the correct shot.

These are the guiding principles from which all strategy and innovation stem, and they are always there for you to return to when the going gets rough.

GENERAL STRATEGIES FOR BATTING

Before we look in more detail at the scenario-specific strategies that should be developed for both one-day and multi-day cricket, it is important to understand that certain tactics are universal to all batters, whether school pupils playing a 30-over match or internationals playing a five-day Test. Many of these tactics straddle the line between technique and strategy (for example, playing spin with soft hands, which not only gives you a better chance of survival, but allows you to score more freely and therefore start imposing your game on the bowler); and many combine common sense with a sound temperament. However, all are worth examining here.

IPS and visualization

In Chapter 2, we introduced the so-called 'ideal performance state' or IPS, known more colloquially as the 'zone' or the 'bubble'. Within the IPS, batting is a barely conscious effort, the subconscious taking over the direct reactions and reflexes that have been practised tens of thousands of times in order to become second nature. All the distractions of the everyday world fade into the background: time itself seems to slow down. The ball, usually a red blur, now appears large and clear, apparently moving more slowly, and giving you all the time you need to choose and play the correct shot. The fatigue in your limbs diminishes, becoming almost irrelevant. Your entire existence is focused in this one moment, this extremely pleasurable and yet disciplined sensation of batting as well as you possibly can.

How you enter your IPS will depend largely on your own personality and current form, but many players have managed to create this state by visualizing a plain white sheet, covering all external distractions, with a red ball coming out of it, clearly outlined against the sheet and moving smoothly and predictably in trajectory towards the bat. There is nothing else in this picture but you, the clean fresh sheet, and the ball.

> The IPS applies to bowlers as well. Of the titanic session of play in the famous Test match between England and South Africa at Trent Bridge in 1998, in which Mike Atherton survived Allan Donald bowling with blistering speed and accuracy, Donald later said, 'I didn't even hear the crowd. It was like there were only two people on the field – him and me.'

Being able to blot out irritations like sledging fielders or hostile spectators is a very useful skill, but one that can require a more dynamic kind of visualization than that of the suspended sheet: a particularly obnoxious wicket-keeper jabbering in your ear can easily intrude into your mental picture, crouching behind the sheet! In these cases, consider trying a tactic Basil D'Oliveira passed on to Bob Woolmer. Instead of visualizing an ideal and uncluttered sheet or blank slate, mentally obliterate distractions. Start by picturing a large table, covered with a white tablecloth, and set for a dinner party with cutlery, condiments, flowers, and so on. Now imagine using your bat to sweep everything off the table, clearing the cloth so that nothing remains except a cricket ball. As soon as anything tries to break into your clean and clear consciousness, such as a particular fielder whose sledging is starting to irritate you, or a bowler who is getting the ball to move uncomfortably, imagine that the fielder or bowler has rudely slapped a bottle of tomato sauce down on the table in front of you. In your mind's eye, take your bat and neatly nudge it off again, leaving everything clean and white again.

Bob Woolmer also remembered Michael Burns of Warwickshire and Somerset speaking of a little man who would perch on his shoulder, urging, 'Go on, hit it for four!' Listening to the little man would invariably lead to impetuous strokes. If you have a rash streak, turn it into a little man on your shoulder, and when he starts piping up, find some way to silence him, perhaps by shrugging so that he 'falls off'.

The final and important psychological tactic to master is that of switching on and off while batting. Whether you wander off to square leg after each delivery, or examine your gloves and grip, or do some 'gardening' on the pitch, it is important to be able to remove your mind from the duel at hand so that you can face the next ball with a 'clean tablecloth'. If the last ball nipped back off a crack, caught the edge and dropped just short of the slips, put it behind you. If you hammered it away for four, put it behind you. The only ball you need to think about is the next one; and you'll only need to start thinking about it when the bowler turns at the end of his run-up. Being able to disconnect from the intensity of the middle will not only allow you to wipe the slate clean after every ball; it will also keep your mind relatively fresh through a long innings.

Danger points

The dangers of approaching, reaching and passing personal milestones are discussed in Chapter 2, but the lapse in concentration that occurs when you reach the high 40s or 90s – or when your pass 50 or 100 – are not the only threats to your psychological discipline.

Never make the mistake of underestimating a change- or part-time bowler. Assuming that you've seen off the worst of the attack and now deserve some easy runs is just asking to nick off. Remain as vigilant as you were against the strike bowler with the new ball, if not more so: remember that the change of pace and action will demand more concentration on your part, not less.

Another extremely dangerous time for all batsmen is when a wicket has fallen. With the rhythm of the batting partnership traumatically and jarringly broken, and the bowler and fielders pumped up and ready to attack a new batsman, another wicket is never more likely than in the next few minutes. It is therefore imperative that the man who is 'in' now assumes the role of anchor, and tries to bat through the innings (regardless of how high or low in the order he is). The new batsman must also recognize his role as initially that of the junior partner, and must give as much of the strike as possible to the batsman already settled at the crease. At the same time, he should be prepared to run twos when necessary, or to keep the strike at the end of overs.

Reading the pitch

All batsmen must be able to read or assess the pitch, either before a match or when they arrive at the crease, and extrapolate with some accuracy the kind of score or run-rate that pitch will allow. This will enable them to pace their innings: knowing that a pitch is likely to slow down later in the day will help the batting team to remain calm and not fret when runs become increasingly scarce. This ability to identify changing pitch conditions, and to interpret them in terms of how to adapt team strategy, is especially valuable.

Running between the wickets

No matter what level of cricket you play, you can always improve this aspect of your batting. Technique and temperament can be superbly developed in a Test batsman, but all it takes is a brilliant piece of fielding or a shaky call to reveal someone with all the judgement and decision-making ability of a rabbit caught in the headlights of an oncoming truck. In fact, running between the wickets is a skill that is learned and developed almost independently of all the other skills of cricket. It is not contingent upon a good eye or great technique, on fitness, or even on strength: a club B-team batter can be a substantially better runner between wickets than a top Test batsman.

The best runners between wickets don't have to call: they learn to trust one another, and react less to commands than to subtle signals in eye contact and body language in their partner. Obviously, this skill is easier to develop in a settled team that plays together over five or six seasons, but the following guidelines can help even novices improve their running.

- Maintain eye contact with your partner.
- Call loudly in large noisy stadiums (here it is vital to keep eye contact).
- Trust your partner's call.
- Do not 'ball-watch' when at the non-striker's end.
- Run the first run quickly.
- Hold the bat in the correct hand when backing up, facing the bowler (so that you can watch out for the run-out by a bowler who has managed to get a hand to the return drive – probably the worst way to be dismissed).
- Always slide your bat into the crease, and always start its slide at least a metre in front of the line: stay low and extended.
- When turning, keep the body low to increase the reach distance, and look at the ball, so that you can make an early judgement about going for a second run.
- Keep alert for overthrows: don't give yourself a follow-through. Jogging away into the distance on a 20-metre follow-through may emphasize to the dressing room how fast you had to sprint for that single, but it won't do you any good if your partner (to whom you have your back) is trying to call you back for a second.
- Run in straight lines and not arcs.
- The non-striker should try to run wide of the batter if you've both decided to run on the same side of the pitch.

Stealing every single, bye and leg-bye on offer (and stealing a few that aren't) will put the opposition under tremendous pressure. Aggressive but sensible running can cause otherwise organized fielding teams to go to pieces suddenly and spectacularly, with throws going wide for overthrows, fielders cursing and yelling at each other, and everyone's mind shutting down in the pandemonium.

BATTING IN MULTI-DAY CRICKET

The five basics of batting outlined above and in Chapter 3 are your touchstone in multi-day cricket. No other form of the game tests your technique and mind as thoroughly, and as in any rigorous examination, you need to be familiar and comfortable with all the basics before you can start elaborating.

We've said it many times in this book: the essence of successful batting is to play each ball on its merits. Wipe both past and future out of your mind. The bowler is asking you a very specific question with each ball, and you need to be in a mental state that allows you to answer the question he sets you. Most batters, regardless of the level of their batting, know that premeditating their shots is a bad move. For years, coaches have told them to play every ball on its merits, and to do nothing silly. But while this advice is rock-solid, if it is not put into the proper context, it can lead, ironically, to a strange kind of mental premeditation. This can be just as dangerous as the more practical equivalent. Coaches who spend most of their time warning their batsmen about what to avoid, instead of communicating the bigger picture, are especially guilty of instilling this bad tactical habit.

COUNTER-INTELLIGENCE: THE NON-STRIKER

Most batsmen develop the ability to 'switch off' between deliveries, a process in which they change gears mentally, going from a high level of alertness and intense focus on the bowler and the delivery to a more relaxed tactical awareness, which allows them to be quietly introspective between deliveries or while standing at the non-striker's end.

As the non-striker, it is important that you centre yourself and concentrate on backing up efficiently, but don't retreat too deep into your own mind: your partner down at the danger end needs your eyes and ears.

Bowlers and fielders often give subtle signs to each other when plotting a particular manoeuvre, signals that are invisible to the batsman who is intently marking his guard or scanning the field. In his position, he is entirely at the mercy of the wicket-keeper, who could be transmitting strategy in semaphore for all the batsman knows. It is therefore important that the non-striker intercepts these codes and warns his partner when necessary.

On the English county circuit during the 1970s, off-spinner Derek Underwood and wicket-keeper Alan Knott conspired to plot the downfall of Alan Jones, a left-handed Glamorgan batsman. Knott developed a sense for when Jones wanted to advance down the wicket, and agreed on a subtle eye-signal to Underwood in these cases. As a result, whenever Jones came down the track to Underwood, he found the bowler spearing the ball down the leg side past him, with Knott triumphantly completing a stumping. Jones fell for the tactic surprisingly often; but with a watchful non-striker alert to any unusual facial tics or winks from Knott, he might have been forewarned.

Bob Woolmer recalled how he was saved from almost certain dismissal by non-striker Dennis Amiss at Perth in 1977: 'Dennis Lillee was steaming in, and was halfway through his run-up when Dennis [Amiss] suddenly stuck his bat across the umpire and into Lillee's path – much to the annoyance of the fiery Australian! My partner had spotted Doug Walters moving in the field, quietly back-pedalling from square leg as the bowler ran in, a clear sign that I was about to be bounced and lured into hooking a ball into an area I had assumed was fielder-free. Today, this strategy is frowned upon as not being in the spirit of the game, but in 1977, all was fair in love and war: thanks to my partner, I avoided the trap. Not surprisingly, the next few deliveries were somewhat lively!'

An example of this would be the batsman who walks out with his head full of 'helpful hints' about what not to do. Taking guard, his mind is a catalogue of cautions and warning signals: 'I mustn't follow the outswinger; I mustn't drive too early; I mustn't show this or that flaw in my technique; above all, I mustn't get out!' If he is wrapped up in negative thoughts and worst-case scenarios, he will be in absolutely no state to play the ball as an all-important once-off event.

We have mentioned that batting can mean entirely different things for various batters, depending on where they bat in the order. We have therefore divided our strategic guidelines into two categories: one for the top order and the other for the middle order. Many of these tactics overlap, and at their heart, they all require batsmen to think and act with focus, precision, calm and speed. Batting is a multi-faceted skill, but it is not complicated or even particularly difficult (given enough practice and a good temperament). In fact one of the best pieces of advice about batting in multi-day cricket, passed on by South Africa's legendary Graeme Pollock, is remarkably straightforward. Pollock's approach was simple: every bowler, no matter how good he is, will send down four or five loose balls in an hour. If a batsman is patient enough to wait for these deliveries, and alert enough to punish them when they crop up, he can expect at least 12 or 16 runs an hour in boundaries alone. In addition, if he picks up singles whenever they present themselves, a batsman can realistically expect to score at around 20 runs an hour, even against the best opposition. If he can keep this up for two sessions, he'll be in striking distance of a century.

Looking at batting in this way makes it seem so simple; and with the correct mindset and a sound technique, it can be. Jacques Kallis and Rahul Dravid are quintessential examples of batters who, possessed of the right mindset and technique, follow this pattern in accumulating huge scores.

BUILDING AN INNINGS

Cricketing parlance talks of 'building an innings' – a potentially misleading phrase, as it might imply that an innings can be built to a point of perfection or completion, at which point the batter can relax and reap the rewards of his hard work, perhaps by smashing a few bonus boundaries. The truth is that as soon as you let your guard down, you're sure to be bustled out. So the reality is that you never finish building your innings, until it all comes tumbling down (courtesy of the bowler or the umpire) or until you walk off at the end of play unbeaten. In other words, there is no such thing as a completed innings. Remember this, and it will help you to 'reset' and start from square one before every ball. 'Building an innings' is therefore just another way of saying 'batting for a long time', and the following guidelines – specific to your position in the batting order – are intended to help you bat for as long as possible.

'Every bowler, no matter how good he is, will send down four or five loose balls in an hour.'

– Graeme Pollock

BUILDING BRICK BY BRICK

As a multi-day batsman, you should be trying to score a century every fourth innings, and a half-century every third innings. However, walking out to face hostile bowlers – especially in pressure situations, such as after the fall of a couple of wickets – can make that 50 or 100 seem a very long way away, and perhaps overwhelming.

You should only be thinking of the next ball, not some vague hoped-for score. By all means anticipate the best, but make short-term plans instead of worrying or dreaming about reaching three figures. So rather than climbing the long, steep road towards the big milestones, break your innings down into small chunks, concentrating on getting the next five or ten runs. The great English batsman and captain Colin Cowdrey called this 'building five bricks at a time'.

First strike: the top three

Taking first strike, or coming in at 'first drop' with the ball still very new and the bowlers fresh, requires an organized mind with a range of strategies to draw upon. Planning and preparation are therefore very important if you are an opener.

- **Practise before the game in a way that suits you.** If, after the team warm-up, you need a short spell in the nets against a specific type of bowler, make sure you've organized this well in advance.

- **Use visualization techniques to prepare yourself for the new ball.** Clear your mind of all external thoughts (as described earlier and in Chapter 2).

- **Select which shots you might want to use during the first period of the game, and consciously discard all those that might be risky.** For example, are you going to cut and hook? Hopefully not: limit your selection to shots in the 'V' until you get used to the pace and bounce of the wicket, and the lateral movement of the ball. (Also remember that the ball may only start swinging once the initial sheen has been knocked off it.)

    The planning phase past, it is time to face the first – and most important – ball. Don't over-think the moment. It is a very important delivery, but you've been here many times before. You know what to do; now just allow yourself to do it.

- **If you're opening the innings, all you have to do is play along the lines of the stumps.** If the ball goes wide, or is bouncing over the top of the stumps, there

STRATEGY AND CAPTAINCY   381

For the first half-hour of the innings, defend with the option to attack; after that, attack with the option to defend.

is absolutely no reason to have a dab at it: your job is to see off the new ball and tire the opening attack, and if the ball isn't directly threatening your stumps or your body, then the bowler is doing your job for you. Leave him to do all the hard work.

- **A disciplined defensive attitude is important early on** (also be ready to play higher because of extra bounce), but don't become stuck in a siege mentality. For the first half-hour, defend with the option to attack; after that, attack with the option to defend.

- **Playing in the 'V' requires a technique that allows you to play straight comfortable and tightly.** If you're prone to pushing away from your body with the bat, try stepping across just as the ball is released so that your back foot is in line with off-stump. This will turn you more square-on to the bowler, bringing the outside edge of your bat back inside the dangerous no-man's-land outside off-stump, and will help you play down the line of the stumps. Even if you now injudiciously chase a wide ball, you'll probably miss it.

- **Never forget where you are in relation to your off-stump.** Take guard again if you feel yourself starting to drift either physically or mentally. Your off-stump is your anchor: lose touch with it, and you are at the bowler's mercy.

- **If the opening bowlers are genuinely fast (140km/h or more), restrict your backlift to give yourself more time to make contact with the ball.** Now more than ever, it is important to watch the ball – a surprisingly large number of batsmen stop trying to follow the ball all the way when they're facing pace or when the pressure is on.

- **The bowler is going to beat you every so often.** This is one of the facts of batting, so don't overreact when it happens. Give the bowler his due if he's just bowled a snorter, and then immediately put it out of your mind.

By this stage, you will hopefully have seen off the opening burst, and survived to face the first change bowlers. With the field starting to spread, and a comfortable cushion of 15 or 20 runs under your belt, you might be tempted to relax and assume that you've got the measure of the pitch and bowler. Resist this temptation: remember, in a multi-day game, you are never 'in' until you've spent three to four hours at the crease.

However, don't translate this lack of security into a conservative or gloomy outlook. Batting is one of life's great pleasures, and having the trust of your captain and team – who believe you are good enough to take on the best of the bowling – should in itself be a thrill. Face the challenge of batting up the order head-on, and relish each obstacle thrown your way. If you've come in with twenty minutes left in the day – a position many pessimistic pundits call a 'no-win' situation – consider the optimistic possibilities: tell yourself you can steal 10 runs and still be there tomorrow.

The heart of the innings: batters 4 to 6

Cricket is very fond of stereotypes, evidenced by a century-old history of portraying fast bowlers as unthinking brutes, spinners as cerebral tricksters, and wicket-keepers as doughty fellows with hearts of oak and hamstrings of rubber. Batsmen too have been buttonholed, with opening batsmen perceived as unsmiling, unimaginative and stodgy, while the middle order has been blessed (often quite undeservingly) with a very favourable public image: it is they who are the sparkling stroke-players, the twinkle-toed cavaliers, the master blasters.

Of course, modern opening batsmen are increasingly defying the stereotype: Desmond Haynes, Gordon Greenidge and Michael Slater were anything but stodgy, and today Matthew Hayden, Virender Sehwag and Herschelle Gibbs can cut a new-ball attack to shreds as quickly as any middle-order showman. But perception is a difficult thing to alter, and too many middle-order batsmen, especially at junior levels of the game, are still buying into the myth of the cavalier who relies on technique and his eye rather that determination and strategy.

The reality is that batting in the middle order takes just as much planning and insight as opening the batting. The bowlers you are likely to face are just as good as the opening pair – is batting at number six and facing Shane Warne any easier than opening the innings and facing Glenn McGrath? – and with the innings now well under way, new tactical concerns will have to be taken into account; for instance whether to attack for a win, or defend for a draw. In other words, do your homework.

- **While waiting to bat, stay relaxed.** Every now and then, do some gentle exercise to prepare your body and eyes for what is to come: hitting a table-tennis ball against a wall can be a good option. Also be sure to stretch thoroughly, paying especial attention to your Achilles tendons, calves, hamstrings and groin.

- **Beware of reading.** As explained in Chapter 4, it accustoms your eyes to short distances and fixed focuses, and can make it more difficult to adjust to a moving ball in bright light. Instead, do some eye exercises, such as switching your focus

The bowlers you are likely to face are just as good as the opening pair – is batting at number six and facing Shane Warne any easier than opening the innings and facing Glenn McGrath?

from an object 3 metres away to one 20 metres away, and back. If you do read, keep looking up at something at least 20 metres away.

- **Study the bowlers you are likely to face before you go in, and come up with methods of scoring against them.** For example, if you're going to face spin, decide if you are going to come down the wicket, sweep, or play off the back foot. Perhaps you'll opt for all three (depending on circumstances), but make this a conscious decision, and then have the courage of your convictions when you finally go out to bat.

    Once out in the middle, much of what we've described for the top order also applies. Opening batsmen are always expected to grind out marathon innings, but there is no reason why middle-order batsmen shouldn't hog the crease as jealously. A four-hour innings should be your goal – again, long enough to get you close to a hundred or even past that significant milestone – but this doesn't mean you can relax and play sloppily once that time has elapsed.

- **Remember that one wicket can lead to another.** Apart from building your own innings, focus on building your partnership. If it is broken, refocus and start again with your new partner. If two or three wickets fall in quick succession, don't start seeing grand designs or demons in the pitch. Simply chalk them up to bad luck, remind yourself that nothing has changed in your own mind or game, and start again.

- **Middle-order batters often have all the shots** – and a penchant for playing them all simultaneously! Don't change your mind about which shot you want to play as the ball is on its way down.

- **Partnerships are key to chasing targets.** If your team is about to chase 300, don't assume that the top six batters all need to make about 40, with the rest chipping in at 12 runs each: such an individualistic attitude won't breed responsible batting. Rather aim for three 100-run partnerships.

- **Rotate the strike as often as you can.** Maiden overs build pressure, and by taking singles – even when you're in a strong position – you slam the door on the opposition. Remember to call loudly and maintain as much eye contact with your partner as possible: run-outs in multi-day cricket are a heinous crime, even if you're involved in a run chase.

Opening batsmen are always expected to grind out marathon innings, but there is no reason why middle-order batsmen shouldn't hog the crease as jealously.

DOMINATING THE BOWLING

Colin Cowdrey always said that the best way to dominate an attack was not to slog the worst bowler out of the attack, but to keep him on. This is fine advice for all but the best teams, who, like the current Australian squad, have the ability to score heavily off the best bowlers in the opposing team as well as the worst.

There are various ways of keeping the bad bowlers on, but one of the most amusing was the method used by Garry Sobers. He'd hit the first ball of the over for four, and then deliberately play and miss at the next few, muttering 'Well bowled!' under his breath. Finally he'd hit the last ball of the over for four more. The hapless bowler would be going for 8 runs an over – taking a hammering, in other words – but at the end of every over, his optimistic captain would come across and say, 'Bad luck, you're bowling brilliantly – you'll get him next time.' Ten overs later, the bowler would have figures of none for 80, and Sir Garry would be laughing all the way to the bank.

This shows that dominating an attack doesn't have to mean lofted drives over cover for six. You'd be mad to try that against a bowler like Glenn McGrath or Curtly Ambrose, and hitting a bowler like Shane Warne for six over mid-wicket simply whets his appetite. In the case of a bowler like Warne, dominance would mean a regular single, changing the strike and forcing him to change his tactics constantly – extremely irritating for someone like Warne, a maestro at applying pressure.

Of course there are times when you'll face bowling of such low quality that a boundary a ball seems possible. However, you must fight this temptation: commentators might talk about 'help yourself time' when particularly weak attacks operate on good batting pitches, but pride always comes before a fall. Any bowler, at any level, can bowl a good delivery out of nowhere. Never bat with a patronizing mindset.

Greed can also be a major threat when facing sub-standard bowling. Even though 16 or 20 runs are apparently on offer every over, be content with a couple of boundaries in an over, and three singles in the next. Major assaults should be preserved for the final overs of a one-day game if you're trying to post a total. Similarly, if you do decide to target the bowling, limit your attack to the weakest bowler, or at least treat the best bowler with the respect he deserves.

BATTING IN LIMITED-OVERS CRICKET

There are three general ideas to keep in mind whenever you walk out to bat in a one-day game. Indeed, if you ever find yourself tending to drift (a cardinal sin when batting in any cricket match, but completely unforgivable in the shortened versions of the game), repeat them to yourself before every delivery:
- pay attention
- one run is all it takes
- every ball is an event.

These three guidelines should keep you focused. But what about the more immediate tactical requirements for scoring quickly from the outset? Being alert and ready to make the most of every ball you face is well and good, but what does this mean in more practical terms?

The range of tactics and strategies at your disposal are discussed shortly; but first we must put them in context. This context is a more psychological than practical, and it is what makes one-day cricket fundamentally different from Test cricket – in short, it is the difference between patience and technique on the one hand, and innovation on the other. Innovation is the foundation of one-day batsmanship, and before you can start practising and mastering the more conventional aspects of one-day batting, you need to have the value and function of innovation firmly set in your mind. Of course, you need to instill the basic principles and rules before you can learn to break them. This book emphasizes the importance of these rules, so before you start breaking them, you need to know why.

INNOVATION AT THE CREASE

Never confuse innovation and premeditation. Premeditation is simply one aspect of being innovative at the crease; and while it is an important one, you must recognize its function. Many batsmen and coaches think that premeditation is about which shot you're going to play (for instance, deciding to slog-sweep before the ball has been bowled), but this is wrong. Instead, it is about what you're trying to do in a more general tactical sense.

The mistake batsmen make is to confuse a specific stroke with a specific intent. Committing yourself to a slog-sweep will leave you rooted to the spot, down on one knee, your eyes fixed firmly at mid-wicket whether or not there is a fielder there; and if the ball nips away or back you're going to edge it, or be out LBW, or even top-edge it into your face. Committing yourself to the principle of hitting it over the top, on the other hand, leaves you a great deal of room to manoeuvre. Mentally and physically

Batters playing in one-day games should never confuse innovation and premeditation.

preparing yourself for a big shot, you are now in a position to play a big shot to whichever ball is bowled: if it's on leg-stump, pick it up over mid-wicket; if it's on off-stump, hit it over the off-side field or straight down the ground.

The irony of innovative and spontaneous batting is that it takes constant practice. Work on keeping your head still for as long as you can, since this will allow you to pick the length sooner, which in turn allows you to innovate or fabricate a suitable shot. Remember, when batting – regardless of the format of the match – never leave anything to chance. Practise innovation until it is as finely tuned as your basic technique.

BATTING 50 OVERS: THREE DIFFERENT BALLGAMES

The tactical demands on the one-day batsman vary dramatically according to the stage of the innings. Early on, conditions usually favour bowlers; next, a change in the condition of the ball and the layout of the field shifts the balance back in favour of those batting; finally, both bat and ball compete in the high-stakes battle of the last ten overs. It is therefore necessary to break these three phases of an innings down, and discuss each as a separate tactical block.

Overs 1 to 15

With the ball hard and the field restricted, there is never a better opportunity to score boundaries than in the first fifteen overs. But with the hard new ball comes often extreme lateral movement, making the opening overs a dramatic time for both batters and bowlers. With this equation offering the potential for both glory and disaster, many batting teams find themselves undone by a lack of strategy – either through trying to score too quickly and losing wickets, or else wasting the opportunity presented by the field restrictions in an effort to conserve wickets. Misusing these initial overs will leave you with a mountain to climb, regardless of whether you've raced to 100 for 5, or crawled to 40 for no loss.

It is therefore important for you as a team to set yourself a target for the first fifteen overs, based on the quality of the opposition's bowling attack, their batting potential later, and what you realistically think you can manage. But what is a fair total? To find this answer, you need to take the conditions into account; and since most cricket matches are played in one of three types of conditions – English, Anglophone and Asian – it is useful to consider each of these arenas separately.

ASIA

Conditions do vary (you are not going to see the same pitches in Pakistan, India, Sri Lanka, Bangladesh and even Sharjah), but generally you can expect lack of grass and pace. So, to supply broad guidelines, we would suggest that the absolutely minimum fifteen-over score in Asian conditions (if you have not lost early wickets) is 75: batting at anything under five runs per over while the field is restricted means you're not taking advantage of conditions that traditionally allow bat to dominate ball. The ball will come onto the bat at a good pace, but with almost no deviation off the seam. And with bowlers trying to extract the only advantage they have – swing – you can expect a very high percentage of deliveries pitched up to you. Limited bounce also means you can simply play through the line of the ball, even if you haven't necessarily got your foot to the pitch. Pitches in Kenya and Zimbabwe are likely to resemble those of the Asian subcontinent, so follow the guidelines given here for playing in those countries.

In other words, scoring a boundary and a single every over should be eminently achievable. To take full advantage of a deck stacked almost entirely in your favour, also pay attention to some of the following hints:

- **In the first five or six overs, play straight, but don't be afraid to lift the ball over the infield.** Playing 'in the V' will prevent you chasing wide swinging deliveries and nicking off. However, if you do flash, flash hard: with the fielders up in the circle, the ball may clear them and race away.

- **Once you've played yourself in and are accustomed to the pace and bounce of the pitch, try innovative shots across the line that use the pace of the ball, such as the leg-side pick-up over backward square leg** (or, if you are timing it well and the bowling is fast, over mid-wicket). These 'whippy' strokes can be particularly rewarding early on, with even mistimed strokes producing threes, as lone boundary riders have to chase the ball long distances.

- **Against particularly accurate new-ball bowlers, try walking down the pitch on the off side and hitting in the arc between mid-on and square leg.** Not only does this force the bowler to change his line and length; it also almost entirely negates the threat of LBW. However, be careful not to go too far outside the line of off-stump: seeing you being bowled around your legs by a straight ball aimed at middle-stump will not please your skipper. And if you do advance, do it early, so that the bowler sees you move and is forced to adjust.

- **Don't give yourself too much room outside off-stump:** balls don't bounce as high on dusty pitches, and having to reach for a delivery that keeps a little low can easily result in dragging the ball onto your stumps.

- **Seventy-five runs is a minimum total for the first fifteen overs, but don't become panicky if you're still falling slightly short of five runs per over after ten overs.** In some conditions, the ball might swing extravagantly for the first ten overs, but it will usually 'die' or 'go to sleep' very soon thereafter. You can then attack with a vengeance, scoring seven or eight off each of the next five overs.

AUSTRALIA, SOUTH AFRICA AND THE WEST INDIES

Bouncier, grassier pitches in these countries have traditionally encouraged the emergence of fast bowlers. As a result, your adversaries in the first fifteen overs are likely to be aggressive quick men, highly skilled in the use of the short ball as both an attacking and a defensive weapon. Bowlers like these will give you almost nothing to drive, pull or cut. Dealing with deliveries pitching short of a length will test your judgement of length, but it can also provide some respite: bowlers who bang the ball in are much less likely to make the most of the white ball's exaggerated swing, so at least you'll generally only have bounce and seam to contend with. However, never assume that seamers won't try pitching it up now and again. Or they might test you with a yorker or outswinger on off-stump.

Because the bowlers will have the overwhelming advantage in the first five overs, your team's fifteen-over target should be considerably lower in Australia, South Africa and the West Indies than it would be in Pakistan, for instance. While you'll encounter a belter with a lightning outfield every so often (some West Indian pitches are as flat and dusty as the flattest Rawalpindi 'highway'), you should generally be looking to score between 55 and 75 runs in your first fifteen overs.

However, this target must be balanced against your main priority in the opening stages of your innings: keeping wickets intact. In these conditions, it is far preferable to be 3 for no loss after five overs than 20 for 3.

- **Keep wickets in hand during the first fifteen overs.** You don't want to be more than two wickets down when the field eventually spreads.

- **Use the first five or six overs to assess the surface and overhead conditions.** Without being overly adventurous, discover which shots are appropriate and which aren't.

- **Play straight.** The cross-batted pick-up shots recommended for Asian conditions will almost certainly be calamitous, as the more pronounced bounce and movement off the seam will open you up to leading edges.

- **Discover which gaps in the field are being left open, and run plenty of singles into them.** Run hard and fast: in low-scoring games a single run can make all the difference. It's long been a truism of the Australian one-day team that whoever runs the most singles, wins.

- **If your team opts for a pinch-hitter, whether at the top of the order or coming in at number three to get things moving, make sure he is a recognized batsman who can survive good bowling.** Losing another wicket cheaply, even if it is that of a tail-ender, will give more spring and venom to the bowling attack.

THE UNITED KINGDOM AND NEW ZEALAND

The Kookaburra ball, used for decades in Australia and South Africa, has recently become the standard choice for one-day internationals. At any lower level of one-day cricket in England, however, you are likely to face either a Reader or Duke ball. The Duke feels and sounds considerably harder than the Kookaburra, and also swings and seams more. The Reader is not quite as batsman-unfriendly, but since Kookaburra have now taken over the Reader company, the construction methods of the latter will no doubt change, with a much more standard ball being produced.

Facing a white Duke ball on a grassy English pitch under grey skies will be the toughest batting challenge you will face in one-day cricket anywhere in the world, and even squaring up to a more amicable Kookaburra in these conditions – whether in England or New Zealand – can be daunting.

Once again, your primary mission should be to keep wickets in hand, and to aim at a fifteen-over total of something between 55 and 75. However, don't be disheartened if you stumble to something like 45 for 3: if you're struggling, the opposition is likely to fare equally badly, and if you manage to limp to 180 or 200, your bowlers should have a serious target to defend. However, do not assume that these standard operating procedures are set in stone: less grass or an extremely dry summer can mean a pitch that might unexpectedly allow a massive total.

Overs 16 to 40

The field is spread, the shine has gone off the ball, and now the game becomes more subtle. Critics of one-day cricket accuse this middle section of the innings of being predictable and dull; but while there is no denying that it has none of the intrigue and flux of a Test match session, one shouldn't make the mistake of mistaking repetition and attrition for inactivity. With the fireworks past, this is the time for level heads, mature innovation, and focus. After all, the middle overs are when you compile the majority of your runs, so you want to take them very seriously.

Geographic location is no longer an issue: the following guidelines now apply to all one-day games, regardless of whether you're playing on a greenish Wanderers pitch in Johannesburg with thunderclouds overhead, or on an Eden Gardens belter under clear (if smoggy) skies. Your run rate may differ by a run more or less, but the overall strategy of your team is now universal: accumulation through pressure.

Waiting for big shots and leaving or blocking dangerous balls is now out of the question. Instead of hanging back for fours, go hunting for singles. Six singles an over will score you 150 runs in this phase of the innings, in itself no mean total; and apart from keeping the scoreboard rolling over, you will be demoralizing the fielding team much more effectively than if you were scoring eight an over with two big hits punctuated by four dicey strokes. Attacking stroke-play always keeps bowlers and fielders interested, even hopeful, but nudging singles into gaps or dropping the ball at your feet for a stolen run deflates them remarkably quickly.

This is not to say that teams shouldn't press home their attack if conditions and opposition allow. The Australians of the last decade or so have been very successful with their tactic of exerting huge pressure on bowlers during the middle overs, hitting through the line of the ball regardless of the spread field. Having Adam Gilchrist bat through most of the innings has been a great asset, since his immense power and timing allowed him to clear the boundaries, rendering boundary riders irrelevant. However, this kind of approach takes huge talent, self-confidence, and a deep batting line-up in case wickets start clattering. In general, the run-a-ball (or at least five runs off six balls) tactic is best.

- **Aim for six singles an over.** Rotating the strike in this way prevents bowlers from settling or carrying out offensive strategies against one or both batsmen.

- **Don't fret if the boundaries dry up: that's why the field has spread, remember?** Your chance will come in the last ten overs. However, be ready to pounce on and put away the bad ball, especially long hops bowled by spinners. Don't get greedy, though – five singles and a four or six is more than enough for one over.

- **Be prepared to run all day.** The middle overs will test your anaerobic and aerobic fitness to their limits: if you end up scoring a hundred, you're likely to run between 60 and 80 shuttles, many of them at a flat-out sprint.

- **Bring up the field by playing a series of soft shots,** dropping the ball at your feet or nudging it into gaps in the inner ring. Once the field closes up, you'll suddenly have opportunities to score boundaries again, either by going over the field, or playing aggressively through it.

Attacking stroke-play always keeps bowlers and fielders interested, even hopeful, but nudging singles into gaps or dropping the ball at your feet for a stolen run deflates them remarkably quickly.

STRATEGY AND CAPTAINCY

TAKING ON THE MID-INNINGS SPIN ATTACK

Spinners are often considered a liability in amateur or junior one-day cricket, but at higher levels of the game, you will almost always encounter at least one slow bowler in the middle overs. Early in his career, Shane Warne was an integral part of Australia's mid-innings plans, and on helpful wickets in Asia, the likes of Saqlain Mushtaq (one of the best one-day bowlers of all time), Anil Kumble and Muttiah Muralitharan have put the brakes on countless opposition batsmen.

However, not all the spinners you face will be match-winning international icons bowling on crumbling dustbowls, so you must therefore look to get after them as much as you can. Aim to take the slow bowler for 50 to 60 runs in his spell, with sensible batting and appropriate innovation. If he throws down the challenge, bringing his long-on and long-off into the ring, take him on once or twice. But don't try to hit him out of the attack if this means playing his game. If you belt him for two sixes in one over and sky one to a fielder in his next over, you will have fallen into his trap. By all means take any bonus runs on offer, but then go back to being content with neatly worked singles. Six runs an over is all you need off the slow bowler.

This point is worth repeating: don't play the spinner's game. He is doing everything in his power to force you to play to certain fielders; and you must therefore understand his tactic, see his bait, and avoid it. For instance, off-spinners will want you to drive the ball to mid-wicket, so work it squarer or straighter instead. But don't simply be reactive: force him to play your game. Slog-sweep him over mid-wicket to force a man back on the fence, and then reverse-sweep on the off side. This kind of batting takes immense mental discipline, but at the elite level it is essential, and can spell the difference between victory and defeat.

Playing a left-arm spinner out of the rough

The ball delivered over the wicket by an orthodox left-arm spinner, which pitches just outside leg-stump, can be very difficult to score off. With no pace on the ball, drives or glances in front of square generally go nowhere, and sweeps risk top-edges or full-blooded aerial shots carrying to short fine leg.

However, there are counter-measures to this particularly nagging approach. The first, and most destructive, was beautifully demonstrated by the enigmatic West Indian stroke-player Carl Hooper. A very fine player of slow bowling, Hooper would come down the wicket outside leg-stump, giving himself room to free his arms, and then lift the ball over mid-off or extra cover. The key to Hooper's success with this tactic was his purpose: when he came down the wicket, he came down a long way, and hit the ball very hard.

A variation on Hooper's strategy is to stand outside leg-stump and then to 'dummy', feigning that you are about to give the bowler the charge. Some batsmen do this by putting their foot down the pitch a long way, or by actually taking two quick steps down the wicket and then retreating equally quickly. Whatever method you try, do it early so that the bowler is forced into changing his line at the last minute. If he tries to spear it wide of you, you'll have room to free your arms, and if he goes for the leg-side stumping, you can step inside it and have it called a wide. You'll have added an extra run to the score, and he'll have to bowl the delivery again.

A final option is the forward defensive push into the gap between backward point and extra cover; however, beware of playing 'on the walk' or thrusting out at the ball, as you can easily walk past the ball and be stumped.

Playing leg-spin

The general guidelines for playing leg-spin as described in Chapter 3 still apply, but with quick scoring now imperative, you will have to improvise a little more. Try moving outside your leg-stump, but staying in your crease. Again look to 'dummy' – this can often elicit a quicker ball from the leggie, dragged a little short, and you can rock back and dispatch it. If he isn't falling for this trick, force him to change his length by coming down the wicket and lifting him over mid-off and mid-on, or by late-cutting him backward of point. Sweeping can also be very effective: if you are wary of the stroke, learn its variations until you find one you feel comfortable playing. This will be very helpful in the long run.

Playing off-spin

The revolution in off-spin triggered by bowlers like Saqlain Mushtaq and Muttiah Muralitharan has made facing this brand of slow bowler somewhat more complicated than it was a generation ago. Increasingly, off-spinners are making the ball go out towards the slips, either by swinging it through the air, or by making it spin like a leg-break with a dramatically altered wrist action. Apart from apparently contradictory angles, the new brand of off-spin can also bounce viciously because of its overspin, which makes playing off the back foot a somewhat more risky proposition.

However, even mystery bowlers can be attacked, and for conventional off-spin, the late cut, the lofted drive over mid-off, and the 'dummy' (pretending to come down the wicket or back away from leg-stump) are three particularly useful tactics. If you're not feeling confident enough to come down the wicket, move across to off-stump – or even outside it – and work the ball square into the gap between the umpire and short fine leg, playing it comfortably under your eyes.

It is important to remind your team that scoring at 'only' a run a ball in the last ten overs will produce 60 runs, only 20 runs short of what would be considered a very creditable finish in international cricket.

Overs 41 to 50

The final ten overs, often called 'the slog', are a dangerous time for inexperienced players or teams. With just 60 balls left in the innings, there is often a great temptation to throw caution – and technique – to the wind, and to start heaving with the long handle at everything in your half of the pitch. Even the best international teams have been known to waste 40 overs of good hard work, losing their heads and throwing away their advantage in just 45 minutes of frankly stupid cricket.

While boundaries are key in these closing overs, never lose sight of your primary mission: see out the innings. Being bowled out short of your allotted overs is unforgivable. Even if your tail-enders squeeze out only three runs an over and nick the odd ball through the slips for four, make sure your team is still at the crease in the 50th over.

Don't lose sight of the bigger picture. The quantity and quality of one-day internationals on television has had the effect of convincing players at lower levels that anything under eight or ten runs an over off the last ten overs is a failure; but younger fans can forget that the games seen on television are played by elite groups of highly skilled athletes. Schoolboy sprinters would be thrilled to run 100 metres in 11 seconds, understanding that even if they are within two seconds of the records of their Olympic heroes, they are physically nowhere near the level of those athletes. Somehow, cricketing youngsters haven't made the same connection; so as a coach or captain, it is important to remind your team that scoring at 'only' a run a ball in the last ten overs will produce 60 runs, only 20 runs short of what would be considered a very creditable finish in international cricket. The following are important points to digest when going out into the frenzy of the slog.

- **Bat only as fast as wickets in hand allow.** Aiming at ten runs an over with two tail-enders at the crease and one wicket in hand is foolish.

- **When premeditating boundary hits, try to score them off the first or last balls of the over.** Hitting the first ball to the fence drastically reduces the pressure on you, and taking four or six off the last ball deflates the bowler, who might have been nearing the end of an otherwise good over.

- **For big hits, use a baseball-style stance:** keep very still, give yourself enough room outside leg-stump to swing the arms, plant your feet wider apart than usual, and watch the ball all the way down.

- **Take into account that the Kookaburra white ball tends to go soft, and can be very difficult to hit a long way in the final overs.** The Duke ball, on the other hand, generally retains its shape and hardness, so look to cash in if you're lucky enough to be facing a Duke.

- **Be ready to face reverse swing.** It may already have started in the late middle overs, but by the final ten overs, the ball is almost sure to be reversing nicely for the bowlers, especially in Asian conditions. Make no mistake: bowlers use reverse swing at the death to take wickets rather than to restrict runs – you are under attack. However, you can't afford to become too defensive. Instead, try using the lines and lengths that reverse swing involves (very full deliveries, usually ducking in towards leg-stump), turning them into scoring opportunities. Move outside leg stump and stay in the crease, so that the yorker becomes a half-volley, and drive it towards mid-off. This way, if you get an inside edge, it will deflect harmlessly to fine leg. You might also try moving across to off-stump and working the ball fine, but this increases your chances of being yorked and bowled or trapped LBW. Use a bowling machine to find which of these two approaches suits you best.

POSTING AND CHASING SCORES

Whether you're setting or chasing a target, you must have the same mindset. In the early overs of the game, do not worry excessively about mathematically-computed targets, or ensuring that your 'worm' (the graph shown on television comparing the runs scored by both sides) matches the opposition's run for run. This attitude means that if you lose early wickets, you might feel anxious and struggle to recover. Rather go out with a mindset that doesn't allow the loss of wickets to upset your game plan. Rather focus on setting yourself up for the last fifteen overs, when you can score 100 to 120.

So a useful target when chasing a score is to plan on arriving at the 35th over no more than 100 runs short of your final target. Then push on – sensibly and intelligently. Bear in mind, however, that once the required rate gets to more than a run a ball, it will quickly begin to get out of hand, unless you attack with one or two big overs.

So what happens when you do need 15 off an over? You're faced with only two options: score 15 runs, or lose wickets trying to score 15 runs! You have to try. This is why it is so important to have wickets in hand.

- **Whether setting or chasing a total, the whole team must share a vision and strategy.** This will allow each batter, from the openers to number eleven, to know how fast he needs to score, and prevents last-minute panic when targets aren't being met.

- **Try to have at least four wickets in hand by the time you reach the 35th over.** If you're fielding six batters, a non-batting wicket-keeper and four specialist bowlers (which is unlikely in the modern one-day game, but club sides generally don't have the luxury of fielding nine all-rounders), aim to have one real batter at the crease who can be supported by the tail.

- **Don't rely on your middle and lower order having to score at more than 4,5 to the over when they first come in.** A number eight or nine will initially find it almost impossible to score at a run a ball, and by the time he ups his rate (if he does), the required run rate will have rocketed.

- **Never assume that the slog will push you up to a good total or get you home to the total you're chasing:** especially when chasing, things can go badly wrong after the 30th over, with lower-order batsmen having to deal with escalating run rates, reverse swing, and a soft ball. This means you should always aim to score the bulk of your runs in the first 25 overs.

- **If mathematical equations start coming into play (for instance, if a rain interruption has adjusted the target), the captain and coach must make sure the team knows the exact permutations.** South Africa's amateurish exit from the 2003 World Cup was entirely due to their failure to understand the figures available to them.

- **If the required run-rate starts to rise, the batsmen at the crease will have to do more than simply score the runs required: at least one big over – 15 runs or more – will have to be ventured.** It is obviously better to take this risk sooner rather than later, while you still have wickets in hand and can regroup if the plan goes awry. If the team decides to try and claw back the rising run-rate with an over or two of premeditated boundary-hitting, the batsmen out in the middle must not get carried away: play percentage shots, hitting into areas that allow for controlled straight- or cross-bat shots, rather than slogging wildly off the stumps. Alternatively, you could try to manufacture a bad ball by dummying.

- **Finally, no matter where you bat in the order, be mentally prepared to 'finish' the innings:** there is no better feeling than being at the wicket and helping to drive the final nails into the opposition's coffin, hitting the winning runs, or backing up for an audaciously stolen single.

PINCH-HITTERS: HIT OR MISS?

Statistics tell us that the tactic of using a pinch-hitter – a batsman moved up the order to attack the bowling with scant regard for his wicket – comes off once in every seven games. Is it worth it? We'll leave that for captains and coaches to decide. If you do opt for this approach, try identifying three potential pinch-hitters. This will allow you to vary them according to the conditions and their own form.

For instance, on very good wickets it makes sense to rely on your front-line batsmen to get stuck in early; but on poor or unpredictable wickets, it can't hurt to gamble on a slogger getting you off to a flying start.

However, one-day cricket is evolving so quickly that this question might well be irrelevant in a season or two. Already the entire idea of a pinch-hitter is looking dated, as high-class batters have moved up a gear and are tearing attacks apart from the very first over. Australian Matthew Hayden is a very good example: one of the most respected and prolific opening bats in Test cricket, he changed very little in his technique or approach to finish as the leading run-scorer in the 2007 World Cup. The belligerent left-hander scored over 100 runs more than his nearest challenger, Mahela Jaywardene, and of the top eight run-getters at the tournament, only one batter scored at a faster rate than him: his opening partner, Adam Gilchrist! In short, new formats of cricket, especially the 20-over format, have shown that class will out: those who score at four runs an over in Tests are the most likely candidates to rattle along at eight per over in short forms of the game.

THE STRATEGY OF BOWLING

In the chapter on batting, we mentioned Peter May's theory of shot selection, which holds that for every conceivable delivery there is an appropriate shot, whether defensive or attacking. This is grim news for the bowler: if the well-trained and talented batsman has an answer for every ball you can send him, it follows that there is no reason why you should ever take a wicket.

But theory and practice don't always mesh in cricket, and while May's theory is a compelling one, it doesn't take into account human nature and human frailties such as fatigue, lapses in concentration, fractionally misjudged movements, and the more complex subtleties of a batsman's emotional and intellectual make-up. Neither does it allow for those entirely arbitrary and decisive accidents and incidents that make cricket so fascinating, whether they be unseasonable showers that suddenly turn a docile pitch spiteful, or a crater forming on a good length thanks to a particularly violent follow-through by a burly bowler.

In other words, batsmen might have an answer for every ball they receive, but whether they produce that answer in time, or at the right time, is an entirely different matter. As a bowler, you will need patience, strength, and stamina – even the greatest Test strike bowlers usually require at least six overs to dismiss a batsman – but the chinks in the batters' armour will appear, and you must be ready to drive home the fatal blow when they do. This section provides some insights into how best to expose those chinks, and how to take advantage of them.

WORKING BATSMEN OUT

> [Bill] O' Reilly is said to have kept a series of notebooks about the play of every leading batsman he faced, and to have entered fresh data there every night after he had finished bowling. His bowling was deadly…. Ferguson, the MCC scorer, makes a graphic chart of each batsman's strokes in Tests, recording every stroke by means of a straight line projected from a point towards a boundary circumference. Bowlers spend hours studying these charts, and analysing the strength and weaknesses of their opponents, before a Test…. Believe me, [such] charts are enormously valuable to the bowlers, and useful to the batsmen also.
>
> Learie Constantine, in Arlott, 1949

When you're marking out your run-up, preparing to bowl to a batsman with a big reputation, whether at under-17 school level or in a Test match, the chances are that you know a little about his game. If you're a dedicated bowler, you've done your homework, and have a fairly good idea that (for instance) he's strong off the back foot, or likes to have a go outside off-stump, or tends to get bogged down if it's straight and short of a length. As for those aspects of his batting that you're not sure of – well, you're about to find out.

But there is one fact you can be sure of, before he's even taken guard: he won't give you his wicket. You're going to have to fight him for it. Simply bowling fast or spinning the ball a long way is not going to be enough. You're going to need to plan his dismissal. Bowling against a good batsman is a test of wits as much as it is of technique and stamina.

The art of bowling, according to former England spinner and coach Ray Illingworth, is the study of batting. Every batsman has a weakness, and it is both a responsibility and a challenge to discover what it is, and then to exploit it. Even Test stars have a chink in their armour, and skilful bowlers learn how to exploit that chink, year after year. Glenn McGrath dismissed Brian Lara and Michael Atherton more than any other bowler, not only because of his uncanny ability to place the

> ## BOWLED, WARNIE!
> Shane Warne's phenomenal career owed much to his almost freakish spin and accuracy, but from early on it was evident that the Australian leg-spinner was also a master tactician, out-thinking batsmen and preying on their insecurities. With perfect control of flight, dip and drift, a favourite tactic of Warne's was to confuse batsmen as to the whereabouts of their off-stump. In his 1997 autobiography, *My Own Story*, he explained: 'My basic plan is to work batsmen across the crease. I might start with a ball on leg-stump, then another, then one on middle and leg, then one on middle, then maybe throw one wide of off-stump. That way you find out whether [the batsman] is prepared to play through the on side against the spin. Or I might work in the other direction [from off-stump to wide of leg-stump]. Normally, I have a plan for every batsman.'

ball exactly where he wanted, but because he recognized (and proceeded to make use of) tiny flaws in their batting.

This careful planning of a dismissal is known as 'working a batsman out'. This is literally and exactly what you do: you work out his game, understand how to undermine it, and then put in the physical work to get him out.

Having a plan for every batsman no doubt kept Warne confident and focused (and it's a safe bet that he and all the other great thinking bowlers had more than just one plan in store, just in case Plan A ended up being hammered through the covers for a quick 50). But as a tactical bowler, he had more than just an ability to hatch plots. To out-think a batsman, the bowler needs to be able to make quick and accurate judgements not only of a batsman's technique, but also his character.

It is important to be able to spot a gap between bat and pad, or to tally a flinch when you slip in a short ball, or a shuffle too far across to off-stump; but it is as vital to be able to sense the batsman's state of mind as you run in. Many batsmen betray their characters and emotional states through small visual clues. Perhaps his eyes are very wide, or he's gripping the bat handle tightly. Some batsmen beat the toe of the bat against the pitch much harder when they're about to hit over the top. A nervous batsman will be a tense batsman, and a tense batsman will be slow to get down to a yorker, or to get his foot to the pitch of a ball swinging away on a good length. Be alert to the signs of tension, and be willing to dominate him emotionally as well as technically.

SPRINGING THE TRAP

In the classic form of the game, which is as much about time as it is about technique, all good things come to those who wait. The hunter must be prepared to be patient for hours – even days – in order to ensnare his prey. Likewise, the bowler hunting wickets should dictate and control the circumstances of play, leaving nothing to chance. Of course, everyone knows what they say about the best laid plans of mice and men.... But as the bowler, you must have a strategy and be in command. Play the batter as you would a fish on a line, giving him slack only to reel him in again. If he gets off strike, you will have to start again, but don't let this worry you. You've got all day, while he can't afford a single mistake.

It is especially in the multi-day forms of the game that tactical bowling ceases to be a battle of techniques, and becomes a battle of wills. You've out-thought the batter, now you need to outlast him. While playing provincial cricket in South Africa, Bob Woolmer remembered bowling under Barry Richards when Ali Bacher came out to bat, a right-hander with a reputation for being a big on-side player: 'Barry told me he wanted me to come round the wicket and bowl at leg stump; accordingly, he gave me a leg slip, three men in the ring, and one man out to save the single. I bowled ball after ball at [Bacher's] legs, maiden after maiden as he worked it off his pads straight to fielders. Slowly it got under his skin: at one point he told me, "You remind me of Trevor Bailey – he was a boring bastard too." Finally, six or seven overs later, he nicked one down the leg side. He'd become frustrated, moved across too far, and got a touch on one.'

The moral of this particularly unglamorous dismissal is simple: be patient, and above all, bowl to your field. Nothing is quite as irritating as seeing two men out on the ropes while the bowler bangs it short of a length and the batters just knock it into the gap for a single. If you're going to have two men out for the hook, then have a short leg or silly mid-on in place to save the single. Now the batter knows he can neither hook nor get the single.

DO YOU BOWL TO THE BATSMAN'S STRENGTHS OR HIS WEAKNESSES?

Early on, it can be a successful ploy to play to the batter's strengths, especially if he likes hitting it in the air. Overconfidence can infect his technique, increasing the possibility of dismissal. However, once he's settled at the crease, bowl to his weaknesses.

Be wary of buying wickets, but don't necessarily discount the value of allowing the scoring rate to increase for a short time: the adrenalin levels of the batsmen are liable to rise, and recklessness can follow. It's a dangerous tactic (because you can lose control of a match within fifteen or twenty minutes), but it has been known to work. Feeding batters short balls to tempt them into hooking can end in disaster – or a flurry of wickets.

Two actions, two modern masters. The difference between chest-on and side-on bowling actions is described in Chapter 5, but in this case two pictures tell a thousand words. The West Indies' Malcolm Marshall **(LEFT)** *took 376 Test wickets and established himself as one of the most dangerous quicks in the game, despite being relatively short; while Pakistan's Sultan of Swing, Waqar Younis* **(RIGHT)**, *epitomized the silky, slinging elegance of the side-on action, generating extreme pace and movement.*

Allegations of throwing have ended careers – and cordial relations between cricketing nations. **LEFT:** *At the MCG in 1995, home umpire Darrell Hair shows Sri Lankan's Muttiah Muralitharan what he thinks a straight arm should look like, no-balling the spinner for throwing and triggering a decade of controversy concerning his bowling action.* **RIGHT:** *South Africa's Geoff Griffin took a hat-trick against England in 1960, but after being no-balled eleven times for chucking, his Test career was over almost as soon as it began.*

The tactics suggested in the pages to come are by no means comprehensive – there have been as many tactics and subtle variations as there have been great bowlers and captains – but they provide an introduction to tactical bowling, outlining some of the more successful plots bowlers have hatched over the years. Experiment with them in the nets, remembering that all tactical success in bowling is based on accuracy. Then have the courage to try them out in the middle when and where it counts.

The following suggestions are predominantly relevant to the longer forms of the game: multi-day games in which you have the time to devise plans and execute them without having to be overly concerned with run-rates and getting through your overs quickly. Naturally, some of them are applicable to limited-overs cricket, but for the sake of clarity, we have added a separate discussion on one-day tactics later in this section.

The tactics discussed below are the following:
1. Bowling in sets
2. Changing pace
3. Changing line or angle
4. Using close fielders
5. What to do in an emergency!

1. Bowling in sets

It was Tom Cartwright, a superb swing bowler for Warwickshire, Somerset and England, who coined the phrase 'bowling in sets'. A 'set' is simply a series of deliveries put together in such a way as to lure or lull the batsman into an error. It might consist of three balls, or three overs – but either way it forms a single tactical manoeuvre, and once completed, the bowler starts another 'set' or changes to an entirely new tactic.

Shane Warne's description of his tactical bowling, quoted on p. 399 above, is a classic example of a bowler thinking and bowling in sets: two balls on leg-stump, the next on middle and leg, another wider. This is a planned and deliberate series of deliveries, and one that will bend the mind of most batsmen.

A set, in other words, gets the batsman doing what the bowler wants him to do, hopefully with a dismissal as its conclusion. Most often it involves a change of line, either tempting the batsman further and further outside off-stump (until he is flashing dangerously far away from his body, with no clue as to where his stumps are); or else getting him used to the ball following one line, and then suddenly spearing it in along another line, perhaps at the stumps.

For example, if you are able to swing the ball, you might send down three overs of dead straight deliveries short of a length, and then slip in a full swinging ball that tempts the frustrated batsman into driving. Some quick bowlers have opted for sets that are nothing more than an outswinger followed by an inswinger: predictable as clockwork, but slight variations in length and line can make this a handful. Alternatively, many bowlers today use the old 'three-card trick', sending down three consecutive short balls before pitching one up on the line of the stumps.

Mike Selvey of Middlesex developed a particularly useful ploy of holding the ball across the seam, and sending down three overs that contained not even the hint of a swinging delivery. He bowled absolutely straight, so all the batsman could do was drop the ball at his feet or knock it to mid-on. Then at some stage in the fourth over, he'd suddenly dish up a wide swinging half-volley. By now the batsman would be thoroughly convinced that it was not a swing day. Seeing yet another straight ball, he'd have a go at what he thought was a full but straight delivery, and nick off. When Selvey dismissed Bob Woolmer this way, he told his victim it had been worth the previous eighteen balls to get that one wicket!

Sudden and unexpected variation is not always necessary. Brian Burgess of Somerset felt that some batsmen were more susceptible to one type of delivery than another, and would simply bowl that one kind of delivery at the batsman until he got him out, perhaps bowling inswing to one batsman and outswing to another.

Swing bowlers must bowl to take wickets – they will invariably go for runs if they don't break through, or aren't landing the ball in the danger zone for the batter. There is no such thing as a defensive swing bowler. For this reason, medium-pacers must be particularly adept at working batsmen out, and must have the nerve to try new tactics all the time.

Genuinely fast bowlers tend to be considerably less resourceful. Fast bowlers take wickets because they can beat your reflexes, and because they can hurt you. Any batter who tells you he is happy against fast bowling is either lying, or has never faced really fast bowling. If the ball hits you, it hurts, which is why the quick men will always have the advantage over their less pacy colleagues.

But the result of this superiority is often mental complacency – or even mental atrophy! Tearaway quicks often bowl too full or too short. It is a pity, because their pace and aggression open up a variety of potential tactics that often go unused, such as the bouncer-yorker combination. West Indian paceman Andy Roberts had a reputation for bowling two different bouncers: he would bowl the first seam-up at a lively (but not unplayable) pace. The next ball would also be short, and the batsman would commit to hooking it, only to have the ball skid through much quicker – Roberts having held it across the seam, which either made it kick (if the horizontal seam hit the pitch), or squat and slide (if the smooth side of the ball hit the pitch). Nasty for the batsman, but an effective form of bowling in sets.

Any batter who tells you he is happy against fast bowling is either lying, or has never faced really fast bowling.

402 THINKING CRICKET

2. Changing pace

Changing the pace of the delivery should be Plan B for every bowler on a lifeless pitch, or on a day on which the ball has gone to sleep.

The basic strategy here is deception: you're trying to trick the batsman's senses. More specifically, you're trying to convince him that the ball is going to arrive much earlier than it really is. The sudden hesitation this causes (both in his mind and technique) is often enough to force an error; or he might remain committed to his original stroke and hit the ball much too early, scooping the ball for an easy catch or even playing over a fuller ball and finding himself bowled or LBW.

There are many varieties of slower ball. Australian all-rounder Ian Harvey would bowl his almost like a leg-break, the ball sitting deep in the fingers and coming out of the back of the hand, the natural spin of the ball sometimes making it deviate away from the bat through the air or off the pitch. Shaun Pollock and Glenn McGrath were masters at cutting their fingers down the side of the ball just enough to take a yard of pace off it, without making it look like an obvious cutter.

However, the standard slower ball is held with a conventional grip and delivered with a classic action. The deception lies in the tightness of the grip, and the motion of the wrist and fingers upon delivery: because it is held in the fingers more tightly than the standard delivery, it comes out more slowly and fractionally later, the additional twist of the wrist sapping the momentum as the ball spins sideways rather than backwards, slowing down even further.

The bottom line for bowling slower balls is common to all variations: you want to throttle your pace back by at least 20km/h without changing your action too

The bottom line for bowling slower balls is common to all variations: you want to throttle your pace back by at least 20km/h without changing your action too much.

> Bob Woolmer recalled: 'Allan Donald could take nearly 17km/h off his slower ball; but sometimes in the four-day game, just a 3 or 4km/h change of pace can be devastating. Of course it doesn't always come off: I remember bowling to Morris Foster in Jamaica on a Sabina Park pitch of shiny mud. Colin Cowdrey saw it wasn't swinging, and told me to vary my pace, so I obliged, carefully setting up the batsman with three good-length balls that he smacked to Graham Johnson at mid-off at a blistering pace. By the fourth ball I could see him getting frustrated, and told Graham to go back fifteen paces, but to do it unobtrusively. He wandered back nonchalantly, and I sent down my best slower ball. It was absolutely perfect – line, length, loop, everything – and Foster was hopelessly beaten and much too early on the shot. Unfortunately he adjusted in the nick of time – and the ball disappeared down Kingston High Street. It's still rolling to this day. I still maintain that it only just cleared mid-off… by about 30 metres.'

The hugely experienced batsman who can play conventional right-arm over-the-wicket bowling almost with his eyes shut, suddenly finds himself in almost uncharted territory as soon as the same bowler starts going around the wicket.

much. And if you can get your slower delivery above the batsman's eye-line, even better: not only will the batsman struggle to judge the trajectory of the ball accurately (discussed in more detail in Chapter 4), he may even lose sight of it against the background.

The moral of this story is that the slower ball can be punished, either if the batsman reads it or has time to recover. But nonetheless, it is a skill that every bowler must master if he is to have any future at higher levels of the game.

3. Changing line or angle

Batsmen thrive on rhythm, predictability and familiarity. All their lives they have practised hitting balls in very specific conditions. Their subconscious decision-making process is finely tuned, and tells them what to do in a microsecond: if the ball comes from over there, and pitches over here, and is travelling at this speed, I play this shot. A straight half-volley on off-stump triggers an immediate response, and the ball rockets to the boundary.

This near-robotic response to certain visual stimuli stands the batsman in good stead, but it also makes him vulnerable. Just like the malfunctioning robot of science fiction who fails to understand a command because it is not phrased correctly – 'Input invalid! Repeat!' – so too can the batsman 'malfunction' if his usual subconscious processes are disrupted or short-circuited.

In other words, the thousands of hours that batsmen spend in the nets have the effect of fine-tuning their subconscious minds; but they also condition them to certain lines and lengths, and thereby make them inherently vulnerable to any sudden changes in those lines and lengths. The vast majority of the balls batsmen face in the nets are from right-arm medium-pacers bowling over the wicket. This means that the hugely experienced batsman who can play conventional right-arm over-the-wicket bowling almost with his eyes shut, suddenly finds himself in almost uncharted territory as soon as the same bowler starts going around the wicket.

In fact, so one-dimensional is most net bowling – and therefore match bowling – that even the slightest variation in line can cause serious problems for batters. Deliver the ball from 30 centimetres wider out on the crease, and watch the batsman's eyes widen and his grip tighten. Similarly, deliver from as close to the stumps as possible, and all manner of emergency lights start flashing for batsmen: they start trying new guards, different stances, shelving certain shots, and so on. All because they don't see enough variations in line in the nets or general play.

But technical shortcomings against unfamiliar lines are not the only hurdle batsmen suddenly find in their way. From being confident in familiar surroundings, many batsmen now find doubt and insecurity creeping into their game: deliveries they would usually have put away easily suddenly seem particularly dangerous. The bowler's tactics and motives also take on a distinctly sinister aspect: what does he know about my technique that I don't? When is he going to straighten it up or make it nip back? Am I being lured into an attacking shot here, and should I therefore tighten up a little more? Or is that what he wants me to do? Suddenly, instead of playing each ball on its merits and shutting himself off to everything else, the batsman is playing the bowler's game.

The psychological impact on batsmen of changing line was well illustrated by the bowling of Glenn McGrath. Thanks to a phenomenal ability to make the ball cut away from the left-hander when bowling around the wicket, the Australian scythed through left-handers in the late 1990s, dismissing the brilliant Brian Lara and other left-handed West Indians apparently at will, and also giving South Africa's doughty left-handed opener Gary Kirsten a torrid time. The upshot of this was that every time he told the umpire he was going to bowl around the wicket, an expectant buzz went around the ground. Whether or not the left-hander on strike experienced a sinking sensation in his stomach we can only conjecture, but certainly as far as the crowd was concerned, a wicket was imminent. This kind of expectation and energy will invariably affect the batsman.

Changing line is not only a good wicket-taking ploy; it can also be extremely effective in slowing the flow of runs, particularly in a one-day game when a good partnership has developed, or the final slog is on. Batsmen looking to slog are often premeditating their shots, and a slight alteration in line – especially if combined with a change of pace – can play havoc with those preconceived big hits.

DON'T OVER-REACT TO ERRORS

Most bowlers react instinctively to their mistakes, often with a drastic – and usually disastrous – overcompensation. Having dished up a short wide ball that was cut for four, you are more than likely to follow it up with a leg-side half-volley: one lapse in concentration has led to another, and you've gone for at least eight in the over. Instead, remember that changes in line can be extremely subtle. The right response to having a wide ball cut to the fence doesn't have to be a ball on the stumps: another short ball 20 centimetres closer to the batsman can easily be pounced upon by the over-eager batsman, who might slash it to gully, or, if his technique is shaky, chop it onto his stumps. However, dangling the bait out there takes courage, and you will need the confidence and encouragement of your captain – and plenty of control – to do this consistently and successfully.

4. Using close fielders

Specific field settings are discussed in more detail on pp. 431–34, but it is important for bowlers to understand the 'why' of the various fielding positions as well as the more traditional 'where'. Both 'why' and 'where' are of course derived from more than a century of experience: fielders stand where the ball is most likely to travel, given the angle and speed of the ball onto the bat. But tradition and unquestioning coaching can also make bowlers and fielders dogmatic about fielding positions, and unwilling to experiment with slight variations on old themes. The modern game is continually changing, and bowlers need to adapt their fields accordingly.

Of course, change isn't always for the better. One of the major changes in modern cricket is the disappearance of leg gully, with most bowlers now being trained to bowl in the 'channel of uncertainty'. It's a style of bowling that can be very effective – since their readmission to international cricket in the early 1990s, South Africa have relied almost exclusively on it – but it also produces limited cricket, and limited thinking. It has also removed one of the great dismissals in the game: the outswinger aimed at the pads, which gets picked up straight to leg gully (or a very agile and brave backward short leg). The advantage of this tactic, apart from opening up the possibility of an extremely satisfying type of dismissal, is that you can bowl straight and not worry about getting hit away on the leg side.

Forward short leg is also a position largely misunderstood and under-utilized by modern bowlers and captains. Many use it 'because that's what you do' early in the innings; others put a man under the helmet because they hope something will happen, regardless of what bowling is on offer. However, the short leg is not there to look impressive or be heroic. He is there to:

- take catches off the pads or gloves
- stop the single
- exert psychological pressure on the batsman.

Given the second 'job description' of the short leg, it is both irritating and confusing to watch modern bowlers and captain push the position ever straighter. In fact, the only time you should ever move your short leg straighter is if he's standing deeper to a batsman who pushes at the ball. Otherwise put him where his title dictates: short and square! The greatest short-leg fielders, especially the Indians of the 1960s and 1970s, all fielded very square, tucked in for the bat-pad catch. Their modern counterparts seem to be more squeamish about being hit, but those greats of earlier generations were extraordinary, standing their ground and taking some appalling blows to the body. Courage is essential in all close fielders, and if you have two brave short legs or silly points in your team, you're going to take a lot more wickets because of their presence.

Most off-spinners shun the short leg entirely, opting for a silly point instead. It's an understandable choice: not only is there the danger posed by the sweep or the slog sweep (which the short leg has no hope of catching in any case), but with the ball turning in to the bat, it's very unlikely that the ball will pop up on the leg side, being far more likely to go straight back down the pitch or up on the off side.

However, those off-spinners who do away with the short leg are overlooking its considerable psychological value. Few fielding positions test a batsman's mental strength as much: batsmen feel far more crowded by a shape in their peripheral vision, breathing on the backs of their legs, than they do by a fully visible silly point. Former England captain Mike Brearley used both close positions masterfully. Posting a short leg and silly point right under the batsmen's noses, he'd tell his bowler to pitch it up, inviting the drive. The batsmen, feeling crowded, and only too happy to try to blast the fielders out of position with a crunching drive, would invariably nick off or be bowled. The pressure of those two figures on either side of the pitch altered the way the batsmen thought, and therefore the way they played.

Bob Woolmer did something similar at a lower level: 'In a club game, I stopped the bowler at the top of his run-up, and quite obviously took myself out of slip and went to silly mid-off. Then I called to the bowler (making sure the batsman heard me) that he should just bowl a good length ball, because I thought the batsman was struggling outside off-stump. The man on strike didn't like that: not only was I in his face, but aspersions had been cast on his ability! He had a go at the next ball outside off-stump, and was caught behind. After the game, he came to me and asked how I'd spotted his weakness. I said I hadn't – I'd just wanted to know how strong he was mentally.'

DIVING FIELDERS: LEFT- OR RIGHT-HANDED?

The skill of a short-leg fielder depends on whether he's left- or right-handed. If he's left-handed, he can stand a lot squarer because he can take catches more easily in his left hand. But right-handed people are far better at diving or moving to their left because their right legs are stronger. Therefore your right-handed short leg needs to favour his right side, odd as that sounds, simply because his weaker left leg won't propel him very far to his right. This is often best illustrated by wicket-keepers: their left legs are generally weaker, so they don't dive as well towards the slips. However, slide the ball down the leg side and they can leap across an extraordinary distance. Adam Gilchrist has taken some blinders in front of his slip cordon, while at times he's looked ordinary dealing with balls down the leg side. The reason? He is left-handed and left-footed, allowing him to kick off much more strongly to his right than his left.

5. Emergency!

You can't always be proactive as a bowler: sometimes plans A, B, C and D have all failed, and you have to be reactive, making the best of a bad situation. However, even at times when you're struggling, there are 'fail-safe' positions to fall back onto, tried and trusted tactical sequences that can dislodge even the most gritty and settled batsman. The following are suggested reactions to some common scenarios you will face as a bowler at various stages in your career.

A BIG HITTER IS GOING ON THE RAMPAGE:

- Don't panic, and remain patient. Keep bowling tight lines and give him nothing.
- Keep subtly changing your pace.
- Try to get him to hit low to the fielder. Bowl fuller so he can't get under the ball: if he's in the mood to keep clubbing it, he'll try to slog it anyway, and could be caught low at extra cover or mid-off.
- Big hitters need their front foot out of the way, so try to get the ball as close to his front leg as possible.
- If it's a tail-ender laying into the bowling with the long handle, just bowl full and wider: tail-enders don't generally move their feet, so he's likely to end up hitting it straight into the air for a catch.

A LEFT-HANDER IS SETTLED AND SCORING AT A RUN A BALL:

- Don't be frightened by the fact that he's left-handed: he's no different to a free-scoring right-hander (see box on p. 410).
- Left-handers thrive on width – give him nothing.
- It sounds obvious, but bowl in such a way that he'll hit the ball in the air where the fielders are. Matthew Hayden likes hooking, so some teams let him hook, but put a man back for the catch. When someone like Adam Gilchrist is on strike, it's best to bowl very straight, trying to hit middle and leg, swinging the ball into him and changing the pace: he's not quite so devastating when the ball is close to him and he's playing off the back foot.
- Above all, don't let him feel settled.

THE BALL IS OLD, THE PITCH IS DRY, AND THEY'RE ON 300 FOR 1:

- Pray.
- Change your pace.
- Place all your fielders in front of the wicket, and bowl straight with the odd change of pace and cutter, to force the batsman to hit the ball in one area

only. You'll have fielders both short and long, which should limit run-scoring opportunities – if he wants to run it down or cut it backward of square into the open area behind the wicket-keeper, he risks a nick or chopping it onto his stumps, especially if the ball is keeping low.
- Assume a holding mode, and wait. Either he'll get out, or the new ball will arrive, or they'll declare!

HE'S A SOLID NUDGER WHO WON'T PLAY EXPANSIVE DANGEROUS SHOTS:
- You can get him out by manipulating your field.
- People hit the ball in the air in certain places. The South Africans of the mid-1990s noticed that the New Zealand batsman Ken Rutherford, who mixed steady accumulation of singles with the odd boundary (but nothing flashy), liked to play square of the wicket, into the gap between Jonty Rhodes at point and whoever was at cover. So the South African side would 'give' him that area. However, after several overs, the two fielders on either side of this gap would start 'crabbing' (walking in sideways): as the bowler ran in the hole was open, but by the time the ball reached the batsman, the hole had suddenly closed. Rutherford wasn't sure what had gone wrong, or why he was no longer scoring in that area. Frustrated, he would try to hit the ball in unfamiliar directions and get himself out.

TACTICS FOR SLOW BOWLERS

Slow bowlers can take awful punishment, but they can also get away with murder: even the most innocuous pie-chucker is often dead-batted away respectfully. No doubt some of this respect is a result of a batsman too timid or conservative to give the bowling the treatment it deserves; but perhaps it also stems from the almost universally shared belief that spinners are somehow more cunning and wily than any other bowler. Just where this cliché comes from is a mystery. Perhaps the challenges posed by slow bowling (how to deal with drift and loop and side-spin) seem more intellectually loaded than those posed by pace or seam, which tend to be more about physical survival than games and tricks with perception.

Certainly, the best spin bowlers have the air of a conjurer, pulling rabbits (or ducks) out of their hats with a twirl of their fingers, a flourish of their arms, and an enigmatic grin. But just as spectators get lost in the trick in the circus tent, so batsmen can forget the basic truth about conjuring: there is no such thing as magic. There is a logical – and often very simple – explanation for the apparently baffling apparitions they see. Indeed, the stage on which the trick is being performed should

THE SOUTHPAW MENACE

Left-handers make up around ten per cent of the global population. If one person in every ten is left-handed, it should follow that one in ten cricketers is left-handed; and since there are only six or seven batsmen in a team, almost every third team should feature no left-handers whatsoever. Yet the most cursory glance at international batting line-ups reveals what seems to be an almost phenomenal prevalence of left-handers; and where there's a record, there's usually a southpaw. Brian Lara notched up the highest Test and first-class individual scores, and at the time of writing, owned the overall runs aggregate record as well; Saeed Anwar's record for the highest one-day score has stood for over a decade; Allan Border was the first batsman past 10 000 Test runs; and Graeme Pollock averaged more than any other batsman after Bradman, and has only recently been surpassed by Australia's Michael Hussey – another southpaw.

From Sir Garfield Sobers, Neil Harvey and Graeme Pollock to Brian Lara, Adam Gilchrist and Matthew Hayden, left-handed batsmen seem to have dominated like no other cricketing demographic, an apparently freakish achievement given that they form such a small minority in the global population.

Even at lower levels of the game, they have proved a thorn in many bowlers' sides. Ask almost any right-arm seamer or fast bowler, and he will tell mournful tales about being driven on the up through the covers, the left-hander blissfully immune to LBWs as the ball pitches outside his leg-stump. The left-hander, it seems, is a freak of nature, blessed with a gift that makes him considerably more potent and fluent than his right-handed teammates. So is it true that the southpaw is always a better cricketer?

The answer is no. The problems that arise when bowling to left-handers are not the result of some freak ability of the batsman; they are entirely due to the bowler's failure to adapt.

The cause of all the panic is the angle of the bowler's body. In the early stages of your career, you will bowl to far more right-handers than left-handers, and by the time you enter your late teens or early twenties, your body is thoroughly used to bowling in a channel that is appropriate to right-handed batsmen. When a left-hander takes guard, your body is settled into that channel: the result is that your first couple of deliveries will be angled into his pads, or at least aimed at his middle stump, an easy ball to time away through mid-wicket for four.

Having now realized that you need to adjust, you make your second mistake: overcompensation. Determined to get the ball outside his off-stump, you go to a great deal of effort (and therefore break your rhythm) to push it wider of him, only to push it too wide. Left-handers love nothing more than width, and you've been crashed for four more. You've now bowled three or four balls, gone for eight runs, and you and your teammates are once again buying into the myth of the left-hander as a fast-scoring batting genius – all because you're not getting your body in the right position.

The solution to this is simple: run in and bowl as you usually do, but as you leap for your gather, turn your body very slightly and open up your front foot a little more than usual. That's all it takes to move the ball those nine inches to the right.

be very familiar to batsmen: it is exactly the same stage on which the fast bowlers are also performing!

What is common to both varieties of bowler is a grasp of tactics. And although they get considerably more credit for their intelligence and plotting than their speedier colleagues, slow bowlers are using precisely the same tactics. Bowling in sets, varying their lines and lengths, slowing down and speeding up their deliveries – these are all familiar subterfuges, and the slow bowler who has mastered them all can advance to the top in cricket. Just add 'prodigious spin' to this list, and hey presto: you have Shane Warne and Muttiah Muralitharan.

There are, however, certain nuances of these tactics that apply specifically to slow bowlers. The following suggestions are thus not so much 'tactics for spinners' as variations on themes that suit the general tactics of most slow bowlers.

The golden rule: changing your pace

This has already been dealt with thoroughly, but where spin bowling is concerned, you can never try it enough. The key to bowling spin, in all forms of cricket, is to change your pace almost constantly, while keeping your length consistent. You should be looking to change up or change down by just four or five kilometres per hour – bowl a couple of deliveries with more loop, then bowl the standard ball, then push one through slightly flatter. However, it is crucial that you land them all in the same area: ideally, about a square foot of the pitch, the size of a handkerchief. This prevents the batsman from ever settling, not least because he is seeing your superb control first-hand. The niggling suspicion that he is playing your game begins to creep up on him.

Be bold. Dominate. Remember, every spinner in the history of the game, whether Grimmett, Laker, Warne or Muralitharan, has had his slower flighted delivery smashed back over his head for six and his flatter one cut past point for four. Boundaries come with the territory. It is how you respond to these attacks – whether you retreat and start spearing them in more quickly, or dare him to repeat the shot by tossing it up even further – that defines you as a bowler. Remember, you have nothing to lose (except six more runs added to your figures): he has his wicket to lose.

Watching the batsman

We have already discussed how important it is that bowlers 'work out' batsmen. Central to this is a close and insightful surveillance of everything the batsman does at the crease. As a spinner, you will have considerably more time to observe everything the batsman does, partly because you will be steady and alert much sooner after delivering the ball than a fast bowler (who is thundering down the pitch – or trying to get off it – in his follow-through), and because you do not have to walk back 20 or 30 metres to your mark. Indeed, as you start your approach, you should be in a prime position to notice every nervous movement or facial expression of the batsman.

The ideal angle for a finger-spinner

As discussed in Chapter 5, off-spinners are an endangered species. Fantastic batting surfaces, covered wickets, shorter boundaries, heavier bats and more attacking batsmen have turned the predator of the pre-war era into the prey of the modern game. With leg-spin now almost universally considered the more penetrative and glamorous form of slow bowling, the art of off-spin has gone into retreat. And as with all retreats, the rich traditions and tactics of off-spin have become somewhat confused and jumbled in the general scramble to start bowling the ball out of the back of the hand rather than out of the fingers.

This is evident in many school games: the leg-spinner, having Warne as the perfect copybook, is slow and deliberate in his approach, knows to go over the wicket with his stock delivery, and to come around when footmarks have developed outside leg-stump. He also knows either to stay close to the stumps like Warne, to get the ball to drift to leg, or to bowl from the middle of the crease like Danish Kaneria, who likes angling the ball towards leg-stump and forcing batsmen to play around the spin. But without decisive and insightful coaching, the young off-spinner is in the dark, mind full of questions. Do I copy Muralitharan and go over the wicket and wide on the crease? Or should I go around the wicket, and try to straighten it for the LBW, with the arm ball or doosra thrown in every so often? What if I can't bowl a doosra? Shouldn't the arm ball then be bowled from over the wicket to open up possibilities of a catch behind, an LBW and a potential bowling?

Not surprising in all the confusion – and with all the hoopla about off-spinners trying to bowl wrist-spin and make the ball leave the bat – the basic wisdom of line has been forgotten. And it is basic: as an off-spinner, all you want to be doing is bowling over the wicket, getting as close to the stumps as you can, drifting the ball out slightly, and turning it back to hit off-stump. If it's turning a lot, go round the wicket to straighten it back into the pads or go through the gate. But on most modern pitches, particularly those outside the Asian subcontinent, you could be asking for trouble using this line. Without big turn, you're as easily driven through the off side as you are swept or slog-swept on the leg side (especially since you'll probably be pitching it outside leg-stump, making the batsman immune to LBW).

Don't be influenced by what you see Muralitharan and Harbhajan Singh doing on television. Both of these spinning maestros can afford to bowl from wide on the crease because (a) they can turn the ball an exceptionally long way; and (b) they're

As an off-spinner, all you want to be doing is bowling over the wicket, getting as close to the stumps as you can, drifting the ball out slightly, and turning it back to hit off-stump.

usually bowling on extremely helpful pitches. Once again, Grimmett offers sound advice on the value of bowling straight:

> *It is much harder to score off balls on the wicket than those on the leg or the off.*
>
> *The batsman is forced to take risks in trying to get the ball away when it is likely to hit the stumps.*
>
> *To keep down runs at any time it is best to bowl at the stumps. The resultant stroke should be between mid-on and mid-off, unless, as I mentioned before, the batsman takes risks – and this, obviously, is what the bowler wants him to do.*
>
> *It is not meant that a bowler should not bowl off the wicket occasionally. This introduces variety into his attack. But, as a general rule, it is far better to attack the batsman. This can only be done by forcing him to play each ball. And the only way to force him to play each ball is by bowling to hit his stumps* (1934, pp. 47–48).

Left-arm spinners

If off-spinners are endangered, left-arm tweakers are almost extinct. The first reason for this is a technical flaw in their game that is not being sufficiently corrected by coaches. The second is an evolutionary change in the game itself.

Most left-arm spinners angle their bodies too wide at the point of delivery. Almost to a man, they plant their front foot pointing at backward point, and then try to bowl around their bodies, with an almighty pivot of their trunks. Instead, they should be pointing their feet much straighter: they do need the angle in order to create the pivot (which generates spin), but this angle should be fairly small. In fact, if you consider the line between the bowler and the batsman an arc of 180°, the front foot should turn by no more than 30°.

But while this technical error can be corrected, the second threat facing the left-arm spinner is unfortunately not going to go away anytime soon. Ever-improving batting pitches are forcing him to bowl over the wicket into the rough outside leg-stump, because it's the only purchase he can find on the wicket, and it's the only place he'll be relatively safe: pitch it any further towards the off, on the best part of the wicket, and modern batsmen are simply going to smash him to all corners, whether on the off side, straight down the ground, or over mid-wicket.

It's a far cry from the high noon of left-arm spin, when left-armers bowled around the wicket on uncovered, damp wickets, gaining prodigious turn and exposing the batsmen to a host of terrors, from being bowled off the pad or through the gate, caught behind, LBW, or even caught down the leg side at leg slip or leg gully. Later in the match, as the pitch dried, it would crumble, producing a surface just as useful for the finger-spinner. In conditions like these, Kent's Titch Freeman took 304 wickets

> *'Always stand exactly where the captain has positioned you. Nothing approximate will do. Mark the spot with your spikes if you are uncertain.'*
>
> *– Jonty Rhodes*

in county cricket in one year (1928), of which 97 were stumpings. Admittedly, these were in the days before tail-enders had to be able to bat, so numbers nine, ten and eleven were 'help-yourself' wickets, who usually just ran past the ball!

This change in the game is another reason why it is so difficult to compare slow bowlers of this generation to past great players. O'Reilly, Grimmett and Laker were excellent bowlers, but they often played on surfaces that gave them a great deal of assistance. Similarly, they also bowled at batsmen who played them much more conservatively than today's hard-charging Test stars. For example, for nearly a century, almost nobody practised or played the sweep: footage of Sir Donald Bradman shows him pulling spinners rather than sweeping them.

Cricket historians will no doubt always treasure the exploits of those former greats of slow bowling; but given the advantages they had, we can't help feeling that Warne and Muralitharan are the greatest the game has ever seen, and will see for a very long time.

Bowling to your field

Once again, this is something we have already discussed, but because the dynamics of spin bowling are so different to those of pace bowling (batsmen have far more time to react to poor balls, and generally tend to be more aggressive in their responses), slow bowlers and their captains have even less margin for error in field placings.

The key to setting the appropriate field as a slow bowler is surprisingly simple: wherever you decide to put your fielders, make sure they stand precisely there, and not anywhere else. It's a necessity reiterated by two great players called Rhodes – Wilfred and Jonty.

The former, the famous Yorkshire slow bowler, told the story of how he'd moved a young fielder to a certain position, and how the youngster, getting restive, kept wandering off the spot. The bowler marched across, and boomed, 'You stand on that mark and don't move!' The very next ball was slogged straight to the young man, who did exactly what he was told from then on.

Two generations later, possibly the greatest infielder of all echoed the Yorkshireman's words almost exactly when he said, 'Always stand exactly where the captain has positioned you. Nothing approximate will do. Mark the spot with your spikes if you are uncertain.'

BOWLING IN LIMITED-OVERS CRICKET

Your role in multi-day cricket can vary depending on what your captain wants, but your chief task is always to take wickets: four-innings matches can only be won by bowling out the opposition. One-day cricket, on the other hand, is all about building pressure through slowing the scoring rate. Wickets are a bonus, of course, but with only 50 overs to play with, no captain or bowler can afford the luxury of attacking fields in the hopes of running through the batting line-up – unless his side has posted an enormous first innings score, and is possessed of exceptionally penetrative opening bowlers.

Most of the following guidelines are therefore variations on a single crucial theme: restriction. There is still room for planning, but the long-term strategies of multi-day bowling, such as working batsmen out with sets, are simply too dangerous in one-day games, with batsmen looking to score off every delivery. Indeed, you should only be thinking one ball ahead, and trying to make sure the batter doesn't score off that one ball.

Adapting to conditions

How you bowl in one-day cricket, whether in a 40-over school match or a one-day international, will be greatly influenced by where you are playing. Grounds in Asia (and some in the West Indies, Zimbabwe and Kenya) are almost always rough and dry, with unforgiving grassless pitches that take the shine off the ball very quickly. By the time the innings is halfway through, the ball will have turned a dull greenish-brown. By contrast Australian, English (and to a lesser extent South African) grounds offer grassy pitches and fast, lush outfields.

It is therefore important to adapt your usual game to the prevailing conditions. For instance, if you are a seamer who likes to bang the ball in hard short of a length, you will need to change both your length and your pace in Asian conditions: with seam movement almost non-existent, and the ball not coming off the pitch as quickly as usual, batsmen will have a licence to hit across the line, whether with an improvised pull or a front-foot pick-up backward of square. Likewise, if are a spinner who relies on turn rather than flight and control, batsmen on Australian or South African pitches can simply hit through the line of the ball, giving you a severe hiding in the process.

Getting the best out of the new ball

Bowling in the first fifteen overs in Asia requires all the skills of bowling 'at the death' elsewhere: give the batsman no width, and make sure you don't allow him to get under a length ball and hit it for six. While the varnish on the leather is still relatively intact, try to get as much swing out of the ball as you can, since the batsman will probably be camped on the front foot, looking to drive on the up against anything evenly vaguely pitched up. Remember, dropping short with the new ball is a cardinal sin in one-day matches, as the field is up, and it's a free hit to the fence.

There will be periods when it is important that you take some pace off your bowling throughout your spell.

In England and New Zealand, the new white ball will swing and seam prodigiously. This was never more evident than during the 1999 World Cup in England, in which many teams regularly found themselves floundering at 50 or 60 after fifteen overs, often with three or four wickets down, the bowlers completely dominant until the shine left the ball. As a bowler in these conditions, it is very easy to get carried away: bowl negatively, and let the ball do the damage. Remember that you don't need to swing the ball out from leg-stump to second slip to be unplayable – a six-inch deviation is more than enough.

Changing pace

Changing your pace is vital in preventing the batsman from setting himself to slog. When combined with a change of length, it can not only prevent a boundary; it can force an error that leads to the batter's dismissal – the best kind of restrictive bowling there is. However, being able to 'change down' – bowl a slightly slower ball without losing your line or length – is not only important as a means of mixing up your pace. There are often periods – or entire matches, depending on the conditions – when it is important that you take some pace off your bowling throughout your spell. This is especially true of slower pitches, where batsmen much prefer the ball coming onto the bat with some pace. After all, the faster it comes onto the bat, the faster and more effortlessly it goes off the bat. There is often nothing more frustrating – and therefore dangerous – for a batsman than to be timing his shots well and hitting the ball sweetly, only to have it dribble away to the cover fielder, or to smash it and see it bobble away into the outfield for just a single. Remember that in many instances, less is more. However, be doubly careful about your length: dropping the ball short while bowling at three-quarter pace gives it a one-way ticket into the stands.

Manipulating fine leg

For batsmen who like coming down the wicket and moving outside off-stump, bring your fine leg up, and move square leg deeper. Now bowl just back of a length. This will allow the batter nothing more than a single to the sweeper out on the leg side. However, be careful: pitching the ball up with your fine leg in the circle can give the batter a free hit, usually a leg-glance for four. Keep the ball back, and don't be disheartened if he picks one up over backward square for four or six – in fact encourage this kind of risky stroke. The chances are you'll win that particular duel.

Reacting to the batsman

As already explained, bowling is as much a battle of wills as it is a physical clash of skills. You should always be watching the batsman, looking for chinks in his armour;

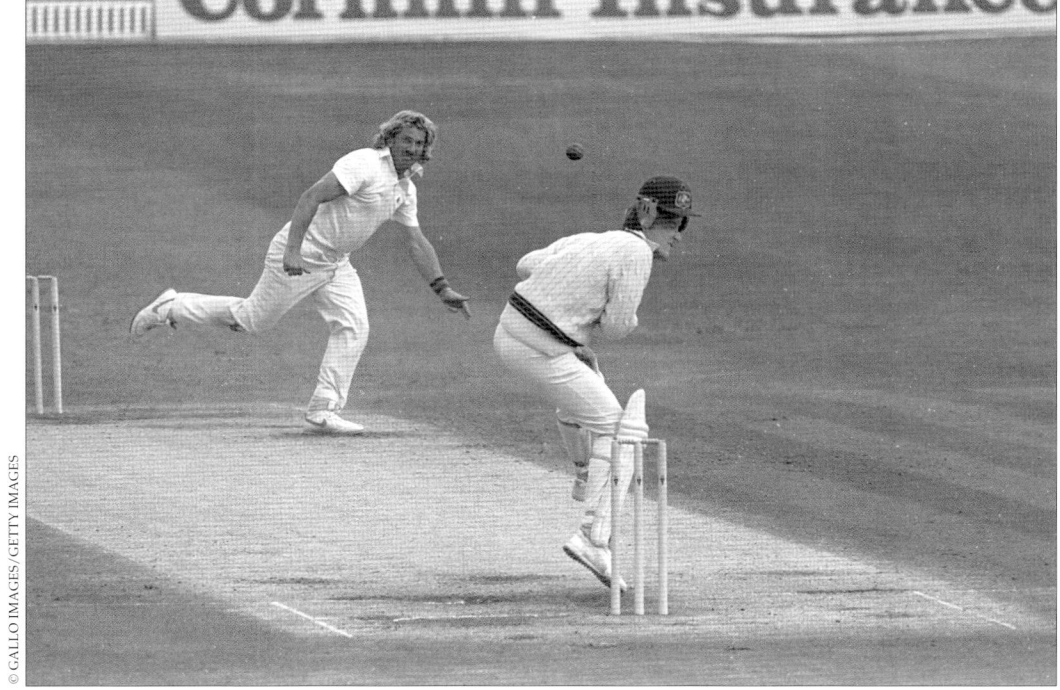

A lesson for every budding quick bowler: don't dish it out if you can't take it. At Headingley in 1981, as a helmetless Ian Botham hooked and cut his way to a legendary match-winning 149 not out, Australian paceman Geoff Lawson let fly with some short stuff at the England all-rounder. Botham, who claimed to enjoy bouncer wars, clearly made a mental note: four years later at the same venue he returned the favour to Lawson with interest.

When passions run high and the pressure is on, tempers can fray. **TOP:** *West Indies' Michael Holding kicks down the stumps as an appeal is turned down in New Zealand, while at the WACA in Perth* **(BOTTOM)**, *Australian and Pakistani macho men Dennis Lillee and Javed Mianded get stuck in after Lillee engineers a mid-pitch collision. Lillee claimed he'd been struck by Javed's bat, while Javed alleged a kick, and the handbags swung thick and fast.*

but watching the batsman as you run in is crucial for another reason: you need to be able to react to his movements as you deliver the ball. The best one-day bowlers in the world do this superbly, watching the batsman's feet and following them as he tries to move around in the crease to give himself room or disrupt their line.

If he backs away, aim at the base of off-stump: if he misses, you hit, and if it's full enough, he won't be able to get underneath it, and at best can just squirt it away for a single. But be careful: if you aim it too wide, there's always the chance of an outside edge flying wide of the wicket-keeper.

The other option when an aggressive batsman backs away is to bowl wide and full: he may be expecting you to follow him, and won't expect to have to reach for the ball a foot outside off-stump. Indeed, he may even give himself too much room, and be unable to reach the ball at all.

Reacting to aggressive intent doesn't have to be a one-on-one duel. Batting teams can get off to a flying start, even if they've lost a couple of wickets in the process, and as the bowling team, you should have a strategy prepared. A common defensive measure used in international one-day cricket is to go into a completely negative mode between the eleventh and fifteenth overs, before the fielding restrictions have been lifted. Set yourself the target of bowling 24 dot balls before the field spreads. Batters will suddenly feel extra pressure to make the most of the fielding restrictions, and this in turn can lead them to play a rash shot and get out.

Slow bowling

Spinners can go for plenty in one-day cricket, but they also have the potential to be unusually economical, if they are given the right fields, and bowl to those fields. It is accepted that most medium-pacers who make up the fifth bowler in one-day internationals will be worked around for between five and six per over; but if you bowl the right lines, vary your pace, and read the batsmen properly, you can aim to go for no more than 40 or 45 off ten overs.

Earlier we discussed how to deal with a hard-hitting batsman on the rampage – getting the ball as close to his foot as possible, to cramp him – but when bowling spin, it is also very important to get your length right so that he can't get under the ball and lift it into the stands. In unhelpful conditions, your goal should be to force the batsman to play the ball along the ground by bowling fuller and straighter.

When off-spinners bowl at left-handers (or left-arm spinners bowl at right-handers), many prefer going around the wicket and spearing the ball into the pads, with the hope of straightening it up for the LBW chance or a leading edge that might pop back for a caught-and-bowled. However, they should consider going over the wicket and bowling a much straighter line at the pads, and then spinning it across the batsman.

THE STRATEGY OF FIELDING

As a fielder, you are the eyes and hands of your captain and bowler, but this does not mean that you should relinquish responsibility to those two leaders. On the contrary, the great fielder is always captaining the side in his mind, working out strategies and trying to anticipate not only what the batsman will do with the next ball, but what kind of trap his captain will set next.

The area of the cricket field of concern to the batsman and bowler is fairly small: they are both primarily concerned with the pitch – indeed, only those few yards closest to the batsman. But your playing field is not only extremely large, but also multi-faceted. In fact, you play in three different fields simultaneously, each of which demands different skills and responses. These three fields are:

- **the close catching ring around the batsman**
- **the inner ring** (visibly demarcated in one-day cricket)
- **the outfield, also called the outer ring.**

It is important to understand how each of these differs, to find the one that best suits your abilities, and to learn and understand the specific skills required to be an asset to your captain and bowler, wherever they decide to put you.

The close catching ring

This high-risk, high-reward area has become the domain of true specialists. The good slip catcher, short leg or silly point is a breed apart. These fielders rely on considerable natural skill and a great deal of courage, speed and focus to pull off the often remarkable catches and saves they perform under pressure. It is therefore not really possible to discuss the tactics of the close catching ring: either you catch them or you don't. Since skill and practice are much more valuable here than any strategy, all we can do is suggest you revisit the practical guidelines in the chapter on fielding!

The inner ring

If you've ever watched a cat hunting, you'll know what to emulate as you patrol the inner ring. Staying low to the ground, and stalking sideways ('crabbing') are excellent starting points; but speed off the mark, flexibility, safe hands and a hard and accurate throw are also essential. Coaches or players in need of a demonstration need look no further than footage of Jonty Rhodes, who was almost perfect as a fielder in the inner ring. His only weakness, perhaps, was that he didn't hit the stumps quite as often as his rival, Ricky Ponting.

The following are some general guidelines to work on.

- **At some stage you're going to have to dive to catch or cut off a ball.** Therefore try to stay as low as possible as you walk in, as if you're a goal-keeper waiting for a penalty.

- **Anticipate.** This doesn't refer only to being ready to take catches, but also means that you should be ready to sprint into a new position. For example, if you're fielding at extra cover, be aware that against certain types of bowlers and in certain game situations, a single might be taken to your left, through the gap between backward point and extra cover. Therefore, take a calculated risk, and walk in heading towards your left.

- **Practise hitting the stumps from all angles.** Make sure that you pick up the ball correctly, and get into a good throwing position. When practising your throwing, take pride in it and remember that one good throw can change the course of an entire match. (It could be argued that Hansie Cronje's sensational turn-and-throw from wide mid-off, running out Shane Warne, was the difference between defeat and a famous victory for South Africa in Sydney in 1994.) When you throw, especially if aiming for a run-out, let it rip: have faith that your teammates will be backing up.

- **Back up all the time.** Wherever you are in the inner ring (or even in the outfield), always be thinking of where you need to be to back up a throw. Slip fielders are also not exempt from backing up or fielding in front of the wicket. Remember, you can never have too many fielders backing up: the classic example is mid-wicket having to run across to square leg to field, and throwing at the bowler's end. In this case, both the bowler and the mid-on should be trying to get back to the stumps, while mid-off and cover should be backing up. Both are needed to field possible ricochets off the stumps.

- **When throwing to the bowler's end from inside the ring, try to bounce the ball in to keep it at stump height,** which gives the bowler or fielder a better chance of breaking the wicket cleanly and quickly.

The outfield (outer ring)

Those who patrol the outfield or the boundary (sometimes called boundary riders) are the long-range artillery of the fielding unit. They need speed across the ground, flexibility, and the ability to judge a high ball while shutting out all distractions, such as the approaching boundary rope, crowd noise, or the odd missile thrown their way. Most of all, they need a great throwing arm. Being able to rifle in a flat throw over the stumps from 40 or 50 metres out is an extremely precious asset, and one that will take wickets for your team.

- **A ball heading for the boundary must always be chased by two fielders:** one for the slide and pick-up, and one to relay the throw in if the ball is flicked up inside the rope.

- **Call loudly and clearly, whether you're calling for a catch, or telling another fielder which end to throw to.** If you're the fielder who has collected the ball and everyone is yelling at you – 'Bowler! Keeper! Run him out!' – remain calm, take in the situation with a quick glance at the batsmen, and get the ball in to the more exposed side.

- **Look after your throwing arm:** a weak shoulder can end your career, or prevent you from starting one in the first place. Maintain strength and flexibility, and practise throwing at every net. However, don't over-do long-range throws: you can damage muscles and ligaments (see Chapter 10 on the risk of injury here).

- **When throwing from any position in the deep, make sure that your body weight is directed at the target.** This will help you to get the throw in flat, hard and accurately; an essential skill, as simply getting the ball airborne is no longer a particularly great deterrent to top players.

- **When you field the ball on the run while skirting the boundary, don't twist and throw, or try to get the ball in side-on:** you'll have very little power on the throw, and run the risk of severe injury. Instead, continue running, but turn infield towards your target.

CAPTAINCY

Top-order batsmen grind out scores that put their side at an advantage, middle-order batsmen can save matches, strike bowlers win them, wicket-keepers chivvy their team and effect dismissals; but it is the captain who is the most important member of any team.

It is the captain who leads his troops on the field, who weighs up the conditions and the opposition, who chooses the tactics and makes the difficult decisions, who takes the big risks; and, when things go badly, it is his head on the block.

The great international captain is born, not made. Most club or first-class skippers are good team men, solid organizers and talented players who command by committee, taking the advice of their coach and senior players, and weighing it against their own understanding and experience of the game. But the thoroughbred Test captain stands out from an early stage: often an all-rounder at school (sometimes academically as well as athletically) he is a born leader, equally comfortable in company or alone, who knows not only his own mind but those of his players. Command comes naturally (if not always effortlessly) to him, and in many cases he is already being groomed for his future role long before he presses a claim for international selection.

However, even though the international captain is the pinnacle of the cricketing hierarchy, he is hardly representative. After all, there are only nine (ten if Zimbabwe are readmitted to Test cricket) Test captains on the planet at any given time, which leaves more than half a million cricket teams that need skippers! Just because you're not internationally renowned as a deep thinker and brilliant tactician, doesn't mean that you aren't a fine captain, respected by your team and prized as a valuable tactical weapon. If captaincy of the average cricket team were some pre-ordained gift or calling, there wouldn't be much we could say in this section. The truth is that captaincy is a skill like any other. Some are instinctively better at it than the rest of us; but for those not destined to lead Test sides, there is tremendous scope for learning and improving the skills of leadership and responsibility.

THE QUALITIES OF THE CAPTAIN

Captaincy is a curious balancing act. On the one hand, the cricket captain must be a strategist, thinking coolly and objectively about the massive chessboard on which he finds himself, and how best to use his eleven pieces, some of them pawns, others kings and knights. On the other hand, he must be a friend, a mentor, a psychologist

It is often said that a captain is only as good as his team, but this is a cop-out: a team is only as good as the captain wants them to be.

and a confidant; a 'people person' who is in touch with the human foibles and psyches of his players. This tension between being a cerebral puppet-master and an intuitive human being is often difficult to get right, and captains must take time to think about their roles and responsibilities, both as leaders and as human beings.

In the heat of battle, both sides of his personality must be able to function at full capacity simultaneously. For example, when planning the dismissal of a batsman, he might have to balance his desire to set a particular field against his bowler's discomfort with that field: if he can explain his needs to the bowler so that the latter goes to his mark inspired rather than apprehensive, it is one sign that he is a true leader.

It is crucial to retain your humanity while leading a team. When things go wrong, or a game starts slipping away from you, it is easy to blame your team and retreat into a superior sulk, silently lamenting your misfortune to lead a team of no-hopers. It is often said that a captain is only as good as his team, but this is a cop-out: a team is only as good as the captain wants them to be. If your team has folded under pressure, look to yourself first, and ask what signals you've been transmitting to them through your body language, tone of voice or facial expressions.

Being able to laugh at yourself is a great trait (not only in cricketers, but in humans in general). In the case of a captain, it can be priceless. Bob Woolmer recalled a match in which Warwickshire (under Dermott Reeve) had completely lost the plot. The opposition were grinding out a huge total, and no matter what the skipper tried, nothing seemed to be working. Finally he decreed that the final session of the day would be dedicated to self-ridicule. The good-natured taunts flew thick and fast ('Hey Gladstone, see if you can get a wicket before Christmas!' – 'Okay, this year or next?'), and very soon the tension had been broken, the fielding team's spirits had lifted, and most importantly, the batsmen's concentration had been shattered by this unusual barrage of banter. Wickets fell, and Warwickshire were back in the game.

Understanding human nature and personal quirks is also essential for captains in their most important relationship on the field: that with their bowlers. Both captain and bowler need each other, and yet their individual needs often get in the way of that mutual symbiosis. For example, even the most macho fast bowler needs to feel respected and appreciated by his skipper, and even the most innocently disparaging remark by a captain can be interpreted as a lack of faith. Similarly, some bowlers become almost obsessed with looking after their averages, all but refusing to attack the stumps or pitch it up, despite their skipper imploring them to attack. The bowler who decides that 2 for 25 off fifteen overs is good enough will become an immovable lump in the hands of his captain once he's taken his second wicket. Of course, sometimes you'll be blessed with a bowler or two like Ian Botham, Malcolm Marshall or Dennis Lillee, tenacious fighters who were desperate to bowl all day, every day. Trying to persuade your bowler to *stop* bowling is one of a captain's more pleasant battles, but unfortunately not all are so lucky!

You can't be a Dermott Reeve all the time. There is a place for the tough, silent captain, the 'hard-as-nails bastard' who expects his team to sweat blood for him – and leads them to thumping victories in return. Australian captains have traditionally adopted this more aggressive posture, with Allan Border and Steve Waugh giving absolutely no quarter and expecting none in return. However, remember that toughness is an ingrained attitude, not a performance: encouraging your team to sledge the opposition constantly, for instance, proves nothing about your leadership, but does point to some rather unflattering truths about your personality. While sledging has its place in the game (up to a point), remember that real intimidation comes from how well you play, not how colourful your vocabulary is. Clive Lloyd's world-beating West Indian side never said a word. They didn't have to. Where Dennis Lillee and Jeff Thomson would let rip with some choice expletives, Michael Holding would just smile, flashing his vampiric incisors, and then walk away, leaving the batsman far more unnerved than if they had been on the receiving end of a string of insults.

We've noted that cool intelligence and humanity are crucial, but these attributes are somewhat vague. So what are the specific qualities needed by a captain? The following list is by no means comprehensive, but it includes the psychological and mental attributes most commonly found in good skippers.

- **Leadership:** A captain must have the ability to lead by example and thereby gain the respect of his players. He must not shirk any of the 'dirty' duties, such as standing in as twelfth man when he does not play.

- **Man-management skills:** He must know what makes each member of his team tick so that he can motivate them to perform to the best of their ability. This also translates into practical on-field skills, such as being able to position fielders or move them around in such a way that they don't get bored or drift. (Efficient movement of players is also key: having players running the full length of the field from fine leg to fine leg, or scurrying across the pitch after every over, should be the preserve of the primary-school captain. Even at the lowest levels of the game, this kind of inefficiency is unacceptable.)

- **Sound tactical skills:** He must know when to attack and when to defend. He must be able to ascertain batsmen's weaknesses and exploit them, and have complete control of all the possible field placings.

- **Knowledge of the laws and competitions:** Often a certain law or a recent change in competition rules can have a profound effect on the game. The captain must have all these at his fingertips, so that he can make the correct decisions, and react appropriately to rain rules and similar mathematical or technical permutations.

- **Discipline:** There are times when the captain has to crack the whip – for example, if a player begins to argue with an umpire. He must ensure that the game is conducted in the right spirit.

- **Compassion:** Occasionally players fail and have to be dropped. The captain must be able to handle these and other tricky situations with diplomacy and understanding.

- **Ruthlessness:** When he has the opposition on the run, the captain must have the focus and killer instinct to finish the match, not giving his opponents a moment's respite or reprieve. This is what really separates the good captain from the one whose side nearly always wins.

- **Administrative capabilities:** Depending on his club's administrative structure, a captain may be called upon to see to a number of important tasks, such as putting the team list up on the notice-board, ensuring that teas and lunches are organized, arranging transport for away games, and, on match days, assessing the wicket, attending the toss, posting the batting order, motivating the team, and communicating his initial ideas and strategies to them.

ROLE IDENTIFICATION

In a team consisting of eleven players and a twelfth man, there are twelve different jobs that need doing, and as a captain, part of your job is to let the other eleven players know what their jobs are. Simply pointing to a batting list, or telling a bowler that he's going to be coming on first change, is not good enough. You need to identify and assign roles to your players, but in the process, you also need to explain your thinking so that your team has a clear picture of your overall strategy, and feel that they are an integral part of your scheme. It may be obvious to you that they are – but some captains can neglect their players' egos.

For example, you and the coach might decide to move a player up or down the order. However, instead of simply telling him and walking away, remember that being shunted around the order can be extremely upsetting for many batsmen. Not only will the player have to deal with the usual stresses of adapting to new tactical conditions, but he will understandably wonder whether his head might be on the chopping-block. International cricket provides him with a frightening array of precedents: players who were yanked all over the order, who failed once or twice in their new positions, and were then unceremoniously dumped from the team, never to surface again. Sharing the bigger picture with the player and the team will not only reassure the batsman, but also smooth any potentially ruffled feathers of other players – who might feel that their own personal ambitions are being threatened by switches in the order.

In fact, identifying roles or tasks for your players is much more about communicating your strategy than it is about appearing decisive or dynamic as a leader. All too often, mediocre captains wander up to their medium-pace swing bowler, announce 'You're on next change from the pavilion end,' and stroll away, leaving their bowler with nothing but questions. Compare this to the kind of instruction former England captain Mike Brearley would give in identical circumstances. Approaching with purpose – making it clear to the bowler that it was he Brearley needed, and no-one else – the England skipper would say something like, 'I need you to hold this end. You'll have a defensive field, and I know you're worth five maidens.' Not only could the bowler now focus and plan his spell, but his confidence was sky-high, knowing that his captain had so much trust in him.

It is important to remain consciously flexible and creative when assigning tasks to your team. Even as you explain your strategy and 'think outside the box' in terms of field placings and bowling orders, you run the risk of taking certain things for granted or falling into the trap of cliché. For instance, if you were lucky enough to be handed fielders of the calibre of Jonty Rhodes and Ricky Ponting, you would probably automatically stick them straight in to field at point and cover. This would be a sensible decision in principle, but danger would lie in the fact that you'd acted automatically, without stopping to think through all the possible permutations. Perhaps you might be better off considering whether Rhodes might be more effective on the leg side, given that Ponting would provide a good off-side deterrent.

Finally, always remember that you are in charge. By all means listen to suggestions and bounce alternative strategies off players whose opinion and experience you trust, but your team must be under no illusions about who is boss. Mid-pitch debates with half a dozen players arguing the toss are unacceptable, and occasionally in recent times, the Indian side have taken this kind of on-field democracy much too far – with four or five players crowding around the captain all pointing in different directions while batsmen try not to lose their focus and precious minutes slip past. This is not only extremely poor form, but also suggests a team that doesn't respect the captain's judgement, and whose members are not clear on their individual tactical roles.

Never move a player up or down the order without communicating the bigger picture not only to him, but the rest of the team. If everyone understands the thinking behind this decision, it will reassure the batsman, and also smooth any potentially ruffled feathers of other players.

MIKE BREARLEY ON LEADERSHIP

Australian fast bowler Rodney Hogg once said that Mike Brearley had 'a degree in people', and while Brearley's academic achievements were impressive – he studied psychology at Cambridge – it was his unwavering ability to read not only the game of cricket, but the people who played it that made him one of England's most respected captains.

In 1985 Brearley wrote *The Art of Captaincy*. One of the first concerted efforts to put into perspective the complex nature of leadership in sport, it soon came to be accepted as the definitive text on the nuances of leadership in sport; and remains current to this day, having been updated in 2001. As is often the case with classic texts, its insights have found a wider audience than cricket: Oscar-winning director Sam Mendes applied its teachings to his film crew while making *American Beauty*; and it remains a valuable source of guidance to anyone in a leadership position, or who works with a close-knit group of colleagues or subalterns.

The book should be compulsory reading for all those who want to understand cricket captaincy, but we sum up some of Brearley's thoughts on leadership here: not to mention them would leave this book incomplete.

Leadership, says Brearley, requires the creation of the best possible morale and working attitude. This requires that the captain 'be able and willing to take in and think about the anxiety of those who work in the team. Sometimes it is a matter of getting to the bottom of an anxiety that has already been covered over. It then has to be conveyed, often subtly, to those in the team that their predicament and anxieties are bearable. If this is done, the team is less likely to resort to damaging states of mind such as defeatism, lack of initiative, or complacency. Nor will it be so likely to split into antagonistic factions. This function, of containing anxiety and handing it back in a form that can be thought about, is based on that offered both by our first nurse – the mother to her baby – and subsequently by both parents throughout childhood and adolescence' (2001, p. 4).

To be able to achieve this, the captain must be interested 'in what makes people tick, particularly when they seem to be difficult or withdrawn or under-achieving' (p. 4). But in order to be effective, he must also stand back from the emotional release of being 'one of the boys, indulging in the dramas of gossip, and having a go at the boss…. In a team, the pull may be to get the person in charge to join in a mood of delinquency or persecution in ways that undermine the performance of the task' (p. 5).

Brearley suggests that this pressure may be directed with the hope of turning the captain into 'a tyrannical boss who relieves the others of the need to think for themselves. Or he may be required to become passive and cringeing before a powerfully bullying process [that may be] predominant in a group at that particular time.' But should the captain succumb to this pressure, he will find that 'the clarity that leaders need to do the job properly has then been hijacked. Power now lies with the unconscious of the group' (p. 5). In other words, the captain no longer leads the team. The rogue team, no longer wanting to confront the anxieties about its collective ability, will be much more likely to subtly give up 'by becoming passive and depressed'. It will 'leave things to someone else and look to a star or the captain to do or initiate everything' (p. 5). Such teams may also be characterized by a lack of mutual respect. 'It is the captain's job to try to unify the team, and the first step in such integration will be his awareness that it is lacking' (p. 57).

Brearley therefore considers that a crucial function of the captain and coach is 'to deal creatively and effectively with these self-defeating attitudes that arise individually or collectively as a result of their anxieties' (p. 6).

For Brearley, the art of leadership is an often instinctive skill, and one that when practised well, can bring about harmony and unity: '[T]he capacity to take in and take on the pressures of a team, both individually and collectively, and then enable the team to reach creative solutions without denying these anxieties – underlie much of what good leaders do, more or less naturally. If we add shrewdness, tenacity and a tactical flexibility to the mixture, players will be more and more likely to give their best. A productive cycle, quite the opposite of the malign cycles in teams where leadership is insensitive or weak, results. The need for such qualities is universal, applies to all walks of life, and is unchanging. However technically and financially sophisticated we become, there is no substitute for the leader's capacity to bring people together in a common task, so that people come to take pleasure in their joint and individual work' (p. 8).

This is not to say that a good leader is someone who dishes out hugs to all and sundry. Brearley points to the Australian tradition of captaincy, which, to him, 'seems to be a tradition in which ruthlessness and efficiency are, at best, allied to a detailed and unsentimental appreciation of the tactics of the game'. This system, he says, is a 'democracy of ideas' in which junior players have traditionally been 'immersed in a shrewd approach to the game as a whole' (p. 8).

Leadership, he concludes, calls 'for universal, but also complex and individually characterized qualities, qualities that are inherently in tension with each other. We could speak of antinomies of leadership – passion and detachment, vision and common-sense, an authoritarian streak and a truly democratic interest in team and points of view. One requires conviction, but also the capacity not to rush to answers but to be able to tolerate doubt and uncertainty' (p. 8–9).

The introduction to *The Art of Captaincy* gives the last word to the ancient Greek historian Xenophon, who summed up what he considered the essential qualities of a Greek general, and which we consider the ultimate definition of the ideal cricket captain. He should be: 'ingenious, energetic, careful, full of stamina and presence of mind... loving and tough, straightforward and crafty, ready to gamble everything and wishing to have everything, generous and greedy, trusting and suspicious' (p. 9).

SETTING A FIELD

As pointed out in the chapter on fielding, fielders have always had the benefit of past generations' trial and error. Today we know where to put the gully when the fast bowler is on because that's where the gully stood in 1980, and he stood there because that's where the gully stood in 1960, and he was copying the gully from 1930, who was probably emulating the poor fellow who first had his nose broken by standing too close or had his captain bellow at him for standing too far back. In other words, fielders stand where they do because that's where the ball goes, and has gone ever since overarm bowling reached the speeds recognizable to a modern cricketing audience.

As such, field placings in the modern game are more about learning by rote than by experimenting. This is not to say that you shouldn't improvise; but moving your fine leg very square or moving your mid-off across to extra cover, just for the sake of experimenting, is fairly pointless: the ball will go where it has always gone, and as a captain, it is your duty to make sure there's a fielder in the way.

The analogy of a chessboard has already been referred to, and it is a good one: as in the game of chess, the cricket captain must understand the tactical value of each player, and how best to use them. Just as it makes little sense to endanger a rook by sending it to take a pawn, it is a waste of skills to put a fast runner with a powerful throwing arm in the slips. The captain must know how to set an attacking field and a defensive one, as well as more subtle variations (like an attacking defensive field, for example, where a wicket is captured by frustrating the batsman and forcing him into a rash shot). Finally, he must be able to communicate his wishes and plans to his team quickly and clearly, so that everyone is working towards the same goal.

How you run your team in the field is your business: if you've found a brand of captaincy that is successful and sustainable, change nothing. However, the following general hints should be considered by all skippers of fielding teams.

- **Run the game from a prominent and central position, such as slip, mid-wicket or mid-off.** If you choose the last option, bear in mind that most mid-off fielders have a tendency to stand too close to the bat. Since you won't be able to see your own position as you would that of another player, remember to move a couple of steps backwards every so often.

- **Make sure fielders aren't running unnecessarily long distances between overs** (for example, from fine leg to fine leg).

- **Always encourage accuracy from your bowlers:** you can't set a field to a bad ball.

- **Put specialists in specialist positions:** these include the slips, short leg, and cover point.

- **Don't whip a fielder out of position if he drops a catch or fumbles a save.** Not only does this demoralize him and make him more likely to err again, but it gives the batsman a sense that he's won a little mental victory and gained a psychological edge.

- **Don't get carried away trying to emulate what you see on television:** giving your opening bowler three slips, two gullies and a short leg will make him feel fantastic and will make you look like the commander of a team of champions, but if he's not particularly quick or accurate, you'll end up looking silly. Similarly, Mark Taylor's 'Star Wars' field (men clustered on every square inch of pitch around the bat) was extremely stressful for batsmen when they faced a young Shane Warne, but if you give the same field to your left-arm spinner who turns it two inches, the most likely outcomes will be a seriously injured fielder and a batsman hitting boundaries at will.

THE THREE-RING FORM OF THE CRICKET FIELD

Before we show standard tactical fielding placements, it is important for captains and players to break the field down into its three basic components:

- the close-catching circle, where the blokes with big hands and quick reflexes crouch;
- the inner ring, where your Rhodeses and Pontings roam, cutting off singles, saving boundaries, and taking stinging catches;
- and the outer ring, where the big men with the cannon throwing arms lurk.

Each of these fielding areas is a distinct space that requires very specific skills, a fact forgotten by many amateur captains, who have a tendency to shuffle fielders around, leaving them stranded in vague positions (the backward-cover-mid-off-sweeper being a common error). Be crisp in your thinking and your field placements. The three illustrations that follow (on pp. 430–31) will help you to gain a clearer picture of the distribution of skills and workings of the fielding team.

The close-catching ring.
A generally comprehensive list of the attacking fielding positions captains can employ. Most of these positions come into play when the new ball is taken, or when captains are trying to knock over a tailender.

1st, 2nd and 3rd slips • • WK • Leg slip
• • Leg gully
Gully •
Silly point • • Bat-pad
Silly mid-off • • Silly mid-on
Short extra cover • • Short mid-wicket
Mid-off •
• Bowler

The inner ring. *Note the 'V' formation of the positions; this effectively cuts off most of the angles for batters. It also means that when it comes to having a shy at the stumps, there is usually someone backing up behind the stumps more or less opposite the thrower.*

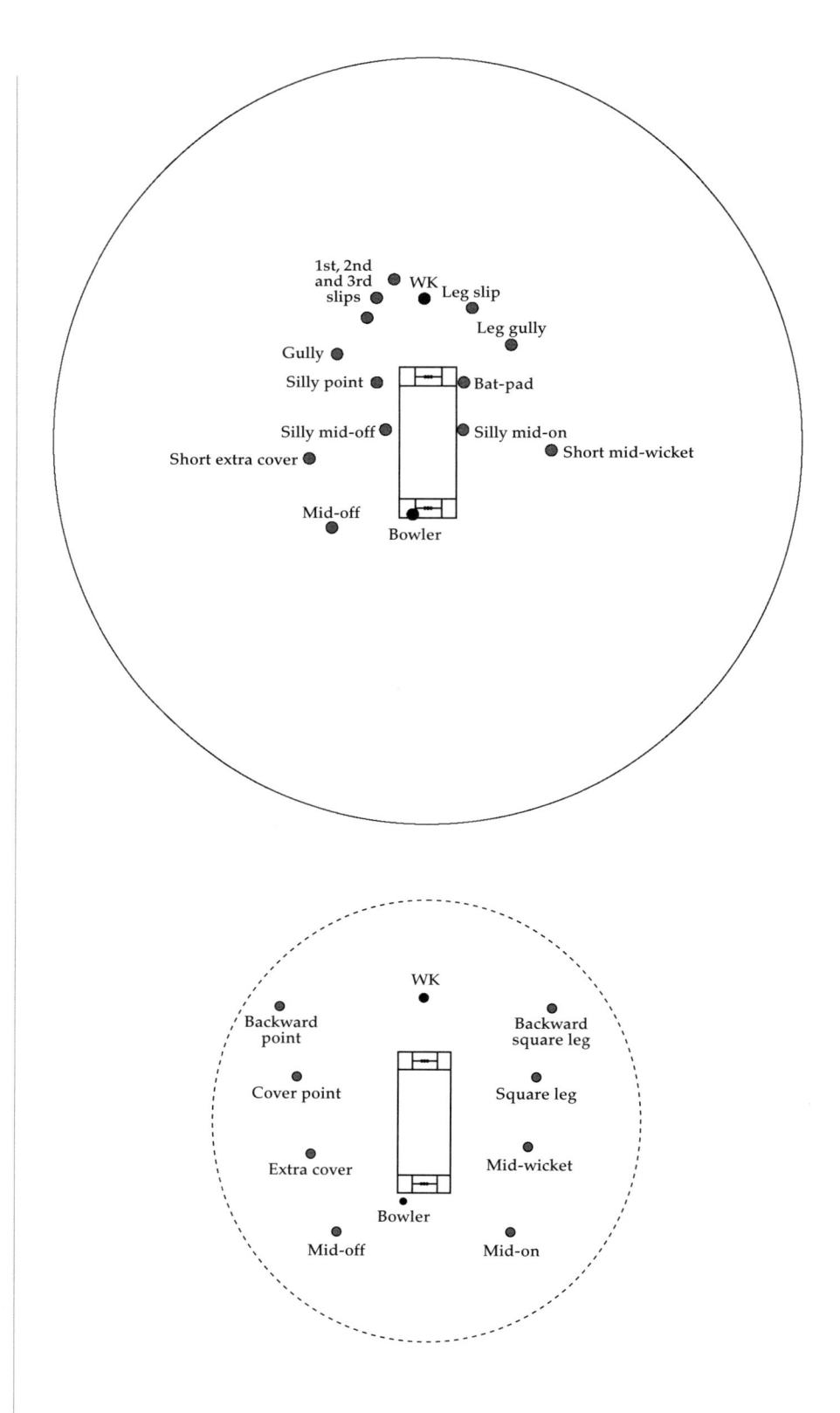

• WK
Backward point • • Backward square leg
Cover point • • Square leg
Extra cover • • Mid-wicket
• Bowler
Mid-off • • Mid-on

430   THINKING CRICKET

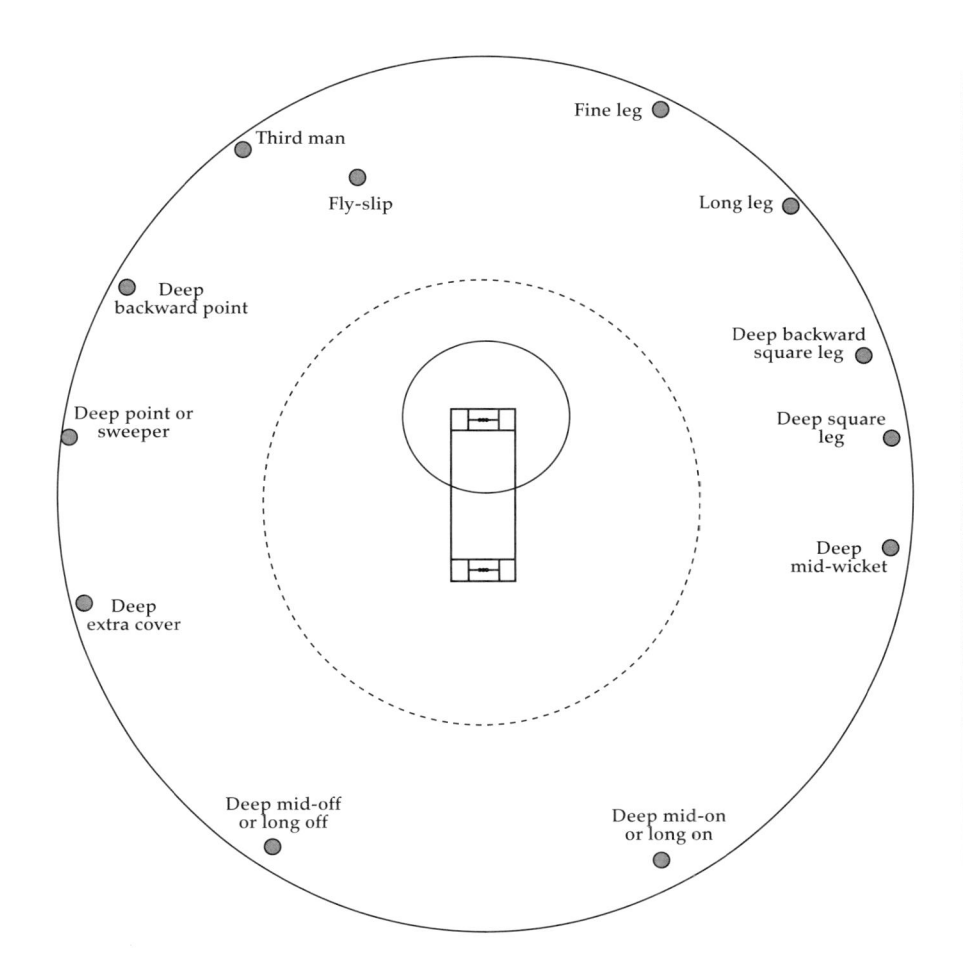

The outer ring. *Almost all of these positions can be altered or adapted to suit game conditions; don't simply put everyone in the deep on the boundary rope. The fly-slip, for example, is not a boundary-rider, but rather a floating fielder who waits for the top-edged slash (or, nowadays, the mistimed reverse hit), positioning himself according to the batter, the pace of the bowler and the pitch, somewhere between a conventional slip and third man. Likewise, in the shorter game, it can often be useful to have fine leg up in the marked fielding circle.*

CLASSIC FIELD SETTINGS

There are as many potential field placings as there are captains with novel ideas about how best to take wickets. However, the diagrams of basic field settings that follow on pp. 432–33 are gold standards, illustrating tactics that have been tried, tested and proven over generations. Use them as starting points and adapt them to your own bowling attack, the prevailing conditions, the strengths and weaknesses of the batsman on strike, and the state of the pitch.

A right-arm fast bowler attacking a right-hander with the new ball. Consider a mid-on if your quick bowler spears the ball into the pads like Makhaya Ntini, or is not getting away movement. However, if he is troubling the batter with a line into the pads or body, don't sacrifice your leg slip by posting him at mid-on: you don't want to stop potential singles played into the 'V' only to see a gloved chance or a strangle off the face of the bat fly through a vacant leg slip area.

An outswing bowler drying up runs while still trying to break through with an older ball. With a softer ball, its varnish hammered off, you're looking to bowl tight lines and keep a lid on scoring, but without sacrificing your wicket-taking options. If your bowler isn't swinging it well on a good line and length, and if the batter is settled, the second slip might be a luxury you can't afford, but don't go defensive too soon. The leg gully is also an optional extra, but don't discount the benefit of having a man in there, especially if your outswing bowler can start the ball on leg-stump and bend it back towards middle; many a batter has perished running an outswinging leg-glance off the face of the bat straight to that position.

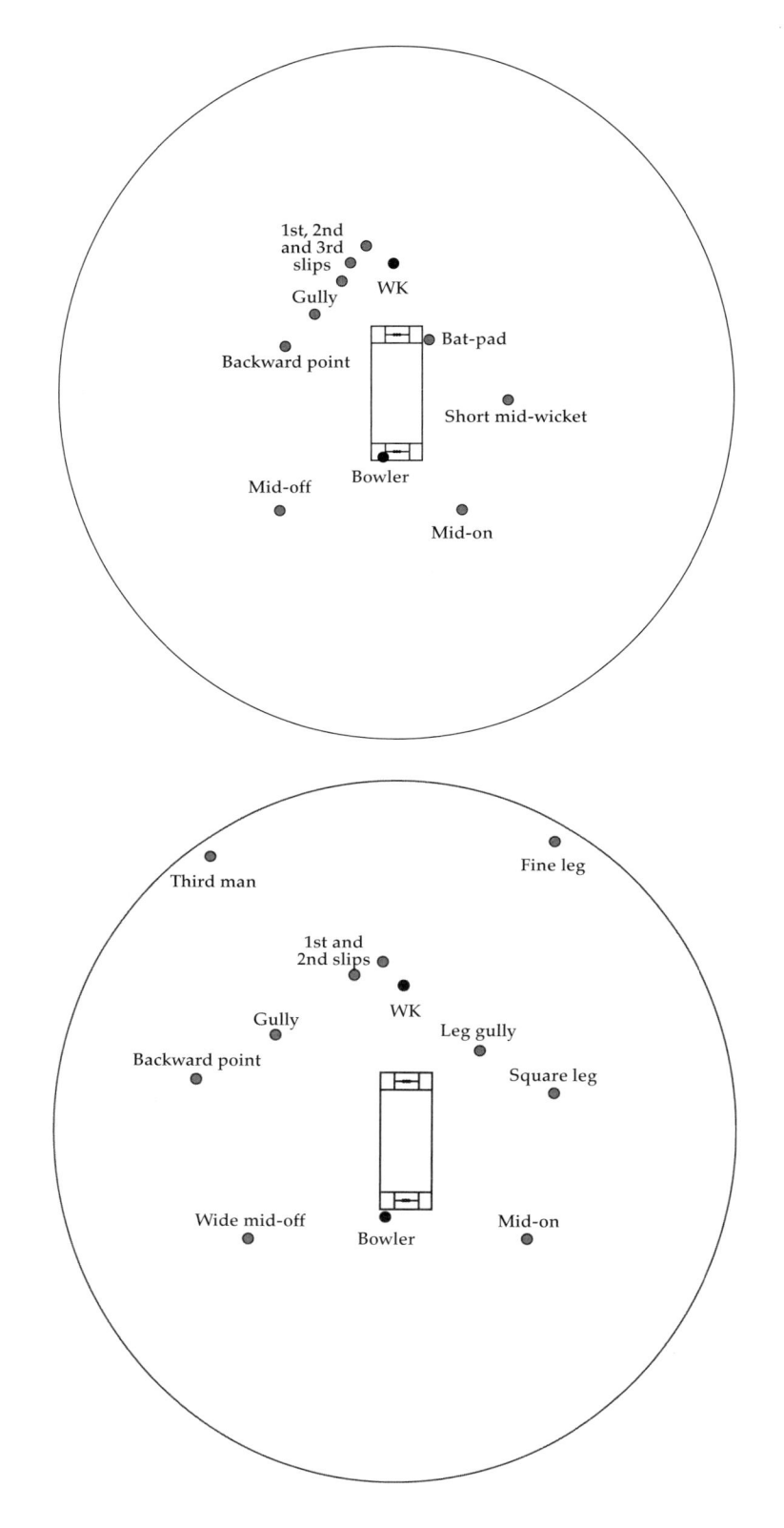

432 THINKING CRICKET

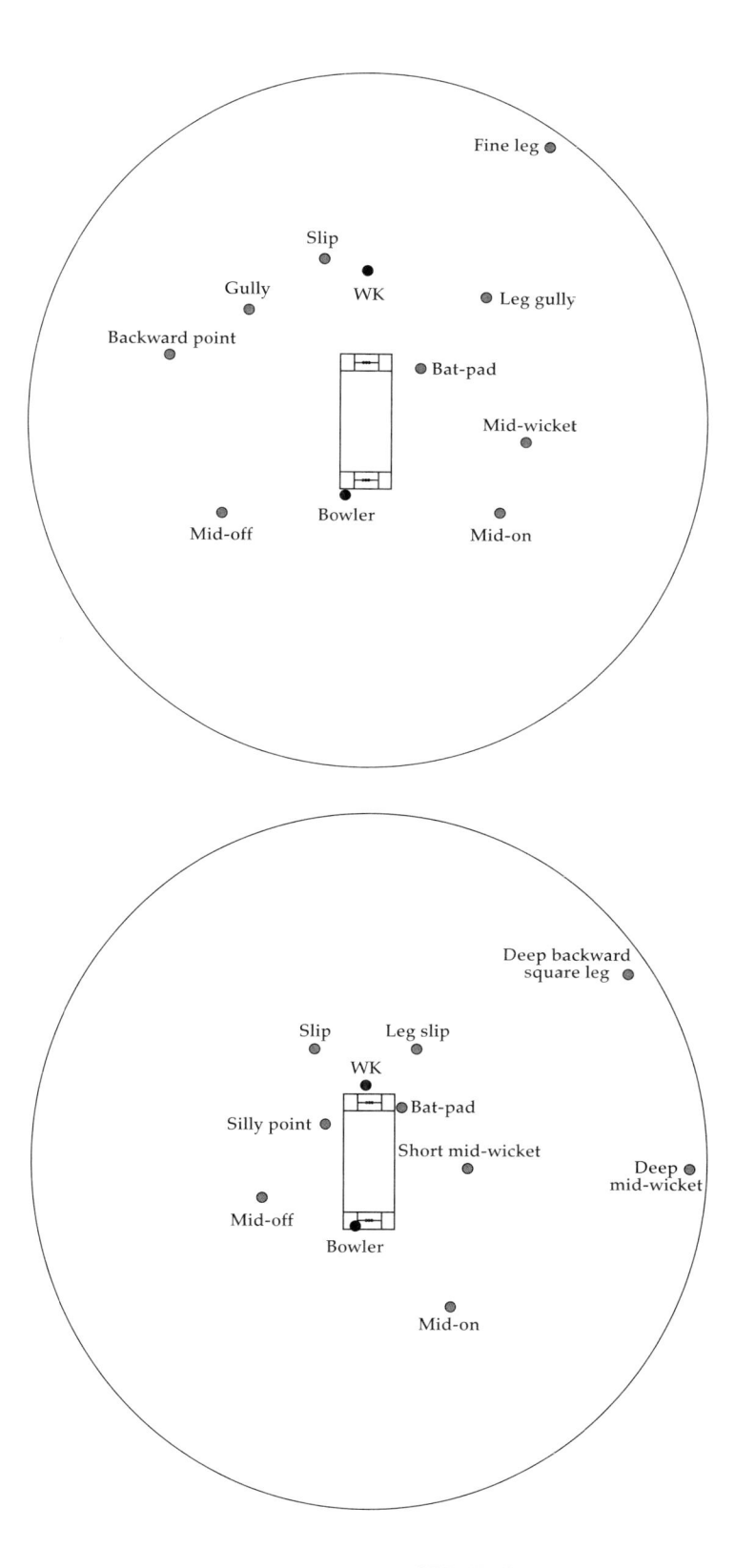

A fast bowler swinging the new ball in, or spearing it into the pads and body. In this configuration, your wicket-taking positions are the bat-pad catcher, leg gully, and mid-wicket. Mid-on should be standing slightly wider than usual, since the ball will be going squarer (and there's nothing you can do about a batter able to drill on-drives down the ground, other than to tell your bowler not to dish up drive-length deliveries). Don't remove your slip too soon; even if your paceman is peppering middle stump, there's always the chance of a leading edge or even a miscued pull flying to slip.

An off-spinner attacking on a good batting wicket. Not a particularly glamorous field, but an important and effective one nonetheless. Silly point, short mid-wicket and the man under the helmet at short leg apply huge pressure, and if your plan works, the batter decides to remove one of these close fielders with an aggressive drive straight at him – and nicks off, or is bowled. Meanwhile, catchers in the deep wait for slightly more circumspect (but less well hit) chances.

STRATEGY AND CAPTAINCY

FIELD SETTINGS: THE INEXACT EXACT SCIENCE

Field settings in the modern game have more or less shaken themselves out into reliable and easily repeatable formulae that can be depended on by most captains. But just because history has taught you how to set a trap, doesn't mean that your prey is going to waltz into it. A great catch in the outfield is often the result of a carefully executed plan, but equally often it takes more than strategy and intelligence to make a vital breakthrough. And this is where cricket science gives way to art: the unquantifiable, unteachable and unrepeatable flash of genius, luck or skill – or all three – that come together to make captains look good.

Such a moment cannot be pulled out of a hat at will, and too many captains know the agony of a well-set batter trampling their plans into dust. You can tweak your field as much as you like, but sometimes all you can do is watch and wait. In the 2008 *Wisden Almanack*, former England captain Mike Atherton described one afternoon's memorable torture at the hands of Brian Lara: 'Eleven fielders were never enough; there were always gaps to plug. When he scored his 375 against my England team, I remember moving first slip out when Lara had scored 291. He edged the very next ball right where first slip had been. I'd love to know whether it was deliberate; I always doubted it, simply on the basis that such a level of genius was beyond my comprehension.'

But even the greats get caught, and via conventional fielding positions too. Sachin Tendulkar was on 169 against South Africa at Newlands in 1997, having just dragged India from 58 for 5 to 359 for 9. In perfect conditions he was scoring at will, either finding gaps in Hansie Cronje's field, or lofting shots over the fielders. A double century looked likely, and when Brian McMillan banged in a short ball, it seemed certain that Tendulkar was about to help himself to six more over square leg. But the Indian maestro was aghast to see the stocky Adam Bacher soar into the air at deep backward square to cling onto a one-handed stunner. Tendulkar stood his ground in disbelief – and then trudged off as Bacher pinched himself.

But you cannot rely on moments of brilliance. Have a plan, and place your field accordingly. If the plan backfires, regroup and adapt. Use fielders' strengths, and minimize their weaknesses (Bacher was probably posted on the rope because he was less than gazelle-like.) As Mike Brearley wrote rather mischievously in the *Observer*, 'When Monty appears at short mid-wicket, it's more Python than Panesar.'

THE CAPTAIN AND THE SELECTORS

'My God, look what the selectors have sent me!'

The captain bemoaning his misfortune was Archie MacLaren, the opposition was Australia, and the year was 1902. In over a century, nothing has changed. Modern captains still stare in disbelief at the teams they've been handed, and journalists still know in which direction to vent their spleen. Indeed, of all cricket's contentious figures, perhaps no group causes as much animosity, controversy and general rancour as the panel of selectors. Regarded with almost universal suspicion in their own country – and totally ignored by the rest of the world – they rarely receive public recognition or acclaim when their team gets it right. And they're fired at the drop of a hat when the team starts losing.

How much say the coach and captain have in selection at international level remains a thorny issue in some countries. But as a captain or coach at lower level – especially in junior cricket – it is a burden that you will have to carry. Be warned: ambitious parents, low-level politicking and backroom string-pulling will often make it a much more murky and stressful job than it should be, a case of being damned if you do and damned if you don't. However, it is important to try and find as much common ground as possible. This is especially true for the captain and the selectors: there are few things worse for a skipper than going out onto the field with a team he is uncomfortable with. If he isn't happy with who he has been given to work with, the selectors need to explain their thinking and reasons for selecting players very carefully indeed.

Selection versus the needs of the captain can be a high-stakes game. In 2003, when South Africa hosted the World Cup, they arrived in Durban needing to beat Sri Lanka to stay in the tournament. Unfortunately, Allan Donald seemed to have reached the end of his long and exceptional career, with some sub-standard performances in the earlier matches. The media were making disparaging noises about this being a 'bridge too far' and a 'World Cup too many' for the paceman. On the eve of the crunch match in Durban, it was clear to insiders that Donald should play – he'd always managed to lift himself for big games, and besides, he'd always wanted to avenge his shock omission from the 1996 World Cup quarter-final team, a selection error (even though it seemed the right decision at the time) that had ended South Africa's campaign in the championship. More importantly, his protégé and current captain, Shaun Pollock, wanted him to play.

But pressure from both the media and political circles seemed to have the final word when Donald was dropped in favour of a promising but entirely untested young black fast bowler, Monde Zondeki. In political terms, this was a coup for South African cricket, and the potential cost of Donald's omission was forgotten in a flood of emotional and jubilant reactions to Zondeki's selection. That the Chair of selectors reportedly wept with joy should have served as a warning – emotional fans have absolutely no business selecting make-or-break World Cup teams – but in the mood of the day, the country pinned its hopes on Zondeki, and looked forward to him grabbing this huge opportunity with both hands.

The results were predictably disastrous. Desperately tense, overcome by big match nerves, and having to fill the biggest boots in South African cricket, Zondeki cracked under the pressure, his body unable to stand the strain. He bowled six overs for 35 runs, and took no further part in the game. Sri Lanka amassed a daunting 268, and the rest is history. Donald left international cricket unavenged, and far worse, Pollock was summarily dumped as captain.

Cricket is a business, and in any business, failures require that heads roll. It was inevitable that Pollock would be used as a convenient scapegoat, despite having a win rate of over 60% as a one-day international captain. But his treatment once again highlighted the great unspoken injustice that lies at the heart of a captain's relationship with the selectors: if a captain is personally accountable for his team's success, it seems only fair and logical that he should be given whichever team he wants in order to hunt for that success.

Reading between the lines, Pollock was sacked for bungling the mathematical permutations of the rain rules late in the game, but he should not have been in that position in the first place. If he'd had Donald, as he wanted, Sri Lanka might not have scored such a significant total, and the critical match might not have come down to a tie. In effect, Pollock was sacked for an error in selection – a selection in which he had absolutely no say.

All that being said, there is no doubt that selectors are far more professional and diplomatic today than in the past. Horror stories abound of teams being decided upon over drinks in the selectors' homes, and then passed on to the coach and captain, with not a word about likely conditions, fitness issues, or indeed any observable logic at all. Bob Woolmer recalled that in his early days of playing for Kent, 'it was often up to the thirteen players in the squad to buy a scorecard at the box office to see if they had made the final eleven. Indeed it was not unusual for twelve players to take the field, with one eventually being sent off!'

Whether or not you as a captain are involved in selection, it is nonetheless worth knowing something about its processes, if for no other reason than peace of mind. The following are the basic principles of selection – whether picking an Under-10 team or a World Cup squad.

Understanding the goal

At international level, winning the next game must be the sole criterion: pick the best possible team to win. This is the first principle of selection; however, international selectors may well come under pressure to make politically correct choices. This is a red-hot debate in present-day South Africa, but as usual, there's nothing new under the cricketing sun: the Trinidadian intellectual C.L.R. James wrote his peerless 1960 book on cricket, *Beyond a Boundary*, partly to press for the captaincy of the West Indian side to be given to their most talented and experienced player, Frank Worrell – who happened to be black. Less than 50 years ago, there was an unspoken rule that the captain of the West Indian side had to be white – hence James' eloquent indignation. While these and other considerations, such as the need to give younger players experience at the top level of the game, have their place, the bottom line is that to win, the best very available players must be picked.

The right team for the right job

Who you select, and in which position, is largely dependent on the type of game you're going into. A three-game one-day series at home will need entirely different players and temperaments to those demanded by a five-Test away series. Likewise, some individuals can experience problems with touring specific destinations, or can be particularly strong in others. Daryll Cullinan was a huge asset in every country he toured except Australia, where he was a liability. Steve Harmison, while a world-beating fast bowler at home in England, has struggled to make an impact overseas: on England's tour of South Africa in 2005, his regular comments about being homesick and miserable did nothing to boost his teammates. A selector who omitted a fit Sachin Tendulkar from any squad would not only need his head read, but would no doubt have his house burnt down. And yet the Indian superstar's record on tours of South Africa has been uncharacteristically poor: while not omitting him, selectors should consider taking an extra batsman, or an all-rounder to facilitate the inclusion of that extra batsman, on tours to South Africa at present.

The composition and balance of teams has also changed over generations, as the game itself has developed. For example, Test cricket has seen regular shifts in emphasis:

- **five batsmen, five bowlers, specialist wicket-keeper** (England, 1960s)
- **six batsmen, four fast bowlers, wicket-keeper-batsman** (West Indies, 1976–1991)
- **six batsmen, three fast bowlers, one spinner, wicket-keeper-batsman** (Australia 1986–present)
- **five batsmen, one all-rounder, three fast bowlers, one spinner, wicket-keeper-batsman** (England, 2005).

THE IDEAL TEST SIDE

All-rounders can be very valuable, but the way to win Test matches is through pace and good spin. The West Indians won with the former, and Australians have dominated with a combination of the two.

Having said that, all Test teams know that they need to score 500, either to force a win or guarantee a draw – and for that you either need a phenomenal top six, or seven very good batsmen. Australia's success over the last decade has owed much to Shane Warne and Glenn McGrath, but the presence of Adam Gilchrist at number seven has been a huge asset. Not only did he score as prolifically as some of the greatest specialist batsmen in the game's history, but he did so at a lightning pace, opening up great swathes of time in the match for his bowlers to get properly stuck in. This format – seven world-class batsmen and four bowlers – will probably be considered ideal for the foreseeable future.

The emergence of excellent all-rounders in the last decade or so has also been a factor. The presence of Jacques Kallis, Shaun Pollock and Lance Klusener in the South African squad of the late 1990s allowed for successful experimentation while providing an extremely deep batting order. And there is no doubt that the explosive flourishing of Andrew Flintoff for England in the 2005 Ashes series will filter through into the development and future selection of more Test all-rounders.

The race to find classy all-rounders may be hotting up again in the Test arena, but it is nothing new to the one-day game. Every year, wicket-taking ability becomes less important in limited-overs cricket as tactics become ever more sophisticated in terms of restricting runs. This shift in emphasis has seen a dramatic move away from 'thoroughbred' specialists towards multi-dimensional players, who, while not necessarily as stellar as their Test team counterparts, can bat, bowl, and above all field well enough to fit into the machine that is the one-day squad. The ideal one-day player is no longer the fast bowler who can bowl outswing at 150km/h and hit batsmen on the body, or even the batter who can grind out a big hundred. It is the man who can score 40 anywhere in the order at slightly more than a run a ball, who can bowl five overs for 20 runs and burgle a wicket, and who can fling himself around in the infield, stopping anything that comes his way.

In other words, what selectors might pencil in as a good one-day team would look completely unintelligible to a selector of 30 years ago: nine batsmen, six bowlers (three of whom bowl medium-pace deliveries that do almost nothing through the air or off the pitch, but which land on a nagging length), and often not a 'proper' opening batsman or attacking spinner in sight!

The demands of touring away and playing at home

The ideal one-day squad, for most series or competitions, seems to comprise fourteen players. This group contains the eleven players most likely to play on any given day, plus three reserves who cover potentially vulnerable aspects in the team. Reserves will vary according to a tour's specific demands, but selectors tend to favour those who can replace an injured fast bowler or a frontline batsman, and have value as a general utility player – usually a great fielder who can bowl.

Test tours are invariably much longer than one-day competitions, and these squads tend to contain sixteen players, although the exact number obviously depends on the length and destination of the tour. A long tour to Pakistan and India, which are traditionally rough on Western players and can therefore have a high attrition rate, will need sixteen players, whereas a short tour to somewhere 'cushy' like England or South Africa may only call for thirteen players. However, the sixteen-man squad is fairly standard, and is based around the best eleven players, with five reserves making up the numbers. At least one of these back-up players is a youngster being groomed for future action, who is extremely unlikely to play any international matches. However, there should be enough depth in the reserves to cover crucial positions should any key frontline players – such as an opening batsman or a wicket-keeper – get injured. (Opening batsmen are specialists, and a hole at the top of the order can be fatal: on their 1994 tour of England, South Africa found themselves with two out of three opening batsmen so badly out of form that they might as well have been walking wounded. South Africa ended up losing the three-Test series largely because their side was invariably one wicket down at the beginning of almost every innings of every match.)

The balance between youth and experience

Cricketers mature at different rates. For example, most Test batsmen mature between 26 and 32 years of age (which itself is a fairly large range), while spinners sometimes don't come into their own until their thirties. Fast bowlers, on the other hand, mature physically long before they mature mentally. Their bodies are capable of bowling full tilt from 25 onwards, but they usually start thinking carefully about their game only in their late twenties or early thirties. The 'shelf life' of players also varies greatly: batsmen can last twelve and even up to fifteen years at the top level, while fast bowlers rarely make it past ten – and by the end of that decade, they have usually turned into medium-fast seamers with shortened run-ups.

Australia's dominance over the last decade has owed much to individual talents coming through at just the right intervals (Allan Border and Mark Taylor, followed by Michael Slater and the Waugh twins, followed by Matthew Hayden and Adam

Gilchrist; and on the bowling side, Craig McDermott and Tim May, followed by Glenn McGrath and Shane Warne). But it has also perfected the mix of youth and experience, offsetting ambitious, exuberant young talent with level-headed veterans: the Waughs were Border's foil, just as Brett Lee drew on McGrath's experience; and Mitchell Johnson is no doubt being mentored by Lee in turn.

The current England team, which first began gelling in 2004, is another good example of this principle. A good spread of old hands on the one hand, and blooded youngsters on the other – with the overall balance slightly tipped in favour of age – was what won them the Ashes in 2005. The Australian team, on the other hand, was perhaps fractionally too old: only a few players in their squad were under 30, and those were barely younger than 26 or 27.

Nevertheless, the average age for a great Test team is not 22 or 23, but somewhere between 28 and 30. In fact, most captains and coaches will take maturity and experience over similarly experienced but younger players any day. You need people who have been there before, who know where to put the ball, who know how to bat through gruelling sessions. Those who coach at school level see this time after time; how a first team who has been together for two or three years copes so much better than a squad that has only just been formed.

It may sound glaringly obvious, but you can only handle situations comfortably if you've handled them before. If you drop two nineteen-year-olds into a scenario they've never encountered before, they literally won't know what to do.

However, youth must not be neglected: as the West Indies discovered so disastrously in the early 1990s, if you simply play a small pool of great cricketers year after year, without blooding enough youngsters, there comes a day when you suddenly find that you have a terribly young, and terribly vulnerable team. Had it not been for the phenomenal staying-power and pride of Curtly Ambrose and Courtney Walsh, who played on for two or three years beyond the point at which most fast bowlers would have retired, and the once-in-a-generation genius of Brian Lara, the West Indies would have plummeted to the bottom of world cricket even faster than they did in the mid-1990s.

Judging talent

This is perhaps the most important task of any prospective selector, and it should be based on the fundamental understanding that Test cricket provides a far more hostile and searching examination of technique and skill than first-class cricket does. It is therefore important that selectors be extremely cautious about thrusting a player enjoying good domestic form into the Test arena: this is what 'A' teams and Under-24 national teams are for. This is not to say that form isn't a useful guide: a player who performs consistently well at every level should eventually be afforded an opportunity to play at a higher level, but only if the player he replaces is not performing or coming to the end of his career.

Similarly, selectors must never listen to the public's calls for a player to be 'given a chance' at international level. An international cap is neither a right, nor something to be handed out as charity. Selection must be earned. Once caps are awarded as experiments rather than safe bets, one is on a slippery slope towards calamity. If anyone in the selection committee even mentions capping someone 'to see if he can handle it', haul them in smartly.

Of course, not all selections are safe bets. Some are long-term gambles, the selectors seeing the promise of great talent that may only flourish in a year or two. The challenge is then to know when to give up on the player if he isn't fulfilling that promise. England's selectors always hoped that the prodigiously talented Graeme Hick would translate his first-class dominance into Test stardom, and persevered with him for years. Similarly, Mark Ramprakash, another Englishman who seemed superb on the first-class circuit, was given endless reprieves when he was clearly out of his depth at Test level.

These two examples illustrate how important it is to have fixed time frames in mind as a selector. Neither Hick nor Ramprakash seemed to have any time constraints within which they had to either improve their game or step aside. However, if selectors have decided to give a player a certain period of grace early in his career, they should not be put off by a string of poor performances. Jacques Kallis was identified as a class act early in his career, and the South African selectors were unflustered by the unimpressive start he made to his Test career. Knowing that he was not playing for his place in the team after just one or two innings, Kallis had an opportunity to learn without having to defend himself against the selectors – and he has amply rewarded them, growing into South Africa's greatest post-apartheid batsman. And remember once again the case of Shane Warne, whose first outings as a Test player were dismal.

Dropping players

Dropping players is not new, but telling them the bad news face-to-face is a new aspect of the game – and not an easy one. Three decades ago, if players were dropped from the national team, all they heard was a deathly silence: there was no communication whatsoever, and the 'unselected' player simply had to slink away and accept his fate, often not even entirely sure why he had been dropped.

Today, however, it is vital to keep dropped players in the loop, as this allows them to stay focused and to fight their way back into contention without becoming embittered, or too far removed from the team's spirit and processes. Sometimes a word of encouragement from a coach or selector can make the world of difference. Of course if the selectors, coach and captain do not think a player has a future in the team (which can suggest an earlier error in judgement by selectors), he needs to be told; but too many players disappear into the cricketing wilderness without knowing why, or where they stand.

Communication

A final word concerning captains and selectors, and once again, it may seem obvious: both sides have to make an effort to keep channels of communication open. The input and influence of the captain concerning selection remains extremely vague, even at the highest levels of the game, but his needs and concerns should be taken into account. After all, it is he who is expected to win matches – and as Shaun Pollock and many before him have discovered the hard way, it is he who will be held responsible if things go horribly awry. It seems both sensible and humane to invite him to share his thoughts.

THE JACK CHEETHAM REVOLUTION

It seems only right to end this section on captaincy, and indeed this chapter, with a story of triumph over impossible odds. We already know that at lower levels of the game, the captain is often little more than a glorified secretary. In junior teams, where the coach calls the shots both on and off the field, the young skipper is often simply a figurehead, put in place to accustom the other players to being led in the field, someone who can be relied upon to put up lists and do head-counts.

But as a captain's responsibility escalates, so too does his capacity to take charge of the team and mould it into something new. Allan Border was hugely influential while he led Australia, grafting his personality onto the team and transforming a wilting and unfocused squad into an outfit that would dominate the cricketing world for decades to come. Of course, too much respect for and authority granted to a captain can lead to the beginnings of a personality cult – and at times, this can exact a terrible cost, something South African cricket learned when it emerged that Hansie Cronje's 'untouchable' status in the administration had hastened his decline into corruption.

But when a captain knows his own mind and has only the best interests of his team at heart, he can be not only a winning leader, but a reformer and revolutionary – and you can aspire to become these even at the lower levels of the game.

South Africa's Jack Cheetham was such a captain. Largely overlooked in both his own country and abroad, he was almost solely responsible for transforming his country into a major cricketing nation.

Cricket was exported to South Africa and Australia at more or less the same time, as colonial Britain decided to help itself to South African gold and Australian pastureland during the nineteenth century. But by the dawn of the twentieth century, the development of the sport in the two colonies was proceeding at dramatically different rates. Where Australia had assimilated cricket into an embryonic culture of nationalism and independence, South African players still considered themselves to be essentially British, their team simply a particularly far-flung subsidiary of the MCC. As the century progressed towards the First World War, South African cricket was far slower than its Australian counterpart to cast off the habit of colonial genuflection to all things British. Williams, one of Bradman's more erudite biographers, writes that at the end of the First World War, 'Australia turned to spectator sport as the prime vehicle for the aspirations to national identity which the War had produced' so that 'sports in Australia thus became an integral part of politics… it both encouraged and disciplined the egalitarian individualism that was emerging as an identifiable Australian characteristic. It was to be Australia's way of showing the rest of the world that the continent was not just an appendage of the British Empire but a real and living nation' (1996, p. 7).

By contrast, cricket historian Luke Alfred (2001) suggests that it was only after the Second World War that South African cricket began its own emancipation from the imperial parent. The crucial event was the South African tour of Australia in 1952/3 under the leadership of Jack Cheetham and the management of Ken Viljoen (Cheetham, 1956). Prior to its departure to Australia, the team was considered to be so inferior to the Australians that the tour was nearly cancelled, and continued only when the South African Cricket Association agreed to underwrite the financial risk of the tour. In the words of John Arlott: 'No critic, however sympathetic to the side, could find any evidence to arouse optimism about the venture' (1972, p. 124).

But under Cheetham and Viljoen, the South Africans reinvented themselves. In the second Test at Melbourne, they became the first team in the history of Australian cricket to win a Test, batting second, in which the first innings had produced more than 500 runs. (The Springboks won by six wickets.) Off-spinner Hugh Tayfield took more wickets (13 for 165 in that Test alone) than any other visiting bowler in Australian history, and the tourists were unanimously considered to be the best fielding team to have visited Australia to that date. So what was the secret of the Cheetham-Viljoen success?

In Arlott's opinion, the following factors were crucial:
- An emphasis on fielding, with an intensity and frequency of fielding practice far transcending anything ever attempted before by international teams – sustained for the full five and a half months of the tour.
- Cheetham's 'addiction to late homework, poring over the figures and charts of Bill Ferguson, the scorer'.
- Cheetham's commitment to his father's motto: Determination, Concentration and Application.
- Cheetham's conviction that his team could beat Australia. To communicate this to his side, he first had to overcome the entrenched inferiority complex of the South Africans, expressed especially in the defensive approach of the South African batters.
- Cheetham's faith in his players, especially in two youngsters, Tayfield and Russell Endean, whose previous performances had been unremarkable, but

who ended the tour as South Africa's leading bowler and batsman respectively. Arlott reports that 'On the sea voyage [from South Africa to Australia] Cheetham kept telling Tayfield what a fine bowler he was. Within a few days Tayfield was telling Cheetham what a fine bowler Tayfield was'.

- Cheetham's ability, by nurturing an intense team spirit, to make players 'rise above themselves'. Arlott concludes that 'The biggest single factor in the Springboks' rise to fame was the spirit of the side which, from the moment it assembled, began conscientiously, persistently and determinedly to apply itself to a formidable undertaking. It was a spirit that made its members play with their hearts when their technical talents were not equal to the task' (1972, p. 124).

The final great quality of Cheetham's leadership – his subtlety – is revealed, ironically and perhaps sadly, by the manner in which his country's players and fans have forgotten him: 'There are no plaques to mark his [Cheetham's] share in the structures he left for future generations. Nor is there anything in the statistical records of cricket to suggest that it was he who started a revolutionary build-up in the play of his countrymen. It was accomplished... by invisible captaincy which led him to become the originator of one of the fables of South African sport' (Arlott, 1972, p. 131).

The magic of exceptional captaincy in this case might have become invisible in past decades, but it would have been anything but invisible to the victorious team and to a national sport galvanized by success. In the next few decades, South Africa was to become a powerhouse of international cricket – but this prowess was to be interrupted by the insanity of the apartheid government. At home, South Africa's cricketing structures were required by law to be organized along strictly racially segregated lines (which led many fine players to boycott the recognized structures), and abroad, the country was banned from playing international cricket. Many of its greatest players were forced either to leave their homeland (one thinks of Barry Richards, Basil D'Oliviera, and many more – at times during the 1970s and 80s, a remarkable number of cricketers playing for England and Australia had South African accents!), or barred from the Test arena where they belonged (one thinks of Graeme Pollock). Or, like Omar Henry, they were prevented even from representing their provinces because of the ban on 'inter-racial' cricket. But through all the madness, the Cheetham legacy of building team spirit and pride has remained. It is there for the taking, by any team.

CHAPTER EIGHT

STATISTICS:
A VIEW OF THE FUTURE?

INTRODUCTION

One of the great characteristics of the game of cricket has been the careful collection, archiving and publication of vast masses of figures in the form of cricketing statistics. Yet in spite of this extensive recording, relatively little use has been made of these statistics to understand the nature of the game and the factors determining successful team performances – for example, in one- and five-day cricket Test matches.

Perhaps some of the reasons for this reluctance can be gleaned from *Moneyball – The art of winning an unfair game*, by Michael Lewis (2003). In this book, the author analyses the success of a Californian baseball team, the Oakland A's. Their rise took place after careful statistical analyses to determine exactly which players were being undervalued by conventional and traditional scouting techniques. As a result, the Oakland A's could use their limited financial resources to purchase these undervalued players – a move that enabled them to compete successfully against teams with almost unlimited financial reserves. How did they do it? By replacing subjective assessment of players with objective data produced by mathematical statistics, thereby eliminating the subjective bias that is a cardinal feature of almost all 'expert' analyses of games like baseball and cricket. This subjective approach is characterized by the belief that any player's performance can be evaluated simply by watching it. In contrast, the objective (scientific) approach uses hard data, the predictive value of which can be evaluated.

The initial drive for the objective measurement of brilliance in baseball came from Bill James, who first published his annual *Baseball Abstract* in 1977. James was driven to understand what really determined a baseball hitter's effectiveness: 'And for the answers I go to the record books… what is remarkable to me is that I have so little company. Baseball keeps copious records, and people talk about them and think about them a great deal. Why doesn't anybody use them? Why doesn't anybody say, in the face of this contention or that one, "prove it"?' Sadly, James eventually concluded that his efforts to promote objective analyses in baseball were pointless: 'When I started writing I thought if I proved X was a stupid thing to do that people would stop doing X. I was wrong… a great proportion of the sport's traditional knowledge is ridiculous hokum' (Lewis, 2003, pp. 75, 94).

One of the many reasons for this resistance, and the clinging to traditional knowledge, is the culture of anti-intellectualism that dogs American baseball (and indeed much else in American political and social life). But such anti-intellectualism (which is certainly not restricted to baseball, much less America) offers opportunities for those prepared to question it. Challenging convention and tradition produces new insights, and these in turn suggest new and improved methods of seeking hard truths. Lewis and before him, James, present a challenge to lovers of any game: 'Think for yourself along rational lines. Hypothesize, test against the evidence, never accept that a question has been answered…. Don't believe a thing is true simply because some famous player says that it is true' (Lewis, 2003, p. 98).

When applied to cricket, this objective approach poses a number of questions:

1. To what extent does batting performance contribute to a cricket team's success?
2. To what extent does bowling and fielding performance contribute to a cricket team's success?
3. How are individual contributions to a team's batting, bowling and fielding prowess best measured?
4. Finally, how can each player's individual contribution (in batting, bowling and fielding) to the team's success be measured?

At present, there are few answers to these questions, although they provide rich opportunities for eager researchers of the future. What we do know so far forms the basis of this chapter.

ASSESSING THE CONTRIBUTION MADE BY THE BATTER TO HIS TEAM'S SUCCESS

Common sense tells us that a cricketer's batting average cannot provide an accurate measure of his performance, given that this figure changes very little once the batter

> 'Think for yourself along rational lines. Hypothesize, test against the evidence, never accept that a question has been answered. Don't believe a thing is true simply because some famous player says so.'
> – Michael Lewis

has completed a large number of innings. While it has merit as a yardstick for comparing batsmen over a career, it provides little information about a batsman's *current* state of form. Current state of form is better assessed by a rolling average, in which a series of innings are averaged – for instance, the last eight innings the batter has played. As each new innings is completed, the average is recalculated on the basis of the last eight innings. In this way, the player's average is calculated on recent performances; if his form improves, the 'rolling eight average' will increase progressively. A dip in form will produce the opposite result.

BATTING PERFORMANCES IN ONE-DAY CRICKET

A novel method for analysing a batsman's contribution to his team's performance, especially in one-day cricket, was developed by Professor Brian Kantor, formerly of the Graduate School of Business at the University of Cape Town, South Africa.

Kantor adapted the traditional business model of reward and risk to the analysis of batting and bowling performances in one-day cricket. His measure of reward was the batsman's strike rate (runs scored per 100 deliveries faced), with the measure of risk the number of times the batsman was dismissed (also per 100 deliveries faced). By plotting these variables on a graph with the y (vertical) axis as the reward and the x (horizontal) axis as the risk, he was able to discern and compare the 'efficiency' of different batsmen. Furthermore, he could show that teams with the most efficient batsmen (those producing high reward at low risk) were the most successful (provided they were teamed with bowlers able to produce high rewards at low risk – discussed in the next section).

His first analysis was of the batters in the 1996 Cricket World Cup held in the Asian subcontinent (see Figure 8.1). This showed that the best batsman in that competition was Arjuna Ranatunga (on the basis that he achieved the highest strike rate of 112 runs per 100 deliveries, at the lowest risk of being dismissed (approximately once per 100 deliveries). Sanath Jayasuriya had the highest strike rate (>130 runs per 100 deliveries), but achieved this at greater risk (more than 3,5 outs per 100 deliveries).

The 1996 World Cup competition was won by Sri Lanka, which had three batsmen (Ranatunga, Jayasuriya and Aravinda de Silva) who achieved strike rates in excess of 100. The strike rates per 100 deliveries of the four top batsmen in the Australian side that lost the final – Mark Waugh (86), Stuart Law (87), Steve Waugh (78) and Ricky Ponting (69) – were substantially

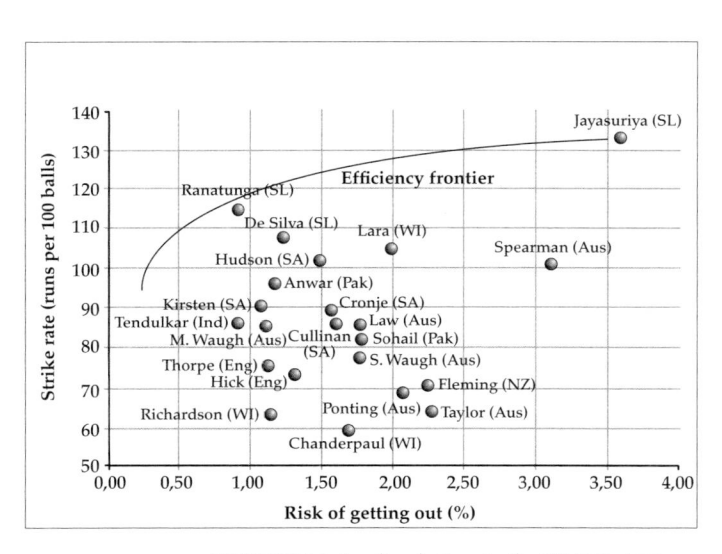

FIGURE 8.1: *Leading batters in the 1996 World Cup*

more modest. Moreover, only Mark Waugh had as low a risk of being dismissed as Ranatunga and de Silva.

We applied the same analysis to the 1997 Wills Quadrangular Tournament in Pakistan (see Figure 8.2). This competition was won by South Africa, which, like Sri Lanka in the 1996 World Cup, had three batsmen (Lance Klusener, Jonty Rhodes and Hansie Cronje) batting near or above a strike rate of 100, with Daryll Cullinan close behind with a strike rate of 87. In contrast, Sri Lanka had only two batsmen with similar strike rates, with Arjuna Ranatunga falling to a strike rate of less than 80.

More recently, Kantor applied his system of analysis to the 2007 Cricket World Cup. His comparison of the teams (see Figure 8.3) clearly reveals the superiority of the Australian batsmen, confirming the opinion of their coach, John Buchanan, who said that the difference between the Australians and the other teams was 'like night and day'.

Figure 8.3 shows that in Matthew Hayden, Stuart Clarke and Ricky Ponting, Australia fielded the three best batsmen at the 2007 World Cup. Each achieved strike rates close to or over 100, with a very low risk of being dismissed (less than 1,5 dismissals per 100 deliveries, indicating that their average innings lasted at least 66 deliveries and that their batting averages would also have been in the 60s. Also notable is the progress that Ricky Ponting has made as a one-day batsman in the past decade (compare his position in Figure 8.1 with that in Figure 8.3).

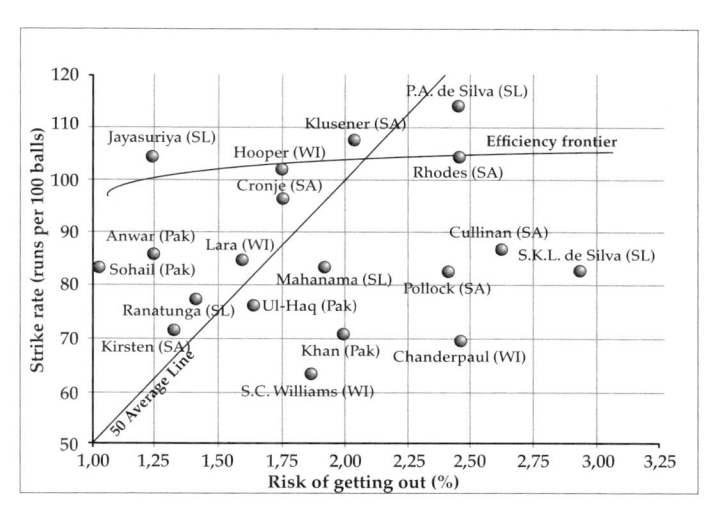

FIGURE 8.2: *Leading batters in the 1997 Wills Quadrangular Tournament*

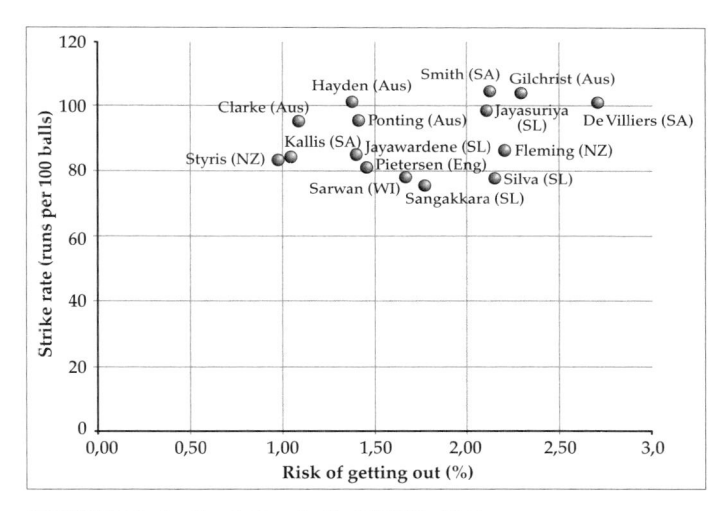

FIGURE 8.3: *Leading batters in the 2007 World Cup*

Figure 8.3 also shows that the only batters whose performances approached those of the three Australians were Scott Styris of New Zealand, Jacques Kallis of South Africa, and Mahela Jayawardene of Sri Lanka.

This analysis clearly shows how batting performances in one-day cricket can be accurately measured; likewise, the contributions of specific batsmen to their team's success. It is clear that to win major one-day competitions in Asia or the West Indies, it is absolutely vital to have three batsmen able to achieve strike rates of 100 or more, while maintaining a dismissal rate of less than 1,5 per 100 deliveries.

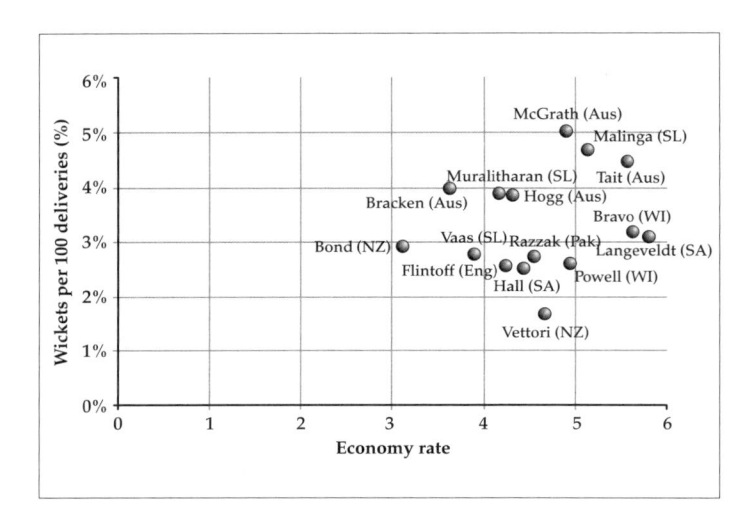

FIGURE 8.4: *Leading bowlers in the 2007 World Cup*

BOWLING PERFORMANCES IN ONE-DAY CRICKET

The method for analysing bowling efficiency (or efficacy) is opposite to that used for measuring batting. In this case, the reward component is the frequency with which the bowler dismisses batsmen (wickets per 100 deliveries), and the risk is the economy rate (runs per six deliveries).

Figure 8.4 sets out the bowling data for the 2007 Cricket World Cup. It shows that Glenn McGrath had the highest strike rate, whereas Shane Bond was the most economical bowler. Four Australian bowlers (McGrath, Tait, Hogg and Bracken) feature in the top group, showing that they were not only the best batting team, but also had the most effective bowlers.

BATTING AND BOWLING PERFORMANCES IN MULTI-DAY CRICKET

So it seems that we may have a formula for shorter forms of the game, but for five-day games, the question of exactly how a batsman's real value to his team can be measured has yet to be puzzled out.

In addition to strike rates and probability of dismissal, the average number of runs scored by his team while each batsman is at the crease is probably essential. This would provide an indication of the batter's ability to develop partnerships. For example, a batsman with a low personal batting average might have a much higher 'partnership' batting average, indicating that he has the ability to contribute more to his team's success than is indicated by his personal or even his 'rolling' batting average.

Evaluating bowling performances in five-day games is still more complicated, given that Tests can only be won by bowling all members of the opposing side – twice. The ratio of dismissals versus the run rate would not be as simple an equation, as the role of a bowler in determining a victory instead of a draw would need to be factored in.

THE ADVANTAGES OF OBJECTIVE MEASUREMENT AND ANALYSIS

American baseball has progressed to the point where an individual's contribution to his team's success can be more accurately quantified. As a result, training interventions can be introduced that maximize those skills most relevant to the team's success. Moreover, a team can be selected that includes the balance of skills most likely to produce success in differing forms of the game, and in the context of the conditions. Players can also be employed (or declined) on the basis of the extent to which they fulfil objective and measurable criteria. Clearly, this all applies equally to the game of cricket.

The statistical study of cricket is an exciting new field of research, with a growing number of useful findings being published. Some of the more intriguing studies that will likely influence the future development of cricket – and which will be embraced by those who favour objectivity over anti-intellectual tradition or subjective opinions – are briefly summarized below. They are of particular value to captains and coaches, but as we have said before: never assume that the hard work of strategic calculations in the game of cricket can be left to someone else. South African cricketers in particular are wincingly aware of the consequences of team members remaining blissfully ignorant of the permutations of rain rules, for instance. Lack of information can cost you a shot at the World Cup! It is your responsibility to keep abreast of statistical information that can help you plot and plan in the field or during your innings. This kind of knowledge can greatly boost your mental strength as well – so it is well worthwhile doing your homework.

HOME ADVANTAGE AND THE VALUE OF WINNING THE TOSS

Many cricketers, commentators and spectators believe that winning the toss is an important determinant of the match outcome. But an analysis of 427 one-day international matches in the 1990s (up until July 1997) revealed that winning the toss provided no competitive advantage. However, what did emerge was clear evidence of home advantage (De Silva and Swartz, 1997). Other studies have confirmed that winning the toss had no effect on the outcome of either one-day or five-day international matches, although the evidence for home advantage was clear (Allsopp and Clarke, 2004). If anything, a study by the latter found that it was an advantage to bat second in five-day Tests, suggesting that the choice to bat first in response to winning the toss may sometimes be the wrong decision. (See pp. 79–80 in Chapter 2.)

FINDING THE TRUE STRENGTH OF INTERNATIONAL CRICKET TEAMS: GOING BEYOND THE WIN/LOSS RATIO

In his 2005 PhD thesis, Paul Allsopp made the point that the true dominance of a team batting second cannot be determined, as at the completion of their victory in either one- or five-day cricket matches, they still retain 'unused run-scoring resources' in the forms of deliveries remaining and wickets intact. He therefore argued that the true superiority of a cricket team that wins when batting second cannot be determined (since different measures of success – runs for the team batting first and wickets for the team batting second – are used, depending on whether the winning team bats first or second). To correct this anomaly, Allsopp and colleague Paul Clarke developed a method of measuring the superiority of the winning team, regardless of whether they batted first or second.

Using the Duckworth/Lewis method to predict the additional runs likely to be scored by the batting resources remaining unused at the moment of victory, these authors formulated a rating system for the relative batting and bowling strengths of all countries currently playing international cricket at the end of the 1997/98 and the 2002/03 cricket years.

These results are shown in Table 8.1. According to this, a team with 'average' ability would score a rating of 100.

TABLE 8.1: Comparative ratings of batting, bowling and combined strengths of national cricket teams in 1997 and 2002

TEAM	1997 BATTING RATING	1997 BOWLING RATING	1997 COMBINED RATING	2002 BATTING RATING	2002 BOWLING RATING	2002 COMBINED RATING
Australia	112	118	130	126	116	142
South Africa	107	116	123	118	120	138
India	116	103	119	95	88	83
West Indies	110	101	111	87	108	95
Pakistan	98	103	101	103	96	99
England	101	84	85	91	97	88
Sri Lanka	88	91	79	104	99	103
Zimbabwe	85	91	76	75	78	53
New Zealand	83	92	75	101	98	99

SOURCE: ALLSOPP, 2005

The study established that by 2002, Australia was by far the strongest team in world cricket in both batting and bowling, and that only three teams (Australia, South Africa and the West Indies) showed above average bowling strength. During the five-year period, the performances of Australia, South Africa, New Zealand, England and Sri Lanka improved, whereas the remainder declined – with India, the West Indies and Zimbabwe showing the most alarming drop.

These figures were then used to develop a model to predict the probable outcomes of five-day Test matches played between the different nations when playing either at home (Table 8.2) or away (Table 8.3).

TABLE 8.2: Estimates of the winning probabilities for the home team at the end of the 1997/98 – 2002/03 period (to convert the numbers to percentages, multiply by 100)

HOME TEAM	AWAY TEAM									
	AUS	ENG	IND	NZ	PAK	SA	SL	WI	ZIM	AVE
Australia	**0.46**	0.71	0.81	0.80	0.72	0.62	0.70	0.75	0.91	**0.75**
England	0.22	**0.46**	0.60	0.58	0.47	0.36	0.44	0.51	0.77	**0.49**
India	0.14	0.32	**0.46**	0.44	0.33	0.24	0.31	0.37	0.66	**0.35**
New Zealand	0.15	0.34	0.48	**0.46**	0.35	0.25	0.33	0.39	0.67	**0.37**
Pakistan	0.22	0.45	0.59	0.57	**0.46**	0.35	0.43	0.50	0.77	**0.48**
South Africa	0.30	0.56	0.69	0.68	0.57	**0.46**	0.55	0.61	0.84	**0.60**
Sri Lanka	0.23	0.47	0.61	0.59	0.48	0.37	**0.46**	0.53	0.78	**0.51**
West Indies	0.19	0.40	0.54	0.53	0.41	0.31	0.39	**0.46**	0.73	**0.44**
Zimbabwe	0.07	0.17	0.27	0.26	0.18	0.12	0.16	0.21	**0.46**	**0.18**
Average	**0.19**	**0.43**	**0.57**	**0.56**	**0.44**	**0.33**	**0.41**	**0.48**	**0.77**	**0.46**

SOURCE: ALLSOPP, 2005

For example, Table 8.2 predicts that Australia had a 75% probability of winning tests played at home against all other nations. This probability varied from 62% when playing South Africa to 91% when playing Zimbabwe.

TABLE 8.3: Estimates of the winning probabilities for the away team at the end of the 1997/98 – 2002/03 period (to convert the numbers to percentages, multiply by 100)

HOME TEAM	AWAY TEAM									
	AUS	ENG	IND	NZ	PAK	SA	SL	WI	ZIM	AVE
Australia	**0.08**	0.20	0.31	0.29	0.21	0.14	0.19	0.24	0.50	**0.26**
England	0.03	**0.08**	0.13	0.12	0.08	0.05	0.08	0.10	0.26	**0.11**
India	0.02	0.05	**0.08**	0.07	0.05	0.03	0.04	0.06	0.17	**0.06**
New Zealand	0.02	0.05	0.09	**0.08**	0.05	0.03	0.05	0.06	0.18	**0.07**
Pakistan	0.03	0.08	0.13	0.12	**0.08**	0.05	0.07	0.09	0.25	**0.10**
South Africa	0.04	0.12	0.19	0.18	0.12	**0.08**	0.11	0.14	0.35	**0.16**
Sri Lanka	0.03	0.08	0.14	0.13	0.09	0.06	**0.08**	0.10	0.27	**0.11**
West Indies	0.02	0.07	0.11	0.10	0.07	0.04	0.06	**0.08**	0.22	**0.09**
Zimbabwe	0.01	0.02	0.04	0.03	0.02	0.01	0.02	0.03	**0.08**	**0.02**
Average	**0.02**	**0.08**	**0.14**	**0.13**	**0.09**	**0.05**	**0.08**	**0.10**	**0.27**	**0.11**

SOURCE: ALLSOPP, 2005

Table 8.3 shows that the probability of winning away from home drops substantially, even for Australian teams. Australia therefore had only a 26% probability of winning away from home, ranging from a probability of 14% when playing in South Africa to 50% when playing in Zimbabwe. Table 8.3 also indicates that Zimbabwe had only a 7% probability of beating Australia in matches played in Zimbabwe, indicating that the balance (43%) of these matches could be predicted to end in a draw. Similarly, when Australia plays South Africa in Australia, the predicted outcomes, for Australia, would be 62% wins, 34% draws and 4% losses. But when South Africa plays Australia in South Africa, the predicted outcomes for South Africa would be 30% wins, 56% draws and 14% losses. Since according to this analysis, Australia and South Africa were the two top teams in five-day international cricket, this shows that the strength of the Australian side during this period provided them with a remarkable capacity to win a majority of home matches with few losses, and to inflict a much larger number of defeats and draws when playing away from home, thereby restricting their number of losses.

These studies also determined that the following factors were highly likely to lead to a successful outcome in five-day Test matches:

- **The team's first innings batting and bowling strength.**
- **The magnitude of the first innings lead.** The two most successful teams during this period, Australia and South Africa, were the two teams likely to have the greatest lead at the end of the first innings.
- **Home advantage (which increased the likelihood of developing a first innings lead).** The home advantage translated into 1 run in 11 scored by the home team, or 32 runs in a score of 350 runs (Allsopp, 2005). In one-day matches, this advantage was 1 in 13 runs, or 19 runs in a score of 250 runs.
- **Batting order, with the team batting second enjoying a significant advantage** (Allsopp and Clarke, 2004). This was due to the relative dominance of the team batting second in their final innings. Allsopp concluded that 'the dominance of the team batting second cannot be overestimated and the results clearly describe an unexpected trend that has emerged in Test cricket. The results strongly advocate that to improve their winning chances, teams should expose their particular strength, whether that be batting or bowling, in the final rather than the penultimate innings. This puts paid to the mythical notion… that when given the opportunity, teams should elect to bat first' (2005, pp. 273–74). This is an excellent example of the subjective opinions of the traditional pundits being proved wrong by statistical analysis.

And there's more: these tables can be used to determine if the 'correct' team wins championships like the Cricket World Cup. Allsopp speculated that the outcome of a one-day international match could be influenced by random factors, especially if the teams were evenly matched. Yet, paradoxically, the design of the Cricket World Cup involves playing many games in the initial (round robin) phase of the competition, when teams of very different abilities often play each other. Yet when more equally matched teams enter the Super Six phase of the competition, fewer games are used to distinguish between the different teams' abilities. In other words, random factors during the Super Six phase could lead to the 'wrong' team winning the World Cup – or rather, the 'best' team might lose.

However, Allsopp and Clarke showed that Australia and South Africa's performances during the 1999 World Cup were identical, whereas in the 2003 World Cup, Australia had a rating that was substantially superior to the other countries. But the other finalist, India, was rated second. Thus in both 1999 and 2003, the team that performed best in the tournament was the eventual winner, and, at least in 2003, the two top performing teams reached the final.

No additional analysis is required to confirm that the best team won the 2007 Cricket World Cup (given the administrative shambles that accompanied the final, this was just as well). The statistical analyses (see Figures 8.3 and 8.4) show that the Australians had the best batsmen and the best bowlers by some way.

MODELLING THE PERFORMANCES OF A SINGLE NATIONAL CRICKET TEAM IN ONE-DAY INTERNATIONALS

Meanwhile, research on one-day games has not been neglected. Thomas Gilfillan and Nozuko Nobandla of South Africa's Council of Scientific and Industrial Research studied 81 one-day internationals played by South Africa between January 1994 and April 1997. (This overlapped with Bob Woolmer's tenure as team coach.)

The authors profiled each of the South African players on the basis of his performance, which was measured in eleven batting and bowling categories in the five preceding matches. It was found that six variables had predictive value:

- maximum number of matches in which the players had batted
- maximum average runs the players made
- number of centuries made by the team
- maximum number of wickets taken by the bowlers in the team, divided by the number of bowlers
- minimum deviation in the team's batting order
- whether it was a 'home' or 'away' match.

On the basis of the model they devised from these variables, the authors found that they could accurately predict 79% of South Africa's winning matches.

THE TIMING OF THE DECLARATION IN FIVE-DAY TEST MATCHES

A key feature of the model of factors determining the outcome of one- and five-day Test matches developed by Allsopp and Clarke (2004) and Allsopp (2005) is that the further the game progresses, the more accurately their model predicts the outcome. They suggest that this information would be of value to those involved in the betting industry, both bookmakers and gamblers. Whichever group – bookies or punters – first adopts these predictive models will have a greater chance of beating the odds, and thus a distinct (if arguably unfair) advantage.

Is there any advantage to cricketers, however? It would seem that the answer is yes. These models can also be used to time the declaration in the third innings of a Test match. Using data from recently completed Test matches, Scarf and Shi (2005) have developed a model to predict the probable outcome of five-day Test matches at any potential declaration points. The outcome probability is based on the target and the required run rate. The authors suggest that their model has 'the potential for practical use in Test matches'.

CALCULATING THE OUTCOME OF RAIN-INTERRUPTED ONE-DAY MATCHES

At present, the Duckworth/Lewis method is used to calculate the revised winning totals for the team batting second in rain-interrupted one-day international matches. The basis for the Duckworth/Lewis method is that it uses historical data to predict the average rate of scoring that would have occurred during the missing overs, on the basis of the number of wickets remaining for the batting side when the rain interruption occurred. This average, times the number of overs lost, is then subtracted from the total achieved by the team batting first and becomes the (rain-revised) target for the team batting second.

Two New Zealand scientists, Carter and Guthrie (2004), have presented an alternate model based on what they call the 'iso-probability rule'. Their model attempts to calculate what the probability is of the team batting second winning the game at any time that the rain-interruption occurs.

Their argument is that as their innings evolves, the probability that the team batting second will win, fluctuates. A few high-scoring overs increases the probability of victory, whereas a few poor overs, especially if wickets are lost, reduces that probability. Their model aims to preserve any winning advantage or disadvantage that the team batting second had acquired at the time of rain interruption, so that this advantage/disadvantage remains when the game resumes. Figure 8.5 illustrates their model.

The bottom (horizontal) axis represents the overs remaining for the innings that begins in the top right-hand corner of the graph. The vertical axis represents the number of runs required to win – i.e., the runs still needed to outscore the team that batted first.

The top curve is known as the winning iso-probability curve for the team batting second. Provided that team remains one run below that curve, by the time they reach the end of the innings, depicted at the bottom left hand corner of the figure, they will have won the match. On the other hand, if they drift above that curve, the probability that they will win is reduced. A closer look at the example used by Carter and Guthrie will help to explain this figure.

Let's assume that the team batting second begins its innings at point A (Figure 8.5; top right-hand corner). They begin by scoring runs freely, so that their scoring 'worm' progresses well below the iso-probability curve required to win the game (indicating that they are well ahead of the run rate needed to win the game at that point). However, they may have used up valuable 'run-scoring resources' (in the form of lost wickets) to achieve this apparently advantageous position. Carter and Guthrie's point is that the team batting second should not have to sacrifice that more advantageous position in the event of a rain interruption, any more than a team which is progressing poorly should be advantaged by a rain interruption. (The Duckworth/Lewis method uses historical data from multiple previous one-day international games to determine how many runs the team batting second might have scored during the overs lost to rain in the current match. But the Carter/Guthrie model tries to calculate this only on the basis of what has happened in the specific match being played.)

However, in this example, rain interrupts the game at point B and continues until point C causing a specific number (B_1–C_1) of overs to be lost.

Carter and Guthrie argue that when the game recommences, the batting team should restart with the same probability of victory as was the case before the rain interruption (Point B). So, when they resume the innings at point C, they should continue on the same iso-probability curve (D–Di) that they had reached at the moment of the rain interruption. This new iso-probability line predicts that the number of runs that must be subtracted from the other team's total is determined by Br–Cr (left axis of Figure 8.5). The further progress of the team is tracked by their

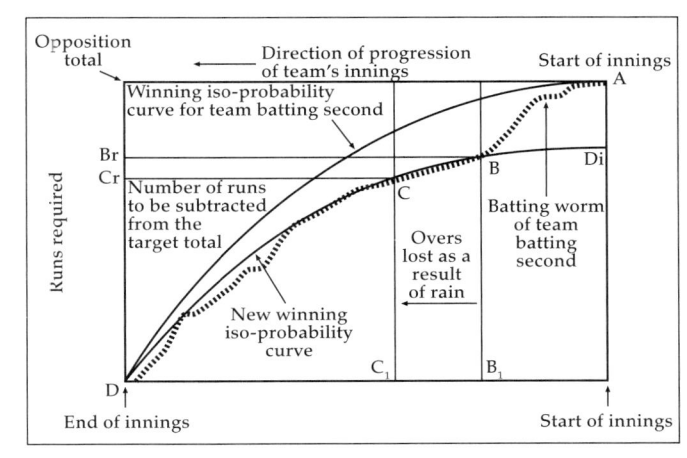

SOURCE: CARTER AND GUTHRIE, 2004

FIGURE 8.5: *The Carter and Guthrie model for calculating the outcome of rain-interrupted one-day matches*

'worm', which generally lies below the iso-probability curve, indicating that the team batting second should have won, according to this method.

Carter and Guthrie acknowledge that their system is likely to pose a more challenging target for the team batting second than the Duckworth/Lewis rule, which tends to increase the probability that the team batting second will win rain-interrupted matches. So it seems that the search for the ideal method to calculate how many runs must be subtracted from the score of the team batting first in a rain-interrupted game is by no means over. New methods will be formulated and tested, but as all are necessarily based on assumptions about what would happen in the rain-interrupted game (some, all or none of which might have occurred), they will always be open to criticism.

Using the Duckworth/Lewis method to predict the likely final score of teams

One feature of the Duckworth/Lewis method is its ability to predict how many runs will be scored in the remaining overs, depending on the number of wickets remaining (Figure 8.6).

Figure 8.6 predicts the average number of runs that are still obtainable, based on the number of overs and wickets remaining. The top curve predicts the number of runs (vertical axis on left) that will in theory be added to the score at any point in the innings by a team that retains all ten wickets for the duration of the innings. Thus, for example, with twenty overs remaining, this particular model predicts that a team with ten wickets intact at that point could expect to add a further 140 runs, whereas a team with only three wickets remaining could expect to add only a further 60 runs.

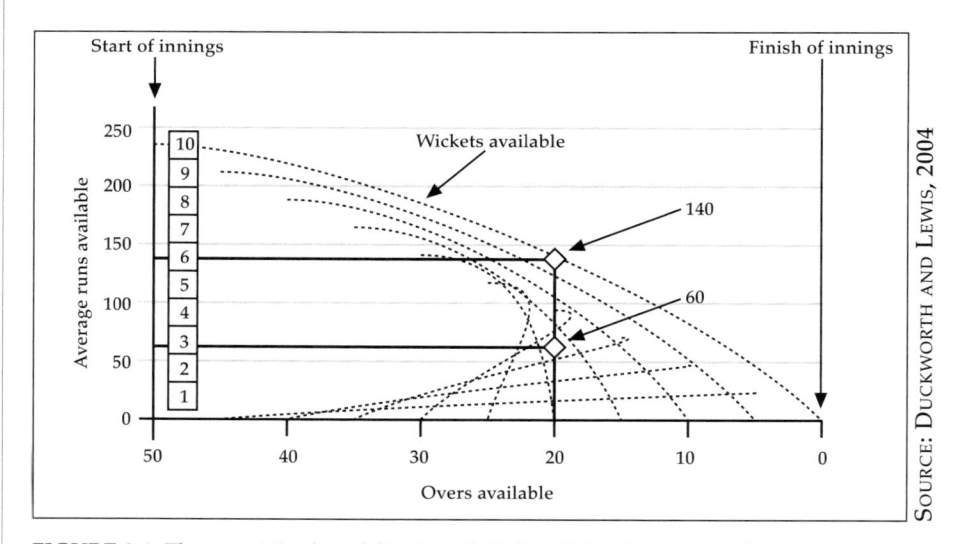

FIGURE 8.6: *The current Duckworth/Lewis method of predicting the outcome of rain-interrupted one-day matches*

458   THINKING CRICKET

PREDICTING THE OPTIMUM BATTING ORDER FOR ONE-DAY CRICKET INTERNATIONALS

While it's obvious that someone handy with a calculator is essential when deciding what to do in one-day games shortened by rain, Swartz and colleagues (2006) wondered if science could help to determine the optimum batting order in one-day cricket. They chose the 2003 Indian World Cup cricket team for their analysis, noting cheerfully that for a team of eleven players, 40 million possible batting orders exist. Far from reducing them to despair, this finding prompted their conclusion that 'even sceptics ought to concede that there may exist undiscovered yet promising batting orders. This is the essential motivation of our work'. (They make a good point, although the notion of Allan Donald or Glenn McGrath striding out to open the batting boggles the mind somewhat.)

By studying India's batting performances in 71 one-day international first innings, they produced predictive models of the batting abilities of thirteen Indian international cricketers. Next, they found that their model was able accurately to predict the actual outcomes of Indian batting performances, based on the players

WHO WERE THE WORLD CHAMPIONS OF TEST CRICKET BETWEEN 1994 AND 1999?

Brooks et al. (2002) published their predictive analysis of which Test sides performed best between 1994 and 1999 – the period during which Bob Woolmer coached the South African cricket team.

They developed a model of each team's batting and bowling performances in Test cricket during this period from measures of overall batting performance (runs per wicket), batting strike rate (runs per over), overall bowling performance (opposition runs per wicket) and bowling strike rate (opposition runs per over).

Using this model, they were able to predict the winning team in 71% and the losing team in 81% of all Test matches played during this period, and in which there was an outcome other than a draw. But they found themselves able to predict correctly only 57% of drawn matches.

Interestingly, Australia's success during this period was based on its bowling performance, while South Africa's success was based on both bowling performance and a high batting strike rate.

According to their model, the South African team under Bob Woolmer had the highest probability of winning and the lowest probability of losing, followed by Australia and Pakistan in the rankings. However, in a 'world championship' contest between Australia and South Africa, Australia would be more likely to win more and lose fewer competitions, confirming the impression that during this period Australia had a psychological hold over South Africa not achieved by any other nation.

ORDER	BATSMAN
1	Dravid
2	Tendulkar
3	Ganguly
4	Sehwag
5	Mongia
6	Y. Singh
7	Khan
8	Kaif
9	H. Singh
10	Agarkar
11	Srinath

chosen and the order in which they batted. They concluded that the Indian batting order shown on the left would produce the highest number of runs (256) in a one-day international.

They also noted that the batting order of the men coming in at seven to eleven had less effect on the outcome than did the order of the first six batsmen.

DECIDING WHEN TO USE A NIGHT WATCHMAN

Clarke and Norman (2003) crunched the numbers to discover the value – if any – of using a night watchman to protect a recognized batsman at the end of a day's play in the multi-day form of the game. They considered two different options – a stonewalling and a slogging night watchman.

Their calculations showed that the use of a night watchman was not usually a good idea. The practice was more defendable if the batting side still had several recognized (about four) batsmen, as well as an equal number of less good batsmen. But if there were few recognized batsmen remaining and few overs to play, it was a better policy (statistically) to send in the next recognized batsman. But if a night watchman was dismissed, it was usually better to send in another night watchman. They also concluded that it was best to leave the night watchman to his own devices, rather than giving him instructions to either slog away, or to stonewall. Here, figures and mental strategy dovetail – it is probably not wise to weigh down the batsman chosen for this unenviable task with a barrage of directives.

BATTING WITH A TAIL-ENDER: TO RUN OR NOT TO RUN?

A few years earlier, Clarke and Norman (1999) used the same mathematical techniques with which they scrutinized the decision to use a night watchman to develop a model showing when batters at the crease with tail-enders should choose to run, and when they should desist (even if a single was on offer) in order to maximize their team's run-scoring potential. They concluded that the problem currently defies a simple answer. However, they did note that statistics suggest that the 'common practice of refusing runs to protect weaker batsmen from the strike has been shown to be sensible under certain conditions' (p. 545). So it would appear that science and traditional practice have their moments of concurrence.

SCIENCE AND STATISTICS: SUMMING UP

A feature of modern human thought is our ability to accept 'truth' without stopping to consider the nature of the evidence that proves this 'truth'. Many choose subjective opinions over objective evidence. These then become truisms ('But it's always been that way!') or dogmas, and any challenges are met with great resistance. It does take effort, and an enquiring, even restless mind, to insist on objectivity and to question popular beliefs. And this is not an attitude that is always promoted or valued in modern education or culture, including in the so-called developed world.

So science, which is understood to be a search for objective truth, is considered by many to be a specific subject – like physics, chemistry, biology or trigonometry – last encountered at high school and remembered with dim alarm. It is not understood as an attitude, or an approach to life in which there is a continuing search for the objective evidence that underpins 'truth'.

The game of cricket, as has been mentioned before, casts a long historical shadow. The richness of its traditions carries a burden: its lore is largely defined by the subjective opinions of its most influential figures. According to baseball statistician Michael Lewis, young baseball players acquire almost all of their early knowledge of the game from television commentators. It is extremely likely that in the case of cricket, the general public in all the cricket-playing nations acquire most of their knowledge and opinions about cricket from television and radio commentators, most of whom are former players. But there is no guarantee that playing a sport, especially if one has a natural talent for that game, will instill the ability to be objective about it. It is far more likely that the natural bias in these cases will be towards subjectivity. After all, if you were successful at the game, surely your opinions are likely to be correct?

Lewis describes the American baseball culture as follows: 'The problem with major league baseball is that it's a self-populating institution. Knowledge is institutionalized. The people involved with baseball who aren't players are ex-players. In their defence, their structure is not set up along corporate lines. They aren't equipped to evaluate their own systems. They don't have the mechanism to let in the good and get rid of the bad. They either keep everything or get rid of everything, and they rarely do the latter' (2003, p. 241).

This is partly why in this book, we have tried to use science to shed light on many aspects of the art of cricket. More than that, we endorse a mental attitude to the game of cricket that constantly questions received or established wisdom; that constantly strives to find better and clearer answers, even when these fly in the face of tradition.

We endorse a mental attitude to the game of cricket that constantly questions received or established wisdom; that strives to find better and clearer answers, even when these fly in the face of tradition.

This short chapter alone has shown how objective statistical analysis of cricket, although a new branch of cricket science, has already produced findings that challenge the prevailing wisdoms of the day. These are worth repeating.

- **The toss has a significant influence on the outcome of one-day matches:** No statistical data can be found to support this.

- **The team winning the toss and batting first has a significant advantage in five-day Test matches (because they do not have to bat last on a crumbling wicket):** Not so, according to the statistics. In fact, statistical analysis shows that the team that bats last in a five-day Test match is at an advantage (although the numbers don't reveal why this is so). But this finding does suggest that there are advantages to batting second that outweigh the risk of having to bat last on a crumbling wicket.

    Perhaps this is because batting in a five-day Test match is easiest on the second and third days, when the team batting second is more likely to be at the crease. Another possibility is that wickets 'crumble' less frequently than is generally believed – or too few modern bowlers are able to exploit a crumbling wicket – or perhaps modern batsmen are getting increasingly skilled at batting on crumbling wickets!

    What is of concern is that because the notion that whoever wins the toss must bat first has become so ingrained, the captain who has called correctly has little option but to send out his opening pair. If his side goes on to lose the Test, no-one (other than a handful of geeky statisticians) will ever accuse him of making a stupid decision. But should he lose the Test after winning the toss and electing to bat second, any number of subjective 'experts' will announce that this outcome was entirely 'predictable', and call for his head.

As we have also seen, the study of cricket statistics has more to offer selectors, coaches, captains and players than the overturning of received wisdoms. The findings so far can be briefly summarized as follows.

- **The relative batting and bowling strengths of the national teams of cricket-playing countries can be measured on the basis of their Test records over a number of seasons.** This analysis can also be used to predict the outcome of matches between those countries when played either at home or away. This means that eventually the real value of individual player contributions to the team's performance will be measurable. When this happens, team selection will become an objective science, rather than the subjective and untested opinions of selectors entrusted with a task involving no small amount of guesswork.

- **A statistical model has been developed with the capacity to help captains make a decision as to when they should declare in five-day Test matches.**

- **Scientists have developed a 'winning iso-probability model'** (see Figure 8.5 on p. 457) that provides teams and match officials (and let's not forget commentators) with the capacity to determine, at any moment in a one-day international game, exactly which team is in the ascendancy. However, this model ignores the batting resources that have already been used up by the team batting second in order to achieve that position. In other words, a team might enjoy a (temporary) spell of ascendancy through adventurous batting that has cost too many wickets – and which is likely to come back to haunt them in the later part of the innings.

    Because the Duckworth/Lewis model accounts for the effect of 'already used batting resources' (i.e., wickets lost) in predicting the final score of the batting team, it is probably a more accurate model for estimating the team's likely final score at any time during their innings. But the bottom line is that no predictive model is ever going to be able to calculate with absolute accuracy what might have happened, had the rain never come down. Scientists are nevertheless likely to continue developing and refining methods of calculating scores in games where overs are lost to rain.

- **Statistical models have been developed to evaluate optimum batting line-ups,** to establish if and when a night watchman should be used, and how best to bat with tail-enders at the crease in order to squeeze the maximum number of runs out of the partnership.

All these are just some of the findings established by scientists using mathematical tools to analyse aspects of a game they find to be intriguing. It is unlikely that any of them embarked on these studies with the specific intention of boosting the performance of their national cricket teams! However, there is little doubt that in the future we will see increasing use of statistics by first some (and then possibly all) cricketing nations in order to gain a competitive advantage or edge over their rivals. This will mean a steady movement towards objective data and tested hypotheses, and less reliance on 'cricketing lore' – the ingrained and subjective opinions of famed figures of the game.

CHAPTER NINE

COACHING

INTRODUCTION

I telephoned Sir Donald Bradman and said I thought coaches should wear concrete boots and be chucked into Sydney harbour. The Don's reply? 'It's not deep enough!'

Arthur Morris, Australian Test batsman 1940–1955

For many who grew up in the game before the professional era, the idea of a professional coach is abhorrent. The notion summons up visions of an officious little man enlisted to confuse good players with obscure, over-complicated technical jargon, psychobabble, and endless lectures on game plans and personal goals. As a result, many younger followers of the game tend to be ambivalent or at least non-committal about the role of a coach. All it takes is a slump in their team's performance for all the old-fashioned prejudices to come out, and for Morris and Bradman's concrete boots to be dusted off.

Many of the criticisms and questions levelled at coaches tend to be non-technical. 'What are you doing about lifting morale? Aren't the lads over-confident? Why isn't the team fitter? Why is the media saying that the team is over-fit and has peaked too soon? Why didn't you select X when he's the fastest bowler in the country? Why did you select X when he's the fastest bowler in the country – and always bowls short?' And so on ad infinitum. Indeed, it is this fairly unsophisticated level of questioning that underlines the role of the coach. Anyone can criticize, but it takes skill, training, and years of observation and practice to become a coach capable of finding and implementing *solutions* to problems like those listed above and many, many more.

Perhaps this was best summed up by Richie Benaud and Dennis Lillee, two of the game's straighter shooters, in their thoughts on coaching (their writings on the subject are well worth tracking down). A coach is doing his job, wrote Benaud, when he is able to not only spot but *correct* errors:

Detection of an error is the easy part. There are approximately a million television viewers watching a match every day and ninety-nine of every hundred of those watchers are able to detect the errors the players are making. No more than one in the hundred, if that, would be capable of proper correction (1998).

Lillee, who was instrumental in developing the Indian Fast Bowling Academy in Madras, echoed this view:

I've lost count of the number of times I've heard a coach say, 'You're falling away – stand up straight.' It just makes me laugh because nobody deliberately tries to fall over when attempting to bowl. The reason they are falling away is because, mechanically, something is wrong. If you cannot explain to the player why it's happening and show him how he can fix the problem, it will not go away. He might be able to stand straight for a couple of balls, but inevitably he will start to fall away again. It was band-aid coaching, not corrective teaching.

Even now we need more people to become more involved in the mechanics of bowling, to find the reasons why an action clicks or why some bowlers bowl continually down leg side when they are trying not to. You cannot just tell the player; you have to show him and explain so he can understand the mechanics, and then work it out for himself by watching a video of his action. Thus the coach coaches himself out of that particular job and moves on to the next one. Some coaches don't want to work that way, but I do. Get in, do the job, and get out (2003, pp. 303–4).

The modern coach has to be more than an analyst, and considerably more than a repairman or cricketing mechanic. The game must survive in the face of increasing competition from many other sporting activities and pastimes; and in order to survive it must not only be taught, but be taught well. Yet while the coach has a vital role to play, he (and increasingly, she) must never imagine that they are indispensable, or start thinking about their abilities and skills as marketable assets in a growing industry. The coach is there to help the players first and foremost. He is nothing without them, and the job is primarily about them. That is why Lillee's words are good ones to remember: if this chapter is about anything, it is about getting in, doing the job, and getting out.

'Get in, do the job, and get out.'

– Dennis Lillee

COACHING AND THE ART OF CRICKET

For many of the greatest artists, perfection or technical mastery was impossible: they considered themselves life-long students, working into old age towards some ultimate goal they knew they could never reach. For them, satisfaction with a particular work was unthinkable: each piece, even if it was declared a masterpiece by the public, was simply another step, another lesson learned.

Cricket has produced more than its share of artists, men who have entranced the public with apparent mastery and grace, subtlety and genius. But like the artists of past centuries, many of these players recognized that they were simply students of a greater art, apprentices to an eternally demanding master. The humility (often coming across as off-hand disdain for their careers) of men like Donald Bradman and Garfield Sobers is the product of a cricketing soul that is never satisfied; that always wants to do better.

Cricketers should never stop learning. Those who reach a point where they think they know it all – or even know enough – are simply proving themselves unwilling or unable to learn cricket's greatest lessons. Bob Woolmer recalled: 'I was attending the Level 4 coaching course in the United Kingdom along with seven international players. After my lecture on batting I was approached by one of the senior players. "You know," he told me, "I've played cricket for nearly two decades, and I didn't know any of that." Here was a player who had clearly made a success of his career, but whose intellectual grasp of batting was far from solid. In other words, he had not come close to fulfilling his potential. He was living proof of one of the game's oldest truths: just because you can play cricket, it doesn't mean that you understand the technical side of the game. That technical aspect of cricket is an intricate combination of art and science – and indeed you can have some success without understanding the game – you can be an artist without grasping the science.'

But to be truly great, an artist must engage with the science of his craft. Leonardo da Vinci was as much an engineer and physicist as he was a painter; the Dutch Masters, who included geniuses like Rembrandt and Vermeer, were fascinated by optics. In fact, most great painters were and are experts in colour theory or perspective or chemistry. Cricket is no different. The greatest players have been both artists and scientists, relishing the aesthetics, the passion, the assertion of individuality that the game allows, but also always researching and pushing the boundaries of the science of the game.

Of course not all great cricketers are alike, nor are they driven by the same desires and motivations. The mix of art and science is not always equally balanced in these players: sometimes it is science that prevails, producing an economical, workmanlike technique that is endlessly repeatable and enormously reliable; sometimes it is the art that triumphs, creating a mercurial unpredictability and emotional highs and lows. Sir Donald Bradman was the consummate scientist, indeed perhaps one of the few cricketers whose art was his science. At the other end of the scale, the elemental geniuses have rampaged and fizzled, thrilled and disappointed – men like Keith Miller, Garry Sobers, Javed Miandad and Jeff Thomson. The pressures of the modern game, with its need for consistency, and its large financial rewards at the elite level, have had a mediating influence on these two extremes, and in more recent times the scientists have become more fluent and expressive (Sunil Gavaskar, Allan Border and Steve Waugh spring to mind), while the artists have tried to exercise more control over their instincts, as evidenced by batsmen such as Viv Richards, Brian Lara, Inzamam-ul-Haq; and bowlers such as Dennis Lillee and Richard Hadlee. A perfectly balanced combination of science and artistry is surprisingly uncommon in the game, but when it occurs, the results are spectacular: Sachin Tendulkar and Shane Warne have perhaps come closer to this balance than any other players in the game's history.

WHO AND WHAT IS A CRICKET COACH?

The modern professional coach is a diagnostic and corrective specialist, someone who is paid to see problems and fix them. But the handful of full-time contracted coaches is dwarfed by the tens of thousands – perhaps even hundreds of thousands – of dedicated amateurs coaching cricket around the world. So in considering a profile of the average coach, perhaps it is more useful to describe this huge majority.

All coaches, whether they are parents, schoolteachers, retired players, volunteers in disadvantaged communities, or simply enthusiasts, share three basic traits:
- They are willing and able to teach the game of cricket;
- They love cricket and want to pass its traditions on to the next generation;
- They recognize the social, emotional and psychological benefits of playing cricket well, and want to give children the best possible chance of enjoying these benefits.

Playing cricket should always be a pleasure, regardless of victory or defeat, and it is this love of the game that should be the ultimate motivation for learning and playing the game. Coaches therefore have a responsibility to foster that love: the coach who thinks that cricket is about winning – especially at junior levels – has entirely missed the point, and would be better served finding another line of work – perhaps as a stockbroker or a debt-collector!

Playing cricket should always be a pleasure, and this should be the ultimate motivation for learning the game. Coaches have a responsibility to foster love of the game: the coach who thinks that cricket is about winning – especially at junior levels – has entirely missed the point.

In many of South Africa's primary schools, the dedication women teachers show in coaching cricket means that the school team usually includes both male and female players. This will contribute to a growing pool of women able to coach cricket as adults in southern Africa in the future.

It is an unfortunate reality, however, that the broad church of cricket contains many thousands of coaches who are not suitably equipped to instill a love and respect for the game, or to diagnose and correct faults. This may be due to a lack of either technical skills, or social and intuitive ones. It is important to acknowledge one of coaching's greatest truths: an ability to play does not always translate into the ability to teach.

Moreover, strange inversions can happen in cricket. Just as a great player can be a wretched coach, someone who has never played the game can prove to be a highly successful coach at lower levels of the game. Similarly, a dour and taciturn coach might be able to reach and positively affect both sensitive and outgoing players, while a jolly 'people person', someone who is liked by everyone he meets, might have no impact whatsoever as a coach.

It is also extremely important to note at the outset that cricket coaching is certainly not the preserve of men. In South Africa's townships, for instance, most schoolteachers are women, especially at primary-school level. As a result, many of those coaching junior players are these same women. And this pattern is seen in many less affluent South African high schools as well, where sometimes the only teachers willing or available to coach cricket are female. We have met many women coaches whose desire to learn, teach and pass on the game is as intense as that of semi-professional male coaches. The enthusiasm of these women for cricket, and their diligence in studying matches on television and on the field, is doing wonders both for their charges and the game. In many of South Africa's larger and poorer primary schools, the dedication women teachers show in coaching cricket means that the school team usually includes both male and female players, and this will contribute to a growing pool of women able to coach cricket as adults in southern Africa in the future. Similar gender trends are likely to be seen in coaching in the Caribbean (where everyone is a cricket coach!) and elsewhere in the cricket-playing world.

Indeed, some top-flight coaches could learn a thing or two from these low-level teachers about humility and the eagerness to learn as much as one can: no matter how high you go, there is always more to learn, especially about technique. Bob Woolmer said he sometimes listened in dismay as he heard great cricketers of the past – and sometimes of the present – saying that this coach or that one was 'too technical':

This kind of thinking does the game a grave disservice, and limits the potential of both coach and players. There is no doubt in my mind that every single coach in the game today should make himself as technically adept as possible. As Benaud points out, anyone can identify errors. But it is only those who are walking encyclopaedias of technical knowledge who will be able to correct those errors.

The coach is thus many things to many people, and we will discuss his or her numerous roles shortly; but perhaps the single most important skill of coaching is the ability to coach all age groups. The demands and techniques involved in coaching ten-year-olds are hugely different to those of coaching an international Test team, and the coach who can do both without having to make fundamental changes to his methods and personality has clearly worked out a consistent and successful coaching philosophy. Exposing yourself to as many levels as possible is also a sure way to encounter your own limitations; and insight into your personal limitations is one of the most valuable assets you can have, as this will give you the humility and flexibility to ask for help from other sources.

Having said that, you can't be a great mentor, facilitator and teacher if you are relieved of your position as coach! How secure your position is depends largely on the perception of those who employ you. You might be doing wonders with young minds and characters, and you might be pulling a wretched team back from the brink, but the people who appoint and pay coaches want one thing, and one thing only – victories. If you take over a team that loses every match by 100 runs, and turn them into a team that loses every match by only 20 runs, you're still going to be considered a losing coach. Therefore in order to keep doing what you're doing – to stay on board, in other words – you will need to privilege two aspects of coaching above all others:

- You will have to make sure that your players improve both technically and mentally;
- You will have to help bind them into a team.

These two tasks will have to come before all else if you are going to start winning games and keep your job.

THE ROLES OF A COACH

The primary role of the coach is simple: as outlined by Richie Benaud and Dennis Lillee at the beginning of this chapter, they must be able to diagnose technical problems, and more importantly, they must be able to correct them.

However, the modern coach is called upon to perform a host of secondary functions across all aspects and disciplines of a cricket team's existence. He can never please all the people all the time, but he should at least be equipped to try. The following is a brief outline of the most important – and most common – of these roles.

1. Manager

Whether your management position is official or not, you will need to organize practice sessions and games down to the most minute detail, from venue to equipment to time-keeping. It is your job to ensure that everyone knows what time they should arrive and what time they can go home, what to bring and what to wear. You must see that everyone knows the venue, the bus routes, the train timetables, and the route to the practice or game. You will have organized practical details (meals or drinks for the players, somewhere to change, a first-aid box) and have the thank-you speech prepared. A good manager ensures that the practice runs with discipline and forward momentum.

2. Communicator

Something that will become increasingly evident in this chapter is the need for all coaches to be able to communicate clearly, logically and sensibly. Being able to transmit information to a player so that he understands it immediately – on an intellectual as well as emotional level – is a priceless asset for any coach.

Not only should you be able to find the best way of putting ideas into words, but you should also try to learn how best to use questions: a good question, carefully timed and clearly asked, can cut through years of instructions and blather. Bob Woolmer recalled: 'Playing against Australia, I had scored a fifty and two hundreds, but somehow in the next Test my feet were all over the place. I should have been in the best form of my life, but in the nets all I could do was defend. Because this was before professional coaches became a fixture, I had to turn for help to the next best thing: a seasoned veteran, in this case, Geoff Boycott. I told him that my feet were going in all the wrong directions, and he asked me what I normally did. I had no idea, except that I normally went back and across. Then he asked me what I usually did with my front foot, and once again I had no clue.' So bear in mind that by asking questions, you can prompt a player to consider and identify gaps and problems in his technique. However, note that it is your job to stick around and help him answer the questions you've posed.

3. Guidance counsellor

Every player is different. Some come from broken homes, some are overloaded with teenage testosterone, and some may be struggling with poverty. Whether they are quiet, rowdy, introverted, extroverted, sensitive or insensitive, you need to put time and effort into getting to know your players so that you can get the best out of them. The more time you spend with them, the more involved you will become, and the better equipped you will be to read each player's technical or emotional needs. Often you become the players' sounding-board, someone to turn to at difficult moments. They will want your advice, even if they don't always take it. A word of caution: be careful to maintain a balance. Don't let players get too close to you or rely on you too much, because when they step across the ropes onto the field, it is they who have to perform, not you.

4. Diplomat

If traditionalists and amateur critics are to be believed, sport and politics shouldn't mix. All right then, *you* try to coach South Africa or Pakistan without cultivating allies or knowing the unwritten rules and complicated policies of administrators and politicians – and see how far you get! Certainly politics (whether international or at club level) shouldn't affect what goes on on the field, but during your coaching career you will need to form alliances with those who can help you and whom you trust. You will also need to be able to say the right thing at the right time: brutal honesty can sometimes turn bosses and players against you.

Be very aware that coaching can be a no-win proposition: success can lead to jealousy, but failure means the sack. It is also very difficult to measure success and failure as a coach: a series of wins sees you touted as the best in the world; a shock defeat instantly demotes you to a no-hoper has-been. Bob Woolmer had first-hand experience of how easily this happens: 'When I coached South Africa, the media were typically clumsy in their judgements, deeming me to be a great one-day coach because our success rate was 75%, but indicting me as a failure in the Test arena because South Africa won 51% of their Tests. I was adamant in stressing the differences in the two codes, and fortunately I was allowed to keep doing what I had been doing for longer than some.'

5. Historian

All too often coaches point to modern changes in the game, and claim that the past has little to contribute. The reality is that cricket's history can act as a fundamental guide to why the sport has reached its current position, and can even hint at future developments. For instance, if you are aware that cricket has always changed its rules to neutralize bowlers and favour batsmen, you can make a fairly educated prediction about the next step in the game – more fielding restrictions, heavier bats, tighter lines for bowlers, and so on. Cricket's history is also a treasure-trove of coaching tips, mostly written far more eloquently than many of today's corporately-produced manuals. For instance, it was a book written by the great C.B. Fry in 1912, *Cricket (Batsmanship)*, that first got Bob Woolmer thinking about the biomechanics of batting. Fry called it the 'mechanism' of batting, but no other writer Woolmer had ever read has been as succinct or clear:

> *In trying the shot, he must feel that there is a point (or short arc) where the bat swings freer and cleaner and faster. Clearly this is the point that bat should meet ball.... It is imperative that the ball must be hit at a definite and exact point to effect perfect timing.*

If traditionalists and amateur critics are to be believed, sport and politics shouldn't mix. All right then, you try to coach South Africa or Pakistan without cultivating allies or knowing the unwritten rules!

Bob Woolmer could not speak highly enough about the quality of Fry's thought processes. 'My very first manual, given to me in 1952, contained not a single mention of timing or hitting areas. Fry was indisputably ahead of his time, and the coach who overlooks these gems of past generations is doing himself a disservice. He might never encounter another of Fry's great lines: "He must take the ball as he sees it; and he must see it as it is. He must neither assume nor guess." Magnificent!'

6. Social worker

Depending on where in the world you are coaching, this might well become a significant part of your role. Bob Woolmer recalled his years of going into the South African townships of Langa and Kewtown to help coach the junior sections of two clubs:

> *It was here that it became abundantly clear that a coach had to attend to far greater problems than just those related to cricket: collecting boys with no transportation, finding food and drink, and helping them at home all became part of the deal. I remember boys from poor families asking for food – a salutary experience for me. This is where a coach has to be part of his community so that he can make more considered decisions about how he coaches his children. For example, many coaches, including myself, demand punctuality; but if a child has to catch three trains and a bus, and then walk quarter of a mile to cricket practice, it is hard to admonish him for being late.*

Of course, the cricket coach cannot save the world, but as the above story shows, it is often necessary to bear the practical implications of harsh or impoverished circumstances in mind. Coaches should not scold untidily dressed youngsters, wilting fielders or tardy children without considering the context. Do not despair, however: in South Africa, the sterling work being done by thousands of coaches and teachers (including the armies of women who have never even played the game themselves) on bumpy fields or dustbowls, with precious few resources, is testament to the importance of coaching in tough socio-economic circumstances. Remember that the sport you are coaching will enrich lives that often have little enough recreation or pleasure – and don't assume that this is true only of developing countries. In a rough ghetto of Los Angeles, a homesick Jamaican began teaching gang members cricket in an effort to divert them from crime – with astonishingly successful results. And this is only one of hundreds of similar tales. So maintain a sense of humour and flexibility, and concentrate on doing as much as you can, regardless of how daunting the circumstances.

7. Paramedic

Although nobody expects you to act as a qualified doctor, you will play an important role in preventing and treating injuries, especially if you coach children. All coaches, regardless of the age group they manage, should be trained in CPR techniques and basic first aid: the former is particularly important, as the impact of a cricket ball striking a player's chest can in rare circumstances disrupt the heartbeat. So be prepared!

It is also your job to establish whether any of your charges have medical conditions such as epilepsy, diabetes, asthma and anaphylactic shock response to insect stings. Remember that there is no reason at all why those afflicted in these ways should not be able to play and enjoy cricket, as long as you are prepared for an emergency, and know how to proceed in case of one. It may be helpful to tell children who have these and other problems that their heroes have also faced similar challenges. For example, Jonty Rhodes played cricket with a mild form of epilepsy, Wasim Akram with insulin-dependent diabetes, and Michael Atherton with a rare and painful spinal disorder; but none of these elite players allowed their 'disabilities' to disrupt or even negatively affect their stellar playing careers.

Finally – and here you do not want your charges to emulate the elite players they watch on television – do not let children suck sweets or chew gum while playing or practising. This is extremely unwise, as a sudden unexpected movement or even a lapse in concentration could lead to choking. As a precaution against this happening while you are in charge, you should brush up on the Heimlich manoeuvre (the clasp used to relieve choking).

8. Scientist

The purists and traditionalists may fuss, but the reality of modern sport is that science is here to stay. The modern international coach needs to have a solid grasp of medical terminology and the latest techniques for avoiding injury or treating it when it arises; he must be comfortable handling audio-visual equipment and the data it provides; and he must be willing to experiment with new technologies as soon as they arrive. Bob Woolmer considered himself lucky in this respect: 'I was especially fortunate to be able to enlist the help of my co-author, Professor Tim Noakes, in helping the South African team into a new era in the mid-1990s. To me it was no surprise that Australia's rise to dominance in all sports coincided with their public embrace of scientific methods, while South Africa's decline over the last five years – especially in one-day cricket – started after that country's administrators decided to abandon Noakes as an advisor and assistant.'

There is no reason why children with epilepsy, diabetes and asthma should not be able to play and enjoy cricket, as long as you are prepared for an emergency.

9. Motivator

Bob Woolmer remembered South Africa's tour to Pakistan in 1994 as a hard one: 'It was my first assignment as coach, and we lost all six one-day games we played. It was there that I asked Australian coach Bob Simpson for some advice about this international coaching lark. For example, what did he recommend for keeping the team motivated? He answered my questions with a question: "If you're not enthusiastic, ask yourself who is?"'

Another great self-motivator, Steve Waugh, will tell you that players should not need to be motivated by a coach to play for their country – that honour should be all the motivation they need. But international cricket is not always about glory and honour and inspiration. Endless one-day tournaments in far-flung parts of the world can sap the enthusiasm of even the most dedicated self-motivator. Sponsors' junkets, television interviews, banquets, ridiculous tour itineraries, all while players are getting increasingly fatigued and missing their families, can make the coach invaluable as someone who can lift spirits and focus minds. Don't bang on tables or spout motivational one-liners: try to understand what it is that motivates your team. Try to reach their hearts rather than their minds. For example, Australian coach John Buchanan took his team to Gallipoli, the battlefield in Turkey where thousands of Australians and New Zealanders, fighting under the ANZAC banner, had died in the First World War, and where so much Australian and Kiwi pride and national identity had been forged.

If you can't afford to fly your squad to Turkey or the equivalent, team-building weekends can be just as good, providing you with the opportunity to bond with your players, and to remind them that cricket is supposed to be fun.

10. Publicity agent and media liaison officer

The professional coach's relationship with the media is a complex – and not entirely comfortable – one. There's an old adage in journalism: if it bleeds, it leads. Bad news sells, and in countries that are passionate about their sport, a team's problems or failures can sell newspapers far more effectively than their successes. Thus journalists and media people often look for a flaw in the coach or team where none exists, or try to rile the coach into saying something newsworthy. Finding that their statements have been published out of context, whether deliberately or because of misunderstandings, is a problem most high-profile coaches will face at some stage. They will also have to cope with the resulting fallout.

Bob Woolmer experienced this first-hand when Shane Warne was dominating South African batsman Daryl Cullinan: 'The Australian and South African media asked me whether Cullinan had a "psychological problem" with the leg-spinner. I

Journalists sometimes try to rile the coach into saying something newsworthy. Finding that their statements have been published out of context is a problem most high-profile coaches will face at some stage – as well as the resulting fallout.

said, "He may, but if he does, then it's our job to put it right." The next day the headlines were ten inches tall: "Woolmer says Cullinan has psychological problems playing Warne!" Obviously Daryll was incensed – which didn't help our relationship as player and coach.'

This kind of treatment causes many coaches and players to become taciturn or cautious in their statements. The media immediately latches on to this and touts it as evidence of a conspiracy or an unpleasant personality. A good example of this in recent times was the treatment meted out to England captain Michael Atherton, an extremely intelligent, affable and well-spoken man – not to mention a brave and tenacious batsman. Nevertheless, his reluctance to gush to the press earned him the nickname 'Captain Grumpy'. Any grimace he made was plastered all over the tabloids as proof that he was a miserable wet blanket, and when he lost his patience at press conferences – as anyone would, given the sustained level of hostility the media directed at him – he was declared a graceless boor, a bad ambassador for Britain, and no asset to English cricket. A no-win situation, and one he was probably relieved to escape when he relinquished the captaincy.

So as an elite coach, you're not only expected to be a friendly face, delighted to provide the press with cheerleader sound-bytes at every turn; you are also expected to communicate your policies, methods and goals in an eloquent and accessible way to the country in general. But this can go too far. 'When I coached South Africa,' Bob Woolmer warned, 'Dr Ali Bacher was very keen that I be an open and approachable coach who would keep the world informed about what we were trying to do. In many ways this was the ideal, but it also became a burden: the more I gave, the more the press wanted. Soon I found I was neglecting the team in favour of being a spin doctor, publicist and cricketing missionary.'

The best thing a coach can do is to remember that the media is an industry, one that needs copy more than it needs accuracy, truth or objectivity. And as any spin doctor – or experienced cricketer – will tell you: today's news is tomorrow's wrapping for fish and chips. The public can have an extremely short memory. Just ride out any storms, and keep looking forward.

11. Disciplinarian

Cricket demands discipline if it is to be played well. This means a disciplined technique and physique, but also a disciplined mind: natural talent and flair all too often come to nothing when combined with a poor attitude or a refusal to conform to certain basic social norms. It is your job as coach to mark the boundaries of what is acceptable behaviour and what is not. Indeed, at lower levels, this is one of your primary jobs. You must do it sensitively and without prejudice – lead by example, using a carrot-and-stick approach rather than traditional top-down stand-and-bellow discipline. At higher levels of the game, players should be self-disciplined, but of course there will always be those who test you and who push the limits of what is acceptable. In these cases, the influence of their peers should be enough to set them straight – in a one-on-one battle with a player you are likely to come off second-best, because he may see himself as indispensable, while you are merely the 'hired help'.

Instill respect in your squad: they should respect you, the team and the game in general. If this means cracking the whip and resorting to restrictions such as curfews, so be it. Hopefully, you're on good terms with your team, but don't forget that you're their coach first and their friend second. Steve Waugh said it best: 'I believe that as a coach, if you are doing your job correctly, you can't possibly be liked by everyone. You must make the difficult calls to get your team to where you want them to get to.'

A PRACTICAL SUMMARY

The longer you coach, the more clearly you will understand these roles, and the more easily you will recognize the practical behaviours that are required by each. Remember, common sense, clarity of thought and speech, and sensitivity will see you straight in most cases. However, if you are still uncertain about how to act in front of your team, or what your primary focus should be, use the following as a rough guide:

- Try not to show anxiety when the side is batting or fielding.
- Try not to overstate your views – especially negative or despairing ones – in front of the twelfth man and others in the dressing room; it will undermine players' confidence if it gets back to them that you make sharp comments about their performance while they are in the field.
- Try to refrain from visible shows of negative emotion (shaking your head or tut-tutting); however, showing positive emotion (applauding, cheering milestones, etc.) will be picked up and appreciated by the players.
- Try to focus the team's energies on the job at hand.
- Always be supportive of the team's efforts.
- Communicate your thoughts through the captain wherever possible.
- If you have a point to make, make it with the individual concerned. Do not discuss an individual problem in front of the team.
- Approach a problem with reason and discussion (it may not always end like this!).
- Attempt to create a balanced atmosphere of calm and relaxation in the dressing room – there will already be plenty of tension, so aim to counterbalance this.

Above all, don't allow any discipline or internal problems to get into the media: the whole thing will instantly turn into a circus, and the issue at hand will spiral out of control.

THE INEXACT SCIENCE OF COACHING

Cricket prides itself on being a 'school of hard knocks'. Veterans of past generations take great glee in sharing war stories and explaining how rough they had it, how nobody held their hand or showed them the ropes. They were told to shape up or ship out, to stay out of the kitchen if they couldn't stand the heat, and all the other macho clichés favoured by ageing sportsmen.

This tradition stems largely from English cultural norms of the late nineteenth and early twentieth centuries, in which toughness, duty, discipline, resilience and stoicism were prized, and experimentation and emotion were generally suppressed. The national character of keeping a 'stiff upper lip' and 'taking it on the chin' saw the English nation through some grim times, but it also led to the unthinking perpetuation of certain practices long after they might otherwise have been adapted or discarded. Traditional cricket coaching methods are a good example of this: all too often, players were told to do X and Y, and no deviation from those norms was tolerated. Challenging the orthodoxies of the day would be seen as signs of weakness or at least eccentricity, and so the majority found it easier to toe the line and say nothing. Of course older and more successful players, who, in the eyes of the patriarchal culture, had earned the right to speak their mind, could experiment as much as they wanted – W.G. Grace's outrageous disregard for many of cricket's Laws is a case in point – but youngsters were expected to be seen and not heard, and to respect their elders and betters. Querying their instructions was considered insolent.

This school of thought survived almost intact for most of the twentieth century, preserved by particularly Anglophile cricket cultures in South Africa and, to a certain extent, Australia and New Zealand. But the evaporation of the old English order and its way of life has coincided with the demise of that autocratic coaching system. Today's coach can no longer bark orders or haul players over the coals for deviating from the manual. Discipline and respect are still essential, but today they need to be earned, not demanded and enforced by yelling.

The demise of rigidly prescriptive coaching has allowed the development of 'discovery learning' (discussed in more depth later on pp. 510–13), a method of getting players to find which techniques suit them best – and that there may be more than one 'right' way of playing.

'I believe that as a coach, if you are doing your job correctly, you can't possibly be liked by everyone. You must make the difficult calls to get your team to where you want them to get to.'
– Steve Waugh

As a coach, always remember: the game is a science, but not an exact science.

However, discrediting the autocratic methods mentioned above, and the flourishing of a teaching style more focused on the player than the manual, shouldn't be confused with a lack of respect for the traditions and technical constants of the game.

An article that criticized many of the traditional coaching and batting drills used by modern coaches as being biomechanically incorrect, and therefore dangerous or potentially destructive, went too far for Bob Woolmer's liking: 'While I accept that science has plenty to teach us, one cannot disregard methods that have been successful for the last 60 years: surely what was good enough for Bradman, Sobers, Richards (Viv and Barry!), Hadlee and Warne, can benefit modern players as well.'

And it is here that the art and science of coaching part ways just a little. Sports science research continually strives to produce the perfect player, but an experienced coach might suggest that there is no such thing as a perfect cricketer – and there never will be. Technique can indeed be perfected, and certainly the coach must treat that as his Holy Grail, but a strictly scientific approach – in which a perfect technique is grafted onto a suitably talented player – would have robbed the game of some of its greatest stars, technically unorthodox players like Graeme Pollock (who didn't get to the pitch of the ball), Lance Klusener and Muttiah Muralitharan.

Therefore, as a coach, always remember: the game is indeed a science, but not an exact science.

ACTIVE AND PASSIVE COACHING

The days of the old-fashioned 'stand behind the nets and holler' coach are over. Whether his methods are active or more passive, the modern coach is far more involved than the retired English professionals of past generations who dispensed wisdom and advice while having a smoke on a nearby bench.

The active coach will run nets, throw well over half a million throw-downs in his career, work with the bowling machine, and take an active part in fielding drills. The passive coach – who is no less effective – will generally take on a more managerial role, but also provide tactical and technical input for the players.

Bob Woolmer warned against being too active a coach: 'Players are quick to take advantage! I remember having batsmen queuing up in a net, waiting their turn to get throw-downs from me. Soon my arm felt as if it was falling off, and I had to call a halt. That day taught me that my limit was three players a day; I made the rest of the batsmen pair off and throw to each other.'

PHILOSOPHIES OF COACHING

What do people mean when they talk about their 'personal philosophy'? While academically trained philosophers might take exception to the phrase being used so loosely, the majority of those who use this phrase would concur that a personal philosophy is a set of beliefs worked out and adopted over time. Sometimes it can be a moral or practical code we apply to certain situations. Sometimes it is simply our set of opinions; but of course the word 'philosophy' sounds considerably more impressive and authoritative than 'opinion'!

However, most personal philosophies have one thing in common: they are vague and undefined. Ask most people to write down, in point form, everything that they believe in or live by, and they'll soon start running dry. Ask them to defend their opinions logically, and they'll start stumbling within seconds, reverting to emotion and gut feel: 'I don't know why I think X is wrong – I just know it is!'

Bob Woolmer freely admitted that for years, he fell into this category: 'I had a philosophy, but couldn't define it – or even declare with any certainty that it was a philosophy at all. It took a long time for that diffuse collection of ideas to come together: I recognize that my philosophy of coaching forms a compact bundle of insights, a unit of ideas that I can add to or subtract from as my outlook on the game, and the game itself, changes. Some ideas will no longer work; and others will work eternally.'

A set of beliefs does not come from nowhere. Perhaps with the exception of a few spectacularly gifted Greek philosophers, German astronomers and English physicists, we are all a product of our emotional and intellectual influences, as a lifetime of experiences slowly compound and solidify into a view on the world that we like to pretend is 'ours'. While cricket has produced a handful of geniuses – the likes of Bradman, Sobers, and Warne come immediately to mind – these gigantic strides forward are almost always seen on the field of play itself. To the best of our knowledge, none of cricket's advances has ever come in a flash of brilliance to a coach or tactician sitting in the dressing room or mulling over a game through a sleepless night. The philosophies of cricket are cumulative, each building on months and years and decades and indeed centuries of trial and error, punctuated by the aforementioned leaps – courtesy of once-in-a-generation superstars.

This is where the role of the coach as historian and custodian of the game becomes so important. Bob Simpson, Mike Brearley and Richie Benaud are among those who have written specifically about coaching philosophies, gathering the wisdom of others wherever they found it useful and applicable. Some have more formally studied what systems might work for the cricket coach. Bob Woolmer was particularly impressed by the practical philosophy of coaching developed by

Michael Fordham, based on the different learning preferences of individuals. Bob; who always insisted that it was both a duty and a privilege to pass on the insights he had received from others, stated, 'My philosophy of coaching was formed by two other philosophies I discovered and adopted, which in turn were no doubt the result of extensive reading and experience. These are the "Six S's for Success", introduced to me by the late Mel Siff of Pretoria University; and the "Core Covenant", developed by Pat Riley, who coached the LA Lakers basketball team for many seasons. His book, *The Winner Within*, should be compulsory reading for every coach. Both systems put into words and pictures the type of education young players need for their futures; and no small part of this education should be reminding young players that the knowledge they are absorbing was gleaned the hard way by cricketers of past generations, and that they have the opportunity to gain those insights without pain.'

THE SIX S'S FOR SUCCESS

This system represents a basic method for a coach and player to work in harmony. The points it outlines are essential for all sports, not just cricket, and provide a sound framework in which both coach and player can get to grips with the crucial aspects of the sport.

1. Skill (a prerequisite for any game)

Cricket is the most technical of sports, but should be taught in a way that is not complicated. As a coach, therefore, you will need to understand technique at its most basic levels in order to make it uncomplicated. Likewise, a player will be more confident if he knows his own game better.

2. Speed

This includes speedy physical reactions, running between the wickets, getting to the ball in the outfield and speed of thought (reacting quickly to situations). And speed is of course the vital ingredient for fast bowlers. Not being physically quick should not prevent people from playing cricket, but players should always try to improve their speed.

3. Strength

Power in shot-making is gained through timing; but stronger players will be able to hit the ball harder and further. Strength is also vital for bowlers, in preventing injury, enabling them to bowl more quickly, and to do so for longer spells. Fielders who dive and throw themselves around need to be strong in order to escape injury and improve recovery time. Mental strength is also essential to both bowlers and batters:

every single name in the top ten of the game's run-scorers and wicket-takers belongs to a man with legendary mental toughness.

4. Stamina

Of all ball sports, perhaps only a four-hour game of gridiron football can rival cricket in terms of the demands it places on players' stamina, and even that sport has passed the stamina buck by employing two teams, one on offence and another on defence. Whether it is bowling 25 overs a day on two consecutive days, or batting for four hours, or simply fielding for six hours a day, cricket can wring a player dry. While bowling is an obviously exhausting activity, batting can be no less draining: given that most Test batsmen will face three balls an over, and that an over lasts around four minutes, he is likely to score just over 22 runs an hour. In other words, an 'average' century (if a Test hundred can ever be called average) takes four and a half hours to compile. When Michael Atherton famously saw off the South African attack to force a draw at the Wanderers in 1995, he batted for just under eleven hours, one of the longest Test innings ever. Until relatively recently, Tests were separated by two or three weeks, and usually included a rest day; but in the crowded modern schedule it is not unusual to see a Test start three or four days after the previous one has finished.

5. Suppleness

The more supple a player's body, the fewer injuries he will suffer. Never underestimate stretching, not just before games, but during and after as well. But physical suppleness is only half the picture: mental suppleness should be encouraged as strongly. As a coach, try to develop an attitude that says, 'I want to learn. I will listen and try out everything to see if it works.' This will rub off on your players. Remember, the player who clings too tightly to what he feels comfortable with will suffer in the long run.

6. Spirit

The most important 'S' of them all. Cricket is a team game, but heroes inevitably rise out from the group, whether they are Test stars stroking double-centuries, or nine-year-old batters developing a reputation for crafting solid scores of 30-ish. But individual heroics are impossible without a group effort: the batsman who scores 250 needs at least two of his teammates to dig in at the other end; and the bowler who takes 500 wickets in a Test career needed a safe pair of hands under at least 250 of those balls. Support from teammates, coaches and friends is all-important for player development. Also, don't wait for team spirit to materialize, either as a coach or a player: it is *you* who creates spirit, not anyone else.

THE CYCLE OF SUCCESS

Pat Riley, one of the most influential coaches in America, made his mark coaching that nation's most fabled pro basketball teams. In his book, *The Winner Within: A Life Plan for Team Players*, even his chapter headings are illuminating, and below we have adapted some of those specifically for cricketers.

Every coach can benefit from Riley's wisdom, and every coach will have observed similar patterns in the ebb and flow of their own teams. Bob Woolmer summarized his approach to Riley's philosophy with the diagram below to reflect the various stages of the cycle he observed as a coach.

Beginnings

This is when a team 'gels' and achieves success for the first time. It all seems so easy in the euphoria of the moment; tributes pour in, along with attention and flattery. It's tempting to assume you can just go out and do it again on the basis of sheer talent….

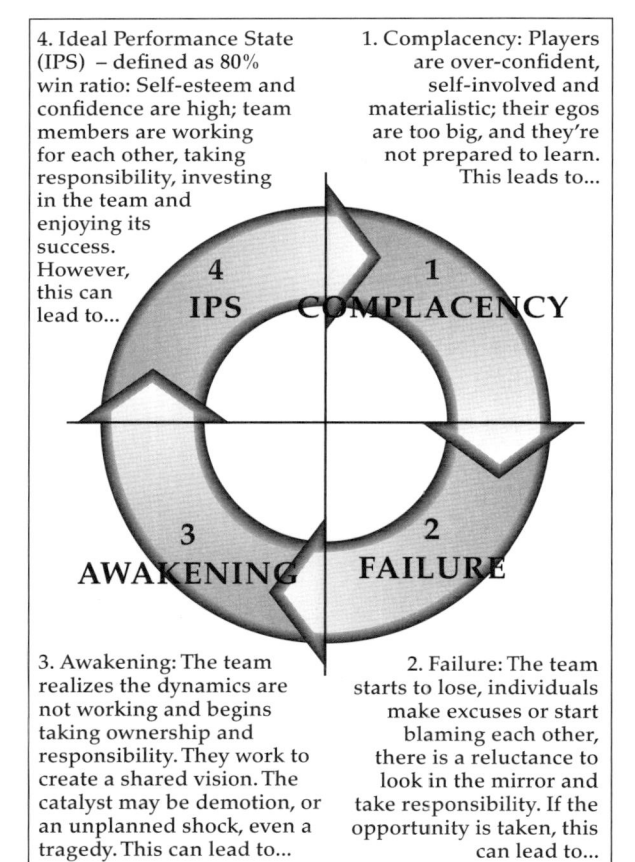

4. Ideal Performance State (IPS) – defined as 80% win ratio: Self-esteem and confidence are high; team members are working for each other, taking responsibility, investing in the team and enjoying its success. However, this can lead to...

1. Complacency: Players are over-confident, self-involved and materialistic; their egos are too big, and they're not prepared to learn. This leads to…

3. Awakening: The team realizes the dynamics are not working and begins taking ownership and responsibility. They work to create a shared vision. The catalyst may be demotion, or an unplanned shock, even a tragedy. This can lead to…

2. Failure: The team starts to lose, individuals make excuses or start blaming each other, there is a reluctance to look in the mirror and take responsibility. If the opportunity is taken, this can lead to…

Complacency

We've seen it so often: winning can be a positive force, but also a negative one. Success can lead to complacency, and a good score is often followed by a sub-standard performance. In the case of amateur golfers, a birdie is often followed by a double bogey. In cricket, the stage of complacency is often revealed when the team coasts, feeling that they can leave the hard work to certain individuals. At the same time, individual players become arrogant or resentful of the pressure on them. The team begins losing, but refuses to take collective or individual responsibility.

It is vital that a coach leads his team away from complacency, insisting they focus on the job in hand at the same levels of intensity in every game they play. Australia's success can be attributed at least in part to the team almost never falling into the trap of complacency.

Choking

These are those frustrating moments when a team has the talent and opportunity to succeed – and yet at the last minute, they apparently fold under the pressure. Among Bob Woolmer's challenges during his tenure as South Africa's coach was the pressure of this label.

'I had to deal with the media tagging us as "chokers". It started in Sharjah just after the 1996 World Cup, where we had lost to the West Indies in the quarter-final. Tony Greig of Channel 9 in Australia interviewed me and suggested we had choked. I was amazed, but from then on, the media latched onto Greig's throwaway line whenever we failed to win a final. It was a tactic that Steve Waugh used every time Australia played South Africa. Eventually I began wondering if the team had come to believe the myth! The truth was that we made more finals than most sides won games. Of course, this fact was always ignored, and so the team became known as a team of chokers.

'It was only much later that I realized that choking or losing important games happened to a team that was making its mark, as Riley points out in his book. Unfortunately the team and I had parted before I came to this conclusion. But our quarter-final defeat against the West Indies, our loss to Australia in the Carlton & United Series finals in 1997, the loss to India in the Titan Cup 1996, and the tied World Cup semi-final in 1999 were the four games (out of many) that got us the tag. At one stage we had an 80% win ratio – but we were still called chokers. It was hard to accept, but it was part of the team growing together. Australia's ability to pull games out of the fire with the right blend of experience and youth also showed me that the South African team of that era was still improving. Another lesson the choking label brought home to me was that coaches need time with their teams to work through the various stages – but as we know, sports coaches are bustled out after defeat so fast their heads must spin – look at what is happening on the world soccer stage.'

Disasters

These are the unforeseen disasters beyond our control. On the way to success, one of the most frustrating things a coach is likely to face is a major injury to his most influential player. Ultimately, it is not the injury that becomes the problem, but how the team deals with it. A strong, committed team will rally around the less experienced replacement, while taking on extra responsibilities. Bob Woolmer remembered: 'Allan Donald broke down with a foot injury in Calcutta in 1996. I asked Lance Klusener, Brian McMillan and the other bowlers to come to the party, and Klusener in particular rose to the challenge by taking eight wickets, while McMillan made the vital breakthrough. The result was a great and morale-boosting victory for the team.' Thunderbolts are inevitable, as Riley points out. They can only be weathered if the core of the team is stable, and if every member is prepared to pitch in and make the extra effort.

Creating team ethics

In cricket – and in life – this is when the team pledges to a covenant to which every single member of the squad is committed. Bob Woolmer explained: 'This is most

> *'If you are not for yourself, who will be for you? If you are only for yourself, what are you? If not now, when?'*
>
> *– Mike Stakol*

effective when it starts with the natural leaders in the team, people whom others will want to follow. At this stage, the following questions, passed on to me by a friend, Mike Stakol, are useful for the team to contemplate: "If you are not for yourself, who will be for you? If you are only for yourself, what are you? If not now, when?" A good coach has to be able to develop the strategies necessary to improve individual players, while at the same time creating a team ethic that will hold all his influential players together. Occasionally the player will have to go if he cannot adapt, or the coach or the captain cannot find the right path for him. The right attitude is critical.'

Getting back on track

This is self-explanatory: a team apparently in the doldrums will suddenly be galvanized into action. Sometimes this is triggered by an external event; sometimes it is a moment of collective realization by the team. Bob Woolmer had his own take on the phenomenon: 'Some people might call it fate; others say that you make your own luck. But every now and again something happens that will have a profound effect on a team. In 2002, Warwickshire received a thunderbolt when one of their best players, Mark Wagh, suffered a knee injury that would keep him out of the team for three months at least. As a result, a young second-team player, Jim Troughton, was given an opportunity to play first-team cricket. Within a year, he had been selected for the English Academy team and then for England. His whole life changed. But the most significant effect was that on the other members of the squad. Suddenly, the team could see that undreamt-of success was possible; that when a chance is given and taken, it was possible to make the most of it. The effect on the young players around him was staggering and led to an improved team performance. The inspiration for success was provided by that first thunderbolt. It led to a breakthrough that affected team performance positively.

'Strange as it may seem, inspiration can come from a tragedy within the team, with the members striving harder than ever. For example, the Surrey County cricket club knuckled down and achieved astonishing success the year following the untimely death of one of their bright young stars, Ben Hollioake. They were already a good side; but suddenly they found that little extra to make them even more powerful.'

Ideal Performance State

Here the sense of excellence runs much deeper than success; it is the process whereby a team overtly sets out to be the very best at that level, to become the acknowledged overall champions. The West Indies did this during the 1970s; Australia has done it for over a decade. The sum of the team is greater than the total of the parts; there is a fantastic work ethic, and everything seems to be running smoothly. But beware that this does not lead back to complacency!

COACHING: POWER DYNAMICS AND ADMINISTRATION

Your age as a coach will largely inform your methods. If you're an energetic 30-year-old coaching little boys, you'll no doubt be demonstrating run-ups, throwing balls, leading the pack around the field on fitness jogs, and so on. If you're a 60-year-old veteran whose knees have done a few hundred shuttle-runs too many, and whose fingers have been dislocated once too often, you're likely to be less fond of demonstration, and more interested in communication, analysis and investigation, with a particular fondness for video analysis – the advent of which has given a new lease of life to the older coach!

While energy and a willingness to muck in with the squad are admirable, the coach must be appointed first and foremost according to his ability and talent in identifying and correcting problems. (Those appointing him are, after all, appointing a coach and not a cheerleader.) And the reality of the coaching profession is that quality comes with experience, and experience usually comes with age. This is not to say that 30-year-olds can't make excellent coaches; but it is almost certain that they'll find themselves stumped at some stage on some technical or strategic matter, simply because they haven't encountered that particular problem before, or haven't encountered it often enough before to test whether or not their diagnoses and solutions are effective.

But cricket is a youngster's game, and no team likes to be coached by an old codger who sits in the shade peering at a laptop. A coach must be fit and strong enough to put in the hard yards with his squad, throwing hundreds of deliveries or feeding players dozens of catches. This is why the ideal mix for an international side – or a lower-level team, if it has the financial resources – is a combination of wisdom and youth, perhaps a senior coach backed up by an assistant, or else a manager backed up by a younger coach. (We stress that this is the ideal – many schools or clubs in poorer areas all around the globe have to take what they can get where coaches are concerned. As we've mentioned above, many enthusiastic and hard-working coaches in South Africa's townships, for instance, are women who have never once played the game.)

This balance also depends on the age and experience of the captain, and his influence within the team. If the captain has been allowed the time and authority to stamp his personality and vision on his team, then the coach must consider himself very much a right-hand man. This relationship, and the positions of coach and captain, should be carefully defined and thrashed out, so that both know their specific roles, and are comfortable with allowing each other into those grey areas where the territory is less clearly defined.

The reality of the coaching profession is that quality comes with experience, and experience usually comes with age.

Remember, you are not there to captain the team. Even at under-10 level, you are there to advise, not instruct. However role-identification remains one of the most difficult aspects to get right, and you're always bound to step on someone's toes. Rely on common sense, diplomacy, and above all, communication. The worst thing you can do is become territorial and touchy.

To help you and the captain to get along smoothly, and to develop confidence in each other's capabilities, try sticking to the following two basic guidelines:

- The captain runs the show on the field. No arguments!
- The coach prepares the players, and organizes that preparation. No arguments!

However, even here you should both be open to suggestions. For instance, the captain may want to work on a specific drill, and you'll need to prepare that drill accordingly, or explain why it is important to practise what you had planned. Once again, clear and open communication is the key, without ego or hostility.

THE FOUR LEGS OF THE TABLE

Coach and captain form only half of the leadership of any modern international team: the head of the selectors and Chief Executive Officer are also inextricably linked to the morale and success of the group. Bob Woolmer used the analogy of a table, standing squarely on four legs; coach, captain, the head of the selectors and CEO all providing a firm foundation for the team. The more solid the table legs, the more stable the team.

But table legs aren't only solid; they need to be of equal length. If one leg is longer or shorter, the table will rock. Ideally then, the four key role players in the team's administration should work together as equals. Of course, they don't always have to agree. In fact, healthy – often heated – debate and constructive criticism from all four corners is important for a team to progress. Always remember that a happy team, free of politicking, self-interest and hierarchies, is a successful team. Take advantage of the growing number of seminars and conferences that teach the principles of good management, and learn how to stamp out divisive elements as soon as they emerge, or else prevent them from developing in the first place.

If this 'table' structure is so successful, why aren't there more great teams, with stable squads and management teams, dominating at first-class or international level? The answer to this lies in human nature. A table with four equal legs is a fine image and ideal, but the difference between theory and practice is all too often exposed by human frailty and insecurity. Someone holding one of the key management positions can become greedy, egotistical, or even bored. Perhaps he fears for the security of his position, or perhaps he is obeying political masters, trying to curry favour with them to advance his own future career. If one of the legs begins to give way or changes its length, the table grows unsteady or tilts, and the team starts to slide off.

This was clearly illustrated during South Africa's tour of Australia in 2001/02, when the South African government imposed a political agenda on the selection of the team, demanding a larger representation of black players. The quota system it enforced may well have been justified, and its desired outcome was certainly admirable, but from that moment onwards it was clear to anyone close to the team (which, of course, the politicians weren't, being thousands of miles away) that the rug had been pulled out from under every player. None of them had any direction, or even any idea what the next day would bring. Not even the new racially-based selection policy provided any stability, since it seemed so vaguely defined and poorly communicated: even as it was being implemented, politicians back home denied that it was foregrounding race over talent. Almost overnight the winning culture of what was the second best team in the world disappeared, to be replaced with a suspicious, nervous outlook and anxiety about the future – which translated into miserable performances on the field. Despite its formidable personnel, South Africa had turned into a team of losers.

WHEN LESS IS MORE

While four key administrative figures have proved a winning combination for most, many teams at club level shy away from having too many leaders, perhaps worrying that 'too many cooks spoil the broth'. Certainly at school level, players often get away with murder by blaming conflicting signals from various coaching figures: ask a batter why he is moving his feet in a particular way, and he might answer that Ms Davids told him X in primary school, Mr Brown told him Y in high school, and Mr Khan told him Z during the summer holiday training camp. Now the poor little chap is completely confused and can't be blamed for his cheap dismissal!

On the one hand, this is a classic case of a child making excuses and refusing to take responsibility; but on the other it is also the result of coaches not explaining their role fully enough. The coach is there to provide information. What the player does with that information is his own business; and the child who claims he has been confused by too much coaching is failing to organize his knowledge effectively. But it's highly likely that he hasn't been given a choice in the matter: too often coaches take a dogmatic view, implying that their knowledge is definitive. No wonder then that players become confused when presented with three quite different coaching philosophies, with each coach insisting that theirs is the only truth. Both coaches and players must be aware that coaching is a buffet of ideas. Players should help themselves to ideas and techniques, and leave behind whatever is not appropriate to

Both coaches and players must be aware that coaching is a buffet of ideas. Players should help themselves to ideas and techniques, and leave behind whatever is not appropriate to their game.

their game. Don't force-feed players, but equally, don't let them get away with only picking up the 'sweets', the easy, fun aspects of the game.

In teams who haven't worked out their relationships with the coach, more than one coach can contribute to a 'cooks spoiling the broth' mindset; but in more settled or mature teams, a coaching entourage can be a valuable asset, to both coach and players. (Unfortunately cricket is still comparatively poor in comparison to Rugby Union, football, and all American sporting codes; therefore only the most wealthy teams will be able to consider an entourage. This makes the doubling-up of positions vital; for instance, physiotherapists can find themselves helping with throw-downs in the nets!) However, coaches need to remember that assistants and entourages are a luxury, rather than a basic requirement. You should be able to handle all aspects of the game yourself; to demand a bowling or batting or fielding coach is absurd.

Having said that, Bob Woolmer's experience taught him that one coach simply cannot give all fifteen or sixteen players on a tour the one-on-one time they need, which is why it can be a very good long-term strategic move to employ a younger assistant: 'This not only provides the coach with invaluable help; it also trains the assistant, and is an investment in the team's future, as well as the future of the game as a whole.'

There are other steps you can take to invest in the future that will not involve an expansion of coaching staff. For instance, nurture a vice-captain, as well as a senior player and a junior player who show the potential to be leaders. Remember that leaders don't necessarily have to become captains, and can sometimes remain far more valuable to a team without the burdens of formal leadership. Jacques Kallis is a superb example of a natural leader in the South African team. Ray Jennings (the team's coach at the time) recognized this in 2005 when he tasked Kallis with being a mentor to the team's youngsters. Kallis obliged, showing himself eager to share his experience and knowledge.

MANAGING THE SQUAD

The ideal situation for any coach managing a squad of fifteen players is when he knows that any eleven he selects will be the best possible team for the day. But even at international level, this is not always a likely scenario, and as you coach at lower levels, it becomes increasingly tricky to manage your squad.

The chief criticism you'll face (although it's seldom explicit, but rather whispered by disgruntled players, teachers and often parents) is that you haven't selected the best eleven. Often this criticism is entirely true, but not for the reasons the critics think: at lower levels, there are often only seven or eight useful players you can choose, and for the rest, you're simply making up the numbers, selecting a team that is far from textbook. Naturally, every individual thinks he should be playing – this isn't necessarily ego, but confidence and a desire to perform – but in general, the more experienced player will deal with being left out. If he's a fighter with a good temperament and steady personality, he'll just work harder to get back into the team.

In junior cricket, the hostility over selection takes on a slightly more worrying aspect: not only are you dealing with hugely ambitious or insensitive parents, but you're also handling an extremely impressionable child with a fragile ego. An eight-year-old doesn't understand the principle of 'horses for courses' or the need for squad rotation. All he knows is that he hasn't made the team, and from this omission he can all too easily conclude that he is a rotten cricketer, a bad pupil, and a waste of everybody's time – especially if he has perfectionist parents or gifted older siblings.

Bob Woolmer dealt with this tricky situation by insisting that at the most junior levels, the most important aspect of practising and playing cricket is not technique, winning or losing, but fun and inclusiveness: 'If you've got a squad of twelve, all twelve must play, getting a chance to bat and bowl.' If necessary, get them playing rounders, a less equipment-intensive game in which everyone gets to bat.

DROPPING PLAYERS

One of the least enviable of the coach's jobs is dropping players from the team. And at some stage, every coach will be confronted by a player who believes he is being victimized. When this happens, you need to tell him two things:

- That you're not victimizing him – you don't do favourites.
- The reason he's been dropped. Be frank. If he's not good enough to stay in the team, or not fit enough, or is considered a back-up player, then tell him so.

Dropping players is difficult for any coach, but in the end you want to be left with fifteen people in your squad who have the right credentials and attitude. Those players who deal best with being dropped can often provide an extraordinary amount of spirit and professionalism in a squad. Australia's Andy Bichel would sit out game after game, finally get a cap, bowl beautifully, and then be dropped again to sit out another Test- or one-day series. And yet he never complained, never let his shoulders drop, and never let his stop-start career affect his performance when he finally did play. Any team with a player like Bichel in the squad, whether on or off the field, will be tough, professional and inspired.

Bob Woolmer was no stranger to the delicate problem of dropping players: 'When South Africa's selectors dropped Daryll Cullinan because he wasn't making enough runs, they asked me to convey the bad news to him. I told him privately and he stormed out of the room because he didn't agree. When he came back, he started reciting his statistics for me, defending himself with his very impressive past record. But the reality was that Daryll's form had taken a dip, and he just needed a break.' Gary Kirsten, a doughty opening bat for years for South Africa and now a provincial coach, is firm on this fact: even the most experienced and successful players need a break from time to time.

The example of Cullinan is important for another reason: sometimes you just have to drop a player not only for his own sake, but for the sake of the entire side. By the time South Africa toured Australia in 1997, it had become popularly accepted that Cullinan struggled when facing Shane Warne's bowling. Whether Cullinan's relatively poor performances against Warne were because of a psychological problem, a technical problem, a temporary dip in form, or simply the immense pressure fuelled by the media, is still open to discussion; but whatever it was, the results were disastrous. When he walked out to bat at Melbourne in the second innings of the first Test, South Africa were fighting to make up a big deficit, but were looking relatively relaxed at 88 for 2.

As Cullinan set foot on the edge of the field, the mood changed. The Australians all headed for the wicket, forming a wedge-shaped arrow as they rushed to sledge him, hurling verbal abuse his way. They weren't alone: 80 000 people in the stands were dishing it out too. For the next 25 minutes, Australia's cricket was intensely aggressive: having been hot and bothered, and effectively out of the game for part of that session, they were suddenly all over the South African batsmen.

No player can survive in that kind of environment, and not only was Cullinan crumbling under the pressure, the poor bloke at the other end suddenly found himself in an entirely different Test match! Peter Pollock, the chair of the selectors at the time, told Woolmer very simply: 'We can't play him again.' Clearly the Australians found Cullinan's presence on the field enraging – it was like a red rag to a bull. By removing the red rag, the bull was less aggressive: a simple tactical decision.

PRACTICAL COACHING

THE COACH'S TOOLBOX

When he discussed the issue of practical coaching, and the skills the modern coach would need, Bob Woolmer spoke of the coach's 'toolbox'. Coaching is a hands-on activity, much like fine-tuning an engine or fixing a particularly tricky length of plumbing: as we have mentioned, the days of the old pro standing behind a net and calling 'Well bowled, youngster!' are well and truly over. A toolbox seems the ideal image for you to take forward as you develop as a coach: a large collection of different, often extremely specialized tools or techniques, each perfectly adapted to address its own specific problem on the cricket field.

Many of your most basic tools seem too simple to be effective. In the age of video technology, where virtual reality helmets seem just a season or two away, it is easy to overlook tools, mistaking them as being obsolete or ineffective because they don't feature high-tech gadgetry. However, never forget that in cricket, the basics rarely change; and the same applies to coaching. For example, some of the methods described in Chapter 3 on batting are used right up to international level. These include:

- **Slowing down the lesson you are giving or skill you are demonstrating and honing.** Especially with younger players, it is easy to forget that even information you regard as extremely obvious might be new to your players. For instance, you know what you mean by 'getting your foot to the pitch of the ball', but your batters might need it explained to them in more detail. Don't rely on jargon or familiar phrases: take some care, and some time, and make sure they understand what you are trying to convey.

- **Hitting a stationary object.** In batting, this could mean hitting a stationary ball (on a particular length, to break down the batter's technique in a particular shot, or on a batting tee); while in bowling this could be as simple (or difficult!) as landing the ball on a marked area on the pitch or hitting a single stump.

- **Rolling the ball, slowly.** The essential stage between the stationary ball and the flying ball: skip it at your peril.

MIRROR MIRROR ON THE WALL...

...Who has the fairest forward defensive of them all? Perhaps the most low-tech of all, the humble mirror can be extremely useful, whether you are showing a player himself and explaining what he's seeing, or whether you've given him some homework and he's in his bedroom at home. Indeed, if neither coach nor players have access to video technology (see opposite), the mirror can be a splendid substitute at any level: Alan Knott was a skilled batter who used to perfect aspects of his technique in front of a full-length mirror.

- **Throwing underarm.** Again, part of building up towards match pace and match-condition reflexes. Throwing underarm produces an unrealistic trajectory for the batter, but it begins to accustom eyes, hands, and most importantly, feet, to dealing with an onrushing ball.

- **Throwing overarm.** A more realistic pace and trajectory: if you don't have a bowling machine, prepare to go home with a sore shoulder!

Once you have come to grips with these simple but vital skills, and if you have enough resources, you can graduate to two of the most essential tools in modern cricket: the bowling machine, and video analysis.

BOWLING MACHINES

Bowling machines are splendid toys for many coaches, but the primary use of this machine is repetition, enabling the player to groove the same shot over and over until it becomes second nature. Remember, it takes roughly 10 000 repetitions before an action or skill penetrates the subconscious – and your throwing arm just doesn't have that kind of life span.

Never use a bowling machine as a mechanical bowler, varying line and length with every ball: this does nothing to improve technique, and a ball accidentally aimed a fraction short can send your star batsman to hospital.

The greatest asset of the bowling machine is not that it can bowl pace and swing (and rudimentary spin), but that it can bowl hundreds of balls per session. Where once coaches ruined their arms providing 50 or 100 throw-downs for one player, today three or four batsmen can each face 600 balls, practising individual shots hundreds of times over. This conditioning is invaluable, and enables batsmen to react instinctively in match conditions.

It takes roughly 10 000 repetitions before an action or skill penetrates the subconscious.

Those coaches and clubs wanting to invest in a bowling machine should first take stock of their nets: uneven or rutted pitches can be dangerous when facing pace, and netting must be intact, especially if batsmen are practising leaving the ball – there is nothing more dispiriting than trudging off across a field or rooting in a hedge looking for balls that have shot through the back netting. The ideal bowling machine net should:

- have a true surface with even bounce
- allow balls to return to the machine (or at least the person feeding it) automatically
- ideally include an automatic feeder system, so that batsmen can practise alone and free up the coach to help other players.

If your club can afford it, it might be worth investing in the second two features listed above: gutters or a slope collecting balls and rolling them back towards the feeder can entirely remove the slog and back-ache of collecting balls.

VIDEO ANALYSIS

David Leadbetter's dictum 'In golf, there was coaching BV and AV' (before video and after video) applies equally to cricket.

The use of digital video, computers and visual aids has supplemented the teaching methods of past decades. Cricket now has the benefit of many advanced computerized analytical systems that aid and enhance coaching, if used properly. Systems such as the Silicone coach and the Quintic system are capable of showing in fine detail where one can make technical adjustments and assist in fine-tuning top-class players. These programmes highlight the importance of the biomechanics of the game. They also allow players to see rather than guess what the coach is trying to tell them. For example, learning bowling is as much about feel as anything else. One often hears bowlers say that 'I don't feel quite right' or 'Something is out of synch'. Watching oneself on video allows players to add visualization to these feelings, and fast-tracks understanding.

However, beware of allowing coaching to become overly focused or reliant on sophisticated technology with plenty of bells and whistles. Cricket remains a developing sport, played all around the world, often in areas that can only dream of the latest technology. The old-fashioned methods of coaching are thus extremely important in the early development of the player. Technology is not only expensive, it can be difficult to use if you have not been brought up in the computer era or have not had access to computers, and financially it is beyond the reach of the vast majority of coaches.

GARY KIRSTEN ON VIDEO ANALYSIS

Bob Woolmer was not 'brought up in the computer era', and was all too aware that technology was an unimaginable luxury for many, but there is little doubt that he understood the value of video and digital aids. He assembled an extensive library of footage over his years as cricket coach and thinker. It is fitting, then, that one of the brightest stars to emerge during his tenure as South Africa's coach should be working to push forward the use of video analysis in modern cricket.

Gary Kirsten played 101 Tests for South Africa, scoring 7 289 runs at an average of over 45. Until Graeme Smith scored 277 against England in 2003, Kirsten shared the South African record for the highest individual score in Tests with Daryll Cullinan (275), and was sole owner of the record for the highest individual score for South Africa in one-day internationals (188* against the United Arab Emirates), as well as the most runs in an ODI calendar year by a South African (over 1 400 in both 1996 and 2000). Kirsten was only the third South African (and the first post-isolation) to score a century in both innings of a Test; and to date Jacques Kallis is the only South African to have surpassed his tally of 21 Test hundreds.

Before being appointed India's national coach, he set up the Gary Kirsten Cricket Academy in Newlands, Cape Town, where he established himself as an ardent lobbyist for the use of video technology in cricket coaching. Specializing in diagnosing and correcting – or simply improving – batting techniques, Kirsten used commercially available software to analyze batters' technique and explain their flaws to them.

'In my opinion, video analysis has become one of the most crucial components of developing, correcting or improving batting or bowling techniques,' says Kirsten. 'It allows both coach and player to go through the entire technique, from head to toe, frame by frame, and breaks down in a very visual way the specific components that must be identified and worked on – for example, a batter's stance, set-up, execution and follow-through.'

When a batter comes to Kirsten, he first watches him go through his repertoire of strokes in the nets. 'Watch him as objectively as possible, so it's clear you're not passing judgement.' He says some faults become immediately apparent. 'For example, maybe his weight transfer isn't good, for instance, he's not getting his head into a good channel when he's going forward. Seeing it is simple, but then you have to break it down and figure out what's causing the problem. Is it his set-up position? His stance? Is he in a weak position in his stance that's causing him to run out of time when trying to get into a position where he can transfer his weight properly?'

After this initial session, which contains almost no coaching, Kirsten brings the batter back for a video analysis session. 'At this time I do some detailed work on what I see, and what solutions I think I can offer.' But, says Kirsten, the most important part of this session is that the player is able to see his own faults for himself. 'From that point, the process of coaching is to take that technique the player has seen on the monitor, and to ask, "Where do we want this to go?" The answer to that question must be a joint decision between coach and player. Yes, you're the coach, but the player still has to feel, to understand what you mean.'

As part of this process, video technology is essential. Most players are aware of where they are going wrong, but showing them themselves on video is vital to helping them understand the difference between where they are, and where they need to be. One effective way of doing this is to show them on-screen comparisons: footage of themselves is aligned in split-screen mode with footage of a top international player executing the same shot, giving them an instant reference. 'It gives the player a clear picture of the fundamental problem,' says Kirsten. 'This isn't a question of changing his style: he's playing the shot in this way because the fundamentals are not in place.'

Coach and batter now go into the nets and work through a series of drills, first with a stationary ball, then a very slowly moving ball, a quicker ball, and finally the ball moving at match-simulation speed. 'If he can apply what we've developed to his technique in every match simulation,' says Kirsten, 'then he's in the clear.' Getting to that point, however, can take time. The younger the player, the more quickly he can develop: Kirsten says twelve-year-olds can make good progress over a winter of perhaps eight to ten sessions. Older batters tend to need a longer process – he estimates sixteen to twenty sessions for players aged eighteen and up.

Kirsten says one of the easiest problems to solve through video technology is that of alignment. 'It's easy to see. If he's backing away and not getting his body behind the line of the ball, he'll see it immediately on the video.' But not all weaknesses in technique will be instantly recognizable. 'It's difficult when you get someone who's hitting the ball really well, but is hitting it from what I term a weak position,' says Kirsten. 'He's striking it sweetly, but his position of execution is not ideal, whether it's because his weight is too much on the back foot, or because he's hitting more of a baseball-type shot. If the bowler is intelligent and puts the ball in the right place, the batter's going to be found out. But convincing him of that fact – that he is not currently equipped to deal with the next level up – can often be a struggle.'

But what about the millions of young players who don't have access to someone like Kirsten or the software he uses, but who still have the use of a video camera? 'If he is watching himself bat or bowl, and he doesn't fully understand the finer points of technique, the best thing he can do is to compare his footage with what he sees on TV. For example, if he's a batter, he can record Jacques Kallis making a hundred in a Test, and ask himself, "What am I doing, and what is Kallis doing, and how can I look more like him?"'

Familiarizing yourself with video technology early on, whether as player or coach, can only have benefits in the long run, says Kirsten. Today, video is an integral part of teams' pre-match preparation. 'The more knowledgeable you are about the opposition's strategy and their bowling trends, the better off you'll be.' Kirsten says that while other sports, such as Rugby Union and American gridiron football have been using video exhaustively for years, cricket has lagged behind.

'If I was opening the batting in a Test tomorrow, I'd take video footage of the six bowlers I was going to face, and break each one down individually. What are his preferences? How does he bowl to left-handers? Does he swing it up front? What are his weak deliveries, and where does he put them? People talk about "paralysis by analysis", but the more information you have, the more informed your cricketing decisions are going to be.'

The ideal modern cricketer, says Kirsten, is one who is able to use video technology fully, and who can do his own analyses. 'He should be able to go to his hotel room with a digital dossier of information on the opposition, and be qualified to play around with that information to maximize his preparation. The modern player must be willing and able to do his own homework.'

Kirsten says people should not be worried that video and similar technologies are going to obliterate traditional methods: Bradman's *The Art of Cricket* has pride of place on his bookshelf, and he is quick to point out that most of what Bradman described and endorsed is still being applied all over the world today. Instead, he says, technology should supplement and bolster tradition. 'Bradman's technique was as clean as you could ever wish to see; but why can't we unpack it in a scientific way, with the technology at our disposal? People get scared that you're tampering with flair. But we just want to find out what flair is.'

COMMUNICATION: THE COACH'S MOST VITAL TOOL

The toolbox of the coach has been unpacked above, but a toolbox is worthless if it cannot be opened. And so the final, and perhaps most important, skill in the coach's repertoire is his ability to communicate, including his command of, and sensitivity to, language.

When one talks about communication, many people glaze over, and perhaps with good reason. Communication in the modern world often seems to revolve around seminars full of talking heads, PowerPoint presentations, reams of impenetrable documents, and an overall suspicion that nothing of any value is actually being said.

But the coach must be a true communicator, someone who understands that communication in its purest sense is about connecting minds. So it is vital that the language the coach uses is based on the understanding of each cricketer. Fortunately, the language of the game is pretty commonplace; however, clear communication, patience and flexibility are necessary if the message is to get across. This will naturally alter according to the age of the audience and their level of intellectual understanding.

For instance, a child of eight can absorb enormous amounts of information, but only if presented in a way he can understand. In cricket terms, telling him that he needs to work on his back-foot shots because bowlers are going to start bowling short at his body, will make almost no impression on him, simply because he's never faced a bowler who could get the ball up above waist-height. However, if you tell him that working on his back-foot shots will allow him to score more freely – or will allow him to finally use that pull-shot he's been dying to learn! – he will absorb your coaching like a sponge.

Obviously if you have a child who is besotted with the game, reads about it, and follows matches on the radio and TV, it is far easier to communicate with him than a child who has no exposure to the game at all. But never assume anything when dealing with young players. Bob Woolmer spoke of a humbling experience at one of his coaching courses: 'A young boy looked at my T-shirt with the slogan "Bob Woolmer Coaching" and asked, "Excuse me, sir, who is Bob Woolmer?" He came from a society that had very few visual aids or literature on cricket, so he had no idea who I was. In the circumstances, it was a natural question!'

In cases like these, when dealing with youngsters with little or no exposure to cricket, a coach has to develop the trust of his charges regarding knowledge and how he communicates it. He will also have to teach his pupils the terminology of cricket, and change or explain it as necessary. For example, a coach might say 'step forward', only to see his new player doing exactly that, not realizing that in cricket stepping forward means moving sideways towards the bowler. Don't assume he knows what you're thinking. Explain, explain and explain – and do so clearly and patiently.

Finding the way to impart your knowledge so that the player 'takes it on board' is thus the true test of the coach, and especially crucial when coaching junior age groups. It is a sensitivity that the good coach has to develop, a feeling for each player and each situation: he must understand that three seventeen-year-old right-handed batsmen from the same school might need three completely different approaches of forms of communication, simply because they come from very different backgrounds.

A young boy looked at the T-shirt with the slogan 'Bob Woolmer Coaching' and asked, "Excuse me, sir, who is Bob Woolmer?"'

NETS AND MIDDLE PRACTICES

Whoever thought of stringing netting around a pitch should have been knighted.

The nets are the office of every coach, his laboratory, his workshop. It is here that he has the control and time to iron out the wrinkles he has spotted, or has been asked to correct; and it is here that he will spend much of his career.

But although nets have changed very little in almost a century, the coach shouldn't assume that they are a perfect coaching tool. They may have worked for Bradman, but don't assume that you can use them like an automaton. Always aspire to innovation and adaptation. It is sad but true that the vast majority of coaches are given sub-standard nets, and for many, this is an excuse to do no more than go through the motions. Cracked concrete pitches, ragged or flapping nets, and deeply eroded and rutted run-ups often elicit a shrug from coaches unwilling to think outside the box, and an endless and pointless barrage of throw-downs.

Of course, administrators often leave coaches in the lurch as far as facilities are concerned. One of the most infuriating cop-outs bandied about by administrators is the hackneyed phrase 'Make the most of what you have', with its unspoken but implied conclusion – 'Because that's all we're going to give you!' – often driving coaches to distraction.

THE IDEAL PRACTICE SESSION

Nets are important, but only up to a point. Players at higher levels need to practise specifics in conjunction with the basics, which means they must be able to switch from nets to middle conditions and back to nets easily and efficiently. In other words, nets are not an end in themselves: regard them as an adjunct to middle practices, which, though often unwieldy for inexperienced coaches, are always the ideal.

The ideal layout of a practice venue, therefore, would feature a bank of six nets on the edge of a field with two high-quality pitches out in the middle – one for spinners, one for seamers – as well as a separate area where players can safely practise specific skills with the help of a bowling machine.

Nets strung out in various fielding positions could more effectively simulate match conditions (in nets, most batsmen simply blast the ball into the side-netting, regardless of whether or not they would have picked out a fielder in real match conditions), and the wicket-keeper and slips are afforded much more valuable practice than simply facing a coach and catching balls. You and the batsmen need to decide how long each of them stays out in the middle, but once their time is up, they can immediately cross over to the bowling machine to groove five or six particular shots over the next few hours.

Just as you need to be creative when organizing standard net practices, so too should you try to structure middle practices that are focused and intense, as well as entertaining. For example, if you have the time and resources, allow each pair of batsmen to bat for two hours. Break that time into four half-hour sessions, in which they experience different scenarios. What these will be will depend on the level of your team and what you're practising for, but four very useful modes of play are:

- leaving the ball
- playing normally (each ball on its merits)
- tip and run
- hitting over the top.

Nets are not an end in themselves: regard them as an adjunct to middle practices, which are always the ideal.

Add your own specific exercises as you see fit. For instance, you might consider having a middle practice (or a half-hour session) in which everyone works on sweeping the off-spinner. To add an extra element of fun and competition, introduce your own scoring system to these half-hour sessions, and then reward the best pair. Whatever you do, don't allow the practice to degenerate into a pointless circus of batsmen carting bowlers all over the park.

The benefits of this technique are various (very few coaches, for example, allow tail-enders the time to focus on hitting over the top, and yet still expect them to walk out and hit the winning boundary every so often), but the most important asset in this case is the intensity a middle practice brings to general practice. We believe that the best possible practice is one that simulates the pressure situations of a match out in the middle, and then allows players to retreat to the nets to groove their shots, much as golfers do. However, this relies very heavily on having the right facilities and willing ground staff, which in turn depends on the finances of your club or administration. And of course you also need the faith of your employers: the purse strings will remain tight if they don't believe that these (admittedly lavish) demands for entire fields and banks of nets will have any impact on performance!

Note that even the best facilities and practice schedules are useless without intensity and focus. Every practice, wherever it takes place, must have a specific goal. Having a net for the sake of having a net is a destructive syndrome, and one that should be stamped out smartly.

THE FAR-FROM-IDEAL PRACTICE SESSION

Very few teams can afford the facilities on our practice 'wish list'. Most clubs have one or two fields, a row of antique nets, and perhaps some worn rubber mats over the run-ups; and that is as good as it is going to get. But even these conditions are often unattainable: for the vast majority of children and coaches, net practices in the real world consist of thirteen or more children in a dustbowl or bumpy field, two rickety nets, five old, soft balls, and 90 minutes to get through everything. So how do you get the most effective practice out of these fairly dire circumstances?

First of all, have a reason for practising. Simply having the bowlers run in and the batsman play aggressive shots is a waste of everyone's time. At school level, your primary motive should be participation: everyone must bat and bowl, and all must have an innings of equal length. If you're practising simply to keep everyone's eye in and to get them involved in the sport, then enjoyment must go hand-in-hand with participation. Perhaps introduce a competitive element: every time a batsman is dismissed, he loses five runs, and whoever ends with the most runs gets a cricket ball to take home or other small prize from the coach.

For the vast majority of children and coaches, net practices consist of thirteen or more children on a bumpy field, two rickety nets, five old, soft balls, and 90 minutes to get through everything.

If, on the other hand, you want to teach a skill, your session needs to be far more focused, and the player/coach ratio needs to be fairly small – not more than six players to one coach at any time (the logistics of this will be discussed shortly). However, with limited time and resources, you will need to focus on a smaller range of skills. For example, begin by teaching the shot for half an hour to the whole group. Next, start with the first batter and throw six relevant balls to him so that he can practise the shot. Move to the next net, and let the bowlers (ideally no more than three in each net) continue dishing up balls that encourage the shot. Once you've thrown to each batsman – in other words, thrown 36 deliveries if there are six nets – it's time for the next set of batsmen to pad up, and the drill repeats. This way each batsman is guaranteed at least six high-quality deliveries, as well as the personal attention of the coach, even if this is brief.

The above is a useful 'real world' practice session, which takes into account players' needs for one-on-one coaching balanced against the time constraints and lack of facilities.

THROW-DOWNS

Never do throw-downs from closer than 15 metres. Remember that you're trying to simulate real conditions as far as possible. The ideal distance is thus around 18 metres, with a little skip before the throw. This skip gives you some momentum and lessens the chance of your injuring yourself, while also allowing the batsman a roughly simulated glance at the bowling action, which he needs in order to time his trigger movements and bat-lift. Also be sure why you're throwing; only use throw-downs to groove one specific shot, or to train the batsman in picking length.

However, there is a third scenario in which throw-downs can be your only option: when you're trying to condition your batsmen to a variety of bowling that none of your net bowlers can replicate. For pace, a bowling machine can't be beaten, but what happens if you're facing a leg-spinner this weekend, and none of your bowlers can bowl leg-spin? In this instance, some simulated leg-spin throw-downs can go a little way to removing some of the mystery. If your leg-spin bowling is only accurate over 8 metres, this will have to do: bowl from 8 metres away.

When South Africa was preparing for a Test at Sydney, knowing that they would have to face their nemesis Shane Warne pitching it into the rough outside leg-stump, they practised by batting against leg-spin bowled into the rough at the bowler's end of the net.

A CRICKET CURRICULUM

If you are fortunate enough to have the resources, facilities and time to organize efficient and intense practice sessions, always remember that the ideal player/coach ratio is 1:1. However, reality – even well-funded reality – intrudes, and in most cases you will have to be satisfied with a ratio of six players to one coach. Although this is not the ideal, it is more than acceptable in most instances.

The ideal practice (for a first-class or international team) has already been described, but in comfortable amateur conditions – such as are found at traditional sporting schools or suburban clubs – what are the most effective drills, given the ever-present time-constraints on players and facilities?

If you've got twelve children in your squad, and a standard two-hour practice, don't plunge straight into the nets. Remember, you're having a net for a reason, usually to develop a skill. So spend the first half-hour explaining the day's new skill, demonstrating it, and answering any questions your charges might have. Now that everyone has been briefed, and has a reason to bat, it's time to let them into the nets. Aim to have them work on the new skill for a total time of around one hour (half an hour each if you've got six nets, ten minutes each if you've got two).

Then get everyone to warm down with some fielding practice, followed by a discussion of last weekend's game, with an analysis of both the successes and failures. This should fill up the final half-hour.

You have now created a neat two-hour cricket lesson. But to be truly effective, lessons need to be part of a larger curriculum. It is therefore important that you devise a curriculum, as would any teacher of maths or history. In fact, we recommend that players should be assessed every so often with written and practical assignments to gauge their progress; coaching is a long-term project, and it is very useful to record and track long-term progress.

How you structure your team's curriculum will depend on their age group and the regularity of practices, and the example on the following page is by no means a rigid prescription. However, it is a particularly comprehensive cricket syllabus, and players can only benefit from being exposed to all its elements.

If you've got twelve children in your squad, and a standard two-hour practice, don't plunge straight into the nets. Remember, you're having a net for a reason, usually to develop a skill.

WEEK	PRACTICAL SKILL	TACTICAL SKILL	THEORETICAL LESSON	FUN TIME
1	Skill assessment			
2	Bowling (fast)	Length and bowling in sets	The action	Bowling at a stump competition
3	Grip, stance and backswing	Changing grips to suit shot placement	Learn ten Laws of the game	Playing cricket tennis
4	Forward defensive	Field placings	Scoring	Throwing drills
5	Forward drives	Attacking field placings	Scoring	Close catching drills
6	Backward defensive	Defensive field placings	Umpiring	Tip and run
7	Cut and pull	One-day field placings	Learn ten Laws of the game	Inner-ring catching drills (diving)
8	Sweeps	Running between the wickets	Read a book on cricket	Throwing drills
9	Hitting over the top	Playing with soft hands	Umpiring	Hitting the ball for six
10	Back-foot drives	Changing to the field to pressurize the batter	Historical stats presentation	High catching drills
11	Bowling (spin)	Backing up in the field	Umpiring	Defending stumps (using an incentive)
12	Skill assessment		Learn ten Laws of the game	

The positive effects of such a curriculum are numerous.
- Players are guaranteed a learning experience.
- The coach becomes accountable, and also feels he is achieving something.
- Parents are able to get feedback on how their child is progressing.
- Provincial, county or state bodies are able to get feedback on better players.
- The results of a structured coaching system are easy to capture and store on databases: with statistics (such as ages, personal scores and match results) easily accessible, players would not be lost in the system or 'fall through the cracks' as is currently the case in many countries.

FIELDING DRILLS

The revolution in fielding brought about by the one-day game has also had a major impact on fielding drills. Indeed, until as recently as the 1980s, fielding drills were laborious and dull. The Australians were the first to introduce fielding drills, which have now become close to an art form. Good fielding drills incorporating a variety of game situations under pressure have lifted fielding techniques to another level. These also add a very necessary element of fun into the business of practising and getting fit.

The following three drills incorporate the skills needed to improve throwing and game awareness. There are of course many more, but Bob Woolmer had great success with these three, which combine entertainment and education.

1. THE SIX-POINT THROWING DRILL

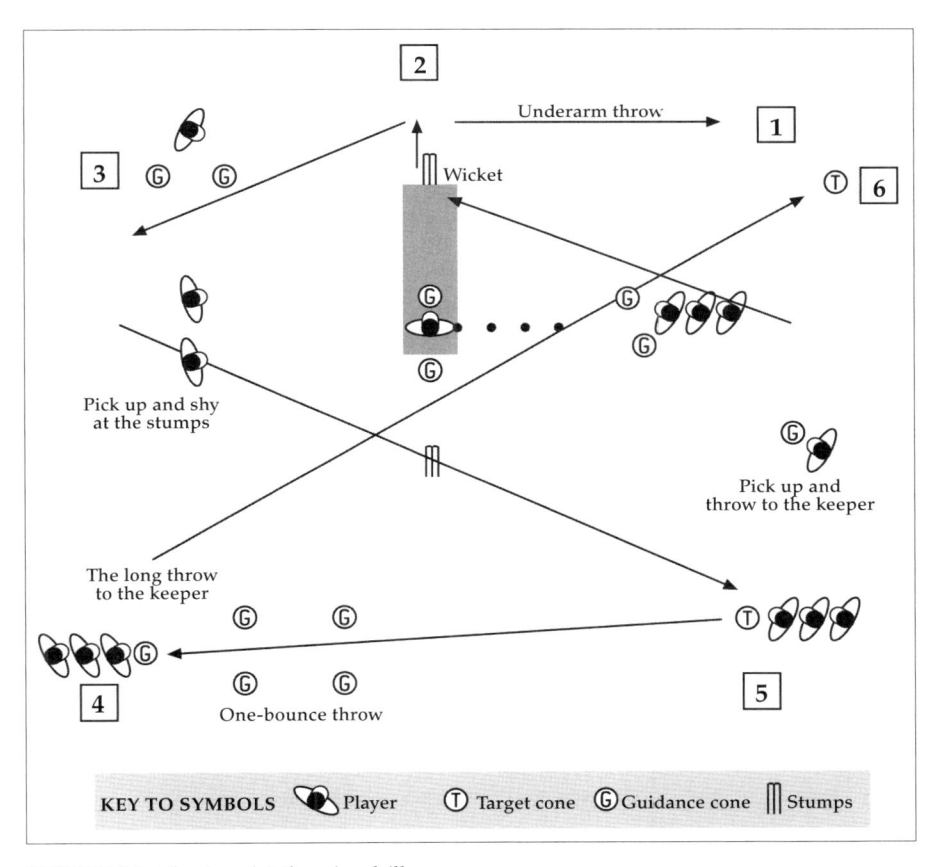

FIGURE 9.1: *The six-point throwing drill*

The value of this drill is that players are able to practise at high intensity all the throwing skills associated with the game, specifically the one-day game. As this is also a high-activity drill, it can be used in order to maintain fitness levels. The intensity levels are the key, and this very much depends on the players and how much they need to improve.

Execution is as follows:

1. **The drill starts at point 2.** The player rolls the ball along the ground to point 1, and the player at 1 collects the ball at speed and throws the underarm pass firmly to the player at 2, who effects a run-out.

2. **As soon as the player at 2 effects the run-out, he turns and rolls the ball at the cone at cover point (his target cone).** The player at 3 then swoops on the ball before it reaches the cone, picks it up and shies at the stumps at the bowler's end. (In the event of a ricochet, the coach or coach's helper will roll another ball towards 5.) The player at 5 will be backing up and collects the ball from the shy.

3. **The player at 5 in turn now throws the ball with one bounce to the player at 4, who will effect a run-out from in front of the stumps.** He then moves towards 6 and will collect a rolling ball (or a hit catch) and throw the ball to the wicket-keeper at the stumps.

4. **The player at 4 then makes a long throw to 6** (a wicket-keeper or coach with a baseball mitt).

5. **The keeper next to 2 will lob the ball back to the player at 2,** who continues the above cycle.

Start with just one ball, so that each player gets used to doing each skill; then introduce two balls, and finally three for the full skill effect. Three balls create greater pressure. For optimum intensity levels, every throw should be done at match speed, and as though there is a run-out opportunity at every station.

If possible, there should be a coach with a supply of extra balls to maintain continuity at the bowler's end. Also if possible, the stumps should be similar to the ones used in Action Cricket (mounted on springs and attached to a single plate), since these reduce the amount of ricochet, and rebound into position easily.

2. THE 'ROUND THE CLOCK' THROWING DRILL

The 'round the clock' drill is designed to help players throw at the stumps from the six different angles that most players are likely to experience during a game.

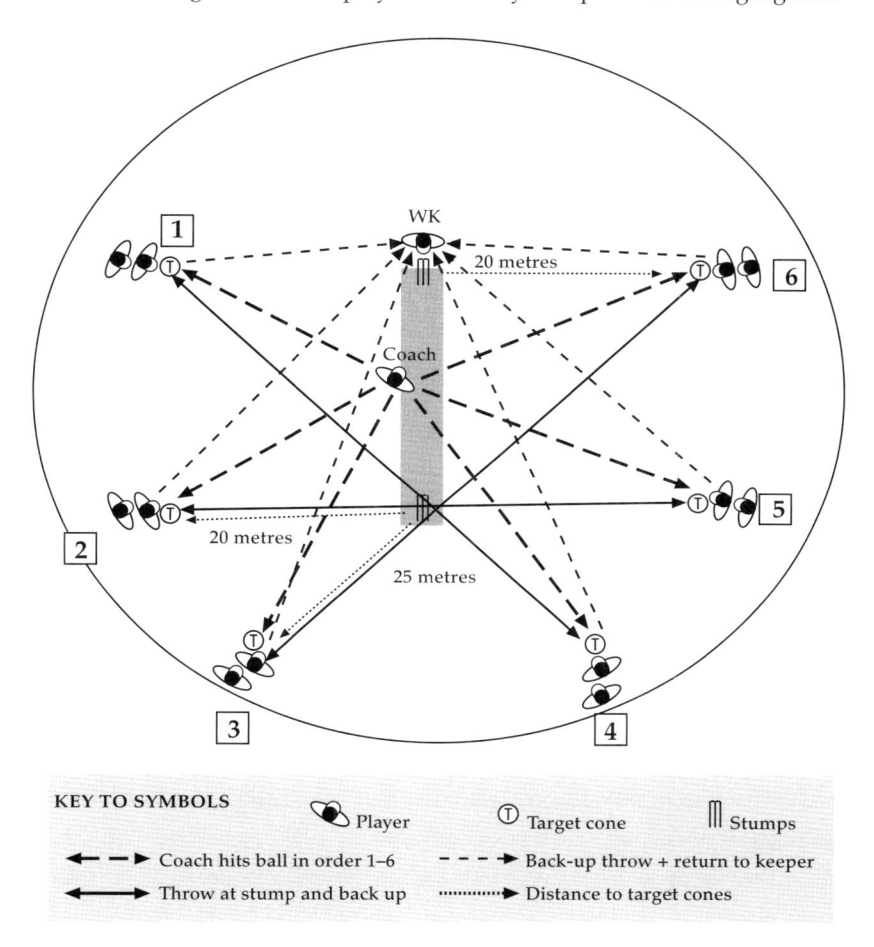

KEY TO SYMBOLS

- Player
- Target cone
- Stumps
- ←--▶ Coach hits ball in order 1–6
- ---▶ Back-up throw + return to keeper
- ←—▶ Throw at stump and back up
- ·······▶ Distance to target cones

FIGURE 9.2: *The 'round the clock' throwing drill*

The game starts with the coach hitting the ball to point 1 (cover point). The player picks up and shies at the stumps, with the player at point 4 (mid-on) backing up. The player at 4 returns the ball to the keeper over the top of the stumps. The player at point 1 then moves to the back of the queue at point 2.

The game continues 'around the clock' in an anti-clockwise direction. It is important to note that the player only moves on once he has shied at the stumps at the bowler's end.

Since the uprooting of the stumps or ricochets will interrupt the game and become irritating, we once again recommend Action Cricket stumps.

The skills here are obvious: they include hitting the stumps at pace, backing up, and returning the ball to the keeper. This drill has to be done at game intensity if it is to be meaningful.

The coach is in the firing line for many returns, so be on the alert! Deft footwork and the use of peripheral vision will be necessary!

Introduce a competitive element – award a prize to the best pair, or a financial incentive if you are feeling generous. Another option is to build in a time limit in which the stumps have to be hit a certain amount of times – this is also useful as a team-building exercise.

Introduce two balls, but stop once the stumps are knocked over. Insist on quality and accuracy. The ball can also be hit along the ground, or with a bounce, or as a catch, introducing catching and throwing as the skill to be practised.

3. RUN-OUT DRILLS

The following run-out drills are specific to the one-day game. They are designed to help the bowlers and fielders identify what tactics are needed in those few seconds in which the batsmen are floundering in the middle of a wicket-threatening mix-up. Too often the batsmen aren't the only ones panicking: fielding sides become over-excited and flustered as they see the chance of a run-out developing, and the bowler doesn't get back to the stumps or the ball is thrown to the wrong end.

Communication is the key, and there are a number of important skills in this drill that will help the fielding side when confronted with a scenario like the above in a game situation.

The drill takes the form of a game, which has three teams: the batting team, which creates the pressure for the fielding side by simulating a mix-up; the bowling team, which simulates the follow-through of the bowler; and the fielding team, which has to communicate and get the ball back as quickly as possible.

Skill 1 – 'Hit the bowler'

The coach rolls or hits the ball out to extra cover for the first drill, while the batsman and bowler move on the throw. The batsman goes just over halfway down the pitch and then simulates being sent back. The fielder sprints from about 4 or 5 metres, picks up and throws to the bowler, who is making his way back to the stumps at the bowler's end. The aim of this drill is to get the ball to the bowler at waist-height on the move and at pace. The bowler then has to remove the bails before the batsman can get back to the crease.

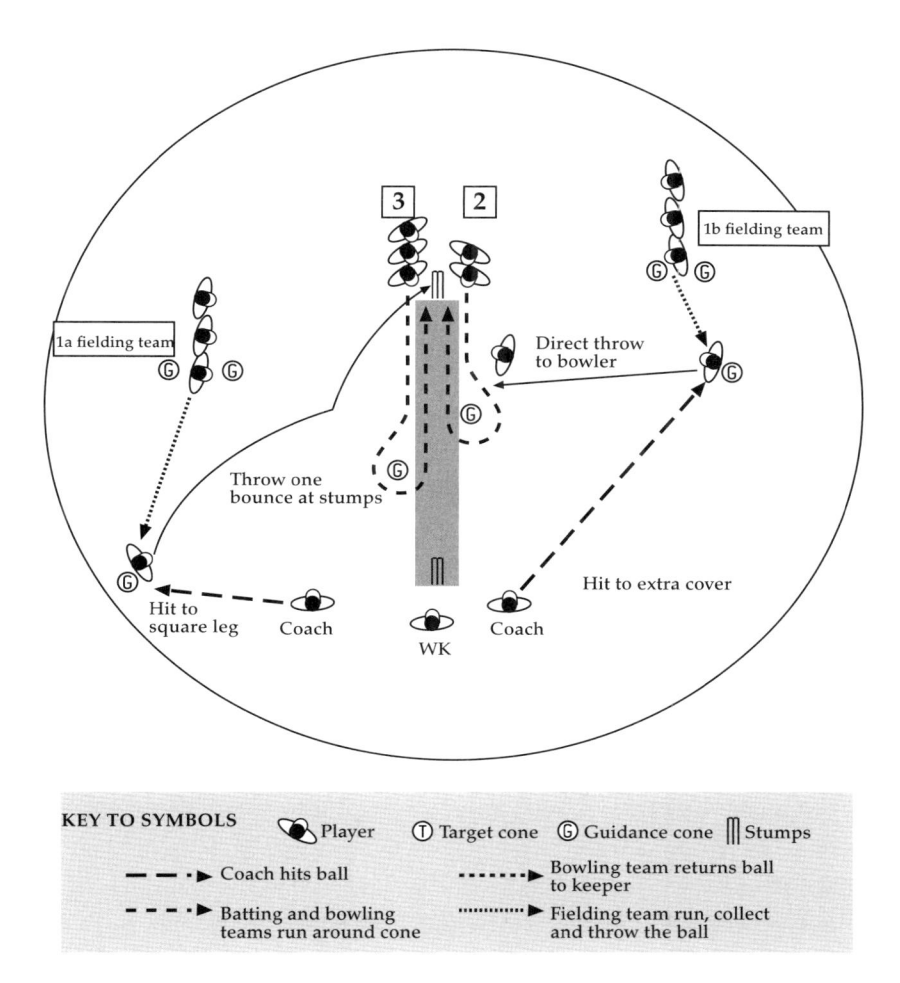

FIGURE 9.3: *Run-out drills*

Skill 2 – Throw on the turn, shy at the stumps with one bounce

The coach rolls the ball to the player at square leg. Meanwhile, the batsman at the bowler's end runs towards the other end, then simulates being sent back. The fielder picks up the ball and throws on the turn, making sure that he bounces the ball about 4 or 5 metres in front of the stumps, with the intention of a direct hit. The bowler attempts to get back as close to the stumps as possible, and either shepherds the ball on to the stumps, or, if it is wide, collects it and takes the bails off.

In both these drills, the batsman is creating pressure. The game can also be played by using the batsmen to simulate a turn and touch practice, sliding in first with the left hand and then with the right hand, improving the turning speeds.

Like any of these drills, it is easy to expand or reduce the number of stations or points, and create a smaller drill, or a number of smaller drills. Remember that all drills should be match-specific and repeated as often as possible, so that the skills they teach become second nature. While it is good to think on your feet, it helps if the subconscious has an idea what to do!

MASS COACHING

As we have explained, one-on-one coaching is the ideal. But in many cases, limited time and resources make it necessary to coach exceptionally large groups: development programmes in countries such as South Africa, Pakistan, Sri Lanka and some of the islands of the Caribbean often require coaches to deal with 20, 40 or even 60 players at any one time.

The official term for this kind of coaching is currently 'group coaching', a somewhat euphemistic description that conjures a cozy picture of a huddle of about fifteen players, all within earshot of the coach. However, we have chosen to call a spade a spade and opt for 'mass coaching', since this will leave you as a coach in no doubt as to what to expect!

The first thing to note about mass coaching is its specificity. You are not there to facilitate a huge net session, or to allow 60 people to have a good time. You are there to teach a particular skill. However, which skill you teach will depend on two key factors:
- the general levels of physical maturity and skill in the group
- the facilities you have been given.

For instance, it is no use teaching skills that require a lot of verbal explanation to a large group of children who need more practical demonstrations, and who might not be able to hear you properly (either because they are too far away, or are straining into a strong wind). Similarly you are going to struggle to demonstrate the nuances of seam bowling if you've been given an indoor sports hall with a hard shiny floor.

Mass coaching requires the ability to improvise and adapt quickly. Make sure you have a Plan B, C, D and E.

Mass coaching therefore requires the ability to improvise and adapt quickly. Because it is mostly used for underprivileged groups of cricketers, often in townships or at the local community centre, be ready to have plans dramatically changed at the last minute as the inevitable organizational mishaps leave you with fields double-booked, halls locked, facilities occupied by other age groups, and so on. Make sure you have a Plan B, C, D and E – you are likely to need them. Be sure to remain cheerful and flexible in all circumstances, as your charges will pick up on your mood. If you take the attitude that the exercise is a fun challenge, they are likely to share this sense.

HOW DO YOU MAKE A BATSMAN BETTER?

Question: How many psychologists does it take to change a light bulb?

Answer: Just one, but the light bulb must want to change.

It's an old joke, but one with an important truth at its core. Change is almost impossible if we don't see a need for that change. We've known for 40 years that current pollution levels are changing our climate and threatening the future of the planet, and yet only after dramatic increases in the oil price in the last few years have people started talking seriously about renewable energy sources. Until we start feeling climate change in our pockets, many of us simply won't care.

So to make a batsman better, you first need to ask him if he really wants to get better. If he does, then carefully examine his shots, his particular approach to batting and his style: this will set you on your way to identifying what will make him better. However, just because *you* know what will improve his game, it doesn't mean he'll necessarily agree with your diagnosis or your recommendations. Your final responsibility, therefore, is to 'sell' him your advice, explaining it in such a way that he will see the logic and the potential of what you're suggesting. At this stage, you don't want to get too caught up in technique, because you're trying to present a more holistic or bigger picture.

You'd expect that all batsmen would answer in the affirmative when asked if they want to improve, but this is not always the case. Many batsmen honestly don't see that they have a problem, and in these cases your skill as a communicator will be tested to the limits as you explain the severity of their predicament to them. Usually it will boil down to a simple choice – either he accepts that he has a flaw and fixes it, or he can get used to sitting on the bench – but this need not be an acrimonious confrontation. He might not want to accept your diagnosis at first, but he can't dispute the fact that you are being paid as an analyst and 'technique doctor', and that he is therefore in the minority if he thinks you don't know what you're talking about!

You can approach the task of improving your players another way, of course. When Bob Woolmer was appointed coach of the Pakistani team, he started by asking the players what they wanted him to do. 'They all answered that they wanted me to find their faults and remove them: a clear sign of a long history of top-down, authoritarian coaching and passive players. In their minds, they were flawed, and could get better. A refreshingly modest approach, you might argue; but in a country in which even a modest lapse in form or minor error by a player can result in massive popular protest, Pakistan's players needed all the self-belief they could get. I therefore put it to them that perhaps, instead of having a variety of faults, they only had one: they believed they were flawed. Instead, I told them, I was going to find their strengths, and make those better.'

COACHING YOUNGER PLAYERS

Those who choose to coach young and beginner cricketers are the unsung heroes and heroines of the game. If you are one of this enormous group of very special people, you are contributing not only to the health and recreation of the children of your school, community or nation; you are teaching your young charges important life skills.

While it is a cliché (although no less true) to say that cricket will teach youngsters the importance of teamwork, the truth is that playing a team sport that involves skill is one of the few non-scripted activities left to modern children. Ours has become a world in which wealthy children have hovering 'helicopter parents' anxiously supervising every interaction lest their precious child should experience disappointment or upset, while poor children are slipping in ever-growing numbers through the widening holes left in the social networks responsible for their care. Cricket can offer children from every walk of life a realm that is both safe from the pressures and hardships of daily life, as well as refreshingly 'real': if you offer a lazy shot, the ball is likely to hit you, or you might lose your wicket. Cricket is a relatively safe world in which to learn that actions have consequences, and that no tantrum is going to change the fact that you're out!

So those who are dedicated to passing on their passion for and knowledge of the game of cricket to beginners are also building citizens. Your task is both fun and challenging; and probably the most important attribute is your ability to communicate, as we have discussed earlier.

USING THE DISCOVERY LEARNING MODEL

While every child in every age group must be treated as an individual, there are some general guidelines you can follow when structuring practices. The most important of these is to make practices for ages eight to ten more focused on fun than technique. Children of this age need the stimulation of a fun and intense learning experience. So-called 'Discovery Learning' can be highly effective with younger children, not just for learning sports, but in all other educational spheres, because it allows the child to learn skills as if discovering them for himself. This intensely personal learning experience has a much more immediate and long-lasting impact on the child than traditional methods, in which children are effectively told, 'This is the way you do it.'

Of course, some traditional teaching tools are essential: children who are left to discover arithmetic and language for themselves are headed for disaster. Visual learning, for example, is something teachers and their pupils have relied upon for centuries, as well as the spoken word. Both variations are also ideally suited to sports coaching, as you can demonstrate a particular stroke or movement, while describing it and explaining why you are doing what you're doing. This combination of traditional methods and Discovery Learning provides a thorough foundation for youngsters, and also allows for differing personalities and learning styles: some children respond best to spoken instructions, others to being shown, and some prefer to go off by themselves and work it all out from first principles.

What your players discover – and what they learn – will be largely a result of what you expose them to. Don't underestimate the educational value of even the most mundane aspects of cricket technique, things you might overlook as being too simple to dwell on.

- Instead of prescribing one particular grip for batsmen, allow the batter to hit the ball off the face of the bat while experimenting with various grips. Once he's found a comfortable one, identify where the hands are, and what they're doing.
- Break preconceptions by hitting the same ball an equal distance with an entirely different grip.
- Get batsmen to hit the ball leaning into it and leaning back in the shot, so that they can feel how different the two are, and can understand why the latter is less desirable. Get them to try to keep the ball on the ground when leaning back in the shot – they'll soon discover how difficult it is.
- Give all players the feel of watching the ball, insisting that they watch a rolling ball down the pitch without blinking, then a ball thrown underarm, and finally a bowled delivery. Players don't in fact watch the ball all the way onto the bat (a physiological process discussed in more detail in Chapter 4), but at this stage the *intention* to watch it all the way is enough to give players the feel for doing so.

How old is old enough?

One of the basic tenets of early childhood development is the fact that the earlier you learn something, the more completely you will master it. Our capacity for learning is immense when we are babies, and this ability to absorb information and skills like a sponge slowly deserts us as we get older. It takes us just five years to learn our mother tongue, but we are as capable of learning two or four or six languages equally well in that time. Compare this to the halting efforts of adults learning a foreign language in their twenties or later.

In other words, the earlier you learn something, the better you become at it, the faster you master it, the more deeply you understand it. It must be a huge temptation for new parents who are cricket fans to buy a tiny bat for their newborn sons or indeed their daughters. Bob Woolmer's father famously placed a bat in his infant son's crib – with the desired effects. Bob was playing cricket by the time he was three

'There have been times when I want to grab the bat or ball, plant a player's feet in the right spot, and say, "Come on! I know what I'm talking about, so just listen to me!" But remember that learning by discovery is both important and successful, so take a deep breath, smile and go back to square one.'

– Bob Woolmer

years old, and the rest is history. This might not work for everyone, but it did give Bob a head start over players who only took up the game at the age of fifteen.

But children have physical and emotional limits. Below the age of six, children are simply not able to hit a ball with a bat, no matter how light the bat or large the ball. Similarly, sports like cricket were designed by adults for adults, with adult conceptions of time and rhythm. Five days in the life of a Test cricketer is a single game, a heartbeat in his career, but to an eight-year-old it can seem the equivalent of an adult month. Very small children will not see the point of the game, and become distracted or bored. Most young children, if they are interested at all in ball sports, simply want to hit or kick the ball as hard and as far as they can, with scant regard for technique or direction. Insisting that a very young child holds the bat or shifts his weight correctly will usually lead to irritation and then tears, and can turn him against the game for good.

SPOTTING AND NURTURING TALENT

Bob Woolmer met Jacques Kallis when the future star was about fifteen years old, playing cricket for Wynberg Boys High School in Cape Town. 'He had some small problems with his technique,' said Woolmer. 'He was moving his feet at the wrong time, which upset his shot selection, but his talent was unmistakable in the way he brought his bat through beautifully straight. He looked extremely organized and correct for someone so young.

'A good coach must be able to identify and develop latent talent in young cricketers, but as this example of the teenage Kallis shows, it is not especially difficult if you know what to look for. Watching Under-10 batsmen, for instance, I'm not looking for high hands or a straight bat: at this age, the prospective stars simply need to show good hand-eye co-ordination, good balance, and athleticism. Precocious talents do come along fairly often – I met an eight-year-old South African with every shot in the book, slog sweep included! – but at this level, their skills are generally undeveloped.

'Technique and body strength become much more crucial as young batsmen reach their mid-teens. The best fifteen-year-olds will display a great technique and good athleticism, but also a range of well-grooved attacking strokes, and perhaps most importantly, good judgement of length and shot selection. The most organized teenagers are often those headed for greater things.

'Whether players are ten years old, or have been playing Test cricket for ten years, some are faster, quicker, better at catching, and have sharper reflexes than their peers. In any group, there are stand-out players who are better organized than others, and above all have not only the physical ability for cricket, but the mind as well. Remember, natural ability does not exempt a player from hard work, nor does it exempt a coach from giving his stars the development and time they need.'

When to start teaching the more formal aspects of cricket is therefore once again a case of being sensitive to the child you're coaching. Some pick up the game naturally, and beg you to play with them or coach them; others come to it much later. But whenever you start, and however developed or undeveloped your young players are, it is important to work slowly and methodically. For instance, spend a day each on the forward defensive, backward defensive, the drive, and so on, so that they have time to assimilate it all while retaining some sort of forward momentum in their learning. Go too fast and they'll become frustrated and bored; go too slowly and they'll drift.

TEACHING THE BASICS TO BEGINNERS: BOWLING, BATTING AND FIELDING

Each of these disciplines is discussed from first principles in their respective chapters, so coaches should not hesitate to refer directly to those specific chapters. However, the golden rule of teaching young players is worth repeating here: whatever you tell your charges, from whichever source (whether our book or another, or your own experience of the game), make sure you communicate it in a way that makes sense to them, and that gives them time to absorb what you're saying.

A practical example of this might best illustrate the point. Let's say that you've been coaching primary-school children, and you're fairly comfortable with teaching the mechanics of the drive; however, you feel you should give your players a few more basic pointers.

Instead of talking about hitting through the line, or playing with high hands, or using other phrases that a young child might misinterpret ('through the line' might logically be confused with playing across the line, while 'high hands' sounds as if you're being held up in a bank robbery), break down the drive into easily understandable chunks as follows:

- Swing the bat back with the aid of a front shoulder rotation.
- Cock the wrists at the top of the backswing.
- Judge length accurately (in case the ball is swinging and moves late, or in the case of a spinner, dips and causes a change in length).
- Move the front foot into a position next to the ball, allowing the hands and bat room to make square contact with the ball. (An important point during the drive shot is to visualize the ball on one line and the front foot on another parallel line, resembling tramlines or railway lines.)
- Allow the ball to travel along that line until it arrives next to your foot. This allows you a chance to use the power of the bat swing and follow-through. If your foot gets too close to the ball, the bat swing is hampered by the foot being in the way.

Whatever you tell your charges, make sure you communicate it in a way that makes sense to them, and that gives them time to absorb what you're saying.

- The front leg then straightens and moves back and inside the line so that the bat moves in towards the leg, 'closing the gate'. This out-to-in movement also guards against in-to-out strokes, i.e., the bat moving from a line close to the legs to one away from the body, which can result in inside edges, outside edges, lifting the ball into the air and uncontrolled slices rather than full-blooded drives.

The following are all common sense guidelines, and most coaches will have an instinctive feel for them at higher levels; but when coaching children you can never take anything for granted, and you must always be aware that you are shaping, rather than polishing, players. Think about what you're doing, and accept the responsibility.

You'll also notice that bowling gets far more thoroughly covered here than batting or fielding. This is because the mechanics of bowling need to be taught much more rigorously to young players than batting technique. A fourteen-year-old batsman with technical faults will experience only frustration and poor scores; moreover, he can be taught correct technique in as little as a year. But a bowler of the same age with a faulty action may already be well on the way to chronic injury – and it will be extremely difficult to correct his technique. Also bear in mind that the action of bowling is counterintuitive to many young players, who will want to throw the ball, or be unable to co-ordinate the five separate movements discussed in the chapter on bowling. Batting – hitting a ball with timing – is a far more visceral and intuitive action.

Bowling

The bowling action and its five component aspects are discussed in more detail in Chapter 5. As with most aspects of coaching very young children, you will need to find effective ways of communicating those five steps. The following is a basic guide to teaching bowling to a child who has never done it before in his life: any omissions or gaps here can be filled by applying the discussion of the action in Chapter 5 to your coaching.

Bowling the ball with a straight arm, as opposed to throwing it with a bent elbow, is an unnatural and apparently difficult action for young players. Keeping the arm straight is often a bridge too far for those learning to bowl for the very first time: if you've ever watched young children trying to bowl, you'll have seen a rough approximation of the gather and unwind (see Chapter 5 on bowling), often a quick shuffle of the feet as they realize they've got their left and right feet mixed up, and then a more or less conventional delivery – until their bowling arm reaches the vertical! At that point, because they've been going fairly slowly and don't have enough momentum, or because they suddenly think that the whole action feels silly or wrong, they bend their elbow and throw the ball.

This series of confused actions – passable gather, mixed-up delivery-stride, cop-out and throw – is often the result of confusion. As seen in Chapter 5, the five component aspects of the bowling action are highly specialized motions that take years to perfect. To expect a child of eight to string them together in quick succession after one or two demonstration deliveries, and still manage to send the ball in the direction he wants it to go, is asking much too much, too soon.

The key to coaching bowling to children, therefore, is a method of progressive training, building small skills slowly and steadily, one on top of the other. Start with the position of the feet, and progress to the movement of the lower body. A mat marked with footprints for right-arm and left-arm bowlers can be very useful in this regard, as the children learn where and how to position their back foot, how to rock onto their front foot, and how to turn into their follow-through.

Next, graduate to the arm movements of bowling, and keep repeating all the steps learnt until the child is able to co-ordinate all the motions from a stationary position. Then add a ball into the mix, and work on how to run, jump and turn, from about 4 or 5 metres. Finally, run through the entire action, with an emphasis on smoothness and momentum. The whole progression should thus look something like this:

- position of the feet
- movements of the legs and hips
- arm movements
- introduce a ball
- run, jump and turn
- the completed action.

In the chapter on bowling, we use an image that may be very useful in communicating to your young bowlers what they're trying to achieve: get them to imagine that the path of their arms during their delivery should trace the edge of a large coin or wheel, rolling in a straight line towards the target.

However, don't leave them with only the idea of a rolling wheel in their minds. The power of the delivery comes from the rapid rotation of the hips after the delivery stride, and you will need to make sure that they are turning far enough, and with enough speed. This is a full 180-degree rotation, with the front shoulder facing the target at the start of the delivery, and the back shoulder (or bowling arm shoulder) facing it after release.

Remember that some children will be better co-ordinated than others in the group, and you will always have one or two who lag behind. Be patient; as the action is bound to crystallize in mind and body at some stage.

> *The more the front knee bends, the harder it is to rotate the hips and follow through; and this leads to further twisting of the back as the player forces his body into a downward motion. The pressure on the spine and the back muscles from this kind of action is horrendous.*

GETTING THE ACTION RIGHT EARLY

Whether a bowler ends up with a side-on or chest-on action (discussed in more detail in the chapter on bowling) is largely dependent on whatever makes him comfortable; but whichever he chooses, it is very important that he be taught the basic action properly. Young children who are just beginning their cricketing life must be fully equipped with an action that they can develop and rely on, and that won't end up damaging them irreparably – also discussed further in the section on preventing injuries in Chapter 10.

Most crucial at this early stage is to get the young bowler to keep his front knee straight as he delivers. Many youngsters bend their knee as they bring their bowling arm over, and while this cushions the force of the delivery stride and makes the bowler more comfortable, it puts the rest of the action in danger. The more the front knee bends, the harder it is to rotate the hips and follow through; and this leads to further twisting of the back as the player forces his body into a downward motion towards the ground. The pressure on the spine and the back muscles from this kind of action is horrendous, and if repeated enough, will almost certainly lead to stress fractures or back injuries – and the implications for a child or teenager are disastrous.

Young bowlers must learn to use their front knees as a lever to propel the body through the action: the straighter it is, the better. It might be useful to explain the role of the front knee in terms of a pole-vaulter's pole. In order to gain height and get over the top of the bar, the pole-vaulter needs the pole to straighten and remain straight as he goes over, the pole remaining 'locked' into position. However, not only does he need a 'locked' pole, he needs enough momentum to go over the top. Too slow, and he'll get halfway to the top and then fall back, or topple over the side as he reaches the bar. Too fast, and he'll be slung at speed through the bar without having the time to pause and arch over it.

Arriving at the crease with enough momentum and balance allows the bowler to pivot up and over his front leg, and to keep his original line. Grooving this action from early on will not only reduce injury, but will give a young bowler the best chance of bowling to his full potential.

Also consider using the analogy described in the chapter on bowling of 'bowling downhill' or bowling down a flight of steps. If you have steps near the field, use them: it will give young bowlers a sense of what it feels like to brace their front leg and bowl over it.

From time to time you'll get older boys coming to you who have already settled into their action. Think long and hard before attempting to change a settled action: if in doubt, don't touch it. In fact, the only reasons a coach should ever try to change an action are:

- it is 'mixed' and therefore putting him in serious danger of injury

> ### STOP CHRONIC INJURIES BEFORE THEY START
>
> Most coaches want to win matches, and so it is only natural that they often want their best bowlers to stay on for as long as possible. The top bowlers in the team are only too happy to bowl long spells, generally being fitter, stronger and more ambitious than their teammates, and eager to reward their coach for his faith in them.
>
> Unfortunately most young bowlers are simply not strong enough to cope with the demands of repeated long spells, and stress fractures are becoming increasingly frequent among players aged between twelve and eighteen.
>
> Chapter 10 on physiology discusses this issue in more depth, and coaches should pay special attention to the guidelines recommended there, whether their bowlers are boys or Test stars. However, the bottom line when coaching young bowlers is to err on the side of caution: if one of your bowlers has back pain (especially if he is your star whom you've been over-bowling!) take him for an X-ray or to a sports medicine doctor immediately.
>
> Over-eager bowlers and coaches can also conspire to cause injuries in another way. Every coach wants a fast strike bowler, and every fast-medium twelve-year-old wants to knock heads off and hit the keeper's gloves hard; but trying to manufacture a fast bowler, or push a boy towards bowling fast when he's not suited to it, can be disastrous. Remember the old adage about pace: fast bowlers are born, not made. While scientific training and good nutrition mean that we can identify potential fast bowlers earlier and earlier, don't get carried away. An over-emphasis on speed can often encourage young bowlers to strain themselves, which simply sets them on the path to chronic injuries that much earlier.

- it is not settled because the bowler has never been properly taught
- a technical glitch has crept into the action.

Remember, no matter how unorthodox or odd-looking an action, if it is getting good results and does not pose an injury threat, you should help the bowler develop it. A good example of this is Paul Adams of South Africa, who possesses probably the most unorthodox action of any international cricketer in the game's history. Most coaches would have taken one look at his 'frog in a blender' action – head pointing at the ground, eyes shut and facing cover point at the moment of delivery, back leg turned upward at a 90-degree angle – and told Adams to start from scratch; but his coaches at school and club level were wise enough to recognize that he was getting good results with it, and helped him work on it.

So adapt your advice to fit the bowler's natural action, not the other way around.

LEARNING TO 'FEEL' LENGTH

'It is obvious that these things, especially length, cannot be taught if the distance he was to propel the ball is beyond him' (Grimmett, 1934).

Bob Woolmer got a shock when first coaching in South Africa: 'I was astounded to discover that eleven-year-olds were playing on the same length of pitch as adult men. This was entirely counterproductive, since the bodies of young players only begin to develop in terms of strength around the age of fourteen or fifteen. Batsmen can graduate to full-length pitches a bit earlier, since they don't need to be as strong as bowlers (I first began playing on a standard pitch when I was thirteen), but bowlers can be thoroughly wrecked by forcing them to bowl beyond their abilities in this way.'

In other words, the first thing to do when teaching young players to bowl is to shorten the length of the pitch according to their physiques. This boosts their confidence, as they are getting the ball up to the bat nicely, with some decent carry to the wicket-keeper or into the back net; it prevents them from over-straining and injuring themselves; and most importantly, it allows them to develop their accuracy.

Bowlers deliver the ball almost entirely by 'feel': very few are still looking at the spot on the pitch they are aiming at as they deliver the ball. Each delivery in their arsenal has been practised so often, and experienced so many times, that each has an unmistakable feel. The moment the ball leaves the bowler's fingers, he knows exactly on which length it is going to pitch, simply because he recognizes the feeling of the delivery. Indeed it is not uncommon for bowlers across the whole cricketing spectrum (from amateur pie-chuckers to Test fast bowlers) to cry out in disgust or alarm as the ball leaves their fingers – a reaction to the delivery before it has even pitched, because they know where it will go, thanks to feel.

Young bowlers need to develop this feel for accuracy in conditions that will simulate those they'll encounter as adults. If an eight-year-old learns to bowl on a good length on an adult pitch (which is frankly impossible), he would grow up to find that his 'good length feel' is hopelessly off target, and will no doubt have a penchant for bowling waist-high full tosses or beamers.

Shortened pitches present no danger to young batters as young bowlers are unlikely to be able to get the ball through dangerously fast. In fact they will offer young batters the chance to develop their reactions more effectively.

The ideal pitch lengths for different age groups are therefore as follows:
- 7 – 10 years old: 15 yards
- 10 – 13 years old: 18 yards
- 14 and upward: 22 yards (full-size pitch).

The first thing to do when teaching young players to bowl is to shorten the length of the pitch according to their physiques.

Don't compromise on these reductions, or assume that your young bowlers are doing fine just because they're getting the ball generally straight and over halfway up on a full-size pitch. If a young bowler can regularly pitch the ball on a good length (for his developmental stage) from an early age, he has already laid the foundations of a successful career.

WHY COUNTRIES FAIL TO PRODUCE GOOD SPINNERS

The pitches and cricketing cultures of Asia have always encouraged the development of good spin bowlers: from Bhagwat Chandrasekhar, Bishen Bedi and Anil Kumble in India to Abdul Qadir and Saqlain Mushtaq in Pakistan, slow bowlers have often been responsible for the successes in international cricket of subcontinental teams. Indeed, no team in the game's history has relied on one single bowler – with such continued success – as Sri Lanka does on Muttiah Muralitharan.

But as fertile as Asia has been for the development of good spinners, so South Africa, the West Indies and New Zealand have been barren. The number of match-winning spinners produced over the last 130 years by those countries barely reaches double figures: Hugh Tayfield was South Africa's last great spinner, half a century ago, while half a century before him Aubrey Faulkner and Albert Vogler were masters of the googly. A generation also separated the West Indies' Lance Gibbs from Sonny Ramadhin and Alf Valentine, while Daniel Vettori is surely the only world-class Kiwi slow bowler in living memory. Why are these countries such wretched nurseries for spin?

As far as the West Indies is concerned, the answer probably lies in the island federation's reliance on fast bowling. With lethal pace quartets winning Tests throughout the 1970s and 1980s, there was no need to develop spinners, and even with the team in decline in the 1990s, fast bowling never went out of vogue: the retirements of the last great quick men of the Caribbean – Curtly Ambrose and Courtney Walsh – simply triggered a hunt for new fast bowlers. Experiments with spin, in the form of leg-spinners Dinanath Ramnarine and Rawl Lewis, were brief and disastrous; but instead of learning from the mistakes made, slow bowlers were dumped rather than developed. As pitches continue to slow down in the Caribbean and loose-limbed tall fast bowlers remain an increasingly scarce commodity, the value of slow bowling may be rediscovered.

The case of South Africa and New Zealand (and, in the last two decades, England) is a bit more complicated. While pace or seam has traditionally also been favoured by these nations, they have never been averse to spin, and have from time to time embarked on major drives to unearth a world-class slow bowler – usually after a particularly heavy mauling by an Asian or Australian spinner!

In recent seasons England and South Africa have blooded two good fingers-spinners in Monty Panesar and Paul Harris, but both emerged largely unheralded. Both countries have struggled in recent times to produce wicket-taking spinners, and it is not coincidental that they share two structural details: hard green covered pitches, and an emphasis on limited-overs cricket at school level. This is the fastest way to kill spin. English spin bowling especially was dealt a body blow by the move away from uncovered, watered pitches. Whereas 'South African spinners' had been something of an oxymoron, aside from Tayfield, English tweakers like Fred Titmus, Jim Laker, and 'Deadly' Derek Underwood had plied their trade for generations, helped by 'sticky' wickets.

When Bob Woolmer coached South Africa, a programme of three-day games at Under-19 level was initiated. It was agreed that Nuffield Week (the annual representative championship for schoolboys, now called the Coca-Cola Week) would keep its 50-overs-a-side format – sponsors have to be kept happy, after all! – but Woolmer insisted that three-day cricket was vital for the development of various cricket skills, not least spin bowling.

One-day cricket provides a steep learning curve for spinners in certain respects – for instance, they can learn valuable lessons about changing their pace and counteracting a batsman intent on using his feet. But it can also ruin young spinning talent, as bowlers are encouraged to focus on accuracy rather than on turn, on restrictive trajectories rather than on flight. The shortened version of the game also puts enormous pressure on the spinner to produce results immediately: young captains tend to over-attack too soon with their spinner (no doubt conjuring fantasies of Shane Warne and Muralitharan running through top orders), instead of allowing the bowler to defend for some time before finding his line and length and starting to attack. The result is a flurry of runs off an uncertain spinner, and a premature end to his spell or his role in the match. Being hammered for eight or ten (or worse) an over in a four-over spell will almost certainly put a severe dent in any slow bowler's confidence, and his next outing may be even worse as he tenses up and tries to make amends in the eyes of his coach and captain.

Once you've damaged (or destroyed) the art of spin bowling in a particular country, a new problem emerges: mediocre spinners rising quickly through the ranks of first-class cricket. The dearth of good spinners means batsmen have been unable to develop their techniques against spin, and any slow bowler who can land it on a length and turn it a little bit will find himself taking plenty of wickets. This problem is particularly prevalent in South Africa, where it starts at schoolboy level, with young batsmen coming down the wicket to slog spinners.

South Africa's weak record in this regard has become a self-fulfilling prophecy: with no world-class spinners retiring to become world-class spin coaches, the cycle is perpetuated. Worse still, real talent can often be destroyed by ignorant coaches. One young South Africa leg-spinner with real ability was wrecked by a retired senior player (who bowled off-spin!) on a tour of Sri Lanka. The old pro insisted that the young leggie bowl outside off-stump with a 7-2 off-side field. Offered an almost deserted leg-side field on a platter, the Sri Lankans simply clobbered the leg-spinner over mid-wicket, as free hit after free hit was served up. This 'coach' wasn't knowledgeable enough to give the youngster the most basic guideline for leg-spin bowling: always bowl at leg-stump.

Batting

The guidelines and drills that hone technique described in Chapter 3 are universally applicable: whether your batsman is eight or thirty-eight, he is physically capable of moving his hands through the ball along the right line, and of moving his feet according to the length of the delivery headed his way.

Of course, you might need to find more accessible ways of communicating these techniques and drills to a much younger player (who may not see the point of playing straight, given that he simply wants to whack the ball over mid-wicket), but all the principles discussed in Chapter 3 stand, and therefore don't need elaboration or illumination here.

However, young batsmen do need special attention in certain areas that older players don't. The first and most fundamental thing for a coach to remember is that young boys have not yet developed much strength in their arms and hands. It is therefore crucial that they play with a bat they can easily manage. Nothing will kill a child's enthusiasm faster than not being able to use his bat deftly: if he's letting the bat lean in towards him at an angle, and is holding it as if it's a sledge-hammer or pick-axe, then he is clearly struggling with its weight. Finances can be a concern, but try to explain to parents that children must never 'grow into' their bats – bats are specialized tools of an intricate trade, and as such need to be perfectly suited to the person using them.

When do you introduce technique?

This is less a question for coaches than it is for eager parents. Most dads who played cricket in their youth will know the pleasure and hope that is bound up with giving their three-year-old a little wooden or plastic bat, and spending time rolling or gently tossing soft balls that may or may not be hit away to the leg side. But baseball-style slugging, with no grip, stance or footwork, can only be left unguided for so long, and many parents – and coaches – start wondering when to formalize the game as their children reach five or six years of age.

So when should you start imposing batting technique on informal games? The simple answer is: when the child is capable of understanding it. Insisting that a four-year-old adopt a proper stance and grip will simply end in tears – and speaks volumes of a pushy parent hell-bent on living vicariously through his child. However, you do need to be invasive quite early on with regards to the grip. Be insistent without being domineering, perhaps simply explaining that the new game you're both playing has certain fun rules, and one of them is to hold the bat in this particular way. Even then, if he or she shows resistance or irritation, don't harp on it for too long, or you'll cause the child to lose interest.

Children should never have to 'grow into' their bats.

When should you start imposing batting technique on informal games? The simple answer is: when the child is capable of understanding it.

There is definitely a need for a children's bat with a moulded-grip handle, but until this innovation is mass-produced, the best way to get young children to change from their 'woodcutter' grip (one they would use for chopping wood) to a correct cricketing one is to put a ball on a cone, and get them to hit it between two other cones or some other demarcated area. This new twist on the game suddenly becomes extremely difficult with the old or 'natural' grip, and children quickly begin experimenting and adapting as they strive to guide the ball where they want it to go: discovery learning in action.

COACHING LENGTH

After the basic physical skill of picking up and wielding a bat, the most important skill for all young batsmen to develop is that of judging length. This means that you should dedicate yourself to finding effective and entertaining ways of coaching this aspect of batting, giving it more time in practices than more mechanical actions like hitting the ball.

One very useful method for coaching length is to throw the batter variously coloured balls, and then to ask him to point to where they landed. For example, throw him a red one, a blue one and a green one, and then ask where the blue ball landed – the colours make the sequence and position of the balls easier to remember.

Actively trying to notice and remember lengths is an important drill for batters at all levels. Bob Woolmer recalled being in the nets in South Africa, watching an Eastern Province player who was then in a severe slump. 'The net bowler delivered the ball, and without giving the batsman prior warning, I asked him to point to where that delivery had pitched. He didn't have the faintest idea! I told him to focus on the point where the ball was pitching, and he faced another delivery, and this time went down the track to show me the spot. He was six inches off target, both in line and length. So now we knew the problem: he was literally not registering where the ball was pitching. From there, it was a short leap to deducing that he was moving as the ball was delivered. We got him to keep still, and suddenly he was judging length superbly.'

Fielding

The basics of fielding are all discussed in Chapter 6, and many of them can start being taught very early on. Getting the 'long barrier' down behind the ball, catching with two hands, walking in with the bowler, watching your captain at all times; all these apply at all age groups, and the drills described in Chapter 6 are effective at almost all age groups.

Speed, agility and anticipation cannot be taught. However, they can all be encouraged or given the opportunity to develop, by exposing the child to an active and healthy lifestyle. All three are biologically ordained and primal assets, and unless actively hindered (by a sedentary lifestyle or poor diet), they can emerge in any person genetically predisposed to them, anywhere on the planet.

Catching, however, is not quite so ingrained. Older children and adults can learn to catch, but there is always a slight hesitation, a hardness of the hands, and very rarely that almost instinctive swiftness and co-ordination seen in the truly great catchers. To produce good catchers, who can take balls at most angles and speeds, you need to start training them early.

The young child faces two obstacles when trying to catch: fear of being struck, and a lack of co-ordination. Even the softest ball, thrown very gently from two feet away, can make toddlers or young children clutch wildly with stiff arms and hands while they simultaneously flinch and close their eyes in defence. It is therefore important to develop both motor skills and confidence gradually.

Start by simply dropping a ball into the child's hands from above. Start small, perhaps no more than a few centimetres, slowly lengthening the drop. This will eventually remove the child's last-minute panic, that almost universal clutch that causes nearly every young child to drop the ball at first. Allowing the ball to come into the hands is a skill that will ultimately help the Test cricketer take a stinging catch at slip.

Once the child is more confident, and no longer clutches at the ball, try rolling the ball down a short length of pipe, into his waiting hands at the bottom. The actual flight of the ball may be even shorter than the initial drops (he may hold his hand just one or two centimetres under the mouth of the pipe), but this technique conditions him to anticipate the arrival of the ball: seeing the 'flight' of the ball all the way down the pipe, he learns when to start preparing himself to take the 'catch'. Then raise the pipe, or lower his hands, so that the ball drops a short distance into his hands. Once this is happening, the child will soon be ready to start taking gentle catches from increasing distances.

WRAPPING UP

From all of the above, it will be clear that teaching long-term athlete development is very important for all coaches, just as it is important to encourage co-ordination and timing in young players. Even if most of your youngsters never play beyond school-level, the fitness and physical skills you teach them, and the reflexes you train, will stand them in good stead throughout their adult lives. Above all, you will have given them immense pleasure; there are few childhood joys greater than deep absorption in a game or sport when you are fit, well-prepared, and thus able to get the most out of the experience.

PART FOUR

CRICKET SCIENCE

CHAPTER TEN

PHYSIOLOGY AND FITNESS

INTRODUCTION

The idea that one needs to be fit to play cricket (or indeed team sports in general) is a relatively new one. Anecdotes abound about Test cricketers in the 1960s avoiding the nets altogether, or practising half a dozen drives before heading indoors for a pie and a cigarette. Yet even traditionally more physical and mobile sports were slow in realizing the potential of fitness, a fact exposed and exploited by the champion rugby teams of New Zealand and Australia. Indeed, until 1987, when the Rugby World Cup was established, the popular wisdom was that you became fit for a team sport by playing that sport.

However, after the All Blacks won the World Cup in 1987 and the Wallabies claimed the championships in 1991 – both teams having paid attention to physical fitness – it became clear that fitness training had arrived for good. Since then, fitness levels of international players have showed a marked improvement, to the point where the physical demands placed on professional rugby players in today's game are close to the limits that the human body can tolerate.

But is this really relevant to cricket? By citing the example of rugby in a manual on cricket, aren't we comparing apples and oranges? Besides, doesn't cricket have a grand tradition of stars who did not appear to be particularly athletic, and whose success at the crease suggests that cricketers can get away with carrying a few extra kilos, as long as they have talent?

From W.G. Grace to Arjuna Ranatunga, Inzamam-ul-Haq to Shane Warne, players have stepped onto the international stage hounded by amused comments about their more generous figures, before going on to suggest – through consistently superior performances – that their excess weight was not a handicap. Grace's batting stood head and shoulders above that of his contemporaries; Ranatunga captained the winning team in the 1996 World Cup (and scored a rapid unbeaten 47 in the final against Australia); Inzamam topped the batting ratings in 1998, and averaged just over 50 for more than a decade; and Shane Warne became the greatest wrist-spin bowler in the history of the game, eclipsing even the performances of such legendary players as the West Indies' Lance Gibbs, England's Jim Laker and Australia's Richie Benaud.

Yet even these examples need closer scrutiny. Grace was no sylph, but he did not have to be: in the 19th-century game, a good eye and an intimidating personality went a long way towards keeping the score ticking over, and less than restrictive bowling kept the running of singles to a minimum.

For Warne's part, as he became older, the leg-spinner increasingly realized that his unique skills would not be enough to retain his place in the ultra-competitive and unforgiving world of Australian cricket. Only by achieving and maintaining a high level of physical fitness would he be able to sustain his career as he aged. As a result, at age 33, he embarked on a rigorous diet in an effort to lose weight – and was not above seeking short cuts, as is discussed elsewhere in this chapter.

But perhaps the most telling attribute of this very small handful of successful overweight players is that none of them is a fast bowler. As this book illustrates, bowling fast is one of the most demanding activities in world sport: to reach the pinnacle of the game, and to prosper there, modern fast bowlers must be among the most athletic of humans.

In other words, in the modern game of cricket, it is not enough to play yourself fit or rely on your skill. To achieve your personal best, you need to pay as much attention to fitness as you do to the perfection of batting, bowling and fielding skills. The demands on the modern player, especially those posed by the sheer volume of cricket played by contemporary professionals (see Table 10.1, for instance), require that anyone who intends taking their game seriously must be committed to becoming and remaining as fit and healthy as possible. Bob Woolmer believed that Test cricketers of the future would have to be as fit as world-class tri-athletes if they are to play their best and reduce their risk of serious injury.

But this advice should not apply only to elite players: club and school cricketers will maximize both their potential and the pleasure they get from the game if they are both physically fit and following a healthy lifestyle.

THE INCREASED DEMANDS ON INTERNATIONAL CRICKETERS

During the 1998/99 cricket season, the South African cricket team played eight five-day Test matches, 17 one-day international games and were eligible to play in eight four-day and ten one-day provincial (county) cricket matches. This made a total number of 99 days on which they could be asked to play.

In contrast, in 1970 (before South Africa was banned from the international sports arena), the South African national cricket team played a total of four five-day Test matches and no one-day international matches. Players were also eligible to play four three-day and three one-day provincial matches during the season, giving a possible season total of 35 days of cricket. In the three decades between 1970 and 2000, the demands on elite South African cricketers have thus increased by 280%. An analysis of international cricketers in the other Test-playing cricketing nations would show very similar increases.

Since it has been the fast bowlers who have borne the brunt of this increasingly crowded playing schedule, it is worth noting how their bowling loads have changed over time. The table opposite lists some of the world's best pace bowlers over the past 120 years, and shows the number of overs they bowled in their careers; how many overs they bowled each year; the number of overs bowled per match; and how much one-day cricket they played compared to multi-day forms of the game.

This table shows the dramatic increase in the number of overs bowled in an average season in the last few decades. Note that there does not appear to be as significant an increase for English fast bowlers – this is because county cricket involves their playing far more first-class (but not necessarily international) cricket than is the case in any other country.

Yet even though English bowlers like Bob Willis did not bowl substantially more than Fred Trueman and Alec Bedser, Willis believes that the number of overs bowled is not the real measure of how the game has changed: 'Fred and Alec only ever played three-day county matches, all at the same pace. They never came on in one-day matches and bowled fifteen yorkers off the last 18 balls while batsmen were trying to slog them out of the ground' (*The Zen of Cricket*, p. 140).

The point is that modern cricketers are now expected to perform under much more trying conditions. It is certain that only the best physically prepared cricketers will perform better, more consistently, with fewer injuries and, as a result, will enjoy longer careers. It is for this reason that it is essential to understand the physiological demands of modern cricket, initially for the benefit of individual players and teams, but eventually for the survival and growth of the game itself.

Where figures for early cricketers are missing, the number of balls bowled throughout first-class careers has been estimated, based on the rough average of 150 deliveries bowled per match.
1. Total number of balls bowled includes both six- and eight-ball overs; overs per year calculated as for six-ball overs.
2. Barnes' career was interrupted by the First World War.
3. The careers of these four cricketers were interrupted by the Second World War.

TABLE 10.1: Increase in volume of workload carried by elite fast bowlers

PLAYER	TEAM	YEARS OF CAREER	CAREER LENGTH (YEARS)	TOTAL BALLS IN CAREER	TOTAL 5-, 4- OR 3-DAY MATCHES	1-DAY MATCHES	OVERS PER YEAR[1]	OVERS[1] PER MATCH
Spofforth	AUS	1874–1888	15	34 778	173	0	386	33,50
Barnes	ENG	1894–1930	36[2]	39 400	160	0	182	41,04
Gregory	AUS	1920–1929	10	24 932	153	0	415	27,15
Larwood	ENG	1924–1938	15	62 996	382	0	699	27,48
Voce	ENG	1927–1952	26[3]	91 860	453	0	588	33,79
Miller	AUS	1937–1959	23[3]	38 531	281	0	428	22,85
Bedser	ENG	1939–1960	22[3]	122 036	536	0	924	37,94
Lindwall	AUS	1941–1962	22[3]	56 865	289	0	430	32,79
Trueman	ENG	1949–1972	24	115 865	670	18	804	28,06
Statham	ENG	1950–1968	19	118 002	629	15	1 035	30,53
Heine	SA	1951–1965	15	13 040[1]	75	0	144	28,97
Adcock	SA	1952–1963	12	26 099	125	0	362	34,79
Hall	WI	1955–1971	17	36 029[1]	218	2	353	27,29
Pollock, P	SA	1958–1972	15	26 082	155	8	289	26,66
Griffith	WI	1959–1966	8	21 212	124	2	441	28,00
Snow	ENG	1961–1980	20	82 399	395	191	686	23,43
Nawaz	PAK	1968–1985	18	83 592	354	273	774	22,22
Willis	ENG	1969–1984	16	83 921	398	357	874	18,52
Lillee	AUS	1969–1988	20	57 444	268	165	478	22,11
Imran Khan	PAK	1970–1992	23	111 265	470	600	806	17,33
Thomson	AUS	1972–1986	15	51 078	238	138	567	22,64
Hadley	NZ	1972–1990	19	111 806	428	433	980	21,64
Holding	WI	1973–1989	17	69 692	282	351	683	18,34
Garner	WI	1976–1992	17	71 687	272	354	702	19,05
Kapil Dev	IND	1976–1994	19	102 742	406	534	901	18,21
Marshall	WI	1978–1995	18	121 736	489	576	1 127	19,05
Walsh	WI	1982–2001	20	148 165	561	645	1 234	20,47
Wasim	PAK	1985–2003	19	120 923	361	955	1 060	15,31
Ambrose	WI	1986–2000	15	97 397	337	505	1 082	19,27
Donald	SA	1986–2003	18	105 779	388	624	979	17,42
Waqar	PAK	1988–2003	16	88 071	315	680	917	14,75
Gough	ENG	1989–2007	19	83 811	297	585	735	15,83
Pollock, S	SA	1992–2008	16	98 734	290	728	1 028	16,16
McGrath	AUS	1993–2007	15	99 767	313	557	1 108	19,11

THE NEW FACE OF SPORTS FITNESS

Achieving the appropriate level of fitness for one's chosen sport, as well as the specialized routines that will hone one's fitness for batting, bowling or fielding, at the same time reducing the risk of injury, is now acknowledged to be a complex enterprise – the realm of the professional fitness/exercise specialist. Fitness training routines must be tailored to fit the individual – the bad old days of PT training where everyone, regardless of their fitness, runs aimlessly round and round the sports field, are over (or at least they should be).

But honing the physical component of cricket skills comprises much more than simple fitness training. It now also combines a detailed knowledge of sports nutrition (including an understanding of the largely detrimental effects of alcohol, tobacco, recreational drugs and prescription medications on performance), together with knowing how to cope with frequent exhausting travel and (for elite cricketers) living away from home for much of the year. A basic grasp of the biomechanics of the game is necessary, and knowledge of the cause, prevention and treatment of injuries is vital for the coach, the team physiotherapist and the exercise specialist – and indeed for each cricketer, since the modern cricketer must take ultimate responsibility for everything that happens to him or her.

Fortunately, a number of factors, most especially the growth of the sports sciences in the past few decades, have produced one of the most profound revolutions in the history of cricket. The cricketing community has finally realized that, to be successful, modern cricketers require considerable expert input from fitness/exercise specialists (biokineticists), nutritionists, physiotherapists, and a host of others within the disciplines of sports science and sports medicine.

Although traditionalists will continue to wonder what has happened to the 'good old days' when one simply played the game and had no need of a gaggle of doctors and scientists, the reality is that the future of cricket lies with those who embrace science and the systematic approach to success. Australian cricket was galvanized by the systematic, scientific and uncompromisingly exact approach initiated by Bob Simpson in the 1980s; English rugby was revolutionized in the late 1990s by the methodical approach of coach Clive Woodward, himself a graduate in sports sciences. There is no doubt that the great cricketing nations of the future will be those that adopt similar approaches, as Australia has done with the appointment of John Buchanan, an exercise science graduate, as national coach. Those who choose to remain 'traditionalist' in their approach to the sports sciences will sadly see cricket in their countries fade into the sunset in an increasingly competitive and technologically advanced world.

Above all, there are two compelling reasons why those who wish to maximize their ability need to embrace all that these various disciplines can offer cricket and cricketers. Firstly, they will enable all participants to play better cricket; and secondly, they will make the game safer. We will explore these claims in detail in the sections that follow. But the bottom line is that by utilizing the best that all these experts can offer, cricketers can play better for longer, with a reduced chance of injury and re-injury, and a more rapid rate of recovery when they do suffer those injuries that are an unfortunate consequence of any activity that places extreme demands on the human body.

But perhaps all of this is summed up with two simple questions: are there any advantages to being unfit? If so, what are they? We've yet to find any.

PHYSIOLOGY OF FITNESS FOR CRICKET

Even though cricket is one of the oldest organized sports, there are very few studies of the physiological demands of cricket or of the specific physiological, biochemical or anthropometric (body shape and size) attributes of exceptional cricketers. Perhaps this reflects the tradition of the game and its devotees, who are more likely to be interested in the 'how' of cricket than in the 'why'. Indeed no less a cricketing icon than Richie Benaud has expressed his distrust of scientific enquiry, famously writing, 'I know we have a real problem if I see a media hand-out which begins, "Research in sport has shown..."' (1998, p. 213). But this sentiment is clearly not shared by many of his compatriots, or at least those actively involved with Australian sport: of all the cricketing nations, it is only the Australian Cricket Board (so far) that actively employs at least two scientists, whose full-time responsibility is to undertake scientific research that will improve that country's cricket. Much of Australia's dominance, not only in cricket, but in other sports as well, is a result of a clearly defined and well-funded programme of methodical and scientific training and research.

No doubt their response to sceptics would be much the same as ours: if the game is continually to advance, and to compete with a growing number of sports vying for the attention of players and public alike, it is essential that the 'why's' of cricket should be answered.

THE FLETCHER STUDY: SLOW-MOTION CRICKET

Perhaps the earliest attempt to study and analyse the physiological demands of Test cricket was made by Fletcher (1955). Collecting his data during the Ashes series of 1953 in England, he attempted to predict the average energy expenditure of the international cricketers involved in that series.

He calculated that if all the activity that occurred during the five Tests of the

There are two compelling reasons to embrace all that sports science can offer: firstly, this will enable the participants to play better cricket; and secondly, it will make the game safer.

1953 Ashes was divided equally among the 22 players on both sides, the mean daily physical activity for each player would have been the following:

- the average Englishman or Australian would bat for 38,5 minutes per day, scoring 14 runs (no doubt a less than thrilling experience for the spectators);
- he would bowl for 14 minutes for a total of 4,2 overs;
- he would field for a duration of 116 minutes, during which he would retrieve 16 deliveries;
- The remaining 191,5 minutes each day would be spent resting in the pavilion.

As a result, the mean rate of energy expenditure worked out at 86,4 kcal/m^2/h.[1] For an average cricketer with a body surface area of 1,8m^2, this would translate into an energy expenditure of approximately 650 kJ per hour.

These calculations, added to other measurements of the energy expenditure of cricketers practising in the nets, showed that the mean energy expenditure for the average Test cricketer was slightly more than that required simply to stand. Although mean energy expenditures when batting or bowling were somewhat higher, each was still less than that required to walk at the leisurely pace of 6km per hour! Only when bowling or batting in the nets did the mean energy expenditure exceed that achieved while playing tennis.

Those who find these figures hard to accept will be reassured to hear that these findings underestimate the true effort involved in playing cricket.

Studies such as Fletcher's no doubt contributed to the perception that cricket is a physically undemanding sport. Frankly, however, the players and administrators of the game were doing a splendid job of spreading that message all on their own. A year before Fletcher released his findings in 1955, the MCC had toured Australia and New Zealand, adhering strictly to the fitness guidelines laid down by its captain, Sir Leonard Hutton:

Each player is responsible for his own fitness. He must stay well rested and must not overstrain in practices. He should exercise only very mildly on 'off' days, during which he may swim or play tennis or golf in the early mornings only; and he must stay out of the midday sun (cited in Woolmer, 2000).

---

1 The term kcal/m^2/h means the amount of energy (kcal) expended every hour (h) – in this case, while playing cricket. To standardize for differences in body size (heavier, taller individuals expend more energy when exercising at the same speed and intensity than lighter, smaller people), the rate of energy expenditure is also corrected for body surface area in metres squared (m^2). Note that 1 kcal = 4,2 kJ (kilojoules).

These sedate suggestions seem amusing and quaint to the modern professional (and might explain the old American barb that cricket is the only sport in which you can put on weight while actually playing). But before we congratulate ourselves on how far we've come, it is worth pointing out that Sir Leonard's views on training with circumspection and getting adequate rest were still held up as a gold standard three decades later. The 1986 edition of the Lord's Taverner's Cricket Clinic made some remarkably tame recommendations regarding fitness:

- To develop stamina, cricketers were advised to run, skip or cycle for ten to twenty minutes in the session.
- To develop strength, they were encouraged to do push-ups, sit-ups and to 'swing the cricket bat'.
- To enhance their mobility, they were advised to perform wide-stride sitting, toe-touching and head and shoulder circling.

Of course, sceptics might argue that if that great player of the 1980s, Ian Botham, could become one of the greatest all-rounders in the history of the game with only the most haphazard and basic scientific support, how much can that support really offer? But this would be to misunderstand the value of a scientific approach to training. Pointing out that athletes like Botham and many others scintillated without access to trained exercise scientists is to ignore the possibility that they might have reached even greater heights if they had had this kind of support. With it, Botham might at least have avoided some the numerous surgeries he had to undergo towards the end of his career – and indeed after it ended.

NOT JUST A WALK IN THE PARK

It was 47 years before another study attempted to provide a more accurate calculation of a cricketer's energy expenditure. In 2002, Candice Christie and her colleagues at Rhodes University in Grahamstown, South Africa, measured the amount of oxygen used by batsmen facing seven six-ball overs on an outdoor turf pitch. During each over, the batters sprinted four single runs of 18 metres each (regardless of where they had hit the ball), running a total of 28 runs from the 42 deliveries, an average scoring rate for a one-day international. The researchers found that the batsmens' energy expenditure was 2 536kJ/m^2/h or about 300kJ/m^2/h, substantially more than the value calculated by Fletcher for the 1953 Ashes (Christie et al., 2003).

They also found that the batsmens' heart rates increased from 126 beats per minute in the first over, to between 149 and 155 beats per minute for the fourth to the seventh overs. Given that these heart rates are similar to those measured in recreational runners during 21km and 42km running races, this is further evidence of the physical demands made on the modern batsman. Indeed, four runs an over is quite sedate in terms of the modern game; one-day batsmen need to be ready and able to sprint at least 12 runs an over during the closing stages of an innings.

Christie's findings indicate how much the game has changed since Fletcher conducted his survey 50-odd years ago. For example, calculations of the estimated peak physical activity in batting during one-day cricket in a player who batted for 100 runs (and who batted with a partner who also scored 100 runs in the same period) show that each batter would run about 3,2km in about eight minutes (spread over his innings). The average running speed would be 24km per hour and the number of decelerations (in which the batter must slow down either at the end of a single or in order to turn when running twos or threes) would be a minimum of 110. To put this into perspective, the world speed record for the half-marathon is 21,6km per hour – slightly slower than the speed measured by the world 10km record-holder!

Bowlers will naturally look at these figures and, in the time-honoured tradition of the workhorse seamer, claim that batsmen don't know the first thing about being tired or working hard. Certainly the out-and-out fast bowler might have a point. Consider the estimated physical activity of a one-day seam bowler, based on the assumption that a faster bowler might deliver around 64 balls (60 legal, with 4 wides or no-balls) in 40 minutes. During this period, he would be expected to run 1,9km in about 5,3 minutes, which translates into an average speed of 21,6km per hour – the same as the world half-marathon record mentioned above! Furthermore, the delivery action would require approximately 64 seconds of strenuous upper body action as well as the sudden lower body deceleration at the end of each delivery.

All of which might explain why Dennis Lillee wrote that at the end of a hard day of bowling, he felt so drained that 'I might have been shovelling gravel all day. It is then that I know all about the component parts of a fast bowler. The aches and pains all over my body remind me in no uncertain manner' (1982, p. 31).

While the physical demands of cricket have clearly increased, especially with the introduction of one-day cricket, at the same time young people today are getting less habitual exercise than ever before. The lives of our parents and grandparents involved far more manual labour or daily physical effort, and considerably more walking, than is usual in the average urban lifestyle of today. Harold Larwood, the great English fast bowler who was at the heart of the Bodyline crisis, wrote, 'I never had any training routines at all. I did a lot of walking exercises as during my career from 1925 to 1938 one had to walk a lot – no cars and buses' (Lillee, 1982, p. 35). Dennis Lillee agrees: 'That about sums it up. Technological advances in the shape of motorcars, elevators and a softening of man. The answer for the athlete is to supplement a fairly sedentary normal existence with a quite active training programme' (Lillee, 1982, p. 30).

In the past, most people played sport for pleasure, relaxation, and 'to get fit', although few realized that their chosen sport simply increased a certain baseline of fitness that was already present. However, because our modern lifestyles are significantly more sedentary than they were even two decades ago, there is a much greater need, especially for younger athletes, to spend more time in physical preparation. We already know that good cricketers are invariably skilled or naturally gifted at the game; but, as is being increasingly recognized, the best players are also mentally tough and physically fit.

The topic is continually under investigation because the perfect formula for helping today's cricketers reach and maintain peak match fitness has yet to be reached. Have coaches, fitness trainers and team physiotherapists kept pace with the physical demands of the modern game? We feel that the answer is no. There is still a long way to go, especially at the top level of the game, where there is a need to mesh fitness training into the excessively demanding rigors of playing and travelling internationally. Under these conditions, a fine line exists between too much training – which produces fatigue and an increased risk of injury – and too little training, which also predisposes to injury. The reality is that modern cricket at the international level is as demanding as any other sport, and as such, it carries a significant risk of injury. The complete elimination of such risk is not possible on the basis of our current knowledge. So much investigation still needs to be undertaken in terms of research and study.

At this point, you might want to assess your own attitudes to fitness by answering the following questions. Be honest with yourself, and consider what your motivations and goals really are.

- Are you satisfied with your current level of fitness?
- Are you strong enough?
- Are you flexible enough?
- Are you working on the specific physical requirements of your particular game?
- Are you prepared to devote more time to improving your fitness?
- In an analysis of your game, in what areas are you most effective? Is this a reflection of your fitness?
- Do you record all your fitness training in a logbook?
- Do you record your performances in each game or analyze how you felt?
- When you train, do you work hard and with enthusiasm, or do you merely go through the motions?

Your answers will illustrate the extent to which you believe that fitness determines your cricket performance, as well as the degree to which you are prepared to commit yourself to a more complete (and, if necessary, rigorous) training programme in the future. Remember, regardless of whether you want to be promoted from the second eleven to the first, or want to play Test cricket one day, the requirements are essentially universal: spend as much effort in the pursuit of fitness as you do in the perfection of skills for batting, bowling and fielding. Fitness is the foundation on which all your other skills are built.

THE BASICS OF EXERCISE PHYSIOLOGY

Just as cricket continues to evolve, so too does our understanding of how the body works during exercise; how training improves performance and reduces the risk of injury; and how best to produce beneficial changes with training. Many new ideas have developed in the past decade, and we begin by reviewing some of these novel concepts.

1. THE CLASSIC CARDIOVASCULAR/ANAEROBIC/ CATASTROPHIC MODEL OF EXERCISE PHYSIOLOGY

Most who have done some biology at school will have been taught that the most important factor limiting exercise performance is the production of 'poisonous' lactic acid in the exercising muscles. We have named this the cardiovascular/anaerobic/ catastrophic model of exercise physiology (Noakes et al., 2004).

This classic model holds that there is an exercise intensity or workload above which the output of the heart reaches a limiting maximum. As a result, when the exercise intensity exceeds that maximum, the muscles must continue to contract (work) even though they are no longer getting an adequate blood and oxygen supply. Faced with this shortage of blood and oxygen, the active muscles must contract 'anaerobically'; that is, in the absence of an adequate oxygen supply. As a consequence, the exercising muscles must revert to the partial breakdown (metabolism) of their major carbohydrate energy source (glycogen) into lactic acid (lactate). It is argued that this partial breakdown of glycogen produces 'poisonous' metabolic by-products, especially lactic acid. This lactic acid then impairs muscle function by increasing muscle stiffness, producing fatigue, and ultimately, the termination of exercise (Noakes et al., 2004).

A popular interpretation of this classic model was described by Webster (1948) as follows:

First the sprinter very quickly creates what is termed an 'oxygen debt'; and secondly, the valuable glycogen inside the muscle fibres is turned into poisonous lactic acid, the muscles become tired and stiff, dwindle in power, and finally refuse to function until the lactic acid has been turned back to glycogen during the recuperative processes of rest.

This concept has given rise to the popular notion that the heart (because it is responsible for supplying the muscles with an adequate blood and oxygen supply) ultimately determines exercise performance. Following this, it seems logical that the main focus of training must be to increase the capacity of the heart, so that it can pump yet more blood to the exercising muscles, developing so-called 'cardiovascular', 'aerobic' or 'endurance' fitness. Since running, swimming, squash, rowing and cycling produce the greatest stress on the heart, proponents of this model would argue that cricketers wanting to develop optimum cardiovascular or endurance fitness need to spend a reasonable amount of time performing one or more of these activities.

But does cardiovascular fitness (as defined above) contribute to or indeed determine the performance of a cricketer in the field? If this model is applicable to cricket, does it mean that the fielder, batter or bowler feels tired at the end of a hard day's cricket – a long innings or bowling spell – because his heart is no longer able to provide his muscles with sufficient oxygen? And if it does, would more endurance training of the heart reduce that fatigue and improve performance in all these areas?

Many famous bowlers and batsmen attest to the importance of endurance training, usually in the form of running, in their cricket preparation: Englishmen Bob Willis and Graham Gooch and Australian Dennis Lillee ran almost daily for at least 30 minutes, and sometimes up to 60 minutes. However, if we compare Willis' 30 minutes of running a day to the two to three or three to six hours a day spent in training by elite distance runners and tri-athletes respectively, we see that these cricketers were deriving comparatively little 'cardiovascular' benefit from their running. So where were these Test stars getting the necessary training to reach and maintain their optimum levels?

One answer might be that as professional cricketers, they would have spent at least another one to three hours a day training their special skills. Furthermore, the average match would demand six or more hours of fielding per day (for multi-day matches) and about three and a half hours during one-day matches. Repeated often enough, such matches are in themselves endurance training sessions, a point that is often overlooked. Often, it is competition that provides the optimum training for competition. But this does not mean that you don't need to get fit to play sport. For instance, bowlers will need to develop muscle strength and muscle balance to offset the injury risks associated with bowling.

STARTING YOUNG

Bob Simpson, Australian Test batsman and the first official coach of the national team, played a significant role in the rise to dominance by the Australian cricket team in recent years. His views on why many players break down closely mirror those of Larwood and Lillee already discussed: 'I really believe that a lot of players have injury problems – and from an early age – because of the easy lifestyle we all enjoy. When I was a kid I walked everywhere, climbed trees and jumped fences for fun. I did a lot of physical work without ever thinking it had anything to do with fitness or conditioning. When I see modern players suffering from back troubles, stress fractures and the like, I can't believe that they are caused simply by the physical demands… kids don't get the physical conditioning they developed naturally years ago… their bodies are not trained, in the widest sense, for physical exertion.'

While this may not be the whole picture, scientists agree that it's a vital clue. One only has to consider how many of England's fast bowlers of days gone by were labourers, builders or miners in the off-season – to the extent that the saying went, 'If you need a paceman, stand at a Yorkshire pithead and whistle!'

There is no doubt that 20 or 30 years ago, most children spent at least some of their recreational time climbing trees, clambering over rocks, walking or riding bikes to school, sailing or rowing, or building tree-houses. The generations that grew up in the 1940s and 1950s also lived with far fewer cars, and could spend their weekends playing informal sports matches in streets that today are congested.

Middle-class children of a generation ago also generally lived in much safer environments (enabling them to walk to school, for example), and had access to more open spaces for play, whether big gardens, parks or forested areas. Certain sports that many Western children of several decades ago used to enjoy on holidays and weekends have become the exclusive province of the wealthy (ski-ing, sailing, horse-riding); security considerations have greatly restricted others.

Children under fifteen are not usually allowed to join gyms, so we recommend that young children who want to get fit for cricket should be encouraged to combine aerobic exercise (hiking, swimming, cycling) with strength training by climbing ropes, or ideally, a safe climbing-wall or rock face. Young people cannot get maximum benefit out of weight training until after puberty because they lack the specific hormones required for muscle development; but general training can do just as well, since it increases the strength of bones and tendons as much as muscles. Indeed, there is now good evidence that ultimate bone strength is influenced to a great extent by the amount of exercise (bone loading) that is done between the ages of ten and fourteen. This means that running and jumping are especially valuable because they both load the bones, as do gymnastics and the jumping component of aerobics.

Perhaps one conclusion is that cricketers need to undertake some endurance training to supplement their skill-specific training, but that they do not need to undertake anything close to the amount required of elite runners or tri-athletes. This in turn suggests that the factors limiting cricket performance are not simply cardiovascular fitness and fatigue of the heart according to this traditional model.

2. THE ENERGY SUPPLY/ENERGY DEPLETION MODEL OF EXERCISE PHYSIOLOGY

This popular model of exercise physiology is a subtle modification of the first. It suggests that muscle performance is determined not so much by the rate of oxygen supply, but rather by the rate at which the exercising muscles are able to produce energy from the sources that are available (either directly in the muscle or supplied through the bloodstream).

Accordingly, it argues that knowledge of the different energy-producing pathways that provide fuel during activities of different intensities and durations should allow one to predict which energy fuels are likely to limit performance in any activity. This knowledge is then used to determine the most appropriate training methods for any specific activity, according to the energy fuels that are likely to be most used during that activity.

Figure 10.1 explains how this line of reasoning is often used to develop specific training methods for different sporting activities. It shows the relative contributions of the different energy systems during exercise of different durations. According to this model, performance during maximal exercise lasting six seconds or less is limited by the muscles' capacity to produce energy from its direct energy stores, known as the phosphagens (Adenosine triphosphate [ATP] and Phosphocreatine [PCr]) and from the breakdown of glycogen to lactic acid (lactate) in the absence of oxygen – a process known as oxygen-independent glycolysis (or incorrectly, anaerobic glycolysis). Some argue that the exceptional ability of great sprinters can be explained by their superior ability to generate energy from these metabolic pathways.

Along the same lines, it is argued that maximal activity that produces fatigue within 120 seconds maximizes energy use from the complete breakdown of glycogen to carbon dioxide and water in the presence of an adequate oxygen supply, with the remaining 35% of the energy derived from oxygen-independent glycolysis, causing the production of some 'poisonous' lactic acid. Accordingly, the inability of these two pathways to provide energy quickly enough in the active muscles is considered to be the main limitation for maximal activity lasting about two minutes. This effect is compounded by the accumulation of the 'poisonous' by-products of rapid glycogen breakdown, especially lactic acid.

Conversely, exercise of 60 minutes or longer is considered to be limited by depletion of body energy, especially carbohydrate reserves. These reserves exist in the liver and the muscles. Depletion of glycogen reserves in the liver causes blood glucose concentrations to fall, reducing the ability to concentrate, as well as the desire to continue exercising, whereas depletion of the muscle glycogen reserves is said to limit exercise by reducing the rapidity with which ATP can be generated within the muscle. It is argued that ATP cannot be generated fast enough from the alternative muscle fuel (fat), so that the exercise intensity must be reduced or else muscle rigor will develop.

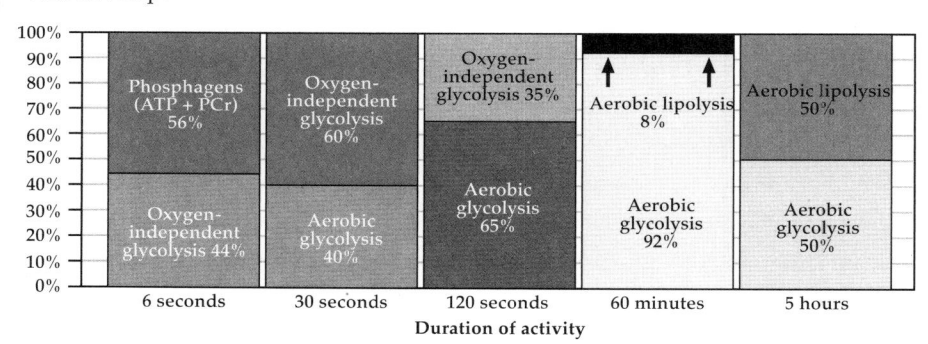

Duration	Energy sources
6 seconds	Phosphagens (ATP + PCr) 56%; Oxygen-independent glycolysis 44%
30 seconds	Oxygen-independent glycolysis 60%; Aerobic glycolysis 40%
120 seconds	Oxygen-independent glycolysis 35%; Aerobic glycolysis 65%
60 minutes	Aerobic lipolysis 8%; Aerobic glycolysis 92%
5 hours	Aerobic lipolysis 50%; Aerobic glycolysis 50%

FIGURE 10.1: *The sources of energy provision during exercise to exhaustion lasting from six seconds to five hours*

This energy depletion model is usually used to explain the fatigue that develops during prolonged exercise, such as is seen in marathon or ultra-marathon running, in which high rates of energy expenditure are sustained for prolonged periods of at least two hours. Calculations suggest that it is possible to deplete all the body carbohydrate stores within approximately two to two and a half hours of very vigorous exercise. However, the energy expenditure in cricket is too low to suggest that athletes could deplete their body carbohydrate stores during one or more days of cricket.

Indeed, the more modest rates of energy expenditure, especially during a three-to-five-day cricket match, suggest that the fuel most likely being used by cricketers during most of their activities (except for fast bowling) is fat. Even batsmen and fielders would use mainly fat, as the energy for their sprints would come from the breakdown of phosphagens (with the restitution of their muscle phosphagen concentrations occurring as they recovered) produced by the burning of fats (in the presence of an adequate oxygen supply). This leads to interesting speculation as to whether depletion of body fat stores is likely during a cricket match.

Nevertheless, even though the physical demands of cricket (in terms of the frequency of international competition) have clearly increased in the past 30 years, it is clear that the only cricketers at risk of developing whole body energy depletion are those who deliberately choose to do so.

This means that these models are not that relevant to cricket physiology, as most activities in the game are of reasonably short duration, lasting perhaps a maximum of ten seconds, and are seldom of the all-out variety that demands complete energy depletion. The longest uninterrupted distance a cricketer might run fast would be a matter of 30 metres in the fine leg area, or perhaps 50 metres (at a leisurely jog) at the end of overs. In addition, cricketers are protected from the risk of developing liver glycogen depletion, leading to low blood glucose concentrations (hypoglycaemia), by the scheduling of tea or lunch breaks at approximately two-hourly intervals.

Most players and coaches know that the speed and accuracy of fast bowlers decline after six to eight overs, and that batsmen are often extremely fatigued by innings in which they score 100 or more, especially if they do so in a frenetic one-day match. But the physiological reality is that neither the fast bowler nor the limited-overs centurion is likely to be suffering from total, whole-body energy depletion. This practical observation of the game suggests that the models currently used to explain the physiology of fatigue are unsatisfactory when applied to activities like cricket, in which there are short bouts of high-intensity exercise interspersed with prolonged periods at much lower exercise intensities. Clearly some other explanation is required.

3. THE INTEGRATED MUSCLE RECRUITMENT (CENTRAL GOVERNOR) MODEL OF EXERCISE PHYSIOLOGY

A key feature of the muscles that connect to the skeleton – the skeletal muscles – the contraction of which allows us to run, throw, bat and bowl, is that not all the muscle fibres (cells) in a muscle are active each time that muscle contracts. So when we lift a light weight, only a few of the muscle fibres in that arm need to be active. This is determined by the brain, which sees the object that must be picked up, calculates its likely weight, and then recruits the number of muscle fibres that, from experience, the brain believes are needed to lift that weight in a controlled manner.

In addition, once the weight is picked up, the brain receives sensory feedback from multiple organs informing it whether it has made the correct decision, or whether it needs to either increase or decrease the number of muscle fibres that it has recruited. In other words, sensors in the muscles and tendons measure the actual weight of the object that has been picked up: if they sense that the weight is too heavy, they will immediately inform the brain that more muscle fibres must be recruited. This typically happens, for example, when an abnormally heavy object is picked up. (A good example of this is a gold bar – which is seldom encountered! – and which is

It is competition that provides the optimum training for competition. But this does not mean that you don't need to get fit to play sport.

Towards the end of a period of exercise, the best athletes are able to increase the number of muscle fibres that are active – the so-called 'end spurt' phenomenon.

very much heavier than any equivalently-sized object.) Once the object is being picked up, the rate of its movement can be sensed both by the eyes and other muscle and joint sensors that measure rates of joint movement. In this way, the brain always chooses just the right number of muscle fibres that are needed to complete any particular task, be it gently lobbing the ball back to the bowler, or throwing it in as hard as possible from the boundary.

The relevance of this to fatigue is that the key assumption of the cardiovascular/anaerobic/catastrophic and the energy depletion models are that *all* the muscle fibres in the active muscles are active at exhaustion. In other words, according to these two models, less than 100% of the available muscle fibres may be active at the start of exercise; and as the exercise continues, progressively more muscle fibres are recruited until, at the point of exhaustion (either in exercise of high intensity and short duration, or during prolonged exercise of lower intensity), every available muscle fibre must have been pressed into action.

Certainly, this is the way it feels. Regardless of whether you exercise to exhaustion within a few minutes or a few hours, the feeling at exhaustion is that every single muscle fibre in your body is working as hard as it possibly can; that there is nothing left in reserve. This is what the exhausted bowler feels as he launches into the final overs of a long spell. Surely he has exhausted every single muscle in his body, which would explain why each delivery seems to require everything he can give.

But it has now been shown that all the muscle fibres in all the muscles in the active limbs are *never* all active at the same time at exhaustion. Rather, especially during prolonged exercise, exhaustion may occur even when less than 50% of the muscle fibres are active (St Clair Gibson et al., 2001). This raises the question of why the brain does not simply recruit some of the 'lazy' 50% of fibres – those that are inactive at exhaustion.

Equally interesting is the finding that, towards the end of a period of exercise (such as a race), the best athletes are able to increase the number of muscle fibres that are active – the so-called 'end spurt' phenomenon. So an athlete who recruits only 25% of his muscle fibres during an activity that lasts two to three hours, may suddenly be able to increase this number to 30–35% as he speeds up during the last 5% of the exercise bout. If this is the case, why was he unable to use 30–35% of his muscle fibres during the first 95% of the exercise bout?

The answer appears to be that the ultimate function of the brain during exercise is to ensure that the body does not come to any harm. Were the brain to recruit more than 50% of the available muscle fibres during prolonged exercise, any of the following might happen:

- the muscles themselves might run out of fuel, causing the development of

irreversible skeletal muscle rigor – the state of muscle contraction that occurs after death;
- the body might run out of fuel prematurely, leading to liver glycogen depletion and hypoglycaemia (low blood glucose concentration);
- the body might overheat;
- there might be irreversible damage to the structural elements of the overstressed muscles; these elements maintain the integrity of the muscles and the damage they sustain when stressed explains why humans develop muscle soreness 24–48 hours after an unusually intense bout of exercise – so-called delayed onset muscle soreness.

It makes no sense for any animal, human or otherwise, to exercise willingly to the point of total muscle- or whole body damage, and our evolution on the plains of Africa as a relentlessly athletic hunter seems to have equipped us with a 'circuit breaker' or safety brake. And so it is that when the batsman, bowler or fielder feels completely exhausted on the cricket field, he does so because he is experiencing the actions of this protective mechanism. In other words, fatigue should be seen as a protective mechanism activated by the brain to ensure the survival not just of the individual, but of the entire athletic species.

However, the cricketer's brain faces especial challenges in protecting him from developing severe heat injury, which requires that there be both high rates of energy expenditure and taxing environmental conditions (heat and humidity). Three- to five-day cricket is sometimes played in extreme environmental conditions in Africa, Australia and especially India and parts of Pakistan. Under these conditions, the only way to protect against dangerously high body temperatures is to exercise at low intensities. However, this might not be possible when batting and bowling, in one-day cricket in particular, in the heat and humidity of the Asian subcontinent, so there is a real possibility of developing heat illness under such circumstances. Fast bowlers bowling for more than an hour under hot and humid environmental conditions, or a batter in a one-day international forced to run a large number of singles in the hot and humid conditions that exist during the summer daylight hours on the Asian subcontinent and in Australia, might well be at risk. To prevent this, they need somehow to rest more systematically between runs or overs.

Nor is it likely that the cricketer is ever at risk of developing whole body energy depletion, as the evidence is clear that cricketers should be able to play cricket without energy depletion for days on end, even if they were not eating. So what is the brain protecting the cricketer from?

Our human evolution on the plains of Africa as a relentlessly athletic hunter seems to have equipped us with a 'circuit breaker' or safety brake that prevents us from exercising to the point of physical damage.

4. A POSSIBLE SOLUTION TO THE PUZZLE: THE ROLE OF ECCENTRIC MUSCLE CONTRACTIONS IN CRICKETER'S FATIGUE

Most people with a lay knowledge of physiology know that when they ask their muscles to work – whether to lift, push, or simply to move the body and limbs – the muscle in question contracts. But this description can be misleading, because it implies that the muscle shortens, and this is not always the case. Indeed, when a muscle contracts, it can either shorten or lengthen.

Shortening will occur if the force the muscle produces is greater than the opposing force (for example, the force of gravity acting on a cricket bat that is picked up from the ground). Provided the brain recruits sufficient muscle fibres, the muscle will shorten, and you will be able to pick up the bat. This form of muscle action is known as a concentric contraction.

However, if the force acting on the muscle is greater than the force produced by the muscle under those circumstances, the muscle will lengthen even though it is contracting. The speed of the lengthening will also be determined by the discrepancy between the loading force and the force that the muscle is able to produce. This form of muscle action is called an eccentric contraction. An example of a powerful eccentric muscle contraction occurs with each delivery of a fast bowler whose knee bends at front foot strike. The knee does not collapse completely because of the powerful eccentric contractions of the upper thigh (quadriceps) muscles. These act as shock absorbers, soaking up the forces (between four to nine times those caused by gravity) experienced during the bowling delivery. There is now solid evidence that skeletal muscles are poorly designed to cope with repetitive eccentric contractions, repeated continuously over minutes (if the contractions are very powerful, as they are in fast bowling) or over many hours (if the contractions are less powerful, as they are with each episode of turning and changing direction while batting and fielding).

So this model proposes that repetitive eccentric muscle contractions alter the way in which the brain recruits the muscles involved in those eccentric contractions. We know that the pattern of recruitment of the lower limb muscles changes even during running events that last as little as fourteen minutes (Nummela et al., 2008). In particular, the muscle becomes less able to store the energy of landing, and therefore less able to recover that energy for the consequent push-off phase of the running stride. The result is that the brain must now either choose to recruit more muscle fibres to produce more work during the push-off phase of the running stride in order to maintain the same running speed, or else accept a lower running speed. Although these studies have not yet been conducted on cricketers, the relevance

The pressure game. **TOP:** *With a packed 'leg trap' in place, Bill Woodfull ducks under a bouncer from England spearhead Harold Larwood at Brisbane during the infamous Bodyline series in 1932/33.* **BOTTOM:** *In this remarkable picture, pressure pays off as the entire England team, crowding the bat, appeal successfully to win the fifth and final Test at the Oval in 1968. The successful bowler is 'Deadly' Derek Underwood, who took 7 for 50.*

While limited facilities are frustrating, don't use them as an excuse: the best in the game have made do.

TOP: *Dennis Lillee of Australia uses what's available to warm up before a match at a county ground.*

BOTTOM: *England's Geoff Boycott gets his eye in on a goat-pasture in St Vincent in 1981.*

to fast bowlers is obvious. As the bowler runs in and bowls more deliveries, the way in which his muscles are recruited will change because of this natural bodily protective mechanism. Yet the bowler must strive to produce the same end result even though his muscles will not be acting in the same way throughout his bowling spell. Interestingly, as the (subconscious) brain is making these choices, and altering the way in which it recruits the muscles, it also begins to flood the conscious brain with the sensations of fatigue.

According to the integrated neuromuscular recruitment (central governor) model, the role of these sensations of fatigue is to dissuade the athlete from continuing to exercise, thereby ensuring that the exercise bout will end before irreparable bodily damage occurs. Applied to the cricket fast bowler, this model would suggest that he develops fatigue during an eight- to ten-over bowling spell because of changes in the recruitment patterns in his leg muscles as a consequence of their being forced to absorb the massive landing forces with each delivery, as well as in the muscles of his bowling arm, which are stretched maximally during each delivery. The 'fatigue' that he perceives is the conscious brain's signal that to continue this activity could potentially be dangerous, as it might produce muscle damage that could take days, weeks or months to repair. Over a fast bowling career, this damage could be irreversible and similar to that measured in veteran marathon runners, who show premature aging of their muscles as a consequence of repeated severe bouts of eccentric muscle damage.

So perhaps the real stress of cricket results from damage (Morgan and Allen, 1999) caused by repeated eccentric muscle contractions that occur particularly in fast bowling, but also in the repeated decelerations that occur when turning during batting or fielding. Indeed it is established that shuttle running, which simulates the acceleration, deceleration and turning required in running between the wickets, is sufficient to induce muscle damage (Thompson et al., 1999).

If this theory is correct, then the best way to cope with the physical stress of cricket and its repeated eccentric muscle contractions would be to substantially increase eccentric muscle strength in the muscles most generally used in cricket. This is because high levels of eccentric muscle strength are the best means of reducing eccentric muscle damage.

The 'fatigue' that the fast bowler feels after an eight- to ten-over spell is the conscious brain's signal that to continue could potentially be dangerous, as it might produce muscle damage that could take days, weeks or months to repair.

THE CENTRAL GOVERNOR MODEL, HEROIC MOTHERS AND 'HUMDINGER' ONE-DAY GAMES

The central governor model outlined on pp. 541–43 possibly explains the superhuman efforts that people can make under extraordinary emotional circumstances. Most have heard tales of slight mothers who perform feats of remarkable strength under duress: the most common story is that of the mother who is able to lift a heavy vehicle to free her child trapped underneath it. In the process she usually suffers significant injury, most likely fracturing one or more of her vertebrae, as her spine is unable to withstand the enormous load caused by lifting such an impossible weight.

The easiest way to explain this is through the central governor model of exercise. This predicts that humans never recruit all their available muscle fibres in any muscle contraction; and the example of the heroic mother explains why: when all the muscle fibres are active, they can produce contractions of such power that they can cause bones to crumble. This has been known for centuries: those unlucky enough to die of tetanus, in which the muscles go into uncontrolled contractions, usually suffer bone fractures caused by these excessively powerful muscle contractions – which cannot usually be produced by will.

So one reason why all the muscle fibres in any muscle can never be allowed to contract fully at the same time is because this would cause bone and perhaps muscle damage. The role of the central governor is to ensure this never happens (although as we have seen, moments of extreme emotional duress can momentarily override it).

Another feature of the central governor model is that it predicts that all exercise will end before damage (the catastrophe) occurs. For this to happen, the brain needs to know before the exercise begins, when that exercise bout will end. Only with this information can the brain 'set' the appropriate exercise intensity that will use up the available fuel and generate heat at the correct rate so that the exercise terminates before the body's energy reserves run out or it overheats. The brain does this by establishing the correct pacing strategy early on in the exercise session. This pacing strategy is established on the basis of the athlete's physiological potential, the expected duration of the activity, the environmental conditions, and the athlete's previous experience of that particular type of exercise.

Of course, another form of pacing occurs in cricket – the pacing of the innings in one-day games. In particular, the team batting second has the luxury of knowing the pace they must set in order to win the game. This often results in an interesting problem – that of 'pacing paralysis'. Why is it that so many one-day matches are decided in the final few overs, and often off the final delivery or two? Surely knowing what the target is should be such an advantage to the team batting second that, if they are to win the game, they should be able to polish the match off well before the final over or delivery?

It's clear that those batting second become subconscious slaves to the total they must reach and the number of deliveries remaining, to the extent that they are often unable to adopt pacing strategies other than one that produces victory off the final few deliveries. Some might argue that this is the safest way to pursue victory (it is certainly more thrilling for the spectators), but it might not be the best technique for developing a team that consistently produces pacing strategies that win one-day games, whether batting first or second.

The winning team in the 1996 World Cup, Sri Lanka, were successful because they adopted a pacing strategy that involved their openers going flat out from the first ball, safe in the knowledge that if they failed, they had rock-solid middle-order batsmen, all fairly conventional run accumulators, in reserve. They followed this pacing policy regardless of whether they batted first or second. (They were aided by self-belief – that they could outscore any opposition under any conditions, and advantaged by the batting conditions of the Asian subcontinent – which perhaps favour this pacing strategy. A similar strategy might well prove risky in English conditions, for example, where the late movement of the ball makes it more of a gamble, as seen in the 1999 World Cup.)

Nevertheless, the future of the one-day game, as portended by the development of 20-over cricket, suggests that successful teams will be those that follow more aggressive pacing strategies – for instance, planning to hit not one, but two boundaries an over from the start. The Australian pacing strategy, as seen in the last two World Cups, is to score at six runs an over by having two dashing left-handers at the top of the order, and then a middle order of creative attackers. The latter can hit sixes when necessary, but can also score singles off a seaming or spinning ball.

THE PRINCIPLES OF EXERCISE TRAINING

There are at least eight fundamental principles that a cricketer or coach needs to consider when preparing a physical training programme.

1. PROGRESSIVE OVERLOAD

The human body adapts to the level of physical stress to which it is exposed. Being sedentary prepares you only for continued sedentariness. On the other hand, the body also needs time to adapt to any change in the level of habitual stress to which it is exposed. Thus if the stress is excessive, the body fails to adapt and breaks down instead.

A good example is the response of the bones of the back and lower limbs to the added stress of either running or fast bowling. If too much stress is imposed too quickly without an adequate period of adaptation, the bone undergoes a period of demineralization, potentially leading to the development of either a bone bruise or a stress fracture (see pp. 621–25). But if the added stress is imposed gradually over a period of months or years, the bone becomes progressively stronger and at a reduced risk of injury. As a result, a fast bowler who has, for example, enjoyed regular long-distance running in his adolescent years would be at a reduced risk for the development of a stress fracture of his lower limbs when beginning to bowl more intensively in his twenties.

The principle of progressive overload thus holds that the stresses of training must be increased gradually during the athlete's career, beginning with fairly gentle training, and reaching maximum values only when the athlete's body is physically mature (in his middle to late twenties). Similarly, during the cricket season, the physical loading in training will initially be quite mild, increasing as the season progresses.

2. SPECIFICITY

The body adapts to the specific stresses to which it is exposed, but does not adapt to those stresses to which it is not exposed. This gives rise to the idea that the more closely the stresses imposed during training mimic those that will be encountered in competition, the better prepared the player will be for that competition.

Cricket's traditional training methods ignore this crucial law almost entirely. Most cricket training around the world consists of net practices, yet it would be difficult to imagine a training method less like a real cricket match! Consider the following typical aspects of a session in the nets:

- **Unless you are a Test batsman practising at an international venue,** it is extremely unlikely that the net pitch will have the same characteristics as the match pitch.

- **New balls are seldom if ever used, reducing speed and swing.** In most cases, especially at schools level, balls are in a worse state than they would ever be in a match: not only does this rule out the possibility of variable movement off the pitch (except for low bounce), it can also teach fast bowlers physiologically damaging habits as they strain for extra pace and bounce. This also robs batters of the opportunity to hone their reactions and technique, especially off the back foot.
- **Fast bowlers do not bowl at their top pace,** and even medium pacers tend to bowl off a shortened run-up at a slower pace, and without the usual swing expected in the match situation.
- **Not many coaches insist on their bowlers obeying no-ball rules in nets,** resulting in the almost universal phenomenon of seamers overstepping by anything up to a metre, thereby playing havoc with their own rhythms and batsmen's trigger movements.
- **There are no fielders, which means that bowlers don't have the opportunity to bowl a specific line to a specific field,** while batters are unable to practise shot placements.
- **Bowlers do not bowl six consecutive deliveries to a specific batter,** to be relieved by a second bowler who does the same. Instead, the batter may face every possible type of bowler in sequence – the opposite of what happens in the match situation!
- **Batters can only be out bowled and perhaps LBW,** if the coach acts also as the umpire. They can't be caught, run out or stumped.
- **Batters don't get to practise running between the wickets.**
- **Batters seldom bat for longer than 20 minutes,** during which they are expected to practise every conceivable cricketing shot. Yet in a match they would be expected to bat conservatively for the first 20 minutes, and only then start playing more adventurous shots. More importantly, practising for only 20 minutes at a time conditions the batsman to bat for only 20 minutes during the match situation. To get accustomed to the concept of an innings that lasts for hours, batsmen should bat in the nets for hours at a time. (Obviously there are practical considerations here; see Chapter 9 for more on how to conduct effective net practices.)

These practical constraints and realities clearly fail to simulate the actual physical demands of cricket, and therefore fall well short of providing optimal physical preparation. Using the principles described in the previous section of a slow and steady progression in training, a fast bowler should gradually increase his fitness until he is capable of bowling 20 overs in six hours on two consecutive days – conditions that, unlike the sporadic and half-hearted deliveries at unmotivated and unfocused batsmen seen all too often in a concrete net, could actually occur in a real match.

Likewise, batters need to develop fitness so that they can maintain unbroken concentration and not became exhausted during an innings that may also last six hours, or, in exceptional cases, six hours a day for three days, as has been the case in Test matches where batsmen have occupied the crease for days, posting massive scores in the process.

As stated in the introduction to this chapter, it is not enough to play yourself fit, but the reality is that match-play is the main method for maintaining and improving fitness. However, we believe that additional training is necessary to reach a sufficient initial level of fitness so that players can perform to their optimum levels in match situations, and thereby get the most out of the 'on the job' fitness training that a match provides.

In other words, treat matches as you would a focused, intensive training period. Telling yourself that the match is the reward for your training is a sure-fire way to relax, play an injudicious shot, lose your line and length, and be removed from the game (either by dismissal back to the pavilion or, if you are a wayward bowler, by being posted to field at fine leg).

Think of it this way: the more you train, the longer you'll stay in the game, and the longer you stay in the game, the more you'll train.

3. QUANTITY FIRST, QUALITY LATER

When you begin training, whether at the start of a sporting career or at the start of the new season, it is important to put the training emphasis on the quantity (volume) of training rather than the quality (intensity or speed). This is because quality training is so demanding that it cannot be performed unless the body has first been properly prepared by a large volume of more gentle training.

The more gentle volume training is also known as *base training*, while the quality training is known as *peaking training*. It is also important to understand that while low-intensity base training can (and should) be continued more or less indefinitely throughout one's athletic life, high-intensity peaking training can be kept up only for relatively short periods (six to ten weeks, depending on the individual) – and in fact should not be attempted for longer than this.

Typically, athletes preparing for a major competition on a specific date will begin base training many months before that competition date, and will then spend a period of six to ten weeks doing high-intensity training before reducing their training (tapering) for the last two to three weeks immediately before competing.

4. REGULARITY OF TRAINING

Regular daily training, with perhaps a single day's rest during the week, is the minimum that is required for the development of optimum fitness levels. However, the need to train one's skill levels as well means that cricketers have less time available for pure fitness training than do those athletes whose sports, like marathon running, involve purely physical preparation, with little need to practise skills. Cricketers should probably aim for daily skills practice and fitness training every other day.

So what happens at international level? Dan Keisel, former fitness coach and physiotherapist for the Pakistan and Sri Lankan national teams, believes that international players should follow a fitness regime specifically tailored for their individual cricketing needs for two and a half hours a day, six days a week, all year round, barring a few weeks vacation. He admits, however, that this is the ideal not the reality! But this kind of regime would lead to burnout and even collapse in practice. We recommend that at elite levels, players should train this hard for three to five months before and during the season, followed by eight weeks rest, and then three months of gentler base training leading up to competition once more. This means that the competitive sporting season should not last longer than seven months.

Recommended fitness regimes and timetables are discussed on pp. 554–59 below.

5. VARIETY

As anyone who has ever dragged himself off to the nets on a blustery and chilly evening knows, it is not always easy to find the motivation to practise and to train with the necessary intensity and focus. However, varying the activities, the venue, and the group leader or instructor can all help. Otherwise, there is the risk that players will merely go through the motions. For suggestions on running effective and stimulating practices, refer to Chapter 9.

6. INDIVIDUALISM

Perhaps one of the greatest mistakes any coach can make is to assume that there is one training method that fits all. Every cricketer is unique, not only physically, but mentally, and requires a slightly different training approach. We know that there are considerable variations in the extent to which humans can adapt to a specific training programme. Indeed, some unfortunate souls are simply incapable of adapting to physical training like running or cycling. Consequently they never become 'fitter', regardless of how hard they train. Others, world-class athletes in particular, adapt to a remarkable degree and may, for example, increase their capacity for maximum oxygen consumption (a measure of fitness) by as much as 70% compared to the more normal (average) increase of about 15% with appropriate training.

Furthermore, the rate at which different athletes adapt to the same training programme also differs substantially. Some adapt very quickly, needing only a relatively short period of training to greatly increase their fitness; others take much longer to achieve the same changes.

We don't know of any studies that have tried to measure whether the same applies to the acquisition of specific skills (for example, judging the trajectory of a cricket ball hit to the deep fielder, or judging the length of a rapid delivery), but it seems very likely that this is the case: some will never be able to attain these skills, whereas top international players will have acquired them with relative ease and with the highest possible degree of refinement.

So while it is important to have group activities, and for all players to be involved in these (so that motivation can be enhanced through competition between players), it is also important for each cricketer to follow an individualized programme that caters for his specific physiological and psychological needs, as well as his current and required fitness and skill levels. Bear in mind that this will also vary according to whether the player is principally a batter, a bowler or a wicket-keeper. Those who show themselves to be particularly adept at specific fielding positions also need to be catered for.

7. WARM-UP AND COOL-DOWN (STRETCHING)

Look at almost any international sport and you will find too many players with too many injuries. In the past, this situation has perhaps been accepted as inevitable; but today's professional teams need to play as a unit, with more or less the same personnel, for as many years as possible. Most of the great Test teams of the past had a core of seven or eight players who turned out for every match, year after year – a clear illustration of the fact that prevention or minimization of injury risk is crucial to a team's ultimate success.

Reduce the risk of injury by using proper warming up and warming down procedures, both before and after each practice and at all matches. This can be as simple as a 15-minute jog before beginning practice or starting the game, doing the essential stretching, and then conducting a skills warm-up. At the end of a training or practice session, repeat the jogging for ten minutes, and do another five minutes of stretching.

It is absolutely vital for a cricketer to follow a set routine of stretching exercises before beginning any exercise routine or game, as well as afterwards. This cannot be stressed enough. However, one often sees athletes stretching in a manner that may do more harm than good. The correct stretching techniques are discussed on pp. 553–54, and it is important that these are followed.

8. EVALUATION

Measuring and evaluating progress is essential to ensure that players remain motivated. Self-evaluation also encourages individuals to compete against their own sense of 'personal best', and gives them concrete goals. All players should keep logbooks, which they fill in daily (or in the case of schoolchildren, weekly), recounting what exercise/practice they did, how long they did it for and at what intensity levels, how they felt during and after, what problems or injury niggles they encountered, and so on. If cost allows, regular external tests (pulse rates, body-fat measurements and so on) should also be done and entered into each player's log. (This is essential at higher levels of the game.) At regular intervals, the coach (or the team fitness coach, if you are lucky enough to have one) should meet with individual players to discuss their logs, and the progress they are making. Keeping a log will often help a player to articulate what's bothering him when it comes to a one-on-one session with the coach. It will also enable them to set milestones, especially in terms of fitness – cricketers can be inclined to focus on practising their skills rather than achieving fitness, so it's helpful (for instance) for a fast bowler to decide to run X number of kilometres per week, and to be able to log this.

SPECIFIC TRAINING PROGRAMMES FOR CRICKETERS

The following training programmes have been designed specifically for professional cricketers by Justin Durandt and his colleagues at the Discovery Health High Performance Centre at the Sports Science Institute of South Africa in Cape Town. This team has worked closely with provincial and national cricketers from South Africa, Holland, Kenya, Namibia and Canada, including overseeing the physical preparation of those teams for various international competitions and the Cricket World Cup. However, the principles on which they are based apply to all cricketers, whatever their level of performance. The goals of these training programmes are to improve endurance and sprint fitness, muscle strength, and flexibility specifically to improve performance and reduce the risk of injury.

Before you attempt any of what is to follow, remember to stretch thoroughly:
- **Move into each stretch slowly and smoothly** – never fling or wrench yourself into position.
- **Hold the stretch to a point of tension** (never discomfort or pain) for a minimum of 20 seconds – 30 seconds is optimum. Longer stretches do not produce any additional gains in flexibility (Hughes et al., 2003).

For fast bowlers, the benefits of running seem to be largely psychological, in that their training seems to prepare their subconscious brains to accept bowling spells lasting 30–60 minutes.

- **While holding the stretch, breathe correctly** (see Chapter 2 for details on belly-breathing, in which you breathe down into the belly, rather than taking shallow gasps into the chest – your diaphragm should move, not your chest).
  As you breathe, the stretch should lengthen, but don't force this.
- **Release the stretch slowly.** A ground rule for almost all stretches undertaken while standing or sitting is to maintain a pelvic tilt and soft knees during the stretch: this protects the lower back and knee joints.

Ask your local fitness centre, an experienced athletic coach, a physiotherapist or biokineticist to demonstrate or supply a full set of stretches that warm up all the muscles of the body likely to be used during exercise, as well as the stretches most beneficial after exercise. These are widely available (including in many illustrated books on exercise), but should be followed carefully and accurately, always following the basic principles above.

1. ENDURANCE (AEROBIC) AND SPRINT (ANAEROBIC) FITNESS

Endurance fitness for cricketers is best achieved by running for up to 30 minutes at a time at a comfortable pace. The value of running is that it adapts the body for weight-bearing exercise, which is essential since the cricketer must carry his body weight in all activities other than the time he spends sitting in the pavilion. So while cycling and swimming can provide valuable training variety, they fail to adapt the cricketer's body for the prolonged weight bearing that is a major feature of the game.

By contrast, after the body has been exposed to prolonged weight bearing, especially the demands of fast bowling or a long stay at the crease, non-weight-bearing activities like cycling or swimming are ideal forms of training during recovery. In fact, running during this recovery period should be contraindicated, as it would delay recovery from the eccentric muscle damage produced by these activities. (In other words, if a fast bowler has bowled his heart out in a match, he should not go for a long run the next day – a few sessions in a heated pool are a much better idea.)

However, all running must be approached with care since there may be some players for whom running may not be especially helpful, and might even be detrimental. Those for whom running may be detrimental include cricketers with bones that adapt poorly to the stresses of running or bowling, for example, and who develop persistent shin, ankle or foot pain (indicating the presence of bone bruises or stress fractures). Any running that such players undertake must be carefully controlled under the supervision of an exercise specialist.

Fast bowlers should not assume that running will help their bodies adapt and adjust to the pressures of the delivery stride: the landing stresses involved in normal running are only about 30% as intense as those experienced during the explosive landing of the delivery. In fact, for fast bowlers, the benefits of running seem to be largely psychological, in that their training seems to prepare their subconscious brains to accept bowling spells lasting 30–60 minutes (the time they would usually spend running).

In other words, the feeling of physical preparedness they enjoy, and the delayed onset of exhaustion, flow directly from the central governor model of exercise (see pp. 541–43 above), which holds that their brain must first be convinced that the performance is possible before that performance will be realized. By running regularly for 30–60 minutes most days, they will have 'convinced' their brain that the effort is possible, and this in turn allows them to keep performing for that time – until they reach 'uncharted territory' and the brain hauls them up by flooding them with a sense of physical exhaustion.

Sprint training, on the other hand, recreates conditions that more closely mirror what actually happens in cricket: bursts of activity of high intensity, but lasting less than five to ten seconds. Such training can be incorporated into general practice sessions by having team members running as fast as they can between wickets. During these sessions, the idea is to perform with maximal effort – i.e., to a point that would rapidly lead to total exhaustion if continued for more than several seconds. The advantage to the cricketer is that this mimics match conditions: where the fast bowler must give it all he's got, or where a batter has to run for his life to avoid a run-out, or steal two runs where only one looked possible. But from an athletic point of view, sprint work plays a role in strengthening the quadriceps muscles in particular, as well as lower-leg muscles – significant for the cricketer who spends all day on his feet. It is also believed that sprint training increases muscle contractability and thus power (Noakes and Granger, 1995).

2. POWER AND STRENGTH TRAINING

Power and strength training using either machines (if you have access to a gym) or free weights is extremely important, because it can lessen the risks of injury and speed up rehabilitation following injury. A circuit on toning machines or a session with free weights should focus on developing strength in all the major muscle groups of the body, with special attention to any problem areas. Note that the idea is to create strength, not bulk – fast bowlers who have pushed heavy weights in the past have found this counter-productive, as they have become 'muscle-bound'. The trick is to focus on repetitions rather than on constantly racking up heavier weights or levels of resistance on the machines. It is crucial that when performing these exercises,

The idea is to create strength, not bulk. Focus on repetitions rather than on constantly racking up heavier weights or levels of resistance on the machines.

> ## STRETCHED TOO FAR
> A failure to warm up and stretch properly before his innings might explain why Steve Waugh suffered a match-ending tear of his left calf muscle as he played the first ball he received in the second innings of the Third Test in the 2001 Ashes series (Orchard et al., 2002). Using video footage from the stump camera, the authors concluded that the injury occurred when the left calf muscle was suddenly loaded as Waugh took off for a run. In that position the muscle was fully stretched, carrying Waugh's full weight and just beginning to shorten to propel Waugh forward.
>
> The study was important because it seems to establish exactly when these injuries occur (at the moment the muscle begins to shorten following stretching to its full length). Interestingly, Waugh had played an exhibition squash match a week before the start of the Test and had subsequently experienced calf muscle tightness (delayed onset muscle soreness).

the entire body is correctly aligned and positioned – exercises performed with the incorrect posture or movements can be pointless or, even worse, result in an injury. Always consult a specialist before beginning any routine that involves free weights or machines, and ask him or her to check your entire body for correct positioning or alignment.

Of special importance is the development of adequate strength of the core (abdominal and lumbar) muscles. Here a specific routine needs to be developed in consultation with an exercise specialist, one that includes a full range of movements that strengthen the core muscles. These include sit-ups and pull-ups, but all too often, athletes 'jerk' themselves through a rapid set of sit-ups, exercising only one set of abdominal muscles. Players need to be able to identify and 'isolate' their deep abdominal muscles and learn how to strengthen them in targeted exercises, using very deliberate and specific sets of movements, Pezzi (sports) balls and other aids if necessary.

Fortunately, almost any qualified fitness instructor or physiotherapist will be able to help, given that core strength benefits everyone, and is essential to those recuperating from or at risk of back injury. The thinking, from a lay perspective, is to develop a supportive 'corset' of muscle around the lower spine, especially around its area of most constant flexion. Anyone who has worn a brace around the waist to relieve lower back pain will appreciate this concept. Core strength training, along with a very specific stretching programme that targets certain muscles, is critical in the prevention of back and hamstring injuries in batters and fielders, and especially fast bowlers.

PRE-SEASON STRENGTH PROGRAMME

This first programme is designed to build extra strength and prepare your body for the rigors of the coming season. Start it four to six weeks before the start of the season. (This is also the time to incorporate cricket-specific exercises into the gym routine or on the playing field.)

MUSCLE GROUP	EXERCISES	SETS	REPS
Trunk	Sit-ups	2	20–50
	OR leg raises	2	20–50 (each leg)
	OR trunk rotations	1	30
Legs	Full squats	4	12, 10, 8, 6
	OR leg raises	2	15, 15
	OR hamstring curls	2	15, 15
	OR lunge/split squats	2	10, 8
Chest/arms	Lateral raises	4	12, 10, 8, 6
	Rowing	4	12, 10, 8, 6
	Shoulder presses	4	12, 10, 8, 6
	Back lifts (with Roman chair)	2	Max. 15 (then add weight)
	Tricep pull-downs	4	12, 10, 8, 6
	OR tricep thrusts	2	Max. 12 (then add weight)
	Bicep curls	4	12, 10, 8, 6
	OR wrist curls	2–3	12, 10, (8) (each wrist)
	OR reverse wrist curls	2–3	12, 10, (8) (each wrist)

IN-SEASON STRENGTH PROGRAMME

This programme maintains your strength levels during the playing season. Abdominal, rotational and light weight work are essential parts of the in-season schedule. Bowlers in particular should concentrate on light shoulder work, for example, exercises for the deltoid muscles using weights.

MUSCLE GROUP	EXERCISES	SETS	REPS
Trunk	Sit-ups	1	20–50
	OR dead man's lifts	1	15–20
Legs	Squat thrusts	2	10, 8
	OR step-ups	1–2	10, 15 (each leg)
Chest/arms	Bench presses (light)	2	10, 8
	OR pull-ups	2	10, 10
	Lateral pull-downs	2	10, 8
	Wrist curls	2	12, 10 (each wrist)
	Reverse wrist curls	2	12, 10 (each wrist)

OFF-SEASON STRENGTH PROGRAMME

This programme is designed to strengthen and balance all the major muscle groups of the body. Consult an exercise specialist about varying the exercises in the programme to correct particular muscular weaknesses or to correct any muscle imbalances.

MUSCLE GROUP	EXERCISES	SETS	REPS
Trunk	Sit-ups	2	12–15
	OR leg raises	2	15–25
	OR trunk rotations	1	15–30
Legs	Leg raises	3	12, 10, 8
	Hamstring curls	3	12, 10, 8
	OR squats	3	12, 10, 10
	OR groin flexes	2–3	12 (each leg)
	OR hip flexes	2–3	12 (each leg)
Chest/arms	Bench presses	4	10, 10, 8, 8
	Lateral raises	3	10, 10, 8
	Shoulder shrugs	3	14, 12, 10
	Upright rowing	4	10, 10, 8, 8
	Tricep curls	4	10, 10, 8, 8
	Bicep curls	4	10, 10, 8, 8
	Wrist curls	3	12, 12, 10

Note that the programmes opposite refer to the Northern hemisphere cricket season; players in the Southern hemisphere should substitute the appropriate months: June or July (depending on when the competitive season starts) for January, and so on. These programmes are also extremely broad and general, and you will need to fill in the details with your coach or exercise specialist, according to your specialist skill, your level of fitness, your genetic strengths and weaknesses, and your fitness goals.

Endurance work will include training to improve fitness for long spells of bowling, one-day batting and fielding; strength work will include work with weights and resistance machines (if you have access to a gym) to build core strength and specific muscle strength; flexibility will include a carefully-worked out programme of stretching; and circuit training refers to the all-over workout, including endurance and strength, afforded by completing a circuit workout – once again, if you have access to a gym. Sport refers to recreational games or participation in sports other than cricket, and maintenance usually refers to a light-to-medium workout or exercise session, focusing on the most important aspects of your fitness regime.

PRE-SEASON TRAINING WEEKLY PLANNER

	JANUARY	FEBRUARY	MARCH	APRIL
Monday	Endurance Flexibility	Strength Flexibility	Sprint Flexibility	Flexibility Nets Fielding
Tuesday	Strength Flexibility	Strength Skills Flexibility	Endurance Strength Skills Flexibility	Flexibility Nets Fielding Circuit Maintenance
Wednesday	Endurance	Sprint Flexibility	Sprint Flexibility	Flexibility Match
Thursday	Strength Flexibility	Strength Skills Flexibility	Strength Skills Flexibility	Flexibility Nets Fielding Circuit Maintenance
Friday	Endurance Flexibility	Endurance Flexibility	Endurance Flexibility	Flexibility Match
Saturday	Free (sport)	Free (sport)	Free (sport)	Match
Sunday	Rest	Rest	Rest	Rest

FITNESS YEAR PLANNER (PER WEEK)

	JANUARY	FEBRUARY	MARCH	APRIL
Endurance	– run 7 km (x 3) – cycle 1 hour (x 3) – swim 30 minutes (x 3)	– as for January – plus run 6 x 400m (x 2)	– as for February, but reduce all work to x 2 – run 6–10 x 50m	– as for March – pre-season training 'cricket fitness'
Strength	– weights: work on shoulders, knees, back and ankles – general programme	– as for January	– as for February – plus step or hill climbing (20-second intervals)	– as for March
Flexibility	– yoga or stretching (x 3)	– as for January	– as for February	– as for March
Skills	– use video camera to analyze techniques	– as for January	– specific skills practice	– emphasis on fielding – match build-up

MAY	JUNE–SEPT	OCTOBER	NOVEMBER	DECEMBER
Flexibility Pre-season matches Maintenance training Days off Fielding practice	SEASON IN PROGRESS	Rest period Holiday with leisure activities	Light training Running, cycling, swimming (x 3)	Light training Running, cycling, swimming (x 3)

NUTRITION AND FLUID INTAKE

Because cricket is played over one or more days, meals (lunch and tea) are part of the schedule of the game. The visiting side is invariably at the mercy of the host caterers in terms of what food they will be offered to eat. In other words, players may have very little (if any) say in the choice of food provided during a match and, as a result, may feel obliged to eat whatever is put in front of them. This could range from sandwiches, chips and cake to a hot three-course meal. The chances of such meals being carefully planned to cater for the special dietary needs of athletes are usually quite slim.

What is more, team rituals are an inescapable part of the game and these often take place around food and drink. Matches often end either in the pub, or around the *braai* or barbecue fire. Players who avoid these social occasions, which almost always involve eating and drinking, might experience difficulty bonding with other team members, especially those who set great store in this form of social interaction. The player who stands around with a bottle of mineral water and carrot sticks is also unlikely to endear himself to his teammates; at the very least, he risks some serious leg-pulling if the culture of the team does not stress health promotion and performance enhancement. However, choices have to be made if the goal is to optimize one's genetic endowment through correct training and a helpful (not destructive) lifestyle.

Alan Knott, possibly England's best ever wicket-keeper, was one of the first English players to follow a strict regime of healthy eating. Far from considering whether his diet played any part in his consistent success as a player, Knott reports that his teammates mostly scoffed. (Of the attitudes to nutrition at that time, county player Simon Hughes noted the following: 'A controlled diet meant you consumed three rather than four packets of chocolate bourbons before the match, rejected a second plate of cheese after a three-course lunch, and ate just the filling in the sandwiches.') Unlike many other modern sports, whose athletes brag about the scientifically calibrated and balanced diets they follow to the point of obsession, the motto of some cricketers still seems to be 'eat, drink and be merry'.

Another factor affecting the diet of not just cricketers, but most athletes, is the role played by families and spouses. Although we live in a world that promises gender equality and sharing of household tasks, the reality is that many male cricketers (and younger cricketers of both sexes) still have their meals provided by wives, girlfriends and parents. Furthermore, meals at cricket matches are often provided by good-natured 'cricket widows', many of whom are wedded to the social dictates of hospitality, but who have little knowledge of the exact dietary requirements of cricket players.

> 'A controlled diet meant you consumed three rather than four packets of chocolate bourbons before the match, rejected a second plate of cheese after a three-course lunch, and ate just the filling in the sandwiches.'
> – Simon Hughes

For the love of the game. International cricket is the top of a giant pyramid, at the base of which are millions of players and hundreds of millions of fans. **TOP:** *The flair and noise of the Sabina Park crowd in 1986, the heyday of West Indian cricket.* **BOTTOM:** *A premeditated sweep offers up a sharp chance to leg slip in the streets of Colombo in Sri Lanka.*

V.V.S. Laxman and Rahul Dravid savour the Kolkata evening sun, and the adulation of the Eden Gardens crowd, having batted for a full day against Australia in 2001. At the end of a perfect summer day, when everything has gone your way, and bat or ball have obeyed your every whim, there is no more beautiful game than cricket.

As a result, the table might well be groaning with poor-quality protein items, high-fat snacks and fried dishes (samoosas, pies, sausage rolls, hamburgers, fried crumbed chicken, sausages and other processed meats), served up with an earnest desire to please and impress, together with the vague notion that 'sportsmen need lots of meat'. Similarly, professional caterers may also have little if any specialist knowledge of cricketers' special nutritional needs – their focus will be on producing something tasty within a budget. Once again, this leads to meals high in fat and salt. The result is that regardless of who produces the food, players are all too often inadvertently 'nobbled' by a heavy lunch menu.

Those cricketers fortunate enough to have someone else shopping and cooking for them sometimes give absolutely no thought to what they find on their plates, and have little basic nutritional knowledge. Even if they do have a general sense of what constitutes 'good' and 'bad' food choices, not knowing how healthy foods should be prepared may still undermine their choices. For example, they might turn down a lean steak in favour of a deep-fried chicken drumstick coated with batter, on the grounds that 'white meat is better than red'. Other common mistakes are eating salads swimming in mayonnaise or oil, or pasta dishes with a high meat and cheese content (such as lasagne and ravioli), because 'salads and pasta are good for athletes'. Players and those who prepare their food require some knowledge of basic nutrition, as well as education about the particular nutritional needs of athletes.

The good news for those cricketers who neither buy nor prepare their own food is that most parents and spouses are increasingly keen to promote healthy eating patterns. However, as this is a cricket book, not a recipe book or a tome on nutrition, we advise readers to study a few good books on basic nutrition, preferably those geared to the needs of sportsmen and women. Cecily Fuller and Shelley Meltzer's *Eating for Sport*, written especially for professional athletes, is one of the most helpful. Written by two South African specialist sports nutritionists (Meltzer provides nutritional advice to elite cricketers through the Sports Science Institute of South Africa), it provides advice on topics such as what to order in restaurants and what to eat before a specific sporting event. And Louise Burke's *Sports Nutrition* provides a list of recipe books that cricketers and their families will find useful.

However, avoid slavishly following 'health' books offering dietary advice or recipes that guarantee miracles or make dubious medical claims, especially those guaranteeing instant weight loss within days or weeks. Real, permanent and safe weight loss is never quick, regardless of the promises made by hundreds of products flooding on to the market. Most of these regimes will result in the loss of muscle and water from the body. This may spell disaster for the athlete who follows them, as he or she may consequently have a higher ratio of fat to muscle, and feel weak

'A dangerous meal, lunch. I have known men bowl like angels before it, and roll onto the field like gorged pythons afterwards.'
– N.A. Knox (Surrey), 1907

from the loss of muscle mass or even dehydration – this will clearly be detrimental to performance. Players who are genuinely overweight in the opinion of their coach or doctor, or who are confused by conflicting advice on diet, or who wish to fine-tune their nutritional intake in an effort to boost their performances, are best advised to consult a registered dietician – preferably one with a special expertise in the management of the nutritional needs of athletes. Note that commercial weight-loss lifestyle programmes (those based on limiting calories) that may do wonders for lay people may be unsuitable for elite athletes, as there is no guarantee that their staff understand the body composition or nutritional needs of athletes. Nevertheless, the following general guidelines are of value, especially for those coaches whose pupils are unlikely to have the means to consult experts.

1. FOLLOW A BALANCED DIET

Until very recently it was believed that a balanced diet was one that is high in complex carbohydrates, fibre, fruit and vegetables, and low in fats and refined sugars. However, in the last few years, researchers and scientists have adapted this slightly. In particular, the emphasis has shifted from a low-fat, high-carbohydrate diet to one that is still low in saturated fats but which now allows a reasonable amount of fat in the form of unsaturated fat.

There is also no doubt that in general, we consume far too much carbohydrate, particularly refined and processed carbohydrates. While complex carbohydrates are essential, and should indeed form the majority of food intake, the consumption of white flours and processed starches (in the form of chips, crisps, white bread products such as pizzas, baguettes, rolls, biscuits, cakes, pretzels and pastries, refined maize-porridge, tortillas and so on) on a massive scale has led in Western countries to a near-epidemic rise in type-two (adult-onset) diabetes, in which the body is flooded with so much glucose over such a long period that it becomes insulin-resistant. Worse still, this epidemic is spreading to developing countries, which are often targeted for aggressive marketing campaigns extolling the virtues of refined and processed foods. The current food pyramid, revised in line with recent findings (see Figure 10.2), shows the basic food groups from which the diet should

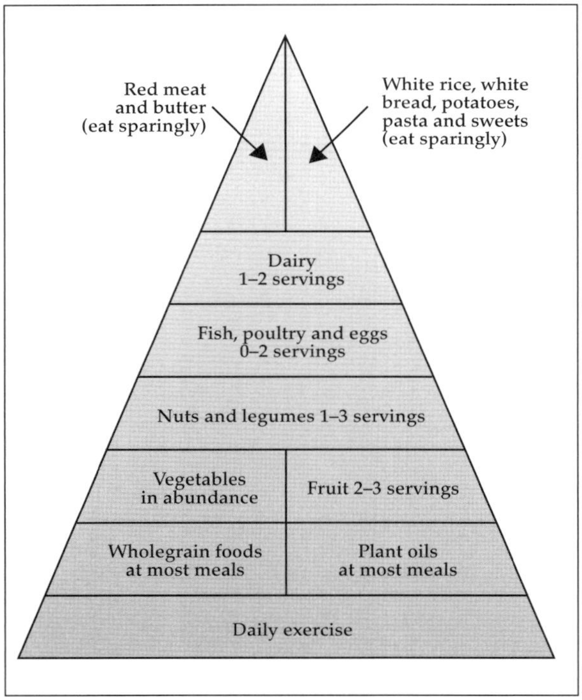

FIGURE 10.2: *Food pyramid showing ideal proportions of food to be taken daily*

be chosen, as well as the proportion in which they should be taken. The emphasis should be on the foods at the base of the pyramid: complex carbohydrates, grains and legumes, supplemented by large amounts of fresh fruits and vegetables. At least half of the fruit and vegetable intake should be eaten raw. Foods at the top of the pyramid should be eaten only sparingly. Protein from animal sources should be high quality and low in fat: for example, choose chicken breasts, lean red meat and fresh fish instead of sausages, hamburger patties, chicken nuggets, fish cakes, polony, processed cheese spreads, and so on. Too much in the way of poor-quality animal proteins and fat is often consumed. Rather use high-quality protein almost as a condiment (cutting a small quantity of lean meat or chicken into strips and stir-frying with vegetables, for example), or serve it as a weekly roast chicken or joint. Fish (preferably a species that is not overfished) should be eaten at least once a week. Beans and other legumes, seeds and nuts are excellent sources of proteins, and should be included among the protein food choices: seeds and nuts contain unsaturated fat, but these vegetable oils are generally good for you.

2. LEARN TO COOK (HEALTHILY)

The real secret to healthy eating is to learn how to use healthy cooking methods – even wholesome celery can be dipped in batter and deep fried, or served with a heavy cheese and cream dipping sauce, turning a fat-free, high-fibre vegetable into a high-fat savoury snack! Educate yourself about low-fat, low-salt recipes – there are some excellent books and cooking courses available. This dictum applies to both sexes: do not take it for granted that Mom or the tour manager or the hotel will always provide for all your nutritional needs.

3. READ WHILE YOU SHOP

Most products in supermarkets now list the ingredients of the foodstuff somewhere on the packaging. These will usually indicate how much sugar and saturated and unsaturated fat the food contains. Make a habit of checking how many grams of fat are present in what you might consider to be a healthy snack; also keep track of how much sugar and salt your favourite products contain. Products that contain long lists of added chemicals should also be treated with caution. As with cooking, don't assume that someone else will always do it for you: teach yourself to shop intelligently.

4. WEST IS NOT BEST

The average Western diet is one of the unhealthiest on the planet. Middle-class (and increasingly, poorer) Westerners as a rule eat a diet that is far too high in poor-quality

Real, permanent and safe weight loss is never quick, regardless of the promises made by hundreds of products flooding on to the market.

You would do well to follow the Asian sub-continental example, where the staple protein meal is dhal (a spicy stew made out of lentils or split peas and poured over rice or naan bread). It is a rich and delicious source of protein, complex carbohydrate and fibre, and is virtually fat free.

protein, saturated fat, refined starches, and sugar, and much too low in fibre. Foods are often refined and treated, a process that often strips them of vital nutrients while potentially harmful chemicals are added. Excessive consumption of salt, tea, coffee, sweeteners and alcohol is standard, although not enough water is taken, and not nearly enough fruit, vegetables, grains and legumes are eaten.

Many rural or peasant cultures, by contrast, have far healthier diets. These are usually centred on a staple complex carbohydrate (wheat, maize, rice, potatoes or barley), supplemented by vegetables, fruits and seeds. This basic diet is seasoned with small amounts of good-quality meat, chicken, fish or dairy products and vegetable oils (olive, peanut, or sesame). Western-style diseases such as diabetes, heart disease and various cancers are almost unknown in communities that still follow these ancient eating patterns.

In other words, to perform like a prince, we recommend that you eat like a peasant. Learn from other cultures: Indian, Chinese, Thai, Vietnamese, Mediterranean, North African, Arab, Mexican and other exotic cuisines are delicious, surprisingly easy to prepare, and fun to experiment with – as well as far healthier than the average Western diet. And don't be fooled by Western versions of those ethnic diets: Chinese cuisine does not necessarily include deep-fried pork and mountains of fried rice, just as Mediterranean doesn't mean deep-dish pizza with lashings of cheese.

5. ENSURE THAT YOU DRINK ENOUGH WATER, ESPECIALLY WITH THE EVENING MEAL

Training in hot weather increases fluid requirements because of increased sweat losses needed to cool the body. Thus cricketers training and playing especially in warmer conditions need to ensure that they have unrestricted access to fluid before, during and after play. Since the body corrects any water deficit incurred during the day at the evening meal, it is especially important that generous amounts of fluid are available, specifically with the evening meal, when training and playing in hot, humid conditions such as those found in Australia and the Asian subcontinent. Generally, thirst is the perfect guide to how much you should drink. Provided you are not thirsty, you will not be seriously dehydrated, notwithstanding the misleading aggressive marketing campaigns for sports drinks which announce, 'By the time you're thirsty, it's too late!' More information on the fluid requirements of cricketers and the dangers of excessive alcohol consumption is provided later in this chapter.

6. GO GREEN

While sceptics consider the marketing of some organic foods as yet another means of persuading the consumer to part with their cash, in the case of meat, chicken and

JUST HOW DANGEROUS IS JUNK FOOD?

One of the problems that cricketers on tour face is the temptation to send out for a pizza, or to pick up a hamburger, especially if the hotel food is bland or unfamiliar. The problem with highly processed and branded food products is that they usually have high concentrations of salt and additives, as well as being high in 'hidden' fats. Mass-produced deep-fried foods are particularly unhealthy, not least because oil that is repeatedly heated to high temperatures is believed to become carcinogenic (cancer-causing). The protein content of these meals is often poor, relying on intensively processed meat from animals reared and bought in bulk as cheaply as possible. Yet these foods have enormous appeal, partly because they are easy to procure and eat, and partly because of aggressive advertising campaigns. Another reason for their appeal is that these foods are mildly 'addictive'; the fats and sugars they contain act to satisfy psychological needs, offering short-term relief from depression and anxiety – so-called 'comfort eating'.

If you bear the following rules in mind (almost none of which guidelines are observed by the fast-food industry), it quickly becomes apparent why you should give junk food a wide berth:

- carbohydrates should be complex (baked potatoes with their skins on, not chips or French fries; wholewheat bread and brown rice, not white)
- animal protein sources should not be processed (no hamburger patties, chicken nuggets, etc.)
- fats and oils should not be processed or heated to the high temperatures seen in commercial mass-production of food.

However, the threat of lawsuits in the US has meant that some of these franchises have added healthier options to their menus – although this claim has been contested by many. Also note that it is no good asking for salad instead of chips with your burger if this simply means a tub of coleslaw doused with mayonnaise.

But there is another hidden danger regarding junk food; it enables, even conditions us, to 'eat on the run', and to eat whenever the urge seizes us, rather than waiting until lunch- or dinner-time. We cram easily purchased food into our mouths as we walk, drive or work at our desks. The old etiquette of not being seen eating in public has gone out the window, and while we are not concerned about manners here, there are sound physiological reasons why we should eat at set times, at a table, focusing on that activity only. We eat more, and are more likely to make poor food choices, when combining eating with other activities, such as working or watching television. Anyone who has wondered how they managed to consume a packet of peanuts, a bowl of popcorn and two bags of crisps while watching a rugby match on TV will recognize this phenomenon. Eating at a table that has been set, and not allowing any other activities for the duration of the meal, means eating more slowly, which aids the digestion process. Most importantly, because this allows time for the brain's appetite regulation mechanisms to kick in, we are much less likely to overeat.

dairy products, and especially fruit and vegetables, it is wise to purchase organic products if they are available and if the budget allows (in some countries, organic foods are still costly, but their prices are dropping as they gain wider acceptance). Given the high levels of antibiotics and hormones pumped into animals intensively farmed for meat and dairy products, and the quantities of pesticides used on food crops, it seems sensible to choose organic produce. But while this may be generally good advice, is it specifically relevant to athletes? More research needs to be done, but it seems that organically grown fruit and vegetables have much higher nutrient values than their conventionally produced counterparts. In addition, palatability is often significantly improved – anyone who eats organically produced tomatoes, spinach, carrots, pears, grapes and strawberries will find it very hard to revert to the regular kind. Athletes and young players who battle to 'eat their greens' will benefit from fruit and vegetables that are tastier and more nutrient-rich.

7. PUT A LEMON ON THE TABLE (AND CUT BACK ON SALT)

As a general rule, Westerners eat far too much salt, an excess that has been linked to the development of high blood pressure in some people who carry a genetic susceptibility for the condition. The human body's daily salt requirements are small (about 1g a day), whereas the average daily salt intake from the typical Western diet is at least 4g and as much as 10–15g in those who heavily salt their foods. The body's need for the sodium found in salt can be met by eating normal foodstuffs – there is no need to add extra salt even when playing cricket in hot, humid conditions that lead to high rates of sweat loss. The amount of salt lost in sweat is still far less than the amount present in the diets of even those who try to restrict the amount of salt they ingest. But even if you were to eat less salt than you were losing in your sweat – a condition that has yet to be documented in free-living humans with unrestricted access to salt-containing foods – your appetite would ensure that you rapidly discovered and ate foods with a high salt content. As soon as your salt balance was restored, your appetite for salt would again normalize.

FOOD IS FUEL

All too often it is assumed that fuelling the human body is as simple as filling up the petrol tank in a car. In reality, it is a somewhat more complex process. Energy stores in the body occur in three main forms: sugar (glucose) in the bloodstream, glycogen (a form of starch made from the combination of multiple glucose molecules, and which is stored in the liver and muscles), and fat. Some forms of fuel are harder to access than others: energy cannot be summoned from these sources like switching on a tap. To use a well-known analogy, blood sugar is like money in your pocket – it is immediately and readily available – but it soon runs out. Glycogen is like money in a current account: without too much inconvenience your body can make withdrawals from it, but once it has been used up, another source has to be found. Fat is like money that has been invested: it is difficult to access, and cannot be drawn on in emergencies. Strategies for breaking down fat are thus always long term – another fact for would-be dieters to ponder.

In the earlier section on the basics of exercise physiology, we discussed the so-called energy depletion model of exercise physiology, which holds that muscles fail when they run out of fuel. But in reality, muscles never completely run out of their fuel reserves – there is always some energy remaining. Which is just as well, for without that remaining energy, the muscles would go into rigor – a state of irreversible contraction. Instead what appears to happen, as discussed in relation to the central governor model, is that the brain calculates the amount of glycogen that is available at the start of exercise, and then adapts the exercise intensity to ensure that exercise stops before complete glycogen depletion can occur. In layperson's terms, it rations the muscle glycogen, making the exercise increasingly more uncomfortable as the fuel is progressively used up. Eventually the athlete becomes so uncomfortable – in physiological terms, he experiences a very high 'rating of perceived exertion' – that he scales down the exercise to such a low intensity that it can be fully covered by energy derived from his invested fuel reserves – his body fat stores. Or, if he is like most amateur cricketers, he calls it a day and heads out of the nets for the pavilion!

Of course, it is not only the falling muscle glycogen concentrations that contribute to the rising ratings of perceived exertion during very prolonged exercise. A rising body temperature (Tucker et al., 2004) or, especially in the case of the fast bowler, the associated muscle damage caused by repeated eccentric muscle contractions during a 20-over day, will have exactly the same effect. The function of these symptoms is self-preservation; they try to dissuade the athlete from continuing to exercise to the point at which irreversible bodily harm might occur. Nevertheless, these symptoms can be reduced if the cricketer begins each match day with muscle glycogen stores that are as full as possible.

How then to maintain glycogen supplies? The most efficient way to top up the glycogen stores is to consume carbohydrates at regular intervals during the day, especially immediately after the end of the day's play. Ingesting either fat or protein will not re-stock the glycogen stores; only carbohydrate provides the glucose molecules that are the building-blocks from which glycogen is made. This is why

Fat is like money that has been invested: it is difficult for the body to access, and cannot be drawn on in emergencies. Strategies for breaking down fat always have to be long term – another fact for would-be dieters to ponder.

it is so important that cricketers should snack on high-carbohydrate, low-fat foods. To further complicate the matter, some foods and carbohydrates will top up blood sugar levels speedily, while others do so at a slow, steady rate. The speed at which food supplies glucose to the body is known as its glycaemic index. Any athlete who needs to perform consistently over a long period of time therefore needs to eat a combination of high (releases glucose rapidly) and low (releases glucose slowly) glycaemic index foods (see the chart below).

VERY HIGH GI	HIGH GI	MODERATE GI	LOW GI	VERY LOW GI
cornflakes, glucose, rice cakes, white bread	bananas, rice, carrots, sweetcorn, oats, corn chips, potatoes, raisins, wholewheat bread	tinned beans, oranges, peas, potato chips, pasta	apples, dried beans, lentils and other legumes, peaches, pears, milk, yoghurt, rye bread	eggs, meat, fish, nuts, soya beans, green vegetables

Sports nutritionists recommend that athletes eat a diet based on low glycaemic index foods, and that high glycaemic index foods be eaten only in combination with foods that release energy slowly, so as to achieve a balance between instant and constant energy delivery. This, however, refers to the athlete's everyday diet. Where knowledge of low and high glycaemic index foods really becomes useful is during matches. During a break, you might choose a hasty snack such as a handful of raisins or a banana that will almost instantly boost your blood glucose concentrations. (See the next section for suggestions on snack choices for players during matches.) These are also good choices at the end of the day, when high glycaemic foods should be eaten as they cause a more rapid re-stocking of depleted muscle glycogen stores. Later, at the evening meal, low glycaemic foods should be eaten, as they sustain the re-stocking of glycogen reserves throughout the rest of night, thereby ensuring that the glycogen stores are topped up at the start of play the next day.

REFRESHMENTS BEFORE, DURING AND AFTER THE MATCH

We have now covered the general guidelines on what the aspiring or established cricketer should eat and drink. Yet following a sensible and healthy diet still does not solve the problem of what to eat and drink *during* a match or very long practice sessions. To further complicate matters, players' needs for food and drink will change according to the circumstances, such as the weather. For example, on warm, dry days, cricketers will need far more fluid than on chilly, overcast and windy days. On a grey day in early spring in England, with a cold breeze blowing, players are likely to want hot soup for lunch; on a very hot, humid and windless day in Melbourne or Mumbai, perhaps all they will be able to face at the lunch break is salad and fruit (both of which will provide valuable fluid and energy replacement). Moreover, during a match, the nutritional needs of fast bowlers and wicket-keepers will be different from those of the batsmen waiting in the pavilion.

Since there are no specific studies on cricketers and nutrition, we have to assume that, for optimum performance, fast bowlers and wicket-keepers will need to follow roughly the same dietary guidelines as distance runners, as the studies already mentioned suggest that total energy expenditure of fast bowlers, wicket-keepers and one-day batters during a day's play or intensive practice are probably similar to those of a long-distance runner in training or competition.

Assuming this is correct, on the evening before a match, fast bowlers and wicket-keepers (as well as any confident batters who plan to spend several hours at the crease) should eat a meal that consists largely of complex carbohydrates with little fat or protein. Pasta with vegetables or a tomato-based sauce, baked potatoes with low-fat toppings, or rice dishes such as paella would be good choices. On the day of the match itself, another high-carbohydrate meal should be taken at least two hours before playing. For example, a breakfast of cornflakes or oats with skim milk, bananas, and plenty of toast with honey (skip the butter, though) would be an appropriate choice.

GO BANANAS

Without further research on the impact of the nutritional choices made by players, especially during matches, we cannot know for certain how various foods aid performance. Most of the information available to us is anecdotal. For example, when Steve Waugh was pushing towards a series-winning double century under punishing conditions in the Caribbean in 1995, the physiotherapist and fitness coach for the team, Errol Alcott, allowed him only fluids and bananas throughout the day's play. Bananas have a high glycaemic index, they contain substantial amounts of water, and are highly palatable and easy to eat; but it's possible that the comfort factor and sensory input of eating bananas might have been just as important as the nutritional value they provided Waugh.

However, it is possible to follow a basic rule of thumb: eat high glycaemic index foods during the match, and a balanced mixture, with the emphasis on low glycaemic carbohydrates, in the evening after the match. Before play the next day, choose high glycaemic foods once again. Save the steak or barbecued meat until the match is over.

Fast bowlers and wicket-keepers (as well as any confident batters who plan to spend more than a few hours at the crease) should eat a meal the night before a match that consists largely of complex carbohydrates with little fat or protein.

GOOD SNACK CHOICES FOR CRICKETERS DURING MATCHES
Rice cakes, raisins, dates, oatcakes, carrots, bananas, grapes, low-fat corn chips, chilled melon wedges (especially on hot, humid days)

POOR SNACK CHOICES FOR CRICKETERS DURING MATCHES
Potato chips, peanuts, dried and highly-spiced meat products, biscuits, muffins, scones, cheese wedges, pies and sausage rolls, chocolate

RUNNING DRY: HOW MUCH TO DRINK

There are few studies of the fluid requirements of fast bowlers. However, according to Gore et al. (1993), the rates of sweat loss of fast bowlers bowling in hot, humid conditions are equivalent to those of long-distance runners, and can be as high as 1,5 litres per hour. Under cooler conditions, sweat rates proved to be less, about 500 millilitres per hour.

It is not possible for a fast bowler to replace 1,5 litres per hour: this would require that he drink 200ml at the end of each over. While this might be manageable for the first few overs, by about the fifth over, he would be running in feeling distinctly bloated and uncomfortable. This is because, under the stress of fast bowling, the peak rate of absorption of fluid by the intestine (usually well above 1,5 litres per hour under rest conditions) would be substantially reduced, causing most of the ingested fluid to be retained, unabsorbed, within the intestine.

Fortunately, humans evolved to cope well with mild levels of dehydration. It has been found that tri-athletes can lose up to 12% of their body weight (close to 8kg) during a 224km Ironman Triathlon, yet perform extremely well and not show any obviously detrimental effects (Sharwood et al., 2004). In other words, if a fast bowler does not have access to water, and has lost 1,5kg over 60 minutes, he should not be overly concerned that his performance will be adversely affected. But he could continue comfortably for more than an hour under these conditions only if he had free access to fluid whenever he required it between overs.

Provided athletes drink according to the dictates of their thirst, they will drink appropriately (Noakes, 2003). After all, thirst is a control mechanism that has evolved over millions of years specifically to ensure that all creatures drink only as much as they require – no more and no less. Interestingly, no-one ever advises animals and other creatures how much to drink; they seem to cope quite well without the complex guidelines that have been evolved to help ensure that apparently more intelligent human athletes do not become 'dehydrated' during exercise. It is worth pointing out that humans apparently lost their ability to judge how much they should drink at exactly the same time that the sports drink industry began to develop, especially in the United States: after all, it is simply not in the interests of any beverage manufacturer to have humans drink only according to their thirst. Unfortunately, there is no scientific justification for the marketing hype that suggests that athletes 'drink as much as you can tolerate'. In the US, at least ten marathon runners and military personnel who followed this advice have died as a result of hyponatraemia, a condition that develops when far too much liquid is consumed. (This is discussed in more detail on p. 572.)

Cricketers should therefore be advised to drink according to the dictates of their thirst. This will usually be between 200–500ml per hour, depending on whether the player is fielding, bowling, batting or keeping wicket. Obviously the more running the player does, the greater his fluid requirements will be. Fluid requirements increase in hot, humid and wind-still conditions. The main problem for cricketers is the availability of fluid. It is much better to drink small amounts often, say 150ml every 15 minutes, rather than larger amounts less frequently (400–500ml every 60 minutes), as is the current practice. Providing fluids more often, especially to fast bowlers but also batters in one-day cricket played in hot conditions, would make these players more comfortable.

This need to provide players with small but frequent drinks presents new logistical problems for cricket matches. While the standard pattern of drinks breaks (taking place every hour) works very well in moderate climates such as in Britain where the game developed, such infrequent breaks do not allow appropriate consumption of fluids in hotter conditions, as might be found in the Southern hemisphere, Asian subcontinent and Caribbean islands. In typical English conditions, which seldom become extremely hot or humid, players consume moderate quantities of fluids during drinks breaks – amounts that can be tolerated without causing discomfort or a sense of bloating during the next session of play. Yet these quantities are sufficient to prevent the development of thirst before the next drinks interval. But in hot climates, players who try to drink as much as they need to quench their thirst and prevent the development of progressive dehydration during the next playing session risk intestinal discomfort and impaired performance as a result.

Cricket administrators seriously need to consider new means of structuring the drinks intervals so that players in hot countries are able to drink more frequently during matches. At present, a parched batsman in dire straits can usually signal for a drink along with fresh equipment, such as new gloves. However, umpires are unlikely to tolerate a fast bowler holding up play every twenty minutes while calling for a drink from the twelfth man! Currently, there is an informal system in place whereby drinks are brought onto the field for those who need them whenever there is a break in play – at the fall of a wicket, if a player needs new equipment, if the umpires are consulting, or if a player is receiving on-the-spot medical attention. Although this is sensible and should be encouraged, it has the obvious disadvantage of being haphazard – in one session, no wickets might fall, and in the next, all kinds of interventions might interrupt play.

So far, no foolproof solutions for this problem have been proposed. Any solution must provide bowlers and batters with the option of drinking between overs from their personal fluid containers. But where such containers could be stored during play is the problem that needs to be addressed.

As for which drinks should be taken, in the past the only option was to drink water, usually straight from the tap. But the increasing variety of bottled and mineral waters currently available provides a much greater choice. In general, there is little to choose between different fluids. The key is to replace lost fluids as they occur and to drink whatever you personally find most tasty. Since it is the liquid replacement that is crucial, the nature of the fluid ingested is less important than the volume that is ingested.

HOW MUCH FLUID IS TOO MUCH? WHAT ROLE DOES SALT PLAY?

These two questions are related and have recently been asked with increasing frequency, especially since a number of female marathon runners have died in the United States from the medical condition known as hyponatraemia (low blood sodium concentrations). In this condition, the concentration of sodium in the blood falls, with the result that water moves from the bloodstream into all the cells in the body, particularly the brain cells. The result is brain swelling, loss of consciousness and even convulsions, leading ultimately to death, due to the cessation of either heart, lung or brain function. Although this condition is exceptionally rare outside of hospitals, its incidence in sport has increased in the past fifteen years ever since the idea has been circulated that athletes need to 'drink as much as they can tolerate' during exercise in order to prevent the supposedly lethal risks of dehydration (Noakes, 2003). As a result several runners, hikers and army personnel involved in exercise lasting at least four hours (mostly in the United States) have drunk vastly in excess of their fluid requirements, becoming 'waterlogged', ultimately suffering from convulsions, and in a few cases, dying if not treated appropriately.

However, this scenario is completely preventable, if athletes simply drink only as much as their thirst dictates. There is no need to ingest sodium (salt) tablets since the condition is not caused by salt deficiency, even though the blood sodium

Cricketers and other athletes should drink according to the demands of their thirst – there is no truth whatsoever in the slogans 'drink before you're thirsty' or 'by the time you're thirsty, it's too late'.

concentration is reduced. The excess fluid in the body simply dilutes the blood salt content, causing the hyponatraemia. Taking extra salt does not address the primary problem, which is the excess body water. Thus drinking only the amount of fluid that your body requires as opposed to the maximum amount that it can tolerate, will ensure that the condition never happens.

The good news for cricketers is that it is extremely difficult for them to reach this level of 'saturation': you would have to sit in the pavilion drinking 1,5 to 2 litres of fluid per hour for at least four hours. Difficult as this might be beyond the boundary, it is impossible on the field of play, since there simply is not enough fluid available out in the middle to supply you with 350–500ml every fifteen minutes for six hours! And even if you somehow managed to drink that much, you would then have to excuse yourself from the game every few minutes to urinate.

In addition, it is clear that only certain genetically predisposed individuals will develop hyponatraemia when they drink too much fluid (Noakes et al., 2005). For most of us, there are sufficient physiological safety measures in place to ensure that if we drink too much fluid, the rate at which we produce urine increases, thus protecting us from developing hyponatraemia.

WHAT ABOUT SPORTS DRINKS?

The value of sports drinks is that they provide both fluid and energy replacement, along with a touch of electrolytes. They are also flavoured to improve palatability and are usually served cold, which is attractive to players during or after a hot and sweaty innings.

Sports drinks were designed initially for long-distance runners, cyclists and tri-athletes who require both fluid and energy replacement during exercise, as they do not have the opportunity to consume food while competing.

However, because cricket matches are structured so that players can take meals and refreshments in the course of the day's play, there is no absolute necessity for cricketers to consume sports drinks. They can be handy for players who struggle to choose the correct snacks during breaks, or can't face solid food during a match, or find that excessive heat has killed their appetite. Sports drinks do provide more carbohydrate than most other drinks (except for fruit juices) and can therefore assist in the process of carbohydrate replenishment following a long day of fielding, bowling or batting.

Cricket administrators seriously need to consider new means of structuring the drinks intervals so that players in hot countries are able to drink more frequently during matches.

CRAMPING YOUR STYLE

At the Wanderers stadium in Johannesburg in 1997, Steve Waugh, while batting through a partnership in which Greg Blewett made his maiden double century, became so stricken with cramp that at one point he was falling over every time he tried to play off the front foot. Why did this happen? Was Waugh simply not fit enough? Was the extreme heat a factor? Or is there something about batting in Test conditions – where a player can spend up to twenty nearly motionless minutes defending, then suddenly have to race two or three runs as fast as possible, a sequence that can take place repeatedly during an innings – that predisposes towards cramps? Then there is the question of individual susceptibility – some players are prone to cramps while others are largely immune.

A popular theory is that muscle cramps are caused either by 'dehydration' or salt deficiency, or both. This theory has been seized upon by sports drinks manufacturers, as it suggests that drinking such products (which contain both water and salt) will prevent the condition. However, the truth is somewhat more complex. We still do not fully understand what causes cramps, but we have some ideas. Sports medicine specialist Dr Martin Schwellnus argues that the reflexes that inhibit excessive muscle contraction become inactive in those muscles that contract repeatedly over prolonged periods of time. The muscles that are particularly vulnerable to this are the diaphragm, the hamstrings, the quadriceps and the calf muscles. There is a very simple solution – lengthening the muscles (through stretching) activates the muscles' own protective stretch reflex. This suggests that in the case of the Wanderers match, Steve Waugh might have been able to avoid being all but paralysed by stretching for a few minutes between each over.

The Schwellnus theory of muscle cramps

According to this theory, muscle cramps occur when fatigue leads to abnormalities in the mechanisms that regulate muscle tone and contraction. Type 1a and 11 muscle spindles (top panel) react to the stretch of the muscle by sending signals to the anterior horn cells that produce muscle contraction. This means that a sudden stretch of the muscle can produce a reflex contraction. In contrast, the Golgi tendon organ detects stretch in the tendon (top panel). If the tendon is overstretched, the organ tendon sends an inhibitory impulse to the anterior horn cells, inhibiting muscle contraction. During a normal muscle contraction (middle panel), excitatory and inhibitory signals to the anterior horn cells are in balance. But in a fatigued muscle, spindle activity increases and Golgi tendon organ activity decreases, resulting in increased muscle excitability, and this can lead to cramping (bottom panel). Cramping is more likely to occur if the muscle contracts continually in a shortened range without being fully stretched to its maximum length. One technique to prevent cramping is repeatedly to stretch the muscle to its longest length. This may reactivate the Golgi tendon organs and reduce muscle excitability.

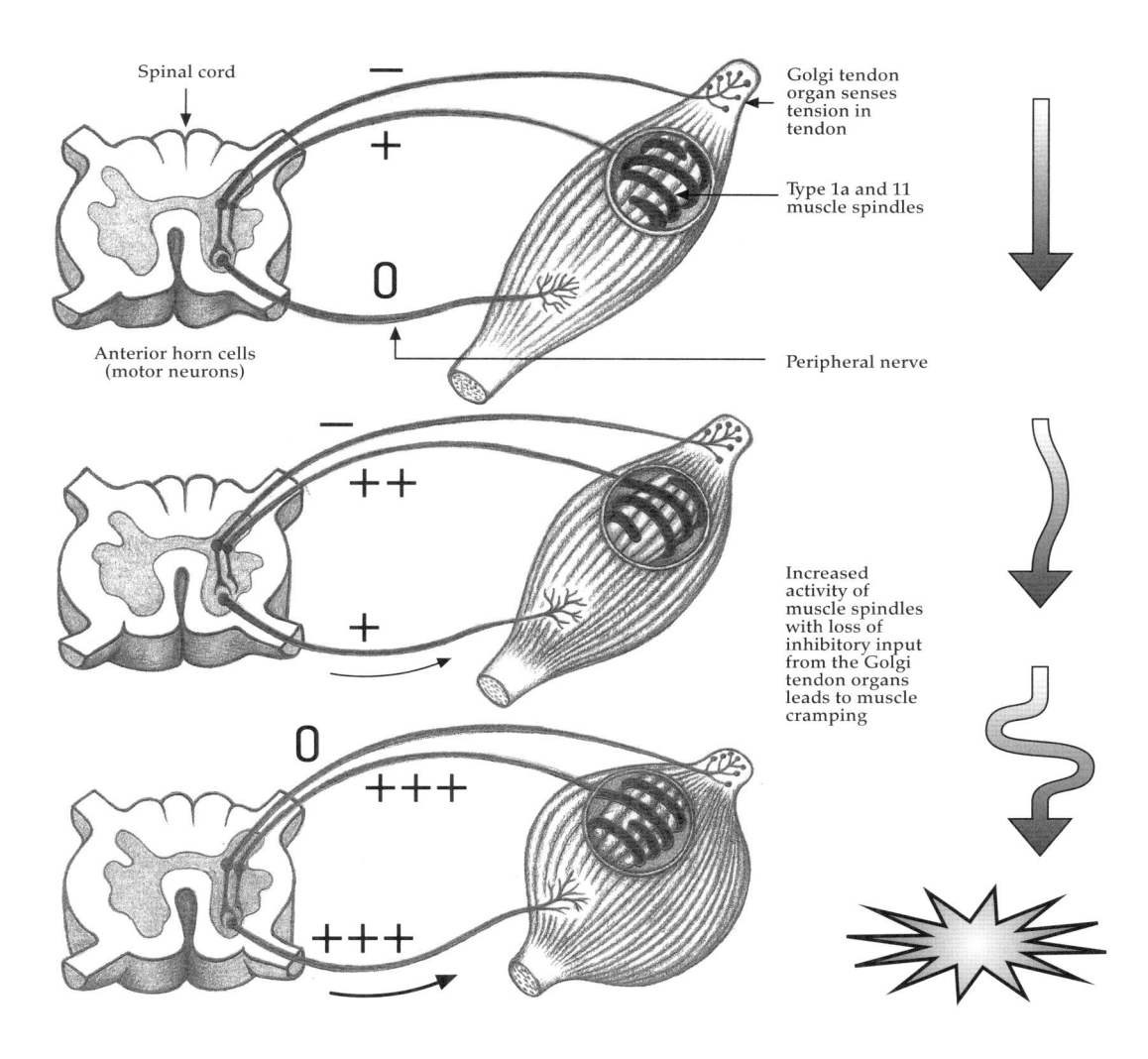

FIGURE 10.3: *The Schwellnus theory of muscle cramps*

TEXT AND FIGURE ADAPTED FROM: SCHWELLNUS, *PHYSICIAN AND SPORTSMEDICINE* (1999), PP. 109–115; NOAKES, *LORE OF RUNNING* (2003) P. 1 073

MEDICATIONS AND RECREATIONAL AND PERFORMANCE-ENHANCING DRUGS

The banning of Australian leg-spinner Shane Warne for twelve months after he was found to have used a diuretic during his recovery from surgery prior to the 2003 Cricket World Cup put the issue of drug use in the sport squarely in the spotlight. More specifically, it raised questions about which drugs cricketers are using to treat illness or injury, or to gain a competitive advantage, as did the cases of Pakistan bowlers Shoaib Akhtar and Mohammed Asif, who tested positive for a banned steroid in 2006.

Research suggests that drug use among cricketers rarely extends beyond taking vitamins and prescription drugs such as anti-inflammatories for the treatment of medical conditions. According to the Australian Sports Medicine Federation, quoted by Stretch and Bartlett (2000), the following drugs and medications are the most widely used: vitamins and food supplements (used by 34% of cricketers), anti-inflammatories (32%), painkillers (21%), medication for asthma and nasal congestion (17%), sedatives and tranquillizers (5%), stimulants (3%), anabolic steroids (1%) and weight-loss drugs (1%). This suggests that relatively few players are resorting to the use of illegal performance-enhancing drugs such as stimulants and anabolic steroids.

In fact, cricket seems to be relatively untainted by the drug scandals that have rocked other sports like cycling, football and athletics. This is not necessarily because most cricketers are squeaky-clean, but rather because of the uncertainties of the game and its reliance on skill and experience rather than pure strength or speed. Using a stimulant might not be of much use to the batsman who has no way of knowing for how long he will be at the crease; whether or not the stimulant will impair rather than improve his concentration; or for how long the stimulant will be active before its action wears off, leaving the batter more mentally fatigued than if he had not used it in the first place.

However, a real threat is posed not so much by stimulants, but by the possibility that anabolic steroids will jump the Atlantic, crossing from baseball into cricket. Baseball in the United States has recently seen a remarkable increase in the number of home runs hit every year, and it appears that strength- and speed-enhancing steroids have played a major role in this: stronger pitchers throw faster pitches, stronger batsmen put more into their swings, and the result – when sluggers make contact – is a ball soaring high into the bleachers. Anabolic steroids also decrease the risk of injury, and the speed of recovery time after injury, which similarly contributes to home-run records: fewer injuries, or shorter lay-offs, mean more games, and more opportunities to bat.

The medicinal attributes of anabolic steroids are already posing major ethical dilemmas for doctors treating injured athletes, since there seems to be a legitimate argument that withholding anabolic steroids could delay the patient's recovery. The ethical problem now becomes that there is almost no distinction between a steroid used to expedite recovery from injury and one used to unfairly increase athletic performance. Add to this the modern phenomenon of huge numbers of sports injuries, and one has to wonder whether the permissible medical use of steroids wouldn't result in a free-for-all of continuous use by leading athletes in many sports.

Are cricketers likely to try to get away with steroid use? (See the cautionary tale of Pakistani fast bowlers Shoaib and Asif in the box on p. 578.) Sceptics might say no, claiming that cricket relies far less on brute strength and far more on timing than baseball does. Similarly, they might point out that even fast bowlers aren't necessarily helped by greater strength: legendary strike bowlers like Curtly Ambrose, Joel Garner and Glenn McGrath hardly have weight-lifters' physiques.

But the reality is that strength – particularly in the upper body – has always helped cricketers. In the modern game alone, it has revealed its worth in the powerful batting of the likes of Andrew Flintoff, Matthew Hayden, Jacques Kallis, Lance Klusener, Inzamam-ul-Haq, Chris Gayle and Andrew Symonds. And the sport's history is full of burly men whose strength gave them the edge over their competitors. Ian Botham leads a field that includes greats like Fred Trueman, Sir Vivian Richards and Dennis Lillee.

Furthermore, ever-lengthening playing seasons and increasingly frenetic touring schedules mean that more cricketers than ever need to recover quickly from injuries: their current income and future careers depend on it. For these reasons, it is essential that cricket authorities pay special attention to the issue of drug use, especially of anabolic steroids, in the sport – they can no longer assume that cricket will remain as untainted as it has been.

Another matter for concern is the fact that nearly every season, a few elite players are found using recreational and illegal drugs, usually marijuana and cocaine. This must be strenuously discouraged, not least because the use of recreational drugs is often associated with other destructive lifestyle behaviours, in particular excessive alcohol consumption. Further negative consequences are obvious, and can range from tabloid media frenzy and scandal to extremely unpleasant legal penalties. Professional cricketers travelling in foreign countries need to be like Caesar's wife where illegal drugs are concerned – not only beyond reproach, but seen to be as such.

> *The medicinal attributes of anabolic steroids are already posing major ethical dilemmas for doctors treating injured athletes.*

STEROIDS, SUPPLEMENTS, SHOAIB AND ASIF

In October 2006, a messy saga unfolded in Pakistan cricket when two fast bowlers, Shoaib Akhtar and Mohammed Asif, were found to have traces of the anabolic steroid Nandrolone in their systems following internal drug tests by the Pakistan Cricket Board. The status of both players remained uncertain as various internal and international tribunals set bans, overturned them, appealed and counter-appealed. The PCB first banned the bowlers from playing, a decision promptly reversed by an appellate committee, while the World Anti-Doping Agency demanded leave to appeal the overturning of the ban. The ICC was drawn in, and after much shuffling around, the players did not play in the 2007 World Cup, even though they had been included in the original squad. Meanwhile the debate raged as to whether they had taken the banned medication deliberately, or inadvertently as ingredients in their nutritional supplements. The matter was further clouded by Shoaib's habit of consulting personal rather than team doctors.

Nandrolone itself is controversial as a banned substance, as the human body produces it in very tiny quantities. It increases muscle mass, apparently without some of the dangerous side-effects of some steroids, and a number of elite athletes (sprinters in particular) have tested positive for the drug in recent times, leading to speculation that the testing process itself might be flawed. But this might well be a defensive argument.

This case, like that of Shane Warne (see p. 581 below), serves as a warning of the complexity of the issues, and the need not only for a zero-tolerance approach to banned substances, but for careful player education on what 'medical' treatments constitute banned drug usage. Handing out a pamphlet is not enough!

We should be under no illusions: drugs in sport are here to stay, whether legally or not. Less good players will still try to cheat by using drugs, and countries that place great store on athletic success will continue developing their state-sponsored programmes of drug use (Hoberman, 1992). How long will it be before a drug is developed or discovered that improves batsmen's selective attention and the speed at which they process information about advance cues? Probably not long: South African scientist Professor Richard Stretch and his colleagues (2000) have shown that the stimulant fencamfamine (2-ethyl amino-3phenyl-bicyclo 2.2.1-heptane), found in a popular South African 'tonic', improved the ability of batters to strike a cricket ball delivered at a speed of 28,6m/s (103km/h) in the centre of the bat. They hasten to add that their research interest in this topic is not to promote or suggest the use of stimulants, but to point to the potential dangers of brushing this explosive issue under the carpet.

MEDICINAL DRUGS

The research cited here has shown that as many as 33% of cricketers may regularly use some form of medication to reduce pain, inflammation and swelling caused by injuries. These drugs range from over-the-counter painkillers (such as aspirin, paracetamol and ibuprofen) and gels to prescription painkillers and non-steroidal anti-inflammatories (NSAIDS). The continuous use of painkillers (both over-the-counter and scheduled) and NSAIDS is not without risk, however, and can cause damage to the intestines, liver and kidneys if used continuously for prolonged periods.

Yet the practical reality of the game is that many players swallow these medications in order to continue playing while injured. While it is acceptable and often necessary to take appropriate drugs to reduce discomfort, cricketers should never see their pills as a 'cure-all' that will enable them to continue playing in spite of an injury. However, occasionally, there may be situations in which the stakes are so high at elite levels of the game that players may take pain-killing drugs (especially in the form of topical preparations or injections) to enable them to participate or to continue playing in crucial matches. This is not the ideal, and should be seen very much as the exception rather than the rule. Coaches and managers should absolutely desist from placing pressure on key players to resort to such actions: 'playing through the pain' can have devastating short- or long-term health consequences. This course of action should only ever be taken with the informed consent of the player, after he has been fully advised of all the possible health implications and consequences, and in conjunction with his medical advisor.

A somewhat more unusual approach is to use drug-free medical procedures to enable injured players to continue playing. For example, Dr Dan Keisel, for many years the Pakistan team physiotherapist, follows the novel approach of using primarily shiatsu, acupuncture, osteopathic and chiropractic manipulations to treat players and manage any physical discomfort that might be hampering their performance. This was part of the ongoing medical management of the team during his tenure, but first-hand observation revealed that when Pakistan players left the field for treatment during matches, they were more likely to receive a quick osteopathic or shiatsu procedure than a pain-killing injection. (The sight of Dr Keisel, not a tall man, hoisting six-foot bowling maestro Wasim Akram into the air to loosen his spine made for an unforgettable picture.) This is certainly a route that other cricket-playing nations might like to explore.

Yet, while this approach may have fewer potential drawbacks than the continuous use of drug therapies, it is still not ideal. An injured player should be rested until he has made a full recovery, not wheeled back onto the field 'propped up' by drugs or other pain-killing strategies. This is especially important since the most accurate predictor of future injury risk is a previous injury. It is a logical conclusion to draw, since many players return to the game before fully recovering from their initial injuries; because the injured tissues have not entirely healed, they are at high risk of re-injury. Thus the best approach is to ensure that the injured tissues have a chance to heal completely before the player returns to practice or competition at full pace.

The relatively frequent use of medications that relieve asthma and nasal congestion caused by hay fever are probably related to the fact that cricket is played in the spring and summer when the pollen count is high. Moreover, it is played on grass, and in hot climates there may also be a fair amount of dust around. Fielders also tend to have plenty of contact with the playing surface.

However, players should be aware that taking decongestants for more than several days may cause 'rebound' congestion (in which the original condition comes back worse than before), an obvious drawback, while many hay fever and cold medications have a sedative effect and can cause drowsiness; clearly not ideal for the player who needs to remain alert at the crease or in the field.

Finally, the incidence of sedative and tranquillizer use by cricketers reported earlier (5%) might seem rather high until we consider that, in the case of elite players who travel frequently, sleeping pills are extremely useful on long-haul flights, as well as for helping them to adapt to a new sleeping pattern in a different time zone, or when they are jet-lagged.

NUTRITIONAL SUPPLEMENTS

'Healthy' and 'natural' medications have become big business over the last decade, and many athletes have swallowed the marketing, investing in a chemical soup of herbal remedies, vitamins, minerals and other nutritional supplements. Are these 'alternative' drugs effective?

The answer is simple, and no doubt disappointing to many who want a quick fix: there is no reputable scientific evidence that any but a very few of these products are of any special value to those who are eating a varied diet that provides the required amount of energy (calories). If you are taking in enough calories from a range of food sources, you will automatically be getting the vitamins and minerals you need.

In other words, the only people who might need vitamin and mineral supplements are those whose diets are inadequate in energy, either because they choose to starve themselves (as in the case of those with the disorder anorexia nervosa), or because they lack the financial resources to buy enough food. Athletes who expend more

If you are eating a sufficient number of calories from a range of food sources, you will automatically be getting all the vitamins and minerals you need.

DIET PILLS AND DEBACLES

Shane Warne made headlines – again – when he was sent home on the eve of the 2003 World Cup, and subsequently banned from playing cricket for a year, after testing positive for a banned diuretic drug. Professional athletes are banned from taking diuretics for the very good reason that because they stimulate the kidneys and increase urine output, they can mask the presence of other drugs in the body. There was speculation that Warne, who was recovering from a shoulder injury, had perhaps taken steroids to speed up recovery, although there was no evidence that this was the case.

Warne claimed indignantly that he was the victim of 'anti-doping hysteria' and that he had been guilty of nothing worse than vanity – allegedly taking several Moduretic tablets (a prescription drug) at his mother's behest, in order to reduce his weight and 'look good for the television cameras'. While it seems unlikely that there was any sinister purpose in his taking the medication, he was disingenuous in his claims that he did not know he was taking a diuretic (he referred to the drugs as 'fluid pills') or that diuretics fell into the category of banned drugs – the Australian Cricket Board's steady education efforts notwithstanding.

The simple moral of Warne's sorry tale is that cricketers (and other athletes) should not take weight-reducing medication, except in extremely rare circumstances, and then only at a doctor's behest, and under strict medical supervision. Diuretics have their place in the treatment of certain medical conditions, but should not ever be used for weight loss, as they cause water loss only – which is replaced as soon as the pill-taker drinks fluids. Many diet pills contain drugs that are unsafe (including ephedra) and have recently been banned for human consumption and withdrawn from the market. There is no reason to believe that those weight-loss drugs that are still on the market will prove to be any safer in the long term. No pills can substitute for a sensible nutritional regime that is low in fat and high in complex carbohydrates.

---

energy than sedentary folk will also take in more calories, and are therefore even less likely to be at risk of developing vitamin and mineral deficiencies than those who are sedentary. This is exactly the opposite of what marketers would like us to believe: that athletes are in special need of supplements.

When considering supplements, the role played by marketers and salespeople should not be underestimated. A billion-dollar industry has been built on the anxiety about body image so assiduously cultivated by Western marketers, an anxiety exported all over the globe with frightening speed in the last few decades. People are afraid of ageing and ill health, and this vulnerability has long been a source of quick profit. (The aggressive and indeed deceitful marketing of special vitamins as a treatment and even 'cure' for HIV/Aids in South Africa, a country that is staggering under the impact of this pandemic, is a good example of this phenomenon at its most extreme.)

When we see a product being supplied to or even endorsed by professional athletes, we assume the athletes in question have been approached because they are ideal test subjects for the product. But they are in fact a target market just like any other.

Even if professional athletes do not use the product they are given, an impression is still created that the supplement must be worth using, simply because it might be used by the sporting star. This 'endorsement by association' is a goldmine for marketers, as international athletes (including cricketers) are constantly in the limelight, adding glamour to everything they touch. Of course, the real prize is to get a sporting star to actively endorse a product. A clear example of this occurred in South Africa in the late 1990s, when the popular rugby player, Bob Skinstad, in response to a question about how he had become more muscular, said that he had been taking creatine. Within six months, South Africa, a developing country with a relatively small population of about 47 million people, had become the world's fourth largest market for creatine. This was in spite of the fact that there was little scientific evidence for the beneficial effects of this dietary supplement, which, given its high cost, was probably an option only for elite athletes.

So beware of miracle products that promise to change your life and grant you dynamic health and awesome new sporting powers – especially if they are very pricey. Such advertisements are common, and a player clutching at straws may well be tempted to investigate. But rip-off merchants abound and you have little protection, either as a consumer or as an athlete. Worse still, these products could even put you at risk of a positive sports doping test.

Similarly, think twice before taking a product because your batting partner or brother-in-law or a friend of a friend swears by it. No two individuals (or cricketers) are the same, and what helps your friend or relative may have no effect on you. Rather follow the guidelines in this section, and consult a professional dietician (one who is independent and has no affiliation with the supplement industry) if you feel that you really would benefit from the use of a nutritional supplement.

ALCOHOL

For better or worse, alcohol appears to be very much part of the culture and social rituals of the game of cricket. Post-match analyses take place over a 'cold one', team-building exercises, travel, and even just relaxing in the dressing room are almost unimaginable without alcohol in some form. For cricketers on tour, who are often bored and lonely, alcohol can provide a means of relaxation, as well as a source of schoolboy fun: one thinks of Steve Waugh's wry 'morning-after' remark during a tour of the Caribbean – 'Some of the guys were looking for the numbers of the trucks that had run them down the night before.'

Bonding between members is essential if a team is to be successful; yet Western society offers men few rituals for bonding and establishing togetherness that do not involve propping up a bar. Cricketers who are teetotal (such as South Africa's first post-isolation captain Kepler Wessels, whose dour but sensible dictum was 'You can't be a star in the bar and on the field') often have to work twice as hard to earn the respect of their peers. Holding back on alcohol intake is still sometimes seen as 'sissy' or a sign of a lack of team spirit. In spite of widespread general knowledge of the negative impact of regular or excessive alcohol intake on both health and sporting prowess, managers and coaches still sometimes regard heavy drinking with an indulgent eye, or as a bit of 'harmless fun', the 'lads letting off steam' and so on. For example, one cannot condone the indulgent, if not actually admiring, tone used by Australian coach Bob Simpson and later Dennis Lillee to describe the various attempts by players, including Doug Walters, Rodney Marsh and David Boon, to drink in excess of 44 beers during the international flight from Australia to England. Lillee's account reflects the entrenched view:

> *Eventually as we were 20 minutes out of Heathrow, he [Marsh] was clearly struggling, but the betting was that he was going to make it. I asked one of the stewardesses if she could make an announcement that Rod was about to break the record, as I thought this would be the spur a competitive man like him would need. The entire aircraft soon found that Australian wicket-keeper Rod Marsh was bidding to break the record for the flight. Proud man that he was, he was clearly determined to finish it…. After finally reaching for the last can and drinking it down just as we came in to land at Heathrow, he collapsed…. Maybe it was stupid, but for me it showed the strength and character of the man and the fact that he loved a challenge, especially as it was his best mate Douggie [Walters] who held the record…. The crew and the pilot joined in with all the passengers, who clapped him when he broke the record before he collapsed, proving it was harmless* (2003, p. 44).

This last claim is emphatically not true. Alcohol is a toxin, and there is a blood alcohol concentration that will prove lethal. Fortunately, Marsh lost consciousness before his 'strength and character' helped him commit suicide. But Lillee is not alone in the attitude illustrated above – after the 2007 World Cup, Ian Botham sprang to the defence of England player Andy Flintoff, whose carousing in the Caribbean had led to calls for crackdowns on excessive drinking by members of the England team. Botham spoke

'You can't be a star in the bar and on the field.'

– Kepler Wessels

FROM PINTING TO PONTING

Australia has long been a country with an ingrained tradition of combining cricket and heavy drinking. The use of alcohol by Australian cricketers during the latter half of the nineteenth century was considered so normal that 'it was common for the drinking of alcohol to influence the course of a game. Champagne lunches were frequently held, even if they delayed the game's commencement. Some newspaper reports of intercolonial and local games gave nearly as much space to the celebrations and after-match festivities as they did to the match itself' (de Moore, 1999).

Yet the opening years of the twenty-first century have seen a dramatic turnaround in attitudes towards cricket and alcohol in Australia at the elite level. This has largely been due to the personal battle with alcohol of one of the world's most gifted batsmen, Ricky Ponting. His towering talent meant that the Tasmanian cricketer was playing for his country at an extremely early age. However, his early international career was marred by rumblings about his predilections for gambling and alcohol abuse – which were showing signs of becoming full-blown addictions – as reflected in his media nicknames at the time, 'Punter' and 'Pinting'. The turning point was a sordid brawl in a Sydney nightclub, in which Ponting was knocked unconscious. In his subsequent public apology, he acknowledged that he had an 'alcohol problem'. His mentors and minders were intelligent and humane enough to give him their full backing and support in tackling his problem. Of course, both sides were acting shrewdly. The Australian Cricket Board had no intention of losing one of the game's brightest stars; and Ponting knew that no matter how glorious his stroke-play, if he kept up a lifestyle of drinking, gambling, clubbing and late nights, he would squander his chance of inheriting the mantle of captaincy of the Australian side from an ageing Steve Waugh.

Ponting was lucky, however, to be tackling his demons in a new and ever more competitive era in Australian cricket. Even before the Tasmanian renounced alcohol, Brett Lee had done the same; not because of any perceived personal problems, but for the purely pragmatic reason that his coach at the time had read an article alleging that fast bowlers who drank alcohol were more likely to rack up injuries than those who abstained. Lee, one of the world's fastest bowlers, was prepared to try anything that might protect his body from injury, and promptly decided to take a two-year vacation from alcohol.

Meanwhile, with all the zeal of the reformed addict, Ponting has been cracking down on the culture of excessive drinking by Australian cricketers: he famously barred the gifted Andrew Symonds from playing in an international one-day game when the latter showed up for the pre-match exercise bleary-eyed and smelling of alcohol. In an interview, Ponting claimed that what 'made him see red' was Symonds' alleged defence that he had played in this condition before!

This shift in attitudes towards alcohol by the world's toughest competitors hopefully presages a move away from the long and unhappy marriage between cricket and the pub so prevalent in the twentieth century.

for many when he argued that going out for a 'few drinks' was a normal response to defeat, and an integral part of being a 'fired-up' all-rounder and fast bowler.

But why do cricketers have this seemingly juvenile fascination for alcohol? Perhaps it is because the game has always attracted individuals who require alcohol to support or express some aspect of their personality. This need is then bolstered by an environment in which excessive alcohol consumption is accepted. Perhaps it is simply part of the historical culture of cricket, especially in its country of origin. (See the box opposite for more on the profound shift in attitudes to alcohol by Australia's cricketing administration and elite.)

But perhaps it is also because the shift in the perception of cricketers as athletes is not yet complete: the entrenched notion – that good cricketers are gifted individuals who can eat, drink and party all night without their natural talents being in the least bit affected – has only in the last decade or so begun to give way to the idea that elite cricketers are athletes whose God-given flair for the game can be improved by honing physical fitness and maintaining their bodies in top condition, in the same way that top-class runners, cyclists, swimmers and tennis-players might do.

Yet there is no doubt that 21st-century cricketers will have to be elite athletes as well as cricketers: the pressures on the modern player and the punishing schedules followed by first-class cricketers will increasingly handicap the gifted player who is sloppy about physical maintenance – and that includes alcohol consumption. As this shift takes place, there will be less and less pressure on cricketers to 'live it up' and more support for increasingly abstemious lifestyle choices.

The following are useful guidelines for adult cricketers who are confused about how to combine alcohol with cricket in a way that is both sensible and enjoyable.

1. Understand the genetic predisposition to alcoholism

Alcoholism has cut a swathe through international cricket: like the high incidence of suicide among former players, it is one of the sport's darkest secrets. It is one of the most demeaning illnesses there is, thanks to the nature of alcohol's action on the brain. Within a few days of the onset of heavy regular drinking, the subconscious brain's function is permanently altered (the basis of all addictions), so that the focus of the alcohol-dependent person's existence becomes the search for those environments (including the pub at the cricket ground) where alcohol can be found and consumed, preferably among 'friends' in an environment that encourages the drinker to reject the 'nagging' and 'killjoy' advice of true friends and family. Eventually all other social and other functions become subservient to this addictive need.

The genetic basis for alcohol addiction is extremely strong: those unlucky enough to have the genetic predisposition will have inherited a subconscious brain function that is more easily 'switched' by alcohol (and indeed other drugs). Thus those who are either abstemious or who drink only occasionally have very likely inherited brains that lack that crucial chemical 'switch' through which alcohol exerts its devastating effect. Without this chemical 'switch', alcohol is unlikely to become an addictive influence.

The point is that young cricketers who have one or more family members with a history of alcoholism, alcohol-dependence or heavy drinking, including binge-drinking, need to understand that they may have inherited the alcohol-specific switch in their brains. If so, they need to be aware that even a single drink could trigger that switch and propel them down a path of heavy drinking, ending in alcohol dependence, alcoholism and the misery that this addiction usually causes. A significant problem is that it takes perhaps 30 years of heavy drinking before the real physical carnage of alcoholism becomes apparent, long after the cricketer has stopped playing cricket. Thus the young cricketer who begins drinking heavily is unlikely to experience any overtly negative consequences of his incipient addiction, and will have little incentive to stop. But 30 years down the line it will be too late, as the damage will have been done.

The safest way to prevent alcoholism is not to start regular drinking in the first place. Since this is not a practical option for many cricketers, the next step is to be able to detect the first signs that the brain has 'switched'. These warning signs include the need to drink regularly as part of a fixed and unbending behaviour pattern and, frequently, to the point of drunkenness – in other words, to be unable to stop drinking until one is completely inebriated. Once these behaviour patterns become fixed (if not before), it is essential to seek professional help. The more quickly help is sought, the more likely the results will be positive.

2. Understand the physiological impact of alcohol on your body

Many believe that alcohol is a bit like chocolate cheesecake – perfectly harmless, and even beneficial as long as it is taken in small quantities, a belief that is bolstered by medical research showing that a few glasses of red wine a week may reduce the risk of heart attacks. But drinkers need to understand that it is not the alcohol in any alcoholic beverage that is beneficial, but rather other ingredients, such as the anti-oxidants found in red wine. Alcohol is a toxin; in other words, a poison. The body therefore has to eliminate it via detoxification by the liver, and it is this organ that bears the brunt of heavy alcohol consumption. So unlike a cream doughnut, which contains nothing that is not nourishing (in very small quantities!), alcohol is always toxic to the body.

3. Switch to low-alcohol or 'lite' drinks

If you would like to cut back on alcohol intake, but do not fancy ordering Perrier in the pub, change brands. One of the simplest ways to keep on enjoying a drink at the post-match gathering with a clear conscience is to switch to a beverage that has a lower alcohol content. If your usual tipple is spirits, change to wine or beer. If a glass of wine or a couple of beers are part of your unwinding routine, try one of the new low-alcohol brands. (For those who are watching their weight, these have the added advantage of containing fewer kilojoules.) Experiment with 'spritzers' – wine that has been diluted with soda water or mineral water – but don't knock these back when you're thirsty. Younger players especially should not assume that the so-called 'alco-pops' – commercially bottled or canned drinks that combine fruit juices and sweetened beverages with spirits – are a low-alcohol option. These taste and look like soft drinks, and are thus easily quaffed or glugged down – but they have a high alcohol content and should be avoided.

4. Don't drink alcohol to quench thirst

If you're thirsty, drink either water or a sports drink. Never come in from an energetic practice or a long, hot day in the field and grab a beer. Drink water, fruit juice or iced tea to quench your thirst, and keep the beer for savouring later, once your thirst has largely disappeared.

5. Count your drinks

Always keep track of how much alcohol you are consuming. Don't keep topping up your wine glass – empty your glass before refilling it. It is a good idea to decide ahead of time how many drinks you will have at any occasion or function, such as a benefit dinner. Then stick to this; do not allow your teammates or peer pressure to derail you. Remember, if you lose count of how many drinks you have already had, you've had too many.

6. Avoid binge drinking

Athletes in training, especially if partying after a game or event is a fixed feature of the team's behavioural culture, will often abstain from alcohol all week, or while training, only to cut loose at the weekend or after a match. The justification sometimes offered is that it is acceptable to save up one's drink 'ration', and then to consume the lot in one glorious 'booze-up'. However, it is far more harmful to the body (and thus to performance) to drink seven beers in one evening than to consume one each day for seven days. One or two drinks a day is relatively harmless, as the liver is able to detoxify the ingested alcohol fast enough to prevent blood alcohol concentrations reaching toxic levels. But binge drinking produces toxic blood alcohol levels from which it will take the body several days to recover fully. There is no truth whatsoever to the notion that one can prepare one's liver for the onslaught by first abstaining for a certain period.

7. Don't drink alcohol when flying

Long-haul international flights, especially across time zones, disrupt the natural sleep-cycle, a disturbance that is worsened by excessive alcohol consumption. The cabins of aircraft are also notoriously dehydrating zones, an effect exacerbated by alcohol. For the speediest recovery from the strain of flying and jet-lag, stick to water and other non-alcoholic beverages when in the air.

8. Be sensible about drinking and playing

It may seem obvious that heavy (and sometimes even moderate) drinking the night before a game or during a match will handicap players, yet one keeps hearing anecdotes about cricketers who indulge on the eve of (and sometimes during) important matches, to the detriment of their performances. Clearly this is unacceptable in the professional era. So perhaps it is wisest to ban alcohol – or ask players to refrain from drinking – for the duration of a match.

ALCOHOL AND THE CRICKETER – TROUBLESHOOTING

All the guidelines listed above raise one or two ticklish issues. A talented player who persistently drinks to excess during the course of matches and at other inappropriate times might be harbouring emotional problems, and is definitely showing the first signs of alcohol dependence. Alcohol abuse might be his only means of expressing dissent or coping with unhappiness. Players on a long, gruelling tour may drink as an antidote to loneliness and boredom, while young or immature players might wish to prove their 'manliness' to other players by drinking excessively. In certain parts of the cricket-playing world, alcohol consumption is illegal, or frowned upon for cultural and religious reasons. Less worldly-wise players from those areas might never have drunk alcohol before and may be curious, or attracted to it because of its 'taboo' status.

The coach or manager has to tiptoe through all these minefields without coming across as a martinet. While he should make sure that players in his charge do not break any laws – under-age drinking and driving under the influence of alcohol should never be tolerated – he should not find himself having to play the role of Chief Alcohol Prohibition Enforcer. Rather than clamping down on players' drinking, the coach (or the medical advisor to the team) should explain candidly what effect alcohol is likely to have on players' performance, suggest practical guidelines for the safe and sensible use of alcohol, and enlist the support of older and (hopefully wiser) team members in guiding younger players.

In the case of international teams, it might be worth pointing out that players are both ambassadors for their country and role models for millions of children. If a player seems to have an ongoing problem with inappropriate drinking, professional help must be enlisted as tactfully and as early as possible if the long-term and destructive scourge of alcoholism is to be prevented.

Early detection of inappropriate alcohol consumption and swift intervention is crucial if a culture of appropriate alcohol consumption is to be introduced to international cricket. This is vital if we are to prevent the devastation alcohol will cause many cricketers in their later lives. At present, we lack specific data on the

SPONSORSHIP DILEMMAS: HAVE A COLD ONE – BUT FOR HOW MUCH LONGER?

One interesting conundrum that has arisen in recent decades is the sponsorship of cricket – ironically – by tobacco and alcohol manufacturing giants. This has led to all kinds of difficulties, especially during international tours where legislation controlling this kind of advertising differs from country to country. Several years ago, Indian and Pakistani teams, sponsored by a leading brand of cigarettes in the subcontinent, were asked to tape over the company's logos on their bats in Australia, where tobacco advertising is illegal.

In South Africa, where tobacco advertising – but not alcohol advertising – was banned some years ago, the Test team is heavily sponsored by a giant beer company, which raises all kinds of ethical considerations, not least for the players themselves. When Hashim Amla, a devout Muslim, joined the team, he could not in conscience wear the sponsor's brand on his cricket outfit, and was excused from doing so on religious grounds. But his was not the only dilemma. Devout Jewish and Christian cricketers may also feel uncomfortable 'promoting' alcohol, and any recovering alcoholics in the team will feel compromised. Players may come under pressure to consume the sponsor's product in public, or it may be freely supplied – possibly the last thing the coach and players need to contend with.

But to cloud the issue even further, there is the tricky question of perceived hypocrisy. Amla's decision not to wear the South African team sponsor's logo was lauded by many, but others pointed out that even as he took a moral stand, he nevertheless benefited from having his kit, accommodation and transport paid for by the very same sponsors. The issues are complex, but players who wish to rock the sponsorship boat must be very clear on their principles and boundaries, and must also understand that playing sport for a living sure beats working! These and other tricky debates may soon be academic, as it is likely that new legislation will bar both tobacco and alcohol advertising and sponsorship of national sports teams in the not-too-distant future.

effect of alcohol on cricketers' performance, their careers and their lives. Until we know more, it seems that total abstinence is probably the best option, at least if an elite athlete wants to play it absolutely safe. Nevertheless, this is not always practical. Moreover, the psychological sense of hardship or deprivation could also outweigh the physical benefits of abstinence. But in all cases, the most sensible option is to keep alcohol consumption to a minimum.

TOBACCO

The hazards of smoking have been scientifically proven beyond any doubt. The findings are emphatic and grim: in general, smokers lop ten years off their lifespan compared to non-smokers, largely because of the premature development of heart and lung diseases, or of cancer. In addition, smoking interferes with exercise performance, most dramatically in endurance sports like long-distance running or cycling.

However, cricket relies more heavily on skill than on supreme physical fitness, and some exceptional cricketers, for example Shane Warne and Ian Botham, have been able to rack up extraordinary performances while continuing to smoke.

We assume that those reading this book are aware of the reasons why no serious athlete (or anyone else) should smoke, so it is probably not necessary to make a case for giving up – or better still, never starting the habit. However, coaches might like to take the following pointers into consideration:

- **At first-class level, few batsmen or fast bowlers will be smokers, simply because attaining and maintaining physical fitness is easier for non-smokers than smokers.** This logic seems simple, but it is worth noting that those who do smoke at this level would indeed enjoy improved fitness and might have longer careers if they kicked the habit; but they will not necessarily become better cricketers the moment they quit.

- **Any serious cricketer who does smoke will almost certainly be under pressure from his doctor, coach, manager, teammates, and family to kick the habit.** The question then arises as to why he continues to smoke. It is important to understand that whereas not everyone who drinks alcohol is an alcoholic, every smoker is an addict, whether or not he or she acknowledges this. Nicotine is one of the most powerfully addictive drugs there is: one study has claimed that nicotine is as addictive as cocaine and even more addictive than alcohol. Although many smokers claim that they smoke for pleasure, almost every regular smoker continues puffing because the cravings triggered by nicotine withdrawal cause real physical and emotional discomfort.

- **For this reason, it is not much use continually to nag players to give up tobacco, any more than the same approach is likely to be helpful in the case of alcohol abuse.** It should also be recognized that in a game such as cricket (which has such a significant mental component), the comfort or relaxation value of that post- or pre-match cigarette can be sufficiently important to a player that efforts to pressure him to give up might even be counter-productive. Rather, any player who sincerely wants to kick the habit should be given appropriate medical advice and plenty of support.

- **Many smokers who are trying to give up cigarettes complain that they receive little or no social or structured support.** There are no supportive organizations with free membership along the lines of Alcoholics Anonymous for them. In addition, while it is considered bad form to flaunt alcohol in front of recovering alcoholics (and positively criminal to press drinks on them), ex-smokers receive no such special treatment. Instead, when they attend parties and other social events, they will all too often be exposed to others smoking freely. Be aware of how hard it is to kick the habit, and be sensitive to the ex-smokers on your team.

- **The good news for those who wish to give up smoking (especially athletes) is that normal lung function is restored fairly quickly,** with quitters commenting, sometimes ecstatically, on how much better and fitter they feel within weeks of giving up the habit. In this respect, ex-smokers are much better off than recovering alcoholics, who sometimes have to live with the consequences of irreversible physical damage caused by heavy drinking in the past.

- **It is now recognized that it is extremely difficult to go 'cold turkey' where nicotine is involved.** Doctors can prescribe nicotine patches and recommend commercial programmes (such as SmokEnders) specifically designed to wean smokers off tobacco as painlessly as possible. Research shows that those who gradually cut back on their cigarette intake are the most likely to quit for ever. There is good news on the horizon: certain SSRI (selective serotonin re-uptake inhibitors) anti-depressants, which act on serotonin levels in the brain, have shown promising results for compulsive and addictive behaviours, including smoking. It is quite likely that smokers who are serious about quitting may in future be able to do so with the help of this family of medications.

- **Smokers should not be given free rein to inflict their habit on their teammates** – the dangers of passive smoking are now well documented.

- **Although (as pointed out in the section on alcohol) it should not be the job of the coach to police or nag players, those responsible for coaching cricket at junior and senior school level should be alert to the tremendous peer pressure that might induce young players to experiment with tobacco.** Most children who start smoking do so out of simple curiosity, because of the allure of the forbidden, or because 'all their friends are doing it'. Coaches should be proactive in educating youngsters about the addictive properties of nicotine. Gloomy statistics about the medical dangers of smoking are unlikely to have much impact on the average fourteen-year-old (who believes, deep down, that he is immortal, and to whom long-term health issues are much less important than appearing cool). When talking to teenagers, it might be more effective to point out that smoking will almost certainly jeopardize their sporting prowess. Positive role models who give youngsters the message that it is not cool or clever to smoke are vital. For this reason, those elite players who have reached stardom in spite of their habit should make every effort to avoid being photographed while smoking.

THE SUN

All cricketers face an implacable enemy more dangerous in the long run than the most ferocious pace bowler. This is the sun – or to be more precise, the UVA and UVB bands of the ultraviolet rays in sunlight, which extract a catastrophic toll on the human skin, increasing the rate of ageing, and the risk of skin cancers, including the usually fatal, malignant melanoma (cancer of skin moles). UVA rays are less harmful, although they are responsible for damaging collagen fibres in the skin, causing it to age. It is UVB light, however, that causes cancer, including the lethal melanomas. It is important to remember that these skin cancers are highest in those parts of the world like Australia and New Zealand, South Africa and the southern states of the United States, where the sun shines fiercely for most days of the year, where a significant number of the population is light-skinned, and where young people spend many hours during the day out-of-doors.

Furthermore, most of the skin damage caused by exposure to ultraviolet rays is accumulated in the first 25 years of life, precisely the time that most cricketers are in the sun. To make matters worse, cricket is usually played during the days when UVA and UVB rays are at their most intense – between 10am and 4pm.

Parents and coaches therefore have a responsibility to ensure that players consistently take sensible precautions against the sun. These can include broad-brimmed hats, long-sleeved cricket shirts with collars that turn up to cover the back of the neck (these are often worn by Australian players, who hail from a country that is more educated about the dangers of skin cancer than most), sunscreen with high protection factors in lavish quantities, and sunglasses if possible.

Although the more fair-skinned a player is, the more vulnerable his or her skin is to sun damage, this does not mean that darker-skinned players can skip basic precautions against sun damage. Also note that measures must be taken against the sun on cloudy and overcast days as well; UVB rays (the ones that do the damage) are present even if the sun is masked by cloud. If you are coaching youngsters, be aware that they are likely to forget to take precautions, and be vigilant on their behalf: research now shows that one type of skin cancer (malignant melanoma) in later life can stem from just a single episode of severe sunburn during childhood.

Players should wear a sunscreen with the highest protection factor that is available. All sunscreens should offer protection against UVB rays – the ones that trigger sunburn and melanin production. Choose a brand that is waterproof or especially designed for athletes, so that it will be harder to sweat off. Remember to apply to the most vulnerable and exposed body areas (especially the nose and the tops of the ears). Many people tend to put on only half the required amount of sunscreen, so when in doubt, 'slop' it on; in the words of the famous Australian sun education campaign – 'Slip, slop, slap: slip on a shirt, slop on the sunscreen, slap on a hat.'

One problem that some athletes have reported is that sunscreen stings if it runs down from the forehead into the eyes. If you find this is happening to you, switch to the chalkier zinc sun blocks (first used by surfers). These often come in bright colours, and are much less likely to melt than creams. These zinc sun blocks that players like Allan Donald and Shane Warne daubed on their faces have become trademark 'war-paint' – known to strike fear in opposition players!

Another common mistake is to apply sunscreen and then forget about it for the rest of a long day's play. It needs to be frequently re-applied, according to the protection factor. Fair-skinned players must use a sunscreen with a protection factor of at least 30 (preferably higher) and re-apply every two hours.

Remember also that the use of long-sleeved shirts has the double advantage of not only cutting out some of the sun's rays, but offering the diving fielder a little extra protection for the elbows. Beware of wearing fabrics that allow UVA and UVB rays to penetrate – if you can see your hand through the fabric of your shirt, it's too thin. The fabric of cricketing togs generally offers good protection from the sun, but when coaching younger players, ensure that they wear clothing that does indeed block out the sun.

Another potential danger to bear in mind is that UVA and UVB rays are considered to be one of the causes of cataracts, a clouding of the lens of the eye that ultimately leads to blindness. Although this can be treated by surgery, prevention, as always, is better than cure. UVB rays can also cause keratitis, which is effectively sunburn of the eye. It has been found that wearing a hat filters out about 20% of rays that are damaging to the eye. The good news is that almost all cricketers wear hats, helmets and caps with peaks or brims. However, sunglasses that specifically filter out these rays should be also worn. The University of Maryland Medical Center notes that cosmetic sunglasses block about 70% of UVB rays and 60% of UVA rays, and considers that this is insufficient for athletes or indeed anyone who spends a lot of time outdoors in a sunny climate. At the very least, they should purchase sunglasses with labels that indicate that they block UV radiation up to 400nm. However, special-purpose sunglasses that block at least 99% UVB and a minimum of 60% UVA rays are optimal. In many countries, these are marked with a national Cancer Foundation stamp of approval. These special-purpose sunglasses should wrap around the head and block light coming from above, below and alongside. In Australia, it is possible to buy special anti-cancer sunglasses that have a second, smaller set of lenses alongside the eye, rather like blinkers for horses – these exclude almost all UV rays. All sunglasses worn by athletes should fit snugly and comfortably on the nose, and in the case of cricketers, should be lightweight and made of shatterproof plastic.

SPECTATORS AT RISK

It is not just cricketers who need to take the sun seriously; cricket spectators should also protect their skin from accumulative sun damage – the result of days spent at the grounds. Cricket poses more of a risk to spectators than many other outdoor spectator sports once again because of the time factor – instead of sitting in the stands for 90 minutes, even a one-day match can mean an entire day spent broiling in the sun – and Test matches, especially in warmer climates, pose an even more serious risk as the sunburnt fan returns to the grounds day after day.

A study of 246 cricket spectators, including 40 women, at the 1990 Boxing Day Test in Melbourne found that 34% wore an appropriate broad-brimmed hat; 29% had no form of cover for their heads; 20% wore long-sleeved shirts, and 72% short-sleeved shirts. Eight per cent either wore bikinis or were topless. Most disturbing of all, 45% of spectators did not use sunscreen, although women were more likely to do so (Broadstock, 1991).

So on or off the field, when enjoying cricket, make sure to take the proper precautions against sunburn and long-term sun damage.

INJURIES: CAUSE, PREVENTION AND TREATMENT

Sports medicine practitioners divide the injuries players can receive (or are at risk for) into two categories: extrinsic and intrinsic. The following section will provide an overview of these two categories, as well as suggestions for prevention and treatment. However, fast bowlers are at greater risk of intrinsic injuries than any other category of cricketer, largely because of the extreme stress the bowling action places on the human frame. While Chapter 5 explains the critical importance of correct bowling technique and action, here we pay attention to the cause (often incorrect action), treatment and rehabilitation of intrinsic injuries to bowlers. This is one area where even junior or 'weekend' coaches (and in fact, parents of young cricketers) need to understand both the technical and the physiological issues involved, as a few early errors in the action of a young bowler can have serious long-term health consequences. This is why we pay so much attention to intrinsic bowling injuries in the following sections – all bowling coaches and young bowlers should read these in conjunction with Chapter 5.

EXTRINSIC INJURIES

As the name implies, extrinsic injuries arise from an external force that is 'applied' to the body (or which the body encounters), and are most likely to occur in contact sports (such as boxing), or those that involve frequent 'collisions' (such as rugby). However, cricket also carries some risk of extrinsic injuries, since it features a hard ball travelling at great speed towards the human body. However, the external force that injures a cricketer doesn't necessarily have to be the ball: it might be another body, the ground, advertising hoardings, on rare occasions a bat, or, if you are former South African off-spinner Pat Symcox on the boundary in Sydney, a frozen chicken.

Most at risk of extrinsic injuries are batsmen, followed by wicket-keepers and close fielders. Other fielders don't have an easy time of it either, as they often have to dive for the ball, hitting the ground (and sometimes the advertising boards). Some of the most high-profile injuries to cricketers in recent years have been those to fielders: South Africa's Paul Adams broke his spinning finger colliding with advertising boards; and Australia's Steve Waugh and Jason Gillespie were hospitalized after colliding under an attempted catch in 2000. Waugh was lucky in that he only broke his nose (and on coming round from having it reset under anaesthetic, he promptly demanded a helicopter to take him back to the game!); but Gillespie's broken leg stole years from his career as a fast bowler. Sadly, fielders in the deep can also be struck by missiles thrown by spectators – an abhorrent practice that should never be tolerated.

While bowlers are as much at risk as any other fielder, the risk of acquiring an extrinsic injury while actually bowling is fairly small. However, they can slip during their gather, or turn an ankle during their delivery stride (usually the result of worn footwear or a greasy pitch). Craig Matthews and Waqar Younis are two examples of world-class bowlers whose careers were set back after they picked up severe ankle sprains during their delivery.

DEALING WITH EXTRINSIC INJURIES

Athletes are by no means the only people who suffer from extrinsic injuries: bumps, scrapes, sprains, blows, cuts and nicks are a part of everyday life, and even the most determined couch potato has at some stage been hit by a moving object or fallen down the stairs. As a result, modern medicine is extremely adept at dealing with this type of injury, and the cricketer suffering this kind of injury can be treated by any trained medical professional, not necessarily one versed in cricket and sports medicine. Naturally, a specialist should be consulted if surgery is required, and once the rehabilitation stage is reached.

Fortunately, most extrinsic injuries will require no more than swift treatment according to the RICE (or PRICER) formula. This sequence of responses requires no special equipment other than icepacks and bandages, and can be practised by anyone, including the player at home.

The core of this method is RICE:
- **Rest**
- **Ice**
- **Compression**
- **Elevation.**
  (PRICER is used to indicate Prevention and Rehabilitation in addition to the other four components.)

Sometimes you, as player or coach, will have to do more than follow the RICE sequence. For instance, if there is heat and/or marked swelling in the affected part of the body 12 to 24 hours after faithfully following the RICE formula, or if the player remains in considerable discomfort, or shows strong disinclination to use the injured part of the body, further diagnostic techniques will be needed. If you suspect a fracture, X-rays will be necessary. If in doubt, always consult a medical advisor. The earlier an injury is diagnosed and treated, the better the prognosis for recovery.

THE RICE RESPONSES

Rest

The moment you sustain an extrinsic injury that causes real discomfort and reduces your range of movement, you should rest the affected part of your body. This does not only mean that you should stop playing cricket: if you have injured a hand or leg, for example, that limb should be rested as much as practically possible, and not be used to perform other activities. If you think a crutch or sling might be necessary, seek medical advice.

Ice

The value of applying ice to any injury is that it reduces not only heat but swelling, as the cold constricts the adjacent blood vessels. Any chemist can supply you with icepacks to keep in the freezer (the flexible gel kind are particularly comfortable), or you can make your own: simply place a generous handful of ice cubes in a plastic bag, seal, wrap in a towel, and apply. An ingenious and inexpensive improvisation that is particularly good for wrapping round limbs is a bag of frozen peas. However, do not ever apply ice to the naked skin – always wrap in a towel or dishcloth first, making sure that there is a layer of fabric between the ice and the skin. Once the ice has been applied to the injured area, hold it or tie it in place. Leave it on for as long as possible, or until the ice melts: you will need to replace the pack every twenty minutes or so.

Compression

This is carried out through bandaging, and works on a similar principle to icing an injury, in that it compresses the blood vessels, thus preventing swelling. It also gives the injured player a sensation of relief, and helps with management of discomfort. Preferably use a sports bandage made out of a natural fibre, and wrap the injured area snugly, but not too tightly.

Elevation

Here the idea is to encourage blood flow away from the injured area, so that it does not pool and exacerbate swelling. Ideally, the injured part of the body should be elevated to a higher level than the heart, if possible. In the case of injuries to the lower limbs, sit or lie down with the leg comfortably raised on cushions.

The most serious extrinsic injuries experienced by batsmen are generally those to the face, head and fingers, which will be discussed in more detail later. Blows to the face and head are usually the result of missed or top-edged pulls or sweeps – or the batsman

Boundary lines should be marked with ropes or other moveable markers to prevent sliding fielders from colliding with fixed fences on or just outside the boundary.

has taken his eye off a short ball and has started turning his back to the ball. Anyone who has ever taken a sickening blow to the side or back of his head, or had his nose rearranged by a ball spitting up off the top edge will understand the value of a helmet. Remember to make sure that the gap between grille and visor is too narrow for the ball to squeeze through – South African tailender Meyrick Pringle had his international career derailed after being felled this way by a delivery from Javagal Srinath.

Extrinsic injuries to the lower leg (with the exception of toes crushed by yorkers) are seldom caused by being struck with a cricket ball: the most common kind of injuries here are pulled muscles caused by suddenly setting off on a swift run, or slipping while running between the wickets. We hope that this brief account has motivated you to wear full protective gear at all times.

WHEN THE CRICKET BALL STRIKES!

No discussion of cricketing injuries would be complete without focusing on the most obvious – and to many players, the most daunting – type of injury inherent in the sport: the impact of a small hard ball on a soft (or not so soft!) body part.

Being hit is part of being a batsman, and yet being 'pinged', 'sconed', 'nutted' or 'zapped' often fires up batsmen into a combative rage, as if the bowler has delivered the most stinging insult imaginable, rather than simply slipped a fast ball through his defences. This reaction is understandable: for many bowlers, the short ball *is* a personal matter, a challenge to both the batsman's technique and his personality. Whichever player wins the encounter – whether it is the bowler, forcing a rushed defensive stroke or a rueful rub of a bruised body part, or the batsman, pulling the ball to the fence or stunning it stone dead at his feet – feels that he has done more than simply gained a cricketing advantage: he has bent another person to his will.

This is the gladiatorial aspect of cricket, and it is this very real danger of physical injury and pain that often provides audiences with their most vivid memories: a helmetless Ian Botham hooking a Dennis Lillee bouncer inches off his face; Mike Gatting getting it wrong and blowing fragments of bone out of his shattered nose in Jamaica in 1986; Devon Malcolm butchering South Africa at the Oval in 1994 and sending a dazed Jonty Rhodes to hospital; Steve Waugh and Michael Atherton surviving (only just!) Allan Donald's two most hostile bowling spells.

But sometimes the fine line between the personal and the sporting is overstepped, and hostile bowling becomes a calculated attempt to hurt and disable opposing batsmen. In the fourth Test against the West Indies at Kingston in 1976, Indian captain Bishen Bedi declared his team's innings at the fall of the sixth wicket, both out of protest against the appallingly green pitch, and against bowling that Sunil Gavaskar called 'barbaric'. Simon Wilde (1994) recalls that fast men Michael Holding, Wayne Daniel and Vanburn Holder consistently bowled short, aiming for the green tufts that had sprung up on the first night of the Test. The results were predictable: Viswanath had a finger fractured and dislocated, Patel edged a pull into his mouth, and the bespectacled Gaekwad was hit over his left ear. The West Indies finally needed just 13 runs to win the Test, and when India took the field, their captain Bedi was notable by his absence, a clear protest against what he considered play that had hugely overstepped the bounds of what was acceptable as sport.

Indeed, the acrimony produced by hostile fast bowling and the consequent threat of injury has at times spilled over into the realm of international diplomacy. This was never more evident than during the notorious 'Bodyline' tour of England to Australia in 1932/33. Faced with the dismal prospect of yet another defeat at the hands of the world's greatest batsman, Donald Bradman, England's fast bowlers (under the direction of captain Douglas Jardine) adopted a policy of aiming their short deliveries straight at the Australian batsmen's bodies, with seven fielders on the leg side, and a total of five men in a ring of close catching positions. While the outraged Australian public and press dubbed this tactic 'Bodyline', Jardine preferred the term 'leg theory' to describe his strategy. The results were very effective: the MCC won the series 4–1 and restricted Bradman to a batting average of 'just' 56,6 compared to his career average of 99,9.

With the deep sense of betrayal following the cynical use of Australian troops by the Allies during the First World War still fresh, international relations between the two countries soured to the extent that the Australian Prime Minister had to intervene to avoid the threat of trade boycotts. The Laws of the game were almost immediately modified to enable the umpire to halt any bowling tactic aimed at injuring the batter, and within the next two decades, leg theory was rendered illegal with the introduction of the rule that only two fielders may be placed behind square on the leg side. (Another outcome was the modification to the LBW law, which subsequently allowed a batsman to be out LBW to a ball that pitches outside the off stump and to which no shot is offered. At the time of the Bodyline series, the batsman enjoyed the unfair advantage that he could be given out LBW only to a ball that pitched in the line of the stumps.)

Of the Australian batsman struck by the English quicks during that notorious series, few suffered more than the captain Bill Woodfull, who was struck above the heart in the Third Test match at Adelaide, and the Australian wicket-keeper Bert Oldfield, who edged a Larwood delivery into his head in the same match – a passage of play that almost led to rioting in the stands. Oldfield's skull was fractured, and

It is essential that at every single cricket match, someone who is familiar with CPR techniques must be present. Why not you? Anyone can learn the basics, and courses are often offered for free by charities like the St John Ambulance Foundation.

although he took the blame for top-edging the ball, he famously announced to the England manager, 'There are two teams out there. One is playing cricket and the other is making no attempt to do so' (Frith, 2001, p. 180).

A heavy blow to the chest from a cricket ball travelling at speed can produce the fatal heart rhythm disturbance known as ventricular fibrillation. It claimed the life of Australian cricketer Martin Bedkober during a grade match in Queensland, and an identical tragedy was only narrowly averted when another Australian, Rick Darling, was struck by a rising delivery from English fast bowler Bob Willis. The life of the unconscious Darling was saved only by the quick action of English bowler John Emburey and match umpire, Max O'Connell. This is why it is essential that someone present at every single cricket match needs to be familiar with CPR techniques; and at higher levels of the game, paramedics with the equipment and expertise to administer electrical shock to the heart – cardiac defibrillation – should always be present.

BATTING GLOVES TO PREVENT FINGER FRACTURES

In theory, it should be entirely possible to avoid the finger fractures incurred by batsmen struck on the hand when facing deliveries from fast bowlers. The finger fractures when it is jammed between the rapidly decelerating ball and the handle of the bat. Unless the padding in the glove is able to absorb sufficient energy or to deflect the ball, the energy in the ball will be transferred to the soft tissues of the hand, causing the fracture.

Alexander et al. (1998) surveyed 59 English county cricket batsmen and found that 24 of them had sustained a total of 44 finger fractures while batting. Twenty-five of these fractures were to the bottom hand, usually to the thumb and first finger, and 19 were to the top hand, usually to the little finger. This suggests that batting gloves should be strengthened in the areas protecting the small finger of the top hand and the thumb and first finger of the bottom hand.

Alexander and his colleagues concluded that the foams used at present in cricket gloves are insufficient to prevent injury from balls delivered in excess of 140km per hour. New materials were required to solve this problem, and they suggested the incorporation of a pre-bent Kevlar insert to protect the vulnerable fingers, and a Kevlar sheet over the back of the hand.

Meanwhile, South African sports scientist Richard Stretch and his colleagues (Stretch et al. 1995; 1998) have been studying the shock absorption characteristics of batting gloves and pads. Their key finding was that gloves and pads produced by different manufacturers differ in their ability to absorb shock and, in the case of pads, in the amount of rebound they impart on the ball. Sadly, as in so much of life, it seems that what you pay for, is what you get. Players should purchase the best quality protective gear that they can afford.

PREVENTION IS ALWAYS BETTER THAN CURE

Many of the alarming injuries mentioned here could have been prevented. The following are some basic guidelines on how to avoid extrinsic injuries:

- Always wear the correct protective gear, even during the most relaxed practice or informal game.
- Ensure that your helmet is in good condition: most manufacturers insist that the helmet should not be worn after it has been cracked, since another impact can easily shatter the shell. Your helmet should always include a visor.
- Appropriate eyewear should be worn (for example, night-vision glasses that enable players to pick up the ball against a dazzle of lights). Players who wear prescription spectacles need to ensure that these are made from shatterproof plastic.
- Bowlers must pay close attention to footwear; studs must be screwed in tightly, and should not be worn down.
- Coaches should make certain that young batters (especially tail-enders) master appropriate defensive techniques.
- Safety precautions should always be taken in the nets – never turn your back on a net in which a batsman is playing shots.
- Bowlers should try to get down to balls hit back past them rather than trying to stop them with their feet: the slightest bounce or miscalculation could earn you a nasty blow on the ankle.
- Fielders on the boundary should dive or slide to stop the ball, and not try to put their foot in front of it: accidentally stepping on the ball can result in a rolled ankle, or worse.
- Never take your eye off the ball when playing shots. However, don't 'ball-watch' either when running between wickets, since this can lead to mid-pitch collisions like the one between Australians Mark Waugh and Matthew Elliott in 1997, which severely damaged Elliott's knee.
- Fielding techniques that enable fielders to 'roll with the punches' should be taught, especially to young players.
- Umpires and coaches must check that the wicket and pitch are safe to play on: the delivery crease should be kept dry (use sawdust if necessary), and bowlers' run-ups must not be soggy or too uneven.
- Umpires and coaches must ensure that play does not take place or continue in poor light.

INTRINSIC INJURIES

If extrinsic injuries are caused by 'outside' forces, it follows that intrinsic injuries are the result of problems and failures 'inside' the body. However, unlike extrinsic injuries, which happen suddenly and dramatically, with immediate pain, intrinsic injures are characterized by a gradual or even slow onset of discomfort or loss or lack of mobility.

By and large these are 'wear-and-tear' injuries, generally caused by the repetition of certain movements to the point that damage is done to the internal muscles, joints or bones involved. Biomechanical factors, genetic weaknesses, insufficient fitness and incorrect sporting techniques can all be contributing factors to this kind of breakdown, although among athletes who give an inordinate amount of time to sports that involve repetitive movements, plain 'over-use' can be the cause of the injury.

In the case of intrinsic injuries (especially those that arise from a specific sport), specialist medical advice is almost always needed: physiotherapists and sports medicine specialists are usually in the front lines for diagnosing and treating such conditions.

Unlike extrinsic injuries, intrinsic injuries must always be diagnosed before an appropriate treatment regime can be embarked upon. While the RICE formula may have some limited use in alleviating symptoms, it is not appropriate as a means of treatment for intrinsic injuries. The reason precise diagnosis is so important is because if the root cause is not addressed, the injury will simply keep on recurring until the player breaks down once more – and sometimes for good. (One study of international cricketers showed that 20% of the injuries sustained during a tour were prior intrinsic injuries that were aggravated and therefore flared up again.) Diagnosis should always be undertaken by an expert, preferably a sports medicine practitioner if at all possible.

INTRINSIC INJURIES TO BATTERS

Batsmen are fortunate in that they suffer a relatively low degree of intrinsic injuries. These are most likely to be back, neck and shoulder injuries, as a result of their posture at the wicket. However, coaches should be warned that intrinsic injuries to the feet and lower leg (previously the preserve of fast bowlers), are increasingly being found in both batsmen and fielders who play at the elite level, a direct result of the sheer volume of cricket being played today.

> ## THE ROLE OF THE PHYSIOTHERAPIST IN A CRICKET TEAM
> No physiotherapist can prevent injury, and can only help in the rehabilitation of injuries. The true worth of a team physiotherapist is in keeping players on the field by seeing to the constant niggles that come with playing a sport in which players spend the best part of six hours a day on their feet, by turns running, sprinting, walking, jogging, bending, stretching, turning, and being sedentary. A physiotherapist who treats elite cricketers must understand modern training methods, and keep an open mind on other methods of treatment such as osteopathy and chiropractic treatment.

INTRINSIC INJURIES TO BOWLERS

Unlike their batting and fielding colleagues, bowlers, especially the quicks, are far more susceptible to intrinsic injuries than extrinsic injuries. Worse still, these intrinsic injuries will often plague the bowler much later in life, long after he has hung up his bowling boots. It is therefore critical that coaches strive to prevent these kinds of injuries in their charges, and this is why we set so much store by correct technique and action (see Chapter 5).

Here we will examine the most common kinds and causes of intrinsic injury in bowlers, as well as investigating how to manage these injuries and rehabilitate affected players. First, however, it will be handy to revise the biological and physiological principles of fast bowling.

The biology of fast bowling

An excellent review of this topic has been written by Professor Roger Bartlett (presently at the University of Otago, New Zealand) and his colleagues (Bartlett et al., 1996) and many of the ideas presented here originated in his article.

The typical length of a fast bowler's run-up varies from 15–30m, with the peak speed being achieved 8–16m from the popping crease, with progressive slowing prior to the pre-delivery stride. Run-up speeds immediately prior to delivery vary from 3,9 to 5,5m/sec, with average values of about 5m/sec (Bartlett et al., 1996) – similar to values measured in javelin throwers. Generally, run-up speeds are faster in front-on than in side-on bowlers (Elliott et al., 1986). A study of four of the fastest bowlers of the 1970s reported their run-up velocities and bowling speeds during the Second Test between Australia and the West Indies in December 1975 as shown in Table 10.2 on the next page.

TABLE 10.2: Run-up and delivery speeds of four fast bowlers of the 1970s

BOWLER	RUN-UP SPEED (M/SEC)	RUN-UP SPEED (KM/HOUR)	DELIVERY SPEED (KM/HOUR)
Jeff Thomson	5,0	18,0	160,5
Michael Holding	7,8	28,1	148,5
Andy Roberts	8,0	28,8	150,7
Dennis Lillee	9,3	33,6	139,0

SOURCE: LILLEE, 1982, PP. 29–30

Note that the run-up speed for Lillee appears to be implausible, given that this approaches speeds reached by elite sprinters during the 100m dash. It is also interesting that the slowest run-up speed produced the fastest delivery (Jeff Thomson).

The pre-delivery stride separates the run-up from the delivery stride. For the right-hand bowler, the pre-delivery stride begins with a jump off the left foot, the right foot passes in front of the left foot in the side-on bowling action and next to the left foot in a front-on bowling action. In the side-on bowling action, the hip and shoulders will also rotate so that both point straight down the pitch. (The classification of the different bowling actions is given in Chapter 5.)

The pre-delivery stride is about 0,42m (22%) longer than the preceding stride as a result of the need to decelerate and 'gather' for the delivery. It is believed that front-on bowlers do not need to jump as high in the pre-delivery stride as side-on bowlers. The higher the jump, the greater the landing (ground reaction) forces will be.

Three key events occur in the delivery stride: back foot strike, front foot strike and ball release. Figure 10.4 shows the reference system used to define the alignment angles of the feet, hips and shoulders at the three key points during the delivery stride.

Note that the reference angles are calculated in an anti-clockwise direction, and that the angle is taken from the side from which the ball is delivered – the right side in this figure.

For perfect positioning in the side-on position, the rear foot should be perfectly parallel to the popping crease, that is, with a defined alignment of 270°. However, most bowlers have a back foot angle greater than 270°, indicating that the hip angle is also likely to be greater than 180°.

At back foot strike, the bowler's body leans away from the batsman. In the side-on action, the lean is due to lateral (sideways) flexion of the spine, whereas in front-on bowlers, the lean comes from the hyperextension (backward) bend of the spine.

Vertical forces through the body vary from 2–3G at back foot strike and these double to between 4–6G at front foot strike (Hurrion et al., 2000). The magnitude of these forces appears to be independent of the type of bowling action.

The length of the delivery stride is, in part, determined by the speed of the run-up and is greatest (up to 1,7m) in bowlers with the fastest run-up speeds.

Three different patterns of the front knee angle have been reported during the delivery stride. Some bowlers, like Allan Donald, maintain the knee in a fully or almost fully extended position at front foot strike and maintain that position until ball release. This is known as the straight leg technique. Its value is that it maximizes the ball release speed (Bartlett et al., 1996) and the height of ball release. Its disadvantage may be that the forces through the knee joint and perhaps also through the complete lower limb, including the hip, may be increased, as the muscles of the thigh will have a reduced capacity to absorb the forces of landing if the knee is completely straight.

In the second type, the knee is flexed to about 150°; this reduces landing stresses as the thigh muscles will absorb some of the energy. However, such shock absorption requires powerful eccentric contractions of the quadriceps muscles, potentially increasing fatigue as a consequence of muscle damage. There is also a loss of energy that might have been used to increase the velocity of the delivery.

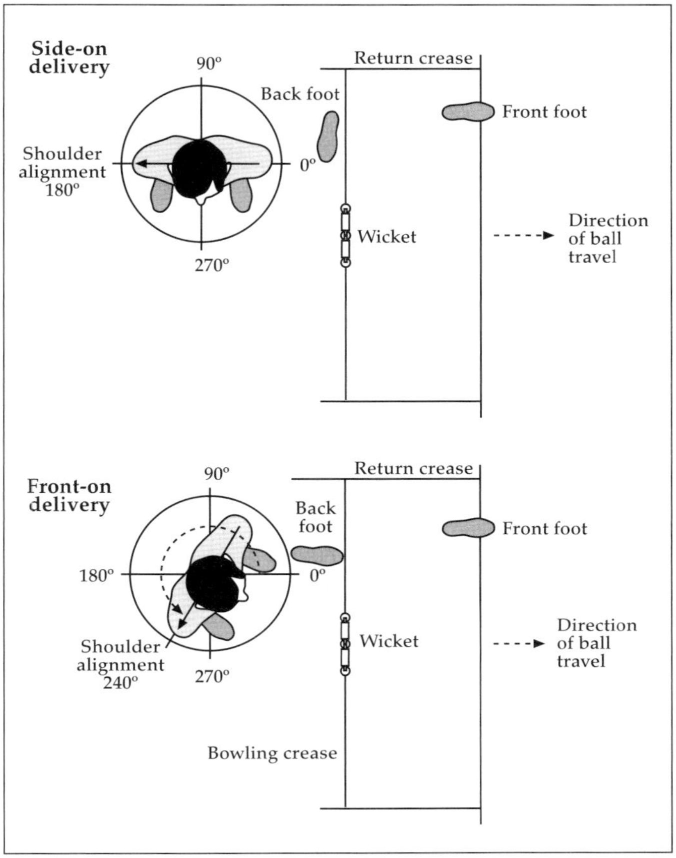

FIGURE 10.4: *The criteria for classifying bowling action on the basis of shoulder alignment at either back or front foot strike. The upper panel shows a side-on bowler whose shoulders are aligned at 180°, whereas the lower panel shows a front-on action with the shoulder alignment at 240°.*

The third type involves slight flexion of the knee with subsequent extension. While this technique is considered to be optimal, as it allows for shock absorption without losing delivery height, it is an uncommon method (Bartlett et al., 1996).

If we look at the action of the non-bowling arm and the trunk, depending on the bowling action, the head will look either outside (side-on action) or inside (front-on action) the vertically orientated arm during the delivery stride. The arm then accelerates downwards and backwards due to the powerful contraction of the shoulder muscles, as the trunk begins to rotate and flex towards the batsman.

A key feature of the action leading up to ball release is the action of the elbow and the definition of what constitutes a 'throw' in bowling. (See Chapter 5 for a far more detailed discussion of throwing.)

A significant feature of the follow-through is that ground reaction forces are even higher than during the delivery stride.

Three studies have evaluated the contribution of movements of the different body parts to the generation of velocity at ball release (Davis and Blanksby, 1976; Elliott et al., 1986; Glazier et al., 2000). Their findings are laid out in Table 10.3.

TABLE 10.3: Contribution of different components of the bowling action to ball release speed

ACTION	% CONTRIBUTION TO BALL RELEASE VELOCITY		
	DAVIS AND BLANKSBY 1976	ELLIOTT ET AL. 1986	GLAZIER ET AL. 2000
Run-up	19	15	16
Leg action and hip rotation	23	0	2
Trunk flexion and shoulder girdle rotation	11	13	6
Arm action	42	50	62
Hand action	5	22	14

This clearly shows that it is the arm action that contributes the most to the generation of ball speed. This is important when one considers the issue of throwing and the addition of internal rotation of the forearm to the circular movement of the shoulder for the generation of ball release speed.

Glazier et al. (2000) found that the length of the arm may be an important determinant of ball release speed. This makes sense according to the concept that as one moves from the centre of the body towards the hand, the velocity generated by the movement of the different body segments that contribute to the final ball speed are added together. This means that relatively small anatomical differences in the proportions of the arm will influence the final speed disproportionately.

Glazier et al. (2000) therefore concluded that a 10cm increase in the length of the radius bone in the forearm would increase the final delivery speed by 12km/h. This would be sufficient to change a bowler's classification from fast (130–145km/h) to express (>145km/h). The authors suggest that such long limbs may be a feature of West Indian bowlers, and might explain the preponderance of West Indians among the fastest bowlers of all time.

Portus et al. (2000) have also reported that chest composition seems strongly related to ball release speed. They found that bowlers with larger and leaner upper torsos bowled faster. However, their study did not measure limb lengths, so the effect they observed might have resulted from the longer limbs associated with taller, leaner individuals.

Now that we know exactly what parts of the body are involved, and how they operate during bowling, we need to consider the more vulnerable sites, and how to prevent and rehabilitate injuries in these areas.

Back injuries in fast bowlers: the case of Dennis Lillee

It is only in the last 30 years that any real understanding of the factors causing low back injuries in fast bowlers has been achieved. Perhaps it was the back injury to legendary Australian fast bowler Dennis Lillee that triggered interest in what was at the time an unknown injury in fast bowlers. Lillee was lucky in some respects; many fast bowlers who break down with apparently crippling back injuries disappear from view, never to be seen again. However, his became almost a test case for how to rehabilitate an injured fast bowler, and his story is worth studying in detail.

Lillee is from Perth, Western Australia – another lucky break, and one that explains why many of the findings emanating from his case come from Professor Bruce Elliott's research team at the University of Western Australia and the team of scientists who eventually cured Lillee. They enabled Lillee to extend his Test career by another eleven years after what appeared to be a crippling injury in 1973; eventually, thanks to their intervention and his determination, he retired the world's leading wicket-taker in Tests at the time.

Lillee first drew attention as a fourteen-year-old opening fast bowler in club cricket in Perth, Western Australia. Interestingly, he did not play cricket at school. This is worth noting: all too often, talented schoolboy fast bowlers are expected to play school, club, provincial and even international cricket in the same season. This produces excessive demands on their growing but still delicate spines, potentially leading to crippling injuries that may stifle future progress in their chosen sport. Not playing cricket at school may have been another of Lillee's strokes of luck. He wrote of his action at the time: 'Because I was twisting so much in my action, I was always aware of having a sore back' (Lillee, 2003, p. 18). While still a schoolboy, he first met Dr Frank Pyke, a man who would play a crucial role in his future career. (Dr Pyke recently retired from his post as Director of the Victorian Institute of Sport in Melbourne, Australia, a crucial component of the hugely successful programme of Australian Sports Institutes.)

At age sixteen, Lillee was promoted to play first-grade cricket; in 1969 he played his first Sheffield Shield game for Western Australia, and in 1970 was selected for the Australia A team. His debut for Australia was in the sixth Test at the Adelaide Oval in 1971. Next stop was England, where he played in the Lancashire League before returning to Australia to play three Tests against the touring Rest of the World team in 1972. However, during the final Test in Sydney, he broke down. He chose to rest rather than continue playing, but travelled to England for the next Test tour. Here his back pain recurred whenever he bowled fast; nevertheless, he had a successful Test series, taking 31 wickets, a record at the time. He returned to Perth feeling 'very tired', just in time for the start of the new season in Western Australia. He faced the daunting task of playing nine matches in nine weeks, including five Sheffield Shield games, a state game against England, followed by three Tests in successive weeks against the visiting Pakistan team. This was to be followed by a tour of the West Indies starting in February 1973. In the six matches leading up to the first Test against Pakistan, Lillee bowled 207,2 eight-ball overs (1 658 deliveries), taking 44 wickets. (That Lillee's early career coincided with the exhausting experiment of eight-ball overs is no doubt also a significant factor.)

In the first innings of the third Test against Pakistan in Sydney, Lillee's back gave way, as he experienced shooting pains in his back, buttocks and legs. He came off the field, but went back to bowl in the second innings. Ten days later he left on a tour of the West Indies, bowling 32 overs in the first Test. By this stage, his back was so painful that he was unable to play again on that tour. Finally, in Barbados, radiologist Dr Rudi Webster, a former bowler from Perth who had himself suffered back injuries, performed a series of special highly focused X-rays, known as tomograms, that showed the presence of three fractures – which had not been picked up by a conventional X-ray examination. Once the diagnosis had been made, Lillee was placed on the first ever specialized rehabilitation programme for his condition, overseen by his old mentor, Dr Frank Pyke.

The important lessons from what appears to be the very first description of the development of a stress fracture in a world-class fast bowler (Lillee, 1982, p. 137), was that the injury began when Lillee undertook an impossible bowling workload without adequate periods of rest. Then the correct diagnosis was missed, simply because the medical techniques for diagnosing the condition were not fully developed at that time. Fortunately for Lillee, the story did not end at this point – but it is sobering to contemplate the fate of others in his position, many of whom simply faded from the game for lack of proper diagnosis and rehabilitation.

When Lillee returned from the West Indies in 1973, he was placed in a plaster cast that prevented any movement of his back for six weeks. Then, after a further three weeks rest, he began an exercise training programme designed by Frank Pyke, then at the Department of Physical Education at the University of Western Australia. The 18-month programme aimed to return Lillee to first-class cricket by November 1974.

The programme began with trunk stabilizing exercises for two to three hours every second day in the evenings after work. Lillee started running again, which had always been part of his routine – as a Sheffield Shield player, he had run six days a week in the pre-season, covering 4–6km a day, with a 10–12km run once every two weeks. He included some sprints in these runs. During his recovery, he began by running for twenty minutes, three times a week at 80% of the maximal speed he could normally sustain for that running time (twenty minutes). Later he supplemented this with sprints of five seconds, alternating with fifteen seconds rest.

His training also included strengthening exercises involving bench presses, biceps curls, dumb-bell flys and inclined sit-ups. He performed three sets of eight repetitions with a load that produced fatigue after fifteen repetitions. This was supplemented with routines that used pulleys to simulate the bowling action, using a resistance of 10kg. He also bowled with a lightweight (2kg) 'medicine' ball.

He also performed flexibility exercises of his trunk and thigh extensors, his arm extensors, arm horizontal adductors, and his trunk lateral flexors and thigh adductors. After the first nine weeks of the programme, the results were impressive. Lillee had increased his maximum oxygen uptake by 9%, his arm strength by 15%, his arm power by 23%, and his flexibility by 350% (Pyke et al., 1975).

As Lillee says: 'I firmly believe that sport is well and truly into an era of scientific calculation. Highly qualified men are studying the human body, charting its reaction to training routines, stress and match conditions and coming up with a whole book of answers which were never even dreamt of a quarter of a century ago. I first got an inkling of the impact of this scientific approach in the winter of 1974 when I was rebuilding for a comeback to first-class cricket after breaking down in the West Indies. Thanks to a team of men at the University of Western Australia's Department of Physical Education and Recreation, I was put through a most successful programme of scientifically prepared and monitored exercises and tests. They brought me from a crippling back injury to a strength and fitness greater than I have ever known. As far as I know this was a pilot scheme in the history of cricket, and its success has convinced many people that performance in our sport can be greatly improved by a scientific approach to the individual's preparation.'

The immediate results were that Lillee played in six Sheffield Shield games during 1974/75, and in five Test matches against England in the same season. In these matches, he averaged 18,5 overs an innings, taking 55 wickets. His bowling speed had returned to his pre-injury speeds, and together with Jeff Thomson, he dominated the English side in an impressive display of pace and aggression. The effects on his career were that in his four seasons of first-class cricket before his injury, Lillee took 243 of his 882 first-class wickets. So after an injury that was considered likely to end his career (and probably would have done anywhere else in the world at that time), Lillee took a further 639 first-class wickets in fourteen seasons before retiring in 1988. In Test matches, he took 51 wickets before his injury in 1973, and the remaining 304 in the final ten seasons of his Test career – which ended in 1983.

Recurrence of the injury in 1977 forced him to miss a tour of England and five Tests. However, in his entire career, injury prevented him from playing in only eighteen Tests. His experiences of injury taught him to listen to his body: 'Early in my career I would not accept those warnings, even if they came from a doctor who knew a lot more about my problems than I did. Now I am more inclined to hear the signals loud and clear and take a breather if it is needed' (1982, pp. 135–36).

Prevention of low back injuries in fast bowlers

Several things are clear from Lillee's tale of warning and triumph. There is no doubt that if young fast bowlers bowl many overs during their formative years (10–21 years) while their spines are still immature, and especially if they use a mixed action, they will develop degeneration of their lumbar vertebral discs with the possible development of pars interarticularis bone bruises or fractures, as illustrated in Figure 10.7 on p. 622. While these fractures are likely to heal fully if the injury is properly managed, the long-term consequences of the lumbar disc degeneration are not known, as there are no retrospective studies of famous fast bowlers who had long careers at international level. Yet it seems likely that any accelerated degeneration at a young age must have unpleasant long-term consequences.

The easiest way to prevent such degenerative changes in young fast bowlers would be to ban fast bowling – defined as any bowling for which the wicket-keeper must stand back from the wicket – until the bowler's spine has matured sufficiently to reduce the probability of such damage. This would occur after the early twenties. Of course, such a drastic measure is unlikely. It would mean materially different games being played at youth and senior level. One result would be that fast bowlers in senior cricket would rapidly become rare beasts, if not actually endangered.

In fact, the reality is that the current system penalizes young fast bowlers – who are less rather than more likely to be able to continue their careers at the senior level.

It is worth noting that many of the more famous fast bowlers in the history of the game achieved international success after beginning to bowl fast only in their late teens or early twenties. Some good examples are the West Indian Wes Hall, who started bowling fast only at age eighteen, but played Test cricket one year later; Malcolm Marshall, who began at nineteen; South African Mike Procter, who was a spin bowler at school and began bowling fast only in his early twenties. Perhaps most famous of all, Curtly Ambrose only began his fast bowling career at the ripe old age of 26. Wes Hall has expressed the opinion that many of the most successful West Indian fast bowlers began their fast bowling careers relatively late in life.

So if we are not to ban young players from bowling fast, then what is to be done? The most effective and practical intervention would be to reduce the probability that fast bowlers use the mixed action. This could be achieved by ensuring that young bowlers are coached in such a way that they do not ever adopt or learn to use the mixed action – we discuss this in more detail later, as well as in Chapter 5.

A still more sensible step would be to understand how young bowlers learn to bowl, and why some adopt the side-on or front-on action. We do not yet know why so many young bowlers adopt the mixed action, even though there is no evidence that this action produces faster bowling speeds. If it were fully understood how young bowlers learn their bowling techniques, it would be easier to ensure that they did not adopt the mixed action.

Another priority would be to ensure that coaches fully understand (a) how to teach young bowlers to adopt either the side-on or front-on actions; and (b) how to teach those who have adopted a mixed action to change to either side-on or front-on actions. This, of course, requires that coaches be capable of teaching the front-on and side-on actions; that they can correctly identify those bowling with a mixed action; and that they have the necessary coaching skills to correct the mixed action.

Since these two theoretical ideal goals – the elimination of the mixed bowling action at every level of the game and the restriction of fast bowling to players over the age of twenty – are most unlikely to be adopted in the near future (if ever), numerous cricket administrators, led by the Australian Cricket Board (ACB) have developed rather more conservative guidelines for the prevention of low back injuries in fast bowlers. What we have provided here is a composite set of principles put together from the ACB guidelines, the United Cricket Board (UCB) of South Africa guidelines – to which one of the authors, Tim Noakes, contributed – and the further guidelines for South African cricketers compiled by Richard Stretch and Janine Gray (1998).

The guidelines are based on Table 10.4, which links the mechanisms believed to cause injury. In fact, not all the identified factors, in particular, the listed physical characteristics, are known definitely to cause low back injury in fast bowlers.

Many of the more famous fast bowlers in the history of the game achieved international success after beginning to bowl fast only in their late teens or early twenties.

TABLE 10.4: Model of factors that may predispose to back injuries in fast bowlers

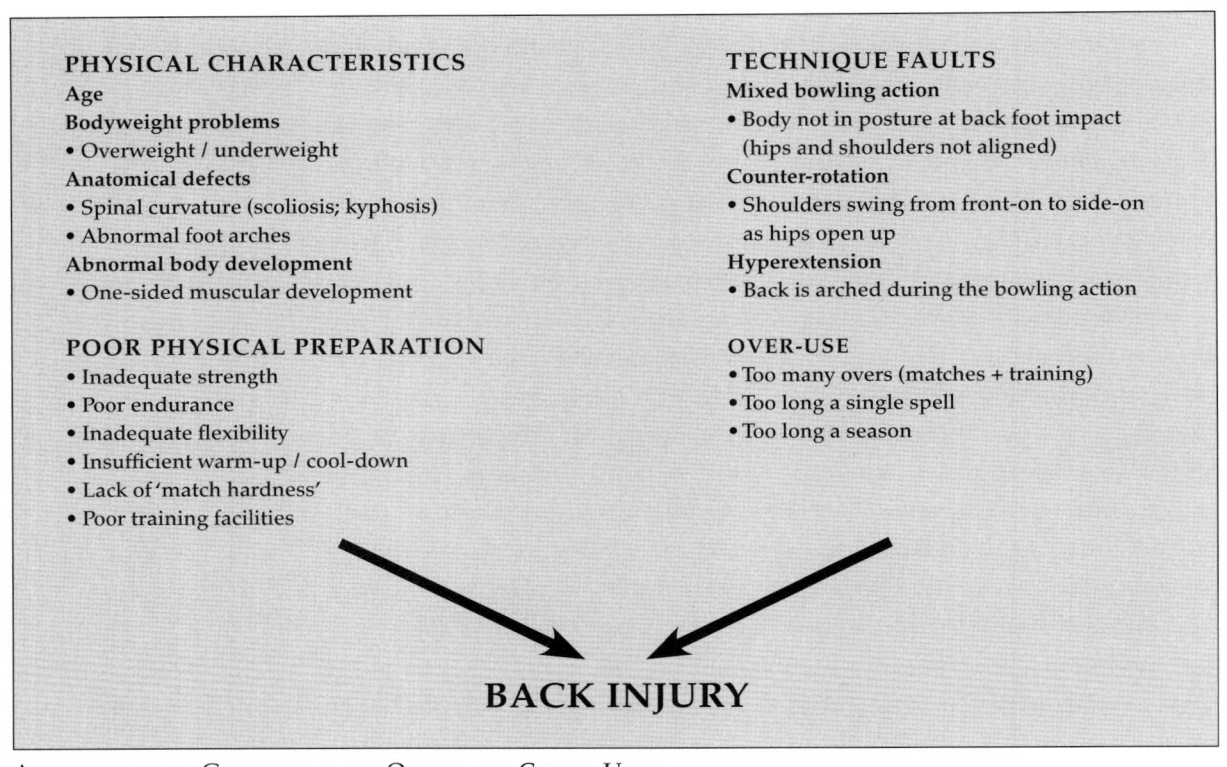

PHYSICAL CHARACTERISTICS
Age
Bodyweight problems
• Overweight / underweight
Anatomical defects
• Spinal curvature (scoliosis; kyphosis)
• Abnormal foot arches
Abnormal body development
• One-sided muscular development

POOR PHYSICAL PREPARATION
• Inadequate strength
• Poor endurance
• Inadequate flexibility
• Insufficient warm-up / cool-down
• Lack of 'match hardness'
• Poor training facilities

TECHNIQUE FAULTS
Mixed bowling action
• Body not in posture at back foot impact (hips and shoulders not aligned)
Counter-rotation
• Shoulders swing from front-on to side-on as hips open up
Hyperextension
• Back is arched during the bowling action

OVER-USE
• Too many overs (matches + training)
• Too long a single spell
• Too long a season

→ **BACK INJURY** ←

ADAPTED FROM THE GUIDELINES OF THE QUEENSLAND CRICKET UNION

The programme developed by the ACB is called the SPOT programme, an acronym for Screening, Physical Preparation, Over-Bowling and Technique.

Screening: This involves the detection of possible risk factors for lower back injury. Possible factors include age (given that the risk is highest for the immature spine), either overweight or, conversely, underweight, the presence of spinal abnormalities, a previous cricket-related back injury, abnormal foot arches (either too high or too low), or abnormal body development – in particular, over-development of the lumbar muscles.

It has been shown that asymmetrical development of the paraspinal back muscles, particularly the quadratus lumborum, is found in young fast bowlers with lumbar stress fractures or other radiological changes (Elliott, 2000). The importance of these muscles is that they stabilize the back during the delivery stride. Abnormal development of these muscles may either cause an unbalanced load on the spine, or it may indicate that such an imbalanced load exists.

Physical preparation: Inadequate physical preparation includes inadequate strength, low endurance, inadequate flexibility, insufficient warming-up and a lack of 'match hardness' at the start of the cricket season. The guidelines state that correct warming-up and stretching are essential before play starts and after each break in play or practice. The development of physical fitness requires the development of endurance fitness achieved through activities such as running, cycling, swimming or rowing; speed through interval-type training; strength with a specific weight-training programme; and flexibility with the range of stretching exercises (see pp. 553-54 above). It is especially important to strengthen the abdominal and lumbar muscles that dissipate forces away from the spine, thereby reducing the risk of injury. Fast bowlers especially need to ensure that they have optimum flexibility of the hamstrings and the lower back.

Over-bowling: The injury to Dennis Lillee occurred after he bowled more overs during a nine-week period than in his entire career up to that point. Over-bowling is indeed relative to the individual: some players are able to absorb much greater bowling loads than others. Nevertheless, less rather than more fast bowling is appropriate during adolescence. Specific guidelines for young bowlers have thus been introduced. However, it may be that similar guidelines should also be developed for adult fast bowlers, especially those at international level, and upon whom the advent of limited-overs cricket has placed an ever-increasing bowling burden.

In fact, a related problem presented by the modern international game is the lack of a real break between playing seasons. We believe that the career durations of fast bowlers will be substantially prolonged if they are able to rest completely for at least two months each year, and if the cricket season does not exceed seven to eight months, thereby allowing two months rest and two months of pre-season training.

Fast bowlers may be exposed to excessive bowling loads for a number of reasons, which may include any or all of the following:

- Over-zealous coaching, especially of talented young players by coaches who do not understand the dangers of exposing the immature spine to fast bowling.
- Bowlers, especially adolescents, practising and competing at a number of different levels, for example, school, club, province (state or county) and international levels.
- Better players dominating the bowling because they are more likely to help their team 'win'. This short-term goal is not in the long-term interests of the individual adolescent fast bowler.

Other factors to consider when determining bowling loads include the following:

Physical maturity: Individuals grow and develop at different rates. Coaches need to consider the individual maturation levels of each player and adjust the training and competitive workloads to suit their maturity level. During the growth period ('shooting up'), the young fast bowler is more vulnerable to injury as the forces associated with fast bowling are unable to be absorbed, causing damage to the immature tissues, including bones, ligaments, lumbar discs and joints.

Level of physical fitness: Fitter players will be able to bowl more overs without loss of bowling technique. Fatigue increases the extent to which bowlers with both the front-on and mixed actions counter-rotate during the delivery action. Fatigue will also reduce the extent to which the thigh (quadriceps) and trunk muscles are able to absorb the shock of the delivery stride and follow-through, potentially increasing the forces to which the vulnerable structures in the back are exposed. On the other hand, extremely fit young players will tire less easily, and will thus be able to bowl many overs, increasing their risk of injury. In some instances, it is those young fast bowlers who are apparently tireless that may be at greatest risk precisely because they are able to 'push' their bodies the hardest.

Bowling speed and effort: The amount of effort the fast bowler produces will determine the number of consecutive overs that the player is able to bowl and the number of spells that should be bowled. The greater the effort that the fast bowler puts into a delivery or bowling spell, the greater the stresses placed on the body – and the more quickly fatigue sets in. In cases like these, the coach should encourage a reduction in the number of overs per spell, while increasing the recovery time between spells.

Playing conditions: As described in the earlier section on the biology of bowling, during the run-up and delivery, the fast bowler must absorb large ground reaction forces during each delivery, irrespective of whether a side-on, mixed or front-on action is used. During the run-up, forces of about three times the bowler's body weight are generated. This increases up to about six times the body weight at back foot landing. Concrete offers 0% force absorption, whereas a hard turf pitch offers about 35% force absorption, and grass can offer up to 75% force absorption. As a result, the risk of injury is greatly increased when bowling on hard surfaces such as solid concrete. Good bowling boots and an efficient delivery stride will reduce the effect that these reaction forces have on the body. Further, when practising on harder surfaces, ground reaction forces can be reduced by using appropriate mats, and ensuring that the length and intensity of practice sessions are modified according to the nature of the surface on which the game is being played or practised.

Technique: The mixed action increases risk of back injury because it is associated with a counter-rotation of the shoulders and hyperextension of the back, as described in greater detail in Chapter 5. Techniques for teaching the bowling action correctly, for diagnosing the type of action that a specific bowler uses, and for correcting a mixed to a pure front-on or side-on action, are also described in Chapter 5 and in the sections that follow.

To return to our guidelines, in order to control and monitor the amount of overs bowled, international experts recommend rigorous enforcement of the fast bowling guidelines laid out in Table 10.5. The bowler's logbook (Table 10.6) should be kept to record all deliveries bowled by both fast and slow bowlers in matches and practices.

TABLE 10.5: Recommended fast bowling guidelines (based on guidelines of the Australian Cricket Board) as adopted by the United Cricket Board of South Africa

LEVEL	MATCHES	PRACTICES
Under 12	A limit of two spells of four overs with approximately a one-hour break	2 x 30-minute practice sessions per week 5-minute short run-up – reduced pace 20-minute match pace – coach controlled 5-minute specific technique development
Under 16	A limit of two spells of six overs with approximately a one-hour break	2 x 40-minute practice sessions per week 5-minute short run-up – reduced pace 25-minute match pace – coach controlled 10-minute specific technique development
Under 19	A limit of three spells of six overs with approximately a one-hour break	3 x 40-minute practice sessions per week 5-minute short run-up – reduced pace 25-minute match pace – coach controlled 10-minute specific technique development
Seniors	A limit of three spells of eight overs with approximately a one-hour break	3 x 60-minute practice sessions per week 10-minute short run-up – reduced pace 40-minute match pace – coach controlled 10-minute specific technique development

SOURCE: STRETCH AND GRAY, 1998, P. 24

TABLE 10.6: The bowler's logbook – to be kept by all bowlers throughout their careers

NAME:.................... SCHOOL:.................... CLUB:.................... COACH:....................

	SUNDAY	MONDAY	TUESDAY	WEDNESDAY	THURSDAY	FRIDAY	SATURDAY	TOTAL	TOTAL	SIGN
WEEK 1 Date.........	Practice...... Match.........	Practice...... Match.........	Practice...... Match.........	Practice...... Match.........	Practice...... Match.........	Practice...... Match.........	Practice...... Match.........	Practice...... Match.........		
WEEK 2 Date.........	Practice...... Match.........	Practice...... Match.........	Practice...... Match.........	Practice...... Match.........	Practice...... Match.........	Practice...... Match.........	Practice...... Match.........	Practice...... Match.........		
WEEK 3 Date.........	Practice...... Match.........	Practice...... Match.........	Practice...... Match.........	Practice...... Match.........	Practice...... Match.........	Practice...... Match.........	Practice...... Match.........	Practice...... Match.........		
WEEK 4 Date.........	Practice...... Match.........	Practice...... Match.........	Practice...... Match.........	Practice...... Match.........	Practice...... Match.........	Practice...... Match.........	Practice...... Match.........	Practice...... Match.........		
WEEK 5 Date.........	Practice...... Match.........	Practice...... Match.........	Practice...... Match.........	Practice...... Match.........	Practice...... Match.........	Practice...... Match.........	Practice...... Match.........	Practice...... Match.........		
WEEK 6 Date.........	Practice...... Match.........	Practice...... Match.........	Practice...... Match.........	Practice...... Match.........	Practice...... Match.........	Practice...... Match.........	Practice...... Match.........	Practice...... Match.........		
WEEK 7 Date.........	Practice...... Match.........	Practice...... Match.........	Practice...... Match.........	Practice...... Match.........	Practice...... Match.........	Practice...... Match.........	Practice...... Match.........	Practice...... Match.........		
WEEK 8 Date.........	Practice...... Match.........	Practice...... Match.........	Practice...... Match.........	Practice...... Match.........	Practice...... Match.........	Practice...... Match.........	Practice...... Match.........	Practice...... Match.........		
WEEK 9 Date.........	Practice...... Match.........	Practice...... Match.........	Practice...... Match.........	Practice...... Match.........	Practice...... Match.........	Practice...... Match.........	Practice...... Match.........	Practice...... Match.........		
WEEK 10 Date.........	Practice...... Match.........	Practice...... Match.........	Practice...... Match.........	Practice...... Match.........	Practice...... Match.........	Practice...... Match.........	Practice...... Match.........	Practice...... Match.........		
WEEK 11 Date.........	Practice...... Match.........	Practice...... Match.........	Practice...... Match.........	Practice...... Match.........	Practice...... Match.........	Practice...... Match.........	Practice...... Match.........	Practice...... Match.........		
WEEK 12 Date.........	Practice...... Match.........	Practice...... Match.........	Practice...... Match.........	Practice...... Match.........	Practice...... Match.........	Practice...... Match.........	Practice...... Match.........	Practice...... Match.........		
WEEK 13 Date.........	Practice...... Match.........	Practice...... Match.........	Practice...... Match.........	Practice...... Match.........	Practice...... Match.........	Practice...... Match.........	Practice...... Match.........	Practice...... Match.........		
WEEK 14 Date.........	Practice...... Match.........	Practice...... Match.........	Practice...... Match.........	Practice...... Match.........	Practice...... Match.........	Practice...... Match.........	Practice...... Match.........	Practice...... Match.........		
WEEK 15 Date.........	Practice...... Match.........	Practice...... Match.........	Practice...... Match.........	Practice...... Match.........	Practice...... Match.........	Practice...... Match.........	Practice...... Match.........	Practice...... Match.........		
WEEK 16 Date.........	Practice...... Match.........	Practice...... Match.........	Practice...... Match.........	Practice...... Match.........	Practice...... Match.........	Practice...... Match.........	Practice...... Match.........	Practice...... Match.........		
WEEK 17 Date.........	Practice...... Match.........	Practice...... Match.........	Practice...... Match.........	Practice...... Match.........	Practice...... Match.........	Practice...... Match.........	Practice...... Match.........	Practice...... Match.........		
WEEK 18 Date.........	Practice...... Match.........	Practice...... Match.........	Practice...... Match.........	Practice...... Match.........	Practice...... Match.........	Practice...... Match.........	Practice...... Match.........	Practice...... Match.........		
WEEK 19 Date.........	Practice...... Match.........	Practice...... Match.........	Practice...... Match.........	Practice...... Match.........	Practice...... Match.........	Practice...... Match.........	Practice...... Match.........	Practice...... Match.........		
WEEK 20 Date.........	Practice...... Match.........	Practice...... Match.........	Practice...... Match.........	Practice...... Match.........	Practice...... Match.........	Practice...... Match.........	Practice...... Match.........	Practice...... Match.........		

SOURCE: STRETCH AND GRAY, 1998, P. 25

The logbook should be used to control and monitor the weekly, monthly, seasonal and yearly workload of bowlers.

How to use the bowler's logbook: After bowling at practices and matches, record the number of overs bowled. Total up the number of overs bowled each week. Ask your coach or parents to sign the space provided at the end of each week so that they are aware of how much you are bowling each week. Now plot and shade your totals on the graph (Figure 10.5), taking care to note whether or not you are over-bowling according to the guidelines provided on the right side of the graph. If your workload enters the 'danger area', then you must address this with your coach and reduce the amount of bowling you are doing in practices and matches. (Be aware that these are recommended bowling workloads, and they will vary for different bowlers and at different times of the season.)

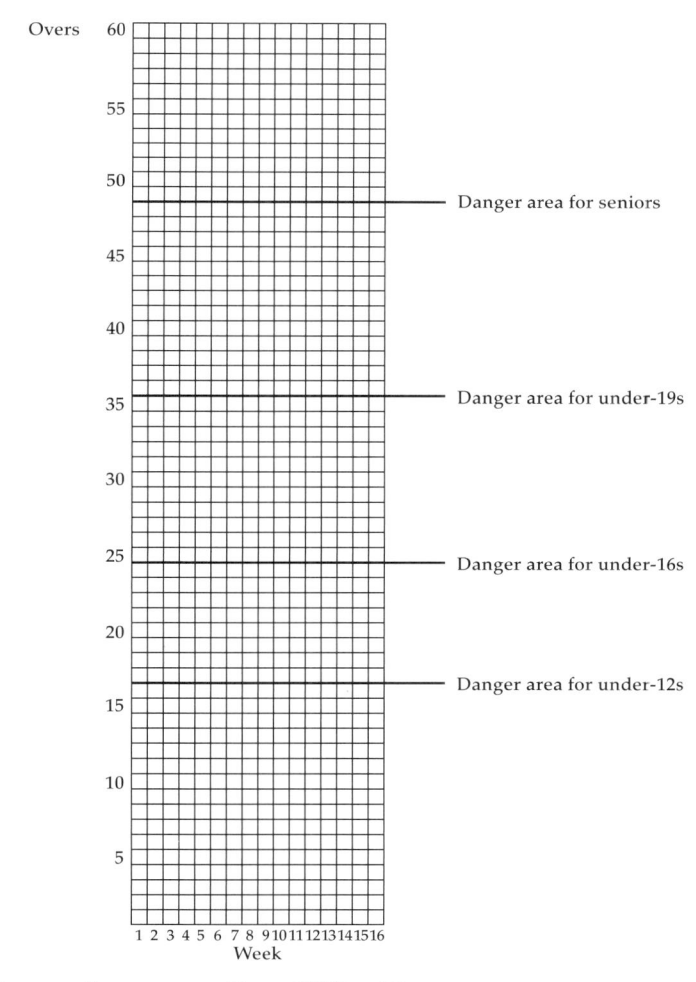

SOURCE: STRETCH AND GRAY, 1998, P. 26

FIGURE 10.5: *Graph of weekly over totals for cricketers, showing danger areas*

BOWLING WORKLOAD AND THE RISK OF INJURY IN ELITE FAST BOWLERS

A scientific criticism of the guidelines listed here are that they have not been tested to determine whether they actually reduce the risk of injury in fast bowlers. It is true that these guidelines have been drawn up on the grounds that they seem likely to work given what we currently understand about these injuries. However, this does not mean that they will definitely reduce injury risk, since our understanding may not be correct.

In order to establish the real factors determining injury risk in any sport, it is necessary to perform a controlled prospective study in which two groups of players are followed for one or more seasons, while the single most important factor considered to cause injury is controlled in the two groups. For example, if bowling workload is considered the most important factor determining injury risk, then an ideal study would be to compare injury risk in two groups of bowlers whose bowling workload would be controlled during the period of the study so that one group bowled significantly less than the other. Then, if the incidence of injury was greater in the group that had bowled more, the reasonable conclusion might be that bowling workload is a factor explaining injury risk.

A less sound but nevertheless scientifically acceptable method is simply to compare injury incidence in a large group of fast bowlers, whose choice of how much they bowl is left up to them. At the end of the study, the injury rate is compared with the amount of bowling done by the different bowlers to see whether any relationship becomes apparent. Our prediction, based on what has been argued so far in this chapter, is that those who bowl the most will have the highest injury rates. The weakness of this approach is that bowlers may choose to bowl fewer or more overs in a season for reasons that may then also influence their risk of injury. For example, healthy, stronger players would naturally choose to bowl more than weaker, less skilled players. So this type of study might lead to the incorrect conclusion that injury risk is highest in those who bowl the least – such are the perils of research!

The first prospective study of a large number of elite state-level adult fast bowlers has been reported from Australia (Dennis et al., 2003). These authors followed 90 of these bowlers for two cricket seasons, and monitored the number of days they bowled each week and the number of deliveries bowled each week. They found that there appeared to be a dual relationship between injury risk and bowling workload – those who bowled with an average of two to five days' rest between bowling sessions were at lowest risk of injury. In contrast, those who bowled either daily or with more than five days between each bowling session were at greater risk of injury.

They also found that bowling more than 188 deliveries (31 overs) or less than 123 deliveries (20,3 overs) per week were both associated with increased injury risk. They concluded that bowlers should be encouraged to bowl two to three times a week, limiting themselves to the equivalent of between 20 and 30 overs a week. Clearly this is a lower frequency of bowling than is advised according to current ACB and UCB guidelines (Table 10.5 on p. 615), which promote bowling on as many as four days a week.

In a similar study performed on elite fifteen-year-old Australian bowlers, the same group (Dennis et al., 2005) found that 25% of these young bowlers developed an overuse injury during a single session, and that 63% of these injuries were to the lower back. Risk factors for bowling injury included: less than three and a half days rest between bowling sessions; bowling on more than two and a half days per week; and bowling more than 50 deliveries per day. The authors concluded that high bowling workload is indeed a significant risk factor for low back injury.

Surprisingly, a comparative study of young English fast bowlers of the same age failed to show a rising injury incidence alongside increasing bowling workload. The authors wondered whether the harder surfaces in Australia (and South Africa) might explain this discrepancy. However, the English study covered only the first three months of the cricket season, whereas the Australian study covered the full season. If the English study had continued through the second half of the season, it is possible that more injuries might have been observed in those who bowled more.

There is a need for more studies of this design to determine whether these findings apply at other levels of the sport, and whether the conclusions are sufficiently different from the current ACB and UCB guidelines to warrant revisions to those guidelines.

Management of the bowler with low back pain

We now know a great deal about the *prevention* of back pain in bowlers. But how do we intervene when a young (or more senior) player complains of pain?

- **An adolescent cricketer, especially a fast bowler, who complains of persistent low back pain must be taken very seriously.** Persistent pain is *not* a normal response to fast bowling. In fact, any young fast bowler who complains of persistent low back pain that comes on while he is bowling, must be assumed to have a lumbar vertebral bone bruise at risk of developing into a stress fracture until that diagnosis is excluded by the relevant examinations. If the pain is sufficiently severe that bowling at normal pace becomes impossible after a few deliveries, then the diagnosis of a stress fracture is more probable. It is safest to assume that the player does indeed have a stress fracture, and he must immediately be treated as if he does indeed have a stress fracture.

- **The bowler must immediately stop playing all sport and be seen by a sports physician with expertise in the diagnosis and management of this condition.** Clinical examination is usually sufficient to confirm the diagnosis – especially if hyperextension when standing only on the leg of the affected side reproduces the pain or discomfort felt when bowling (Figure 10.6). A Technetium bone scan or a CAT scan will confirm the diagnosis, which may not be apparent on a standard X-ray, but may be shown by specialized CT X-rays. (If health facilities are scarce or impossibly expensive, the hyperextension test alone will suffice.) The importance of early detection of a stress fracture is that it allows for an earlier return to the game and a reduced risk of early retirement from the game due to injury.

- **What rehabilitation programme is appropriate for a fast bowler with severe low back pain, whether or not a stress fracture has been diagnosed?** There is some evidence that the degree of pain is a better marker of the severity of the injury and the extent of recovery in a fast bowler than the extent of injury shown by either X-rays, bone or other scans. Thus the presence of continuing pain and discomfort is the best marker of when the rehabilitation programme may begin and how rapidly it can progress. Our approach has therefore been that there should be complete rest (remember the case of Dennis Lillee!) until there is no back pain with any movement, including the hyperextension movement. At this point, a strengthening and conditioning programme specifically designed for that particular bowler, taking into account his age, physiological make-up and

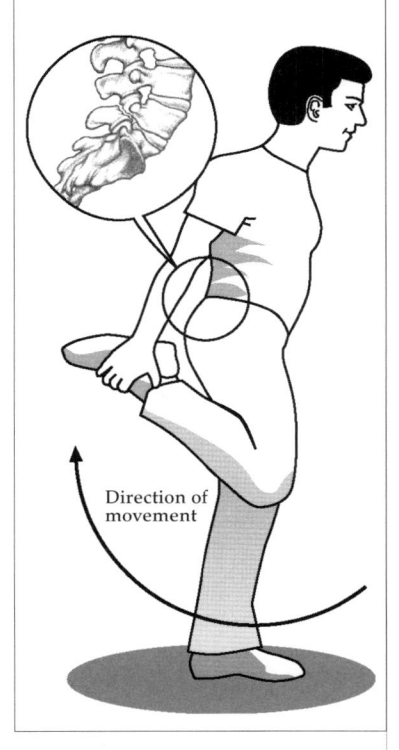

FIGURE 10.6: *Test for discomfort in case of suspected stress fracture in fast bowler*

technique must begin. The return to bowling should be gradual, and must begin with careful analysis of the bowling technique and action in order to check for mixed action. If the latter is present, careful and rigorous corrective coaching of the correct technique must be employed. We explain how the coach should proceed in such cases in Chapters 5 and 9.

- **It cannot be stressed enough that sufficient time and support must be allowed for the recovery and rehabilitation process.** Dennis Lillee's final piece of luck was that (presumably) his cricketing employers (the state) paid his salary during his 18-month rehabilitation period. He was also not expected to meet the costs of his highly specialized recovery programme – which would no doubt be way beyond the means of most in countries lacking a national health system. Many players are not so fortunate: Sandy Gordon, the acclaimed international sports psychologist, noted in 2003 that members of the Indian Test team were often afraid to reveal an injury until it became completely unmanageable, in case this cost them their place in the side. Lillee could so easily have been thrown on the scrapheap – but he wasn't, and the rewards to his country were great.

The pathology of back pain in fast bowlers: vertebral stress fractures, bone bruises and disc degeneration

Bone is a dynamic tissue that is continuously undergoing processes of remodelling in response to stresses imposed on it. The goal of this process is to produce bone that is strongest in the areas of greatest stress. To achieve this, there are two different sets of bone cells: osteoclasts that continuously digest old bone and osteoblasts that lay down new bone, especially along the lines of greatest stress.

Thus the strength of a bone at a particular site is dependent on the balance of the action of the osteoblastic and osteoclastic bones at that site. When the action of the osteclastic cells is dominant, the bone is temporarily weakened. Continual stress at that site produces discomfort that is not yet painful, and which is first felt after exercise. Then as the bone strength declines even further at the site of injury, pain becomes increasingly more noticeable, even during less stressful activities such as gentle training. Before long, pain is present as soon as exercise begins – for example, in the fast bowler's first delivery of the day. At this point, the bone is severely 'bruised' – the activity of the osteoclastic cells is dominant and the bone is becoming increasingly fragile at the site of injury. In fact, pain may signify minute movement within the bone at the site of weakness. Eventually, pain may become so severe that continued bowling is impossible. At this point, the bone has fractured: by now, the

THE PATHOLOGY OF LUMBAR STRESS FRACTURES IN FAST BOWLERS

There are five lumbar vertebrae that join the thoracic (chest) vertebrae to the pelvic bones. The lowest five lumbar vertebrae (L1 to L5) are especially prone to injury in fast bowlers. The area at risk of fracture is the delicate flake of bone on both sides of the midline, known as the pars interarticularis of the vertebrae.

In front, the lumbar vertebrae comprise the solid vertebral bodies that carry the weight of the body from the head to the pelvis. But behind these bodies and forming the spinal canal, through which the spinal cord runs, carrying nerve impulses from the brain to the rest of the body, is a much more thin-walled structure. The pars interarticularis is the especially fragile part of this structure, and the area that is especially prone to bone bruising or fracture in young fast bowlers. It was in this area that the vertebral fractures suffered by Dennis Lillee showed up. Lumbar stress fractures that have plagued subsequent fast bowlers have appeared at the same site.

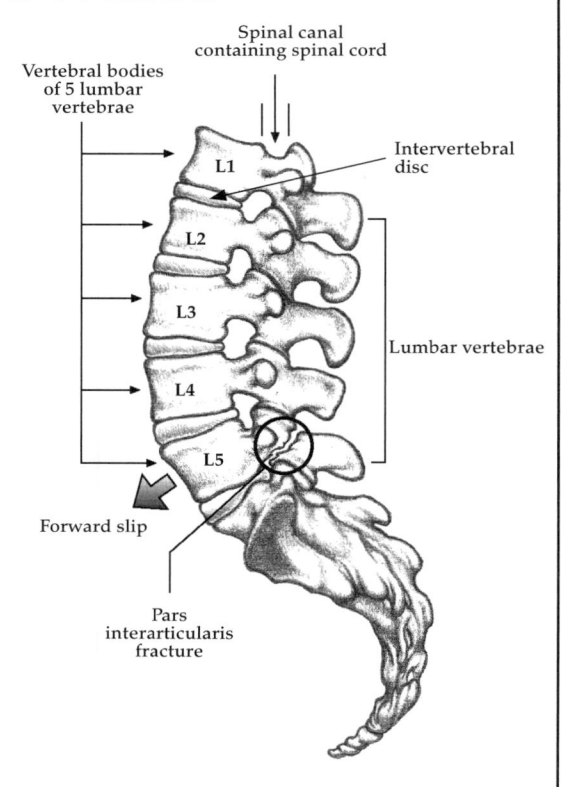

FIGURE 10.7: *The lumbar vertebrae vulnerable to injury in fast bowlers*

---

bone structure is so disrupted that any stress, however minor, causes movement within the weakened bone. This activity is so painful that the surrounding muscles go into spasm, preventing normal movement. At the same time, pain signals the brain to avoid the pain-causing activity. As a result, even if the bowler is still able to run in and bowl, he will not achieve anything near his fastest speeds – the brain, protecting the weakness of the spine, simply will not allow this to happen. It does this by preventing the full recruitment of the bowling muscles and hence the development of a peak bowling speed (see the central governor model, pp. 541–43 above).

Pain usually starts on the side opposite the bowling arm and it is on this side that the stress fractures occur. This indicates that counter-rotation rather than hyperextension is the cause of unilateral injury on the side opposite the bowling arm, as it is the opposite side – the bowling arm side – that is exposed to the greatest amounts of hyperextension (Hardcastle et al., 1992).

When Dennis Lillee suffered what may have been the first recognized vertebral stress fractures in a fast bowler, he went through all these stages over a period of almost a year. At first, he was able to return to fast bowling after a break, indicating that the osteoblasts at the site of injury had become active, temporarily strengthening the injured site. But when he opened the bowling in nine first-class matches in nine weeks at the start of the Australian summer of 1973, the stress on his back was too much and he suffered the fractures later diagnosed by Dr Webster, using what was then the revolutionary technique of X-ray tomography. The development of additional techniques, including bone scanning with radiolabels, MRI and CAT scanning, has greatly increased our knowledge of these injuries. Similarly, the rehabilitation of these injuries, pioneered by the medical staff in Western Australia who assisted Dennis Lillee, has progressed substantially in the past 30 years.

Figure 10.7 opposite shows that the site of weakness in the lumbar vertebrae is the thin sliver of bone that joins the body of the vertebrae with the posterior elements to which the powerful back muscles are attached. It is this anatomical area that is particularly stressed by fast bowling, and which undergoes the process of osteoclastic/osteoblastic remodelling that can lead to the development of pain and ultimately a stress fracture.

Approximately 4–6% of normal young men active in sports (other than fast bowling) show abnormalities of the pars interarticularis (see Figure 10.7). However, the incidence among fast bowlers whose careers last more than five years is around 50–60%, and can be as high as 90% (Hardcastle et al., 1992; Elliott et al., 1995; Gregory et al., 2004). As many as 60% may show degeneration of the intervertebral discs. In another study, Foster et al. (1989) studied the incidence of back injuries in 82 high-performance young (seventeen-year-old) male fast bowlers during one season of club or school cricket in Western Australia. Thirty-eight per cent of bowlers were injured in the season. Eleven per cent sustained a vertebral stress fracture during the season, and 27% sustained a soft tissue injury of the back. Risk factors for injury included bowling with a mixed action, bowling a greater number of overs, and having a greater release height. The study of Hardcastle et al. (1992) also showed that a majority (75%) of bowlers who used the mixed action reported low back pain. Pain, these authors stress, is always associated with a radiological abnormality.

Probably the first structures in the back to be affected are the intervertebral discs (see

Figure 10.7) which shrink in height, or may bulge or herniate into the spinal column, with pressure on the sciatic nerve, causing pain that distributes down the outside of the leg into the foot. Interestingly, as little as 30 minutes of fast bowling causes an acute (immediate) loss of height of about 2,3mm due to shrinkage of the spine caused by loss of fluid in the intervertebral discs (Reilly and Chana, 1994). This shrinkage is not caused by standing or the run-up, but by delivering the ball. It is only during the delivery that the spine is exposed to very large loads. The authors of this study suggest that bowlers need more recovery time between bowling spells in order to allow for recovery of spinal height, along with rehydration of the intervertebral discs.

In contrast to these acute changes, as many as 65% of fast bowlers may show chronic (present for months or years) disc abnormalities (Elliott et al., 1995); and an even higher percentage (70%) has been reported in retired elite fast bowlers (Annear et al., 1992). Another study from the same group at the University of Western Australia (Elliott et al., 1993) studied 24 fourteen-year-old school and club fast bowlers. Twenty-one per cent of the bowlers showed disc degeneration or bulging; these bowlers tended to use the mixed bowling action. No bowler who used a purely side-on or front-on technique showed disc degeneration, in keeping with the finding that the mixed action is more likely to cause lumbar vertebral radiological abnormalities (Elliott et al., 1992). There were no other biomechanical differences that might explain why some young fast bowlers in that study developed lumbar disc damage.

Nineteen of these original 24 fast bowlers were studied again three years later, by which time the incidence of disc degeneration had increased almost three-fold to 58% (Burnett et al., 1996). The number complaining of back pain had also increased significantly.

In order to prove that two factors were associated (lumbar disc degeneration or stress fractures or both, and the mixed bowling action), it was necessary to undertake an intervention trial in which the proposed causative mechanism – the mixed action – was altered and its effect on lumbar disc degeneration was then evaluated. Elliott and Khangure (2002) studied a total of 41 young fast bowlers over four years while they were coached to reduce the amount of shoulder counter-rotation they performed during the delivery stride. The goal was to reduce the extent of the mixed action and convert these bowlers to either a side-on or front-on action. As a result, the number of bowlers who used the mixed action dropped from 81% in the first year to 33% in the fourth year. Of the 49 players who exclusively used the front-on or side-on action, only one (2%) developed a lumbar disc abnormality. In contrast, 21% of the bowlers with a mixed action showed vertebral disc abnormalities.

By the end of the study, during which the number of bowlers with a mixed action was progressively reduced, the number of bowlers with disc degeneration rose from

25% to 33% over four years. This compares to the much greater increase of 58% in the three-year study of Burnett et al. (1996). The authors concluded that even greater efforts at individual coaching of fast bowlers are required if the prevalence of the mixed bowling action is to be reduced, in turn reducing the prevalence of back degeneration in young fast bowlers.

While it is clear that fast bowling produces significant acute and chronic changes to the lower back, the short-term outlook for the injured fast bowler nevertheless appears reasonable. A number of studies confirm that regardless of the severity of the radiological changes, early diagnosis and appropriate rehabilitation of injured players can produce complete functional recovery in the vast majority of fast bowlers (Ranawat et al., 2003; Stretch et al., 2003; Millson et al., 2004). While some bowlers have undergone surgical repair of stress fractures (Hardcastle et al., 1993), there is plenty of evidence that a conservative, non-surgical approach is probably as effective (Ranawat et al., 2003). Just ask Dennis Lillee.

TECHNIQUES FOR MODIFYING THE BOWLING ACTION OF FAST BOWLERS WITH LOW BACK PAIN OR INJURY OR AT RISK OF INJURY DEVELOPMENT

- **Coaches instructing young cricketers should teach a pure side-on bowling technique.** This requires that the back foot be placed parallel to the crease, and that a line drawn through the shoulders should point down the wicket at back foot impact.

- **Any individual adopting a 'mixed' technique should be corrected at an early age** – attempts to alter an already adopted bowling action become increasingly difficult as the player ages and the learned brain/nerve/muscle pathways that produce that technique become 'hardwired' into the brain. The mixed technique, as explained in Chapter 5 and above, can be recognized by a back foot alignment which faces down the wicket and a shoulder counter-rotation away from the batsman between back foot and front foot impact.

- **One method of correcting a 'mixed' technique involves advising the bowler to slow his approach velocity slightly to allow adequate time to adopt a correct side-on foot and shoulder position.** This is unlikely to reduce the ball velocity as the speed lost in a slower run-up is compensated for by the greater linear velocity acquired with the body in a side-on position.

THE KIWIS COME TO THE PARTY

A study similar to those reported here has been written up by Milburn and Nuttridge (1999). Fifty bowlers in senior club and first-eleven schoolboy cricket in Canterbury, New Zealand, were studied for one cricket season. At the start of the season the players underwent a battery of physiological testing to measure their fitness, muscle strength and flexibility. A video analysis of their bowling actions was also performed so that their actions could be classified as either side-on, front-on, mixed, or in-line (according to the New Zealand definition). Players also completed a diary to record their training, number of overs bowled, and their injury status. Players were contacted weekly to determine whether they had suffered injury in the previous week.

The study found that 45% of bowlers used the side-on action; 29% the mixed action; 16% the front-on action; and 10% the in-line action. Injury occurred frequently; 72% of bowlers sustained some form of injury during the season, and 57% were prevented by injury from bowling at some stage of the season. Fifteen per cent suffered back injuries and 42% suffered lower limb injuries. Seven bowlers (14%) developed stress fractures; six had suffered this injury previously. Thirty-one per cent of injuries prevented bowling for periods of more than fifteen weeks – these were typically bone fractures, either lumbar stress fractures or fractures or bone bruises of the lower limb bones (shin splints). Other lower limb injuries included hamstring and groin strains, and knee, shin, ankle and heel pain.

Most injuries (72%) occurred early in the season, usually within the first month. Interestingly, bowling workload was unrelated to risk of injury; the least injured bowlers bowled the most either because they were initially at low risk of injury, or because bowling actually prevented injury. Here it is worth remembering the study of Dennis et al. (2003), which shows that there appear to be two injury thresholds – one at low and one at high bowling workloads.

The findings of the New Zealand study would be explained if the workload of their most hard-working bowlers was below the upper threshold identified by Dennis et al. (2003). Alternatively, that threshold might be higher in this specific group of bowlers than in the Australian study.

In the study of Milburn and Nuttridge (1999), there was no fitness, flexibility or strength variable that was related to the risk of injury; nor did the player's subjective rating of the hardness of the surface on which they bowled influence the risk of injury. Instead, the strongest predictor of injury risk was a previous injury – as is the case in all sports injuries. This serves to emphasize the importance of preventing the very first injury in any sport.

The type of bowling action was also unrelated to risk of injury. This is understandable, since the greatest number of injuries occurred to the lower limbs and it is improbable that the bowling action influences the risk of lower limb injuries. However, thirteen of the nineteen back or trunk injuries, including five of the seven lumbar stress fractures, occurred in bowlers who used either the mixed- or the in-line bowling action.

The authors concluded that more low-intensity bowling in practice may reduce the risk of injury; that all bowling actions are associated with a high risk of lower limb injury; but that back and trunk injuries are more likely in those who use the mixed- or in-line action. Injury was also more likely to occur early in the season and in those who had been previously injured. Inadequate rehabilitation of previous injuries, inadequate pre-season preparation and returning to the game too soon after a prior injury were all likely to contribute to injury risk. The authors concluded that: 'These results confirm the advantage of thorough preparation through controlled build-up of strength and technique and caution against use of pace bowlers early in the season.' They also provided seven recommendations to reduce the risk of injury in fast bowlers:

1. Since the best predictor of injury is a previous injury, special attention must be paid to the optimum management of bowlers with previous injuries.
2. Since the physical tests do not predict injury risk, there is a need to re-evaluate the value of these tests and to develop more effective tests, better able to predict the risk of future injury.
3. It was assumed that the reason why bowlers with the highest workloads were not at increased risk of injury was because they had followed a gradual build-up in bowling intensity and volume in the pre-season (although there may be other explanations). Thus guidelines of bowling workloads (see Table 10.5) should remain in place. In addition, these guidelines should caution against excessive bowling at pace and should emphasize that bowlers do the appropriate 'groundwork' in preparation for bowling fast in the new season.
4. Since the greatest risk of injury was in the first month of the season, fast bowlers need to bowl sparingly during this period until they are fully 'match hardened'. Only then should they begin to bowl at full effort for prolonged periods in matches.
5. The mixed-action delivery technique must be removed from the game.
6. The high risk of injury to fast bowlers requires a better understanding of the physical preparation and management of injured players. At all costs, there must not be a rush to return injured fast bowlers to play.
7. There is presently little that can be done to predict the risk of injury in fast bowlers. Thus more research is required.

- **Once the coach and player have decided on the most suitable action, it will be necessary to go back to the basics of the bowling action in order to effect these changes.** Furthermore, it is important to realize that these changes may take a long time to correct, and should preferably be done during a period when no matches are being played. The following suggested steps should be followed, guarding against rushing into bowling off a full run-up.
    - Without a run-up, stand with the feet in the correct position, and ensure that the wind-up is into the correct position.
    - Stand and bowl with a short follow-through.
    - Walk and bowl.
    - Progress up to a slow run-up.
    - Once this has been mastered, progressively increase the speed of the run-up while ensuring that the side-on action is retained without any counter-rotation of the shoulders.
    - Once a normal run-up speed is achieved, start to increase the bowling speed to the normal maximal speed while continuing to ensure that there is no reversion to the mixed action with shoulder counter-rotation.
    - Increase the number of deliveries bowled at normal speed to ensure that increasing levels of fatigue do not increase shoulder counter-rotation, leading to a reversion to the mixed action.

- **If this change in technique reduces the bowler's effectiveness, then a vigorous back and trunk strengthening programme specifically designed for that player should be prescribed.** A strong co-ordinated muscular system also provides protection by aiding in the dissipation of forces away from the area of the spine most likely to develop a stress fracture.

- **Fast bowlers who do not bend their front leg when bowling should be coached into allowing a small degree of knee flexion to help absorb some of the ground reaction forces.** This may require some additional knee-strengthening exercises to ensure this movement is performed with the required control, so as not to influence the bowling rhythm.

- **Attempts to develop a harness that would encourage the use of the front-on bowling action have proved disappointing** (Wallis et al., 2002) in part because, to be truly effective, a harness would probably make bowling impossible. However, it does seem possible that at some time in the future, training aids that ease the adoption of the side-on bowling action will have to be developed.

Injuries in slow bowlers

Surprisingly, stress fractures also occur in slow bowlers. A study of young English bowlers training at the Centres of Excellence for three counties revealed that, when corrected for an equal number of balls delivered, slow bowlers had about one-third the risk of injury of fast bowlers (Gregory et al., 2002). Although slow bowlers had half the risk of back injuries of fast bowlers, they were about ten times more likely to experience shoulder injuries. In fact, slow bowlers were twice as likely to develop shoulder injuries as fast bowlers were likely to suffer low back injuries. Some of the factors associated with shoulder injuries in bowlers and fielders have been identified (Aginsky et al., 2004; Bell-Jenje and Gray, 2005), including specific muscular weaknesses, in particular in the muscles that stabilize the scapula. The authors advise that biomechanical evaluation and correction of weaknesses is required if these injuries are to be prevented.

THE REST OF THE BOWLER'S BODY

We have here focused on the bowler's spine, because back injury effectively renders the player physically unable to bowl; and more importantly, because the long-term consequences of low back injury can be extremely serious, leading to chronic, disabling pain.

Yet, as the New Zealand study already referred to indicates, bowlers also experience intrinsic injuries to their legs, shoulders and trunks. The physiotherapist to the South African national cricket team between 1991 and 1999, Craig Smith, may have been the first to describe a novel condition that appears to be specific to the ankles of fast bowlers – posterior talar impingement syndrome (PTIS). Bowlers with this condition become increasingly disabled especially when bowling on uneven surfaces, particularly when bowling into the worn foot holes at the popping crease.

Of the 23 South African bowlers studied by Smith, eight developed the condition and five required surgery, which was performed by an orthopaedic foot specialist in Pretoria, South Africa. The results were excellent, with all five bowlers returning to international competition.

Smith theorized that this condition results from repeated episodes of forced plantar flexion of the fast bowler's front foot. Contributory factors include worn foot-holds, a long delivery slide, abnormalities of the talar bone in the ankle, abnormal foot biomechanics – and of course, overuse.

Preventative measures include bowling fewer overs (see the bowling guidelines in Table 10.5 above) and repairing the worn bowling foot-holes both in matches and in the practice nets.

Another South African study has described the first case of a stress fracture of the scapula (shoulder blade) in a 21-year-old professional fast bowler (De Villiers et al., 2005). The discomfort began as night pain in his shoulder (night pain is a common indicator of a bone injury). Eventually there was an acute exacerbation of pain that forced him to have to stop bowling and to leave the field. A computer tomography (CT) scan revealed the fracture, which healed without complications after eight weeks of rest.

Ten cases of lateral trunk muscle injury were studied by Humphries and Jamison (2004). Seventy per cent of injuries were to the internal oblique, the external oblique, or the transversalis muscles at or near to their attachment to one or more of the lowest four ribs on the non-bowling arm side. In six of the ten cases, the injury was a recurrence. The exact biomechanical causes of these specific injuries remain unknown, according to the authors.

INTRINSIC INJURIES TO FIELDERS

Most injuries experienced by fielders are extrinsic, and arise from diving, sliding, rolling, crashing into the advertising boards or another player, being struck by the ball (as a close fielder or because they have taken their eye off the ball) and all the other hazards of trying to intercept a hard ball travelling at speed. However, fielders are at risk of a particular kind of intrinsic injury that is related to the technique they use for throwing in from the deep.

THE DANGERS OF THROWING

One of the easiest ways to do a serious injury to a cricketer is to get him to throw in hard from the deep – repeatedly. However, even a few throws – or just one – can be risky. Most dangerous in this respect is the side-arm throw, because the bicep tendon can pop out of the groove in which it runs. (If this happens, treat it with ice and a vigorous – and excruciatingly painful! – physiotherapy technique known as cross-friction.) Fielders who prefer the side-arm throw-in are most at risk when they are running to their left and throwing with their right arm. They should pay special attention to our advice about trying to get into as strong a throwing position as possible before releasing the ball.

Cricketers have always been guilty of neglecting their throwing arms – a strange oversight given that a healthy and strong arm is a basic requirement for being selected! Even professional players will get treatment for their backs, knees and hamstrings after games, but leave their overworked throwing arm dangling off the massage couch untended. In this respect, elite baseball players are much more enlightened than cricketers: after a game, the entire team (even those whose specialist positions don't require them to throw the ball in from the deep) will don Cryo-Cuffs, a kind of padded shoulder sling that is iced. This pre-empts swelling. They also do plenty of work with Therabands, but at least in this respect cricketers are starting to catch up.

ONCE MORE: PREVENTION IS ALWAYS BETTER THAN CURE!

To sum up, the goal of the cricketer is to avoid developing an intrinsic injury in the first instance. The following are some basic reminders on how to avoid intrinsic injuries:

- Cultivate correct technique.
- Always follow a thorough, sensible stretching routine (warm-up and warm-down) before and after playing.
- Increase overall fitness.
- Include cross-training in your fitness programme.
- Footwear should be closely monitored: appropriate shoes should be chosen that fit your physiological foot-type and gait. If necessary, consult a podiatrist and use prescribed orthotics.
- Regular massage can help maintain flexibility and prevent stiffness.
- Take action on problems while they are still minor; don't ignore them, hoping they will go away.
- Avoid over-training or repeatedly playing to the point of exhaustion.
- Don't forget to rest!

CHAPTER ELEVEN

WHITHER CRICKET?
THE FUTURE OF THE GAME

The game of cricket has a magnificent past and a complex history. Part of what we have tried to communicate in this book is a sense of the legacy of this great game, which has given pleasure to millions. Nevertheless, as we have also noted, because of the centuries of tradition that accompany the game there is a sense that cricket, perhaps more than some sports, has to be dragged into the future kicking and screaming. Almost every innovation in the game – from one-day games ('pyjama cricket') to the use of technology to assist with umpiring decisions – has been met with resistance from cricket purists. Some innovations have indeed been quashed outright – we've mentioned how the Laws of the game were modified to exclude Dennis Lillee's notorious aluminium bat. And when Bob Woolmer, then the South African team coach, communicated with captain Hansie Cronje onfield via a two-way ear-piece in the course of the 1999 World Cup, this practice was hastily – and perhaps unwisely – banned. (Certainly we might see the return of this or similar devices as noise levels at cricket grounds rise steadily. Variations on this theme might include a radio link between the stump microphone and the on-field umpires, to enable them to make better caught-behind decisions, as background noise makes it increasingly difficult to pick up snicks and nicks.)

Some of the new forms that cricket might take this century will give many pause, such as the notion of an all-weather cricket pitch played on an artificial pitch with a stadium roof that can close in case of rain; or the replacement of human bowlers by computer-programmed bowling machines.

Another innovation no longer in the realm of science fiction is the development of a cricket helmet that offers 360-degree protection with an all-round 'veil' of extremely tough but light clear material – something that will eliminate almost entirely the batter's fear of being hit in the face or on the head. Just as the by now almost universal practice of wearing helmets with face guards has increased the number of batters we see playing the hook shot, so changes like this will alter the way the game is played.

So what else might the future hold? There is no doubt that cricket will increasingly come under the scrutiny of scientists, with good prospects for protective devices, equipment, study of statistics for strategic purposes (see Chapter 8 for examples), technology that will aid and support umpiring decisions, and the prevention and treatment of cricket-specific injuries. While cricket has been placed under the microscope by sports scientists in the last several decades, many argue that the newest frontier is that of mental skills, with research here still in its infancy. It could be argued that it is those who crack the riddles of the human mind that will dominate in cricket in the century that lies ahead. While this is true to a degree of many sports, it is especially true of cricket, as we discuss in Chapter 2.

There is also a real possibility – and danger – that those countries with excellent infrastructure, large middle-class populations and explicit research commitments will pull ahead (in cricketing terms) of countries with fewer resources and arguably more pressing priorities. One of the great joys of cricket in the second half of the twentieth century, as we have mentioned, is that developed and developing nations have played each other pretty much on an equal footing: it would be a great pity if this was to become a phenomenon of the past. The issue is not even necessarily one of wealth – subcontinental nations, for instance, have vast sums to spend on cricket – but one of organization and cricket administration. If, as happens in Pakistan, for instance, cricket administrators are chosen by and politically affiliated to whichever regime is in power, then with every change in government, there will be upheaval in cricketing structures.

All this means that regardless of what surprises and ingenuous discoveries science may pull out of the hat concerning cricket, the single most important concern for the future of cricket is the building of strong teams. But this is not a straightforward process, as we shall see.

MANUFACTURING A GREAT TEAM

The notion of a production line in cricket is anathema to many traditionalists. Talent, they insist, cannot be produced by scientific formulas or corporate expenditure, but is rather the happy – and arbitrary – result of good genes, correct temperament and helpful socio-economic circumstances. Indeed, many modern pundits, no strangers to long-term governmental and corporate investment in sport, are sometimes sceptical of the notion of 'manufacturing' cricketers. For example, tradition insists that the West Indies had a 'production line' of fast bowlers in the 1970s and 1980s, and that Australia currently has a similar 'factory' system that churns out world-class batsmen. But it has been over fifteen years since the West Indies capped a genuinely classy quick bowler; and Australia's drubbing at the hands of England in 2005 – which owed much to a suddenly weak Australian batting line-up – seemed to hint that the batting cupboard Down Under was perhaps less well-stocked than the world had assumed.

Certainly some countries are better at consistently producing certain types of cricketers; but those planners and corporate backers who strive for production lines must be cautious, and not misunderstand history: such systems, if they ever existed, would not have stopped producing talent overnight, as some argue that they seem to have done in the case of the West Indies.

The idea of cricketing production lines is dangerous for another reason: it absolves everyone involved of responsibility. The implication is that the process is automated, or at least automatic: talent will be produced with or without the active participation of cricket administrators, coaches and players. Indeed, many commentators have suggested that it was precisely this attitude that crippled the West Indies after their two-decade dominance of the cricketing arena. No-one had planned for the future. Winning had put an end to hard work. And few, it seemed, had considered that the emergence of the famous pace quartets of the 1980s was not the result of a formal and self-perpetuating system, but rather a particularly well-timed flourishing of individual talents.

But even if the past success of the West Indies, for example, owed nothing to production lines, does that mean that the idea itself is inherently flawed? And if it is indeed a workable system, how does one account for some of the greatest players of all time appearing as if out of the blue? After all, Bradman and Sobers didn't grow up playing mini-cricket or being streamed and analyzed by sophisticated administrative software.

These two camps are, like the wise blind men of Hindustan who each only identified a piece of the elephant, both right and both wrong. The reality is something of a conundrum: you can manufacture great sides; and you do rely almost completely on God-given talent appearing out of the blue. However, in order to allow these two ingredients – the administrative and the mysterious – to percolate together, you need the right system in place, and that system is shaped roughly like a pyramid.

Cricket has always relied on a large and sturdy base. First in Britain, and then in its colonies, hundreds of thousands of boys and young men played the game in all weathers and on all kinds of pitches, every weekend or mid-week match providing the building-blocks for future greatness. Today tens of millions play on formal fields, village greens, dusty maidans, and even beaches and streets. (In 2005, a South African investigative television programme profiled a group of Pakistani expatriates who congregate after midnight to play cricket in one of Johannesburg's inner-city squares, their deserted cement and tar field eerily illuminated by street lights.)

But numbers are not enough. If they were, India would be unbeatable, Pakistan a distant second, and the rest of the Test-playing world squabbling for the leftovers. The base of the pyramid needs huge numbers of players, but it also needs a formal structure. This is where schools come into the equation: good coaching at schools is one of the foundations upon which all national cricket is built. Then come clubs and universities, the next stage of the sifting process, physical maturity bringing increased intensity to the game. These clubs then feed the lower echelons of the first-class system (B-teams), which in turn feed front-line first-class teams, which ultimately provide a pool from which cricketers are selected for national honours.

The Australians have been blessed with some phenomenal players over the last fifteen years, but they have also built their international dominance on an extremely solid pyramid. The country's club system is highly sophisticated and well run – many Australian clubs are more professional than some English county teams. And its first-class structure is in turn hugely competitive, providing the most rigorous training available anywhere in the world.

But remove or even disrupt one of the layers of the pyramid, and its pinnacle – Test cricket – will be seriously disturbed. For decades, England's Test team was being fed by excellent counties, which in turn were getting good raw players from both public and private schools where cricket was taught and coached. In the early 1990s, cricket was all but removed from schools, and sure enough, by the mid-1990s, England had become the laughing-stock of world cricket. Their current resurgence owes a great deal to a conscious and intelligent process of rebuilding.

South Africa has been less fortunate. Despite its political isolation, cricket of an extremely high quality was played internally throughout the 1970s and 1980s, with the likes of Graeme Pollock, Clive Rice, Vince van der Bijl and Peter Kirsten all helping to create a highly competitive standard. This was largely thanks to a rock-solid pyramid: good schools investing in sport, well-funded universities, excellent clubs, and a first-class game hugely popular among the country's white sports fans.

But it was success based on a racial fantasy. The advent of democracy in 1994 ended the era of white privilege, and the new government was far more concerned with the harsh realities of a developing country than the state of a sport still considered by many to be a white enclave. New social and economic policies saw major upheavals

Numbers are not enough. Good coaching at schools is one of the foundations upon which all national cricket is built.

in education, with slashed budgets leading to a mass exodus of dedicated teachers, many of them skilled and experienced cricket coaches. Universities also had their budgets reduced. With university competitions diluted, it was inevitable that first-class and international teams would soon suffer. Currently South Africa is relying almost exclusively on the unpredictable emergence of natural talent, and on players produced by the handful of cricketing schools that survive on private or corporate funding.

The failure to organize formal structures – to build the pyramid, in other words – can be extremely frustrating for national coaches. In Pakistan, 20 million children play street cricket at an extraordinarily impressive level – swinging taped balls, spinning tennis-balls, hitting very hard – but the net or filter that is supposed to scoop them up and carry them to higher levels of the game is simply not there.

A sturdy base is essential in developing a winning cricketing nation, but simply having millions of players thumping the ball all over the park every weekend is no use: while the foundation of the pyramid is made up of large numbers of players, much more importantly, it must be made up of large numbers playing multi-day cricket. Four-innings cricket is the great template from which all other varieties of the sport spring; and by reducing it in favour of one-day cricket, countries are condemning themselves to B-grade status.

It is an increasingly common phenomenon that batsmen, even in well-established Test sides like Pakistan and India, no longer know how to spend time at the crease, largely as a result of too much one-day cricket. The situation is considerably worse in some ICC Affiliate countries, where the only form of the game played is one-day cricket. In some of these countries, players struggle to bat out 20 overs, let alone 50.

Multi-day cricket is the answer to this problem. As long as some countries focus on four-innings games, and others play only limited-overs cricket, the gap between the top teams and the minnows will widen.

THE FUTURE MEETS THE PAST – THE QUESTION OF UMPIRING

The role played by cricket umpires, and the skills and training required for the job, warrant a separate book, and we cannot do justice to the subject here any more than we can provide in-depth discussion of scorers, statisticians, groundskeepers, administrators, selectors and the myriad others involved in the game.

Nevertheless, there can be little doubt that the figure of the umpire stands squarely in the spotlight (some might even call it the firing-line) in any contemplation of the future of the game. In the last two decades, technology has come to the assistance of

WHAT SCIENCE CAN CONTRIBUTE TO CRICKET IN THE FUTURE

In many respects, researchers have just scratched the surface of the science of cricket. In the decades to come, it's entirely possible that scientists will be looking more closely into the following areas.

Genetic factors

These determine athletic and cricketing ability more than any other single factor. However, genetic factors for success are not solely related to the specific skills needed for batting, bowling and fielding. Scientists will also be probing the important physical and psychological requirements for success in the game. Will great cricketers of the future need to have the physical gifts of elite athletes as well as the specific skills of the game? This is likely to be the case.

Environmental factors

These include local conditions (such as climate) and playing surfaces. For example, we need to know more about how to prepare players so that they are able to play on many different surfaces.

As far as weather, humidity, altitude and so on are concerned, little research has been done on how these affect cricketers, although several studies have been undertaken on how these affect other athletes. Not just elite cricketers, but also school and club cricketers will benefit from acclimatizing when playing away matches. Not only do these conditions affect the physiological status of the players (less oxygen is available at altitude than at sea-level, for example), but the weather conditions and levels of moisture in the air will dramatically influence the mechanics of the pitch and flight in terms of the way the ball will behave when bowled and after striking the pitch. All of these factors bear further scientific investigation, so that coaches and players can have a greater understanding of these variations and how to cope with them.

Equipment

New materials for cricket pads and gloves are being developed that are better able to absorb shock without being so bulky. Now that run-out decisions are made on the basis of millimetres, it is essential that bulky clothing that slows the batsman must be redesigned. This is vital given that run-outs so often have a dramatic influence on the outcome of games, especially in one-day matches.

Opponents

There should be a more scientific and less subjective analysis of the playing patterns of one's opponents. Scientists have developed techniques for analyzing the playing patterns of individual players and teams in both rugby and cricket. Bob Woolmer was a pioneer in this field, who provided his players with detailed questionnaires and self-assessment forms at regular intervals; he also encouraged careful study of the batters' 'wagon-wheels' long before it became fashionable to do so.

the umpire at an unprecedented rate. Today, the sight of an on-field umpire drawing a square in the air as he signals to the third umpire up in the television box is so ubiquitous that we forget how novel a phenomenon this is in terms of cricketing history. The notion that television cameras and stump microphones could assist in adjudging run-outs and stumpings, and that a third umpire would be needed for matches to scrutinize TV footage and replays, has been around only since the 1990s, when South Africa, eager to dust off the cobwebs of years of sporting isolation, pioneered the use of fixed cameras and television umpires to help adjudicate run-outs and stumpings.

This was an excellent innovation, and one that has led to a much fairer system of judging certain types of dismissal, but at the time many argued that this was the thin edge of the wedge in terms of undermining the authority of the umpire. It is certainly true that the relationship between human umpires on the field and the technology now available to them has remained uneasy, and the boundaries have never been quite clear.

On the one hand, umpires now find that they have superb and impartial technology to assist in all kinds of decisions – such as whether a ball intercepted by a frantically diving fielder did indeed reach the boundary, whether a ball that bounced in deep shade close to the boundary was a four or a six, and so on. Umpires have even called upon their colleague off the field to use television technology to help them ascertain whether a dubious catch was indeed a clean take, or whether the ball was momentarily grounded before sinking into the hands of a fielder.

On the other hand, the rule remains that the on-field umpires remain the arbiters of whether or not to call for such support. An umpire who believes, in his opinion, that a scrambling batter made it back to his crease before a fielder's throw shattered the stumps, and is thus safe from a run-out decision, has to resist strong pressure from the fielding side to refer the decision to the third umpire. What is more, the television broadcasters will immediately replay this incident from every angle – and should the umpire have gotten it wrong, almost everyone around the grounds, including both teams, will know immediately. This has led to scenes where a batter who is given 'not out' by an umpire, but who is shown by subsequent replays to have been out, comes in for aggressive treatment from the understandably aggrieved fielding side.

Given the extremely high stakes involved, not to mention the financial implications at higher levels of the game, on-field umpires are coming under increasing pressure to refer all tight run-out and stumping decisions to the third umpire, whose job is made easy by the various camera shots and angles he is able to scrutinize.

But this goes against the grain of one of the principal tenets of the history of the game; that on the field, the umpire's word is law. The old truism, 'When is the umpire most right? When he's wrong', is still bandied about. Commentators who have the luxury of slow-motion replays that reveal that the umpire made a shocker

THE FORFEITED TEST AND THE HAIR-RAISING UMPIRE

In 2006, during a Test match between England and Pakistan at the Oval, umpire Darrell Hair accused the Pakistan team of tampering with the ball, and resorted to a Law never before used in the modern game, docking them five runs. Indignant, the team remained in the pavilion after the tea-break, discussing what course of action to take. The umpires removed the bails and declared that Pakistan had forfeited the match – the first time this had happened in Test cricket in 129 years. This unprecedented decision was popular with no-one, not even the English team, which was trailing by over an innings at the time.

The resulting furore raged for months: the question of ball-tampering was raised all over again (none of the TV cameras at the ground picked up any activity that bore out Hair's contention that Pakistani players had interfered with the ball); tickets for the final day's play had to be refunded, with losses to the tune of hundreds of thousands of pounds; Hair wrote the ICC a confidential letter offering to resign in exchange for US$500 000, which triggered further scandal; the Pakistan captain, Inzamam-ul-Haq, was censured by the ICC, which in turn was blasted by the Asian bloc – it was an all-round lose-lose scenario.

Andrew Miller, UK editor of the website Cricinfo, made the point that while cricket purists insisted on the umpire's right to make such decisions, Hair's actions showed an extraordinary lack of understanding of the social and political context of the times, never mind the match. The UK was a country still reeling from the aftermath of attacks on the London Underground by suicide bombers – heinous actions that widened and hardened racial and religious divides in multicultural Britain. Even as the Test match that ended in such controversy got under way, Heathrow airport was temporarily shut down in response to credible security threats. Yet, as Miller pointed out, the Test series had been a triumphant display of harmony and goodwill, two countries bonding through sport: 'What an improbable and wonderful time for these two teams to be pulling off such a diplomatic coup…. The global stand-off between East and West has seldom been more pronounced, and yet in the heart of London – a city forever wary of paralysis by extremists – a team from the misunderstood world of Islam has been performing wonderfully well in front of sell-out crowds and appreciative TV audiences.' He wound up with the impassioned words, 'I'll tell you what cricket really is. It's a bridge between cultures that might otherwise have drifted apart without a backward glance.'

No umpire should feel he has to consider the state of the globe and international relations before raising a finger – his job is quite tough enough as it is. However, high-handed and contentious decisions at the highest levels of the game – especially in the absence of factual support for those decisions – are increasingly hampering the game's capacity to act as a 'bridge across cultures'. The outpourings of emotion leading to accusations of racism and even threats against umpires who make seemingly biased decisions, can no longer be brushed aside as irrelevant.

of a decision continue to point out that bad decisions are a part of the game, that they are never malicious, and that for every wrong decision that has a batter trudging off the field even though the replays he is about to watch prove conclusively that he wasn't out, he'll have decisions that go in his favour and allow him to continue playing even when he should in fact be out.

This is not much comfort to the players whose averages are affected, or who might be dropped from the team, or whose rare opportunity to play is cut short by a bad decision. There has also been lively debate about the impartiality of umpires, and whether this is actually possible (see pp. 79–80 in Chapter 2). Umpires have been accused of home-side bias since they first took the field, to the extent that the rule concerning neutral-country umpires was introduced in the latter part of the last century.

HOWZAT?

Nowhere is the debate about the future of umpiring more contentious than around the question of LBW dismissals. In the past ten years, technology has been developed that can prove conclusively whether or not such balls would in fact hit the stumps (it cannot prove quite so conclusively whether the ball did in fact hit the leg or the foot without brushing the bat en route, although close cameras are making this call an easier one).

Yet this is one decision that still lies entirely in the hands of the umpire. Unlike a stumping or run-out decision, help with adjudging a clean catch, or ascertaining whether a ball has reached the boundary rope, where an umpire has the option of asking for clarity from the cameras, the notion of turning an LBW decision over to the third umpire and his barrage of technological support still generates great controversy.

That this seemingly simple and sensible step prompts such furious debate is to hint at the immense emotional complexity of the issue. Many feel the technology is there; there is no reason not to use it; it will make for fairer decisions and take the responsibility off the umpire's shoulders. After all, should he get it wrong, everyone watching the match on television, as well as spectators and players watching the screens now seen at many major cricket grounds, will be aware of this within seconds, as the technology is indeed used – not yet to show the umpire which decision to make, but to show everyone else whether or not he made his unaided, split-second decision correctly. In other words, in cases of LBW and caught-behind appeals, the available technology is used, sometimes rather cruelly, to judge the competence of the umpire and the correctness of his decisions.

Many more, however, feel that to turn LBW decisions (and caught-behind decisions, where technology, in the form of the 'snickometer', has also caught up with and overtaken human umpiring) over to technology is to render the umpire's presence decorative. Besides, when should such decisions be turned over to the third umpire? In every case, or in cases where the umpire is uncertain? If the former, then what is the point of having umpires on the field?

Every debate about the use of technology in adjudging dismissals raises this vision, which millions find disturbing: cricket without umpires. Instead, a Big Brother complex of technological aids, computer programmes, microphones and cameras will make all dismissal decisions – utterly impartially and utterly correctly. If umpires remain, it will be to police player behaviour on the field.

Future changes in the game will certainly involve the role of the umpire, an emotive issue because of his place in the game's history and traditions. For many, cricket is unimaginable without the presence of the white-coated gentlemen whose word is law for the duration of the game. And this reminds us that for cricket, the rich lore of the game continues to function, often simultaneously as both hindrance and help.

WILL PLAYERS CHALLENGE UMPIRES IN THE FUTURE?

Pragmatists have already begun to draw up scenarios in which players who believe an umpire to be in error might ask to have a decision referred to the third umpire. In county cricket, a system has been proposed in which each captain has two options per innings to ask that an umpire's decision be referred to the third umpire – and overruled, if technology proves that decision to be incorrect. The advantage of this system is that it forces such challenges to become part of the captain's strategic thinking: knowing that he is limited to only two makes him consider carefully when to use them – he is unlikely to waste them on borderline calls.

Another sensible proposal on the table is that the individual player – either the batsman who knows that he has been given out incorrectly or the bowler who knows that the batter definitely snicked the ball on its way to the safe hands of the keeper – may ask that an umpire's decision be referred to the third umpire. If the third umpire finds that technology supports his colleague on the field, the challenging player forfeits half his match fee, or otherwise pays a substantial financial penalty. This will prevent spurious or over-optimistic challenges, with the players turning every decision into a free-for-all. It might also bring back the days when the batter who knew he had tickled the ball en route to first slip would 'walk', sparing the umpire the trouble of making the decision. This would end some of modern cricket's less edifying spectacles – batters who have audibly nicked one to the wicket-keeper hanging around at the crease in the hope (sometimes realized) that the umpire has been momentarily snoozing, bowlers appealing vociferously for a catch off the batter's shoulder (the ball having gone nowhere near bat or gloves), and fielders claiming catches that replays show to have been grassed.

In conclusion, however, it is worth noting that most umpires have welcomed the technological advances that now support them or make their decisions for them. If nothing else, these aids remain valuable diagnostic tools for umpires, many of whom appreciate the opportunity to see where they are in error. And the use of technology has also led to calls for stricter controls and measurable criteria (including hearing and vision tests) for umpires at the upper levels of the game. And this in turn reminds us that the great majority of umpires around the world do their job with absolutely no technological support whatsoever – and that there will thus always be a need, at most levels of the game, for umpires able to make decisions with no more support than that provided by their own spectacles.

THE LAST WORD – THE LEGACY OF BOB WOOLMER

It is the history of the game, and the complexity of the challenges it offers all who play, coach and watch it, that inspired this book, which has become a compendium of the life's work of two extraordinary innovators in the realms of cricket and sports science respectively. In the case of Bob Woolmer, this book has become the legacy he left cricket-lovers all over the world after his tragic and untimely death in March 2007, just as the first proofs of this manuscript were being mailed to him.

Bob Woolmer believed passionately that he had a responsibility to pass on all that he had been taught or had gleaned from great players and teachers who went before him; at the same time, he remained acutely aware of the almost daily evolution of the game. Because of this, he felt that regardless of his vast experience – nothing less than a life spent playing and coaching cricket at the highest levels of the game – he remained a student of the game. In the decade that he laboured on this book, he continually revisited and updated his ideas with characteristic enthusiasm and humility. In his original conclusion he wrote, 'We do not feel that this is a final imprimatur, or that we have all the answers. We hope to continue to learn, research and explore the multiple aspects of this most fascinating and rewarding game, and we have no doubt that the game of cricket has more to teach us.'

We are grateful that we have not only the life experience of Bob Woolmer to pass on to future generations of cricketers and fans, but also his example and attitude of enthusiasm and humility – a mindset that befits the great game of cricket, of which Bob was such a faithful servant. We hope that readers will take Bob's words to heart: let us look not only to what we can learn about cricket, but to what cricket can teach us.

SELECT BIBLIOGRAPHY

Abernethy, B. 1982. 'Skill in cricket batting: Laboratory and applied evidence.' *Proceedings of the Kinesiological Sciences Conference* 7: 35–50.

Abernethy, B. and D.G. Russell. 1984. 'Advance cue utilisation by skilled cricket batsmen.' *Australian Journal of Science and Medicine in Sport* 16 (2): 2–10.

Aginsky, K.D., et al. 2008. 'The detection of a throw.' *British Journal of Sports Medicine* (in press).

Aginsky, K.D., L. Lategan et al. 2004. 'Shoulder injuries in provincial male fast bowlers – predisposing factors.' *Sports Medicine* 16 (1): 25–28.

Akram, Wasim (with Patrick Murphy). 1998. *Akram: The Biography of Wasim Akram.* London: Piatkus.

Alexander, S., D. Underwood and A.J. Cooke. 1998. 'Cricket glove design' in *The Engineering of Sport: Design and Development*, ed. S.J. Haake. Oxford: Blackwell Science.

Alfred, Luke. 2001. *Lifting the Covers: The Inside Story of South African Cricket.* Cape Town: Spearhead.

Allsopp, P.E. 2005. *Measuring Team Performance and Modelling the Home Advantage Effect in Cricket.* PhD dissertation, Swinburne University of Technology, Australia.

Allsopp, P.E. and S.R. Clarke. 2004. 'Rating teams and analysing outcomes in one-day and Test cricket.' *Journal of the Royal Statistical Society*: Series A 167 (4): 657.

Andrew, Keith. 1986. *Coaching Cricket.* Ramsbury: The Crowood Press.

Annear, P.T., T.M. Chakera et al. 1992. 'Pars interarticularis stress and disc degeneration in cricket's potent strike force: the fast bowler.' *Australia New Zealand Journal of Surgery* 62 (10): 768–773.

Arlott, John. 1949. *How to Watch Cricket.* London: Sporting Handbooks Ltd.

Arlott, John (ed). 1972. *Cricket: The Great Captains.* Newton Abbot: The Sportsmans Book Club.

Australian Cricket Board. 2000. *Coaching Youth Cricket.* Human Kinetics.

Bahill, A.T. and T. LaRitz. 1984. 'Why can't batters keep their eyes on the ball?' *American Scientist* 72: 249–253.

Bartlett, R.M., N.P. Stockill et al. 1996. 'The biomechanics of fast bowling in men's cricket: A review.' *Journal of Sports Sciences* 14 (5): 403–424.

Barton, N.G. 1982. 'On the swing of a cricket ball in flight.' *Proceedings of the Royal Society of London: Series A* 379: 109–131.

Baum, Greg. 1996. 'What goes in to not getting out.' *The Good Weekend*, 21 December: 26–33.

Bawden, Mark and Ian Maynard. 2001. 'Towards an understanding of the personal experience of the "yips" in cricket.' *Journal of Sports Sciences* 19 (12): 937–53.

Bell-Jenje, T.C. and J. Gray. 2005. 'Incidence, nature and risk factors in shoulder injuries of national academy cricket players over 5 years – a retrospective study.' *South African Journal of Sports Medicine* 17 (4): 22–28.

Benaud, Richie. 1998. *Anything But … An Autobiography.* London: Hodder & Stoughton.

Botham, Ian (with Peter Hayter). 1995. *My Autobiography – Don't Tell Kath.* London: CollinsWillow.

Bown, W. and R. Mehta. 1993. 'The seamy side of swing bowling.' *New Scientist*: 21–24.

Bradman, Donald. 1958. *The Art of Cricket.* London: Hodder & Stoughton.

Brearley, Mike. 1985. *The Art of Captaincy.* London and Sydney: Hodder & Stoughton.

Broadstock, M. 1991. 'Sun protection at the cricket.' *Medical Journal of Australia* 154 (6): 430.

Brooks, R.D., R.W. Faff and D. Sokulsky. 2002. 'An ordered response model of Test cricket performance.' *Applied Economics* 34 (18).

Burnett, A.F., M.S. Khangure et al. 1996. 'Thoracolumbar disc degeneration in young fast bowlers in cricket: A follow-up study.' *Clinical Biomechanics* 11 (6): 305–310.

Campbell, F.W., S.E. Rothwell et al. 1987. 'Bad lights stops play.' *Ophthalmic & Physiological Optics: The Journal of the British College of Ophthalmic Opticians (Optometrists)* 7 (2): 165–67.

Cardus, Neville. 1929. *The Summer Game*. London: Grant Richards & Humphrey Toulmin.

Carter, M. and G. Guthrie. 2004. 'Cricket interruptus: Fairness and incentive in limited overs cricket matches.' *The Journal of the Operational Research Society* 55: 822–29.

Chappell, Greg. 2004. *Cricket: The Making of Champions*. South Melbourne: Lothian Books.

Cheetham, Jack. 1956. *I Declare*. Cape Town: Howard Timmins.

Christie, C.J., L. Todd and G.A. King. 2003. 'Energy cost of batting during a simulated cricket work bout.' In *Science and Medicine in Cricket*, eds. R.A. Stretch, T.D. Noakes and C.L. Vaughan, Second World Congress of Science and Medicine in Cricket.

Clarke, S.R. and P.E. Allsopp. 2001. 'Fair measures of performance: The World Cup of cricket.' *The Journal of the Operational Research Society* 52 (4): 471–79.

Clarke, S.R. and J.M. Norman. 1999. 'To run or not?: Some dynamic programming models in cricket.' *The Journal of the Operational Research Society* 50 (5): 536–545.

Clarke, S.R. and J.M. Norman. 2003. 'Dynamic programming in cricket: Choosing a night watchman.' *The Journal of the Operational Research Society* 54: 838–45.

Constantine, Learie (with C.L.R. James). 1933. *Cricket and I*. London: Allan.

Constantine, Learie (with Denzil Batchelor). 1966. *The Changing Face of Cricket*. London: Eyre & Spottiswoode.

Cook, Geoff and Neville Scott. 1991. *The Narrow Line: An Anatomy of Professional Cricket*. London: The Kingswood Press.

Cooke, J.C. 1955. 'The boundary layer and "seam" bowling.' *The Mathematical Gazette*: 196–99.

Daish, C.B. 1972. *The Physics of Ball Games*. London: The English Universities Press Ltd.

Davis, K. and B. Blanksby. 1976. 'A cinematographical analysis of fast bowling in cricket.' *Australian Journal for Health, Physical Education and Recreation* 71 (suppl.): 9–15.

Dellor, Ralph. 1990. *How to Coach Cricket*. London: Willow Books.

De Moore, G.M. 1999. 'The suicide of Thomas Wentworth Wills.' *Medical Journal of Australia* 171 (11–12): 656–58.

Dennis, R., P. Farhart et al. 2003. 'Bowling workload and the risk of injury in elite cricket fast bowlers.' *Journal of Science and Medicine in Sport* 6 (3): 359–367.

Dennis, R.J., C.F. Finch et al. 2005. 'Is bowling workload a risk factor for injury to Australian junior cricket fast bowlers?' *British Journal of Sports Medicine* 39 (11): 843–846.

De Silva, B.M. and T.B. Swartz. 1997. 'Winning the coin toss and the home team advantage in one-day international cricket matches.' *The New Zealand Statistician* 32: 16–22.

De Villiers, R.V., M. Pritchard et al. 2005. 'Scapular stress fracture in a professional cricketer and a review of the literature.' *South African Medical Journal* 95 (5): 312–317.

Donald, Allan (with Patrick Murphy). 2000. *White Lightning: The Autobiography*. Johannesburg: Jonathan Ball Publishers in conjunction with CollinsWillow.

Duckworth, F.C. and A.J. Lewis. 2004. 'A successful operational research intervention in one-day cricket.' *The Journal of the Operational Research Society* 55: 749–59.

Elliott, B. 2000. 'Back injuries and the fast bowler in cricket.' *Journal of Sports Sciences* 18 (12): 983–91.

Elliott, B., A. Burnett et al. 1995. 'The fast bowler in cricket: A sports medicine perspective.' *Sports Exercise and Injury* 1: 201–206.

Elliott, B., J.W. Davis et al. 1993. 'Disc degeneration and the young fast bowler in cricket.' *Clinical Biomechanics* 8: 227–234.

Elliot, B., D.H. Foster and S. Gray. 1986. 'Biomechanical and physical factors influencing fast bowling.' *Australian Journal of Science and Medicine in Sport* 18: 16–21.

Elliott, B., P. Hardcastle et al. 1992. 'The influence of fast bowling and physical factors on radiological features in high performance fast bowlers.' *Sports Medicine, Training and Rehabilitation* 3: 113–130.

Elliott, B. and M. Khangure. 2002. 'Disc degeneration and fast bowling in cricket: an intervention study.' *Medicine and Science in Sports and Exercise* 34 (11): 1 714–18.

Fingleton, J.H. 1946. *Cricket Crisis: Body Line and Other Lines*. Melbourne: Cassell & Co. Ltd.

Fletcher, J.G. 1955. 'Calories and cricket.' *Lancet* 268 (6 875): 1 165–66.

Foster, D., D. John et al. 1989. 'Back injuries to fast bowlers in cricket: a prospective study.' *British Journal of Sports Medicine* 23 (3): 150–154.

Francis, Tony. 1992. *The Zen of Cricket: Learning from Positive Thought*. London: Hutchinson.

Frith, David. 1990. *By His Own Hand: A Study of Cricket's Suicides*, republished as *Silence of the Heart: Cricket Suicides* in 2001. Edinburgh: Mainstream Publishers.

Fry, C.B. 1912. *Cricket (Batsmanship)*. London: Everleigh Nash & Co.

Gilfillan, T.C. and N. Nobandla. 2000. 'Modelling the performance of the South African national cricket team.' *South African Journal for Research in Sport, Physical Education and Recreation* 22 (1): 97–110.

Glazier, P.S., G.P. Paradisis et al. 2000. 'Anthropometric and kinematic influences on release speed in men's fast-medium bowling.' *Journal of Sports Sciences* 18 (12): 1 013–21.

Goddard, N. and D. Coull. 1994. 'Colour-blind cricketers and snowballs.' *British Medical Journal* 309 (6 970): 1 684–85.

Gore, C.J., P.C. Bourdon et al. 1993. 'Involuntary dehydration during cricket.' *International Journal of Sports Medicine* 14 (7): 387–95.

Goulet, C., C. Bard et al. 1989. 'Expertise Differences in Preparing to Return a Tennis Serve: A Visual Information Processing Approach.' *Journal of Sport and Exercise Psychology* 11: 382–98.

Gregory, P.L., M.E. Batt et al. 2002. 'Comparing injuries of spin bowling with fast bowling in young cricketers.' *Clinical Journal of Sports Medicine* 12 (2): 107–112.

Gregory, P.L., M.E. Batt et al. 2004. 'Is risk of fast bowling injury in cricketers greatest in those who bowl most? A cohort of young English fast bowlers.' *British Journal of Sports Medicine* 38 (2): 125–28.

Gregory, P.L., M.E. Batt et al. 2004. 'Comparing spondylolysis in cricketers and soccer players.' *British Journal of Sports Medicine* 38 (6): 737–742.

Grimmett, Clarence. 1934. *Tricking the Batsman*. London: Hodder & Stoughton.

Guha, Ramachandra. 1994. *Spin and Other Turns*. New Delhi and London: Penguin.

Hardcastle, P.H. 1993. 'Repair of spondylolysis in young fast bowlers.' *Journal of Bone and Joint Surgery (British Volume)* 75 (3): 398–402.

Hardcastle, P., P. Annear et al. 1992. 'Spinal abnormalities in young fast bowlers.' *Journal of Bone and Joint Surgery (British Volume)* 74 (3): 421–425.

Hoberman, J. 1992. *Mortal Engines: The Science of Performance and the Dehumanization of Sport*. New York: The Free Press.

Holmes, Richard. 2003. *Acts of War: The Behaviour of Men in Battle*. London: Weidenfeld & Nicholson.

Hughes, Simon. 1997. *A Lot of Hard Yakka*. London: Headline.

Hughes, Simon. 2001. *Jargonbusting: The Analyst's Guide to Test Cricket*. London: Channel Four Books/Macmillan.

Humphries, D. and M. Jamison. 2004. 'Clinical and magnetic resonance imaging features of cricket bowler's side strain.' *British Journal of Sports Medicine* 38 (5): E21.

Hurrion, P.D., R. Dyson et al. 2000. 'Simultaneous measurement of back and front foot ground reaction forces during the same delivery stride of the fast-medium bowler.' *Journal of Sports Sciences* 18 (12): 993–97.

James, C.L.R. 1963, 1994. *Beyond A Boundary*. London: Serpent's Tail.

Johnstone, P.G. 2003. '"Sledging" – the practice of psychological distraction in cricket.' In

Science and Medicine in Cricket, eds. R.A. Stretch, T.D. Noakes and C.L. Vaughan, Second World Congress of Science and Medicine in Cricket.

Kantor, Brian. 2007. 'A statistical analysis of the World Cup 2007.' Investec Newsletter 11 May.

Keri, J., et al. 2006. *Baseball Between the Numbers*. New York: Basic Books.

Kimber, A.C. and A.R. Hansford. 1993. 'A statistical analysis of batting in cricket.' *Journal of the Royal Statistical Society Series A: Statistics in Society* 156 (3): 443–55.

Kirk, D., T. Carlson et al. 1997. 'The economic impact on families of children's participation in junior sport.' *Australian Journal of Science and Medicine in Sport* 29 (2): 27–33.

Knott, Alan. 1977. *Wicket-keeping*. London: Stanley Paul.

Lamb, Allan (with Jack Bannister). 1997. *Allan Lamb: My Autobiography*. London: CollinsWillow.

Land, M.F. and P. McLeod. 2000. 'From eye movements to actions: how batsmen hit the ball.' *Nature Neuroscience* 3 (12): 1 340–45.

Lara, Brian (with Brian Scovell). 1994. *Brian Lara: Beating the Field*. London: Partridge Press.

Lewis, Michael. 2003. *Moneyball: The Art of Winning an Unfair Game*. New York: W.W. Norton & Company.

Lewis, Tony. 1994. *MCC Masterclass: The New MCC Coaching Book*. London: Weidenfeld & Nicolson.

Lillee, Dennis. 1982. *The Art of Fast Bowling*. Guilford, Surrey: Lutterworth Press.

Lillee, Dennis (with Bob Harris). 2003. *Lillee: An Autobiography*. Sydney: Hodder.

Lloyd, D.G, J. Alderson and B.C. Elliot. 2000. 'A upper limb kinamatic for the examination of cricket bowling: A case study of Muttiah Muralitharan.' *Journal of Sports Sciences* 18: 975–82.

Lyttleton, R.A. 1957. 'The swing of a cricket ball.' *Cricket Journal*: 186–191.

Marshall, R. and R. Ferdinands. 2003. 'The effect of a flexed elbow on bowling speed in cricket.' *Sports Biomechanics* 2 (1): 65–71.

Martin-Jenkins, Christopher. 1996. *World Cricketers: A Biographical Dictionary*. Oxford: Oxford University Press.

May, Peter. 1956. *Peter May's Book of Cricket*. London: Cassell and Company Ltd.

McLeod, Peter. 1987. 'Visual reaction time and high speed ball games.' *Perception* 16 (1): 49–59.

Mehta, R.D. 1985. 'Aerodynamics of sports balls.' *Annual Review of Fluid Mechanics* 17: 151–189.

Mehta, R.D. and D. Wood. 1980. 'Aerodynamics of the cricket ball.' *New Scientist*: 442–47.

Mehta, R.D, K. Bentley et al. 1983. 'Factors affecting cricket ball swing.' *Nature* 303 (30 June 1983): 787–88.

Milburn, P.D. and G. Nuttridge. 1999. *The Nature, Prevalence and Risk Factors Associated with Pace Bowling Injuries in Men's Cricket*. Wellington: Sports Science New Zealand Technical Report.

Millson, H.B., J. Gray et al. 2004. 'Dissociation between back pain and bone stress reaction as measured by CT scan in young cricket fast bowlers.' *British Journal of Sports Medicine* 38 (5): 586–591.

Noakes, T.D. 2006. 'Laboratory research, commercial interests and advice to the public on fluid ingestion during exercise: The development of a fatal foundation myth.' *Clinical Journal of Sport Medicine* (submitted).

Noakes, T.D. 2003. 'Overconsumption of fluids by athletes.' *British Medical Journal* 327 (7 407): 113–114.

Noakes, T.D. 2003. *Lore of Running* (4th edition). Cape Town: Oxford University Press.

Noakes, T.D., N. Goodwin et al. 2005. 'Water intoxication: a possible complication during endurance exercise.' *Wilderness and Environmental Medicine* 16 (4): 221–27.

Noakes, T.D. and S. Granger. 1995. *Running Your Best*. Cape Town: Oxford University Press.

Noakes, T.D. and A. St Clair Gibson. 2004. 'Logical limitations to the "catastrophe" models of fatigue during exercise in humans.' *British Journal of Sports Medicine* 38 (5): 648–49.

Noakes, T.D., A. St Clair Gibson et al. 2004. 'From catastrophe to complexity: a novel model of integrative central neural regulation of effort and fatigue during exercise in humans.' *British Journal of Sports Medicine* 38 (4): 511–14.

Noakes, T.D., A. St Clair Gibson et al. 2005. 'From catastrophe to complexity: a novel model of integrative central neural regulation of effort and fatigue during exercise in humans: summary and conclusions.' *British Journal of Sports Medicine* 39 (2): 120–24.

Nummela, A.T., K.A. Heath et al. 2008. 'Fatigue during a 5-km running time trial.' *International Journal of Sports Medicine* (in press).

Orchard, J., T. James et al. 2002. 'Injuries in Australian cricket at first-class level 1995/1996 to 2000/2001.' *British Journal of Sports Medicine* 36 (4): 270–74.

Oslear, Don and Jack Bannister. 1996. *Tampering With Cricket*. London: CollinsWillow.

Peebles, Ian. 1969. *Straight From the Shoulder: 'Throwing' – its History and Cure*. Newton Abbot: The Sportsmans Book Club.

Penrose, J.M.T. and N.K. Roach. 1995. 'Decision-making and advanced cue utilisation by cricket batsmen.' *Journal of Human Movement Studies* 29: 199–218.

Philpott, Peter. 1995. *The Art of Wrist-spin Bowling*. Ramsbury: The Crowood Press.

Portus, M.R., B.R. Mason et al. 2003. 'Fast bowling arm actions and the illegal delivery law in men's high performance cricket matches.' In *Science and Medicine in Cricket*, eds. R.A. Stretch, T.D. Noakes and C.L. Vaughan, Second World Congress of Science and Medicine in Cricket.

Portus, M.R., P.J. Sinclair et al. 2000. 'Cricket fast bowling performance and technique and the influence of selected physical factors during an 8-over spell.' *Journal of Sports Sciences* 18 (12) 999–1 011.

Potter, Jack and Ashley Mote. 2001. *The Winning Edge: The Secrets and Techniques of the World's Best Cricketers*. Manchester: The Parrs Wood Press.

Pyke, F.S., G.C. Crouch et al. 1975. *The Testing and Training of an International Fast Bowler – Dennis Lillee*. Western Australia.

Ranawat, V.S., J.K. Dowell et al. 2003. 'Stress fractures of the lumbar pars interarticularis in athletes: a review based on long-term results of 18 professional cricketers.' *Injury* 34 (12): 915–919.

Ranjitsinhji, K.S. 1897. *The Jubilee Book of Cricket*. Edinburgh and London: William Blackwood.

Regan, D. 1992. 'Visual judgements and misjudgements in cricket, and the art of flight.' *Perception* 21 (1): 91–115.

Regan, D. 1997. 'Visual factors in hitting and catching.' *Journal of Sports Sciences* 15 (6): 533–58.

Reilly, T. and D. Chana. 1994. 'Spinal shrinkage in fast bowling.' *Ergonomics* 37 (1): 127–32.

Renshaw, I. and M.M. Fairweather. 2000. 'Cricket bowling deliveries and the discrimination ability of professional and amateur batters.' *Journal of Sports Sciences* 18 (12): 951–57.

Richards, Viv (with Bob Harris). 2000. *Sir Vivian: The Definitive Autobiography*. London: Michael Joseph.

Riley, Pat. 1994. *The Winner Within: A Life Plan for Team Players*. Berkley Trade.

Ripoll, H. and P. Fleurance. 1988. 'What does keeping one's eye on the ball mean?' *Ergonomics* 31 (11): 1 647–54.

Rundell, Michael. 1996. *The Dictionary of Cricket*. Oxford: Oxford University Press.

Sharwood, K.A., M. Collins et al. 2004. 'Weight changes, medical complications, and performance during an Ironman triathlon.' *British Journal of Sports Medicine* 38 (6): 718–724.

Scarf, P. and X. Shi. 2005. 'Modelling match outcomes and decision support for setting a final innings target in test cricket.' *IMA Journal of Management Mathematics* 16 (2): 161–78.

Shillinglaw, A.L. 2003. *Bradman Revisited: The Legacy of Sir Donald Bradman*. Manchester: The Parrs Wood Press.

Simpson, Bob (with Terry Brindle). 1996. *The Reasons Why*. Sydney: HarperSports.
Snow, John (with Kenneth Wheeler). 1968. *The Art of Bowling*. London: Stanley Paul.
Sobers, Garfield (with Ivo Tennant). 1996. *Sobers: The Changing Face of Cricket*. London: Ebury Press.
St Clair Gibson, A., E.V. Lambert et al. 2001. 'Exercise and fatigue-control mechanisms.' *International Journal of Sports Medicine* 2 (3): 1–14.
Stretch, R.A., G. Barnard et al. 2002. 'Improving the accuracy and consistency of shot reproduction in cricket batting through a vision training programme.' *The South African Optometrist* 61 (4): 145–150.
Stretch, R.A. 2003. 'Cricket injuries: a longitudinal study of the nature of injuries to South African cricketers.' *British Journal of Sports Medicine* 37 (3): 250–253.
Stretch, R.A., R. Bartlett et al. 2000. 'A review of batting in men's cricket.' *Journal of Sports Sciences* 18 (12): 931–49.
Stretch, R.A., T. Botha et al. 2003. 'Back injuries in young fast bowlers: A radiological investigation of the healing of spondylolysis and pedicle sclerosis.' *South African Medical Journal* 93 (8): 611–616.
Stretch, R.A., E. du Toit et al. 1998. 'The force absorption characteristics of cricket batting pads at four impact velocities.' *Sports Medicine* (October 1998): 9–13.
Stretch, Richard and Janine Gray. 1998. *Fast Bowling Injury Prevention*. United Cricket Board of South Africa.
Stretch, Richard, Tim Noakes, Mike Proctor and Clive Rice. 1997. *Fast Bowling Injury Prevention Strategy*. United Cricket Board of South Africa.
Stretch, R.A. and J. Tyler. 1995. 'The force absorption characteristics of cricket batting gloves at four impact velocities.' *Sports Medicine* (September 1995): 22–29.
Stretch, R.A., J.V. von Hagen et al. 2000. 'The effect of fencamfamine on the accuracy and consistency of shot reproduction in cricket batting.' *Sports Medicine* (November 2000): 21–25.
Swartz, T.B., P.S. Gill et al. 2006. 'Optimal batting orders in one-day cricket.' *Comparative and Operational Research* 33: 1939–50.
Synge, Allen and Derek Anns. 1987. *Masterstrokes*. London: The Kingswood Press.
Tainton, Neil and John Klug. 2002. *The Cricket Pitch and its Outfield*. Pietermaritzburg: University of Natal Press.
Tucker, R., L. Rauch et al. 2004. 'Impaired exercise performance in the heat is associated with an anticipatory reduction in skeletal muscle recruitment.' *Pflugers Archive* 448 (4): 422–430.
Turner, Matthew. 2002. *The Motion of Balls in Sports*. Dept of Mathematics, University of East Anglia.
Tyson, Frank. 1977. *Complete Cricket Coaching*. London: Pelham Books Ltd.
Wallis, R., B. Elliott et al. 2002. 'The effect of a fast bowling harness in cricket: An intervention study.' *Journal of Sports Sciences* 20 (6): 495–506.
Warne, Shane (with Mark Ray). 1997. *My Own Story*. London: Bookman Projects Ltd.
Waugh, Steve. 1995. *Steve Waugh's West Indies Tour Diary*. Sydney: HarperSports.
Webster, F.A.M. 1948. *The Science of Athletics*. London: Nicholas Kaye.
Wilde, Simon. 1994. *Letting Rip: The Fast-bowling Threat from Lillee to Waqar*. London: H.F. & G. Witherby.
Williams, Charles. 1997. *Bradman: An Australian Hero*. London: Abacus.
Woolmer, Bob. 1984. *Bob Woolmer: Pirate and Rebel? An Autobiography*. London: Arthur Barker Ltd.
Woolmer, Bob. 1993. *Skilful Cricket*. London: A & C Black.
Woolmer, Bob (with Ivo Tennant). 2000. *Woolmer on Cricket*. London: Virgin Publishing Ltd.

INDEX

The page references in *italics* indicate illustrations. Entries are listed in letter-by-letter alphabetical order.

Adams, Paul 33–34, 219, 288, 309, 595
administration 485–90
adrenaline 72
aerodynamics of spin 301–7, *302–4*, *306*
aerodynamics of swing 270–71, *271*
  boundary layer 273–75, *274*, *275*
  development of turbulence 272–73, *273*
  different velocities 271–72
  eddying currents 273
  friction 269–70, *270*, 273
  reverse swing 283–84, *284*
  Reynolds' number 275–77, *277*
  See also ball swing, factors affecting
Akhtar, Shoaib 214, 218, 223, 576, 578
Akram, Wasim 45, 70–71, 118, 211, 217, 249, 259, 282, 283, 473
Akram, Huma 45
alcohol 582–90
Alderman, Terry 245
all-rounders 88–89, 438
Ambrose, Curtly 186, 440
Amla, Hashim 31, 589
Anwar, Saeed 410
apartheid 17, 445
Arlott, John 444–45
Art of Cricket, The 172, 175–77, 496
Asif, Mohammed 576, 578
Atherton, Michael 262, 398, 473, 475, 481
autogenic phrase training 43

Bacher, Ali 400
back-foot drive 148–49
  common problems 150
  playing the shot 149, *149*
  practising the shot 150
  when to play it 149

back glance *See* backward defensive and back glance
backswing *See* bat-lift and backswing
backward defensive and back glance 129–30
  common problems 134
  playing the shot 131–33, *131–32*
  practising the shot *133*, 133–34
  when to play it 130
ball strikes 63, 598–600
ball swing, factors affecting 277
  angle of seam 281
  height of the seam 278–80, *278*, *279*
  make of ball 282–83
  speed of delivery 280
  weather 281–82
  wind speed 280
  wobble 281
ball tampering 255, 261–62
baseball 222–23, 372, 446–47, 576–77
basics of batting 93
  judging length 95–96
  keeping the head still 94–5
  moving into position 96
  shot selection 97, 98
  watching the ball 94
bat-lift and backswing 119–22, *122*, 176–77, 182
  Donald Bradman 120, 176–177
batting
  danger points 64–6, 376–77
  hand position 96–102
  left-handed 410
  predicting flight of the ball 185–95, 320
  principles of 92

  psychology of *See* psychology of batting; mental strategies for batting
  science of 93
  straight and across the line 143, *143*
  timing the ball 97–102
  visualization 60, 375–76
  with or against spin 161
  See also basics of batting; batting shots; batting techniques; strategy of batting
batting for beginners 521
  introduction of technique 521–22
  length 522
batting in limited-overs cricket 386
  Asia 387–89
  Australia, S. Africa and W. Indies 389–90
  innovation at the crease 386–87
  overs 1 to 15 387–90
  overs 16 to 40 390–93
  overs 41 to 50 394–95
  pinch-hitters 397
  playing spinners 392–93
  posting and chasing scores 395–97
  U.K. and New Zealand 390
batting order 459–60
batting performance and team success 447–48, 450
  one-day cricket 448–50, *448–50*
batting shots 123, 170–71
  See also back-foot drive; cross-bat shots; front-foot drives; hook, the; pull, the; straight bat shots; sweep shots
batting techniques
  See grip, the; stance; stance, adapting to

bowling; taking guard; 'trigger' movements
beamer 243–44
Benaud, Richie 287, 309, 314, 317, 319, 465, 531
Bevan, Michael 89, 309
Bland, Colin 322, 328
'Bodyline' tour 599
body/mind debate 28
boots *See* equipment
Border, Allan 26, 285, 410, 423, 443
Bosanquet, B.J.T. 311–12
Botha, Johan 229
Botham, Ian 23, 47, 66, 81, 92, 259, 261, 533, 583
bottom hand (batting) 97–102
Boucher, Mark 345, 352
Bouncer Wars era 15, 129, 242
bowling 204
  attributes of bowlers 246–50, 287, 288–89
  history 205–7
  machines 492–93
  misleading the batsman 185–86
  taking aim 245
  See also bowling, basic action of; bowling line and length; bowling rhythm and accuracy; medium and fast bowling; slow bowling; strategy of bowling
bowling and fielding, psychology of *See* psychology of bowling and fielding
bowling, basic action of *208*, 208–9
bowling off the wrong foot 212–13, *213*
dangers of mixed action 211–12
delivery 210, *210*
follow-through 210, *210*

INDEX **649**

run-up, jump, gather 209, *209*
set-up 209, *209*
side-on versus front-on 210–11
unfold 209, *209*
See also run-up
bowling for beginners 514–15
   action 516–17
   injury prevention 517
   length 518
bowling in limited-overs cricket 414–15
   adapting to conditions 415
   changing pace 416
   manipulating fine leg 416
   new ball 415–16
   reacting to the batsman 416–17
   slow bowling 417
bowling length 241, *241*, 320–21
   beamer 243–44
   bouncer 242
   full toss 243
   good length 243
   half-volley 243
   long hop 242
   practising 321
   short of length 242
   yorker 243
bowling line and length 240–41, *241*, 244–45, *244*, *255* *See also* bowling length
bowling machines 492–97
bowling off the wrong foot 212–13, *213*
bowling performance and team success 450, *450*
bowling rhythm and accuracy 237–38
   practising for accuracy 239
   which comes first? 238–39
Boycott, Geoffrey 47, 128
Bradman, Sir Donald 31, 77, 90, *115*, 120, 172–83, 187, 316
Brearley, Mike 47, 48, 162, 425, 426–27

breathing techniques 38–9
building an innings 380–81
   batters 4 to 6 383–84
   dominating the bowling 385
   the top three 381–83
burnout 41

captaincy 421
   Mike Brearley on 426–27
   qualities of the captain 421–24
   role identification 424–25
   selectors and the captain 435–36
   See also selection; setting a field; strategy and captaincy
Carter and Guthrie model 456–58, *457*
catching 333–34
   attributes of catchers 333
   calling for 336
   cup position *335*, 335–36
   high catches 334–36, *335*
   soft hands 334
   See also slip catching
Chanderpaul, Shivnarine 103
Chappell, Greg 190, 191
Chappell, Ian 33, 119
check drive *See* on drive, check drive
Cheetham, Jack 443–45
children
   back foot play 130
   batting 394
   bowling 251, 320–21, 610–11
   choosing a bat 101, 512
   fitness 538
   preventing injuries 610–11
   training 175, 182–83
   See also coaching younger players
choking 482–83
'choking' the bat 108, 111
chucking *See* throwing (bowling)
circle of concentration, the 73–74, *74*
Close, Brian 26

coaching 464–67
   and administration 485–90
   attributes of a coach 467–69
   and captaincy 485–86
   choking 482–83
   complacency 482
   Donald Bradman 172–83
   dropping players 489–90
   Ideal Performance State 484
   managing the squad 488–90
   the science of 476–78
   team ethics 483–84
   See also coach, roles of; coaching philosophies; coaching, practical; coaching younger players
coaching philosophies 478–80
   cycle of success 482–84
   six s's to success 480–81
coaching, practical
   bowling machines 492–97
   coach's toolbox 491–92
   communication 496–97
   curriculum 501–2
   mass coaching 508
   video analysis 493–96
   See also nets and middle practices
coaching younger players 510, 468, 488–89, 496–97
   age 511–13
   Discovery Learning model 510–11
   fielding 522–23
   teaching basics to beginners 513–14
   See also batting for beginners; bowling for beginners
coach, roles of 469
   communicator 470, 496–97
   diplomat 471
   disciplinarian 475–76
   guidance counsellor 470
   historian 471–72
   manager 469–70

motivator 474
paramedic 473
publicity and media 474–75
scientist 473
social worker 472
summary 477
colonialism 13, 16, 443–44
colour blindness 202
coming down the wicket 144
   common problems 146
   playing the shot 145, *145*
Constantine, Learie 94, 290, 331, 398
cover drive 137, *137*
Cowdrey, Colin 39, 46, 118, 129, 381, 385
'cradle' formation 150, *150*
cramping 574–75, *575*
criticism 35–37, 47–48, 76 *See also* mental toughness
Cronje, Hansie 165, 262, 327, 419, 443
cross-bat shots
   See cutting; hook, the; pull, the; sweep shots
crowd *See* spectators
Cullinan, Daryll 36, 52, 62, 66, 437, 474–75, 489–90
cutters (off- and leg) 263–64
   action 264–65, *265*
   grip 264, *264*
cutting (batting) 150
   common problems with *154*, 154–55
   square cut off the front foot 152
   See also late cut; square cut off the back foot

declaration, timing 456
deep relaxation 39–41
   progressive relaxation technique 40
defensive sweep 164–65, *164–65*
development 17, 468, 472, 633–36
De Villiers, Fanie 78
discipline 475–76
D'Oliveira, Basil 376

Donald, Allan 37, 43, 53–54, 62, 218, 248, 249, 375, 403, 435–36
doosra 315
Drakes, Vasbert 217
Dravid, Rahul 22, 346, 380
drives See back-foot drive; front-foot drives
Duckworth/Lewis method 19, 456, 458, *458*
Dujon, Jeff 344, 348
Duke ball 283, 390
drugs See medications and drugs

Edwardian and Victorian periods 13
emotional fatigue 77
endurance (aerobic) and sprint (anaerobic) fitness 554–55
equipment 15, 53–54, 266–68, 362–66, 600, 633
ethics 483–84
exercise physiology 536
 cardiovascular/ anaerobic/catastrophic model 536–39
 energy supply/energy depletion model 539–41, *540*
 integrated muscle recruitment (central governor) model 541–43, 546–47
 role of eccentric muscle contractions in fatigue 544–45
exercise training principles 548
 evaluation 553
 individualism 551–52
 progressive overload 548
 quantity and quality 550
 regularity 551
 specificity 548
 variety 551
 warm-up and cool-down (stretching) 552, 553–54
 See also training programmes
extra-cover defensive shot 127

failure
 fear of 46–48
 Steve Waugh's five lessons of 49–51
 See also loss of form
fans 16, 37, 52, 79
 See also spectators
'groupies' 81
fast bowling
 attributes of bowlers 246–50
 biology of 603–7, *605*, *606*
 the deliveries 251–52
 fitness 527–29, *529*
 kit 266–68
 practising 266
 run-up 217–19
 See also injuries, intrinsic, fast bowlers; seam bowling; swing bowling
fear
 of failure 46–48
 of loss of form 55–56
 of physical injury 53–55
 of success 48, 52–53
fielding 322–24
 attributes of fielders 324
 coaching younger players 522–23
 injuries 630–31
 practice 341–43
 supporting the bowler 332
 throwing 331–33
 See also catching; fielding drills; ground fielding; psychology of bowling and fielding; strategy of fielding
fielding drills 503
 Donald Bradman 174–75
 'round the clock' throwing drill *505*, 505–6
 run-out drills 506–8, *507*
 six-point throwing drill *503*, 503–4
finger-spin 293
 action 295–300, *296*, *297*, *298*, *300*
 grip *294*, 294–95

high arm vs. round arm action 299–300, *300*
 'vertical discus' vs. 'javelin' action *298*, 298–99
fitness 526–36
 children 538
 endurance (aerobic) and sprint (anaerobic) fitness 554–55
 fast bowlers 527–29
 See also exercise physiology; exercise training principles; physiology of fitness; training programmes
flight of the ball 199–201, 291, 319–20
Flintoff, Andy 583
flipper ball 96, 314
fluid intake 564, 570–73
 See also nutrition and fluid intake
focus (for bowlers) 73–74
follow-through
 batting 99–100
 bowling 210, *210*
form, loss of 55–56
forward defensive 124–25, *125*, *126*
 common problems 127–28
 Geoffrey Boycott on 128
 playing the shot 126–27
 practising the shot 127
 when to play it 125–27
Fraser, Angus 262
front-foot drives
 cover drive 137, *137*
 off drive, straight drive 135–37, *135–36*
 the pick-up 148, *148*
 summing up 144
 when to play them 134
 See also coming down the wicket; front foot glance; on drive
front foot glance 147
 playing the shot *147*, 147–48
 when to play it 147
full toss 243

Garner, Joel (Big Bird) 117
Gatting, Michael 26, 31, 160, 305–7
Gibbs, Herschelle 333, 383
Gilchrist, Adam 345, 348, 391, 407, 408, 438
good length bowling 243
good-luck charms 50–51
googly 311–12
 grip and action *312*, 312–13
Grace, W.G. 181, 476, 527
Grimmett, Clarrie 266, 309, 319–21, 413
grip, the (batting) 107
 Alan Knott on 109, *109*
 hingeing 110, *110*
 'O' grip 108, *108*
 orthodox ('V') grip 108, *108*
 Ranjitsinhji 107
 Donald Bradman 175–76
ground fielding 324
 anticipation 330–31
 attacking 325–27, *325*, *326*
 chasing and throwing on the turn 327
 defensive 324–25, *325*
 sliding *328*, 328–29
 trigger movements and stance *326*, 326–27
 what to watch 329–30
 with feet 327
guard See taking guard

Hadlee, Richard 218, 237–38, 249, 250, 266
Hair, Darrell 24, 261, 639
half-volley 243
hand-eye co-ordination See visual-motor system
hand position (batting) 96–102
hard hands 127–28
 See also soft hands
Harmison, Steve 437
Harvey, Ian 403
Hawkeye system 638
Hayden, Matthew 102, 161, 383, 397, 408
Healy, Ian 43, 318, 344, 348, 356

helmets *See* protective
    equipment
Hick, Graeme 441
hingeing 110, 110–11
history 14–15
    bowling 205–7
    coaches and 471–72
    Laws of cricket 14–15,
        206–7, 207
    Victorian and Edwardian
        periods 13
    See also apartheid;
        colonialism; innovation
        and tradition
Hobbs, Sir Jack 316
Hobson, Denys 312
Hogg, Brad 309
Holding, Michael 23, 26,
    214, 248, 423
home advantage 77, 79–80,
    453–54
hook, the 155–56
    common problems 157
    playing the shot 156, 156
    practising the shot 156
    and the pull 155
    and Steve Waugh 158
    and Viv Richards 158
    when to play it 158
    See also pull, the
Hooper, Carl 392
Hughes, Simon 44, 48,
    70, 560
Hutton, Sir Leonard 532

Ideal Performance State
    (IPS) 91, 375, 484
injuries 595
    fear of 53–55
    prevention, young
        bowlers 517
    protective equipment 15,
        53–54, 362–66, 600, 633
injuries, extrinsic 595–96
    ball strikes 598–600
    prevention 600–1
    treatment 596–98
injuries, intrinsic 602
    batters 602
    fielders 630–31
    slow bowlers 629–30
injuries, intrinsic, fast
    bowlers 603, 629–30

back injuries (Dennis
    Lillee) 607–10
biology 603–7, 605, 606
bowler's logbook
    615–17, 616
bowling technique 625–29
bowling workload 618–19
factors affecting low back
    injuries 612–15
management of low back
    pain 620, 620–21
pathology of back pain
    621–25, 622
prevention of low
    back injuries 610–19,
    612, 615–17
innovation and tradition
    632–33
inswinger
    grip 258, 258
    action 258–59, 259
Inzamam-ul-Haq 27,
    62, 323
IPS *See* Ideal Performance
    State

Jayasuriya, Sanath 65, 448
James, C.L.R. 13, 437
Jennings, Ray 347, 488
Jones, Dean 26, 31

Khan, Imran 45, 249, 250,
    259, 262, 283
Kallis, Jacques 63, 125, 126,
    380, 441, 488, 512
Kaluwitharana, Romesh 348
Kirsten, Gary 34, 36, 52,
    55–56, 63, 66, 148, 490,
    494–96
Kirsten, Peter 151, 187
Klusener, Lance 102, 268
Knight, Nick 100–1
Knott, Alan 109, 164, 344,
    347, 349, 349–51, 351,
    353–61, 355, 379, 560
Kookaburra ball 283, 390
Kumble, Anil 50, 312

Laker, Jim 300, 300
Lamb, Allan 53, 80–81, 259
Lamb, Lindsey 80–81
Lara, Brian 52, 75, 77, 90,
    181, 189, 398, 405, 410

late cut 153
    playing the shot 153, 153
    practising the shot 154
    when to play it 153
Laws of cricket
    bowling, history 206–7
    history 14–15
    innovation 632–33
    throwing 224–26
Lee, Brett 223, 245, 584
left-handed batsmen 106,
    118, 410
leg glance *See* front
    foot glance
leg-spin
    action 310–11, 311
    batsman's stance 117
    doosra 315
    flipper 96, 314
    grip 310, 310
    Shane Warne 117
    See also googly
length, judging 95–96
    See also bowling length
light 198
Lillee, Dennis 15, 32–33,
    151, 219, 238, 250, 465,
    534, 607–10
limited-overs cricket 322–23,
    456–58 *See also* batting
        in limited-overs cricket;
        bowling in limited-
        overs cricket
Lloyd, Clive 323, 328
long hop 242
loss of form,
    fear of 55–56

Magnus effect *See*
    aerodynamics of spin
Malcolm, Devon 48
Malinga, Lasith 72
Marshall, Malcolm 26,
    211, 350
Marsh, Rodney 66, 583
Massie, Bob 73, 256
mathematics
    tactics 371–73
    See also statistics
May, Peter 97
McGrath, Glenn 91,
    240–41, 241, 245, 249,
    350, 398, 403, 405

media, the 55, 56, 461,
    474–75, 483
medications and drugs
    576–79
    alcohol 582–90
    diet pills 581
    medicinal drugs 579
    nutritional supplements
        580–82
    recreational drugs 577
    steroids 576–78
    sun protection 592–94
    tobacco 590–92
medium and fast bowling
    246–47 *See also* fast
        bowling
mental fatigue 41
mental skills 29
mental strategies for batting
    building an innings 62–64
    danger points 64–66,
        376–77
    preparing for an innings
        57–60
    sledging 66–69
    waiting to bat 60–62
    Wasim Akram 45, 70–71
mental techniques,
    basic 37
    breathing techniques
        38–39
    deep relaxation 39–41
    visualization 41–44
mental toughness 32
    Australia 34–35
    batters and bowlers 33
    criticism 35–37
    Allan Donald 37
    Daryll Cullinan 36
    Dennis Lillee 32–33
    Gary Kirsten 36
    Graeme Smith 36
    Sandy Gordon 34–35
    Shane Warne 37
    Steve Waugh 35, 37
    See also mental techniques,
        basic; mental strategies
        for batting
Miller, Keith 27, 85
mind/body debate 28
Mitchley, Cyril 23
moving into position
    (batting) 96

Muralitharan, Muttiah 165, 288, *298*, 315, 412
   throwing 223, 228, 234–37, *235*, *236*
Mushtaq, Saqlain 300, 315, 392

nets and middle practices 497–98
   a cricket curriculum 501–2, *502*
   the practice session 498–500
   throw-downs 500
   See also fielding drills
Neuro-Linguistic Programming 37
   breathing techniques 38–39
   deep relaxation 39–41
   visualization 41–44
new ball 415–16
Ngam, Mfuneko 16–17, 254
night watchman 460
Noakes, Tim 172, 187, 191, 473
Ntini, Makhaya 82, 118, 350
nutritional supplements 580–82
nutrition and fluid intake 560
   balanced diet *562*, 562–66
   before, during and after a match 568–73
   cramping 574–75, *575*
   fluids 564, 570–73
   food as fuel 566–68
   glycaemic index (GI) 568
   junk food 565
   organic foods 564, 566
   salt 566, 572–73
   sports drinks 573

off drive, straight drive 135–37, *135–36*
on drive, check drive *138*, 138–39
   common problems 142, *142*
   practising 140–41, *140–41*
one-day cricket *See* limited-overs cricket
O'Reilly, Bill 173, 398

orthodox sweep 162–64, *163*
outfield preparation 20–24, *22*
outswinger 104, 257–58
   action *257*, 257–58
   grip 257, *257*
over-confidence 64–65

pad play 129
peer influence 319
performance state *See* Ideal Performance State
Philpott, Peter 73–74, 238, 313, 319
physical training *See* exercise training principles
physiology 184 *See also* exercise physiology; vision
physiology of fitness 531
   energy expenditure 531–34
   See also exercise physiology
physiotherapists, role of 602
pick-up, the (batting) 148, *148*
Pietersen, Kevin 123, 333
pitch, the
   and outfield preparation 20–24, *22*
   reading 377
   and shot selection 98
pinch hitters 397
politics *See* socio-political context
Pollock, Graeme 36, 47, 79, 181, 380, 410
Pollock, Shaun 249, 350, 403, 435–36
Ponting, Ricky 418, 584
power and strength training 555–59, *557–59*
pre-delivery movements *See* 'trigger' movements
predicting flight of the ball 185–88
   clues from the bowler 189
   flight of the ball 199–201
   latency time (LT) 190
   light 198
   movement time (MT) 190
   reaction time 195–97

saccade heresy 192–93, *193*
   viewing time (VT) 190–91
press *See* media, the
pressure 51, 65
Proctor, Mike 212–13, 214
production line of players 633–34
progressive relaxation technique 40
progressive training 140–41
protective equipment 15, 53–54, 362–66, 600, 633
psyching up (for bowling) 71–72
psychology 27–32
   mental and psychosocial skills 29
   See also mental techniques, basic; mental toughness
psychology of batting 44–46
   fear 46–48, 52–56
   See also mental strategies for batting
psychology of bowling and fielding 45, 69–71
   focus 73–74
   getting psyched 71–72
   staying in the game 74–75
psychosocial skills 29, 76
   emotional fatigue 77
   home advantage 77, 79–80
   sex 80–82
   touring 77, 78
psychotherapy 82, 84
pull, the 158
   common problems 160
   and the hook 155
   playing the shot 159, *159*
   practising the shot 159, *159*
   when to play it 158
push drive *See* on drive, check drive

qualities of a cricketer 88–89

race 30–32
   ball-tampering 261
   fast bowling 246
   selection 36, 436, 437
   sledging 69

rain-interrupted games
   Carter and Guthrie model 456–58, *457*
   Duckworth/Lewis method 19, 456, 458, *458*
Ramadhin, Sonny 315
Ramprakash, Mark 441
Ranatunga, Arjuna 448, 527
Ranjitsinhji 15, 107
Reader ball 283, 390
'ready' position 119–22, *122*
recreational drugs 577
Reeve, Dermott 166–67, 422
relaxation *see* deep relaxation
religion 30–31, 589
reverse hit 169–70
reverse sweep 166–69, *168*
reverse swing 259–60
   action 260
   aerodynamics 283–84, *284*
   ball-tampering 261–62
   grip 260
Rhodes, Jonty 62, 66, 85, 89, 160, 168–70, 323, 326, 328, 330, 414, 418, 473
Rhodes, Wilfred 150, 291, 414
rhythm movements *See* 'trigger' movements
Richards, Barry 400
Richardson, Dave 33–34, 344, 345, 348
Richards, Sir Vivian 51, 54, 61, 65, 66, 97, 102, 181, 316
Roberts, Andy 402
'rock star' syndrome 29
rules *See* Laws of cricket
running between the wickets 377–78
run-up 209, *209*, 214–16, *216*
   adapting to conditions 221–22
   fast bowlers 217–19
   rhythm and speed 220–21
   Shane Warne 215, 219
   spinners 219–20
   working out your ideal 216–17
   See also throwing
Russell, Jack 346, 356
Rutherford, Ken 409

saccade heresy 192–93, *193*
Schwarz, Reg 311–12
science 473, 637
   and art 466–67
   of batting 93
   of coaching 476–78
   and statistics 461–63
   and umpiring 636–41
   See also aerodynamics
     of spin; aerodynamics
     of swing
seam *See* ball swing,
   factors affecting
seam bowling
   action 253
   conditions 253
   grip 252, *252*
   troubleshooting 254
selection 435–36
   communication 441–42
   dropping players 441–42
   home and touring 439
   the ideal Test side 438
   talent 440–41
   understanding
     the goal 437
   youth and experience
     439–40
Selvey, Mike 402
setting a field 428–29
   classic settings 431–33,
     431–33
   three-ring form 429–31,
     430–31
   See also strategy of fielding
sexual behaviour 80–82
   Allan Lamb 80–81
   Ian Botham 81
   Shane Warne 81
Shillinglaw, Tony 120,
   172–83
shot selection 97
   and the pitch 98
Simpson, Bobby 59,
   319, 323, 330–31,
   337, 474, 538
Singh, Harbhajan
   226, 412
sledging 66–69, 423
   racist 69
sleep and visualization 62
sliding (fielding) *328*,
   328–329

slip catching 337
   how and where to stand
     337, 337–38
   practising 340
   taking the catch 339–40,
     339, 340
slog sweep 165–66, *166*
slow bowling 285–86 *See*
   also spin bowling
Small, Gladstone 70
Smith, Graeme, mental
   toughness 36
smoking 590–92
Sobers, Sir Garfield 23, 181,
   187, 214, 316, 385
socio-political context
   16–18, 30–32, 443–44,
   471, 472, 487, 633
   See also apartheid;
     colonialism;
     development; race
soft hands (batting) 111
soft hands (catching) 334
spectators 16, 37, 79, 594
   See also fans
spin bowling 285–86
   attributes of bowler
     287, 289
   basic principles 288–89
   deceiving the batsman
     290–92
   the deliveries *292*, 292–93
   failure to produce
     spinners 519–20
   flight 291
   left-arm spinners 309
   run-up 219–20
   See also aerodynamics
     of spin; finger-spin;
     wrist-spin
springing the trap (bowling)
   399–401
   bowling in sets 401–2
   changing line or angle
     404–5
   changing pace 403–4
   emergency situations
     408–9
   using close fielders 406–7
square cut off the back foot
   playing the shot
     152, *152*
   when to play it 151

square cut off the front
   foot 152
stance (batting) 111–12
   closed 115, *115*
   Donald Bradman 175–176
   feet close together
     115, *115*
   open 114, *114*
   orthodox (sideways)
     112, *112*
   standing tall, high backlift
     116, *116*
   wide stance 113, *113*
stance (batting), adapting
   to bowling 116
   fast and tall 117
   left-handed batsmen 118
   leg-spin 117
   southpaw 118
stance (wicket-keeping)
   347, 347–49
'Star Wars' field 317–18, 429
statistics 446–47
   advantages 450–51
   beyond the win/loss ratio
     451–55, *452, 453*
   Carter and Guthrie model
     456–58, *457*
   debunking prevailing
     wisdom 461–62
   Duckworth/Lewis
     method 456, 458, *458*
   home advantage and
     winning the toss 451
   modelling performance
     of a team 455
   optimum batting order
     459–60
   rain-interrupted one-day
     games 456–58
   and science 461–63
   timing of declaration 456
   using a night
     watchman 460
   See also batting
     performance
     and team success
steroids 576–78
straight bat shots 124
   See also backward
     defensive and back
     glance; forward
     defensive

straight drive 135–37,
   135–36
strategy and captaincy
   370–71
   mathematics of tactics
     371–73
   See also captaincy; strategy
     of batting; strategy of
     bowling
strategy of batting 374–75
   danger points 376–77
   IPS and visualization
     375–76
   multi-day cricket 378–80
   the non-striker 379
   reading the pitch 377
   running between the
     wickets 377–78
   See also batting in limited-
     overs cricket; building
     an innings
strategy of bowling 397–98
   working batsmen out
     398–99
   See also bowling in
     limited-overs cricket;
     springing the trap;
     tactics for slow bowlers
strategy of fielding 418
   close-catching ring 418
   inner ring 418–19
   outfield (outer ring)
     419–20
   See also setting a field
Stratham, Brian 245
stumpings 356, *356*
Styris, Scott 449
subconscious abilities 185
substance abuse 84
suicide 83
sun protection 592–94
superstitions 50–51
sweep shots 160–62
   defensive sweep
     164–65, *164–65*
   Jonty Rhodes 160,
     168–69, 170
   orthodox sweep
     162–64, *163*
   reverse hit 169–70
   reverse sweep
     166–69, *168*
   slog sweep 165–66, *166*

swing bowling 255–56
  Dennis Lillee 256, 281
  inswinger 258–59, *258–59*
  outswinger 104, *257*, 257–58
  reverse swing 259–62
  troubleshooting 263
  and weather 281–82
  and wind 280
  See also aerodynamics of swing; ball swing, factors affecting
Symcox, Pat 25, 37, 83, 255
Symonds, Andrew 584

tactics *See* mathematics of tactics; strategy and captaincy
tactics for slow bowlers 409–11
  bowling to your field 414
  changing pace 411
  ideal angle for finger-spinners 412–13
  left-arm spinners 413–14
  to left-handed batsmen 410
  watching the batsman 411–12
taking guard 102–3
  Shivnarine Chanderpaul 103
  leg stump *103*, 103–4
  middle and leg (two legs) *105*, 105
  middle or centre *105*, 105–6
taking the ball (wicket-keeping) 352
  spinning or medium-pace ball 353–54

Tanvir, Sohail 213
Tayfield, Hugh 444
Taylor, Mark 317, 323
teams
  development 633–36
  ethics 483–84
  production line 633–34
Tendulkar, Sachin 27, 437
tension, physical *see* deep relaxation
Thomson, Jeff 183, 248
throwing (bowling) 222–24
  the great chucking debate 224–37, *226–29*, *231*, *235*, *236*
  Muttiah Muralitharan 223, 228, 234–37, *235*, *236*
throwing (fielding) 331–33, 630
timing the ball (batting) 97–102
tobacco 590–92
toss, winning the 451, 462
touring, psychosocial skills 77, 78
  Steve Waugh 78
tradition and innovation 632–33
training *See* exercise training
training programmes 553–54
  endurance (aerobic) and sprint (anaerobic) fitness 554–55
  power and strength 555–59, *557–59*
  See also exercise training principles
Trescothick, Marcus 245

'trigger' movements 95, 118–19
  bat-lift and backswing 119–20
  rhythm and 120–22, *122*
Trueman, Fred 248

umpiring 14, 24
  Darrell Hair 261, 639
  LBW 640–41
  and technology 636–42
  See also throwing
unweighting *See* bat-lift

Victorian and Edwardian periods 13
video analysis 493–96
Viljoen, Ken 444
vision 184
  colour-blindness 202
  flight of the ball 199–201
  light 198
  See also predicting flight of the ball
visualization 41–44
  autogenic phrase training 43
  Basil D'Oliveira 376
  for batters 60, 375–76
  Viv Richards 62
  the Woolmer way 60
visual-motor system 185–86

Walker, Max 213, *213*
Walsh, Courtney 253, 440
Warne, Shane 37, 51, 66, 68, 81, 96, 117, 215, 219, 285, 288, 305–7, *306*, 309, 315–18, *317*, 332, 385, 399, 474–75, 527, 576, 581

Waugh, Mark 314, 323
Waugh, Steve 35, 37, 49–51, 66, 78, 123, 423, 474, 476, 556, 569, 574, 595
weather 18–19, 592–94
  and ball swing 280–82
  See also rain-interrupted games
Wessels, Kepler 54, 123, 583
wicket-keeping 344–46
  attributes of wicket-keeper 367
  catching 356–59
  diving and rolling 358, *358*, 407
  fitness 362
  kit 362–66
  practising 359–61
  stance *347*, 347–49
  standing back 349–50
  standing up 350–51
  stumpings 356, *356*
  tight lines 354
  wicket-keeper-batsmen 348
  See also taking the ball (wicket-keeping)
Willis, Bob 248, 332, 528
win/loss ratio 451–55, *452*, *453*
Wisden, John *Almanack* 13
women 468
Worrell, Frank 437
wrist-spin 308–21
  See also leg-spin

'yips', the 72
yorker 243
Younis, Waqar 71, 260, 282

Zondeki, Monde 436

ACKNOWLEDGEMENTS

In the case of a project that has lasted twelve years, and has drawn on the life experience of not one, but two men, it is inevitable that many need to be thanked – and equally inevitable that some names might inadvertently be omitted. In circumstances like these, where the principal author was tragically lost so close to finishing his book, the surviving authors were left more reliant than ever on the support of others, while unable to thank everyone who helped Bob prepare this manuscript.

Please therefore excuse the incompleteness of this list of those who helped with comments, suggestions and material for this book. Nevertheless, our thanks go to the following: for being so generous with their ideas and experience, Alan Knott, John Snow, Michael Fordham, Dan Keisel, Richard Stretch, Janine Gray and Justin Durandt; for help with the chapter on mental skills, Sandy Gordon, Steve Bell and especially Huma and Wasim Akram and Clinton Gahweiler – Huma for explaining how she uses Neuro-Linguistic Programming and hypnosis (and Wasim for granting an interview on how he used these tools), and Clinton for reading an early draft of this chapter and providing insightful comments. Any shortcomings in the material are the authors' responsibility, not theirs.

We are indebted to Jacques Kallis, Allan Donald and Jonty Rhodes for doing what they do so brilliantly in front of the camera to illustrate the finer points of batting, bowling and fielding, and to Carl Fourie for taking these photos. We would also like to thank Kamran Akmal, who posed for the wicket-keeping photographs, taken by Bob. Gary Kirsten kindly provided a vital interview that enabled us to finalize the coaching chapter. We are especially grateful to Paul Hurrion and all at Quintic, who not only provided critical images, but went the third mile to help us after their first batch of materials disappeared from the mail. In the final scramble to find outstanding illustrations, Marc Portus, Kerith Aginsky, Paul Muzzell, André Odendaal and Russell Adams were all most helpful. Megan Lofthouse provided invaluable typing support throughout.

This book has a long and convoluted publishing history, and we would like to thank Jeremy Boraine, then at New Africa Books, who first persuaded the authors to publish in South Africa, and Brian Wafawarowa for taking on the challenge. We are grateful to Pete Bosman for his beautiful initial designs for the book, and particularly to Clive During, who managed the project with great dedication for two years – Bob especially enjoyed working with him.

Words cannot express our gratitude to the team at Struik Publishers, and space does not allow us to list everyone there who had a hand in the book. Mention must be made, however, of Brian Wootton, who provided guidance at a critical stage, Steve Connolly, for believing so passionately in this book, and Linda de Villiers, whose calm maternal presence and professionalism made everything run smoothly. We were blessed with another exceptional designer, Beverley Dodd, who crafted the book with love and commitment, and was a pleasure to work alongside during the long, painstaking months of production. Thanks also to the team at Hirt & Carter (especially Martin Jones), for whom nothing was too much trouble, our artist James Berrangé who had the novel idea of designing a glass cricket ball for his drawings of the bowling grips, and Anthony Sharpe, who lost his shirt to get a vital last-minute picture.

We received unstinting support from Bob's wife Gill and sons Dale and Russell, even during the worst crisis of their lives. They allowed us free access to Bob's library, pictures and computer, and were always helpful. We would also like to thank Russell for designing such an exquisite cover.

Above all, we are profoundly grateful to Tom Eaton, who acted not only as an editor, but as a friend, advisor and comforter, especially in the terrible months following the 18th of March 2007. His rapport with Bob meant a very happy collaboration between the two, and his unwavering commitment to realizing Bob's vision for this book made its completion possible. We will never be able to thank him enough.

TIM NOAKES AND HELEN MOFFETT